CENSORSHIP

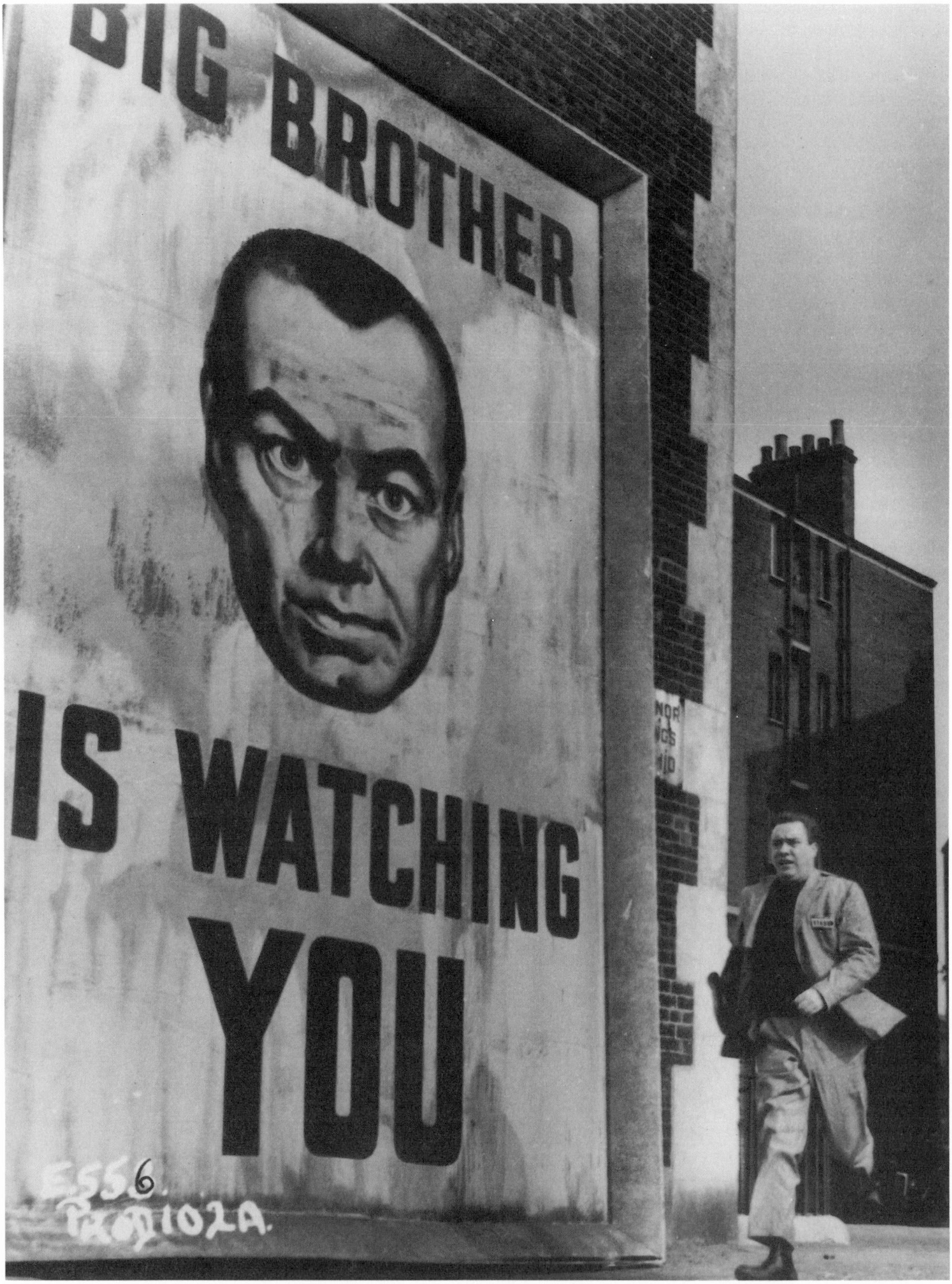
BIG BROTHER
IS WATCHING
YOU
E556.

CENSORSHIP

Volume III
President's Task Force on
Communications Policy – Zouaves

Consulting Editors

Lawrence Amey
Dalhousie University

Timothy L. Hall
University of Mississippi Law School

Carl Jensen
Project Censored
Sonoma State University

Charles May
California State University,
Long Beach

Richard L. Wilson
University of Tennessee at Chattanooga

Project Editor
R. Kent Rasmussen

Salem Press, Inc.
Pasadena, California   Englewood Cliffs, New Jersey

Editor in Chief: Dawn P. Dawson

Managing Editor: Christina Moose   *Project Editor:* R. Kent Rasmussen
Research Supervisor: Jeffry Jensen   *Production Editor:* Janet Long
Acquisitions Editor: Mark Rehn   *Layout:* James Hutson
Photograph Editor: K. L. A. Hyatt   *Proofreading Supervisor:* Yasmine A. Cordoba
Research Assistant: Irene McDermott

Frontispiece: courtesy of Museum of Modern Art/Film Stills Archive

Library of Congress Cataloging-in-Publication Data

Censorship / consulting editors: Lawrence Amey, Timothy L. Hall, Carl Jensen, Charles May, and Richard L. Wilson; project editor, R. Kent Rasmussen

    p.   cm. — (Ready reference)

Includes bibliographical references and index.

    ISBN 0-89356-444-3 (set : alk. paper). — ISBN 0-89356-447-8 (vol. 3 : alk. paper).

    1. Censorship—United States—Encyclopedias. 2. Censorship—Encyclopedias. I. Amey, L. J., 1940-   .
II. Rasmussen, R. Kent.   III. Series.

Z658.U5C38   1997

363.3'1—dc21

97-14245
CIP

First Printing

PRINTED IN THE UNITED STATES OF AMERICA

CONTENTS

ALPHABETICAL LIST OF ENTRIES

Volume I

Volume II

Volume III

CENSORSHIP

President's Task Force on Communications Policy

DATE: August, 1967 - May, 1969
PLACE: Washington, D.C.
SIGNIFICANCE: The task force's 1968 report recommended the removal of unnecessary restraints on private communication initiatives and the encouragement of diversity and innovation in radio and television broadcasting

On August 14, 1967, President Lyndon B. Johnson delivered a message to Congress revealing the formation of the President's Task Force on Communications Policy. The task force, he announced, would study a variety of issues relating to communications technology, including matters relating to radio and television broadcasting. Johnson appointed then Undersecretary of State for Political Affairs Eugene V. Rostow, a Yale law professor prior to his joining the Johnson Administration, to chair the task force.

The task force produced its report late in Johnson's administration. The massive report was the product of sixteen months of work and of the input from fifteen federal agencies and departments. The task force stressed the need to deregulate certain aspects of communications technology and to provide as free a field as possible for private initiative and innovation in communications matters. The task force, whose report emphasized the value of diversity in broadcasting, doubted whether closer supervision by the Federal Communications Commission was a fruitful path to the desired diversity. It saw great promise in the cable industry because the medium seemed poised to generate a broader diversity of programming. The task force also recommended the establishment of an office within the president's executive branch to coordinate the role of this branch in overseeing communications issues.

The report produced by the task force arrived late enough in Johnson's term that his administration took no action to implement its recommendations. The report, in fact, was never officially released by the Johnson Administration, perhaps because its generally procompetition and prodiversity findings were not entirely consistent with the personal financial interests of Johnson, whose family owned a broadcast station in Texas that was the chief source of the president's private wealth. The defeat of the Democrats in the 1968 presidential election may have also blunted any urgency in making public the findings of the task force. A change in presidential administrations had a similar effect. When President Richard Nixon assumed the executive office in January, 1969, political machinations within his administration appear to have temporarily suppressed the task force report. Early in 1969 a White House aid informed the press that the final report of the task force could not be located. Ultimately, in May, 1969, the White House released the report with a disclaimer asserting that the administration did not endorse any of the task force's findings.

See also Broadcast media; Federal Communications Commission; Nixon, Richard M.; Presidency, U.S.

Presley, Elvis

BORN: January 8, 1935, Tupelo, Mississippi
DIED: August 16, 1977, Memphis, Tennessee

IDENTIFICATION: The first great superstar of rock 'n' roll
SIGNIFICANCE: The legendary star often encountered attempts to censor his sexually suggestive performance style

Loud and sexually suggestive, rock 'n' roll music was controversial from the day it was born. It was particularly popular among young girls, who clamored to buy records and photographs of rock 'n' roll singers and to attend any rock 'n' roll performance. The music was quickly condemned by parents, teachers, politicians, ministers, and local police officials. This resistance soon crystalized around the man dubbed "Elvis the Pelvis."

To many, Elvis Presley symbolized rock 'n' roll, which was even denounced by the Soviet Union as an example of the corrupt culture of the West. When his music was played on the radio, stations were swamped with calls from teenage girls pleading for more, and from parents insisting that his music be banned.

It was his live and television appearances, however, that instigated most attempts at censorship. As he sang, Presley twisted his body into suggestive movements and literally beat at his guitar, often breaking strings. His gyrations on stage, as well as his interaction with screaming girls in the front rows, created controversy, and soon cries were heard throughout the country for his music and his performances to be banned. His 1956 appearance in Charlotte, North Carolina, prompted a television critic for the *Charlotte Observer* to label him "obscene." His appearance on Ed Sullivan's popular show the same year was the most celebrated case of censorship in

At the 1956 Mississippi-Alabama state fair held in his home town, Elvis Presley demonstrates some of the "gyrations" that moved critics to call his performances "obscene." (AP/ Wide World Photos)

Presley's career. He was signed for three appearances; in the third show, the camera never showed anything below his waist, because, many thought, his "swivel hips" were deemed too offensive. However, a biographer of Presley declared that this was the exact opposite of censorship, claiming that Presley's performance was purposely photographed from the waist up as a tease, to give the impression that more was going on "down there" than actually was.

Presley ended his stage performance in Los Angeles, California, in October, 1957, in controversy. He threw his arms around a huge replica of the Boston Bulldog (the symbol of his recording company, RCA) and rolled with it across the stage. The next morning, he was called a "sexhibitionist" by the *Los Angeles Mirror-Times*. The following night, local authorities mounted three cameras in the auditorium to monitor his show. As rock and roll became accepted into the mainstream of American society, however, attempts to censor Presley's performances gradually faded away; by the late 1960's, President Richard M. Nixon, a cultural conservative, was happy to pose for pictures with "the king of rock and roll."

See also Beatles, the; Jackson, Michael; Lewis, Jerry Lee; Madonna; Rock 'n' roll music.

Press conferences

DEFINITION: Meetings organized formally to acquaint the media with news or other information

SIGNIFICANCE: Press conferences are often attempts to stage-manage the news in order to mold public opinion through selective dissemination of information

The primary reason to call a press conference is to tell a story one's own way. The media are thus enlisted as potential allies in getting one's message across to the public. Press conferences are not "real" events, such as baseball games, murders, or wars. They are initiatives to gain publicity, influence public opinion, and showcase one's best image. While they can be newsworthy, press conferences are efforts to control what the public knows and thinks. As they are tightly managed events, reporters and others must ask themselves what the sponsors are trying to tell them and what the sponsors are trying to prevent them from knowing and why.

Press conferences are generally called only when something of major importance has occurred or is contemplated. The key to conducting a successful press conference is controlling the content of what appears to be a completely unpredictable forum. In fact, the press conference is a scripted event, with the roles to be played and the topics to be discussed clearly defined. On the surface, a press conference is a straightforward affair. It is a question-and-answer session, with multiple interviewers called to collect news and to question news sources. Reporters are sometimes given special interview opportunities afterward to maximize the impact of the events.

Underneath its theater, press conferences are more than mere meetings with the press to "get ink." Presidents, chief executive officers, religious leaders, scientists, sports figures, and others use them to communicate their plans and policy objectives, and to gain support to achieve them, as well as to launch trial balloons to test public attitudes. Political leaders

and others control the agenda by restructuring reporters' questions to make their points better, by planting questions, and by selectively recognizing friendly reporters. The sponsor decides when a press conference will be called, where it will be held, how long it will last, and what ground rules will prevail. Individual reporters are often limited to a single question each.

Press Conference Ground Rules. Protocols have developed concerning press conference conduct. For example, remarks may be "off the record," which means the information may not be used in a story. "On-the-record" comments may be attributed to the speaker. When information is given "on background," a specific source cannot be identified, although general descriptions of the position such as "a White House source" are permitted. No attribution is allowed if the information is given as "deep background."

The ancestor of the America press conference was the private interview. President Andrew Johnson offered interviews to selected reporters during his impeachment trial because he sensed that the public was reading published interviews more closely than his own speeches.

Presidential Press Conferences. The modern presidential press conference itself began as a news leak. President Theodore Roosevelt pioneered written news releases and "leaking" information to favored reporters to assist in winning support for his legislative program. Any reporter who broke Roosevelt's rules—especially the one requiring that information given in confidence must remain confidential—would be banned from the White House and be denied future access to legitimate news. The president preempted journalistic discretion by retaining control over which stories could be reported and how.

President Woodrow Wilson initiated regular news conferences in 1913, and immediately used the press as a sounding board for U.S. intervention in the Mexican Revolution. A breach of confidentiality at one press conference threatened the future of open press conferences. The White House and the press corps agreed that the corps would be responsible for policing the president's press conferences.

Early press conferences were informal small group discussions governed by special rules. Presidents Warren Harding, Calvin Coolidge, and Herbert Hoover required questions be submitted in advance in writing. No verbatim quotes were allowed without special permission. Reporters were willing to play by the rules because they were given the opportunity of having frank exchanges with presidents willing to take reporters into their confidence. President Franklin D. Roosevelt dispensed with written questions but permitted his staff members to plant questions among receptive reporters. He permitted occasional direct quotations if White House permission were granted, and he required that off-the-record remarks could not be repeated to absent reporters.

On December 16, 1953, President Dwight D. Eisenhower took a historic step in putting the entire news conference on the record. A recording of his December 16 meeting was released to the radio networks, which was the first time the public could listen to an entire presidential news conference. Eisenhower held the first televised presidential news conference on January 19, 1955, after he became upset over negative portrayals of his presidency in the press. He used the conferences to go directly to the people with favorable news so that they would rely less on journalistic interpretations. Eisenhower compelled the television networks to film the press conferences in a pool arrangement and then submit the film to the White House for editing.

The first live telecast of a presidential press conference was conducted by President John F. Kennedy on January 25, 1961. Kennedy continued the protocols of his predecessors. He opened the session with a formal announcement and was followed by recognition of the senior Associated Press or United Press International correspondent. Other reporters were then called upon as—and if—they caught the president's eye. The conferences still ran thirty minutes and ended when the senior news service correspondent said, "Thank you, Mr. President." Kennedy broke tradition, however, by holding special news conferences with publishers and reporters of papers from particular states or regions. Later presidents have thrown reporters off balance by holding impromptu and short-notice press conferences.

Press conferences can be risky for reporters. A television reporter in San Antonio, Texas, for example, was fired in 1992 for being too persistent in his questioning of President George Bush at a news conference following a drug summit with Latin American leaders.

Presidents, business executives, and others have used press conferences to tell stories their way. The press conference may be a pseudo-event; however, it is one that enables the stage management or control of the news.   —*Fred Buchstein*

See also Advocacy; News media censorship; Off-the-record information; Presidency, U.S.; Propaganda; Television.

BIBLIOGRAPHY

Scott M. Cutlip's *The Unseen Power: Public Relations: A History* (Hillsdale, N.J.: Lawrence Erlbaum Associates, 1994) analyzes the practice of public relations in the twentieth century. Samuel Kernell's *Going Public: New Strategies of Presidential Leadership* (2d ed. Washington, D.C.: CQ Press, 1993) discusses the relationship between the presidency and the press. Robert E. Denton, Jr., and Dan F. Hahn provide an overview of presidential communications in *Presidential Communication: Description and Analysis* (New York: Praeger, 1986). Informative articles include Coates Lear's and James Bennet's "The Flack Pack—How Press Conferences Turn Serious Journalists into Shills," *The Washington Monthly* (November, 1991), and Catherine Ann Collins' "Kissinger's Press Conferences, 1972-1974: An Explanation of Form and Role Relationship on News Management," *Central States Speech Journal* 28 (Fall, 1977).

Press-radio war

DATE: 1933-1935

PLACE: United States

SIGNIFICANCE: When the newspaper industry attempted to stop radio news broadcasts during the 1930's, its leaders claimed they were protecting their vested rights, while members of the broadcasting industry believed that the newspapers were censoring radio in order to maintain a monopoly on information

The development of the U.S. radio broadcasting industry in the 1920's was aided by the older newspaper industry. Friendliness turned into animosity by the early 1930's when the National Broadcasting Company (NBC) and the Columbia Broadcasting System (CBS) began comprehensive news reporting. Newspaper owners blamed declining circulations on radio news competition, although the decline was more likely due to the Depression. On April 24, 1933, the Associated Press (AP) decided to stop providing news releases to the radio networks.

Because the new radio networks were in a weaker financial position than the newspapers, they asked for a compromise solution. Paramount in their willingness to compromise was the fact that government licensing in effect granted radio stations limited monopolies within their broadcasting areas. Newspapers had for years resented these monopolies, so they announced their willingness to use their greater economic resources to begin antitrust suits against the two major radio networks, NBC and CBS.

In December of 1933 the networks agreed to the terms of the Press-Radio Agreement, a ten-point pact that in effect made the radio industry subservient to newspapers. One major point of the agreement was the formation of the Press-Radio Bureau, a joint committee made up of five representatives of the newspaper industry and two from radio. Another point of the agreement limited radio stations to two daily five-minute reports. Other major points assigned the first radio news report to 9:30 A.M. and the second to 9:00 P.M., prohibited the radio networks from using news for commercial purposes, and required that the radio networks not enter the news-gathering business.

NBC and CBS were prepared to honor the agreement, but independent stations generally refused, due to the profitability of radio news. Leading a revolt of independents, Trans-Radio Press Service by 1935 proved to the newspaper industry the impossibility of keeping news off the radio. The mid-1930's was an exceptionally eventful period in history. German rearmament in Europe, Japanese expansion in Asia, and sensational events such as the Lindbergh kidnapping in the United States proved lucrative grist for the radio news mills. In April of 1935, in order to prevent further revenue losses in the news business, the major newspaper wire services finally decided to sell news stories to the radio industry. The press-radio war was over.

The Position of the Newspapers. The newspaper industry took the view that the news stories that they purchased from the wire services were their property. Therefore, when radio stations sold time to read that news on the air, they were, in effect, "stealing" the newspaper industry's "property." Silencing the radio news broadcasts was, therefore, not censorship because it was done to protect property.

American newspapers regarded themselves as the guardians of a free press, and it was up to them to ensure the continuation of that tradition. If the radio stations were allowed to broadcast news, freedom of the press would die because of the requirement that radio stations purchase licenses from the federal government. That licensing procedure, the newspapers argued, would allow the government to silence the news if it were allowed to pass primarily to radio—which is what appeared to be occurring at the time.

Prior restraint, the suppression of news before publication, has long been the primary tool employed by censoring agencies. Newspapers were not subject to prior restraint because the government could not prevent the publishing of a paper; they had no licenses that could be revoked. Invulnerability to prior restraint gave the newspaper industry its claim to being the protector of the First Amendment. Radio, on the other hand, could be prevented by the government from broadcasting news stories simply by having their licenses canceled.

The Perspective of Radio. Members of the radio industry took the view that they were not in competition with newspapers, but that they supplemented their news coverage. Radio news broadcasts triggered interest in the news, and that could only benefit the newspaper industry. Drawing on the newspapers for news was not "stealing property," as the newspaper industry claimed, but simply a form of free advertising. Radio was thus the news industry's partner, not its competitor. As partners, radio and newspapers had a common interest in protecting their First Amendment rights from outside censorship. When the Framers of the Bill of Rights saw fit to ensure the freedom of the press and speech in the First Amendment, they were concerned with the freedoms of all Americans, not just those who happened to own vested property rights. If the radio could be silenced, it would only be a matter of time before the newspapers could be silenced.

Complicating the issue was the fact that it was the newspaper industry that was attempting to censor the radio industry, not the government. That not only contradicted the newspaper industry's claim to being the protector of First Amendment rights, it highlighted the possible abuse of the power of the American press. Under the guise of protecting property rights, claimed the radio industry, newspapers were attempting to silence radio news in order to maintain a monopoly in a protected market. The newspaper industry's refusal to supply radio with AP news releases in 1933 constituted the worst kind of prior restraint in that it was done by the press itself.

Press-Radio Cooperation. The deeper issue exposed by the press-radio war was the First Amendment's vulnerability to private, monied interests. The amendment had been written to prevent Congress from passing laws compromising free expression; however, it became apparent in the 1930's that the real danger to free speech came from within the press itself.

As the newspaper industry underwent a process of conglomeration, newspapers became the property of fewer individuals. These individuals became more and more powerful, and were finally able to effect the censorship of the radio industry under the guise of the protection of property.

After the press-radio war, newspaper chains began to purchase radio stations. In light of the fact that increasing numbers of radio stations became the property of newspaper chains, the solution to the press-radio war was more a merger than a settlement. Since no constitutional issues were resolved, the question of the safety of the First Amendment remained.

—Tim Palmer

See also Associated Press; First Amendment; News broadcasting; News media censorship; Newspapers; Propaganda; Radio.

BIBLIOGRAPHY

Information on the press-radio war is difficult to locate. In *Public Opinion Quarterly* (Summer, 1949), Girard Chester offers a basic outline in "The Press-Radio War: 1933-1935." T. R. Carskadon's "The Press-Radio War," *The New Republic* (March 11, 1936), fully explains the important events. David Holbrook Culbert describes the development of radio news in *News for Everyman: Radio and Foreign Affairs in Thirties America* (Westport, Conn.: Greenwood Press, 1976). Although not directly related to the press-radio war, Carl Jensen offers the flavor of censorship in *Censored: The News That Didn't Make the News—and Why* (Chapel Hill, N.C.: Shelburne Press, 1993). Censorship issues are also discussed in Michael Schudson's *Discovering the News: A Social History of American Newspapers* (New York: Basic Books, 1978) and in *A Free and Responsible Press* (Chicago: University of Chicago Press, 1947), by the Commission on Freedom of the Press.

Pressure groups

DEFINITION: Special-interest bodies organized to influence particular public or governmental policies

SIGNIFICANCE: Pressure groups have campaigned successfully to have schools, libraries, and other organizations change policies, alter funding decisions, and restrict access to materials

Allegations of censorship of school materials have been made by both the Left and the Right. Some conservatives believe that certain textbooks purposefully leave out references to such matters as God, creationism, and prayer. Meanwhile, liberals charge that groups such as the Stop Textbook Censorship Committee, formed by Phyllis Schlafly and the Eagle Forum, are not interested in balanced information, but simply in fostering school textbooks slanted in favor of conservative views.

The state of Texas has been the focus of much of the controversy surrounding textbooks. Most textbook companies cannot issue separate editions of their books for individual states, but they are inclined to cater to Texas, which has one of the nation's largest school systems. Once a textbook is approved in Texas, the standard is set for the rest of the country. Until the 1980's a private organization called Educational Research Analysts, led by Mel Gabler and Norma Gabler of Longview, Texas, exerted extraordinary influence over the Texas school system by persuading it to select textbooks it regarded as emphasizing so-called traditional values.

During the 1980's a group of parents in Hawkins County, Tennessee, was awarded fifty thousand dollars when the Concerned Women of America helped bring its case to court. Quoting heavily from one of the Gablers' handbooks, the parents expressed their concern with publisher Holt, Rinehart and Winston's Basic Reading Series, which included material on witchcraft, astrology, pacifism, feminism, and evolution, but nothing about their own religious beliefs or mainstream Christianity. The ruling was later overturned by an appeals court.

Members of a pressure group called the Susan B. Anthony Project tried to force a Florida nude dance club out of business after one of its teenage dancers committed suicide in 1987. (AP/Wide World Photos)

In 1994 parents in Fairfax County, Virginia, asked that the book *Families* by Meredith Tax be removed from the public school curriculum. Written for first graders, this book depicted a variety of lifestyles including single-parent families and homosexuality. The complaining parents were successful when in August of that year the Fairfax school board removed the book from the curriculum. The group also campaigned to have material on homosexuality removed from the Family Life Education Curriculum, although parents were already allowed to have their children opt out of the class. After a panel discussion and a heated argument, the Fairfax County Family Life Education Curriculum Advisory Committee (FLECAC) voted to retain the material. A group of moderate parents then organized a body called FARE, for "Fairfax Alliance for Responsible Education." Claiming to represent majority views, this body opposed school prayer, censorship, and vouchers, and supported teaching responsible sex and AIDS prevention education.

National Endowment for the Arts. The Taxpayer for Accountability in Government (TAG) is a coalition of profamily and conservative groups including Concerned Women for America, the Eagle Forum, the American Family Association, the Christian Legal Defense and Education Foundation, and

the Traditional Values Coalition. In 1990 TAG requested cutting off federal funding of National Endowment for the Arts (NEA) because they regarded some of the art funded by NEA as obscene and sacrilegious. Acceding to pressures from the Right, the NEA denied funding to four performance artists in order to protect itself. The so-called "NEA Four" then brought suit against John Frohnmayer, former chair of the NEA, and won a $252,000 settlement from the federal government. It had become clear during testimony that the Bush Administration had pressured Frohnmayer into denying funding to controversial artists, especially those who work with sexual or religious themes.

The American Family Association. The American Family Association (AFA), led by Donald Wildmon, a Methodist minister in Tupelo, Mississippi, has tried to change practices of the entertainment business by organizing boycotts against advertisers who sponsor shows that contain sex, violence, or profanity. One night in 1977 Wildmon watched television with his family; after changing channels several times and finding something offensive on every channel, he conceived a Turn-Off-TV Week campaign. The press picked up on his idea. Shortly thereafter Wildmon left his church and organized the National Federation for Decency.

A POSTCARD TO MR. EISNER

Many Americans in the religious right disapproved of the Disney Company's permitting the celebration of Gay and Lesbian Day at its Disney World amusement park in Florida. In order to pressure the company into changing its policy, several Christian Fundamentalist groups organized an aggressive boycott of Disney films and products. Among these groups was the American Family Association, which encouraged its members to sign this preprinted postcard and mail it directly to Disney's chief executive officer:

> Dear Mr. Eisner,
>
> I know that thousands of people have written you.
>
> Count me among those who protest Disney's recent moves to undermine my faith and the values I hold dear. **I will not knowingly support Disney until you change your practices.**
>
> I am praying that you will see the tremendous damage you are doing to our society, especially our children, and will change your practices. **I can no longer trust Disney to be the company I thought it was.**
>
> Feel free to pursue whatever social and political agenda you like. **But don't count on my support until you change your present practices.**
>
> Sincerely,_____

Many companies say that Wildmon's attempted boycotts have not effected their sales. However, Wildmon and the AFA have enjoyed some success in pressuring sponsors to withdraw support for certain shows, and in preventing the broadcast of certain material. For example, a few seconds were deleted from a *Mighty Mouse* episode in which AFA claims Mighty Mouse is sniffing cocaine, although the series animator says it was a flower. After Wildmon spoke with a General Motors executive about its advertising of a certain *Wiseguy* episode, the company agreed to pull advertisements from episodes that might be deemed offensive because of gratuitous sex or violence, offenses to religious or racial groups, or presentations of one-sided treatments of controversial issues.

From 1990 through 1995 Wildmon and AFA led a boycott of Kmart stores for refusing to remove *Playboy* and *Penthouse* magazines from the Waldenbooks chain that the company owned. The boycott was called off after Kmart divested itself of the bookstore chain. A Kmart spokesperson acknowledged that the boycott did have a negative impact on traffic in some regions of the country.

Family Friendly Libraries. Dissatisfied over language in the American Library Association's (ALA) Library Bill of Rights, which directs libraries to make as wide a range of opinions available as possible in their collections, two citizens have started a group called Family Friendly Libraries (FFL) as an alternative to the ALA. Family Friendly Libraries issues its own policy documents that libraries may adopt instead of the Library Bill of Rights. The group's goals are to win more local control over libraries and to provide parents with more control over the library materials to which their children have access.

—*Pamela Hayes-Bohanan*

See also American Library Association; Boycotts; Eagle Forum; Gabler, Mel, and Norma Gabler; Library Bill of Rights; National Endowment for the Arts; Textbooks.

BIBLIOGRAPHY

Joan DelFattore's *What Johnny Shouldn't Read: Textbook Censorship in America* (New Haven, Conn.: Yale University Press, 1992) treats textbook censorship in elementary and secondary schools from both liberal and conservative groups. Donna A. DeMac, *Liberty Denied: The Current Rise of Censorship in America* (New Brunswick, N.J.: Rutgers University Press, 1990), surveys censorship from several aspects including in the schools, in libraries and government censorship. Nat Hentoff's *Free Speech for Me—But Not for Thee: How the American Left and Right Relentlessly Censor Each Other* (New York: HarperCollins, 1992) covers a variety of cases involving censorship and book banning. In *Bookbanning in America: Who Bans Books?—And Why* (Middlebury, Vt.: P. S. Eriksson, 1990), William Nobel provides details of censorship in the United States from colonial times through the 1980's. Donald J. Rogers, *Banned!: Book Censorship in Schools* (New York: Messner, 1988), examines book censorship cases in schools during the 1970's and 1980's.

Printing

DEFINITION: Making multiple copies of a document by impression against a tool (for example, type or a plate) covered with ink

SIGNIFICANCE: Printing, rather than copying by hand, made books much easier to produce, and radically altered the relationship between the publisher and the censor

Printing in Europe had a rather positive beginning for those with concerns about censorship. By the time Johann Gutenberg of Mainz, Germany had developed his printing process using movable type in 1450, there had been numerous instances of censorship, especially on the part of the church at the time. With the advent of printing in Europe, however, church authorities labeled the press as a gift of God, seeing it as a device to further the work of the church.

Printing as a Threat. The printing press was soon seen as a threat for the spread of heretical doctrines, and even the scriptures presented a problem, for, if they were made readily available through printing, people everywhere would be reading the Bible and interpreting it in their own way.

Within a few years following 1450, town councils and church authorities were carefully reviewing printed books, censoring those considered dangerous politically or in a religious sense. Bible translations in the vernacular were considered especially dangerous, but there was little concern for printed books that were obscene or sexually explicit. By the beginning of the sixteenth century, censorship was considered a duty for anyone in the leadership of the Christian church, and that sense of duty intensified with the Protestant Reformation.

The introduction of printing with movable type into Europe was a strong factor in the success of the Reformation, and the Roman Catholic church attempted to stem the tide through the issuance of various lists of banned books. An official list of prohibited books was issued by the Catholic church in 1559, under the authority of Pope Paul IV, and this was replaced by Pius V with the *Index Librorium Prohibitorium* in 1564. The premise for such lists was that reading certain works could undermine the faith or morals of Catholics.

Even though there was little consistency for listing books in the index, it remained as a guideline to reading for Catholics into modern times, finally coming to an official end in 1966. Officially, the Catholic church banned books as part of its mission of saving souls. There were others who exercised book banning for quite different reasons. Henry VIII of England issued a list of banned books in 1529. Although this was not an extensive list, it did limit the availability of materials about England, especially those issuing from foreign presses.

Other censorship attempts by European governments usually combined political, religious, and economic motives. Some governments, such as the council in Venice, were striving to control or eliminate competition for officially sanctioned printers. The licensing of some printers, such as John of Speyer and Aldus Manutius, while denying licenses to others, had the effect of controlling what was available to the reading public.

There were European governments that made printing enterprises difficult by trying to control or edit all published materials. The result of overzealous control was the movement of promising printers to other countries or the demise of successful book industry enterprises. An example of the latter is the decline and eventual demise of the highly successful Frankfurt book fair after the event was placed under the jurisdiction of the narrow-minded imperial censorship commission in 1579. The fair survived until 1750, but never with any degree of its former prominence, because censorship had driven the book industry to other markets.

Among the early printers who moved to escape official censors were Johann Froben of Germany and Robert Estienne of France. Froben established himself as a printer in Basel, Switzerland in 1516. There he could print the works of Desiderius Erasmus and other scholarly writers without interference. Estienne experienced great difficulty through repeated censorship attempts, even though his printing enterprise was under the protection of Francis I, King of France. Even his title of Printer to the King did not protect him adequately from attacks instigated by the University of Paris. Estienne was a Humanist who supported the ideals of the Reformation. Relying on early Bible translations, he corrected obvious errors in the New Testament, and this practice drew criticism and sometimes resulted in Estienne seeking refuge in the king's court. In 1550 he moved his press to Geneva to be freed from harassment by theological censors.

Johannes Gutenberg demonstrates the first results of his printing process in this nineteenth century engraving by Adolf Menzel. (Library of Congress)

Heretical and other objectionable writings were the focus of concern in England when Queen Elizabeth I exercised censorship through granting the Stationers' Company a monopoly of printing in 1559, and censorship intensified with the establishment of the Star Chamber in 1585. The licensing of the Stationers' Company was modified and the Star Chamber was abolished through actions of the Long Parliament in 1641, creating for a short time freedom of the press. In 1642 Parliament began to prosecute printers and writers judged to be abusing their freedom. Licensing was again put into practice, and new moves toward censorship inspired John Milton to write *Areopagitica* (1644), a pamphlet objecting to censorship and promoting freedom of the press.

The Threat Spreads to America. With only a few modifications, James Franklin was using the same printing press design in Boston in 1717 as Gutenberg had used in 1450. As long as he and other early American printers devoted their presses to ballads, poems, songs, Bibles, and school books, there was usually little to fear from censors. When American printers employed their presses in the criticism of colonial authorities and the British crown, those in authority attempted to retaliate through censorship. In spite of the limited advancement in printing technology over more than two centuries, the press provided the means for widespread expression of opinion and fact.

John Peter Zenger, a New York printer and publisher of the *New York Weekly Journal* was tried in 1735 for libelling Governor William Cosby. He was acquitted on the grounds that the published statements were true. The printing press allowed Isaiah Thomas to launch bitter, sarcastic, and sometimes fierce criticism against British authority in the colonies. He published the newspaper, *The Massachusetts Spy*, in Boston, but in 1775 had to move his printing enterprise to Worcester because of pressure from the British.

In the nineteenth century advances in printing technology made it increasingly difficult for censors to exercise control of the press. Friedrich Koenig, a German, is credited with the steam-powered cylinder press in 1811. The rotary press was developed by an American, Richard Hoe, in 1846. Ottmar Mergenthaler, a German in the United States, introduced the linotype in 1884, and in 1905 Ira Rubel invented offset printing. With so many presses in operation and the speed with which printing could be done, it became more difficult for the censor to work with any efficiency. The advent of the computer and on-line access has made it virtually impossible fully to control expression, except in isolated cases or by the most extreme measures.

The proliferation of books and other materials through the printing press has, from 1450 to the present, caused concern for the censor. The concerns for the early censor settled on ecclesiastical matters and rapidly spread to a variety of religious, political, and moral issues. Those several areas remain at issue, but printing has made the censor's job more difficult.

—Harlan R. Johnson

See also Book publishing; Franklin, Benjamin; *Index Librorum Prohibitorum*; Licensing Act of 1662; Licensing Act of 1737; Newspapers; Photocopying; Reformation, the.

BIBLIOGRAPHY

Henri-Jean Martin, *The History and Power of Writing* (Chicago: University of Chicago Press, 1994), translated by Lydia G. Cochrane, describes written communication in its various forms and the effects it has had upon civilization. Douglas C. McMurtrie, *The Book: The Story of Printing and Bookmaking* (London: Oxford University Press, 1943), is an overview of early book production and detailed accounts of printers of Europe and early America. George Putnam's *Books and Their Makers During the Middle Ages* (New York: Hillary House, 1962) describes production and distribution of literature from the fall of the Roman Empire to the close of the seventeenth century. S. H. Steinberg's *Five Hundred Years of Printing* (Baltimore, Md.: Penguin Books, 1961) recounts the stories of printers, privileges, and censorship to the twentieth century. Isaiah Thomas' *The History of Printing in America* (New York: Weathervane Books, 1970), edited by Marcus A. McCorison, details the work of printers in North America from the Massachusetts Bay Colony to the years following the American Revolution.

Prior restraint

DEFINITION: Government restraint of objectionable material before its publication, distribution, performance, or broadcast

SIGNIFICANCE: Prior restraint has long been the essence of censorship because it has been one of the most effective tools used by governments to prevent the spread of offending ideas

Government leaders and other authorities have given prior restraint of free expression a bad name, but it is easy to understand why prior restraint is important to them. If authorities wait until after offensive ideas are expressed to punish offenders, the damage has already been done. Even extreme retroactive penalties, including death, may not deter some critics from voicing their opposition. In the Soviet Union, in which prior restraint and severe penalties for expressing ideas were commonplace, there were always holders of dissident views, such as Aleksandr Solzhenitsyn and Andrei Sakharov, willing to write or speak out, in spite of what the regime could do to them after their ideas came to light.

In modern democracies, prior restraint has long been proscribed as one of the best ways to encourage free expression. As early as the mid-eighteenth century, the great British jurist William Blackstone wrote in his *Commentaries* (1765-1769) that "liberty of the press is indeed essential to the nature of a free state; but this consists of laying no *previous* restraints upon publications." Blackstone's *Commentaries* was one of the major sources of law for the American colonists and the early leaders of the United States. Abundant evidence demonstrates that the nation's founders shared a common understanding that freedom of the press meant at minimum no prior restraint. At the same time, prior restraint has been recognized as a necessary part of those forms of expression in which assembly is involved. The U.S. Bill of Rights guarantees only that Congress shall not abridge the right "peaceably to assemble," implying a right to restrain assemblies in advance.

Prior Restraint in the United States. Although the absence of prior restraint is the starting point, free expression has come to encompass a great deal more. Shortly after passage of the Bill of Rights in 1791, laws restricting press freedom became a major issue with the passage of the Sedition Act of 1798. The ruling Federalist Party feared losing the 1800 presidential election to its Democratic-Republican opponents and sought to restrain opposition newspapers by making it a criminal offense to write false, malicious stories about the government or its officials, including the president. The Federalists justified the law by arguing that it did not impose a prior restraint. When adopted, the Sedition Act was used to convict several Democratic-Republican publishers who attacked its reputation for fairness. The ensuing political outcry was so great that the Federalists lost the presidency and never regained it. Thomas Jefferson, after winning, pardoned those convicted. The experience kept the national government from attempting similar acts for more than a hundred years, and added the recognition that restraints after the fact can also limit free expression by what later came to be known as the chilling effect.

Definition of the First Amendment limits was left to the twentieth century U.S. Supreme Court. The first example of an attempted prior restraint on the press came in *Near v. Minnesota* (1931). A man named Near published a newspaper in Minneapolis, Minnesota, that denounced local "Jewish" government officials for graft and corruption. Minnesota authorities sought to use state statutes to stop Near from publishing his anti-Semitic newsletter, since no federal statute existed. After the case reached the U.S. Supreme Court, the Court initially decided that the First Amendment's free press clause applied to the states as well as the federal government by using the Fourteenth Amendment's due process clause to rule that all persons were entitled to equal protection of the laws under their state governments. The Court then ruled that despite the despicable character of Near's views, no state could exercise a prior restraint on a newspaper.

A later case of attempted prior restraint on the press involved a set of purloined documents known as the Pentagon Papers that raised serious national security issues in 1971. Nevertheless, the Supreme Court declined to allow a prior restraint to stop their publication in *The New York Times*. After this case, it became difficult to see what circumstance would justify a prior restraint on the press in the United States.

Prior Restraint and Freedom of Assembly. The First Amendment divides the free expression of ideas into three categories: press, speech, and peaceable assembly. Neither speech nor press is to be restrained as a free expression of ideas, but the amendment's use of the word "peaceably" in connection with the right to assembly means that assemblies can be—and routinely are—subject to prior restraint. Even in cases of assembly, however, prior restraints are only allowed for reasons of time, place, or manner and cannot be used to block expression of ideas.

Freedom of press and freedom of speech differ from freedom of assembly because of their more passive character, although the U.S. Supreme Court has not always consistently and officially said so. Press, in particular, is regarded as a less dangerous medium for the expression of ideas since reading is a more passive activity than speaking to an audience. While speakers have often been known—intentionally or unintentionally—to incite audiences to riot, it is difficult to imagine people reading a newspaper to riot spontaneously.

Because speech is frequently expressed before assemblages, it falls partially under the First Amendment's requirement that unless an assembly is peaceable, it may be restrained. This point rests on a distinction between ideas and actions. Pure ideas as expressed in the press or in speeches to peaceable assemblies are fully protected, but the requirement that an assembly must be peaceable may lead to restraints on speech, even if there are no prior restraints on the press. The essence of freedom of the press is no prior restraint of any protected material before its distribution, but it clearly implies that restraints may be applied afterward.

By the late twentieth century, concern about chilling effect had led the proponents of free expression to oppose the use of libel laws as postrestraints. The cost of litigation meant that many who would otherwise speak out would be restrained. The Supreme Court recognized this by limiting the grounds by which newspapers could be held accountable in libel cases, thereby limiting the extent to which postrestraints apply to newspapers. However, the essence of freedom of expression still rests on no prior restraint or no censorship.

—*Richard L. Wilson*

See also Assembly, right of; Censorship; Clear and present danger doctrine; Demonstrations; *Near v. Minnesota*; Obscenity: legal definitions; *Pentagon Papers, The*; Shaw, George Bernard.

BIBLIOGRAPHY

The best book of general scholarship on the subject is Henry J. Abraham and Barbara A. Perry, *Freedom and the Court* (6th ed. New York: Oxford, 1994). For a thoughtful analysis of free expression, see Kent Greenawalt's *Speech, Crime, and the Uses of Language* (New York: Oxford University Press, 1989). One of the best edited casebooks for general readers is Wallace Mendelson's *The American Constitution and Civil Liberties* (Homewood, Ill: Dorsey, 1981). An interesting survey of freedom of speech generally is Jeremy Cohen's *Congress Shall Make No Law* (Ames: Iowa State University, 1989). Anthony Lewis, longtime critic of censorship, has written extensively about the *Near* case in *Make No Law* (New York: Random House, 1991).

Prisons

DEFINITION: Places in which criminals and suspected criminals are isolated from society and kept under surveillance

SIGNIFICANCE: Persons in prisons do not have the same liberties as other people; prison communities therefore raise interesting questions concerning the extent to which censorship is appropriate and justifiable

Prisons in their current forms are comparatively recent developments. Most historians date their emergence to the late eighteenth and early nineteenth centuries. In earlier times prisoners were held in facilities from which they could not escape;

however, such confinement was enforced while trials were being conducted. Once suspects were convicted, punishments were handed down, which usually entailed either some form of physical mutilation or execution. What characterizes the modern forms of prisons is that they have become the predominant form of punishment. Criminals are punished by spending their time in the prison itself. At the same time, however, the prison becomes the site where, through constant observation and discipline, prisoners can be rehabilitated and returned to society. For this reason prisons are also referred to as correctional institutions.

The Emergence of Prisons. The early nineteenth century was the time when the modern prison came about. One of the more important reasons is that as industrial technologies began to thrive, cities became much more populous. Consequently, prisons emerged as an effective way to deal with lawbreakers in urban settings. Jeremy Bentham proposed what he referred to as the Panopticon. As a design style for the prison, the Panopticon was to allow for the greatest visibility of the inmates while simultaneously keeping guards from sight. The basic design of the building was to be circular or octagonal, with a large interior courtyard with a watchtower in the center. With cells facing onto an inner courtyard, each cell would be easily visible from the central watchtower. Venetian blinds would prevent the guards themselves from being seen. The idea behind this design was that it would instill in the prisoner a sense of being constantly watched. Bentham thought that this would condition prisoners self-consciously to follow the laws of society.

Another final reason for dating the birth of the modern prison to the end of the eighteenth century is that prisons were thought to be more humane forms of punishment in an era when concern for human rights was emerging as a dominant concern.

Prisons and Censorship. A problematic issue arising in the context of the modern prison is reconciling the need to discipline inmates through constant vigilance, while respecting their natural rights as human beings. The general policy of prisons has been that forms of disciplinary intervention such as censorship are justified because they help prevent unrest within the prison community; they prevent inmates from carrying out illegal activities; and they facilitate efficient operation. An important litmus test applied to the activities of the prison is the "clear and present danger" test. According to this test, the rights of prisoners need not be respected when doing so could present a clear and present danger, such as an escape or a riot. The weight of this justification rests upon what is perceived to be a clear and present danger. Prior to 1970 U.S. courts generally sided with the prisons on censorship issues. In 1970, however, a federal district court in Wisconsin ruled in favor of a plaintiff's complaint that previously would have been dismissed. The plaintiff charged that the Wisconsin prison system unjustly refused to forward mail to inmates, post inmates' letters, or allow inmates to subscribe to magazines. In *Odell v. Wisconsin Department of Health and Social Service*, the court ruled that prison officials had not adequately justified the need for censorship because they did not sufficiently show

that their policies were necessary for "prison administration," or that they averted a "clear and present danger." Since this decision, the right of prisoners not to be censored has been affirmed in other cases. However, in many other situations censorship is still perceived to be a legitimate and necessary practice of the prison system.

Censorship and Prisoners' Rights. An important issue relating to a prisoner's right not to be censored involves prisoner access to attorneys. The right to counsel is a basic right of all citizens. However, recent court rulings have allowed for censorship of letters among prisoners and attorneys if the substance of the letters does not pertain to legal defense issues. The courts struck down, for example, the complaint of a prisoner who felt that his access to his attorney was being censored and suppressed. The substance of his mail, however, dealt only with his attitude that homosexual relations among consenting inmates should be allowed. The court believed that since this did not pertain to the prisoner's own defense in any way, the prison administration was justified in refusing to mail his letter.

Another right of prisoners with regard to censorship that has been affirmed concerns communications among inmates and government officials. Prisoners have the right not to endure cruel and unusual punishments, and should be able to communicate to the government if they feel this right is being violated. The courts have therefore allowed prisoners to send mail to government officials when the substance of their mail involves grievances concerning their treatment in prison.

In *Nolan v. Fitzpatrick* (1971) a plaintiff contested the legality of a Massachusetts prison regulation that banned letters from inmates to the news media and banned distribution of prison newsletters written by and for inmates. The reasoning behind the bans was that allowing contacts among inmates and the media would contribute to unrest, and prison security would be compromised. The court, however, ruled against the ban, arguing that prison officials had not adequately demonstrated that real danger to prison security would result from allowing for communication among inmates and the media.

The courts have also generally upheld the rights of prisons to censor and suppress prisoner access to obscene materials. Whether or not one can legitimately argue that obscene material will inflame inmates and create unrest—which is what many prison officials will argue—the fact remains that the courts have long denied pornographic and obscene materials protection. Consequently, they have generally ruled in favor of the right of prisons to censor obscene materials.

—Jeffrey A. Bell

See also Bentham, Jeremy; Clear and present danger doctrine; Courts and censorship law; Criminal trials; Privileged communication.

BIBLIOGRAPHY

Michel Foucault's *Discipline and Punish: The Birth of the Prison* (Trans. by Alan Sheridan, New York: Vintage Books, 1979) is a classic study of the historical conditions and circumstances that gave rise to modern prisons. Foucault explains how prison officials justify their use of censorship. John Palmer's *Constitutional Rights of Prisoners* (Cincinnati: W. H.

Anderson, 1973) is an excellent source for tracing the legal history of the important court decisions that bear upon the issue of censorship. Dick Whitfield, ed., has compiled in *The State of the Prisons—200 Years On* (New York: Routledge, 1991) an excellent collection of essays comparing in a cross-cultural manner the often problematic relationships among prisoners and prison officials. J. M. Moynahan and Earle K. Stewart's *The American Jail: Its Development and Growth* (Chicago: Nelson-Hall, 1980) discusses the history of the prison in the United States. Gordon Hawkins' *The Prison: Policy and Practice* (Chicago: University of Chicago Press, 1976) is a good overview of prison policies.

Privacy, right to

DEFINITION: The right to be left alone; particularly the right not to be in the public eye

SIGNIFICANCE: Censors have often sought to limit privacy or to prevent the private use of objectionable materials

Although one may argue that the First, Third, Fourth, Fifth, Ninth, Tenth, and Fourteenth Amendments to the U.S. Constitution implicitly protect privacy, they do not mention it specifically. Supreme Court justice Louis D. Brandeis described privacy as the most comprehensive of rights and the right most valued by civilized people. Privacy can be conceptualized as what lies within the realm of personal information, conduct out of public view, personal expression, the home and one's person, and the right of association.

Privacy has been described as serving the functions of protecting personal autonomy, permitting emotional release, promoting self-evaluation, and allowing for protected communication. The social and technological complexity of modern civilization has made privacy an important issue in everyday life. Privacy boundaries under the law are sometimes defined in terms of areas in which an individual would have a reasonable expectation of privacy, such as private mail, telephone conversations, and activities within the home.

Privacy Protection. Some authorities believe the right of privacy is a natural right which is independent of written laws or constitutions. Most countries have cultural traditions, many of which are embodied in laws, that recognize personal privacy. However, the degree of protection given to privacy varies widely among different countries. Although the right to privacy is generally protected, the protection is not absolute.

In the United States the right of privacy is not a specifically stated or enumerated right under the U.S. Constitution. United States courts have interpreted the Fourth, Fifth, and Fourteenth Amendments to the U.S. Constitution to contain the right of privacy. In addition to federal and state constitutional and regulatory protection, legal theories have evolved through case law that protect the privacy interests of individuals. These legal theories provide the foundation for private lawsuits to recover damages for intrusion into privacy.

Interference and intrusions on privacy are permitted so long as they are reasonable and supported by a justifiable need.

A New Yorker registers his protest against government spying and censorship by wearing a mock television camera with a label evoking George Orwell's dystopian image of "Big Brother." (Betty Lane)

Justifiable needs usually relate to the protection of the safety, health, and welfare of society. In the United States and many other countries, the determination of whether the intrusion is reasonable is accomplished by balancing an individual's right of privacy with the justification given to intrude on that right.

Privacy and Censorship. The United States and a number of other countries have laws for the protection of expression such as freedom of speech and freedom of the press. These laws promote access to certain types of ideas and information and facilitate the flow of information and open discussion whether public or private. Central to these freedoms is the right to gather, publish, and discuss information and express ideas without restriction. Restraints and limitations on expression can impact freedom of speech and press and may result in a form of censorship.

The conflict between privacy rights and censorship can arise in several contexts: restriction on the publication of private information, the right of individuals to obtain private information, the right to distribute information, the right to solitude, and the right to engage in private activities and private forms of expression. Forms of expression can involve a variety of public and private activities. Censorship can operate to restrain these activities. However, when it operates to restrain private activities, the justification for protection of the public good is generally minimized because private and not public interests are affected. In some instances censorship can protect privacy and in other instances it may operate to invade privacy.

Censorship can invade privacy when it attempts to control or suppress activities that take place in private. Prohibiting certain types of private discussion, private conduct, private association, and other private activities is a form of censorship that intrudes on private expression. Enforcing the prohibitions can involve some form of invasion in private areas in order to determine whether individuals are violating the prohibitions. Intrusions can occur by many methods, including eavesdropping, examining personal records, unauthorized viewing, monitoring communications, and other methods that would be offensive to a reasonable person.

Communications and Privacy. Censorship can also invade privacy in communication. Generally, people have an expectation that the content of telephone and mail communications are private. Prohibiting or restraining discussion of certain ideas or subjects in private communication is censorship. Expectations of privacy can also extend to electronic communications such as electronic mail, data communication, and communication through on-line information services. Suppressing and controlling the content of the communication can have a chilling effect on private communication, the exchange of ideas, and other private forms of expression.

Government restraints and limitations designed to protect an individual's privacy can also have the effect of interfering with the accumulation, transmission, and dissemination of information and ideas within the public interest. For example, a conflict between privacy and freedom of the press can occur in the context of public disclosure of private facts, such as publishing the name of a rape victim in a newspaper. A conflict occurs between the public's right to the information and the victim's right to privacy. The justification for restraining the public disclosure of private facts is generally stronger when it involves publication of private matters in which the public has no legitimate interest. The investigation of items of public interest can also intrude into an individual's seclusion or solitude during the information gathering process. The degree of intrusion relates directly to restrictions on the collection methods.

Suppressing and controlling information can also protect privacy rights by restricting or prohibiting intrusion into solitude and private areas. For example, telephone communication, mail communication, and broadcast communication have a unique ability to intrude on privacy. Therefore, laws that provide for the removal of an individual's name from commercial mailing or telephone solicitation lists upon request and laws that control radio and television programming prevent intrusion into an individual's solitude but operate to restrain expressive activities. For example, in *Rowan v. U.S. Post Office Department* (1970), the U.S. Supreme Court commingled speech and privacy concerns to determine that the basic privacy right to be free from unwanted sights, sounds, and tangible matter outweighed a commercial mailer's right to communicate to an unreceptive addressee.

Advances in technology facilitate the ability of private and public organizations to accumulate, store, and transmit large amounts of personal information. Rules and laws that regulate the gathering, retention, and dissemination of this personal information such as tax and medical records can constitute a form of censorship but may also operate to protect privacy.

—Bruce E. May

See also Biography; Censorship; Courts and censorship law; Fourth Amendment; Outing; Privacy Protection Act of 1980; *Rowan v. U.S Post Office Department*; *Titicut Follies*.

BIBLIOGRAPHY

Sidney G. Buchanan's "The Right of Privacy: Past, Present, and Future" in *Ohio Northern University Law Review* 16, no. 3 (1989) examines the historical development of legal protection for privacy, including protection against arbitrary government actions. David A. Elder's *The Law of Privacy* (Rochester, New York: Lawyers Cooperative Publishing, 1991) gives a thorough analysis of the law of privacy and contains supplementary updates on latest developments. Irwin R. Kramer's "The Birth of Privacy Law: A Century Since Warren and Brandeis" in *Catholic University Law Review* 39 (Spring, 1990) is a scholarly manuscript that reviews the state of the law prior to and after the landmark privacy article written by Warren and Brandeis. Vincent J. Samar's *The Right to Privacy* (Philadelphia: Temple University Press, 1991) examines the objects, concept, and justification for legal privacy with particular emphasis on lesbian and gay privacy issues. Ferdinand David Schoeman's *Privacy and Social Freedom* (New York: Cambridge University Press, 1992) examines privacy in the context of a variety of social dimensions. Raymond Wacks, *Privacy* (New York: New York University Press, 1993) is an edited collection of scholarly essays that examine the common law right of privacy, privacy and free speech, and privacy and the state.

Privacy Protection Act of 1980

ENACTED: October 13, 1980

PLACE: United States (national)

SIGNIFICANCE: This federal law increased protections against unreasonable government searches of newsrooms by requiring officials to secure subpoenas

The United States has never had a national shield law giving journalists special privileges to protect their news sources. The Privacy Protection of 1980 arose from incidents occurring during the 1970's that heightened congressional awareness of the need for greater protection of news gatherers. In 1971 police searching for evidence in a criminal investigation rifled the offices of Stanford University's student newspaper. When the U.S. Supreme Court upheld the power of government to conduct such searches armed only with court-issued warrants, in *Zurcher v. The Stanford Daily* (1978), the nation's press was outraged. President Jimmy Carter responded by proposing legislation to protect newspapers and others from such searches. Fresh incidents of government invasions of newsrooms around this same time moved Congress to pass legislation, which Carter signed into law in October, 1980. The Privacy Protection Act of 1980—also known as the News Room Search Law—went into effect for the federal government the following New Year's Day, and for state and local governments exactly one year later.

Avoiding a problem common to such legislation, the new law did not single out the press for protection. Instead, it offered protection to all persons preparing material for publication. The law specifically forbade government officials from either seeking or issuing warrants to search for, or to seize, any work owned by persons "reasonably believed to have a purpose to disseminate [it] to the public." Its protections covered documentary materials, including magnetically or electronically recorded cards, tapes, and computer media; and any work product materials, created for the purpose of disseminating information to the public. The law exempted cases in which there is "probable cause to believe" that the custodians of the work in question have committed, or are planning to commit, criminal acts to which the materials relate. Also exempted were instances in which seizure of material is necessary to save human life, or in which the custodians would not comply with a valid subpoena, or try to hide or destroy material if a search is not undertaken.

The act established guidelines for federal officers mandating that recognition be given to the personal privacy of those holding the materials sought and requiring that the least intrusive means be used to obtain materials needed by the government. That act further mandated that care be given not to impair confidential relationships, such as those between doctor and patient or attorney and client, and required that except in rare and genuine emergencies, only a government attorney can authorize search and seizure under one of the exceptions built into the act.

Violations of the act are not punishable under criminal law, but aggrieved persons can seek redress against offenders in the civil courts. Damages are limited to actual damages, but the act is weakened by language that says a "reasonable good faith belief in the lawfulness of his conduct" would excuse an officer who violated the terms of the act.

See also Fourth Amendment; Privacy, right to; Shield laws.

Privileged communication

DEFINITION: Communication that is protected by law from being disclosed or from being legally actionable by a third party

SIGNIFICANCE: Assertion of the privilege can be used to prevent access to confidential information and communications

Traditionally, communications made within certain types of relationships are protected by law from being disclosed to a third party. The legal protection that attaches to such communications is called a privilege. The privilege can be absolute or qualified. The types of relationships that are protected by the privilege are generally classified as special or fiduciary relationships. Special or fiduciary relationships are typically based on the existence of a special trust and confidence between individuals. Relationships that usually enjoy the protection of privileged communication include: husband and wife, attorney and client, physician and patient, therapist and patient, and cleric and parishioner. Whether a particular communication between parties in these relationships is actually protected by a privilege is generally determined by the existence of a statute providing for the protection. Privileged communication statutes vary among different legal systems but usually specify the nature and extent of the protection within the relationship. The privilege that attaches to privileged communications can generally be waived by consent or by making the communication in the presence of a party to whom the privilege does not apply.

Privileged communications can promote the public policy of protecting confidential communications within certain relationships, thereby promoting and encouraging freedom of speech. Providing legal protection for communication made within protected relationships contributes to the public good because it encourages open and honest communication in these relationships without the fear that the communication or the identity of the communicator might be disclosed to others.

The privilege can also be used as an instrument of restraint and censorship by preventing access to certain types of information. The privilege can be asserted to prevent public access to records, names, documents, and other information that might be of interest or benefit to the public. Whenever the privilege is asserted, it can deprive another party or the public of information that may be relevant, important, or useful. Thus the privilege can have the impact of restraining access to and censoring certain types of information. The public's right to know can be significantly frustrated when the privilege is asserted to restrain access to relevant information and data.

The law also protects communications made pursuant to certain legal and legislative activities, such as court and congressional proceedings. A statement made by an individual during these proceedings is generally absolutely privileged. Thus, the person who made the statement is protected from liability for defamation. The threat of legal liability for statements can have the impact of restraining the flow of information. Thus, the privilege encourages an open exchange of ideas and debate in judicial and congressional proceedings.

See also Courtrooms; Off-the-record information; Privacy, right to; Shield laws.

Project Censored

FOUNDED: 1976

TYPE OF ORGANIZATION: University-based media watchdog body

SIGNIFICANCE: Since its foundation, this nonprofit body has called attention to censorship in the news media in annual reports

Project Censored was founded at Sonoma State University in Northern California by Carl Jensen, an emeritus professor of communications studies at the university who served as the project's director for two decades. After he retired in 1996, Peter Phillips took over as the project's executive director. The project annually solicits information of national importance on issues that have been largely overlooked by the mainstream news media. From the hundreds of articles nominated each year by journalists, librarians, educators, and the general public, student researchers in a media seminar select the top twenty-five undercovered stories. Criteria used in the selection process include the amount of coverage a story has received, the national or international importance of the issue, the reliability of the source, and the potential impact the story may have.

Twenty-five stories are then submitted in synopsis form to a panel of judges who select the top ten censored stories of the year. The essential issue raised by the project is the failure of the mass media to provide the people with all the information they need to make informed decisions. The primary object of the project is to find, identify, and publicize stories on important issues that have been overlooked or underreported by the major news media. It hopes to stimulate journalists to provide more news coverage of undercovered issues and to encourage the general public to demand more coverage of those issues and to seek information from alternative sources.

Through the years the project has achieved international renown. The project publishes an annual yearbook on censorship—*Censored: The News That Didn't Make the News—And Why*. The project has stimulated discussion of news media self-censorship in journalism publications such as *Editor & Publisher*, *St. Louis Journalism Review*, *Associated Press Managing Editors News*, *The Quill*, *World Press Review*, and *American Journalism Review*. The latter described the project as a distant early warning system for society's problems, a tip sheet for investigative reporting, and as a moral force in American media.

Project Censored was also the model for Project Censored Canada, launched by the Canadian Association of Journalists and the Communication Department at Simon Fraser University in 1993.

See also Airline safety news; Automobile safety news; Journalism reviews; Junk food news; News media censorship; Pesticide industry; Presidency, U.S.; Project Censored Canada; Simpson, O. J., case; Toxic waste news.

Project Censored Canada

FOUNDED: 1993

TYPE OF ORGANIZATION: Nonpartisan collaborative scholarly and public interest research body

SIGNIFICANCE: This project assesses and publicizes significant blindspots in Canada's major national news media on an ongoing basis

Inspired by Project Censored in the United States—from which it is autonomous—and initially funded by the Goodwin's Foundation, Project Censored Canada was founded in 1993 by Bill Doskoch, a representative of the Canadian Association of Journalists (CAJ). Since then it has been directed by Robert Hackett, James Winter, and Donald Gutstein, with Richard Gruneau as a consultant. The project was created as a partnership among the CAJ, the communication department at Burnaby's Simon Fraser University, and (since 1994) the University of Windsor's department of communications studies. Each year students at both universities research hundreds of stories nominated as under-reported that are published in alternative periodicals, major newspapers' back pages, books from small presses, and elsewhere. About twenty such stories selected for their intrinsic significance and validity and for their lack of mainstream media coverage are forwarded to a national panel. Made up of journalists, scholars, and public figures, this panel reduces the nominations to a "top ten" list, which always attracts wider media attention.

Since receiving a three-year grant from Canada's Social Sciences and Humanities Research Council in 1994, the project has broadened its research to identify general blindspots in Canada's news agenda, particularly as they relate to scholarly hypotheses about influences on the media. The project also

---

IMPORTANT STORIES THAT FAILED TO MAKE BIG NEWS IN CANADA

- Tobacco companies and cigarette smuggling
- Media and corporate ties to political power
- Collapse of the cod fisheries and Canadian mismanagement
- Oil company interests behind humanitarian efforts in Somalia
- Canada's relationship with Indonesia's repressive regime
- NAFTA's economic constitution for North America forged in secrecy
- White-collar and corporate crime overlooked by the media
- Canadian arms exports contradict the nation's image as a peace-keeper
- The need of Atomic Energy of Canada Limited for $300 million in tax money to clean up old nuclear sites

Source: Project Censored Canada

produces yearbooks and annual "junk food news" lists, and it has surveyed journalists and interest groups about the news agenda.

The project seeks to raise debate about the extent and nature of censorship in Canada's news system. It broadens traditional notions of censorship as governmental sanctions against publication, to encompass self-censorship within newsrooms, and unwitting structural censorship which may result from concentrated ownership, commercial pressures, or other aspects of media organization.

See also Canada; Junk food news; News media censorship; Project Censored.

Prokofiev, Sergei

BORN: April 23, 1891, Sontsovka, Ukraine, Russia
DIED: March 5, 1953, Moscow, Soviet Union
IDENTIFICATION: Prominent Soviet composer
SIGNIFICANCE: Despite his international reputation, Prokofiev endured periods of official disfavor under Joseph Stalin after he returned to his native Soviet Union

Prokofiev, who has remained among the most widely performed of twentieth century composers, made two fateful decisions: first, to emigrate from the fledgling Soviet Union in 1918, and then to return to it permanently in 1936. During his years in the West, Prokofiev toured the world, winning acclaim as a composer and conductor.

Once back in the Soviet Union, he gained both official approval and censure. His return coincided with Soviet dictator Joseph Stalin's Great Purges, during which many leading artists and intellectuals were harassed, imprisoned, and even executed. A scathing review in *Pravda* of Dmitri Shostakovich's opera, *Lady Macbeth of Mtsensk*, for example, entitled "Chaos Instead of Music," signaled Stalin's assertion of total control over Soviet arts and culture. Twelve years later, in January, 1948, accumulated resentment against Prokofiev erupted at a conference of musicians called by Stalin's minister for the arts. Despite his declining health, Prokofiev had been forced to attend the conference, where he came under attack for his alleged determination to be "modern" and individualistic.

Ironically, Prokofiev died a mere few hours before Stalin's death finally ended the Soviet Union's worst period of cultural and artistic repression.

See also Music; Shostakovich, Dmitri; Soviet Union; Stalin, Joseph; Zhdanov, Andrei.

Propaganda

DEFINITION: Messages that are consciously or unconsciously tendentious or deceptive
SIGNIFICANCE: In its malign forms, propaganda is often intimately interconnected with censorship, on which it depends for its effectiveness

Links between propaganda and censorship can be seen most clearly by tracing the development of three distinct meanings of the term. In 1622 Pope Gregory XV founded the *Sacra Congregatio de Propaganda Fide* (Congregation for the Propagation of the Faith) to provide centralized control of the missionary activities of the church. The word "propaganda" entered the language from this source and initially denoted messages that are consciously tendentious, or "biased," in the sense that they argue for a particular viewpoint. There is nothing intrinsically wrong with the dissemination of tendentious messages. To the contrary, the American political and legal systems are both grounded in a conflict notion of truth that presupposes a clash among biased viewpoints. It is worth noting that nearly all of the most venerated examples of American public discourse, from the Declaration of Independence to Martin Luther King, Jr.'s "I Have a Dream" speech, qualify as propaganda in this sense. Thus propaganda was originally a neutral or even positive term, and this connotation persisted in American usage through the 1920's in fields such as advertising and public relations, as suggested by the title of an influential 1926 article by Bruce Bliven: "Let's Have More Propaganda." Among Marxists "propaganda" is still used in a positive sense to describe a kind of educational activity that, in Georgi Plekhanov's classic formulation, "conveys many ideas to one or a few persons."

Negative Connotations. A second common usage, however, reserves the term "propaganda" for messages that are not only tendentious, but also false or deceptive. This reflects the ancient Aristotelian distinction between two fundamentally different forms of persuasion: rhetoric, which is both rational and ethical, and sophistry, which is neither. Although this wholly negative meaning had emerged by the mid-nineteenth century, it became dominant in the Western democracies only in the aftermath of World War I. As the first "total war," this conflict was unprecedented in its scope, intensity, and destructiveness. Most of its European belligerents resorted to state-sponsored propaganda in efforts to influence world opinion and sustain popular support in the face of extraordinary losses and privations. In particular, British and French propaganda sought to place all blame for the war on the Central Powers, and it often featured lurid accounts of atrocities committed by the brutal and barbaric "Huns." When the United States entered the war in April, 1917, President Woodrow Wilson, who had just won re-election on the slogan "He kept us out of war," was faced with the task of uniting a skeptical and deeply divided public. He responded by establishing the Committee on Public Information (CPI), which blanketed the country with prowar propaganda that often echoed British and French themes. In its brief existence, the CPI distributed more than 100 million pamphlets and posters, provided newspapers throughout the country with a steady stream of ready-to-print articles, editorials, and cartoons, and fielded a force of 75,000 "Four Minute Men" to speak at public gatherings on themes selected by the Wilson Administration. It also organized numerous local "Americanization Committees" to instruct various non-English ethnic minorities on the views deemed appropriate to their new status as Americans.

When hostilities ended in November, 1918, the propaganda activities became the focus of widespread criticism in the United States (and elsewhere) fueled both by the discovery that many claims about responsibility for the war and German atrocities had been false, and by a growing uneasiness among prominent intellectuals, such as John Dewey and Walter Lippmann, about government manipulation of information and public opinion. These concerns were strongly reinforced by the course of events in at least three areas over the next two decades. The first was the rapid growth of the fascist and communist movements in Europe. Both movements openly endorsed the systematic use of propaganda, often including techniques widely seen as deceitful. The second was the introduction and rapid diffusion of radio, an instantaneous mass medium of truly national scope that seemed to offer propagandists unlimited opportunities to mold the beliefs of a defenseless public. Finally, the period after 1918 was marked by the rise to public prominence of the intellectual ideal of objectivity. Closely associated with the phenomenal success and prestige of the natural sciences, objectivity was enthusiastically embraced as an inherently superior alternative to subjective bias, especially in the new "profession" of journalism, where it was enshrined as a core value. The result was that propaganda, whether used to denote deceitful or merely tendentious messages, acquired the universally pejorative connotation that persists in American usage to this day.

Effectiveness of Propaganda. It is generally recognized that propaganda is least effective when its recipients are consciously aware of its persuasive intent, as the message is then subjected to immediate and searching critical scrutiny and propagandists can be held accountable for the veracity of their claims. Accordingly, in those (nondemocratic) societies that have sought to use propaganda to instill uniformity of thought and action in their citizens—most notably Nazi Germany, the Soviet Union, and other Marxist countries—there have been concerted efforts to minimize these factors. In particular, awareness can be blunted by expanding the scope of propaganda to encompass all forms of public discourse and expression, including education, the arts, popular culture, and even religion. More important, critical scrutiny is minimized through the rigorous exclusion of all competing viewpoints, and it is in this sense that censorship is the handmaiden of propaganda. Finally, all significant power is concentrated in the hands of the ruling elite, to whom the propagandist is solely accountable.

Censorship and Propaganda. Such arrangements are typically justified on the grounds that because the "truth" is known (at least to the ruling elite) it is only reasonable to seek to instill it in the masses and to exclude competing viewpoints, which are, by definition, both false and subversive. This attitude contrasts sharply with the view of propaganda and censorship in the United States and other democratic countries. Given commitment to the belief that truth is most likely to be discovered through open debate in the free marketplace of ideas, democracies must tolerate and even encourage propaganda, including some that is putatively deceitful. However, acceptance of propaganda has been grudging at best, and in this century it has often been accompanied by efforts to ensure that the marketplace functions effectively. The principal focus of these efforts has been to prevent the domination of the debate by the views of powerful established groups—especially politicians, government agencies, businessmen, corporations, and advertisers—by working to ensure that exaggerated, self-serving, and deceitful claims from these sources are exposed as such and that the views of the less powerful—especially minorities and marginal groups—are included in the marketplace. These activities, in turn, have fueled a continuing controversy about whether certain views are so obviously false and destructive that they should be excluded from public discourse.

In the period after World War I, concern about the harmful effects of propaganda was greatest among members of the political Left. One result was the "propaganda analysis" movement, an effort by politically progressive scholars to educate the public about the dangers of propaganda, especially the manipulation of news and information by corporate and government interests in the United States and, as World War II approached, by Nazi Germany. After the founding of the Institute for Propaganda Analysis in 1937 under the leadership of Professor Clyde R. Wilson of Columbia University, the movement was highly successful in introducing antipropaganda training in the schools and encouraging publication of a large body of scholarly research on the subject in the two decades following World War II.

A second initiative was the introduction of the new "social responsibility" model of journalism outlined in the 1947 report of the Commission on Freedom of the Press (the Hutchins Commission). Under this view, the principal duty of the journalist is not merely to provide an objective account of the conflict of ideas but to work actively to improve society. This is accomplished in part by seeking out the views of neglected groups, but more generally by conducting a continuous critique of American society in order to call attention to problems, inequities, and failures that must be resolved.

First evident in reports of the Civil Rights movement, social responsibility journalism reached maturity in coverage of the Vietnam War and the Watergate scandal and culminated in the new "corrective journalism" adopted by most of the major national news media in the 1992 presidential campaign. Although most visible in stories explicitly devoted to evaluating campaign advertisements, this approach also figured prominently in routine campaign coverage, with many journalists using the same news story both to report and, on their own authority, to "correct" a candidate's claims.

Finally, the period since World War I has been marked by the introduction of numerous government controls on public discourse. These include restrictions on "foreign" propaganda, the Federal Communications Commission's now-defunct fairness doctrine, and various constraints on commercial speech and advertising imposed by agencies such as the Federal Trade Commission, Securities and Exchange Commission, and Food and Drug Administration.

New Views on Propaganda. Since the mid-1960's discussions of propaganda in America have been dominated by two very different trends. One trend began with the gradual elimination of antipropaganda training and a sharp decline in academic research on deceitful propaganda. Several factors appear to have produced these changes. At the most basic level, the defeat of fascism in 1945 meant that the most egregious new examples of deceitful propaganda came largely from the Soviet Union and other Marxist countries. Perhaps out of sympathy with the general goals of Marxism or a desire to avoid any association with the strident anticommunism of the Cold War and the excesses of McCarthyism, progressive scholars chose not to focus on propaganda from these sources. In addition, the growing acceptance in academic circles of the doctrines of cultural and moral relativism rendered judgments of deceitfulness problematic. But the most important factor was the rapid dissemination of a new "cultural" definition of propaganda. Grounded in the work of the French cultural critic Jacques Ellul, this view expands the meaning of propaganda to include virtually all forms of tendentious communication in a technological society, including, in particular, messages reflecting unconscious biases. Thus, huge areas of social discourse, including much of education, politics, popular entertainment, journalism, and the arts, can be seen as propagandistic because they disseminate unexamined values and assumptions. Broadly compatible with the basic tenets of postmodern criticism and neo-Marxist notions of hegemony and false consciousness, this view has dominated scholarly discussion of propaganda since about 1970.

The second trend is a growing reaction against propaganda among members of the political Right. Initially focused on communist propaganda in the aftermath of World War II, conservative concerns began to shift in the mid-1960's to the activities of what John Corry called the "dominant culture" of the artistic and intellectual elite. In this view, the members of the dominant culture are united by progressive political and social values and a commitment to social activism. More important, they exercise de facto control over most of the major channels of communication in American society. In particular, conservatives argue that social responsibility journalism has produced pervasively biased coverage that is dominated by liberal issues and concerns and systematically distorts or excludes conservative views. They also point to the growth of "didactic entertainment," beginning with the popular television series *All in the Family*, that sought not only to entertain (often by ridiculing traditional values), but also to educate its audience about contemporary social issues and the appropriate new (liberal) attitudes and behaviors that are required to address them.

Finally, conservatives have criticized the growing politicization of education, especially in the arts, humanities, and social sciences, that seeks to impose a revisionist orthodoxy centered on the contributions of women, minorities, and other "neglected" groups and enforced by stringent campus speech codes and required training in the desirability of "diversity" and multiculturalism. Because all these activities combine systematic propaganda with perceived attempts to suppress opposing views, they are now commonly described as manifestations of "political correctness," a term borrowed from totalitarian Marxism.

Responses to political correctness include the proliferation of alternative sources of news and information such as talk radio, widespread calls for a return to "family values" in entertainment programming, and efforts by groups such as the National Association of Scholars to reinstitute traditional ideals of academic freedom, rational scholarship, and liberal education.
—*Ted J. Smith III*

See also Advertising as the target of censorship; Art; Communism; Fairness doctrine; Foreign Agents Registration Act of 1938; Opera; Police states; Political campaigning; Radio Martí; Talk shows; Vietnam War; World War I.

BIBLIOGRAPHY

Richard A. Nelson's *A Chronology and Glossary of Propaganda in the United States* (Westport, Conn.: Greenwood Press, 1995) offers an exhaustive historical overview of American propaganda, while *Propanganda for War* (Jefferson, N.C.: McFarland, 1996), by Stewart H. Ross, focuses on U.S. government propaganda during World War I. *Propaganda: A Pluralistic Perspective*, edited by Ted J. Smith (New York: Praeger, 1989), includes an array of different perspectives on propaganda and studies of several key issues. J. Michael Sproule's *Channels of Propaganda* (Bloomington, Ind.: Edinfo, 1994) provides a history and analysis of propaganda from a progressive point of view. *Propaganda and Persuasion* (2d ed. Newbury Park, Calif.: Sage Publications, 1992), by Garth S. Jowett and Victoria O'Donnell, examines propaganda as a form of communication. Jacques Ellul's *Propaganda* (New York: Alfred A. Knopf, 1965) is the primary source for the cultural definition of propaganda.

Prostitution

DEFINITION: Practice of engaging in sexual activity for payment

SIGNIFICANCE: Although prostitution has existed in most cultures, overt depictions of prostitutes in literature and the arts have only been tolerated in modern times

Sometimes called "the oldest profession," prostitution has existed for as long as written records have been kept. Descriptions of prostitutes have been found in records in ruins of the ancient cities of the Babylonian civilization. It has been found in most cultures, but even where it has existed attitudes toward selling sexual favors have varied widely. Similarly, depictions of prostitution in mainstream works of fiction and in poetry have mirrored larger societal attitudes toward issues such as the differing status of men and women, human sexuality, class differences, and personal freedom.

Prostitution in Literature. Societies have often placed restrictions on how prostitutes may be portrayed in literature, on the stage, and in film. Until the modern age, however, these restrictions were more often informal than formal. That is, formal censorship seldom concerned itself with depictions of prostitution or sexuality, unless such depictions were part of a larger work that government or established religion viewed as subversive or heretical. Following the invention of the printing press in Europe the Roman Catholic church began requiring publishers to submit manuscripts for approval prior to publication. If censors found that a book contained immoral content they could forbid its circulation. Nevertheless, for many decades authorities showed more concern about radical scientific and political ideas than they did about bawdy characters in literature.

Thus, references to prostitutes and houses of prostitution were common in much early modern literature. Elizabethan and Jacobean playwrights included references to "trollops" in their work, often assigning leading roles to characters who were prostitutes. Whether they used prostitutes for comic relief or for dramatic tension, authors generally portrayed prostitutes as unabashedly sensual and free of pretension, far more honest than their supposedly more virtuous contemporaries. Twentieth century literary critics argued over whether matter-of-fact portrayals of whores by writers were meant as subtle condemnations of the moral hypocrisy of their times, or served merely as evidence of the decadence prevalent in seventeenth century England. Whatever the playwrights' intent, however, literary efforts that were bawdy rather than politically oriented generally were free from government censorship, as were the lively eighteenth century novels of authors such as Henry Fielding and Daniel Defoe.

In addition to formal censorship, a society's overall values and beliefs dictate what material the general public will accept in a play or a story and what it will reject. This is one reason why depictions of male prostitutes were rare in material meant for mainstream audiences in both North America and Europe. Depictions of prostitutes that differ too widely from commonly held beliefs about them have generally been relegated to obscurity, or condemned as pornographic. For example, the images of prostitutes in the popular fiction of nineteenth century French author Guy de Maupassant corresponded closely with a reality that many of his readers thought they knew. At the time prostitution was both legal and common in urban areas in Europe. Maupassant's short stories, although occasionally criticized for their frank sensuality, nonetheless enjoyed wide readership on the Continent.

Prostitution in Different Cultures. Not all cultures were as open in their acceptance of explicit depictions of prostitution in literature. By the nineteenth century readers in the English-speaking countries proved much more strait-laced than the French. Authorities in Great Britain and the United States suppressed publication of material they believed offended standards of public decency. Spicy stories that were openly published in France were forced underground elsewhere. Prostitutes in mainstream literature vanished, or were referenced obliquely, appearing only as dissolute fallen women sinking ever lower and shunned by decent elements of polite society. The cheerful whores of Jacobean times became consumptive, opium-addicted victims forced into lives of moral depravity, with death as their only release. Reports in cheap tabloid periodicals, such as *Police Gazette*, reinforced these stereotypes while titillating male readers with salacious details of investigations into "white slavery" rings. Thus, by the beginning of the twentieth century the image of the prostitute that emerged in popular culture in the United States was that of a woman, occasionally good-hearted, forced to sell sex through circumstances beyond her control. Seduced and betrayed by unscrupulous men, or, even worse, kidnapped by white slavers who turned innocent girls into opium addicts, prostitutes were depicted in popular culture as young, female, and, almost universally, as victims.

The image of fallen woman was not easily contradicted. For example, in 1900 when American author Theodore Dreiser painted a picture in his first novel, *Sister Carrie*, of a woman who used her sexual attractiveness to climb socially, readers were so shocked that the book was quickly suppressed. Following the success of Dreiser's subsequent work, his publisher re-issued *Sister Carrie*, but critics still denounced it as unnecessarily coarse.

Prostitution in Films. The development of films in the early twentieth century provided another medium for depictions of prostitution. Self-censorship by the entertainment industry, however, often led to its being mentioned only indirectly, just as mainstream literature had carefully skirted the topic in the past. For many years characters such as saloon women in western movies were never shown engaging in activities that would indicate the historical truth that their duties often included providing sexual favors to male customers.

The sexual revolution of the 1960's contributed to a loosening of restrictions on depictions of prostitution in both literature and film. For example, by the 1980's television scriptwriters even routinely included streetwalkers as background characters in television series such as *Night Court*. In the 1990's *Pretty Woman*, a film that would have been unthinkable thirty years earlier retold the Cinderella story by making its heroine (Julia Roberts) a whore; it was a resounding box office hit. Some feminist scholars deplored the film's adherence to old stereotypes of the female prostitute as a passive victim rescued only because she happened to be beautiful;

Suspected prostitutes eye a potential customer in Rock Springs, Wyoming, in 1978. During the 1980's a greater social tolerance of prostitution made once-taboo scenes similar to this acceptable even on television. (AP/Wide World Photos)

however, other scholars noted that *Pretty Woman* indicated the growing willingness of the general public to accept prostitutes as real people who no longer fit the Victorian stereotype of the "fallen" woman. References to prostitution in popular television series reflected this latter reality as more programs, such as *Wings* and *The John LaRoquette Show* employed plot lines revolving around call girls who more closely resembled school teachers and attorneys than they did the pathetic, foul-mouthed creatures clad in tacky clothing occupying holding cells on *Hill Street Blues* only a few years earlier. Depictions of prostitution still made it clear that selling sex was not socially condoned behavior, but by removing explanations such as a visible pimp or an obvious drug addiction, writers also removed the stereotype of the female prostitute as passive victim.

—*Nancy Farm Mannikko*

See also Adultery; *Catcher in the Rye, The*; Drama and theater; Dreiser, Theodore; *Fanny Hill, The Memoirs of*; Fielding, Henry; *Maggie: A Girl of the Streets*; Maupassant, Guy de; Nudity; Pornography; Sex in the arts.

BIBLIOGRAPHY

The Invention of Pornography: Obscenity and the Origins of Modernity, 1500-1800 (Cambridge, Mass.: MIT Press, 1993), edited by Lynn Hunt, includes intriguing essays on the images of prostitutes in early modern literature, a time period also covered by Anne M. Haselkorn in *Prostitution in Elizabethan and Jacobean Comedy* (Troy, N.Y.: Whitston Publishing, 1983). Nancy McCombs looks at changing images of prostitution in the late nineteenth and early twentieth centuries in *Earth Spirit, Victim, or Whore? The Prostitute in German Literature, 1880-1925* (New York: P. Lang, 1986). James Robert Parish provides information on more recent depictions of prostitutes in *Prostitution in Hollywood Films: Plots, Critiques, Casts, and Credits for 389 Theatrical and Made-for-Television Releases* (Jefferson, N.C.: McFarland, 1992). *Sexual Knowledge, Sexual Science: The History of Attitudes to Sexuality* (New York: Cambridge University Press, 1994), an anthology edited by Roy Porter and Mikulas Teich, reviews attitudes toward sexuality from antiquity to the twentieth century.

Protest music

DEFINITION: Musical work with extramusical significance that criticizes or protests against political, economic, or social factors outside the direct control of the composer or performer

SIGNIFICANCE: Protest music has been censored from the earliest times

Although many people connect protest music with the folk-music revivals of the 1940's and 1960's, and many connect musical censorship with rock 'n' rap lyrics during the 1980's and 1990's, both musical protest and censorship have existed since the beginnings of music itself. The first mention of music as having political and social power was made by Plato in his *Republic* in the fourth century B.C.E. This also may be the first mention of censorship, as Plato advocates prohibiting innovative music because it might hurt the state.

It is difficult to study censorship of protest music prior to the modern technological advances that have enabled per-

formers to record their music because the act of censoring frequently destroyed any documentation of the work or stopped its creation altogether. In addition, the traditional system of economic support for musicians inhibited the creation of any art that questioned or criticized those in power. Little record of politically censored protest music survives from before the twentieth century.

Patronage as Censorship. Much of the Western music written before the nineteenth century was produced under a system of patronage that was not conducive to the creation of songs that could be construed as critical. Literate musicians capable of writing down their songs made their livings either by working for churches or for courts of rich nobles; since their livelihoods depended on the good graces of their employers, few of them would have dared publicly to complain or criticize those in power, or record their complaints in writing. After the invention of the printing press in the fifteenth century, the licensing of printers was another way that political powers had to censor works; those who printed unflattering or otherwise unacceptable works could easily lose their license to print anything else.

Even after patronage ceased to be the major form of economic support for professional musicians, economic and political censorship continued to discourage the creation of works that might be critical. Giuseppe Verdi, one of nineteenth century Europe's most popular composers, both during and after his life, struggled long and hard with the Italian censors before he could stage his opera *Rigoletto* (1851). While the work was not an intentional piece of social protest, it did present an unflattering portrait of an Italian noble. Verdi was upset by the censors, but he nevertheless made the required changes to his story so that it could be performed and he could realize the money he had earned from writing it. This type of censorship inhibited the creation of any types of protest or politically sensitive work. Because professional musicians' livelihoods depended upon the successful productions of their works, musicians were hesitant to create protest work that could not have passed the censors.

Several other countries in Europe maintained strict control over the publication and dissemination of print matter, including music during the nineteenth century. Austria's bureau of censorship, established in the eighteenth century, exercised extensive control over moral, political, and religious topics. Music with even vague political or social connotations was suppressed from both publication and performance. In 1779, for example, the bureau halted the dissemination of a song whose text was unflattering to the king of Prussia and forbade the performance of a work entitled *Friedensymphonie*. Scattered written court documents indicate that specific musical pieces were condemned; however, because of the suppression inherent in acts of censorship, the music itself no longer exists, making it impossible to know how much protest music was suppressed in this way.

Early Music. Although economic forces frequently inhibited professional musicians from composing politically sensitive music, musicians not bound by the patronage system were less subject to censorship pressures. One of the earliest examples of what might be considered protest music is in the medieval work known as the *Roman du Fauvel*, a long satirical poem by Gervais de Bus, a fourteenth century French royal clerk. The name "Fauvel" for a horse or an ass is made up of the initials of the vices *Flaterie* (flattery), *Avarice* (greed), *Vilanie* (villainy), *Variété* (fickleness), *Envie* (envy), and *Lascheté* (lust). The work itself comments on the social corruption of the noble classes. The poem survives in twelve manuscripts, one of which has more than two hundred songs that were included to supplement Bus's social critique.

The unwritten repertoires of the popular wandering minstrels of these early eras also presumably contained much political satire and social critique, and some of the oldest folk songs that have survived present early examples of protest songs. One type of folk song was the broadside ballad, in which new texts written to familiar old tunes were printed on large folio sheets called broadsides. These were popular in England from the sixteenth through the eighteenth centuries, and in America in the eighteenth century. The texts of these songs could be witty, satirical, and critical. In the early years of the broadsides the English monarchy controlled their printing closely through licensing and royal proclamations. Later, when governments no longer controlled the presses, they found other ways to censor the songs.

In 1728 John Gay's *The Beggar's Opera* opened to great popular acclaim. The songs of this work were all broadside ballads, for Gay had written new words to old favorite popular tunes to provide the music for his work. Many of the lyrics were satirical, and many were political, criticizing the government, in general, and Sir Robert Walpole in particular. The satire in *The Beggar's Opera* was subtle enough that it was a month before the press reported on "the most venomous allegorical libel against the G[overnment] that hath appeared for many years past." No immediate action was taken, possibly because of the immense popularity the work enjoyed. However, Gay's next work, *Polly*, a less subtle and more satirical sequel to *The Beggar's Opera*, was suppressed by the government and not allowed to be staged. The government was not, however, able to stop its publication in 1729.

American Folk Songs. The English colonists who settled the new world in the seventeenth and eighteenth centuries brought their traditions of broadside balladry with them. Protest lyrics flourished in this new milieu. Protest songs composed between the eighteenth and the twentieth centuries included anti-British colonial songs, antiaristocracy songs, antislavery songs, antiwar songs, antidiscrimination songs, labor protest songs, agrarian protest songs, and depression-era songs. After the American Revolution and the adoption of the U.S. Constitution, the First Amendment protected these songs and their creators from official political censorship.

For professional musicians, however, money still served as censor. Because ultimate economic powers have traditionally been under the control of the white population in this country, African American musicians have been especially subject to economic censorship. In the twentieth century, publishing and recording companies have been hesitant to handle racially sensitive material. In 1939, for example, at the first height of

Billie Holiday's fame and popularity, her publisher, Columbia Records, refused to record her hit song "Strange Fruit." The lyrics of this song describe bodies of lynched black men as "strange fruit" that hang from Southern trees. After a smaller label, Commodore Records, did release it, many radio stations refused to play it.

African American blues and spirituals in the nineteenth century were not subject to direct censorship since they were only transmitted orally in closed circles. The texts of recorded blues in the twentieth century seem to be primarily apolitical, but this is probably due more to economic forces than creative ones. In 1954 J. B. Lenoir recorded "Eisenhower Blues," which protested the rising unemployment among black workers; no radio stations played the song, however, and it was soon withdrawn. Afterward, no American labels would record Lenoir's blues protest songs.

American Folksingers and the Communist Party. Although politically oriented art has always been theoretically sanctioned and protected by the First Amendment of the U.S. Constitution, in the 1950's, the government came perilously close to state-imposed censorship when the House Committee on Un-American Activities (HUAC) held hearings that blacklisted many outspoken artists. Several prominent folksingers were silenced in this way.

In the late 1930's and 1940's, partly as a result of government-sponsored folk-art collection projects, rural American folk music was becoming more popular in cities. As urban intellectuals turned to the ideals of communism for solutions to social problems, musicians were turning folk songs into social propaganda. Several folksingers with strong communist connections, including Pete Seeger and Woody Guthrie, wrote new texts to old songs in the best broadside tradition, as well as new songs in a folk style, and modern American protest music was born. The federal government officially identified some of these folksingers as "political deviants" as early as 1941. In 1947 HUAC began investigating folksingers. Over the next several years many singers, artists, writers, and actors were accused of being communists. In 1950 the anticommunist magazine *Counterattack* published the book *Red Channels*, which listed the names of many musicians in the entertainment industry. The explicit purpose of this book was as a guide for employers, telling them which entertainers not to hire. Many folksingers lost their ability to work as a direct result.

One of the most dramatic examples of the damage done to performers was the case of the Weavers, four singers, including Pete Seeger, Lee Hays, and Ronnie Gilbert, who joined forces in 1949. Their music combined political and apolitical songs. By 1951 they were a commercial success, with widely selling albums and performances on national television. After the publication of *Red Channels*, however, the group began having problems getting and keeping engagements. In 1951 they lost their booking on a major television program just three days before the broadcast. By the end of 1952 these tactics had effectively destroyed the group, which disbanded, leaving its individual members temporarily silenced. Although the communist "witch-hunts" ended by the late 1950's, their legacy lingered. Network television continued to blacklist Seeger until 1967, when the Smothers Brothers fought their network to have Seeger on their show.

After the late 1950's economic censorship continued to play a role in commercial music production, and most record companies were slow to accept that protest music could sell. While the folk-music revival of the 1960's was far more lucrative than folk music performances had been in earlier decades, initially there was less protest material. After the middle of the decade, students and civil-rights protesters sang many protest songs as rallying cries. Singers such as Bob Dylan, Joan Baez, and the group Peter, Paul, and Mary realized commercial success with mixed repertoires of folk songs, folk-style songs, and protest songs. Older protest singers, such as Seeger, lamented the fact that big commercial music publishers and recording companies were not interested in protest material. Despite the hesitancy of the music industry, some popular and folk-style singers, such as Holly Near and Tracy Chapman, achieved commercial success with predominantly protest-oriented material. Many other popular music, rock, rap, and hiphop musicians have recorded one or more 'socially conscious' numbers as well. —*Robin Armstrong*

See also Baez, Joan; Folk music; Guthrie, Woody; Music; Seeger, Pete; *Smothers Brothers Comedy Hour, The*; Weavers, the.

BIBLIOGRAPHY

Winton Calhoun, "John Gay: Censoring the Censor," *Writing and Censorship in Britain*, edited by Paul Hyland and Neil Sammell (London and New York: Routledge Press, 1992), describes the events surrounding official censorship of John Gay's broadside opera *Polly*, a satirical work protesting governmental corruption. R. Serge Denisoff, *Great Day Coming: Folk Music and the American Left*, (Urbana: University of Illinois Press, 1971), presents a useful introduction to the origins of twentieth century American protest music, the connection between folksingers and the Communist Party in the 1930's and 1940's, and the subsequent activities of the House Committee on Un-American Activities (HUAC). Alice M. Hanson, *Musical Life in Biedermeier Vienna* (London: Cambridge University Press, 1985), gives a thorough analysis of musical life in early nineteenth century Vienna, including a full chapter on the secret police and artistic censorship, and their effects on musicians at the time. *Rockin' the Boat: Mass Music and Mass Movements* (Boston: South End Press, 1992), edited by Reebee Garofalo, contains a set of essays on different types of protest music in the late twentieth century, including music outside the United States. David M. Rosen, *Protest Songs in America* (Westlake Village, Calif.: Aware Press, 1972), contains a discussion of protest songs in a historical context as well as many song texts.

Proudhon, Pierre-Joseph

BORN: January 15, 1809, Besançon, France
DIED: January 19, 1865, Paris, France
IDENTIFICATION: French social theorist
SIGNIFICANCE: The founder of modern anarchism, Proudhon was persecuted in France from the moment that he began to

write, and was imprisoned and exiled during the reign of Emperor Napoleon III

A self-educated man with a peasant background, Proudhon worked as a cowherd in his native Besançon. He then apprenticed as a printer, rising to become managing editor of *L'Impartiale*, a utopian socialist newspaper. However, he resigned after only one day on the job when he learned that each edition of the paper had to pass prior censorship by the prefect of police.

In 1839 Proudhon competed for an award from the Besançon Academy by writing an essay on the creation of the Sabbath as a day of rest by Moses. His essay not only did not win the prize, it was banned from publication by the prefect of police. A year later Proudhon wrote "What Is Property?" in which he coined the nineteenth century revolutionary slogan "property is theft." This work barely escaped public prosecution, but his subsequent essay "Warning to the Proprietors" was seized by the police and resulted in a nine-charge indictment, which included a charge of incitement to hatred of priests and judges. In 1842 a jury found him innocent because he was "working in a field of ideas inaccessible to ordinary people." The trial gave Proudhon both fame and a loyal readership for his anarchistic writings denouncing inequalities caused by property.

During the Revolution of 1848, Proudhon wrote for the paper *Le Répresentant*. After it was suppressed, he wrote for *Le Peuple*, using his columns vehemently to attack Louis Napoleon, the Bonepartist candidate for president of the republic, until its printing presses were smashed by the national guard. Proudhon went on to found a new paper, *Le Voix du peuple*, in which he continued his attacks on Louis Napoleon.

Following Louis Napoleon's electoral victory, Proudhon was charged with inciting antigovernment hatred, attacking property and the constitution, and provoking civil war—mostly due to the contents of his greatest work, *De la Justice dans le révolution et dans l'Eglise* (1858). His trial resulted in a three-year prison sentence, with much time spent in the isolation of solitary confinement.

From 1858 to 1862 Proudhon was permitted to go into exile in Belgium, but all his Belgium writings were banned in France. Ill and living in poverty, Proudhon was permitted to return to France in 1862, as Louis Napoleon—by then "emperor" of France—was undergoing a liberal shift. He received a full pardon, and he lived his few remaining years in Paris.

See also Bakunin, Mikhail Aleksandrovich; France; Goldman, Emma; Prior restraint.

Prynne, William

BORN: 1600, Swainswick, Somerset, England
DIED: October 24, 1669, London, England
IDENTIFICATION: English Puritan pamphleteer
SIGNIFICANCE: A prolific writer, Prynne encountered violent opposition, including torture, in response to his religious and social views

A lawyer educated at Oxford University, Prynne began writing as a young man, criticizing the growth of Roman Catholicism as well as a supposed decline in morals that he identified with the increasing popularity of such entertainments as the theater. Prynne's most famous work, *Histriomastix* (1632), an attack on the theater and female actors, landed him in the Court of Star Chamber in 1634 because it was regarded as critical of the queen. The archbishop of Canterbury, who was fond of the theater and fearful of violence incited by Puritan pamphlets, pushed for severe penalties. Prynne was heavily fined, had part of his ears cropped, and was imprisoned in the Tower of London, where, however, he continued to write. He was tried again in 1637, along with two other Puritan pamphleteers; heavily fined, he had the remainder of his ears cut off, the letters "S" and "L" (for seditious libeller) branded on his cheeks, and was exiled to the Channel Islands.

Many regarded Prynne as a martyr. Released in 1640, he made a triumphal procession to London. During the English civil war (1642-1648), his criticism of the Parliamentarian army that opposed Charles I resulted in his being ejected from Parliament in 1648. Protests against taxes earned him three years' imprisonment without trial. After his release in 1653, he was still critical of Oliver Cromwell, the Puritan leader who had been named lord protector of England. Prynne's last confrontation with authority came during the Restoration, when his attack on the Corporation Act (1662) earned him the censure of Parliament.

See also Courts and censorship law; Crop-ears; Drama and theater; English Commonwealth; Puritans; United Kingdom.

Pseudonyms, male

DEFINITION: Masculine pen names adopted by female writers
SIGNIFICANCE: Male pseudonyms have historically been used by female writers to overcome social attitudes that have discouraged them from writing for publication

Until the late nineteenth century, many Western societies considered it scandalous for women to write for publication. This attitude was more widespread in England and Europe than in America, but it prevailed almost everywhere. Three obstacles confronted women writers: getting their work published, having their published work taken seriously, and suffering reproach from family or society for being writers. For these reasons many women have published anonymously or under pen names. While some women have used female pseudonyms, or such anonymous sobriquets as "A Lady," those who have gone beyond personal narratives or domestic dramas to write about social and political issues have typically assumed male pseudonyms.

Among the best known of such writers is Mary Anne Evans, an English editor and novelist. Writing as "George Eliot," she produced several notable works of fiction, including *Adam Bede* (1859), *Silas Marner* (1861), and *Middlemarch* (1871-1872). Eliot also served as the actual, though not official, editor of the *Westminster Review* for three years, and she published numerous essays. In France, Amandine-Aurore-Lucile Dudevant wrote as "George Sand" during the same era; she created more than a hundred works, including highly regarded novels, plays, and collections of graceful essays and letters. A somewhat later example is the South African writer Olive Schreiner. Using the pseudonym "Ralph Iron," she wrote despite her husband's opposition. She is especially noted for *The Story of an African Farm* (1883), containing a challenge to accepted moral rules, and as an early opponent of apartheid. In America, Louisa May Alcott published *Little Women* (1868) and its sequels under her own name; later she was discovered to have also written lurid adventure stories as "A. S. Barnard."

As prejudice against women writers lessened in the twentieth century, the number using male pseudonyms decreased. On certain subjects and within some genres, however, it remained difficult for a woman writer to be respected. For example, in the 1950's Marijane Meaker wrote crime novels and lesbian romances under the name "Vin Packer." Science fiction in particular remained a male preserve for many years. Some women writers gained acceptance in this field with given names that are used by both sexes (for example, Marion Zimmer Bradley) or by adopting such a name (for example, Andre Norton). In the late 1970's, the well-regarded science fiction writer "James Tiptree" was revealed to be a woman named Alice Sheldon. Sheldon's unmasking at the height of the women's movement embarrassed critics who had praised Tiptree for "his" strong masculine voice.

By the 1980's and 1990's, the most common form of censorship by gender was probably self-censorship. A number of women writers still used pseudonyms—though not always male names—to conceal their writings on sexual or controversial topics from their families, employers, or friends. Curiously, the tables turned slightly as male writers used female pseudonyms to give their romance novels credibility.

See also Family; Literature; Outing; Sand, George; Women.

English novelist George Eliot—whose real name was Mary Ann Evans—was one of the most prominent women writers to use a male pseudonym. (Library of Congress)

Public Broadcasting Act of 1967

ENACTED: November 7, 1967

PLACE: United States (national)

SIGNIFICANCE: Although this law was designed to develop public broadcasting, its content restrictions and failure to designate a dedicated source of federal funding constrained public broadcasting's expressive freedom

The Public Broadcasting Act of 1967 has been credited with helping what had been known as educational radio and television evolve into a mature source of news, entertainment, and education. However, because some legislators were concerned that federal involvement in broadcasting might lead to an "Orwellian" government network used for propaganda purposes, the law also included two important content restrictions.

Section 399 prevented public broadcasters from editorializing or supporting political candidates. Although it allowed individual commentators to express opinions, this section constrained station managements from broadcasting their own opinions. Some congressional advocates of the provision contended that it would help insulate stations from political pressure to support particular issues or candidates. Other supporters acknowledged that they had been the targets of commercial press editorials in the past and welcomed the ability to restrain public broadcasting from editorializing. More than a decade later a consortium of groups challenged the constitutionality of section 399. In 1984 the U.S. Supreme Court voted 5-4 to overturn the provision as a violation of public broadcasters' First Amendment rights in *Federal Communications Commission v. League of Women Voters*. The Court's majority opinion stated that the value of editorial contributions to the marketplace of ideas outweighed any harm that public broadcasters might suffer if their editorials angered politicians.

Another restrictive provision of the Public Broadcasting Act required all programs or series funded by the Corporation for Public Broadcasting (CPB)—which had been created by the act to channel federal dollars to public stations—to maintain objectivity and balance. Demanding such balance was viewed as a means of ensuring that public stations would not serve as propaganda voices for those supporting one side of controversial issues. In 1975 the Federal Communications Commission (FCC), responding to a complaint over two allegedly biased public television programs, held that it could enforce no stronger requirement than the fairness doctrine—an FCC regulation calling for balanced coverage of issues over a station's overall programming. The U.S. Court of Appeals for the District of Columbia upheld that decision, ruling that requiring the FCC to demand balance within individual programs or series would threaten broadcasters' expressive freedom. That case did not end congressional attempts to mandate greater objectivity within public broadcasting.

In 1992 Congress attached an amendment to the CPB funding bill, requiring the CPB to ensure that public television programming was balanced and objective, and to report annually to Congress on its progress toward achieving such balance. Congress' action illustrates the Public Broadcasting Act's greatest threat to public broadcasters' freedom of speech:

its failure to provide for any source of dedicated federal funding. Requiring public broadcasters to depend on congressional appropriations for a significant part of their operating budgets meant that legislators unhappy with public broadcasting programming could manifest their displeasure by reducing the system's funding. This power was exemplified in 1972 when President Richard Nixon, angered by what he perceived as public television's liberal bias, vetoed CPB's appropriations bill.

See also Broadcast media; Fairness doctrine; National Public Radio; Nixon, Richard M.; Orwell, George; Propaganda; Public Broadcasting Service.

Public Broadcasting Service (PBS)

FOUNDED: 1969

TYPE OF ORGANIZATION: Agency created by the Corporation for Public Broadcasting (CPB) to maintain connections among public television stations and to provide programming

SIGNIFICANCE: PBS's dependency on the federal government and corporate donors for funding has limited its broadcasting freedom

The Corporation for Public Broadcasting created PBS to interconnect and serve public television stations. The Ford Foundation was apparently heavily involved in the creation of PBS, and this has led to questions about corporate control over the service from its beginning. There was also potential for government control, since the Public Broadcasting Act of 1967, which chartered the CPB, required objectivity and balance in programming. Nevertheless, from its beginning PBS has offered information and points of view not available through commercial television stations. Regular programs such as *Washington Week in Review*, *Banks and the Poor*, and *Black Perspective on the News* have provided unique perspectives that were often critical of the U.S. government.

In the early 1970's, however, President Richard Nixon became upset with public television, which he regarded as overly liberal and excessively critical of his administration. In 1972 he vetoed the annual appropriations bill for public broadcasting. Fearful of losing funding, the CPB either canceled or toned down many PBS programs that might be regarded as antigovernment or anti-Nixon Administration.

After Ronald Reagan was elected president in 1980, PBS again suffered a tightening of the federal purse. During his campaign Reagan had identified federal spending cuts as a major goal; after his election he made it clear that government spending on public broadcasting would be reduced. Funding reductions in 1981 led PBS to search for alternative sources. Donations from business corporations, always part of the financing of public television, became even more central.

Greater reliance on business money led to greater business control over programming. In the early 1980's, for example, WNET in New York aired "Hungry for Profit," a program about multinational corporations buying up land in Third World countries. Angered by this program, Gulf and Western—which had been a major corporate underwriter for WNET—accused the station of being antibusiness and withdrew its financial support from the station.

A 1986 study of public television in the United States and Britain, conducted by the British Broadcasting Corporation, found that corporate underwriting tended to bias funding toward noncontroversial programs.

By the 1990's PBS was experiencing financial pressures from both business and government. In 1992 Republican senator Robert Dole of Kansas sponsored an amendment to the Public Broadcasting Act requiring PBS and its sister organization, National Public Radio, to review their programming regularly and to report to Congress on their progressing in providing "balanced coverage" as a condition for continued federal funding.

The experience of PBS illustrates a central problem of the electronic media. The costs of television or radio time can render free expression extremely expensive, making financing itself a possible source of censorship.

See also Broadcast media; Fairness doctrine; National Public Radio; Nixon, Richard M.; Reagan, Ronald; Television; Television networks.

Public service announcements

Definition: Advertisements targeted at specific audiences advocating a course of action meant to benefit the public at large

Significance: Because public service announcements are often produced and distributed by government agencies, they can be targets for censorship by those who believe them to conflict with prevailing political ideology

Hundreds of millions of dollars worth of broadcast time and print space are annually devoted to public service announcement (PSA) campaigns. Research has shown that PSAs can contribute to personal behavioral change, provided that they use simple and direct messages targeted at specific audiences. Most public service campaigns present fairly innocuous messages, encouraging members of the audience to do such things as wear automobile seat belts, get regular medical checkups, or stop smoking.

The "America Responds to AIDS" campaign, begun in the mid-1980's by the U.S. Department of Health and Human Services and the U.S. Centers for Disease Control, was criticized for its explicit symbolism. The campaign's "America Responds . . ." radio announcements spoke frankly about illicit drug use and sexual infidelity; a television PSA featured an animated condom that "walked" across a floor and jumped into a bed, where it slid under the covers between the bed's two occupants.

Supporters cheered the campaign's frankness, but others criticized its advocacy of condom use and failure to promote sexual abstinence. The campaign was attacked by conservative members of Congress, who agreed that it was improper for government funds to be used to create PSAs some people found objectionable. Many broadcasters refused to air the spots, claiming they were inappropriate for their audiences.

See also Advertising as the target of censorship; Alcoholic beverages; Birth control education; Political correctness; Smoking; Symbolic speech.

Publick Occurrences

Date: September 25, 1690

Place: Boston, Massachusetts

Significance: The first newspaper published in North America was immediately suppressed by government, ostensibly because it had not been licensed, but more likely because of its political content

Printer Benjamin Harris planned to produce a monthly journal when he launched the first newspaper in America—*Publick Occurrences, Both Foreign and Domestick*—on Thursday, September 25, 1690. But Massachusetts governor Simon Bradstreet and the colony's provisional governing council ordered the suppression of the newspaper four days later, and there was never a second issue.

The officials wrote that the newspaper had been published "without authority," meaning that Harris had not gotten permission from the governor to publish. Before licensing a publication, the governor had to approve or censor each item planned for publication—what was later called prior restraint. But it was more than a technicality that caused the paper's suppression, for the council also announced their "high resentment and Disallowance of said Pamphlet, and order that the same be Suppressed and called in." Harris, they ruled, had published "Reflections of a very high nature: As also sundry doubtful and uncertain Reports."

Harris and associates, such as Puritan cleric Cotton Mather, apparently sought to dispel rumors about perceived unrest in the colony after the overthrow of the royal governor in 1688, and the paper promised to "assist businesses and Negotiations." Some stories were not provocative—for example, an account of a Thanksgiving in Plymouth—but others clearly were. The three-page paper (an additional page was blank) recounted "epidemical fevers" in the area, charged Indian allies of the British with "barbarous" atrocities against French prisoners, and claimed that the king of France had "cuckolded" his son by seducing his own daughter-in-law.

Harris was an opinionated Anabaptist who had faced similar controversies before moving to Boston from London, where authorities ten years earlier had jailed him for seditious libel. Between 1686 and 1730 British rulers instructed colonial governors "to provide by all necessary orders that no person keep any printing press for printing, nor that any book, pamphlet or other matter whatsoever be printed without your especial leave and license first obtained."

See also Boston; Licensing Act of 1662; Newspapers; Prior restraint; Radio; Zenger, John Peter.

Pulitzer, Joseph

Born: April 10, 1847, Mako, Hungary

Died: October 29, 1911, Charleston, South Carolina

Identification: American newspaper publisher

Significance: Using sensationalistic methods Pulitzer built the *St. Louis Post-Dispatch* and *New York World* into financially successful newspapers, independent of political parties and eager to expose official corruption

At the age of seventeen, Pulitzer ran away from his European home and sailed for the United States, where he enlisted in a

Joseph Pulitzer's name has come to be associated with journalistic excellence, but his actions as a newspaper publisher were often questionable. (Library of Congress)

cavalry unit. After the Civil War he moved to St. Louis, Missouri, where he became a reporter for a German-language daily. Naturalization as a citizen in March, 1867, permitted Pulitzer to participate in American politics and hold several minor political offices.

In 1878 Pulitzer purchased the *St. Louis Dispatch* and combined it with the *St. Louis Post*. In short order, he turned two failing newspapers into one whose profits quickly recovered the money that he borrowed to purchase them. Vigorous writing, extensive coverage of crime, and a series of "crusades" against corruption attracted readers and advertising revenue. In an unprecedented exposé, the *Post-Dispatch* published the tax returns of the city, showing that the wealthiest citizens paid the lowest personal property taxes. The paper also publicized a grand jury report on prostitution, listing the names of prominent citizens who rented houses to prostitutes. Other no-holds-barred crusades exposed a lottery racket, a horse-car monopoly, and an insurance fraud. Pulitzer and his editors made so many enemies that they needed to carry pistols for their own protection from those willing to use force to silence the paper.

By 1883 Pulitzer felt that he had outworn his welcome in St. Louis, so he moved to New York and purchased the money-losing *New York World*. Within a single year he re-

peated his earlier success and paid for the paper with his profits. Pulitzer insisted on provocative headlines and tight writing, with active verbs driving short sentences. His front pages featured crime, human interest stories, and sensational stunts. Once more, his crusades drew attention to official corruption and the social ills of the day.

Pulitzer's innovative combination of sensational news stunts, bold coverage of events, cartoons, and crusades against corruption came to be called "yellow journalism"—after the popular cartoon "The Yellow Kid." After William Randolph Hearst came to New York in 1895, he copied Pulitzer's innovations, launching a vigorous intensification of sensationalism that was widely criticized. Many blamed the blaring headlines and invented stories on the Cuban situation for inflaming public opinion and leading to the Spanish-American War.

After 1900 Pulitzer responded to criticism by reducing the stridency of his papers, but he did not abandon his search for official misdoing. For example, a 1908 series of articles accused President Theodore Roosevelt of falsely asserting that the money the United States had paid the original French Panama Canal Company had gone to its stockholders. In response the government indicted Pulitzer and two of his editors for criminal libel, but Pulitzer stood his ground and the case was eventually dropped.

In his will Pulitzer left funds to endow a graduate school of journalism at Columbia University and to establish the annual Pulitzer Prices for outstanding achievements in American journalism, literature, and music.

See also Caricature; Hearst, William Randolph; Newspapers; Spanish-American War; Steffens, Lincoln.

Pulp Fiction

TYPE OF WORK: Film
RELEASED: 1994
DIRECTOR: Quentin Tarantino (1963-   )
SUBJECT MATTER: Incorporating three stories loosely enveloping each other, this film broke traditional rules of linear narrative development to trace the lives of small-time hitmen, drug lords, and others in modern Los Angeles
SIGNIFICANCE: This award-winning film stirred audiences across the United States because of its graphic violence, unique narrative structure, and raw language

Unlike previous winners of the prestigious Palm d'Or award at the Cannes Film Festival, *Pulp Fiction* found a large American audience because of its dynamic storytelling and all-star cast, which includes John Travolta, Samuel L. Jackson, and Bruce Willis. Mixing relaxed humor with graphic and often jarring violence, the film was heavily criticized for its amorality and scenes of sadomasochistic action and drug abuse. Although the film was not formally banned anywhere, it was strongly attacked by conservative and religious organizations. Kansas senator Robert Dole, for example, denounced Tarantino's films as examples of the "bad" work corrupting family values emanating from Hollywood. The film was also criticized for its frequent use of the word "nigger."

See also Film censorship; Gangster films; *Natural Born Killers*; Violence.

Puritans

DEFINITION: Protestant religious dissenters of late sixteenth and seventeenth century England, many of whom migrated to New England to protest the theology and practices of the Church of England

SIGNIFICANCE: Victims of religious persecution in England, the members of this religious movement gained political power in New England that they used to censure religious beliefs that they opposed

Puritans were dissenters within the Church of England during the late sixteenth century and the seventeenth century. They believed that the Church of England had neither sufficiently purified itself of the lingering traces of Roman Catholicism nor sufficiently pursued the theological and ecclesiastical purifications in the church initiated by the Protestant Reformation. Especially during the early decades of the seventeenth century under King Charles I and his ecclesiastical ally, Archbishop William Laud, the Puritans suffered from various forms of censorship and religious persecution in response to their criticisms of the Anglican establishment. This harsh treatment ultimately encouraged thousands of Puritans to migrate to New England, where they attempted to fashion a society according to their own political and ecclesiastical vision. As John Winthrop, an early governor of the colony, described their project, the Puritans had set out to build a "city upon a hill" in the New World, governed by godly principles.

When the Puritans obtained political power in New England, they immediately imposed their own variety of censorship upon those who did not share their religious vision. The Puritans of the Massachusetts Bay Colony, established in the late 1620's, pursued religious liberty for themselves but not for those who disagreed with them. According to Nathaniel Ward, a New England preacher, the only freedom granted to those who opposed the Puritan establishment in Massachusetts was the "free liberty to keep away from us." Religious dissenters who declined to stay away from the Puritans found an inhospitable welcome. In 1630, for example, Phillip Ratcliff was sentenced by the Puritans to a whipping and—after having his ears cut off—banishment for saying "scandalous" things concerning the government and churches of the Bay Colony. Within a few years, the Puritans had banished religious dissenters such as Roger Williams and Anne Hutchinson for vocally opposing particular aspects of the colony's government and official theology. Toward the middle of the seventeenth century, Quakers began invading the colony and immediately earned the ire of the Puritan establishment. After unsuccessfully attempting to banish the Quakers, the Puritans resorted to the punishment of ear cropping for Quakers who violated their sentence of banishment by reentering the Col-

ony. Even this punishment failed to discourage the Quakers, however, and in the 1650's, the Puritans in Boston executed three Quakers by hanging.

See also Boston; Calvin, John; Christianity; Crop-ears; Heresy; Hutchinson, Anne; Reformation, the; Religion; Williams, Roger.

Pynchon, William

BORN: December, 1590, Springfield, London, England
DIED: October, 1662, Wraysbury, Buckinghamshire, England
IDENTIFICATION: Anglo-American writer and philosopher
SIGNIFICANCE: Pynchon wrote against Puritan orthodoxy in the colonies

Pynchon was a controversial Puritan landowner and community leader who actively challenged the theological visions offered by the church. Though his writings had little impact on the religious climate in England, they were important expressions of enlightened inquiry in the New World. A strong believer in individual freedom and intellectual inquiry, Pynchon clashed with the Puritan hierarchy, who ultimately banned his works.

Pynchon was one of the founders of the Massachusetts Bay Company, and he became a prominent farmer and trader in that region. In 1641 he founded the town of Springfield, and served as treasurer and justice in the Connecticut and Bay colonies until 1651. Yet despite his powerful position within the Puritan community, he diverged from the religious orthodoxy and commercial conservatism. As early as 1638 he took a controversial stand on the granting of fur-trade monopolies on the grounds that they curtailed individual determination. He was further branded a renegade after he removed Springfield from the jurisdiction of the Massachusetts Bay government.

These actions contributed to the larger denunciation of the man and his works. In 1650 Pynchon published *The Meritorious Price of Our Redemption*, which attacked the central tenets of Puritan theology by suggesting that Jesus Christ did not pay for man's sins. The book was burned, and a day of fasting and humiliation was proclaimed to purge the colonies of Pynchon's heresy.

Despite the attempts at censorship, Pynchon never made a full retraction. He went on to publish two more editions of his book in 1655, building on his eloquent and well-reasoned rebuttals of extreme Puritan theology. His scholarly reevaluation of theology in the colonies was carried further in Pynchon's *The Jewes Synagogue* (1652) and *The Covenant of Nature Made with Adam* (1662).

See also Book burning; Heresy; Hutchinson, Anne; Prynne, William; Puritans.

R

Rabelais, François

BORN: c. 1494, La Devinière, near Chinon, France
DIED: April, 1553, Paris, France
IDENTIFICATION: French novelist and writer of scatological satire
SIGNIFICANCE: Rabelais' books have been frequently banned for heresy or because they have been considered obscene

François Rabelais had a varied career. For almost two decades he was a monk, leaving a monastery in 1530 to study medicine at the University of Montpelier. During his lifetime, Rabelais published four books: *Pantagruel* (1532), *Gargantua* (1534), *The Third Book* (1546), and *The Fourth Book* (1552). A volume titled *Fifth Book* appeared in 1564 and was attributed to Rabelais, but most scholars doubt that he wrote it.

Rabelais' knowledge of classical languages, theology, and philosophy was solid, and his books reveal his interests in both

To many the name of French writer François Rabelais has come to be synonymous with obscene literature. (Library of Congress)

popular culture and the need to reform Christianity. Although he remained a Roman Catholic, his belief that Christian scholars should read the New Testament in the original Greek and not in the Latin translation of the Bible that the Catholic church had long regarded as official, alarmed many conservative theologians, fearful that Rabelais' view would encourage heretical interpretations. In sixteenth century France, censorship of books on religion was entrusted to the judicial Parliament of Paris and to the Sorbonne, which was then the theological school at the University of Paris.

In all four of his books, Rabelais satirized the pretentiousness and superficiality of theologians, especially those at the Sorbonne, arguing that their restrictive approach to biblical exegesis stifled the creativity of sincere Christians who wished to appreciate on their own the many levels of meaning in the Bible. Many characters in his books discuss biblical passages, and their commentaries are often at odds with traditional Catholic interpretations. All his books were placed on the French Index of Prohibited Books by the Sorbonne and the Parliament of Paris. In 1564 the Council of Trent reaffirmed the French condemnation of Rabelais, and the Roman Catholic *Index Librorum Prohibitorum* described him as a heretic whose entire works were to be banned.

Since the sixteenth century, Rabelais' novels have often been banned because of their crude language and the coarse behavior of certain characters. His works were formally banned in South Africa in 1938, and a ban against his books in the United States was lifted only in 1930 under the provisions of the Tariff Act of 1930, which authorized the secretary of the treasury to permit importation and distribution of "so-called classics or books of recognized and established literary or scientific merit." Efforts to ban Rabelais' novels have been singularly ineffective over the centuries, and his works are still considered classics of French fiction and satire.

See also Bible; Christianity; Customs laws, U.S.; France; Heresy; *Index Librorum Prohibitorum*; Offensive language.

Race

DEFINITION: Classification of human beings into groupings based on their real or perceived relationships and physical commonalities
SIGNIFICANCE: Race has historically inspired a variety of censorship efforts, both by racially supremacist political regimes and by modern opponents of speech that promotes racial hatred

For nearly two centuries conflict regarding race has occupied a central place in American society, and this conflict has been mirrored in many other countries of the world. Challenges to racial supremacy have frequently faced official censorship. Where such challenges have prevailed, they have in turn often aimed their own censorship efforts at racist speech.

Censorship in Service of Racial Supremacy. Societies organized around a principle of racial supremacy have routinely sought to suppress speech threatening to the racist regimes. In the United States, for example, the pre-Civil War South greeted abolitionist attacks on the institution of slavery with profound alarm. Southern authorities frequently persuaded local post office masters to treat abolitionist materials as incendiary and therefore unfit for distribution through the mails. A century later, after slavery had been abolished and Jim Crow segregationism had taken root in the South, civil rights protests faced a variety of censorship efforts in Southern states. In actions ranging from the dismissal of university faculty who spoke disapprovingly of segregation to violence inflicted on African American demonstrators and Northern "agitators," Southern authorities endeavored to preserve Jim Crow against its increasingly vocal opponents.

For example, at the University of Mississippi, opposition to racial segregation during the 1960's was officially censored by state officials. In the fall of 1963 Professor James W. Silver, chair of the university's department of history, delivered an address to the Southern Historical Association titled "Mississippi: The Closed Society," opposing the doctrines of white supremacy and racial segregation. In the public furor that followed this speech, state legislators demanded Silver's dismissal and attempted to ban any further public speaking on his part. Ultimately, the state board responsible for the university charged Silver with promoting racial tension and violence. To avoid further conflict, Silver accepted a visiting professorship at the University of Notre Dame and then consented to retire from the University of Mississippi rather than return there. Three years later the same state board took further steps to suppress antisegregationist speech. After the university's chancellor invited Attorney General Robert F. Kennedy to speak at the university in March of 1966 and National Association for the Advancement of Colored People (NAACP) leader Aaron Henry gave a speech at the University's law school, the board passed an order requiring all Mississippi college presidents to deliver to it in advance the names of proposed speakers before issuing any speaking invitation.

Similar patterns of racial censorship have exhibited themselves elsewhere around the globe. For example, prior to South Africa's democratic revolution in the early 1990's, its apartheid regime suppressed anti-apartheid protests on a variety of fronts. South African critics of official segregation such as Nelson Mandela were jailed or killed, and international critics found their diatribes against apartheid officially banned from circulation. For example, when the black American singer and songwriter Stevie Wonder dedicated to Nelson Mandela an Academy Award won in 1985 for his song, "I Just Called to Say I Love You," the government-controlled South African Broadcast Corporation banned his songs from its broadcast stations.

Hate Speech Codes. The latter half of the twentieth century witnessed a global erosion of legally sanctioned racial segregation and oppression in favor of egalitarian ideals. In 1954, for example, the U.S. Supreme Court ended legally enforced racial segregation in public schools in *Brown v. Board of Education*. Over the following decade Congress enacted sweeping legislation that prohibited racial discrimination in a variety of contexts, including restaurants, hotels, and educational institutions. However, the burgeoning consensus against racism and increasing social distaste for expressions of racist sentiments ultimately collided with free speech principles. Opponents of racism have frequently argued that racially derogatory speech should not escape censure by cloaking itself in the mantle of free expression. Armed with egalitarian zeal, opponents of racist speech have succeeded in producing a variety of "hate speech" codes, especially on university campuses. These codes provide for sanctions against speakers who utter racist comments, and typically include similar sanctions for speech by persons insulting one another on the basis of gender, religion, or sexual orientation. Campus hate speech codes have often been accompanied by a general vigilance against expression deemed racially insulting.

Hate Speech and the Supreme Court. Hate speech codes implemented by government bodies or public institutions such as state universities must survive scrutiny under the First Amendment's freedom of speech clause. The U.S. Supreme Court has never construed this clause to provide absolute protection of speech, and has, in fact, recognized certain categories of speech that either receive no protection at all under the First Amendment or lesser degrees of protection than accorded to other forms of speech. For example, the Court in *Chaplinsky v. New Hampshire* (1942) found that "fighting words"—that is, insulting words likely to provoke public violence—were outside the protection of the First Amendment. Advocates of codes punishing racist speech have sometimes relied on *Chaplinsky*'s "fighting words" doctrine to justify restrictions on racist speech.

In *R.A.V. v. City of St. Paul* (1992), however, the Supreme Court dealt a major blow to advocates of hate speech codes. The case involved an ordinance passed by the city of St. Paul, Minnesota, that banned symbols, graffiti, and other forms of expression likely to offend others on the basis of race, color, creed, religion, or gender. The city relied on this ordinance to prosecute, for disorderly conduct, several teenagers who burned a cross in the yard of an African American family. The Supreme Court held that the ordinance violated freedom of speech. The Court concluded that the "fighting words" doctrine could not be used to single out particular viewpoints—in this case, a racist viewpoint—for criminal sanction, even if government might generally ban all fighting words. Since the First Amendment protects speech only against official sanction, private schools and universities have been able to retain their hate speech codes, even though *R.A.V.* probably prevents governments or public institutions from adopting codes that single out particular kinds of fighting words—such as racist comments—for punishment.

Racism and Literature. The same impulse that has produced hate speech codes has also energized attempts to censor literature thought to glorify racist sentiments or to demean racial minorities. For example, Mark Twain's classic tale of adventure along the Mississippi River, *Adventures of Huckleberry Finn* (1884), has incurred twentieth century protests for its copious use of the racially derogatory term "nigger" and uncomplimentary aspects of its portrayal of Huckleberry Finn's African American companion, Jim. Enemies of anti-Semitism have targeted for protest works no less famous than Charles Dickens' *Oliver Twist*, for its characterization of the Jewish thief Fagin, and William Shakespeare's *The Merchant of Venice*, whose Shylock seems to some readers a form of the vicious stereotyping of Jews at the heart of anti-Semitism.

Not all attempts to suppress a consciousness of race in literature have come from critics of racism. Occasionally, African American authors or works about African American characters have been objects of censorship efforts. Typically, however, criticism of such authors or works has not appealed directly to issues of race, but has leveled condemnation at a perceived moral coarseness in the author or work. Maya Angelou's autobiographical work, *I Know Why the Caged Bird Sings*, for example, has been a frequent target of censorship attempts for its sexually explicit descriptions, its purportedly offensive language, and what some readers have viewed as its religious irreverence. Alice Walker's *The Color Purple* has earned similar opposition to its inclusion in public school curricula for its graphic sexual depictions. Occasionally, however, the subject of racism has drawn complaints of its own. The 1958 children's book by Garth Williams titled *The Rabbits' Wedding*, about the courtship of a white rabbit and a black rabbit, drew fierce public protest and was banned from a variety of bookstores and libraries for the offense of glorifying miscegenation, even if the "miscegenation" clothed itself in the soft fur of bunnies.

Racism and Academic Discourse. As the climate for expression of racist sentiments and stereotypes has chilled in the United States, scholarly attempts to investigate racial differences have met with increasing protest. A protest against an idea does not necessarily entail censorship of that idea; one may freely allow the dissemination of ideas one believes to be objectionable and against which one lodges vigorous protests. Nevertheless, to some observers there are indications that attempts to measure differences such as in intelligence among races may increasingly be subject not only to protest but to suppression. Within the academic community, the suppression of ideas seldom takes the form of blatant calls for censorship. Instead, it manifests itself through assertions that particular theories or investigations are simply beyond the pale of accepted science or thought. *The Bell Curve*, a book published by conservative social scientist Charles Murray and Harvard University psychologist Richard Herrnstein in 1994, contains a chapter concerning racial differences in IQ scores. The book produced a flurry of accusations that the authors had peddled racist pseudoscience under the guise of serious scholarship. The brisk sales of the book tend to counter any accusations that its writers have been censored in a meaningful sense. However, the vehement opposition to the book in academic circles might lead one to wonder whether young scholars, reliant upon favorable assessments by peers for promotions, tenure, and grants, remain truly free to pursue questions involving possible genetic differences among races relating to intelligence.

The American Nazis and Skokie. One of the more combustible intersections between the U.S. constitutional commitment to racial equality and its commitment to free expression seemed poised to occur in Skokie, Illinois, a suburb of Chicago in 1977. Of the town's population of seventy thousand people, forty thousand were Jewish, five thousand of whom were survivors of the Holocaust in Europe. In March of 1977, the president of the National Socialist Party of America announced that the party intended to hold a demonstration in Skokie. The participants, he informed the town, would wear uniforms similar to those worn by Nazi party members under Adolf Hitler, and would wear arm bands or emblems of swastikas. Skokie officials filed suit to prevent the march, claiming that the marchers intended to incite hatred toward Jews and that the First Amendment should not shield this effort to promulgate anti-Semitic racism. In a running battle across various trial and appellate courts, Skokie's attempts to block the marchers, both through court action and by a hastily adopted series of ordinances, was ultimately rebuffed. In a curious climax to the legal warfare, however, the National Socialist Party of America eventually canceled the planned demonstration in Skokie in favor of one in Chicago.   —*Timothy L. Hall*

See also Abolitionist movement; African Americans; Asian Americans; Campus speech codes; Civil Rights movement; Hate laws; Judaism; National Socialism; Native Americans; Offensive language; Political correctness; Skokie, Illinois; Nazi march.

BIBLIOGRAPHY

Nat Hentoff's *Free Speech for Me—But Not for Thee: How the American Left and Right Relentlessly Censor Each Other* (New York: HarperCollins, 1992) offers a spirited criticism of contemporary examples of censorship, including censorship of racist speech. *Illiberal Education: The Politics of Race and Sex on Campus*, by Dinesh D'Souza (New York: Free Press, 1991), is a fierce polemic against campus speech codes. For a defense of government attempts to punish racist and other forms of hate speech, see Mari J. Matsuda's *Words That Wound: Critical Race Theory, Assaultive Speech, and the First Amendment* (Boulder, Colo.: Westview Press, 1993). A similar argument is made by *The Price We Pay: The Case Against Racist Speech, Hate Propaganda, and Pornography*, edited by Laura J. Lederer and Richard Delgado (New York: Hill and Wang, 1995). James L. Gibson's *Civil Liberties and Nazis: The Skokie Free-Speech Controversy* (New York: Praeger, 1985) describes the Skokie incident in detail.

Radio

DEFINITION: A long-range mass communication medium of sound signals sent on electromagnetic carrier waves

SIGNIFICANCE: Radio has traditionally been more regulated—censored—by the government than books

Radio broadcasting has been allowed First Amendment protection, but the government has taken the position that radio's special characteristics demand not only the regulation of the technical aspects of radio but of its content as well. The special characteristics of radio include that it operates across public space; that it travels through private space uninvited; and that it operates on given frequencies, of which there have been, arguably, a limited number. These public concerns have justified the greater amount of censorship that radio has had in comparison to print media, which does not have radio's special characteristics.

Aside from its frequency allocation and licensing functions, the Federal Communications Commission (FCC) is mandated to supervise the ongoing operations of its broadcast licensees. A certain amount of that supervision involves technical matters such as frequency and power level, but the commission also has the authority to regulate the content of radio programming.

No government agency has the authority to tell newspaper and magazine publishers to print a specific amount or kind of material or to provide access to their columns for those with whom they disagree. Many radio broadcasters argue that no government agency should have the authority to control the content of broadcasting either.

Spectrum scarcity has been the most common rationale for the FCC's instituting a number of content-based regulations for radio. Supporters of broadcast content regulation argued that there simply was not enough frequency space for everyone to have a voice on the airwaves. Therefore, the FCC was given the power to regulate radio broadcasting in the public interest by requiring broadcast stations to air certain types of programs and to cover all sides of controversial issues.

Broadcasters who support having full First Amendment rights argue that spectrum scarcity was a legitimate concern during the days when only a few broadcast signals were available, but with the emerging new media outlets such as multichannel cable and direct home-to-satellite links, spectrum scarcity has ceased to be an issue.

Broadcast Content Regulations. Although section 326 of the 1934 Communications Act forbids the FCC to censor broadcasters, the commission has adopted a variety of rules to regulate broadcast content. Also, the Communications Act itself and other federal laws set forth rules governing the content of radio programming.

By the 1980's, the FCC had changed its stance toward regulating broadcast content. The FCC began to move away from treating radio broadcasters as second-class citizens when it came to the First Amendment. It no longer believed it was in the public interest to dictate to radio stations the types of information they should provide to their audiences. Instead, the commission decided that the public interest would best be served by deregulating broadcasting and allowing the marketplace or economic forces to determine what type of programming a radio station would air.

As part of its deregulation efforts, the FCC abolished most of its broadcast content-related regulations. In 1987 the commission abolished its most controversial content regulation, the Fairness Doctrine, which required broadcasters to devote an unspecified amount of time to controversial issues of community importance and to devote time to significant points of view concerning those issues. The U.S. Supreme Court in its 1969 *Red Lion Broadcasting Co. v. Federal Communications Commission* decision had affirmed the constitutionality of the

fairness doctrine, but an appeals court later ruled that the fairness doctrine was nothing more than an FCC policy—not a law codified by Congress. Therefore, the FCC had the authority to repeal the fairness doctrine in 1987.

The commission also abandoned its 1971 ascertainment policy in which broadcast stations must interview community leaders to determine what issues needed to be addressed in their programming. The commission also repealed its guidelines for nonentertainment (news) programming and advertising.

A number of restrictions on broadcast content are still in force, restrictions that do not apply to most other media. Some of those content-based regulations apply to providing access for candidates running for public office.

Political Broadcasting. The key provision regarding political broadcasting is section 315 of the Communications Act, often called the equal time rule or the equal opportunity provision. Section 315 requires broadcasters to provide equal access to airwaves to all legally qualified candidates for a given public office during election campaigns.

Section 315 does not require broadcasters to give politicians free time or campaign advertising. Rather, it merely requires that all candidates for the same election be treated equally. If one candidate is sold airtime for a certain fee, then the equal time rule merely requires that other candidates in the same election be allowed to purchase equal time in the same part of the broadcast day for the same price. According to section 315, if one candidate is given free airtime, then all other candidates for the same office must also be given free airtime. Bona fide newscasts, news interviews, news documentaries, news and public affairs programs, and coverage of news events such as political conventions and debates between candidates are exempt from the equal opportunity provision.

In order to prevent radio broadcasters from meeting the equal time requirement by simply excluding all political advertising, the Communications Act places an additional requirement on broadcasters. Section 312(a)(7) gives the FCC the power to revoke a broadcaster's license if that broadcaster fails to provide reasonable access to candidates in federal elections. The broadcast networks challenged the constitutionality of section 312 in court, and the U.S. Supreme Court upheld the commission's authority under section 312 to order broadcasters to air federal candidates' political statements. The Supreme Court majority ruled that the First Amendment rights of candidates and the public outweighed the First Amendment rights of broadcasters during an election.

Indecent Language. From the beginning of government regulation of radio, the broadcast of obscene, indecent, or profane language has been prohibited. The FCC has the power to revoke any broadcast license if the licensee transmits indecent material over the airwaves. Indecent language is any material that is not legally obscene but too sexual, shocking, offensive, or vulgar for children to hear. Unlike obscenity, which has no First Amendment protection, indecency is constitutionally protected speech.

Although indecent programming is protected by the First Amendment, the government may impose carefully tailored regulations to protect children from indecency.

The 1978 U.S. Supreme Court decision in *Federal Communications Commission v. Pacifica Foundation* supported the FCC's ban on comedian George Carlin's monologue about the seven dirty words that cannot be said on radio. This decision represents the U.S. Supreme Court's break from the scarcity rationale. In justifying its decision, the Supreme Court did not state that because broadcasting was scarce it was improper to hear Carlin's monologue; instead, the Court ruled that radio was an "intruder" in the home, "uniquely pervasive," and "uniquely accessible to children."

In an effort to control indecent language on the airwaves, the FCC had issued a twenty-four-hour ban on indecent broadcasts. An appeals court, however, struck down the twenty-four-hour indecency ban and ordered the commission instead to establish a "safe harbor"—a period during which the number of children in the audience is small and broadcasters may air indecent programming.

Hoaxes. Actor Orson Welles once led a special radio broadcast about the invasion of Earth by Martians. In Welles' program, music was interrupted by authentic-sounding news bulletins that terrified millions of people, especially near the Martians' purported landing site in New Jersey. The story was intended as a radio drama, but many listeners believed the Earth was really being invaded by Martians. As a result of the panic caused by the realistic format of Orson Welles' radio program, the FCC adopted a policy that radio dramas could not portray themselves as radio newscasts.

In 1992 the FCC adopted a new rule restricting hoaxes. The rule was enacted in response to several widely publicized incidents in which radio stations reported fake events. For example, a station in St. Louis reported during the Persian Gulf War that the United States was under nuclear attack; a Virginia station reported that a large waste dump was about to explode. The potential dump explosion created a panic similar to the one caused by Orson Welles' broadcast.

The FCC responded to the radio hoaxes by banning broadcast fabrications about crimes and catastrophes that cause substantial harm to public health and welfare. The FCC's response to banning radio hoaxes illustrates the limited First Amendment rights of broadcasters and raises a variety of censorship issues.

Lotteries, Gambling, and Advertising. United States law and the FCC forbid the broadcasting of material that promotes gambling. Government-run and charitable lotteries may be legally advertised, however, as may promotions and prize drawings by businesses other than casinos. Under the 1988 Charity Games Advertising Clarification Act only casinos and others whose gambling is an end in itself are forbidden to advertise under federal law.

The 1998 federal law left the states free to restrict or ban lotteries and lottery advertising even if the advertising would be legal under federal law. For example, the U.S. Supreme Court has ruled that a broadcaster in a non-lottery state cannot carry advertising for a nearby state's lottery, even if it has a large audience there.

Radio broadcasters are also subject to other laws that govern advertising in general. For example, the federal Truth in Lending Act requires full disclosure of all credit terms for loans. These required disclosures, however, are sometimes so detailed that they cannot be squeezed into a short radio commercial.

Format Changes. The FCC also has become involved in content regulation when a radio station proposes to change a unique programming format. During the 1970's, the only classical music stations in several cities tried to abandon their classical format, triggering protests by classical music lovers. Classical music lovers feared that minority tastes would not be served if all broadcasters were free to tailor their programming for the audiences that are most attractive to advertisers.

After a series of federal court decisions, the FCC began to review format changes when the proposed change would result in the abandonment of a unique format and produce widespread protests. In 1981 in *Federal Communications Commission v. WNCN Listeners Guild* the U.S. Supreme Court ruled that the FCC had the right not to interfere in broadcast format disputes. The Court said entertainment programming was within the broadcaster's discretion. The Supreme Court decision was a victory for the radio broadcast industry, which has wanted market forces, and not the FCC, to dictate format decisions.

—Eddith A. Dashiell

See also Armed Forces Radio and Television Service; Broadcast media; Call-in programs; Canadian Broadcasting Corporation; Carlin, George; Fairness doctrine; National Association of Broadcasters; National Public Radio; Pacifica Foundation; Stern, Howard; Television.

BIBLIOGRAPHY

Wayne Overbeck's *Major Principles of Media Law* (New York: Harcourt Brace, 1995) provides a concise overview of law as it pertains to broadcast regulation and other media. Other sources that provide a thorough historical analysis of the First Amendment rights of U.S. radio broadcasters include: Lucas A. Powe, Jr.'s *American Broadcasting and the First Amendment* (Berkeley: University of California Press, 1987), Hugh C. Donahue's *The Battle to Control Broadcast News: Who Owns the First Amendment?* (Cambridge, Mass.: The MIT Press, 1989), and William B. Ray's *FCC: The Ups and Downs of Radio-TV Regulation* (Ames, Iowa: Iowa State University Press, 1990). Powe, Donahue, and Ray all trace the history of radio regulation and discuss the various viewpoints of how the First Amendment should be interpreted regarding radio regulation.

Radio Free Europe (RFE)

FOUNDED: 1950

TYPE OF ORGANIZATION: International radio broadcasting service sponsored by the U.S. government

SIGNIFICANCE: During the Cold War, shortwave broadcasts by Radio Free Europe were among the only sources of information reaching communist countries that were not censored

Radio Free Europe (RFE) is part of a network of media offices financed by the U.S. government for the purpose of promoting democratic values and American interests abroad. RFE was established in 1950 to broadcast into Soviet-dominated Eastern Europe. Its headquarters were placed in Munich, Germany, and shortwave transmitters were set up in various locations for maximum penetration into Eastern Europe. A similar agency, Radio Liberty (RL), was added in the early 1950's to broadcast into the Soviet Union.

As did Radio Liberty and several similar operations, RFE offered news, information, and commentary as an alternative to that provided by the communist-controlled media in the East European countries. (The Voice of America, which had been created several years earlier, covered a broader geographical area and focused more on explaining American culture, values, and policies.) In its early years, RFE actively advocated popular rejection of the Soviet-backed governments of Eastern Europe. Millions of East Europeans listened, and the uprisings in Hungary in 1956 and in Czechoslovakia in 1968 are at least partially credited to RFE's broadcasts. Engaging in yet another form of censorship, the communist governments periodically attempted to jam the signals broadcast by RFE, but they met with only partial success.

Although it was staffed by émigrés and expatriates from Eastern Europe and was made to appear as a private operation, RFE was covertly funded by the U.S. Central Intelligence Agency. When this fact became public in the early 1970's, critics charged that RFE's CIA-funded propaganda was an unworthy corrective for the government-controlled media in Eastern Europe. As a result of this criticism, RFE's and RL's ties to the CIA were severed and both were placed under an independent Board for International Broadcasting. In 1976 the two networks merged.

Even after the termination of CIA influence, RFE maintained a substantial presence in Eastern Europe. It broadcast throughout each day in a half dozen languages, utilized (with RL) seventeen hundred employees, and received some $100 million in annual funding. With the collapse of the Soviet-sponsored regimes from 1989 to 1991, however, RFE/RL's anticensorship mission was made obsolete. Most Eastern European and former Soviet countries developed relatively democratic governments, and state monopolies on the media were broken. Nevertheless, RFE/RL continued its operations as both a promoter of American values and foreign policy as well as a source of information on the former Soviet bloc for use by western analysts. Its future at the end of the twentieth century was uncertain, however, as the administration of President Bill Clinton attempted to phase out some of the remaining institutions of the Cold War.

See also Broadcast media; Central Intelligence Agency; Communism; Propaganda; United States Information Agency; Voice of America.

Radio Martí

Founded: 1983

Type of organization: Florida-based, U.S.-financed radio service directed at Cuba

Significance: As a propaganda arm of the U.S. government, Radio Martí has been engaged in a communications war with Cuba

Since the Cuban revolutionary hero José Martí died while leading the late nineteenth century struggle for Cuba's inde-

pendence, his name has been synonymous with independence struggles in the Hispanic countries of the Caribbean. It was thus natural that his name was attached to a radio service created by the U.S. Congress in the early 1980's to transmit propaganda to Cuba. First proposed in 1982, Radio Martí was approved by Congress in September, 1983, and was fully operational two years later. Under the control of the United States Information Agency (USIA)—which was also responsible for Voice of America—Radio Martí was mandated to beam to Cuba positive information about life in America, along with anticommunist and anti-Castro propaganda. Its programs have included such material as broadcasts of U.S. congressional hearings, to allow Cubans to hear authentic democratic debate, and interviews with exiled Cubans who have succeeded in American business. Many of Radio Martí's staff members have been members of the Cuban exile community with vested interests of their own in returning home to a Cuba free from Castro's rule.

In 1995 Jorgé Mas Canosa, a millionaire Miami Cuban with strong influence in the Cuban community and in Washington, D.C., began a move to create Television Martí. The U.S. Congress has many ties with the Cuban exile communities. Members of the House and Senate regularly budget funding for Radio Martí and Television Martí.

Fidel Castro countered Radio Martí by having Cuban radio stations broadcast more competitive programming, with a particular increase in rock 'n' roll music. A more ominous response came after Radio Martí began full broadcasting services in 1985; Cuban technicians then started jamming its signals. Cuba's success in blocking broadcasts has caused some congressional members to question the value of paying to broadcast messages that cannot be received by their intended audience. Nevertheless, as increasing numbers of people in Cuba have begun to doubt their government, Radio Martí's influence there has grown. Some have charged that these media are not giving Castro Cubans enough information on the merits of a noncommunist society. As more cuts have been made in funding, the possibility has grown that Radio and Television Martí will either have to find funding from the Cuban American community, or more strongly espouse American ideology.

See also Cuba; Grenada, U.S. invasion of; Martí, José Julián; Panama, U.S. invasion of; Propaganda; Radio Free Europe; United States Information Agency; Voice of America.

Radishchev, Aleksandr

Born: August 31, 1749, Moscow, Russia

Died: September 24, 1802, St. Petersburg, Russia

Identification: Russian author and social critic

Significance: A Western-educated member of the Russian aristocracy, Radishchev achieved a posthumous reputation as the first radical Russian intellectual because of his published critique of serfdom

Radishchev's book *A Journey from Saint Petersburg to Moscow* (1790) criticized the social and political foundations of the Russian Empire so strongly that the government of Empress Catherine II banned the book and ordered Radischev's beheading (a sentence later commuted to exile in Siberia). In condemning serfdom, Radischev also implicitly criticized the autocracy, the established social order, and Russia's claim to full membership in Western civilization. His book was also unappreciated in Russia because it coincided with, and was influenced by, the French Revolution.

Although Radishchev was fully pardoned in 1801, he was demoralized by his exile. His later writings were deliberately noncontroversial. In 1802 he committed suicide after receiving criticism for his work in a state legal commission.

After Radischev's suicide, *A Journey from Saint Petersburg to Moscow* continued to circulate illegally within Russia, where it was interpreted as a protest against tyranny that won Radischev mythic status in the eyes of later social critics. Often called the "father" of Russian social radicalism and the first repentant nobleman, Radischev inspired numerous followers, including Alexander Pushkin, the Decembrists, and Alexander Herzen. His book remained accessible to later generations; it was reprinted in London in 1858, was published in Russia during the reign of Czar Nicholas II, and was reissued by Joseph Stalin's regime in 1935.

See also Nicholas I; Russia; Sedition; Stalin, Joseph.

Raleigh, Sir Walter

BORN: 1552 or 1554, Hayes Barton, Devon, England
DIED: October 29, 1618, London, England
IDENTIFICATION: English courtier, soldier, politician, explorer, writer, and historian
SIGNIFICANCE: Raleigh's *The History of the World* was censored for challenging the authority of kings, and his defense of his life encapsulated key arguments for the rights of individuals against all-powerful authorities

A favorite of Queen Elizabeth I who was awarded numerous trade monopolies in the New World, Raleigh was the object of jealous attacks on his unorthodoxy, tolerance, and intellectual boldness. In 1592 a Jesuit pamphlet by Robert Parsons accused him of heading a "School of Atheism" and denounced his skeptical scientific inquiry as conjuring. An ecclesiastical commission established to investigate Raleigh's baiting of a conventional parson named William Ironside yielded to Raleigh's witty logic, but Raleigh was rarely circumspect. He spoke out, for example, against conducting witch-hunts for religious nonconformists.

All copies of *The History of the World*, a cynical assessment of human history that Raleigh composed during the thirteen years he was convened in the Tower of London, were recalled in 1614, at the command of King James I, who objected to the book's allegorical frontispiece, to the fact that a condemned prisoner claimed authorship, and to its "too saucy" censuring of princes. The *History*'s prefatory "Premonition to Princes" asserted that the power of kings might seem great in the small theater of the world but was little next to the power of God, who would call even kings to account for their sins through Death, "the great Leveller."

Officially executed for plotting to dethrone James, Raleigh was actually executed for his defiance of conventional Jacobean wisdom. Later, Puritans made his condemnation of tyrants in *Prerogative of Parliaments* a cornerstone of their dissent.

See also Atheism; Book burning; Censorship; Death; Exploration, Age of; Intellectual freedom; James I; Puritans.

Rap music

DEFINITION: Style of popular music that evolved from an improvised fusion of dance music and disk jockey calls featuring electronically woven segments of songs and sounds with spoken lyrics that often describe aspects of urban life
SIGNIFICANCE: The lyrical content of some rap songs has attracted protests from antiobscenity, antiviolence, and antisexism groups

Since the early 1980's the style and content of rap music have alarmed many listeners. Although most rap songs deal with subjects familiar to pop music fans in general, a few songs have depicted explicitly sexual or violent subjects. Many of these more controversial songs and acts have fallen under the umbrella known as "gangsta rap," an ill-defined epithet that often excludes them from radio play lists.

Although defenders of rap music have applauded its realism and frankness, and claimed that it is an authentic expression of the experiences of disaffected youth, opponents have denounced it as an unwelcome addition to the cultural scene. Many have argued that some lyrics cross over the line of acceptable speech and qualify as obscenity.

Among the harshest critics of rap lyrics have been cultural conservatives, such as former education secretary William Bennett, who led an effort in 1996 to encourage the Time Warner corporation to divest itself of holdings in Interscope Records, a producer of "gangsta rap" records. Some public figures with more liberal leanings, such as Senator Joseph Lieberman of Connecticut and C. DeLores Tucker, head of the National Political Congress of Black Women, joined Bennett. They specifically castigated Time Warner, Sony, Thorn EMI, Bertelsmann Music Group (BMG), and PolyGram for selling rap music containing "degrading and indefensible" lyrics. The

Rap music star Ice-T addresses a Nation of Islam audience in Los Angeles in May, 1994. (AP/Wide World Photos)

goal of their campaign was not directly to censor controversial music, but to delegitimize it by encouraging major recording companies to drop offensive artists and let smaller companies take them on.

Other efforts, however, have tried direct legal action to discourage the production and sale of offensive rap music. Despite such attempts, as late as 1996 no rap or rock song was ever found legally "obscene," according to the test established in the U.S. Supreme Court's 1973 decision in *Miller v. California*. According to that definition, obscenity is sexually explicit art and entertainment that lacks any serious artistic or other values, is patently offensive, and appeals to prurient interests, as judged by the standards of a particular community. To be found legally obscene, material must meet all three criteria.

Pop music groups charged with obscenity have occasionally lost in trial courts, but have triumphed on appeal. For example, the group 2 Live Crew was convicted of obscenity in Broward County, Florida, in 1990 for their album *As Nasty as They Wanna Be*, but this decision was reversed two years later by a federal appeals court, which found that the album's music possessed inherent artistic value. The U.S. Supreme Court has upheld that ruling.

See also "Cop Killer"; Copyright law; *Miller v. California*; Music; Obscenity: legal definitions; Obscenity: sale and possession; Protest music; Redeeming social value; 2 Live Crew.

Reagan, Ronald

BORN: February 6, 1911, Tampico, Illinois
IDENTIFICATION: Fortieth president of the United States
SIGNIFICANCE: Reagan markedly increased the number of government documents classified as "secret" and wanted all governmental employees with access to classified material to submit to lifetime prepublication review of all their writings and speeches

After a career as an actor, during which he made over fifty films, and several years as a spokesman for the General Electric Company traveling the country preaching a conservative ideology, Reagan attracted national political attention with an emotional convention speech in support of Barry Goldwater's presidential campaign in 1964. He was elected governor of California in 1966 and 1970. After unsuccessful campaigns for the Republican presidential nomination in 1968 and 1976, Reagan won the presidency in 1980, easily defeating incumbent Democratic president Jimmy Carter.

As president, Reagan embarked on a course of strengthening American military power and challenging communism throughout the world. To protect his military and diplomatic initiatives, his administration expanded the classification and censorship operations of the federal government, barring access to "sensitive" information as well as to documents involving national security. Reagan reversed President Carter's efforts to reduce the number of federal documents classified as secret. He multiplied the categories of records that were to be kept secret and authorized the reclassification as secret of documents previously released and published, preventing any further public use.

In March, 1983, Reagan issued a directive requiring all federal employees with access to classified information to submit their future speeches and writings to government censorship through their entire lives. Pressure from Congress led to suspension of the order, however. In 1986 the Reagan Administration required federal employees to sign a form agreeing not to divulge information already classified, as well as "nonclassified but classifiable" information—an uncertain and infinitely expandable category.

Using provisions of the Immigration and Nationality Act of 1952, the Reagan Administration regularly denied visas to foreign critics of American policy. South American novelists, Japanese proponents of a nuclear freeze, and a retired general and former NATO commander who opposed Reagan's nuclear policies, were among those denied admission to the United States.

In 1983 when Reagan decided to invade the island of Grenada to overthrow its Marxist government, he established the most rigid censorship that had ever been imposed on the press in any American war. Keeping reporters away from most of the action and allowing only pool coverage of events meant that knowledge of the war came only from carefully controlled government sources.

A major scandal erupted when Lebanese press reports revealed that the Reagan Administration was secretly selling arms to Iran to secure the release of American hostages held in Lebanon; profits from that operation were then used to support Contra guerrillas in Nicaragua. Each of these operations was of questionable legality and could continue only while information was withheld from the American people and Congress. Meanwhile, Reagan won re-election in 1984 by a landslide and retired in 1989, widely acknowledged as one of the most popular presidents in U.S. history.

See also Bush, George; Classification of information; Grenada, U.S. invasion of; Immigration laws; Iran-Contra scandal; National Security Decision Directive 84; Presidency, U.S.; Prior restraint.

Realist, The

TYPE OF WORK: Magazine
PUBLISHED: 1958-1974
EDITOR: Paul Krassner (1932-   )
SUBJECT MATTER: Social and political satire
SIGNIFICANCE: *The Realist* challenged prevailing standards of decency and conventional thought during the late 1950's and 1960's and occasionally brought calls for censorship

The Realist advocated unpopular and controversial causes, often expressing its views in uninhibited and biting satire. The magazine supported abortion rights, sexual liberation, and religious skepticism, and it opposed American Cold War military policies. *The Realist* also championed controversial individuals, such as comedian Lenny Bruce and atheist Madalyn Murray.

Efforts were made to censor the May, 1967, *Realist* for alleged obscenity. The issue published "The Parts Left out of the Kennedy Book," a literary hoax written by editor Paul Krassner that purported to publish sections of William Manchester's new book, *The Death of a President*, which had been deleted by the publisher. It included a scene on the flight to Washington from Dallas after President John F. Kennedy's assassination, in which the president's widow observed the new president, Lyndon Johnson, engaging in a sexual act with the dead president. The same issue contained a centerfold entitled "The Disneyland Memorial Orgy," which depicted familiar Walt Disney characters in various sexual positions, enjoying the new freedom allowed by the recent death of their creator. Although the magazine's Baltimore, Maryland, distributor removed the Disney centerfold, and charges of distributing obscene material (later dropped) were brought against the magazine's Chicago distributor, attempts to prevent circulation of the issue failed. The most provocative issue of *The Realist* sold 100,000 copies.

See also Censorship; MAD magazine; Magazines; Newspapers, underground.

Recording industry

DEFINITION: The corporations responsible for the recording, manufacture, distribution, and sales of sound recordings
SIGNIFICANCE: Commercial sound recordings have been censored most commonly for obscenity, but also for promoting drug abuse, radical politics, and racial mixing

Indirectly regulated by the Federal Communications Commission (FCC), which regulates the radio, the recording industry is largely self-censored—often leading to confused and arbitrary policies. Commercial sound recordings have generally been difficult to censor. The recording industry is a network of independent producers, record labels, distributors, retailers, broadcasters, and artists. There has been no one point at which to halt the flow of controversial product. In fact, a ban on broadcast of a particular song or album has often translated into retail sales. This type of success has been commonplace in popular music. A radio ban on the Rolling Stones' 1965 single "Satisfaction" seemed only to have lifted sales and to have prompted the band to repeat the tactic, less successfully, with their 1966 release "Let's Spend the Night Together." Even a ban imposed by large retailers cannot prevent the flow of controversial product. In 1992 retail giants Wal-Mart and Kmart refused to stock Nirvana's *In Utero*, whose cover art pictured human fetuses; nevertheless, the album entered the *Billboard* charts at number one.

Indirect Censorship. The FCC is responsible for licensing radio stations and hence exerts indirect control over the content of sound recordings. Rather than directly censor controversial material, the agency has more often issued warnings, imposed fines, or withheld license renewals for offending stations. Yet even with such powerful means at its disposal, the agency's practical censorship powers are limited. In 1971, for example, the FCC attempted to sanction New York's WBAI for broadcasting a recording of George Carlin's famous monologue on the dirty words one cannot say on the radio. In *Federal Communications Commission v. Pacifica Foundation* (1978), the Supreme Court upheld the FCC's right to declare such material indecent; however, the controversy had taken seven years to be resolved.

Unlike its British counterpart, the British Broadcasting Corporation, the FCC is unable to impose nationwide bans on controversial recordings. Instead it must adhere to the doctrine of community standards in determining obscenity. Thus, a song that might have serious literary or artistic merit in New York City might be declared obscene in Bible Belt. Furthermore, the amorphous notion of community standards makes the FCC's role in censoring material largely reactive as it responds to citizen complaints.

Given the lack of consistent federal regulation, most censorship in the recording industry has been self-imposed by producers, record label executives, and artists. For example, in a typically haphazard move, Columbia Records initially included, then deleted the satirical song "Talking John Birch Society Blues" from the album *Freewheelin' Bob Dylan* (1962). Moreover, what is acceptable for one record label may not be for another. RCA allowed the Jefferson Airplane to include the word "motherfucker" on their 1968 *Volunteers*; however, Elektra compelled MC5 to substitute the phrase "brothers and sisters" for the plural version of the same obscenity on their 1968 release *Kick Out the Jams*. At times record labels have created a censored version as a single release while including the uncensored version on the album. The single release of Van Morrison's "Brown-Eyed Girl" substituted the innocuous line "laughing and a-running" for the album version's "making love in the green grass." Many rap artists follow a practice of dual release, providing a cleaner version of a rap for radio airplay.

Sex and Race. In 1954 U.S. Representative Ruth Thompson proposed a bill to ban from the mails any sound recording deemed by postal officials to be "obscene, lewd, lascivious, or filthy." The bill's explicit target was rhythm and blues, the sexually suggestive music of black America, which had become increasingly popular with a white youth audience. In response, crossover stations (stations playing black music for a white audience) began to ban suggestive rhythm and blues songs such as the Midnighters' "Work with Me, Annie" and the Drifters' "Honey Love." Necessarily limited in scope, such measures were unable to cope with rhythm and blues' even more popular derivative, rock 'n' roll. Taking its name from a euphemism for sex, rock 'n' roll extended the transgression of sexual mores and racial boundaries. For the first time, black artists such as Little Richard and Chuck Berry had direct access to the lucrative white youth market. Yet, a form of de facto racial censorship soon arose as white artists began to cover the songs of black artists and supplant them in the marketplace. Especially in the South, many top-forty radio stations played only white covers of black songs and many retailers stocked only the white product. Thus, Pat Boone had a far bigger hit with his sanitized remake of "Tutti Frutti" than the song's originator, Little Richard.

Some white reactionaries, particularly in the Deep South, continued to see rock 'n' roll as a threat to racial segregation. In the late 1950's the North Alabama White Citizens Council declared rock to be the result of a conspiracy, orchestrated by the National Association for the Advancement of Colored People (NAACP), with the design of infiltrating and corrupting

668 / Recording industry

the morals of white youth. While most whites ridiculed such reactionary paranoia, the equation of moral corruption and race mixing went largely unchallenged even in the more racially liberated 1960's. Atlantic Records forced the British band The Who to change the line in their 1966 song "Substitute" from "I look all white, but my dad was black" to the nonsensical "I'm walking forward, but my feet walk back." Janis Ian's "Society's Child," a song about racial mixing, was too controversial for 1967's Summer of Love and effectively banned across the nation.

A New Target: Drugs. From the mid-1960's to the early 1970's censorship groups shifted their focus from sex to illicit drugs. In 1966 *The Gavin Report*, an influential radio programming guide, published a list of current singles that promoted drug use. Included were the Byrds' "Eight Miles High," which the group defended as a description of a transatlantic airline flight, and Bob Dylan's "Rainy Day Women #12 and 35," whose obscure title concealed the refrain: "Everybody must get stoned!" The fabled Summer of Love witnessed the birth of the first psychedelic groups such as San Francisco's Jefferson Airplane and the Grateful Dead. Just as 1950's rockers had used code words to sing about sex, the 1960's groups relied upon code words for drugs. Jefferson Airplane's "White Rabbit" describes psychedelic experience in the imagery of Lewis Carroll's *Alice's Adventures in Wonderland* (1865). While record companies rushed to capitalize on the emerging drug culture, radio stations, prodded by Dallas communications magnate Gordon McLendon, moved toward a ban of all songs that celebrated drug use. This effort was soon undercut by the censors' zealotry in alleging drug references in seemingly innocent material such as Peter, Paul and Mary's "Puff the Magic Dragon" and the Beatles' "Yellow Submarine."

Somewhat belatedly, in 1971, the FCC issued Notice 71-205, which stated that radio stations must be aware of the lyrical contents—including any hidden drug messages—of all songs broadcast. Yet the era of the covert drug song was over. The notice's first victim was Brewer and Shipley's unabashed anthem "One Toke Over the Line," which New York's influential WNBC summarily banned, allowing stations around the country to follow suit. While the notice broadened the practice of printing lyrics on the album covers, critics derided its ambiguity since it made no distinction between songs which promoted drug abuse and those which depicted its dangers such as Bloodrock's "D.O.A.," a graphic account of a drug overdose. Later that year the Illinois Crime Commission published its own list of "drug songs"; however, the attempt to censor drug lyrics foundered in the 1970's. Eric Clapton scored a hit in 1978 with "Cocaine" and the 1980's saw the rise of rap music, which made an icon of crack cocaine.

Political Censorship. To a lesser degree than sex or drugs, radical politics have incited record bans. In the 1950's anticommunists targeted folk musician Pete Seeger. His group the Weavers, who had scored a hit with "Goodnight, Irene," were suddenly blacklisted from commercial radio. However, politically minded censors were forced to use more subtle tactics in battling the 1960's counterculture. In 1965 right-wing groups in California, including the John Birch Society, petitioned the

FCC to ban Barry McGuire's antinuclear jeremiad "Eve of Destruction" on the grounds that it violated the fairness doctrine. The song was effectively blocked from California stations, but the FCC never offered a definitive ruling which would have placed popular music within the authority of the fairness doctrine.

More commonly, political censorship has resulted from local politics. The Rolling Stones' "Street Fighting Man," released in the weeks following the violent 1968 Democratic Convention, was banned by a number of urban radio stations in the fear that it might incite riots. Nor has political censorship always come from the Right. In 1989 Ten Thousand Maniacs enjoyed a Top Ten remake of Cat Stevens' "Peace Train." However, on learning that muslim Stevens supported the Ayatollah Ruhollah Khomeini's death sentence for author Salman Rushdie, the group urged radio stations to boycott its own single.

Cover Art Controversies. As often as not, censorship has concerned product packaging rather than the recordings themselves. The Beatles butcher cover to their Capitol release *Yesterday and Today* (1966) showed the group surrounded by raw meat and headless dolls; after retail protest, an unoffensive cover was simply pasted over the original. Atco was similarly compelled to offer a substitute cover for Blind Faith's eponymous 1969 album: it displayed a bare-chested teenage girl. The same year John Lennon and Yoko Ono's album *Two Virgins*, featuring a frontal nude shot of the pair, was seized by customs authorities at Newark airport. As recently as 1987 Jello Biafra of the Dead Kennedys was prosecuted for obscenity for including a sexually explicit poster in the album *Frankenchrist*. Even liner notes have been subject to censorship: Elektra quietly withdrew the revolutionary cant of White Panther John Sinclair from the MC5's hapless *Kick Out the Jams*.

Rap and Corporate Censorship. The popularity of funk and disco music of the 1970's saw black artists once again crossing over into the white market and seemed to spell an end to racially segregated markets. However, with the emergence of the Music TeleVision Network (MTV) in the early 1980's the racial divide seemed to reassert itself. Only through the pressure of Columbia Records was black artist Michael Jackson able to air his music videos, which proved to be enormously popular with the white youth audience. Even with the admittance of safe black artists such as Jackson, Prince, and Whitney Houston, MTV catered to a largely white youth audience and hence refused to program the controversial black urban music known as rap. In the mid-1980's MTV finally bowed to industry protest and audience demand and began to air rap videos.

Rap music is unrepentantly transgressive of racial, sexual, and political codes, often combining a glorification of gang culture with a pornographic objectification of women. Its new visibility, via MTV, made it especially susceptible to censorship efforts. The first reaction took the form of the Parents' Music Resource Center (PMRC), founded in 1985 by then-Senator Al Gore's wife Tipper. Though Gore's group also attacked white "heavy metal" groups for their celebrations of teen sex, sadomasochism, satanism, and suicide, the PMRC took special aim at rap. At the PMRC's suggestion, the major record companies voluntarily instituted a ratings system for its products similar to the MPAA code for films.

The work of the PMRC stimulated a wave of state and local legislation around the country, particularly in the South. In 1989 the city of New Iberia, Louisiana, passed an ordinance requiring that retailers place any "obscene" recordings out of plain view of unmarried persons under seventeen years of age. The following year state legislatures in Missouri, Maryland, Delaware, and Florida required mandatory warning labels for any recordings judged to be excessively violent or sexually explicit. Antiobscenity activist Jack Thompson protested that Dade County, Florida, record stores were ignoring the new law by selling to underage buyers 2 Live Crew's *As Nasty as They Wanna Be* (1990). Federal district judge Jose Gonzalez declared the rap album obscene and upheld the state's restrictions on its sale. Gonzalez also ruled that local law enforcement officials had been guilty of prior restraint in attempting to control sales of the product prior to judicial review.

In a move that perhaps charts the course for future censorship efforts, censors have directed their efforts at the large communications conglomerates that have controlled the recording industry since the 1980's era of corporate mergers and acquisitions. A group of shareholders led by actor Charlton Heston pressured media giant Time-Warner into dropping distribution of Ice-T's 1994 album *Body Count* which included the unrepentant single "Cop Killer."   —*Luke A. Powers*

See also Carlin, George; "Cop Killer"; Federal Communications Commission; Jackson, Michael; Lennon, John; Music TeleVision; Parents' Music Resource Center; Rap music; Rock 'n' roll music; Seeger, Pete; 2 Live Crew.

BIBLIOGRAPHY

The definitive history of censorship in the recording industry is Linda Martin and Kerry Seagrave's *Anti-Rock: The Opposition to Rock and Roll* (New York: Da Capo Press, 1993). R. Serge Denisoff's *Solid Gold: The Popular Record Industry* (New Brunswick and London: Transaction Books, 1975) is somewhat dated but provides an excellent discussion of a crucial period of record censorship: the late 1960's and early 1970's. Trent Hill explores the roots of censorship in past racial politics in his essay "The Enemy Within: Censorship in Rock Music in the 1950's" in *The South Atlantic Quarterly* (90, no. 4, Fall, 1991). Robert Palmer's *Rock and Roll: An Unruly History* (New York: Harmony Books, 1995) and Joe Stuessy's *Rock and Roll: Its History and Stylistic Development* (Englewood Cliffs, N.J.: Prentice-Hall, 1994) explore the essentially controversial nature of their subject.

Red Badge of Courage, The

TYPE OF WORK: Novel

PUBLISHED: 1894 and 1895

AUTHOR: Stephen Crane (1871-1900)

SUBJECT MATTER: Novel about a young Union soldier's difficult adjustment to the horrors of combat during the Civil War

SIGNIFICANCE: From the first year it was published, this classic American novel has been challenged by various groups

The Red Badge of Courage is a novel in which Henry Fleming, "the Youth," struggles with the question of whether he will fight or run when he sees his first real battle. After it begins, he stands firm for the first charge, then runs when the Confederate forces charge again. He is ashamed, wishing he had a bloody bandage, a "red badge of courage." Eventually, he returns to his outfit and becomes an obsessed fighter.

This book was first attacked when it was removed from the American Library Association list of approved books in 1896. However, its removal was more of a response to author Stephen Crane than to the book itself. As Crane was writing *The Red Badge of Courage*, he published *Maggie: A Girl of the Streets*, a gritty, realistic look at life in New York's slums that brought many calls for censorship against Crane. Also, Civil War veterans objected to a young man with no military experience writing detailed battle accounts. Nevertheless, the novel enjoyed a sustained popularity, occasionally being objected to by religious or antiwar and antiviolence groups. In 1985, for example, the superintendent of schools in a Florida community banned *The Red Badge of Courage* for profanity because it used the word "hell."

See also *All Quiet on the Western Front*; American Library Association; Civil War, U.S.; *Maggie: A Girl of the Streets*; War.

Redd v. State of Georgia

COURT: Georgia court of appeals

DATE: April 6, 1910

SIGNIFICANCE: The Georgia court's decision expanded the definition of public indecency, affirming the right of the state to regulate individual behaviors that society deems indecent

The state of Georgia's 1895 penal code dictated that acts of public indecency were punishable as criminal misdemeanors. The plaintiffs in *Redd v. State of Georgia* had been convicted of public indecency for having deliberately displayed to a woman and her children a view of a bull and a cow copulating in an open field. The plaintiffs argued that their actions did not fall within the legal definition of public indecency, which, they asserted, "relates only to indecent exposure of the human person." Rejecting this interpretation, the court ruled that public indecency encompassed "all notorious public and indecent conduct, tending to debauch the public morals."

The court's interpretation was supported by an earlier decision in *McJunkins v. State*. Quoting from *McJunkins*, the court held that the term "public indecency" had no fixed legal meaning, that it was "vague and indefinite" and could not in itself imply a definite offense. The court's acceptance of this view, coupled with its refusal to limit acts of public indecency to those outlined in *McJunkins*—the inappropriate display of the human body or the production and distribution of obscene materials—allowed it to expand the legal definition of public indecency. The court ruled that the state's statute was "broad enough to cover all notorious public and indecent conduct, tending to debauch the public morals, even though it be unattended by an exposure of the human body."

Having expanded the legal definition of public indecency,

the court went on to state that acts by themselves could not be considered indecent, unless "the time, the place, the circumstances, and the motives of the actors [are] considered." Accordingly, certain acts might be deemed decent in certain contexts and indecent in others. The court ruled that "a fair test to determine whether an act is notoriously indecent . . . is to consider whether the general run of the citizenry . . . would readily recognize it as such (all the attendant facts and circumstances and the motives of the actor being considered)."

Redd determined that individual behavior and the right to free expression were governed by contemporary social norms of decency. It supported assertions that individual behavior is open to public censure when its runs contrary to society's norms. Thus, the court classified the plaintiffs' behavior as indecent and open to censure because their deliberateness in displaying animal copulation to other people ran contrary to society's norms of decency at that time.

See also First Amendment; Morality; Obscenity: legal definitions.

Redeeming social value

DEFINITION: Positive quality of a book, film, or other work that gives it some measure of worth to society as a whole
SIGNIFICANCE: The U.S. Supreme Court once defined this concept as a measure for determining whether works otherwise deemed obscene are worthy of free speech protections
In the evolving definitions of obscenity that British and American courts have used since the Hicklin case in 1868 to determine whether books and other materials should be protected from censorship, the question of whether otherwise obscene materials have some kind of merit that should exempt them from prosecution has arisen repeatedly. In 1957 the U.S. Supreme Court ruled, in *Roth v. United States*, that most "unorthodox ideas, controversial ideas, even ideas hateful to the prevailing climate of opinion—have the full protection" of the First Amendment. Up until that decision any material labeled as "obscene" was automatically regarded as something other than constitutionally protected speech. The presumption was that any material deemed to be obscenity lacked "redeeming social value" because of its obscenity.

In *Memoirs v. Massachusetts* in 1966 the Supreme Court transformed the concept of "lack of redeeming social value" from a description of obscene material to part of the definition of what constituted obscenity. Under this revised definition, any material containing redeeming social value, however slight, could not be labeled obscene. In the opinion that he wrote for this decision Justice William J. Brennan, Jr., advised lower courts facing obscenity decisions to consider "all possible uses" of material before judging it "utterly without redeeming social value," and thus obscene. In *Miller v. California*, in 1972, the Court replaced its social value standard with the requirement that in order to be judged obscene, a work must lack any serious literary, artistic, political, or scientific value.

See also Books and obscenity law; Brennan, William J., Jr.; Family; *Fanny Hill, The Memoirs of*; Hicklin case; *Miller v. California*; Morality; Obscenity: legal definitions; *Roth v. United States*.

Reformation, the

DATE: Sixteenth-seventeenth centuries
PLACE: Western Europe
SIGNIFICANCE: This widespread movement to reform the Roman Catholic church gave rise to Protestant denominations, as well as persecutions and censorship
The Protestant Reformation began in Germany in 1517, when Martin Luther published his theses challenging the Roman Catholic church's practice of selling indulgences. Pope Leo X responded with a decree ordering Luther to submit to the authority of the Church. After Luther burned the decree, the pope declared him a heretic. Luther's writings were then banned by imperial edict, but he had great support among the people and his writings continued to be openly sold. Unable to reconcile with the Catholic church, Luther formed the first Protestant denomination, which took his name and became known as Lutheranism.

After several princes converted to Lutheranism and brought their subjects with them, Lutherans living under Catholic rulers were forced to flee for their lives. However, geographical boundaries could not halt the flow of ideas, as the Holy Roman Empire's ruler Charles V learned when he tried to stop the spread of Protestant ideas in The Netherlands by burning Luther's books in 1522. His attempt failed. Protestantism, the name given to the reformed churches that split from the Roman Catholic church, took hold in The Netherlands and continued to spread across Europe.

But this did not discourage either Catholics or Protestants from employing censorship and violence to advance their own religious causes. In Switzerland the early reform movement was led by Ulrich Zwingli, a Catholic priest who attracted a large following after he began attacking the authority of the Church. He met his death on the battlefield when war broke out between Catholics and Protestants in 1531. Anabaptists often met even crueler fates. Originally followers of Zwingli, they broke away because of doctrinal disputes. Despised by Catholics, Lutherans, and Zwinglians alike, Anabaptist leaders were sought out and killed, along with their families. The preferred method of executing them was drowning.

In England, after King Henry VIII broke from Rome and established the Church of England, both Roman Catholics and Lutherans were executed. Then, when Queen Mary ascended to the thrown and attempted to restore Catholicism to England, she ordered the burning of hundreds of Protestants. However, the tables turned once again when Mary's half-sister, Elizabeth I succeeded her and ordered the execution of Catholics.

Before Protestantism was stamped out in France following civil wars between Catholics and Protestants, John Calvin, a convert to Protestantism, was forced to flee France to escape persecution. He settled in Geneva where he established a theocratic government in which church leaders held supreme authority. From 1541 to 1564 heretics were expelled and executed. All theaters and places of amusement were closed, and a council of church elders inspected every household and examined citizens regarding their religion, dress, love-making, and political opinions.

One of the Catholic church's responses to the Protestant Reformation was a serious attempt to reform itself from within. But it also turned to violence and censorship. In 1542 Pope Paul III founded the Congregation of the Inquisition to seek out and execute heretics. He also ordered the publication of the *Index Librorum Prohibitorum*, which listed books considered dangerous to the faith. Catholics without special dispensation were prohibited from reading books listed in the *Index*.

See also Bible; Calvin, John; Death; Erasmus, Desiderius; Hobbes, Thomas; *Index Librorum Prohibitorum*; Luther, Martin; Paul IV, Pope; Puritans; Richelieu, Cardinal.

Reggae music

DEFINITION: Jamaican popular musical form frequently containing politically conscious lyrics that arose during the 1960's

SIGNIFICANCE: Antiestablishment messages conveyed by some reggae artists have provoked opposition to the performance and broadcasting of reggae, particularly within Jamaica

Reggae is a rock musical form with Jamaican origins that grew out of ska. Many of the artists who popularized a style known as "roots reggae" during the 1960's were from the slums of Jamaica, and their lyrics reflected ghetto life and the concerns of the poor. Most of these same musicians were also members of a religious sect known as Rastafarianism, which holds that this world is the biblical Babylon. Babylon is represented in Jamaica by the government, which Rastas believe is not serving the people, but rather itself. Rasta philosophy, which emphasizes brotherhood and an end to all forms of oppression, is a frequent topic in reggae lyrics, which have a long tradition of political consciousness and opposition to the status quo. These elements have made reggae music and its artists targets of censorship by those who prefer the values of mainstream society.

Until nongovernment-owned Jamaican radio stations, such as IRIE-FM, began operation, little reggae music was played on the radio. What were played typically were love songs with no political content. Many politically conscious musicians had additional trouble in finding producers who would make record albums because of their fear of retaliation by local police. In 1960, the performer Ossie's allegedly "blasphemous" recordings were refused air time on radio stations; however, his Rasta-oriented material was sold in record shops. A 1964 Wailers concert in Kingston was nearly canceled after fights broke out between police and those attempting to gain entrance. Afterward the Wailers were accused of attracting a "criminal element," the Rastafaris.

Reggae performer Bunny Livingston was arrested and convicted in 1967 for possession of marijuana (which he claims he did not have); he spent fourteen months in prison. At the same time his Wailers bandmate Bob Marley spent two days in jail for a traffic offense. Those living in Jamaica's ghettos believed that the police were trying to silence the Wailers and their Rasta message. In 1975 another member of the Wailers, Peter Tosh, released "Legalize It," a single that promoted legalization of marijuana, the smoking of which is a Rasta ritual. Although the song was banned by the Jamaica Broadcasting Authority, it became an underground hit. In 1976 Bob and Rita Marley were shot during a murder attempt on Bob Marley. The gunmen hoped to prevent him from performing a pre-election concert sponsored by the cultural section of the prime minister's office.

A variation of reggae known as "dance hall" became popular during the 1980's. Its beat is faster than that of roots reggae and its artists tend to perform less politically conscious material. Nevertheless, dance hall artists have been charged with communicating a message of violence. In 1992 Buju Banton's single "Boom Bye Bye" was not played by major radio stations in Jamaica and the United States after the Gay and Lesbian Alliance Against Defamation (GLAAD) protested the song for condoning violence toward homosexuals. Shabba Ranks's scheduled performance on *The Tonight Show* was canceled after GLAAD protested his support for Banton's antihomosexual views.

See also Folk music; Music; Protest music; Rap music; Recording industry; Rock 'n' roll music.

Regina v. Cameron

COURT: Court of Appeal, Ontario, Canada

DECIDED: June 23, 1966

SIGNIFICANCE: In rejecting arguments that a work of art is not obscene simply because it has artistic merit, this ruling decreed that the only acceptable standard of obscenity is set by the average Canadian

An exhibit of seven drawings that attracted fewer than forty spectators constitutes the focus of this case. In late May of 1965 the Dorothy Cameron Gallery in Toronto exhibited the drawings, titled *Eros 65*. Police described the drawings as manifesting strong sexual connotations, including acts of lesbianism, heterosexual intercourse, and sexually inviting poses. Because obscenity was a crime defined by statute, the court required the Crown to prove beyond a reasonable doubt that the drawings were obscene, that they were exposed to public view, and that such exposure was done knowingly and without lawful justification or excuse.

Several expert witnesses asserted that their interest in the drawings centered not upon the pictures' "subject matter," but on their artistic merit. While the court accepted artistic merit as one factor to be considered when evaluating obscenity, it ruled that such merit alone could not "obliterate" obscenity when it was as clear and unequivocal as it was in these seven drawings.

The question of whether the exhibit was knowingly exposed to public view was discussed at some length. The court said "knowingly" did not mean that the exhibitor must possess legal knowledge of obscenity. It meant only that the exhibitor be aware of the subject matter and purposely expose it to the public. The posting of an "Adults Only" sign and statements by the gallery owner were cited as evidence of knowing exposure. Among other things, the owner said the gallery was hers and she would run it. She also pressed herself against exhibits with arms outstretched and said, "You'll have to kill me first before you take my pictures."

The element of the absence of lawful justification or excuse introduced a legal complexity by requiring the Crown to prove a negative. The court said that such proof could be inferred by actions of the exhibitor. Since the gallery owner took no actions offering lawful justification or excuse to the magistrate, the court ruled that none existed. The court also commented on the gallery's affirmative defense that its display benefited art students, and helped the public to appreciate art. Expert witnesses asserted that public benefit resides in the form, not the subject matter, of the drawings. The court expressly rejected this argument, however, saying that such a benefit could have been provided without resort to obscene subject matter. Consequently, the court dismissed the appeal and supported the magistrate's ruling that the exhibit was obscene.

See also Art; *Butler v. The Queen*; Canada; Community standards; Morality; Nudity; Obscenity: legal definitions; Seldes, George.

Regina v. Penguin Books Ltd.

COURT: Old Bailey, London

DECIDED: November 2, 1960

SIGNIFICANCE: The court's decision in this first test of Great Britain's newest Obscene Publications Act against a work of art was widely interpreted as fulfilling the act's aim to protect art while clamping down on pornography

This case involved publication of an uncensored paperback edition of D. H. Lawrence's *Lady Chatterley's Lover* (1928) in early 1960. The book had previously been available in Britain only in abridged forms. Penguin Books planned to publish the unexpurgated version in a series marking the thirty years that had passed since Lawrence's death. In order to test the Obscene Publications Act of 1959, Penguin technically "published" the novel by sending twelve copies to the government's Director of Public Prosecutions (DPP), who announced he would prosecute the novel under the 1959 law. To be guilty under this act a book, recording, film, or other work had to be shown to have a "tendency to deprave and corrupt" its likely audience. The trial that followed thus centered on the question of whether Lawrence's novel had such a tendency.

The case came to court in November, 1960, and centered on the novel's profane language and a section in which Lady Chatterley engages in anal intercourse with her husband's gamekeeper. During the trial the prosecuting counsel, Mervyn Griffiths-Jones, uttered a remark that later became notorious in linking censorship with elitist attitudes: He asked the jurors

Pleased by the Regina v. Penguin *verdict in 1960, Alan Lane, the head of Penguin Books, holds a copy of* Lady Chatterley's Lover. (Archive Photos)

whether *Lady Chatterley's Lover* was a book that they would "wish your wife or servants to read."

The Obscene Publications Act contained clauses permitting challenged works a "public good" defence, should the works have artistic merit. Thirty-five defense witnesses, including literary scholars, members of the clergy, and an educational psychologist, testified that Lawrence's novel was of a high artistic standard. The defense also noted that Penguin Books were clearly not pornographers, but publishers of high repute. The prosecution called no witnesses, apparently believing that the book could speak for itself.

After the jury returned a not guilty verdict, Penguin issued 200,000 copies of the book and dedicated its next editions to the jury. There was no appeal. One result of the case was to make available to the general public a wide range of works that had previously been available only in expensive hardbound editions. British publishers were now free to publish works containing obscene language in inexpensive paperbacks. Some people have seen this trial as instrumental in ushering in the so-called permissive era of the 1960's, although later prosecutions under the 1959 Act were successful.

See also *Lady Chatterley's Lover*; Obscenity: legal definitions.

Religion

DEFINITION: Systems of beliefs about the ultimate meaning of life

SIGNIFICANCE: Organized religion has often employed censorship as a means of enforcing correct beliefs and as a means of preventing people from being exposed to activities that are seen as immoral

The early Christians, during the time of the Roman Empire, were deeply concerned with establishing orthodoxy. Beliefs that were not orthodox were heresies. "Heresy" comes from a Greek word that means "to choose": Heretics were those who had chosen to follow their own ideas rather than the teachings of the Church.

The New Testament, in Acts 19:19, provides justification for religious censorship in a passage in which the Apostle Paul praises converts to Christianity for burning their pagan books. The first reported official act of censorship by the Christian church occurred in 150 C.E., when the Church condemned and prohibited a book on the life of Saint Paul that was decided to be in error. The Gnostics, believers in a form of salvation through spiritual self-knowledge, were seen as challenging Christian teachings, and the Gnostics became targets of much of early Church censorship. Church authorities condemned and burned Gnostic books.

The Christians themselves were subject to censorship, as well as other forms of persecution, throughout much of the period of the Roman Empire. In 324, however, Constantine, a convert to Christianity, became emperor. With the exception of the Emperor Julian, all following emperors were Christian, and the Church was able to augment its acts of censorship of unorthodox beliefs and writings with the power of the state. Pope Innocent I, in 405, and Pope Galasius, in 496, issued the first lists of books forbidden within the Christian Roman Empire.

The Middle Ages. Since the Church was supposed to be the sole source of correct teaching during the Middle Ages, the Church was concerned with preventing people from being exposed to ideas that might mislead them. In the early Middle Ages, when books were rare and few could read, the written communication of ideas did not pose much of a problem. By the 1100's, however, books and literacy were gradually becoming more common, although books still had to be painstakingly copied by hand.

Gradually, the Church developed the *Index Librorum Prohibitorum*, or index of forbidden books. The more available books became, the more the Church leadership attempted to control them. In the 1200's, Pope Gregory IX condemned some of Aristotle's philosophical works and ordered all copies of the Talmud, a Jewish religious text, burned. In 1467 Pope Innocent VII commanded that all books should be submitted to local Church authorities before being released to readers. In 1487 this same pope issued a declaration recognizing books as a serious danger to society and calling for alliances between religious and political authorities to suppress ideas that challenged Church teaching, including the ideas of the new Protestant sects, as well as philosophical and scientific ideas. At the Council of Trent in 1545 Church leaders began to draw up a comprehensive plan to control literature and the Church issued the Index of the Inquisition of Rome, the first published list of prohibited books and authors. Throughout the later Middle Ages, not only the pope but also cardinals, bishops, and even parish priests had the power to censor materials that they found objectionable. Church censorship continued to be concerned primarily with ideas that challenged sacred teachings, rather than with obscenity.

Protestantism. As the printing of books made them more widely available in the 1500's, it became easier to spread views that challenged those of the Church. Some members of Protestant sects began to see the suppression of books as a part of the system of religious control of the Roman Catholic church. In England, especially, which broke away from the Roman Catholic church and established its own church under the English monarchs, many people began to see prior restraint, the censorship of books before their publication, as a Roman Catholic practice, since this involved the establishment of orthodoxy from above and did not permit individuals to discover religious truth for themselves. The biblical passage John 8:32, "you will know the truth and the truth will make you free," was seen by many Protestants as scriptural support for opposition to censorship.

One of the most famous early treatises against censorship was the *Areopagitica*, published in 1644 by the poet John Milton. Milton argues that there should be no prior restraint of publication, since the truth wins out over falsehood in the free struggle of ideas. He does, however, recognize the need to criminally prosecute some writings after their publication.

Despite such early Protestant objections to Catholic censorship, when Protestants came to power they often engaged in censorship themselves. The religious regime in Geneva, Switzerland, which was created by John Calvin and which lasted from 1541 to 1564, practiced a much more severe form of censorship than that of the Catholic church. All books that conflicted with Calvinist doctrine or that were considered in any way immoral were banned from Geneva.

During the Commonwealth in England, from 1649 to 1660, the Protestant Puritan government of Oliver Cromwell enforced a rigid program of censorship. At about the same period, the Puritans in America refused to tolerate most forms of graphic art, discouraged nonreligious reading and writing, and understood hymns to be the only type of acceptable music.

Modern Catholicism. Church censorship has continued to be a doctrine of the Catholic church in modern times, although the Church has usually relied on persuasion and moral authority, rather than on force and legal authority. The Church still licenses books that are acceptable and withholds licenses from profane, obscene, sacrilegious, or heretical books. However, the approval of the Roman Catholic church is most often meant simply as a guide for believers.

Some Catholics who are not priests or officials of the church may attempt to suppress materials that are critical of the church or not in accordance with church teachings. Public opinion in Catholic Ireland led to the establishment of official state censorship in that country in 1929 with the passage of the Censorship of Publications Bill. The Censorship Board created by that legislation continued to exist after the Irish Republic was created in 1949.

In the United States, the Catholic National Organization for Decent Literature (formed in 1938) has published lists of objectionable literature. Members of the National Council of Catholic Men were active in urging the House of Representatives Select Committee on the Study of Current Pornographic Materials, often called the Gathings Committee, to recommend legal action against pornography in 1952.

About as soon as motion pictures were invented, the Catholic church became concerned with moral indecency in film. As a result, the church formed the Legion of Decency, which sought to give films moral classifications, based on the treatment of sex, profanity, and religious issues. The familiar rating system that was eventually adopted by the Motion Picture Producers and Distributors Association owed much to the classifications developed by the Legion of Decency.

Censorship in Islam. Much of the opposition to governmental censorship in Western countries is based on the concept of separation of church and state. Those who believe in the separation of the two argue that governments should simply promote the well-being of their citizens and not try to establish the ultimate truth. In this view, governments have no business forbidding the expression of religious or antireligious ideas.

Islam, the Muslim religion, generally rejects the idea that religion and government can be separated. Under Islamic law, human law is the expression of divine will. Therefore, Islamic law does not simply attempt to regulate relationships among people, it also attempts to regulate the relationship of individuals with God and with their own consciences. Some Muslim governments interpret this to mean that they have both the right and the obligation to control sacrilegious expressions of opinion.

The best-known modern act of Islamic censorship in modern times involves the novel *The Satanic Verses* by Salman Rushdie, a British author born in India to a Muslim family. The novel, published in late 1988, contains references to the Prophet Muhammad that many Muslims saw as blasphemous and obscene. As a result, the book was banned in most Muslim countries. Early in February, 1989, the Ayatollah Ruhollah Khomeini, leader of Iran, called on Muslims around the world to kill Rushdie and anyone who, knowing the book's contents, participated in its publication. Anti-Rushdie demonstrations followed among Muslims in many places of the world, including England. Rushdie himself was forced to go into hiding and the British government provided him with protection, as he was a British subject under a clear and believable threat to his life. The Rushdie affair indicated the depth of the cultural conflict between Western political ideals regarding free speech and Muslim views of government as part of a religious system.

The Religious Right. By the late 1970's, many conservative Christians were expressing the belief that the problems of American society were due to America's straying from Christian truth. American schools and the American media, from this perspective, were spreading ideas that were opposed to Christianity and that were undermining the nation's moral character. Therefore, some conservative Christians saw attempting to exercise control over the schools and the media as both a religious and a patriotic duty.

During the early 1980's, attempts at library censorship in North America more than tripled in number, according to the American Library Association, and conservative religious groups were responsible for the overwhelming majority of these attempts. In Escambia County, Florida, members of the Crossroads Baptist Church organized to remove a number of sociology and psychology texts from the schools. Books about evolution, children's books with witches, books that treated homosexuality with anything but condemnation, books with four-letter words, books with elements of magic, and myriad other books became the objects of censorship attacks.

The views that the members of the religious right have seen as dangerous have often been characterized as secular humanism. This term refers to a philosophy that places human beings, rather than God, at the center of human concerns and endeavors, and that sees morality as a relative and human creation, rather than a product of the divine ordering of life. Conservative Christians have long been opposed to sexually explicit literature; with the rise of the religious right, calls for censorship have also been directed at philosophical expressions.

Onalee McGraw's pamphlet *Secular Humanism and the Schools: The Issue Whose Time Has Come* (1966) and Tim Lahaye's book *The Battle for the Mind* (1980) helped to popularize claims that secular humanism has taken over the media and the schools and that the so-called philosophy must be suppressed. One of the most influential figures in the religious right, Jerry Falwell, founder of Moral Majority, has expressed similar views.

Falwell has argued that censorship already exists in American schools: the humanists who control education censor

Release of the film adaptation of Nikos Kazantzakis' novel The Last Temptation of Christ *in 1988 offended the religious sensibilities of many Christians.* (Museum of Modern Art/Film Stills Archive)

Christian ethics and Christian beliefs. In his book, *Listen America* (1980), Falwell argues that education is a means of passing on the values of a society. It may pass on Christian values, or it may pass on non-Christian values. By opting for the perspective that Falwell described as "amoral humanism," educators were removing Christianity from the curriculum and replacing it with a substitute religion that teaches rejection of American society's basic values. Falwell's critics have pointed out that one place to look for American society's basic values is the Constitution, of which the first sentence of the First Amendment states that "Congress shall make no law respecting an establishment of religion." Courts have since decided that public schools, as state-funded and state-supported institutions, likewise are not in the business of supporting any religion. Private schools, in turn, are allowed to support the religion of their choice.

Views similar to those of Falwell motivated the textbook critics Mel Gabler and Norma Gabler to found the group Educational Research Analysis, based in Texas. This group attempts to have school systems reject textbooks that do not promote values its founders consider "traditional" American Christian values. The Gablers dislike being called censors, seeing their work as part of a struggle between two educational philosophies.

Religious conservatives in Canada have formed influential pressure groups to keep books that they see as sacrilegious and profane out of schools. The Fundamentalist Christian organization Renaissance International has organized media campaigns across Canada to protest objectionable schoolbooks. In the late 1970's, Renaissance International supported efforts in several communities to remove from school curricula a prize-winning novel by Canadian author Margaret Laurence.

Christian conservatives have tended to see obscene or pornographic literature as destructive in itself and as part of the general moral decline of North America. In the mid-1980's, the Religious Alliance Against Pornography, under the leadership of its chairman, Jerry Kirk, drew national attention for its attempt to organize leaders of all religious denominations in the United States to fight pornography. Kirk and his associates, such as the Gablers in Texas and the Canadians of Renaissance International, understood their efforts as a cultural struggle against forces threatening basic social values.

The National Endowment for the Arts in the United States became a target of conservative religious efforts to protect basic social values. Evangelical religious groups opposed the NEA because it provided funds to artistic projects that the religious groups believed were obscene and corrupting. Religious organizations were particularly active in opposing museum exhibitions of the photographer Robert Mapplethorpe in 1989, because several of Mapplethorpe's photographs depicted homosexual eroticism. Senator Jesse Helms of North Carolina, a Southern Baptist with ties to many conservative religious leaders, was especially outspoken in his criticism of the NEA and led the movement to cut government funding for the organization.

The U.S. Constitution. The First Amendment to the United States Constitution both forbids the establishment of religion by the government and guarantees freedom of speech and of the press. Religious freedom and freedom from censorship are often virtually the same thing: The right to say what one thinks is the right to express religious views. In some situations, however, there may be conflict between the expression of religious beliefs and the principle that the government and governmental institutions should not be involved in establishing a religion.

Minority religions have found freedom from the censorship of their views in the religious clause of the First Amendment. For example, in 1951, in the case *Niemotko v. State of Maryland*, the Supreme Court struck down the arrest of a group of Jehovah's Witnesses who had been arrested by the police for attempting to hold Bible classes in a city park. When those expressing religious views are public institutions or public officials, however, the courts have tended to see these expressions as violations of the religious clause. In the case *American Civil Liberties Union of Illinois v. City of St. Charles*, in 1986, the ACLU brought suit against the city for displaying a cross on public property during the Christmas season, thus displaying official support for the Christian religion. The court agreed with the ACLU and granted an injunction, forcing the city to take down the cross.

Many of the most heated conflicts between freedom of expression and establishment of religion have involved public schools. The Supreme Court has consistently ruled that school sponsored prayers, even if nondenominational and voluntary, involve the establishment of religion and are unconstitutional. Schools are also forbidden from using religious literature, causing some to argue that the courts are engaging in censorship by decreeing what schools may or may not teach. The prohibition on religious literature in schools may also sometimes raise questions about whether written materials are religious or instructional in nature. —*Carl L. Bankston III*

See also Atheism; Buddhism; Calvin, John; Christianity; *Index Librorum Prohibitorum*; Islam; Judaism; Milton, John; Moral Majority; Puritans; Rushdie, Salman; School prayer; Secular humanism.

BIBLIOGRAPHY

Most books on censorship touch on religion, since religious beliefs provide a fundamental motivation for attempting to control ideas and forms of expression. Eli M. Oboler's *Fear of the Word: Censorship and Sex* (Metuchen, N.J.: Scarecrow Press, 1974) provides a readable overview of the role of religion in promoting censorship in the western hemisphere, from ancient times to the present. The role of the Roman Catholic church in promoting control over films and a rating system for films is dealt with by James M. Skinner in *The Cross and the Cinema: The Legion of Decency and the National Catholic Office for Motion Pictures 1933-1970* (Westport, Conn.: Praeger, 1993). The Ayatollah Khomeini's call for the death of Salman Rushdie brought attention to the issue of censorship in

Islamic societies. An overall view of this is provided by *The Rushdie Affair: The Novel, the Ayatollah, and the West* (N.Y.: Carol Publishing Group, 1990), by Daniel Pipes. The views of Muslim writers who supported Rushdie and opposed attempts to ban his book may be found in the collection, *For Rushdie: Essays by Arab and Muslim Writers in Defence of Free Speech* (N.Y.: George Braziller, 1994), edited by Anouar Abdallah. Many books about the censorship of the religious right have been published. Stephen Bates's *Battleground: One Mother's Crusade, the Religious Right, and the Struggle for Control of Our Classrooms* (N.Y.: Poseidon Press, 1993) is a readable narrative of the war over books in the schools. Arthur F. Ide's *Evangelical Terrorism: Censorship, Falwell, Robertson, and the Seamy Side of Christian Fundamentalism* (Irving, Tex.: Scholars Books, 1986) is a no-holds-barred attack on efforts by religious conservatives to control publications in schools and in the media. For the other side of the argument, readers may consult the Reverend Jerry Falwell's *Listen America!* (Garden City, N.Y.: Doubleday, 1980). Falwell presents his argument that secular humanism in the schools and in the media is undermining basic social values, and that book critics such as the Gablers are defending American civilization. In *Book Burning* (Westchester, Ill.: Crossway Books, 1983), Cal Thomas, syndicated newspaper columnist, maintains that the liberal establishment practices censorship by keeping religious and conservative views out of magazines, libraries, bookstores, and other means of communication.

Religious education

DEFINITION: Teaching of religious doctrines in secular educational institutions

SIGNIFICANCE: Whether public schools should provide instruction in religion has been a subject of heated debate, especially in the United States

Free education has long been available to citizens of most developed nations. The content of that education, however, continues to be controversial. In Europe, for example, the earliest private schools were religious and were intended to produce members of religious orders. Likewise, the schools of the early Puritan colonists of North America were establishments of orthodox Christianity.

The First Amendment to the U.S. Constitution states, in part, that "Congress shall make no law respecting an establishment of religion, or prohibiting the free exercise thereof." During the first century of U.S. independence, religious thought nevertheless was at the heart of American education. The Bible was a textbook, particularly in small schools, in which it was the only printed book available. As such, it was reading primer, history book, math book, science book, treatise on genealogy, and geography text, all in one. The Bible was also the linchpin of the Christian religion. For a young nation born largely of the desire for religious freedom, the Bible was the primary source of ethical standards—the characters in its collection of stories, histories, and parables were looked to, by children and adults alike, as behavior models. The Bible was considered by most to be a historical account of actual events and real people. Until the close of the nineteenth century U.S. education reflected the prevailing view that embracing of strong religious values was basic to intellectual and moral development and that such values were to be disseminated through the schools of the land.

At the close of the nineteenth century, a nationwide reform, spearheaded by educator John Dewey, decreed that the partnership of education and religion should be dissolved in order to remove superstition and narrow thinking from the classroom. Education was to be separated from the influence of possibly biased religious thought and placed firmly in the hands of intellect. In the mid- and late twentieth century, separation of church and state moved more to the forefront of American thought and politics. The issue of whether aid to religious schools should be declared, as a matter a law, a violation of the U.S. Constitution, became one of the most hotly argued controversies in the American legal system.

Whether or not a definitive separation of religion and education was the original intent of the Framers of the First Amendment, formal teaching of religious thought and practices has almost disappeared from modern public classrooms. This separation holds true not only in the United States, but, to varying degrees, in other educated nations of the world community—except in private religious schools and in seminaries.

Views from the Right and the Left. The conservative view of religious education holds that the individual is a spiritual being before all else, and that education, to be effective, must educate the whole person. Intellectual prowess is important, but the spiritual must not be neglected in favor it. According to the conservative view, the main thrust of education must be the molding of the moral and ethical beliefs of the student, because the moral and ethical standards of a nation's citizens are vital to the continuing prosperity of that nation.

According to the educators espousing the liberal point of view, educating an individual should be a process of developing the intellect, without recourse to the use of religious myths, mysteries, or beliefs. The student's mind should be equipped to think, to analyze, to judge, and the development of moral and ethical beliefs should be left to parents and religious institutions attended by choice.

Teaching of the sciences—especially physics, genetics, biology, and anthropology—has occasioned the major part of the controversy. According to biblical account, God created the universe; physicists offer other theories, such as the "big bang." The Bible depicts God as creating humans from the dust of the earth; scientists suggest that humanity descended from earlier primates.

Methods of Handling the Controversy. Court decisions handed down during the late twentieth century have, for the most part, concerned themselves with the state-supported public school systems. Whether religion should form part of the curriculum of state-funded public schools is the legal question at the crux of most hotly contested court cases. A movement known as the National Association for Released Time Christian Education has offered one solution: Students wishing to participate in religious education should be able to leave their regular classrooms to receive religious instruction in off-campus sites from volunteer teachers. Such released-time programs have been found constitutional in the U.S. court systems.

State-supported colleges and universities in the United States have observed the separation of church and state precedents by presenting religion in elective philosophy, anthropology, sociology, psychology, and literature courses. Privately funded religious schools, as they are not supported by state monies, are exempt from the legal fray. —*Barbara C. Stanley*

See also Bible; Education; Evolution; First Amendment Congress; Gabler, Mel, and Norma Gabler; People for the American Way; School prayer; Secular humanism; Textbooks.

BIBLIOGRAPHY

Censorship: Opposing Viewpoints, edited by Lisa Orr (San Diego, Calif.: Greenhaven Press, 1990), contains a balanced consideration of the role of censorship in the business of publishing textbooks. Stephen L. Carter's *The Culture of Disbelief: How American Law and Politics Trivialize Religious Devotion* (New York: Basic Books, 1993), although firmly on the religious right, is a fact-filled review of the role of religion in American education. *Battleground: One Mother's Crusade, the Religious Right, and the Struggle for Control of Our Classrooms*, by Stephen Bates (New York: Poseidon Press, 1993) is an unbiased, accurate, and detailed account of *Mozert v. Hawkins County Board of Education*—the 1986 Tennessee court case dubbed "Scopes II" by the press. John J. Coughlin's "Religion, Education, and the First Amendment," in *America* 168, no. 17 (May 15, 1993), traces the influence of religion on U.S. educational institutions. Charles R. Kniker's "Teacher Education and Religion: The Role of Foundation Courses in Preparing Students to Teach About Religions," in *Religion and Public Education* 17, no. 2 (Spring-Summer, 1990), suggests ways to prepare future teachers to teach about religion in the public schools.

Reporters Committee for Freedom of the Press

FOUNDED: 1970

TYPE OF ORGANIZATION: Nonprofit association created to protect the media's free speech rights

SIGNIFICANCE: The committee supports reporters' right to access and publish information

The Reporters Committee for Freedom of the Press was organized at a meeting at Georgetown University prompted when *New York Times* journalist Earl Caldwell was ordered by a grand jury to reveal his sources in the Black Panthers organization. The resulting committee formed during this meeting wanted to offer frfee legal services to reporters facing infringement of their First Amendment rights.

The committee intervened in a number of free speech battles, including the fight to keep Richard Nixon's presidential papers public. The Reporters Committee for Freedom of the Press has taken part in many significant press freedom cases that have come before the Supreme Court, including *Nebraska Press Association v. Stuart*. The committee claims that it serves two thousand journalists each year and never requires payment for legal aid. It also produces numbers of publications and resources on free speech issues. It publishes a quarterly magazine, *The News Media and The Law*, and a biweekly newsletter, *News Media Update*. The Reporters Committee for Freedom of the Press also publishes handbooks and guides on First Amendment rights, what information is required to be public, and how to access it. In the 1990's it became a leading advocate for reporters' interests on the Internet.

See also First Amendment; First Amendment Congress; News media censorship; Watergate scandal.

Revolutionary War, American

DATE: 1775-1783

PLACE: North America

SIGNIFICANCE: The revolt of American colonists against British rule tested the rebels' commitment to liberty; they suppressed dissent by those who expressed loyalty to Britain or dissatisfaction with armed insurrection

The American war against Great Britain began with the battle at Lexington, Massachusetts, on April 19, 1775, but the struggle by American rebels for the support of their fellow colonists preceded this skirmish. It has been estimated by historians that colonists who remained loyal to the British monarchy may have numbered 20 percent at the most, but the strength of loyalist support varied widely between and within colonies. Disloyalty to the British Crown was not a step taken lightly, and as long as the conflict was viewed as between the American colonies and the British Parliament, many who were later considered loyalists or Tories often supported measured resistance to perceived threats to their liberties by Britain. The lines between American patriots and loyalists began to harden after Lexington, and became fixed after the Declaration of Independence. Actions and even words against the American cause brought swift and often harsh censure.

Continental Association. In 1774 delegates from the thirteen colonies met as the First Continental Congress to seek redress of grievances against Britain that dated back to 1763. After failing in their previous attempts to petition Great Britain's Parliament to rescind what many American colonists considered unjust encroachments upon colonial prerogatives, the Continental Congress set up the Continental Association to put economic pressure on Britain. Effective December 1, 1774, American colonists would cease to import goods from Britain, the British Indies, and Ireland. Effective September 1, 1775, colonists would discontinue their exportation of colonial goods to these destinations. Congress authorized the establishment of committees in every town, city, and county to enforce the association's decrees. All voters eligible to participate in local elections could vote for committeemen. This enforcement apparatus was the first legally sanctioned effort to enforce compliance with the colonials' struggle against the British. By 1775 local committees were summoning violators of nonimportation. They might be fined or have their names published in the local newspaper. The outcome desired by the committees was to have the dissenters sign oaths pledging themselves to the Continental Association.

Committees of Safety. The shedding of American blood at Lexington quickened the pace and resolve of American resistance to British authority. As the rebels brushed aside the governmental structures put in place by imperial Britain, they went about setting up their own governments. On July 18, 1775, the Second Continental Congress recommended the establishment of committees of safety in the various colonies to carry on the functions of government. Among the duties of these committees were the recruitment and arming of troops, gathering pledges of support for the nonimportation of British goods, and the apprehension of Tories opposed to the struggle for American rights. The local committees of safety drew sharp lines between friends and enemies of the American cause. While the phrase "enemies of the people" had been used in the Continental Association to stigmatize those who violated the commercial prohibitions of that document, this negative label was extended to any persons who expressed any disapproval of revolutionary activities or who took any action contrary to the American cause.

As the eyes and ears of American resistance, local committees of safety sometimes created situations to expose Tories. Some local committees circulated defense associations, which were agreements to take up arms against Britain. Persons who refused to sign these agreements were publicly labeled as enemies. Another tactic used to expose the unsympathetic was the official mustering of the local militia. Once the disaffected were identified, they came under the committees' control. Suspects were watched, fined, required to post bond for their proper behavior, disarmed, imprisoned, or forcibly removed to other areas in the colony or to another colony. Sending away dissenters or getting them to flee to areas under British military protection served the purpose of separating the critics of the American cause from their neighbors, whom they might influence

Punishing Loyalists. When the Second Continental Congress declared for independence on July 4, 1776, the necessity for a united colonial front against the British gained urgency. American rebels faced a war against the British military, domestic resistance from colonists opposed to independence, and lack of commitment from Americans who either maintained neutrality or changed their support depending on the latest military situation. Antiloyalist legislation and its enforcement depended on the relative strengths of the competing sides and the threat of the British military to local security. Pennsylvania, New York, and New Jersey each had significant portions of its populations either opposed to or neutral to the American cause.

In Pennsylvania, the legislature took steps to punish non-Associators. Many of these non-Associators were Quakers, whose pacifism kept them from supporting either the British or the Americans. Representing nearly one-third of Pennsylvania's population, Quaker refusal to take up arms caused considerable resentment among the state's militiamen, who pressured the legislature to penalize those not siding with the militia. A fine and an additional tax were levied against persons refusing to serve. In 1777 the legislature demanded that all adult, white male inhabitants take an oath of allegiance. Those who refused lost their citizenship, were disarmed, and could not sue to recover debts or engage in real estate transactions. In 1778 the legislature passed an act allowing the confiscation of property owned by notorious loyalists. During the next three years nearly five hundred were identified, and many lost their property. When the British evacuated Philadelphia in June, 1778, some loyalists failed to leave with the British forces. To make an example twenty-five loyalists were hanged. It is not clear whether all of these Tories aided the British or if some merely held loyalist sympathies.

In New York Tories held a majority in the southern counties of Queens and Staten Island. The loyalists in Queens embarrassed their patriot opponents in November, 1775, during an election to send delegates to a provincial congress. The loyalists refused to send delegates, defeating the patriots by a vote of 747-221. After their electoral setback, the patriots sent twelve hundred troops to discourage the loyalists. About twenty were arrested. In December, 1775, Staten Island loyalists also voted not to send delegates to the provincial congress. After the suppression of Queens's loyalists, the Staten Islanders decided to elect delegates.

A significant part of New Jersey's population did not support the patriots. In the eastern counties, Tories held considerable influence, while neutrals, mostly religious pacifists, were numerous in the western counties. The legislature penalized active Tories, but pacifists in New Jersey did not suffer persecution.

The Press. Censorship of the press during the American Revolution was as swift and certain as was the suppression of individual dissidents. American patriots tolerated no criticism of their cause. The censorship of James Rivington illustrates the various means used to silence opponents of the Revolution. Arriving in America from Britain in 1760, Rivington established a successful bookstore in New York City. In 1773 he also decided to publish books, pamphlets, and a newspaper, the *New-York Gazetteer.* For a time his newspaper carried articles arguing both sides of the dispute between the colonies and the mother country. As the conflict deepened, Rivington began to publish an increasing number of pro-British pamphlets. Meanwhile, he published articles and editorials that satirized the Sons of Liberty. These radical patriots urged people to cancel their subscriptions to the *New-York Gazetteer.* Rivington's pro-British pamphlets were publicly burned. On April 13, 1775, Rivington was hanged in effigy by a crowd at New Brunswick, New Jersey. On May 10, a mob entered his shop, damaged his press and other equipment, and tried to kidnap him. Rivington managed to escape to H.M.S. *King Fisher* in New York's harbor. After Rivington agreed to support the Continental Association, the Provincial Congress of New York agreed to allow him to resume his business. On November 23, an armed mob led by Isaac Sears, a leader of the Sons of Liberty criticized by Rivington, broke into Rivington's shop and destroyed his printing press. This effectively ended publication of the *New-York Gazetteer.* Rivington fled to Britain in early 1776 but returned to British-occupied New York City to begin publishing *Rivington's New-York Loyal Gazette.* This unabashedly pro-British newspaper continued until the British withdrew from New York City.

Impartiality did not fare much better than Toryism. In Boston, the Fleet brothers' *Evening-Post* published news articles and letters from patriots and loyalists. Although denying public claims that they were a loyalist organ, the Fleet brothers ceased publication after the battles of Lexington and Concord. Even a pro-patriot paper could raise the ire of patriots. In February, 1777, the *Maryland Journal,* owned by the patriot William Goddard and published by his sister Mary Katherine Goddard, ran into trouble with the local Whig Club, who misinterpreted a tongue-in-cheek piece anonymously submitted by a signer of the Declaration of Independence. The satirical article advised the acceptance of the peace terms offered by the British ministry. The Whig Club demanded that the publisher leave Baltimore within forty-eight hours. The Goddards stood their ground, and the Maryland House of Representatives backed them. Two years later the *Maryland Journal* came under fire for publishing an article by General Charles Lee, who had been dismissed by General George Washington. The article was critical of Washington and aroused the anger of Washington's friends. William Goddard was mobbed, forced to publish a recantation, and narrowly escaped hanging. Goddard appealed for state protection and published a disavowal of his recantation.

The need to protect military secrets and maintain popular support for the sacrifices of war make censorship common during wars. Censorship during revolutionary or civil wars is usually even more quickly invoked, and the penalties much harsher, than is the case with wars of other kinds. American revolutionaries propagandized to rally their countrymen to arms against Great Britain. They held no tolerance for neutrality nor opposition in their struggle for independence. Local committees of safety held wide powers of censorship that were used against individuals who opposed the war for independence. Despite abuses of power, the penalties were usually invoked to bring dissenters into the patriot camp. Compared to the violent excesses of the French Revolution, and the Russian and Chinese revolutions, the censorship of the American Revolution was moderate; it was ironic, however, that such measures were taken in defense of freedom. —*Paul A. Frisch*

See also Draft resistance; Espionage; Fear; Journalists, violence against; Loyalty oaths; Newspapers.

BIBLIOGRAPHY
Pauline Maier's *From Resistance to Revolution: Colonial Radicals and the Development of American Opposition to Britain, 1765-1776* (New York: Alfred A. Knopf, 1972) traces the evolution of colonial resistance from mob actions to more formal extralegal activities. Arthur M. Schlesinger's *The Colonial Merchants and the American Revolution, 1763-1776* (New York: Columbia University Press, 1918) gives thorough coverage of the Continental Association and the local enforcement committees that served as models for the Committees of Safety. Agnes Hunt's *The Provincial Committees of Safety of the American Revolution* (New York: Haskell House, 1968) was originally published in 1904 and is still the best analysis and overview of Committees of Safety, the Revolution's vehicle for censorship. Robert M. Calhoon's *The Loyalists in Revolutionary America 1760-1781* (New York: Harcourt Brace Jovanovich, 1973) covers loyalist activities and their suppression. Frank L. Mott's *American Journalism: A History of Newspapers in the United States Through 250 Years, 1690-*

1940 (New York: Macmillan, 1942) provides two chapters on the press in the American Revolution.

Richelieu, Cardinal

BORN: September 9, 1585, Paris, France
DIED: December 4, 1642, Paris, France
IDENTIFICATION: French statesman and Roman Catholic cardinal
SIGNIFICANCE: In his drive to strengthen France's monarchy, Richelieu rigidly suppressed religious and political dissent

Richelieu was obsessed with the need to create an ordered and stable France. When he became prime minister of France, the divisive political and religious factions within the country and the external threat of the Spanish Habsburgs moved him to a policy of increasing the monarchy's power. He expanded the extensive network of royal spies and employed a wide range of propaganda methods.

Richelieu also founded the French Academy and controlled both its membership and its publications. He quickly gained control of the *Mercure Français*—an annual political publication—and the newspaper *Gazette*. He eliminated other newspapers and strengthened state censorship of all publications by regularizing lay and ecclesiastical controls. He appointed four permanent censors to the Faculty of Theology. Penalties for illegal publications or ownership of banned works were expanded and included execution for treason.

Under Richelieu's direction numerous books were confiscated and burned. He forced critics such as Mathieu de Morques into exile and executed other political rivals. Richelieu manipulated the judicial process and then destroyed compromising court records. Religious dissent that escalated into political resistance was brutally suppressed. He crushed the Protestant Huguenot uprising and the participants lost many political and religious safeguards. The Jansenist movement was continuously persecuted.

See also Balzac, Honoré de; Book burning; France; Machiavelli, Niccolò; Reformation, the; Religion.

Right of reply

DEFINITION: Guarantee that political opponents, persons with opposing points of view, and those accused of misconduct will be granted access to media
SIGNIFICANCE: This policy fosters the exchange of ideas by requiring the media to provide access for differing points of view

The right of reply encompasses a number of legal doctrines. One is the personal attack rule, providing a right of reply to individuals maligned on the air. Another is the political editorial rule, providing a right of reply to candidates opposed in a broadcast editorial. A third is the equal time rule, which entitles a political candidate to the same amount of airtime granted his or her opponent. A fourth doctrine behind the right of reply was the fairness doctrine, which required broadcasters to treat controversial issues in a fair manner by affording air time to spokespersons of differing views.

In 1987 the Federal Communications Commission repealed the fairness doctrine, largely because it was feared that the doctrine discouraged broadcasters from contributing to public discourse by covering controversial issues and, ironically, curtailed media free speech rights by infringing on editorial judgment. The right of reply was not repealed, however, in the context of personal attacks and political campaigns, although in these areas, too, the right of reply is subject to constitutional challenges based on First Amendment concerns about the chilling effect produced by such government controls over the broadcast media.

See also Fairness doctrine; Federal Communications Commission; Political campaigning.

Rivera, Diego

BORN: December 8, 1886; Guanajuato, Mexico
DIED: November 25, 1959; Mexico City, Mexico
IDENTIFICATION: Mexican muralist
SIGNIFICANCE: Rivera created works in the United States that were censored

Educated in Mexico and Europe, Rivera returned from his overseas study convinced that art was a means of creating a new order in society. He maintained that art should belong to the people, rather than to wealthy individuals who would display it in their homes. In order to make art available to the masses, he began painting large-scale murals in public buildings in Mexico.

The popularity of Rivera's work in Mexico led to invitations for him to create murals in San Francisco, Detroit, and New York. In 1931 his exhibition at New York's Museum of Modern Art broke all attendance records and the museum's director, Nelson Rockefeller, persuaded him to come to New York to paint murals in the Radio Corporation of America building at Rockefeller Center. The young Rockefeller was aware of both Rivera's unflattering depictions of his father and grandfather in other murals and his leftist leanings. Nevertheless, he commissioned Rivera to produce the murals. Rivera then submitted detailed sketches of the proposed work, which he proposed to call *Man at the Crossroads Looking with Hope and High Vision to the Choosing of a New and Better Future*.

Rivera began the mural in March, 1933. In the center of the piece he painted a worker at the controls of a large machine. To the left of the worker he created a world controlled by wealthy elite who were drinking and gambling while the homeless and hungry were being harassed by mounted police. The opposite side of the mural depicted a new order in which power was placed in the hands of the people through socialism. Rivera's original sketches included the face of a labor leader holding hands with a black farmer, a white worker, and a soldier. As the mural evolved, the face of the labor leader was painted as that of V. I. Lenin. When the Rockefellers recognized this face they asked Rivera to substitute another figure. Rivera declined, but offered instead to add the portraits of great Americans, such as Abraham Lincoln. On May 9, 1933, the unfinished mural was surrounded by guards. An official of the Rockefeller Center's management informed Rivera that his commission had been canceled and gave him a check for the full amount of the work.

After news of the dismissal of Rivera became an international event, Nelson Rockefeller assured the public that

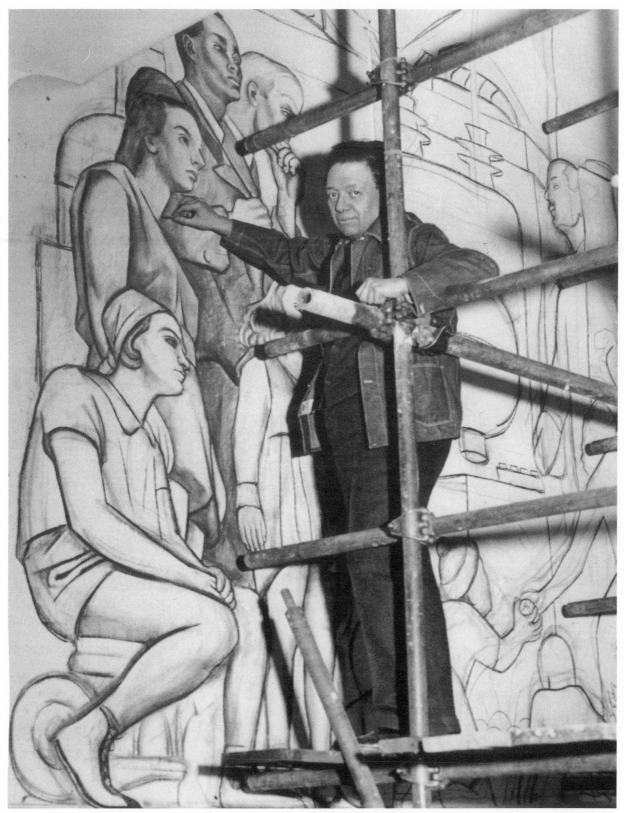

Diego Rivera paints one of his most controversial murals at New York City's Rockefeller Center in 1933. (AP/Wide World Photos)

Rivera's work would not be destroyed, and he began to explore the possibility of having the unfinished work moved to the Museum of Modern Art.

Meanwhile, Rivera and his wife left New York and returned to Mexico with the mural only two-thirds completed. Ten months later, however, the mural was destroyed by hammering its surface until it was removed from the wall and smashed to bits. The event was described at the time as an act of censorship and of cultural vandalism.

See also Art; Communism; Lenin, Vladimir Ilich; Mexico; Mural art; Warhol, Andy.

Robeson, Paul

BORN: April 9, 1898, Princeton, New Jersey
DIED: January 23, 1976, Philadelphia, Pennsylvania
IDENTIFICATION: American actor, singer, and campaigner for civil and human rights
SIGNIFICANCE: Because of his political views, Robeson was banned from appearing on television and forbidden by the U.S. State Department from traveling outside of the United States

Robeson holds the distinction of being not only the most censored African American in the history of the United States but also one of the most censored U.S. citizens of any race. His political views concerning racial equality and human rights were met with condemnation by both the U.S. media and government in the 1950's, leading to measures as extreme as a ban on overseas travel, and as thorough as the removal of his name from a 1918 all-America football team in a 1950 reference book.

The son of a former slave, Robeson first gained fame as a star athlete at Rutgers University, where he earned fifteen varsity letters in four sports. He came to international prominence during the 1920's, not for his athletic ability but for his commanding stage presence as an actor, particularly in the role of William Shakespeare's *Othello*. He later became equally famous as a singer and interpreter of folk songs, most notably African American spirituals. Combining these two talents, he starred in films during the 1930's and 1940's, including a recapitulation of his stage role in the film of Eugene O'Neill's *The Emperor Jones*.

Robeson's political views were not considered controversial until after World War II, at the beginning of the Cold War. At that time his antifascist, anticolonialist, pro-Soviet, and pro-civil rights politics began to attract the attention and criticism of right-wing demagogues in the press and in politics. His 1949 benefit concert in Peekskill, New York, for the Harlem chapter of the Civil Rights Congress was the focus of a right-wing riot that resulted in the hospitalization of 150 people, most of whom were Robeson's supporters. For his efforts on behalf of the Civil Rights Congress, Robeson was denounced on the floor of the U.S. House of Representatives and burned in effigy in at least two southern cities.

The Peekskill riot did not dissuade Robeson from his political beliefs, nor did it dissuade his critics from using all the weapons at their disposal. He became the first American officially banned from television when the National Broadcasting

Paul Robeson's career as a singer and actor was nearly ruined because of his political beliefs. (Library of Congress)

Company announced in 1950 that he would never appear on the network. Later that year, the U.S. State Department lifted Robeson's passport, effectively ending his international acting and singing career. For almost a decade the press collaborated by either denouncing Robeson or ignoring him: His autobiography, *Here I Stand* (1958), garnered no mention at all in *The New York Times*, although twenty-five thousand copies of the book were sold in six weeks. Finally, in 1958 the U.S. Supreme Court, in a five-to-four decision, ruled that the State Department could not deny citizens passports because of their political beliefs. At the age of sixty, Robeson went on a tour of Europe, where he was welcomed as a great artist and activist.

See also African Americans; Blacklisting; Communist Party of the U.S.A.; Television networks.

Robin Hood, The Merry Adventures of

TYPE OF WORK: Book
PUBLISHED: 1883
AUTHOR: Howard Pyle (1853-1911)
SUBJECT MATTER: Modern collection of tales about a legendary thirteenth century English outlaw
SIGNIFICANCE: During the midst of the anticommunist scares of the early 1950's, a member of Indiana's state textbook commission tried to have references to Robin Hood removed from schoolbooks because the legendary outlaw allegedly promoted communist doctrine

The legend of the thirteenth century English outlaw Robin Hood developed during the following century in England's

Yorkshire, Nottinghamshire, and Lancashire counties. Although scholars disagree on whether such a person actually existed, various versions of the legend have long appealed to young people with their exciting tales of a populist outlaw band that struggled against repressive authority in the persons of the Sheriff of Nottingham, Sir Guy of Gisbourne, King John, and King Edward II.

The Robin Hood legend crossed the Atlantic Ocean early in the British settlement of the American colonies, and it received perhaps its definitive schoolyard edition in Howard Pyle's *The Merry Adventures of Robin Hood*, which retold twenty tales and included wood-cut illustrations. Pyle's text stayed in print throughout the twentieth century. In 1953, Mrs. Thomas White of Indianapolis, a Republican member of Indiana's state textbook commission, demanded that references to Robin Hood be removed from textbooks because the legend promoted the communist doctrine of redistributing income by robbing from the rich in order to give to the poor. At the same time White also inveighed against Quakers because she noted that they do not believe in fighting wars. (It is unclear whether White knew that Howard Pyle was, in fact, a Quaker.)

In response to White's statement, Indiana's state superintendent of education, Wilbur Young, agreed to reread *Robin Hood* in order to consider the merit of the charge. However, the Indianapolis school superintendent, H. L. Shibler, refused to ban textbook references to Robin Hood, claiming that he saw nothing subversive about the Robin Hood stories. On November 14, 1953, *The New York Times* printed a response from the current sheriff of Nottingham, who unequivocally stated that "Robin Hood was no Communist."

See also Books, children's; Censorship; Communism; Morality; Textbooks.

Rock 'n' roll music

DEFINITION: Popular music genre associated with youth
SIGNIFICANCE: As a musical form often associated with rebellion, sex, drugs, and protest, rock 'n' roll has often been attacked for its content and its performers' actions

Since the onset of its popularity in the mid-1950's, rock 'n' roll music has remained controversial, largely for its lyrics expressing rebellious themes, sexuality, antiwar and other political opinions, and language deemed offensive by parents and broadcast institutions. During rock 'n' roll's first decade, the blues influence on rock rhythms and the performers' stage acts troubled parents, the broadcast media, and the music establishment, largely on racial grounds although use of rock music in such films as *The Blackboard Jungle* led some adults to associate the new music with juvenile delinquency.

White Fear of Black Influences. Before June, 1951, African American-influenced music had been called "race," or "rhythm and blues," until Cleveland disc jockey Allan Freed started a rhythm and blues radio show for largely white audiences. To avoid racial stigmatizing he coined the phrase "rock 'n' roll." Immediately, white parents reacted against black influences on their children, claiming that stage antics by performers such as Little Richard (Richard Penniman) were too overtly sexual for white audiences. Record companies

responded by giving songs by Chuck Berry, Bo Diddley, and other black artists, to white performers to "cover" for young white audiences. For example, Pat Boone covered Little Richard's "Tutti Frutti" in 1955. Other white groups altered the lyrics of black composers, as when Bill Haley and the Comets covered Joe Turner's "Shake Rattle and Roll." This began a long tradition of altering recorded lyrics in order to appease broadcasters.

Segregationists also turned to violence to suppress rock music, as in 1956, when a director of the Birmingham, Alabama, White Citizens' Council assaulted black jazz singer Nat King Cole in the middle of a concert, thinking him a rock 'n' roll performer. During this period the American Society of Composers, Authors, & Publishers (ASCAP), then the largest royalty-collection agency for songwriters, resisted accepting rock composers into its membership. ASCAP wanted to distance itself from music that it felt was faddish and primitive; it accepted rock musicians only after its primary competitor, Broadcast Music, Inc. (BMI) grew in power by building on the growing financial boom of rock's success.

Radio stations were also quick to ban rock records. For example, three radio networks banned Dot and Diamond's 1956 song "Transfusion," finding the then-popular theme of teenage death inappropriate for airplay. In 1955 Chicago rock stations received fifteen thousand letters complaining of dirty lyrics, and Mobile, Alabama, station WABB promised to exclude black rhythm and blues records from its playlist.

Great Britain. In 1960 the tightly restrictive British Broadcast Corporation (BBC) banned Ray Peterson's "Tell Laura I Love Her" for its theme of young death. Through the subsequent decade the BBC's tight control of broadcast music, including its banning of Gene McDaniels' and Craig Douglas' versions of "One Hundred Pounds of Clay" (1961), helped to popularize "pirate" radio stations, which aired rock music from ships at sea to avoid detection and prosecution. These unauthorized broadcasts were paralleled in the southern United States; Mexican radio stations, notably "Radio X," featured disc jockeys such as Wolfman Jack playing songs banned by American radio stations for American audiences across the border.

The 1960's. During the 1960's rock lyrics expanded to embrace social criticism, more overt sexuality, and more daring onstage performances, which led to continual attempts to censor rock musicians. In 1966, for example, Chicago radio station WLS banned the song "Gloria" by the Irish band Them, and hired the local band Shadow of Knight to cover the song, altering one lyrical line.

Record company clashes with rock artists included Verve's holding up the release of the Velvet Underground's first 1967 album because of its sexual and drug-oriented lyrics. In 1968 the Detroit group MC5 issued their album *Kick Out the Jams*, which contained an offensive line prompting one record chain's refusal to carry the album. Elektra Records issued an altered version of the album and then dropped the group. In 1969 RCA's group Jefferson Airplane had several problems with their album *Volunteers*, which contained lyrics the label found offensive. RCA forced the band to alter printed lyrics on the album sleeve. Originally titled "Volunteers of Amerika," the title was changed at the insistence of the charity organization of the same name. The band then formed its own label, Grunt Records, to avoid future conflicts.

Censorship occasionally occurred because of misunderstood or unintelligible lyrics. In 1966, for example, the BBC banned the Byrds' "Eight Miles High," incorrectly inferring that the song was about drug use. An El Paso, Texas, radio station banned all Bob Dylan songs because their lyrics were "indecipherable" and potentially offensive; however, it did air cover versions of the same songs. Rumors that the Kingsmen's 1963 version of "Louie Louie" contained obscene lyrics inspired in a Federal Communications Commission investigation, which found the song's lyrics were indecipherable, and therefore not obscene.

Anti-Vietnam war music of the 1960's aroused censorship. However, Barry McGuire's 1965 "Eve of Destruction" quickly rose to the top of the charts, despite a nationwide banning of the song that included all of the ABC networks and attacks by the Christian Anti-Communist Crusade. Chicago mayor Richard Daley attempted to ban airplay of the Rolling Stones' "Street Fighting Man" in 1968, fearing it might contribute to the volatile atmosphere surrounding the Democratic National Convention. Ohio governor James Rhodes asked radio stations not to broadcast Crosby, Stills, Nash, and Young's 1970 song, "Ohio" for similar reasons.

Television shows also censored rock music, notably *The Ed Sullivan Show*. Sullivan himself insisted that Elvis Presley would never appear on his Sunday night variety show, but he relented under commercial pressure. However, Presley's third 1956 appearance was censored, as the camera was not allowed to descend below Presley's waist. In 1967 Sullivan ordered the Rolling Stones to alter the lyrics of "Let's Spend the Night Together," and attempted to force the Doors to do the same with their "Light My Fire." However, Doors's lead singer Jim Morrison ignored the request; the band was subsequently banned from the show.

Morrison's frank sexuality in his lyrics and on-stage performances led to arrests in New Haven, Connecticut, in 1967 and Miami, Florida, in 1969 for which he was found guilty of public indecency. The controversy surrounding Morrison's alleged misbehavior resulted in a series of "Decency allies" in the American South, in which religious leaders and performers such as Anita Bryant preached against the evils they felt present in the rock scene. Other Doors recordings banned on broadcast media included 1968's "The Unknown Soldier," an anti-Vietnam War song.

The packaging of rock records was also a subject of censorship, notably the Beatles' *Yesterday and Today* (1966) "butcher boys cover," which Capitol Records covered with a less-offensive sleeve, and John Lennon and Yoko Ono's *Two Virgins* (1969) cover, which portrayed Lennon and Ono nude. Other banned album covers included a 1969 Blind Faith album whose British cover had a Botticelli print of a nude woman. This cover was not accepted by the band's American label, Atlantic Records, which substituted a picture of the band itself.

Religion and Rock Music. Although public furor over rock lyrics subsided in the 1970's, the FCC sent telegrams to rock stations in March, 1971, reminding them that broadcasts of songs promoting or glorifying the use of drugs could endanger their station licenses, but no such challenges resulted. In the mid-1970's various Christian organizations led boycotts of radio stations that aired songs deemed sacrilegious. In 1981 stations in Provo and Salt Lake City, Utah, banned Olivia Newton John's song "Physical," finding it offensive to Mormon audiences.

Broader movements to ban rock songs surfaced in the late 1980's with the rise in popularity of lyric-driven rap music. In 1991 Ice-T issued *Body Count*, which became one of the most notorious recordings in pop history. A Texas police group complained about one album track, "Cop Killer," and threatened to boycott Time Warner, the corporation for which Ice-T recorded. A political firestorm ensued, led by the American Family Association and Tipper Gore, spokesperson for the Parents' Music Resource Center. The U.S. Senate's Juvenile Justice Subcommittee held hearings on "Gangsta rap" at which lyrics determined to be violent or sexist were read by Snoop Doggy Dogg, Ice Cube, Luther Campbell, Eazy-E, and Boss. The National Political Congress of Black Women and the Reverend Jesse Jackson praised radio stations, such as Los Angeles' KACE-FM and New York City's WBLS-FM, which banned songs such as Dr. Dre's "Wit Dre Day (and Everybody Celebratin')," H-Town's "Lick U Up," and Aaron Hall's "Get a Little Freaky with Me."

The pressure groups successfully gained voluntary parental advisory labels on albums with explicit lyrics, although the National Association of Broadcasters resisted these efforts, as did rock composers such as Frank Zappa. However, a year later, "Cop Killer" was removed from *Body Count*, and Ice-T was released from his contract, as were other rappers deemed controversial.

Concurrent with these moves, cable music network Music TeleVision (MTV) began to censor the visuals of music videos, asking artists to obscure or edit anatomical features or controversial subject matter, as in John Mellencamp's "When Jesus Left Birmingham."

During the 1990's several attempts were made in Washington State to criminalize the sale to minors of recordings judged in court to be "patently offensive," appealing "to prurient interest" or lacking "serious literary, artistic, political or scientific value for minors." The Washington Music Industry Coalition fought these measures, beginning in 1992, by using Seattle band Soundgarden for a test case. The state supreme court eventually declared the first statute unconstitutional, although subsequent attempts were made to broaden censorship of all entertainment media in the state. —*Wesley Britton*

See also American Society of Composers, Authors & Publishers; Beach Boys, the; Beatles, the; Jackson, Michael; Lewis, Jerry Lee; "Louie Louie"; Music; Music TeleVision; Presley, Elvis; Rap music; Recording industry; Rolling Stones, the.

BIBLIOGRAPHY

No single work yet focuses on rock censorship, but much information can be found in back issues of *Variety* and *Bill-*

board magazines, the most important trade journals in popular music, as well as in *Rolling Stone*. *Rolling Stone* has also published two indispensable works on rock history: *Rock of Ages: The Rolling Stone History of Rock & Roll* (New York: Rolling Stone Press, 1986), by Ed Ward, Geoffrey Stokes, and Ken Tucker; and *The New Encyclopedia of Rock & Roll* (New York: Rolling Stone Press, 1995), edited by Patricia Romanowski and Holly George-Warren. Both volumes contain a great deal of information on censorship issues. For a list of banned songs, see Edward J. Volz, "You Can't Play That: Selected Chronology of Banned Music 1850-1991," *School Library Journal* (July, 1991).

Rolling Stones, the

FOUNDED: 1962

TYPE OF ORGANIZATION: British rock band

SIGNIFICANCE: The Rolling Stones have persistently challenged accepted standards in their lyrics and their behavior, thereby making themselves targets of censorship

As products of tough working-class neighborhoods in postwar London, the young men who formed the Rolling Stones were determined to be successful in their chosen field of music. At the urging of their first producer, Andrew Loog Oldham, the group violated social mores, record company regulations, and even national law, initially for the sole purpose of recognition. The plan apparently worked as the group gained vast popularity, an accomplishment resulting from their undeniable talent and studied outrageousness. The Rolling Stones sought confrontation and found it, resulting in a prolonged and angry struggle with censorship.

The group's lead singer and lead guitar player, Mick Jagger and Keith Richard, ran into trouble almost immediately concerning the lyrics they wrote. One of their earliest songs was "It's All over Now," which contained the controversial line "half-assed games." This phrase had gotten past their English publishing company, Decca Records, and their American distributors, London Records, but many American disc jockeys cut out the offending line or simply did not play the record. In November, 1966, guitarist Brian Jones showed up for a cover shot for a German magazine wearing a Nazi SS uniform. Not surprisingly, Jones was dropped from the cover, but he gained substantial notoriety.

The most public censoring of the Rolling Stones occurred January 15, 1967. The group had contracted to appear on the American variety program, *The Ed Sullivan Show*. Sullivan had booked the group with trepidation, and he became even more concerned when Jagger told the show's producers he intended to sing the group's current hit, "Let's Spend the Night Together." This song, which many radio stations were refusing to play, worried Sullivan because of its sexual suggestiveness and the possibility that substantial numbers of viewers and advertisers might be offended. Sullivan ordered the Stones to change the offending phrase to "let's spend some time together," or not appear on the program. The group reluctantly agreed to the change, but while performing the song, Jagger rolled his eyes and uttered unintelligible sounds when the song came to the controversial line.

The group also had continuing problems with its record company in reference to album covers. The original cover of the *Beggar's Banquet* (1968) album featured the graffiti-littered wall of a dirty public restroom, but Decca refused to release the album until the cover was changed. Disgusted by Decca's interference, in 1971 the Rolling Stones created their own publishing company and began releasing their own records. The first release was the album *Sticky Fingers*, showing a close up of a male crotch, complete with a working zipper. Even with their own recording company, though, the Rolling Stones could not totally escape censorship, as Spain refused to allow the album into the country.

See also Beach Boys, the; Beatles, the; Broadcast Music, Inc.; Cover art; Music; Presley, Elvis; Recording industry; Rock 'n' roll music.

Roman à clef

DEFINITION: A novel in which historical events and characters are represented under fictional guise

SIGNIFICANCE: The *roman à clef* exposes authors, publishers, and distributors to legal liability, which arguably constrains literary freedom

By thinly disguising actual persons and events, the *roman à clef* blurs boundaries between imagination and reality. Information transmitted through an ostensibly fictional medium can mislead readers into correlating fictional characters with actual people. This correlation directly affects those about whom *romans à clef* are written. Benevolent portrayals rarely breed conflict, but negative ones often incur lawsuits.

Under U.S. law, a successful defamation action requires reputational damage caused by the defendant's intentional or reckless publication of a false statement of fact about the plaintiff. A successful invasion of privacy action requires the defendant's publication of private, embarrassing facts about the plaintiff. A successful infliction of emotional distress action requires the defendant's extreme and outrageous conduct, causing severe emotional distress to the plaintiff. Each cause of action illuminates the internal paradox of the *roman à clef*: The plaintiff essentially argues there is too much (true or untrue) fact in this fiction. The defense asserts the work in question is fiction, not fact.

While libel law softens fear of litigation by constructing rigorous liability standards, fear of an adverse verdict, of basic litigation costs, of reduced productivity, and of the reputation-tarnishing effect of a civil suit can be great. Such fear arguably leads to stifled creativity, heavy editing, and refusals to publish. Such self-censorship inhibits unqualified freedom of speech and the press. The question becomes whether such a chill on expression is acceptable.

See also Chilling effect; Defamation; Dreiser, Theodore; Libel; *Life and Death of Colonel Blimp, The*; Privacy, right to.

Roman Empire

DESCRIPTION: Political system based in Rome that incorporated most of the Mediterranean littoral and much of Western Europe and the Near East from the first century B.C.E. through the fifth century C.E.

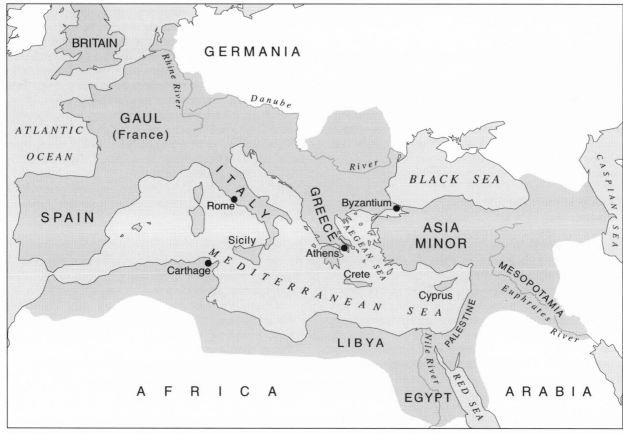

The Roman Empire (dark gray area) at its height in the early second century, C.E.

SIGNIFICANCE: As the first truly inclusive governmental organization in Europe and North Africa, the Roman Empire created the basis for much of Western law and government Ancient Rome had no written constitution. Its politics operated on a set of unmodified principles based in tradition and individual character. Roman candidates stood for election, not on the basis of their ideas or programs, but as men of good reputation and outstanding family. For this reason, the law courts were important forums of political advancement. Through the use of inflammatory rhetoric, leading Romans built their careers by denouncing the immorality and base origins of their political opponents. The right to stand in court and assail one's adversaries was considered an essential privilege of Roman citizenship, a natural right, a demonstration of liberty. No topic, no matter how personal or defamatory, was forbidden.

In a few notable instances audacity and oratorical skill momentarily curbed the excesses of those who exploited the Roman system for their own benefit. Such a case was the famous attack in 70 B.C.E. that the young Cicero made upon the rapacious governor of Sicily, Gaius Verres. By the force of his words alone, Cicero established himself as a rising talent, startling one of the most powerful political machines in Rome and forcing Verres into exile.

The personal nature of Roman politics made it susceptible to demagoguery. As a result, in the century before 27 B.C.E.

Roman society fragmented, political conflicts turned violent and Roman oratory seemed to lose a sense of civility. Verbal attacks became more scurrilous creating the image of a society that had fallen into the hands of thieves and immoral thugs. When Cicero turned his oratorical powers upon the violent excesses of the Second Triumvirate, Marc Antony, one of the triumvirate's members, ordered his assassination.

The reforms of Emperor Augustus, which took hold after 27 B.C.E., consolidated power in the hands of one man. It was justified as a return to the stability of the past, including a return to civility and morality in speech. In this way Augustus could justify such actions as his exiling of Ovid for writing immoral poetry. In the name of order, informers became common weapons against those who resisted the emperor's will, effectively destroying the Senate. The same sort of civilizing arguments were used to justify the suppression of foreign religions in Rome and to rationalize laws sanctioning the destruction of books written by undesirables, who were often labeled as magicians or soothsayers.

The dampening placed upon free speech in the name of the Princeps hastened a rhetoric of praise. Civility became adulation, and the artificial praise of the panegyric evolved as the new medium for oratorical exercise and political advancement. The difference was that in panegyric personal rhetorical skills were employed in the service of the person of the emperor alone.

See also Athens, ancient; Christianity; Cicero; Gibbon, Edward; Italy; Ovid; *Satyricon, The*; Seneca the Younger.

Ronde, La

TYPE OF WORK: Film
RELEASED: 1950
DIRECTOR: Max Ophüls (1902-1957)
SUBJECT MATTER: Ironic comedy set in turn-of-the-century Vienna in which the interlinked romantic pairings among ten characters are followed in a series of vignettes
SIGNIFICANCE: The most explicit sex comedy released in the United States up to its time, this film provoked censorship attempts that led to a U.S. Supreme Court decision expanding freedom of expression in film

La Ronde is based on Austrian dramatist Arthur Schnitzler's comedy *Riegen* (written 1900; performed 1920), which several European filmmakers adapted to the screen before Max Ophüls' 1950 version. *La Ronde*'s array of international talent—from the director to its stars, Simone Signoret, Jean Louis Barrault, and Gerard Philipe—attracted such attention that the sex comedy became a *cause célèbre* after its release in the United States. It was one of the first films shown in the country that depicted casual trysts among multiple characters who were clearly enjoying sexual relationships.

In 1952 New York's state censorship board banned the film, claiming that it "would tend to corrupt morals." When a state appeals court upheld this decision, one of its judges expressed the opinion that the film advanced the view that "life is just a 'round' of sexual promiscuity.'" However, when the case reached the U.S. Supreme Court, that court ruled that films were entitled to constitutional protection from state censorship and could not be banned simply because censors found them immoral. In his concurring opinion, Associate Justice William O. Douglas adopted an absolute standard for upholding the First and Fourteenth amendments, which collectively hold that Congress and the states shall make no law which abridges freedom of speech or of the press. He concluded by noting that "in this Nation, every writer, actor, or producer, no matter what the medium of expression he may use, should be freed from the censor." This important ruling significantly enlarged the freedom of U.S. filmmakers to treat controversial subjects without fear of official censorship.

French director Roger Vadim filmed a new adaptation of *La Ronde*, with the same title, in 1964.

See also *And God Created Woman*; Douglas, William O.; Film censorship; *Moon Is Blue, The*; Morality.

Max Ophüls' 1950 film La Ronde *was the most the most explicit sex comedy released in the United States up to its time.* (Museum of Modern Art/Film Stills Archive)

Rooney, Andy

BORN: January 14, 1919, Albany, New York

IDENTIFICATION: American television journalist and commentator

SIGNIFICANCE: Bowing to pressure from offended groups, the Columbia Broadcasting System suspended Rooney from its program *60 Minutes* for making allegedly racist and anti-homosexual remarks

On February 8, 1990, the news division of the Columbia Broadcasting System (CBS) suspended Andy Rooney, a long-time satirical commentator on its popular weekly news program, *60 Minutes*, for three months without pay. CBS took this action in response to allegations that Rooney had made racist statements in an interview and evidence that he had, during one of his *60 Minutes* segments in December, 1989, linked homosexual unions with the abuse of alcohol, drugs, overeating, and cigarettes as causes of premature death.

The Advocate, the most widely read gay-oriented magazine among Americans, quoted remarks that Rooney made to one of its own reporters in an interview that African Americans had diluted their genes because the least intelligent members of their race were producing the most children. Rooney denied having made such a statement and protested the accusation that he was a racist. He also recanted his statement about homosexual unions, saying that he should instead have referred to unsafe sex.

David Burke, president of CBS News, nevertheless, suspended Rooney, saying that his future with CBS would be

A few unwise words got television commentator Andy Rooney suspended from 60 Minutes. *(AP/Wide World Photos)*

discussed at the conclusion of his suspension. Rooney was reinstated following strident protests from his loyal audience members, including many African Americans and homosexuals.

See also Homosexuality; News broadcasting; Race; Television; Television networks.

Roth, Samuel

BORN: November 17, 1894, Austria

DIED: July 3, 1974, New York, New York

IDENTIFICATION: American book publisher

SIGNIFICANCE: Roth's 1956 obscenity trial led to the definition of a more liberal standard for judging obscenity

Roth migrated to the United States in 1904 and began publishing a literary magazine called *Two Worlds Monthly* in 1925. Five years later he spent sixty days in jail for publishing uncensored portions of James Joyce's novel *Ulysses*. In the 1930's he published two love manuals from India, the *Kama Sutra* and *The Perfumed Garden* and then spent ninety days in jail for violating New York State's obscenity law. A few years later he sold an edition of D. H. Lawrence's *Lady Chatterley's Lover* through the mail and was jailed for three years.

By the 1950's Roth had become known as America's "smut king" and was still facing prosecution for his publishing ventures. In April, 1957, his name entered legal history in a U.S. Supreme Court decision titled *Roth v. United States*. By a 6-3 margin the Court established the "Roth" standard for obscenity. In this view the First Amendment protected all kinds of speech no matter how hateful. It did not, however, protect obscenity because obscene speech was "utterly without redeeming social importance." After this decision a work could be considered obscene only "if taken as a whole" it appealed to the "prurient interest" of the "average person." The idea that the whole work had to be considered, rather than isolated passages, created a more liberal standard for obscenity. Roth's sentence of five years in jail and a $5,000 fine was upheld, however, and he went to jail again.

See also Books and obscenity law; Ginzburg, Ralph; Girodias, Maurice; Joyce, James; *Kama Sutra*; *Lady Chatterly's Lover*; Obscenity: legal definitions; *Roth v. United States*.

Roth v. United States

COURT: U.S. Supreme Court

DATE: June 24, 1957

SIGNIFICANCE: As the first case in which the Supreme Court considered whether obscene materials were protected under the First Amendment, *Roth* began the Court's systematic effort to define the constitutional limits of sexually explicit expression

After Sam Roth, a mail-order bookseller, was convicted of violating the Comstock Act, an 1873 federal statute that prohibited mailing "obscene, lewd, lascivious, filthy [or] indecent" material, his appeal reached the U.S. Supreme Court, accompanied by companion cases, challenging state obscenity laws in California and New York. Roth argued that the Comstock Act violated the free speech and press guarantees of the First Amendment. He maintained that any abridgment of a

First Amendment freedom could be justified only if the material presented a clear and present danger, and that sexually explicit materials presented no such dangers. Justice William J. Brennan, Jr., writing for a bare majority, ruled that obscenity was not within the area of constitutionally protected speech. The purpose of the First Amendment, he reasoned, was to protect the exchange of ideas. Since obscenity was "utterly without redeeming social importance," it did not fall within the First Amendment's protections. The government thus did not need to show a clear and present danger in order to ban obscenity.

If obscene speech was not constitutionally protected, how was it to be distinguished from protected speech? This question provided the Court its first opportunity to define obscenity, and it did so in a way that was more sensitive to literary expression than the prevailing standards of the time. Under the traditional English standard—known as the Hicklin standard—material was considered obscene if even an isolated part of it might tend to excite lustful thoughts. In contrast, the new *Roth* standard for defining obscenity asked whether an average person applying contemporary community standards would regard the dominant theme of the material, taken as a whole, as appealing to prurient interest.

Almost every phrase of this new definition generated public controversy. It raised such new questions as who constituted an "average person"; whether contemporary "community standards" were local or national in character; how "dominant" the prurient theme of material must be in order to contaminate it as a whole; and how an "appeal to prurient interest" was to be determined. The court's majority opinion, that obscenity was "utterly without redeeming social value," added confusion.

Justice Brennan's opinion provoked both concurring and dissenting opinions. Justice John Marshall Harlan, expressing his long-standing concern for federalism, dissented, but voted to uphold the state statutes. To him, the national government lacked any general power to "protect public morality," and its censorship should be limited to prohibiting "hard core pornography." In contrast, he argued that the states had a general police power, and were free to enact whatever reasonable limitations they choose. Chief Justice Earl Warren voted with the majority, but chided his colleagues for focusing on the wrong issue. To him, the behavior of the defendant, not the quality of the book, was the central issue. So far as he was concerned, Sam Roth's real crime was commercialization of sex. Justices Hugo Black and William O. Douglas dissented, and reiterated their position that the words "no Law" in the First Amendment must be taken as an absolute prohibition on laws restricting the freedom of speech or press. Both found the majority's definition of obscenity hopelessly subjective.

The impact of *Roth* was twofold. It established the precedent that obscenity was not protected by the First Amendment; it also initiated a series of judicial attempts to define obscenity in a way that distinguished clearly between protected and unprotected speech. But because this attempt was unsuccessful, challenges to obscenity convictions forced the Court to refine its definitions of obscenity for decades to come.

See also Brennan, William J., Jr.; Clear and present danger doctrine; Comstock Act of 1873; First Amendment; Hicklin case; *Miller v. California*; Obscenity: legal definitions; Pornography; Reporters Committee for Freedom of the Press; Roth, Samuel.

Rousseau, Jean-Jacques

BORN: June 28, 1712, Geneva, Switzerland
DIED: July 2, 1778, Ermenonville, near Paris, France
IDENTIFICATION: French philosopher and writer
SIGNIFICANCE: One of France's most influential writers, Rousseau was persecuted for his writings during his life and many of his writings were banned after his death

The son of a poor Swiss watchmaker, Rousseau spent his youth in various apprenticeships and minor occupations and did not gain any notice he was thirty-seven. That year he won a prize for an essay on science, the arts, and social morality, awarded by the provincial academy at Dijon. Six years later he won wider attention with the publication of *Discourse on the Origins of Inequality* (1755), in which he contrasted the corruption of his contemporary society with the simplicity and goodness of humanity in a natural state.

Rousseau's highly popular *La Nouvelle Héloise* (1761) was published with the tacit consent, rather than formal permission, of the royal censor. Rousseau's next work, *Emile* (1762), which develops a concept of progressive education, was less fortunate. The book's pantheistic stress on education through communion with nature moved the archbishop of Paris to censor it and the parliament of Paris to burn it. Soon anathema to both Protestants and Roman Catholics, *Emma* was burned in Rousseau's native Switzerland, as well as in Rome.

Emile's banning caused Rousseau considerable anxiety. Indeed, the whole issue of censorship threatened the security of Enlightenment philosophers. French censorship laws were tightened after 1757, with the possibility of a death sentence for works published without official approval. More usual punishments, however, were prison time in the Bastille or service on a galley ship. Despite such censorship, a clandestine book trade flourished. Almost any book—including considerable pornography—could be obtained for a price.

Following *Emile*'s classification as subversive of religion, Rousseau avoided imprisonment by going to Switzerland and England. However, as revealed in his posthumously published *Confessions*, he was growing increasingly paranoid about both real and imaginary conspiracies against him. Reflecting on the unnatural repressiveness of society, Rousseau wrote, in *The Social Contract* (1762), "Man is born free, and everywhere is in chains." This seminal work—which influenced both democratic and totalitarian thought—gained Rousseau a quick listing on the Roman Catholic church's *Index Librorum Prohibitorum*.

Rousseau eventually returned to France, a depressed, paranoid, and quarrelsome man. He died in 1778, the same year as Voltaire. Four years later publication of his psychological masterpiece, the autobiographical *Confessions*, won him immortality as one of the eighteenth century's greatest writers. The French Revolution, which ended the censorship of literary works, honored him as "First Citizen." Death did not, however, end Rousseau's persecutions. His bones, along with those of Voltaire, disappeared from their graves in 1814. Rousseau's *Confessions* was banned by U.S. Customs in 1929, and the Soviet Union banned all his books as counter-revolutionary.

See also Book burning; Customs laws, U.S.; Diderot, Denis; France; *Index Librorum Prohibitorum*; Locke, John; Voltaire.

Rowan v. U.S. Post Office Department

COURT: U.S. Supreme Court

DATE: May 4, 1970

SIGNIFICANCE: In a case originating in a mail-order company's complaint that its constitutional right to free speech was violated by a federal postal law empowering people to stop unsolicited mailings, the Supreme Court issued a ruling favoring protection of individual rights to privacy over free speech

Section 4009 of the 1967 U.S. Postal Revenue and Federal Salary Act, Title III, empowers individuals to order companies engaged in mass mailings to stop sending them unsolicited advertisements for material that they regard as "erotically arousing or sexually provocative." The law also permits individuals to order their names deleted from all mailing lists in the mail-order companies' possession. *Rowan v. U.S. Post Office Department* originated in a case brought by the owner of a mail-order company who claimed that the 1967 law violated his First and Fifth Amendment rights of free speech and due process. He also asserted that the law's section 4009 was "unconstitutionally vague, without standards, and ambiguous."

In deciding *Rowan*, the Court examined the subsections of section 4009 that outline the procedures for ordering the cessation of mailings to individual households. One subsection states that mailers can be ordered by private individuals "to refrain from further mailings . . . to designated addressees." Another subsection assigns the postmaster general the duty of issuing requested cessation orders to specified mailers. A third subsection requires mailers to remove the names of complainants from their mailing lists and prohibits the sale, transfer, or exchange of lists bearing their names. Upon determination of a violation, the postmaster general can ask the attorney general to issue a compliance order against the mailer.

The Court decision affirmed the right of private individuals to direct the cessation of mailings and the deletion of their names from mailing lists used in the distribution of unsolicited advertisements. Explaining the Court's opinion, Chief Justice Warren Burger wrote: "Weighing the highly important right to communicate . . . against the very basic right to be free of sights, sounds, and tangible matter we do not want, it seems to us that a mailer's right to communicate must stop at the mailbox of an unreceptive addressee." Burger added that "a mailer's right to communicate is circumscribed only by an affirmative act of the addressee." In sum, the Court ruled that a mailer's right to communicate is not significantly infringed upon when balanced by a recipient's right to be free from unwanted communications.

The Court also held that the appellant's due process was not violated, and that section 4009 of the law was not unconstitu-

tionally vague. Burger noted that "the only administrative action not preceded by a full hearing is the initial issuance of the prohibitory order. Since the sender risks no immediate sanction by failing to comply with that order . . . it cannot be said that this aspect of the procedure denies due process." Furthermore, Burger reasoned that because "appellants know precisely what they must do on receipt of a prohibitory order," the appellant's vagueness argument was ruled invalid.

See also Courts and censorship law; First Amendment; Postal regulations; Privacy, right to; Privacy Protection Act of 1980.

Royal family, British

IDENTIFICATION: Members of the family providing Great Britain's hereditary heads of state

SIGNIFICANCE: The modern royal family has become the focus of such intense media attention that calls have been raised to protect the family's privacy

Great Britain has no written constitution or bill of rights. Press and media freedoms not guaranteed by charter are defined narrowly or broadly by Parliament. For example, the Official Secrets Act of 1911 identified more than two thousand separate offenses of unauthorized disclosure of official information. The 1942 civil service rulebook and the 1985 Armstrong Memorandum prohibited public employees, including members of the staff of the royal family, "serving or retired," from disclosing information about their work without prior clearance.

Britain has no specific laws regulating the press. Most legal proceedings against the press have been libel actions brought by private individuals. The Press Complaints Commission (PCC), which replaced the Press Council in 1991, was established to ensure that newspapers and periodicals follow a code of conduct self-imposed by editors, on recommendation of a government commission, because of parliamentary and public concern over the behavior of members of the press. The code of practice has provisions pertaining to inaccuracy, press harassment, intrusion into privacy, discrimination by the press, and the obtaining of information for publication through such intrusive methods as using high-tech surveillance devices or surreptitiously taking photographs or making tape recordings. The PCC regularly publishes all complaint reports and resolutions.

During the early eighteenth century Henry Fielding's dramatic satirizing of Prince Minister Robert Walpole provoked Parliament to pass the Theatrical Licensing Act of 1737 that required a government officer, the Lord Chamberlain, to approve and license all plays. King George III was the first monarch to hire a court newsman because he felt that too many lies were being written about him, his court, and his often profligate sons. Not until 1919, however, did the royal family consider it necessary to establish a full-time press office.

In the twentieth century the British press's relationship with the royal family has generally been one of self-regulation. During the brief reign of Edward VIII, for example, the press's astonishing discretion and loyalty to the Crown in playing down the role of the American divorcée Wallis Simpson in the new king's personal life was the result of a brokered agreement between Edward and Lord Beaverbrook and other powerful newspaper proprietors. It was only weeks before Edward VIII's abdication in late 1936 that a stunned British public learned about the king's romantic involvement with Simpson.

Between 1945 and 1968 the royal court fed the newspapers stories about the House of Windsor. Personal activities of members of the royal family were restricted to innocuous gossip column items and press stories about royal overseas trips. The British Broadcasting Corporation (BBC) deleted jokes about the royal family from broadcasts, and pictures and articles about the royal family in incoming foreign periodicals that might be considered inappropriate by the British government were typically excised before the publications were sold to the British public. Exceptions included 1955 editorials criticizing the marriage of Princess Margaret to the divorcé Peter Townshend and 1957 articles by Lord Altrincham, Malcolm Muggeridge, and John Osborne attacking the monarchy's isolation, narrow circle, and generally boring national contribution.

The televised investiture of Queen Elizabeth II's son Charles as Prince of Wales in 1968 increased the public's demand for more information about the royals. Allegations began appearing in the British press about matters such as alleged infidelities of the queen's husband, Prince Philip; Prince Charles' drinking; and the adulterous relationships of the queen's Harewood cousins. The spectacular 1981 wedding of Prince Charles to Lady Diana Spencer turned the House of Windsor into a "feeding frenzy" for the British and world press. The scandalous behavior of Sarah, Duchess of York, and the divorces of the queen's sister Margaret and daughter, Anne, frequently garnered greater media attention than parliamentary debates, national disasters, or foreign news.

On June 8, 1992 the PCC released a statement denouncing the British press for its contribution to the breakdown of Charles and Diana's marriage. However, both Charles and Diana themselves were known to have used the press to leak stories about their own versions of their failing marriage. The Princess of Wales's 1995 judgment against a publication for using secretly taken photographs of her gym workouts seemed to be but a temporary setback against a press corps with an insatiable appetite for information about the royal family.

The British press has continued to remain both unregulated and self-regulated. The press has agreed to leave the young princes William and Harry alone while they attend boarding schools. Because the monarchy remains the final social arbiter in the United Kingdom, the royal court's ostracism of anyone who publishes material deemed offensive by the royal family, as evidenced by former royal nanny Marion Crawford for publishing without authorization the rather innocuous *The Lit-*

When Great Britain's King Edward VIII abdicated in 1936, the news came as a shock to the public, who had not been told anything about his romantic affairs. (National Archives)

tle Princesses, remains an effective form of censorship by the royal family against the press.

See also British Broadcasting Standards Council; Censorship; Fielding, Henry; Henry VIII; James I; Official Secrets Act (U.K.); United Kingdom.

Rushdie, Salman

BORN: June 19, 1947, Bombay, India

IDENTIFICATION: British novelist

SIGNIFICANCE: Rushdie's novel *The Satanic Verses* was condemned and forbidden throughout the Muslim world, and the Iranian government called on Muslims to execute him as a blasphemer

To many readers, Rushdie has become the modern world's preeminent victim of censorship. Not only has his novel *The Satanic Verses* (1988) been condemned in many Muslim countries, Rushdie himself was placed under a death threat endorsed by the Iranian government in early 1989. In a startling refutation of the lament of many modern fiction writers that their novels have no consequences, Rushdie has proven that the novel can still wound and inspire outrage. Six years after the issuance of the fatwa (or condemnation) against *The Satanic Verses*, Rushdie's next novel, *The Moor's Last Sigh* (1995), was promptly banned by the government of India, allegedly for its insulting treatment of Hindu beliefs. As ecumenical in his disparagement of the world's religions as he is well traveled, Rushdie has obviously sparked a universal debate on his fictional treatment of a variety of cultures and religions.

Born in Bombay, Rushdie was educated in England at the prestigious Rugby School and at Cambridge University, although he spent his school vacations with his family in Karachi, Pakistan. While working as a copywriter in advertising agencies in England, he began writing his earliest novels. On the strength of the good reviews and serious critical attention his novels have received, Rushdie has frequently been acclaimed as one of Britain's most important novelists and essayists. His early novels, *Shame* and *Midnight's Children*, based on his experience as an Anglo-Indian, won him serious critical attention if not a wide readership. Publication of *The Satanic Verses* in 1988 won him generally positive and sometimes enthusiastic reviews until—quite unexpectedly—the novel was denounced in the fatwa given in the name of the Ayatollah Ruhollah Khomeini, the head of the revolutionary government in Iran.

The Fatwa. Issued on February 14, 1989, Iran's fatwa condemned Rushdie and the publisher of *The Satanic Verses*, calling on "all zealous Muslims to execute them quickly." In a series of subsequent statements from official sources in Iran, Rushdie was depicted as a demonic blasphemer and tool of sinister Western manipulators. The speaker of the Iranian parliament saw Rushdie's novel as the most overt of a series of covert hostile actions against Islam. A report on Iranian radio blamed British intelligence for Rushdie's book, calling it part of a larger anti-Islamic propaganda campaign. Although Khomeini himself was said to have viewed *The Satanic Verses* as a calculated move against religion in general, another leader, President Khamenei, detected a broad cultural conspiracy behind the novel. In Khamenei's view, "aside from being a sin in the eyes of the law, religion and humanity, this dirtying of literature and arts was an ugly deed." Khomeini's statement claimed that God himself had revealed the anti-Islamic nature of the novel and wanted it published in order to expose its poison. The statement of President Khamenei viewed Rushdie inconsistently as both a mere stooge of the United States and a "member of the British royal literary society" who "was forced to write a book."

The Novel's Alleged Offenses. The novel's odd-numbered sections narrate the adventures of two popular Anglo-Indian actors, Gibreel Farishta and Saladin Chamcha, who (having survived the terrorist bombing of their airplane) attempt to resume normal life in modern London. The even-numbered sections concern an imaginary story about the Prophet Muhammad in the fictitious holy city of Jahilia and the apparently doomed mission of the prophetess Ayesha to lead Muslim Indian villagers on a pilgrimage to Mecca. The novel's climax reveals a miraculous parting of the waters of the Arabian Sea and the subsequent apparent drowning of the pilgrims. However, it is possible that the entire sequence is part of a fantasy

Members of the National Writers Union demonstrate against the decision of many U.S. book stores that responded to Iran's execution order against author Salman Rushdie by not carrying his novel The Satanic Verses. *(AP/Wide World Photos)*

in one of the popular religious films ("theologicals") that had made Gibreel an Indian film star.

It is possible that a few particularly vivid episodes in the novel inspired the fatwa against Rushdie. In the section titled "Mahound" (a profoundly offensive derisive name given to Muhammad in medieval English mystery plays), the devil—in the guise of the archangel Gibreel (or Gabriel), gives Muhammad the so-called "Satanic verses" in the Koran. (In anti-Islamic traditions, Muhammad inserted a contradictory passage in the Koran attesting the divinity of three local goddesses in order to secure a community's conversion to Islam.) In another section, "Return to Jahilia," the religious doubts of the scribe named Salman about Mahound and his wives leads the scribe to alter portions of the sacred text of the Koran. Perhaps equally offensive to Muslim readers, whores at a brothel called the Curtain each assume the identity of one of Muhammad's wives, allowing their customers to act out blasphemous sexual fantasies. In the penultimate section of the novel, "The Parting of the Arabian Sea," the pilgrims going to Mecca suffer from internal dissension and the hostility of a Hindu mob. When they wade in the waters and apparently drown, others claim to have seen the waters part miraculously.

Rushdie and Modern Fiction. The novel's "The Parting of the Arabian Sea" passage forms not only the narrative climax to the book, but its emotional highlight. The novel is distinguished both for the Joycean exuberance of its language and the fantastic nature of its plotting, written in the spirit of the Magical Realism of Colombia's Gabriel García Márquez. Because Middle Eastern literature has not developed the range and variety of fiction in the English tradition, it is possible that the Iranian clerics and officials profoundly misunderstood Rushdie's complex narrative strategy, and consequently misread the novel's tone, as did the thugs who beat the Egyptian novelist Naguib Mahfouz.

Although the novel admittedly treats three of the world's great religions as absurd delusions, it also shows the potential for human love, action, and profoundly contradictory behavior. So much of its narrative concerns dreams, fantasies, and dreamlike behavior that it is difficult to identify Rushdie's own attitude toward Islam, beyond an implied playful skepticism about the claims of any religion. Any Western reader willing to read through his complex text would probably concede that he has complicated and perhaps contradictory things to say about race, religion, politics, sexuality, and ethnicity in postmodern society.

The threat of murder by a government against a creative artist with no personal connection or debt to that government is a horrifying demonstration of the worst kind of official censorship. Not only Western intellectuals and proponents of democracy, but also non-Iranian writers and intellectuals have issued sharp defenses of Rushdie's right to write as he pleases, regardless of the offense that he may cause to religious sensibilities, and to live without the threat of bodily harm. The Tory government of Great Britain under Margaret Thatcher was quick to condemn the Iranian fatwa and to supply security and safe housing for Rushdie, although Thatcher herself was one of the prime targets of Rushdie's sharp satire. —*Byron Nelson*

See also Article 19; Blasphemy laws; Death; Iran; Islam; Koran; Mahfouz, Naguib; PEN; Suicide.

BIBLIOGRAPHY

The Rushdie File, edited by Lisa Appignanesi and Sara Maitland (Syracuse, N.Y.: Syracuse University Press, 1990), is a useful compilation of documents relating to fatwa. James Harrison's *Salman Rushdie* (New York: Twayne, 1992) surveys Rushdie's provocative literary career. Two books with similar titles ponder the modern implications of alleged offenses against religion: Leonard W. Levy, *Blasphemy: Verbal Offense Against the Sacred* (New York: Alfred A. Knopf, 1993) perceives the theme of *The Satanic Verses* as "lost faith" and comments thoughtfully on the specific offenses of the novel; David A. Lawton, *Blasphemy* (New York: Harvester Wheatsheaf, 1993), criticizes Rushdie's allegedly oedipal debunking of Muhammad—which Lawton compares to Sigmund Freud's debunking of Moses. A reading of *The Satanic Verses* itself by readers alert to its energy and high comedy is the best refutation of the charge of blasphemy.

Russell, Bertrand

BORN: May 18, 1872, Trelleck, Monmouthshire, Wales

DIED: February 2, 1970, near Penrhyndeudraeth, Wales

IDENTIFICATION: British philosopher, logician, and political activist

SIGNIFICANCE: Russell advocated complete freedom of thought and expression; his 1940 appointment to an American college was terminated primarily because of his views on sexual morality

Although Russell contributed work of permanent value in the areas of logic, philosophy of mathematics, and philosophy of language, his widespread fame was also caused by his radical views on social, political, and religious matters. A classic "free-thinker," he did not believe in God and held that religion did more harm than good. Not only, he thought, were certain religious doctrines (such as the Roman Catholic prohibition of birth control) pernicious, but they also encouraged fanaticism by accustoming people to accept views without regard to evidence. As he wrote in *Why I Am Not a Christian* (1957), the antidote for such evil was "a habit of basing convictions upon evidence, and of giving to them only that degree of certainty which the evidence warrants." His application of this ideal to ethical and political matters led to his adopting radical views, such as his suggestion that college students satisfy their sexual urges by forming temporary, childless "marriages."

Academic freedom, Russell thought, was necessary to prevent a "democratic tyranny" in which the majority abuses the minority. He believed that university professors must not be required to keep silent on controversial issues, because the community benefits from their intellectual training; academic freedom in America, he also thought, was chiefly threatened by the churches and by those who were powerful by virtue of their wealth. In Russell's time, the accusations of communist sympathies were often used to smear innocent people; Russell was characterized as pro-Soviet in an effort to censor his unpopular views, even though, as he later recalled, he had frequently criticized the Soviet regime of Joseph Stalin. Aligning himself with the "liberal tradition," Russell said, "If I held power, I should not seek to prevent my opponents from being heard. I should seek to provide equal facilities for all opinions and leave the outcome to the consequences of discussion and debate."

In 1940 Russell, by then recognized as one of the world's leading philosophers, was appointed professor of philosophy at City College of New York. A tremendous public controversy followed. A bishop of the Protestant Episcopal church led the attack on Russell, asking, in a letter to all New York newspapers, "What is to be said of colleges and universities which hold up before our youth as a responsible teacher of philosophy . . . a man who is a recognized propagandist against both religion and morality, and who specifically defends adultery." Russell was widely denounced as a moral nihilist, a philosophical pagan, and an advocate of sexual deviancy. The college trustees reconsidered Russell's appointment and again approved it, but a certain Jean Kay sued to block the appointment on the grounds that Russell was an alien and an advocate of sexual immorality. The courts agreed with Kay, and Russell never took up the appointment at City College.

See also Atheism; Davis, Angela; Marcuse, Herbert; Morality; Universities.

Russia

DESCRIPTION: Eastern European-Asian nation with deep historical roots that was part of the Soviet Union through most of the twentieth century

SIGNIFICANCE: Russia's reemergence after the collapse of the Soviet Union represents a return to questions of censorship and free speech not addressed since the czarist era

The state of Russia has a long history of censorship. Although the printing press did not arrive in Russia until 1564, and was not employed for secular purposes until the reign of Peter the Great (1682-1725), government policies of censorship rose quickly after the emergence of the press. Indeed, in October, 1720, Czar Peter, expanding upon the Code that Czar Alexis had established in 1649, enacted a law under which the production of any material had to receive prior approval of the Russian Orthodox church. Furthermore, Peter's special police, the Preobrazhensky Commission, had the authority to arrest and torture anyone breaking the censorship code.

Peter's Preobrazhensky Commission lasted until the reign of his son, Peter II (1727-1730). While Peter II continued his father's policy of prepublication censorship of ecclesiastical materials by the church, he transferred the censorship of secular materials to two organizations: the Senate press and the Academy of Sciences. Under this structure, the Senate press was charged with the censoring and publication of all government sources and the Academy of Sciences was responsible for all other secular materials. Furthermore, until 1750, and the reign of Czar Elizabeth (1741-1761), the Senate had the authority to censor all materials published by the Academy. Both the Senate and the Academy, however, permitted little opportunity for publications to promote their opinions without governmental interference.

Catherine the Great. Governmental policies on censorship remained extremely limiting until the reign of Czarina Catherine II (1762-1796), also known as Catherine the Great. Catherine established a commission in 1767 to create a new, more liberal code of laws on censorship. Although the new code maintained state and church monopolies on printing, the general mood of the country moved toward a more open, liberal environment. In 1771 Catherine moved toward decentralization of the press by permitting the creation of the first private press operating under the premise that nothing would be printed which opposed "Christianity, the government or common decency." The decentralization of the press was created in statute in 1783, when Catherine granted a greater freedom of the press, under the monitoring of the police who had the ability to repeal any materials contravening "the laws of God and the state" or considered to be of a "clearly seditious" nature.

Under the more liberal atmosphere, publishing flourished until the government became concerned with acts of sedition due to the French Revolution. In 1796 Catherine abolished the free press established in 1771 and transferred absolute control over all printing to the state. Government offices were established in Moscow, St. Petersburg, Riga, and Odessa to monitor the printing and importation of works, and works deemed "against God's law, governmental orders or common decency" were burned.

When Catherine died in 1796, she was succeeded by Paul I. Czar Paul pardoned several convicted under the censorship laws of Catherine I, but also moved to strengthen the control of the censors. Paul centralized control of censorship in St. Petersburg. All foreign works attacking "faith, civil law and morality" were automatically outlawed, as were all references to the Enlightenment and the French Revolution. The importance Paul attached to censorship is demonstrated by the fact that he personally chaired all inquisition into questionable publications.

Alexander I and the Return of Liberalism. Alexander I (1801-1825) came to power in a coup against his father, Paul. His censorship policies marked a return to the more enlightened era of Catherine the Great. In 1801 Alexander abolished his father's restrictions on foreign press and, in 1803, decentralized the press. Under Alexander's new policies, codified in the statute on censorship law in 1804, control over state censorship was transferred from the police to educational institutions, thereby transforming governmental policies of censorship from repressive to educational functions.

However, Alexander's liberal attitude toward the press was cut short by the war with France lasting from 1805 to 1815. To combat efforts of the French fifth column aimed at the subversion of the Russian government, new committees on censorship were established. In 1811 the newly established Ministry of Police was given control of all security functions within the Russian state, including power of censorship. However, the Ministry of Police was not effective in controlling the press, and in 1819, the power of censorship reverted to the Ministry of the Interior.

Decembrists and the Shishkov Reforms. When Alexander I died in 1825, he was succeeded by his brother, Nicholas I (1825-1855). After the aborted Decembrist coup of December 14, 1825, Nicholas was deeply concerned with the power of the press to influence the peasants and workers of Russia. He instituted more conservative measures, aimed at limiting the influence of the press. These measures, proposed by Admiral Shishkov and adopted into law in May, 1826, included policies aimed at replacing academic censorship with professional bureaucrats charged with monitoring the press. The Shishkov reforms were intended to guarantee that publications would "have a useful or at least not-dangerous orientation for the welfare of the fatherland" and to "direct public opinion into agreeing with the present political circumstances and views of the government." Included in the policy were restrictions on discussion of metaphysical rights of justice and freedom, and elimination of all works which discussed secular or religious dissent.

Although the Shishkov reforms were strongly embraced by the Russian Orthodox church, strong opposition to the strict censorship laws was nevertheless felt across the country. When Czar Nicholas, responding to the opposition, began to weaken the strict censorship laws, Admiral Shishkov resigned his post as chair and chief censor of the Supreme Committee and Chief Administration on Censorship. He was replaced on April 23, 1828 by the moderate Prince Lieven. Under the new censorship laws enacted by Nicholas to weaken the Shishkov reforms, any work which endangered the primacy of the church or the state remained outlawed. However, the ability of the government to hold authors accountable for their works was limited.

Secret Directives of Nicholas I. Despite the new, liberal bias of the czar's censorship laws, Nicholas remained concerned with the possibility of revolution. To that end, he enacted a secret directive on April 25, 1828. Under this directive, a secret section of the chancellory responsible for censorship was created and charged with the responsibility of monitoring any materials which affected the czar's interests and to interfere with their publication as deemed necessary.

The secret directive of 1828 was enhanced by two other secret directives of 1828 and 1831. The combined effect of these directives was to limit the scope and effectiveness of the legal reforms enacted by Czar Nicholas earlier in his reign. The revolutions of 1848 served to prove to the czar that a greater degree of control over the press was necessary to ensure his continued reign. As such, on April 2, 1848, Nicholas created the Committee for Supreme Supervision, and placed it under the leadership of D. P. Burturlin. Although the committee operated secretly, it acted strongly to crush any possible opposition or challenges to the policies of the government.

The Obolensky Commission. Nevertheless, an unofficial, radical press emerged to cater to the increasing demands for newspapers and magazines. Indeed, by the time Czar Nicholas died in 1855, a radical press catering to the intellectuals and bourgeoisie was well established. Thus, when Alexander II (1855-1881) came to power with a hope of emancipating the serfs, or slave-farmers, he hoped to employ the assistance of the new press. Alexander hoped an open dialogue would serve to further his intention to free the serfs, a policy which was strongly opposed by many influential and powerful people in Russia. As such, he appointed A. V. Golovnin as education minister in 1861.

Golovnin, strongly supporting the czar's open policy on censorship, moved quickly to liberalize governmental policies on censorship. He permitted many new publications to be established and allowed them to carry advertisements for the first time. Furthermore, he established the Obolensky Commission to draft new proposals for governmental policies on censorship.

However, as Golovnin and his Obolensky Commission were establishing new policies on censorship, the political and economic situation in Russia was becoming less stable. As the czar became concerned with the stability of Russia, he transferred some of Golovnin's authority to the minister of the interior. Under the czar's directive, the ministries of education and the interior shared responsibility for censorship. Additionally, the ministries could suspend any publication deemed dangerous for up to eight months and criticism of policies of the government was strictly controlled.

In November, 1862, the Obolensky Commission provided its proposals for governmental reforms. It recommended control of censorship be transferred solely to the Ministry of the Interior, while simultaneously embracing the need for a free press, similar to the ones developing in Europe at the time. Although Golovnin strongly opposed the transfer of authority, Czar Alexander, faced with growing opposition and revolutionary sentiment in the country, enacted the proposal in March, 1863.

With his newfound power, Count P. A. Valuev called for new laws on censorship. In April, 1865, his wish was fulfilled and a new law on censorship was enacted. However, the law was not what Valuev had hoped for. Instead, it provided guarantees for the rights of the author and established legal frameworks, Western in nature, for the control of the press. Although the letter of the law was liberal, Valeuv continued his attempts to control the press. He brought many cases to court under the new legal framework, charging authors with libel or with threats to the security of the state, both of which were illegal under the new system.

The Last Czars. Despite Valeuv's efforts, however, revolutionary movements continued to grow. When Alexander was assassinated in 1881, Alexander III acceded to the throne. Alexander III, a long-time supporter of strict policies of censorship, approved temporary measures on August 27, 1882. The temporary measures included provisions which allowed the censors to ban any topic from discussion in the press, and created a new fund which provided the government with cash to bribe newspapers. Nevertheless, the press continued to grow and provide challenges and opposition to governmental policies.

When Alexander III died in 1894, he was succeeded by Nicholas II, the last of the czars. By 1905, however, the press was operating without hinderance. Nicholas had given up his attempts to control the press. However, with the Revolution of 1905, he made one last attempt to regain control. On November 24, 1905, Nicholas passed a law called the charter of freedom. Under the new law, all censorship boards above the provincial level were dismantled. Responsibility for censorship was transferred to the editors, who were supposed to provide a copy of their publications for the local press affairs committee at the time it was released for general circulation. If a publication was deemed to contain illegal materials or deal

In 1906 the German journal Ulk *mocked Czar Nicholas II's strict press censorship policies by depicting him with his head blotted out—like the page on a Russian newspaper—as his children ask where he is.* (Robert J. Goldstein)

with illegal issues, the remaining issues were seized. However, the law was widely ignored and for all practical purposes, the press operated freely until the 1917 Bolshevist Revolution that ended the Russian Empire.

Russia After the Soviet Period. After the Soviet Union collapsed in the early 1990's, the Russian government was faced with countless challenges. Among these problems was the emergence of the mafia powerful enough to control governmental policies. Indeed, the current governmental policies on censorship are quite liberal, yet control over the media and press is nevertheless maintained by the mafia. The problems faced by the Russian state are similar to the problems of the Italian state insofar as the degree of mafia influence and control is quite similar. An example of the degree of mafia control is provided by the assassination of Vladislav Listyev in 1994. Listyev, who was the most prominent and influential Russian reporter, was gunned down in the street for his investigations into the links among the media, advertising, and the mafia.

—Noah R. Zerbe

See also Bakunin, Mikhail Aleksandrovich; Bulgakov, Mikhail Afanasyevich; Censorship; Dostoevski, Fyodor; Gorbachev, Mikhail; Lenin, Vladimir Ilich; Nicholas I; Soviet Union; Tolstoy, Leo.

BIBLIOGRAPHY

Excellent overviews of pre-Soviet Russian history include Ronald Hingley's *A Concise History of Russia* (5th ed. New York: Viking, 1972), Nicholas Riasanovsky's *A History of Russia* (New York: Oxford University Press, 1993), and W. Bruce Lincoln's *The Romanovs: Autocrats of All the Russias* (New York: Dial Press, 1981). For a discussion of the development of Russian conservative and radical intellectual thought, including the issues of censorship, during the reign of Nicholas II, see Theofanis George Stavrou's edited work entitled *Russia Under the Last Tsar* (Minneapolis: University of Minnesota Press, 1969). The reforms of Catherine the Great are discussed in John Alexander's *Catherine the Great: Life and Legend* (New York: Oxford University Press, 1989) and Isabel de Madariaga's *Russia in the Age of Catherine the Great* (New Haven, Conn.: Yale University Press, 1981). Evgenii Anisimov's *The Reforms of Peter the Great: Progress Through Coercion in Russia* (Armonk, N.Y.: M. E. Sharpe, 1993) deals with the changes instituted by Czar Peter. Finally, Joseph T. Fuhrman, Edward C. Bock, and Leon I. Twarog, *Essays on Russian Intellectual History* (Austin: Published for the University of Texas at Arlington by the University of Texas, 1971) includes detailed discussion of the development of critical religious and intellectual thought in Russia and the Soviet Union.

Rutherford, Joseph Franklin

BORN: November 8, 1869, near Boonville, Morgan County, Missouri

DIED: January 8, 1942, San Diego, California

IDENTIFICATION: Leader of the Jehovah's Witnesses

SIGNIFICANCE: Imprisoned for conscientious objection during World War I, Rutherford waged a legal battle that led to greater protection of freedom of speech

Born in Missouri, Rutherford became a member of the Jehovah's Witness society in 1906 and the legal counselor for the organization in 1907. In January, 1917, he was selected second president of the organization and began an extensive proselytizing campaign that resulted in the denial of his own and other members' civil liberties. He and seven other Witnesses were arrested in May, 1918, and charged with sedition. Because of judicial bias the case was ultimately heard by Vermont Judge Harlan B. Howe. Rutherford and six associates were found guilty on four counts of sedition and sentenced to serve concurrent twenty-year terms. A campaign by Jehovah's Witnesses led Supreme Court justice Louis Brandeis to order their release on bail until their appeals could be heard. On May 5, 1920, all seven Witnesses were cleared of judgments.

Until his death in 1942, Rutherford used the judicial system, especially after 1938, to uphold the civil rights of Jehovah's Witnesses as they publicly defined their positions on proselytizing methods, the draft, flag salutes, publications, and blood transfusions. His legal arguments based on the First and Fourteenth amendments were instrumental in strengthening civil liberties in the United States.

See also American Civil Liberties Union; Canada; Communications Act of 1934; *Diary of Anne Frank, The*; Flag burning; Leafletting; Pledge of Allegiance; Sedition.

S

Sade, Marquis de

BORN: June 2, 1740, Paris, France
DIED: December 2, 1814, Charenton, near Paris, France
IDENTIFICATION: French writer and philosopher
SIGNIFICANCE: Sade spent more than a third of his life imprisoned for criminal sex acts and for advocating gaining sexual gratification by inflicting pain—for which his name was later given to the term "sadism"

Born into an aristocratic Provençal family related to the king of France, Sade began a career as an officer in a royal army regiment in 1754. Despite his powerful family and marital ties, he was repeatedly arrested for sexual assault, sodomy, and even murder by means of an overdose of the aphrodisiac "Spanish fly." In 1777 he was incarcerated on order of the king and was later held in the Bastille until the French Revolution began. While in the Bastille he wrote his famous *Les 120 journées de Sodome*, which was not printed until the 1930's. After his release he continued to write plays and novels, including *Justine*, and *La Nouvelle Justine, suivie de l'historie de Juliette*, which were published in 1797. The latter in particular resulted in a second period of imprisonment, under Napoleon Bonaparte, from 1801 to the end of his life in 1814. Much of this time he spent in an insane asylum near Paris.

Sade's writings have always been controversial for extolling atheism and egoism and for extolling murder as a supreme act of virtue. They are also controversial because of their scatology and their detailed descriptions of sexual acts, including sodomy, incest, orgies, coprophagy, and physical torture—particularly that involving clerical figures. Nevertheless, many later French critics and writers—from Sainte-Beuve to feminist Simone de Beauvoir—have ranked Sade among the great writers and philosophers of the eighteenth century Enlightenment.

Although some of Sade's writings are technically still banned in France, a nearly complete edition of his works was published in 1948; a "complete" edition was published in 1966 (a freshly edited edition appeared in 1986). His most erotic writings were translated into English and published in the United States by Grove Press in the late 1960's. Although these writings have neither been banned by the federal government of the United States nor specifically challenged under various obscenity laws, they have not been easily accessible. Public and private libraries have exercised indirect censorship, either by refusing to acquire Sade's works or by keeping them under lock and key.

See also Atheism; Casanova, Giovanni Giacomo; Diderot, Denis; First Amendment; France; Grove Press; Homosexuality; Sex in the arts; Violence.

Sahl, Mort

BORN: May 11, 1927, Montreal, Quebec, Canada
IDENTIFICATION: Canadian comedian and screenwriter

SIGNIFICANCE: Sahl was an innovative political satirist whose publicly stated disbelief of the official account of President John F. Kennedy's assassination hurt his entertainment career

Comedian Mort Sahl introduced a hipster's view of America's Cold War politics to audiences at San Francisco's legendary hungry i nightclub in 1953. Undaunted by McCarthyism, Sahl satirized the House Committee on Un-American Activities: "Every time the Russians throw an American in jail, HUAC retaliates—by throwing an American in jail." Dubbed the "iconoclast in the nightclub," Sahl stood apart from television vaudeville and Las Vegas stand-up comedy. Never obscene and rarely even acerbic, Sahl was still regarded as a dangerous comedian; his free-ranging monologues good-naturedly revealed the emperor without clothes. It was a winning style in nightclubs and on the jazz circuit, but it unnerved the show business establishment, who doubted that Sahl would appeal to mass television audiences. Sahl himself acknowledged that more than any other form of censorship, he "ran into intellectual censorship against the audience . . . the most dangerous censorship of all."

From 1966 to 1970, Sahl assisted New Orleans district attorney James Garrison in his independent investigation of the assassination of President John F. Kennedy. Sahl's unstinting promotion of Garrison cost him television appearances and nightclub bookings, so he turned to Hollywood screenwriting and college appearances. In 1994, he returned to the stage in a one-man show, "Mort Sahl's America."

See also Bruce, Lenny; Carlin, George; House Committee on Un-American Activities; Kennedy, John F., assassination of; Television.

Sakharov, Andrei

BORN: May 21, 1921, Moscow, Soviet Union
DIED: December 14, 1989, Moscow, Soviet Union
IDENTIFICATION: Russian scientist and human rights activist
SIGNIFICANCE: Though greatly respected for his scientific achievements, Sakharov was ostracized within the Soviet Union for his commitment to human rights

Sakharov is known for his contributions in two fields: nuclear physics and human rights issues. His scientific work brought him recognition and honor in the Soviet Union, but by the early 1960's his main interest was becoming his growing concern for human rights and political reform. Disturbed by high-handed government treatment of both ordinary citizens and intellectuals and by several public "show trials" of Soviet writers in the early and mid-1960's, Sakharov began speaking out on these issues. At first privately, and then more publicly by 1968, he raised searching questions about repressive Soviet government policies and the hardships faced by those who sought nothing more than fairness and justice. He signed petitions supporting those who were harassed, arrested, and tried merely for seeking civil rights guaranteed to them in the national constitution.

The Soviet invasion of Czechoslovakia in the summer of 1968 galvanized Sakharov's thinking into a more organized presentation of his views. Such views could not legally be published inside the Soviet Union, since the authorities regarded any support for reform and democracy as seditious and threatening to the state. Sakharov sent his manuscript to the United States, where it was published in 1968 under the title *Progress, Peaceful Coexistence and Intellectual Freedom*. His criticisms of Soviet repression and police harassment—now compounded by this manifesto calling for major reforms—led to his removal from highly classified physics work on Soviet military weapons research. Eventually the government stripped him of the awards, honors, and other privileges he had received as a prominent Soviet scientist.

During the 1970's Sakharov's stature grew among the human rights movement within the Soviet Union, especially after Aleksandr Solzhenitsyn's expulsion in 1974. Sakharov wrote essays, received journalists and foreign visitors, and became the conscience of the reform movement. Meanwhile, the government and hostile media regularly denounced him and his wife, Elena Bonner—who was also a human rights activist. In January, 1980, the Soviet government sent Sakharov and Bonner to Gorky, a city closed to Westerners. This isolation virtually ended Sakharov's ability to communicate freely. For a brief period he and his wife staged a hunger strike to protest their treatment.

Changing leadership in the Soviet Union eventually allowed Sakharov to resume his human rights efforts. Mikhail Gorbachev, the new Communist Party head, permitted Sakharov to return to Moscow in December, 1986. Sakharov resumed writing and giving interviews and was elected to the Congress of Peoples Deputies in 1989. He continued his efforts for democratic reform in his country, and helped to prepare a new national constitution.

See also Communism; Gorbachev, Mikhail; Pasternak, Boris; Solzhenitsyn, Aleksandr; Soviet Union; Yevtushenko, Yevgeny Aleksandrovich.

Sand, George

BORN: July 1, 1804, Paris, France
DIED: June 8, 1876, Nohant, France
IDENTIFICATION: French author of romantic, pastoral, and political novels and plays
SIGNIFICANCE: A feminist libertine who fought for sexual and economic equality, Sand wrote books that were listed in the *Index Librorum Prohibitorum*

A leader in the Romantic movement in literature, a feminist libertine, and a socialist champion of the working class, George Sand advocated freedom of the press throughout her career. Her novels and political writings outraged bourgeois sensibilities and challenged the conventions that the middle class held absolute.

Born to an aristocratic father and a woman of humbler social origin, Sand was raised by her paternal grandmother, then sent to a convent in Paris. At eighteen she married Baron

Dudevant but, finding conjugal life oppressive, left him in 1831 for a young writer, Jules Sandeau, whose surname she adapted for her pen name. Sand's subsequent extramarital liaisons, most notably with Alfred de Musset and Frédéric Chopin, but also with persons of her own sex, scandalized Paris. Her lifestyle was bohemian, she wore men's clothing, smoked cigars, and used her masculine pen name in public.

In 1848 Sand was unofficial minister of propaganda for the republican revolutionaries in Paris. However, she disassociated herself from radical feminist attempts to have her elected to the National Assembly because she deemed political equality for women premature. In the government suppression of radical elements that followed the unsuccessful republican coup, she was accused of conspiracy, but was not arrested. Her popularity suffered, however, and she gave up political writing.

Sand's early novels, including *Indiana* (1832), *Valentine* (1832), *Lélia* (1833), and *Jacques* (1834), established her as a feminist writer who denounced marriage as "one of the most barbaric institutions . . . ever invented." These novels, scandalous in their time, represent a literary landmark in the struggle for emancipation waged by nineteenth century French women. Sand's next works emphasized socialism, Christianity, and humanitarianism. They included *Spiridion* (1838), *The Seven Strings of the Lyre* (1839), *Consuelo* (1842-1843), and *The Countess of Rudolstadt* (1843-1844). A number of pastoral and socialist works followed that idealized rural, working-class life: *The Devil's Pool* (1846), *The Sin of Monsieur Antoine* (1847), *Little Fadette* (1849), *Francois the Champ* (1850), and *The Master Bell-Ringers* (1853). Several less successful novels followed, as well as Sand's twenty-volume autobiography in 1855.

During her lifetime Sand enjoyed a significant readership in Russia, including the authors Fyodor Dostoevski and Ivan Turgenev. The imperial censors, who regularly expunged more conservative works than Sand's, apparently failed to detect her dangerous doctrines in their romantic trappings.

The Roman Catholic church's *Index Librorum Prohibitorum*, however, was more thorough, citing a bookseller's pamphlet of 1871 that represented Sand as "more depraved than Messalina, in fact an utter slave to Lesbian passion."

Sand's popularity generally declined in the twentieth century, but she has gained new interest among feminist scholars. Her influence on the modern, however, may owe as much to her accomplishments as a woman as to her writings. By challenging the double standard, combining a successful career with motherhood, and demanding self-fulfillment as a right, Sand anticipated the modern woman.

See also Dostoevski, Fyodor; France; Pseudonyms, male; Russia; Women.

Sanger, Margaret

BORN: September 14, 1879, Corning New York
DIED: September 6, 1966, Tucson, Arizona
IDENTIFICATION: American nurse and birth control advocate
SIGNIFICANCE: Sanger fought censorship of contraceptive information through her writings, speeches, and establishment of birth control clinics

Sanger's battles with censorship shaped the American birth control movement in the twentieth century. Trained as a practical nurse with a background in radical and socialist politics, Sanger saw the fight for birth control as a free speech issue. When she began her efforts in 1912, the federal law classified sex education and birth control as obscene under the Comstock Act of 1873. Sanger challenged U.S. Post Office censors by publishing a series of articles on sex education in the *New York Call*. Her article on venereal disease was banned.

Undaunted in 1914, Sanger founded her own journal, *The Woman Rebel*, which espoused birth control, feminism, and radical labor politics. The federal government then indicted her for violating the Comstock Act. Unwilling to risk prison, Sanger fled to Europe before going to trial. Once she was out of the country she released *Family Limitation*, a pamphlet providing graphic instructions on a variety of contraceptive methods. She returned to the United States to face trial in 1915, but rather than make her a martyr, federal prosecutors dropped the charges against her in January, 1916.

Sanger then popularized birth control through speaking tours. Her audiences were generally large and receptive, but on occasion local Roman Catholic groups attempted to thwart her appearances by intimidating theater owners or the police—as happened in St. Louis, Missouri, in 1916 and in New York City in 1921. Sanger was arrested in Portland, Maine, in 1916 for distributing *Family Limitation*, but was later released. Despite these efforts at censorship, Sanger managed to reschedule her lectures and attracted more listeners and publicity.

By the end of 1916 Sanger had shifted her focus from free speech agitation to the provision of clinical services. In October that year she opened the first birth control clinic in the United States in Brooklyn, New York, again in defiance of the law. After being convicted of violating New York State's own Comstock law, she spent thirty days in jail. Her efforts to dramatize the event by starring in a silent film, *Birth Control* (1917), were squelched when the film was banned after one showing. In 1919 although Sanger's Brooklyn conviction was upheld on appeal, New York State appeals court ruled that physicians were exempt from obscenity prosecution if they prescribed contraception for the cure and prevention of disease.

After the Brooklyn decision, Sanger focused her efforts on securing for doctors the right to distribute contraceptive information. In 1923 she opened another birth control clinic in New York, staffed by a woman physician, and she encouraged

Birth control advocate Margaret Sanger outside of a Brooklyn courthouse with her supporters in 1916. (Library of Congress)

others to establish clinics across America. From 1929 through 1937 she lobbied unsuccessfully to have doctors exempted from federal censorship of contraceptive information. She also supported a test case, *United States v. One Package*, that challenged customs restrictions on physicians' rights to import contraceptive devices. Sanger fought this case to the U.S. Supreme Court and in 1937 the Court ruled in her favor, reversing a key tenet of the federal Comstock Law. This decision freed the way for medical acceptance of contraception and increased research.

See also Birth control education; Comstock, Anthony; Comstock Act of 1873; Film censorship; Kneeland, Abner; *New York Times Co. v. Sullivan*; Postal regulations; Sex education; Stopes, Marie.

Sapho

Type of work: Play
First performed: 1899
Playwright: Clyde Fitch (1865-1909)
Subject matter: Dramatic adaptation of a novel by Alphonse Daudet detailing the adventures of a French courtesan
Significance: After *Sapho* was condemned as an immoral play, its New York City production was shut down by police

After premiering in Chicago in 1899 *Sapho* opened at Wallack's Theatre in New York City in February, 1900. Featuring a cast of twenty-four with dances arranged by Carol Marwig and settings by Ernest Albert, it ran for twenty-nine performances until the theater was closed by order of the police. English actress Olga Nethersole was arrested for playing a scene in which her lover boldly carries her up a stairway to her apartment.

Audiences of 1900 were reportedly shocked by the production. William Randolph Hearst, publisher of the *New York Journal*, wrote: "We think there exists in this county a respect for decent women and for young girls. We expect the police to forbid on the stage what they would forbid in streets and low resorts." These and similar editorials in other newspapers brought about Nethersole's arrest, a dramatic courtroom trial, reams of front-page publicity, and, ultimately, a not-guilty verdict. In April *Sapho* reopened on Broadway—supposedly in a blaze of box office glory, although critics rated it a very bad play. After fifty-five performances with most of the original cast, a new production at Wallack's Theatre began the following November and ran for another twenty-eight performances.

Sapho was the inspiration for a 1931 film entitled *Inspiration* starring Greta Garbo and Robert Montgomery.

See also Courts and censorship law; Drama and theater; Morality; Obscenity: legal definitions.

Saro-Wiwa, Ken

Born: October 10, 1941, Bori, Rivers State, Nigeria
Died: November 10, 1995, Port Harcourt, Nigeria
Identification: Nigerian author and environmentalist
Significance: After what was widely considered a sham trial, Saro-Wiwa was sentenced to death for his outspoken opposition to oil extraction in eastern Nigeria

A member of Nigeria's Ogoni ethnic group, Saro-Wiwa was educated at the government college at Umuahia and at the University of Ibadan. He later held a wide variety of administrative positions in the government, including education commissioner in Rivers State in the late 1960's, and information and home affairs commissioner during the early 1970's. In addition, he was a publisher and a writer, and he served as president of the Association of Nigerian Authors. His works include two children's books, a collection of poetry, a collection of short stories, a novel, and his last work, *A Month and a Day: A Detention Diary*. Saro-Wiwa also created a popular situation comedy, *Basi and Company*, which satirized the get-rich-quick mentality of Nigerian officials who exploited Nigeria's natural resources.

In 1990 Saro-Wiwa helped found the Movement for the Survival of the Ogoni People (MOSOP). He claimed that the oil revenue from Ogoniland, on the Niger River Delta in eastern Nigeria, was being used to enrich the Nigerian elite and that Ogoniland was being ruined by the consequent pollution. MOSOP planned to boycott the June, 1993, presidential elections. Political opposition developed from within MOSOP over this issue and in May, 1994, a riot occurred at a meeting in Giokoo resulting in the death of four progovernment Ogoni. Although Saro-Wiwa was not present, he was arrested for allegedly instructing his supporters to "deal with" his political opponents. Human rights groups claimed that his methods were based on nonviolence.

Saro-Wiwa and four other Ogoni were tried and convicted by a special tribunal in which the military held a great amount of influence and precluded the possibility of appeal. Saro-Wiwa was hanged with eight other Ogoni activists on November 10, 1995. Afterward several witnesses for the prosecution stated that they had been bribed to testify against him. International reaction was severely critical of the military government of General Sani Abacha. The fifty-two-member Commonwealth, which includes Great Britain and most of its former colonies, threatened Nigeria with exclusion unless democracy were restored; no member had ever been expelled previously. Human rights groups and environmental advocates accused Shell and other oil companies operating in the Niger River Delta of doing little to secure the release of Saro-Wiwa and his supporters and therefore held them indirectly responsible for their deaths.

See also Death; Environmental education; Military censorship; Nigeria; Soyinka, Wole.

Sartre, Jean-Paul

Born: June 21, 1905, Paris, France
Died: April 15, 1980, Paris, France
Identification: French philosopher, novelist, essayist, and political activist
Significance: Awarded the Nobel Prize in Literature in 1964—an honor which he refused—Sartre wrote numerous works that became targets of censorship because of their philosophical and political ideas

A leading figure in French culture after World War II, Sartre exerted an enormous influence on the intellectual life of his times through his development of the philosophical theory of existentialism, the study of the fundamental features of human existence. In his major work *Being and Nothingness* (1943), Sartre claimed that to be human was to be unconditionally free. Whatever meaning there is to be found in existence, he argued, stems from one's own choices and actions, for which one is solely responsible, rather than from existing sources of meaning, such as God's plan for human life. In literary works from the same time period, Sartre dramatized his philosophical ideas through characters such as Antoine Roquentin, the anti-bourgeois, perpetually alienated, hyper-conscious "existentialist hero" of his 1938 novel *Nausea*.

A lecture that Sartre gave on existentialism and humanism in a café in 1945 brought his philosophy to popular attention. In it he identified himself as a representative of "atheistic existentialism," and reaffirmed that the only hope human beings had lay in their own hands. As Sartre's fame grew, and increasing controversy materialized around his views, existentialism attracted the attention of the Church of France, which proclaimed its evils in sermons to parishioners. In October, 1948, Sartre's writings became the object of censorship by the Roman Catholic church when papal authority ordered all of his works to be put on the *Index Librorum Prohibitorum*.

During this same period, the Soviet government attempted to ban performances of Sartre's play *Dirty Hands* (1948) in Helsinki, Finland, on the grounds—which Sartre denied—that it contained anti-Soviet propaganda. But in the early years of the 1950's, although Sartre had previously been a critic of Stalinist communism, he began to move toward re-establishing ties with the French Communist Party (PCF), and engaged in a flurry of political activity, which included a strong defense of the PCF in his essay "The Communists and Peace," and participation in the People's Peace Conference in Vienna in 1952. In 1953, in an infuriated printed attack, which brought him to the attention of the U.S. Federal Bureau of Investigation, Sartre condemned the United States for what he called the "legal lynching" of Ethel and Julius Rosenberg, convicted spies whom he viewed as innocent victims of McCarthyism. Taken with what he found on a visit to the Soviet Union in 1954, Sartre reported in highly favorable terms on social conditions in that country in a series of interviews upon his return to Paris. In the same year, his ties to communism led the United States Information Agency's libraries to remove his books from their shelves. Although Sartre retreated from the PCF following the Soviet invasion of Hungary in 1956, during this time he himself adopted the position that because his play *Dirty Hands* had become a "political battlefield," it should not be performed in any country without the prior approval of the country's Communist Party.

Jean-Paul Sartre (center) and Simone de Beauvoir (left) receive Italy's Tor Margana literary award, as Carlo Levi looks on, in Rome in 1963. (AP/Wide World Photos)

See also France; France, Anatole; Genet, Jean; *Index Librorum Prohibitorum*; Literature; United States Information Agency.

Saturday Night Live

TYPE OF WORK: Television program
BROADCAST: 1975-
SUBJECT MATTER: Comedy monologues, skits, topical humor, and popular music
SIGNIFICANCE: This television program's satire and general irreverence have frequently provoked network censors

Since *Saturday Night Live* began airing on October 11, 1975, with Lorne Michaels as executive producer, it has featured comedians such as Bill Murray, Gilda Radner, John Belushi, Jane Curtin, Dan Aykroyd, Steve Martin, Eddie Murphy, and Phil Hartman. The program's format has typically involved an opening monologue by a guest host, several comedy sketches, and performances by guest musicians. True to its title, it has been broadcast live—in the Eastern time zone—from New York City's Rockefeller Center.

Over the years *Saturday Night Live*'s producers and writers have frequently clashed with network censors. The National Broadcasting Company's (NBC) broadcast standards department has employed an editor to act as censor in the show's control room. The editor has been responsible for enforcing the provisions of the network's broadcast standards handbook and for ensuring that viewers not become overly angry at the show. The standards department has frequently insisted that the show's producer and writers rewrite or eliminate skits that may be regarded as offensive. Sometimes, however, the live nature of the program has given performers opportunities to circumvent the censors. For example, Dan Aykroyd once performed a sketch in which he played a refrigerator repairman whose pants fell low enough to reveal a significant portion of his posterior cleavage each time he bent over. After rehearsals of the sketch, the network censor ordered Aykroyd to cover up, but the actor defied the censor during the live performance. On some occasions when performers circumvented the wishes of censors, the network acted to remove objectionable material before airing the show's taped version to West Coast audiences, or before rerunning an episode of the show.

In 1994 the network censored comedian Martin Lawrence's opening monologue and "bleeped" his language in several skits when the show was rebroadcast on the West Coast. In February, 1981, one of the show's regular comedians used an obscenity in an impromptu line at the end of the show. The network made sure the word was not heard on the West Coast tape-delayed broadcast. This incident may also have contributed to a general purging of *Saturday Night Live* personnel and the firing of the same comedian and the show's executive producer (then Jean Doumanian) the following month.

Occasionally, protests made subsequent to a broadcast have moved the network to revise the show prior to repeating it. In June, 1993, for example, the network deleted a joke about President Bill Clinton's daughter, Chelsea, which had drawn numerous protests from viewers upon its original airing six months earlier. Similarly, that same year, Irish singer and songwriter Sinead O'Connor tore up a picture of Pope John Paul II during her appearance on the show. When the network rebroadcast the show later, it substituted an uncontroversial tape of O'Connor's dress-rehearsal performance for the one in which she tore up the pope's picture.

See also *Beavis and Butt-head*; Murphy, Eddie; O'Connor, Sinead; *Smothers Brothers Comedy Hour, The*; Talk shows; Tape-delay broadcasting; Television networks.

Satyricon, The

TYPE OF WORK: Book
WRITTEN: c. 66 C.E. (English translation, 1694)
AUTHOR: Gaius Petronius Arbiter (c. 20-66 C.E.)
SUBJECT MATTER: The imaginary adventures of three dissolute young Romans in southern Italy
SIGNIFICANCE: This rare surviving example of a Latin picaresque novel, offering an uninhibited look at the excesses of Roman society, was an object of modern censorship in 1922

In classical antiquity prose fiction was regarded as a low form of writing and the arts, not bound by traditions of good taste or proper literary convention. *The Satyricon*, attributed to one of the emperor Nero's courtiers, represents a brilliant mix of prose and verse and of conventional literary idiom and vulgar language. It satirizes and parodies the human absurdities and spectacular failures of contemporary Roman society. Petronius' depictions of his protagonists and their equally disreputable acquaintances are icily drawn; the outrageous, the obscene, and even the monstrous appear as commonplace.

In the summer of 1922 the New York Society for the Suppression of Vice, headed by John Sumner, filed suit to halt publication and sale of *The Satyricon* by the firm of Boni and Liveright. In a comment which well expresses the nature of the controversies which have surrounded *The Satyricon* for centuries, an editor for *The New York Times* remarked in the July 21 issue: "In any ordinary definition of that word Petronius is certainly obscene; and yet he is read by many who are merely annoyed by his obscenities. The extant fragments of what must have been a long book reveal a brilliant talent." The complaint was dismissed in the early autumn of the same year.

See also Books and obscenity law; *Caligula*; Liveright, Horace; Obscenity: legal definitions; Obscenity: sale and possession; Offensive language; Roman Empire; Society for the Suppression of Vice, New York.

Saumur v. City of Quebec

COURT: Supreme Court of Canada
DATE: October 6, 1953
SIGNIFICANCE: This decision overturned a municipal ordinance forbidding the distribution of literature on city streets by Jehovah's Witnesses

This case revolved around the validity of a municipal bylaw of the city of Quebec, Canada, which outlawed distribution of written material on city streets without prior permission of the chief of police. Passed in 1933, the law was generally perceived as being aimed at Jehovah's Witnesses, whose beliefs encouraged them to preach publicly and hand out literature. Witness literature often contained harsh criticism of the Roman Catholic church that offended Quebec's largely Catholic population. In 1947 Laurier Saumur, a Witness, was arrested for distributing such material and fined. Two provincial courts upheld his conviction.

In 1953 the Supreme Court of Canada heard Saumur's case on appeal. Saumur claimed that the city had violated his freedom of religion, which was guaranteed by the British North American Act of 1867 and the Freedom of Worship Act of 1851, a preconfederation law that had been re-enacted by Quebec's legislature in 1941. The city of Quebec, on the other hand, argued that an ordinance to regulate streets was a valid assertion of municipal power and applied to all citizens, not only to Jehovah's Witnesses.

In a narrow decision the Supreme Court of Canada ruled that Saumur's freedom of religion had been violated. However, many legal observers regarded the ruling as confusing and complicated. Four justices had found the bylaw constitutional. They argued that the regulation of streets was a proper concern of municipalities, that Jehovah's Witnesses were not exempt from obeying reasonable civic laws, and that they were not prohibited from the practice of their religion. Four other justices found the bylaw unconstitutional, arguing that such an important right as freedom of religion was under federal and not provincial jurisdiction. They also held that the purpose of the bylaw was to regulate not the streets but the minds of those who used them, and that the bylaw, if upheld, might also justify censorship of newspapers or political pamphlets.

The court's deciding vote was cast by Justice Patrick Kerwin, a Roman Catholic, who held that although the municipal bylaw was constitutional, it could not apply to Jehovah's Witnesses, who were guaranteed free exercise of their religion by the province's Freedom of Worship Act and the preconfederation act of 1851.

Many Canadians believed that the case enshrined freedom of religion throughout Canada; however, civil libertarians were concerned that five of the justices had effectively ruled that civil rights were under provincial, not federal, jurisdiction. Their concern was justified. The Quebec legislature took advantage of the interpretation to amend the Freedom of Worship Act so that it did not protect distribution of literature by Jehovah's Witnesses. The Canadian Supreme Court later upheld this amendment.

See also Canada; Jehovah's Witnesses; Leafletting; Prior restraint.

Savonarola, Girolamo

BORN: September 21, 1452, Ferrara (Italy)
DIED: May 23, 1498, Florence (Italy)
IDENTIFICATION: Roman Catholic cleric who dominated Florence in the late fifteenth century
SIGNIFICANCE: While acting as the virtual ruler of Florence during the late 1490's, Savonarola oversaw the burning of books, works of art, and other morally objectionable objects in the "bonfire of the vanities"; later he himself was burned, along with his own writings

The celebrated dominican friar of Ferrara, Italy, Girolamo Savonarola taught theology at the Dominican priory of San Marco in Florence. His sermons warned against impending doom. In 1490, at the insistence of Lorenzo de'Medici, influential patron of Renaissance art and learning, he became prior of San Marco. His sermons increased in popularity and aimed at restoring religion and morality by attacking the vices and tyrannical abuses of the Medici family.

In 1494 he expelled the Medici government and established a Christian commonwealth in Florence, becoming a virtual dictator. He imposed a program of sweeping moral reforms governing the repression of vice and frivolity. In his desire that Florence become the most Christian city in the world, he asked the inhabitants to make sacrifices by ridding their homes of smut, vanity, and frivolity. Members of a youth squad went from home to home collecting obscene literature, pornographic pictures and paintings, lewd statues, mechanical dolls of impure posturing, and other items designed to incite feelings of lust. These articles were then thrown onto a pyramid erected in the middle of the piazza that measured sixty feet in height. This was the famous pyramid of vanities, which contained mirrors, masks, wigs, cosmetics, perfumes, costumes, playing cards, and dice. In addition, books on astrology, witchcraft, necromancy, and devil worship, and works illustrated by Giovanni Boccaccio and Petrarch were thrown onto the pyramid. In the popular surge of piety many people heeding Savonarola's call to reform and purify termed these items "vanities"—hence the probable origin of the term "bonfire of the vanities." On February 7, 1497 church bells pealed as the pyramid of vanities exploded into flame.

Some historians have called Savonarola a "trail blazer" for John Calvin. Savonarola's belief that he was a prophet of God sent to announce judgment on Italy and on the Church brought him into conflict with Pope Alexander VI on grounds of heresy. In 1497, after Savonarola disobeyed an order to refrain from sermons, the pope excommunicated him from the Church. The Florentine reformer denounced Pope Alexander, declaring his election to the papacy invalid because he had bought the office. After Savonarola denied the pope's power, he alienated many of his own supporters. He was arrested, tortured, tried, and condemned to death for rejecting and opposing Church doctrine. In 1498 he was hanged and then burned at the stake on charges of sedition and heresy. His books were burned along with him.

See also Book burning; Calvin, John; Christianity; Heresy; Religion; Vatican.

Schenck v. United States

COURT: U.S. Supreme Court
DECIDED: March 3, 1919
SIGNIFICANCE: This case established the "clear and present danger" test permitting restrictions on speech that might produce immediately harmful effects

Charles Schenck, general secretary of the Socialist Party, was convicted of violating certain provisions of the Espionage Act of 1917. At the height of U.S. involvement in World War I he had circulated by mail thousands of leaflets urging young men eligible for military service to resist conscription into the military. Arguing that the Conscription Act violated the Thirteenth Amendment's prohibition against involuntary servitude, Schenck did not deny that it was his intention to influence draft-aged young men to obstruct efforts to implement the draft. Despite his intent, Schenck asserted that this is speech protected by the First Amendment to the Constitution.

The fundamental question facing the U.S. Supreme Court in this case was one of congressional authority to restrict freedom of speech, in this case political free speech. Justice Oliver Wendell Holmes, writing for the Court, sought to establish criteria which would carefully limit such suppression of free speech while permitting Congress to protect national security.

The Court held that Schenck's speech urging draft resistance could be restricted. In his opinion, Holmes reasoned that free speech was not absolute. One cannot shout "fire" in a crowded theater, for example, or utter words of threat and expect that all such utterances are protected speech. In this case, Holmes articulated a "clear and present danger" test, which requires the government to demonstrate that the specific speech, the context in which it occurred, and its potential impact create a "danger" which may bring about "the substantive evils that Congress has a right to prevent." The danger must be both substantial and proximate. With the nation at war, Schenck's urging of draft resistance was held to represent a clear and present danger.

Holmes had hoped that the clear and present danger test would be utilized to protect speech. However, in the decade following the Schenck decision, the clear and present danger test was never used to overturn a conviction or prevent restriction of free speech. By 1951, in *Dennis v. United States*, the Court had reformulated the test into a criterion for restricting speech, instead of one designed to protect it.

In *Dennis* the Court argued that advocacy of a dangerous idea could be restricted. The *Schenck* clear and present danger test, the Court concluded, does not mean that government must "wait until the putsch is about to be executed" to respond to the threat. The test was modified to permit restriction of political advocacy. In *Yates v. United States* (1957) the Court drew back from its *Dennis* ruling. In *Yates*, the Court held that advocacy of political ideas could not be restricted unless they amounted to an actual incitement to action. In thus separating advocacy from action, the Court shifted back to Holmes's formulation of clear and present danger. Without actually referring to the test, the Court in *Yates* overturned a conviction and protected free speech in a manner consistent with Holmes's intention in *Schenck*.

See also Clear and present danger doctrine; Draft resistance; Espionage Act of 1917; First Amendment Congress; *Greer v. Spock*; Holmes, Oliver Wendell, Jr.; Leafletting; Sedition; World War I.

Schiller, Friedrich von

BORN: November 10, 1759, Marbach, Württemberg
DIED: May 9, 1805, Weimar, Saxe-Wiemer
IDENTIFICATION: German playwright, poet, and philosopher
SIGNIFICANCE: All of Schiller's plays were censored to varying degrees in the various German principalities

In his play *The Robbers* (*Die Räuber*) Schiller, then a cadet at the prestigious ducal academy in Stuttgart, created Karl Moor, a young German nobleman who turned rebel to combat the injustices and tyranny of his brother, the Duke, and social ills. For this radicalism the French National Assembly awarded Schiller honorary citizenship in 1792, after Schiller himself had been made a nobleman and begun to distance himself from revolutionary politics. Because *The Robbers* could not be staged in Stuttgart, it opened in the somewhat more liberal city of Mannheim, only seventy miles away. Such differences in censorship were typical of Germany in those times.

Throughout the eighteenth century German censorship varied in extent and degree in each of the more than one hundred independent principalities, city states, and territories. Although *The Robbers* could be staged in Mannheim, Schiller had to make significant changes stipulated by the stage director and the Roman Catholic court. He removed offensive language and changed a treacherous "clergyman" into a "city councilor." Moreover, the stage director shifted the contemporary setting of the play to the Middle Ages in order to obscure the play's contemporary political allusions. Censorship of Schiller focused on "good taste" in language, conventional morality, church dogma, and overt political ramifications. Interestingly, censors distinguished sharply between plays' performances and their printed versions, which were generally regarded as less threatening. Thus, *The Robbers* was published almost without alteration in some states months after its first performance.

Schiller's other plays fared similarly. After he became a history professor in Jena in 1789, he wrote historical plays such as the *Wallenstein* trilogy (1798-1799), *Mary Stuart* (1800), *Maid of Orleans* (1801), and *William Tell* (1804). Strongly influenced by Immanuel Kant's philosophy, he depicted heroes and heroines as characters who achieve their

German playwright Friedrich von Schiller was arrested after his play Die Räuber *was banned in Wurttemberg. (Library of Congress)*

high goals by subordinating their personal interests to humanistic ideals.

Schiller had fewer problems with censorship in small states, especially in Weimar (Saxony), where Johann Wolfgang von Goethe became first an admirer and later a friend who shared his humanistic idealism and other views on aesthetics. Nevertheless, both men continued to censor themselves and each other. For example, as stage director of the Weimar Court Theater (1791-1817), Goethe struck out the communion scene in Schiller's *Mary Stuart*. For his part, Schiller rejected for his journal *Die Horen* two of Goethe's *Roman Elegies* because of their eroticism.

Because of their political and humanistic subject matter, Schiller's plays were often censored as political conditions changed throughout the German states, especially on the important stages in Vienna and Berlin. *Wallenstein*, for example, was not staged in its entirety in Vienna until 1848, and while it was normally impossible to stage *Wallenstein's Camp* in Berlin, because it portrayed an army ready to rebel, its performance was permitted and even encouraged after the French occupied Prussia in 1806.

After the National Socialist Party assumed power in Germany in 1933, the Nazis first hailed Schiller as a truly "German" author, because his heroic images lent themselves to misuse; however, they banned performances of *William Tell* in Berlin during World War II because of its positive portrayal of the legendary Swiss hero and of his successful resistance against the oppressor, which came uncomfortably close to describing the oppressive power of the Nazis.

See also Drama and theater; Germany; Goethe, Johann Wolfgang von; Kant, Immanuel; National Socialism.

Scholarships

DEFINITION: Grants given to students

SIGNIFICANCE: Some people have claimed that selection methods used to award scholarships have been used to restrict free expression

Scholarships are awards given to students to assist them financially as they pursue their educational goals. At the graduate and postgraduate levels, scholarships are normally referred to as fellowships. Scholarships may be awarded based on criteria such as academic merit, financial need, or athletic ability. Some recipients may be chosen for an unusual skill, ethnic heritage, or geographical background. The money comes from a number of sources, including governments, schools, foundations, and private donors.

In the United States, the largest single scholarship program is the National Merit Scholarship program, which provides one thousand scholarships annually to undergraduates. It is supported in large part by the Ford Foundation. Among some of America's most prestigious scholarships are the Fulbright and Rhodes scholarships for graduate study abroad, and the Jacob Javits and Andrew Mellon fellowships for graduate study.

Some scholarships may require recipients to perform certain services before, during, or after completion of their studies (such as the national Americorps program scholarships or graduate teaching assistantships). These scholarships are, however, distinguished from loans, which require repayment of the awards.

In most communist countries, the selection of scholarships is based on party loyalty, and any expression against the party or official policies places such financial support in jeopardy. In the Soviet Union prior to the collapse of the Communist Party and the renaming of the country, scholarships were regularly revoked for engaging in opposition activity, and all holders of graduate fellowships were forced to sign an oath of loyalty to the Soviet state. In China, Deng Xiaoping announced that loyalty to China was the principal factor in awarding scholarships to study abroad.

Some American scholarships have been criticized as being politicized. Some have complained that the extremely prestigious McArthur Fellowships, the so-called genius grants, contain a liberal bias. In 1992, Congress voted to eliminate scholarships for Indonesian soldiers, who had previously come to the United States for advanced military training. Congress argued that the Indonesian military's poor human rights record justified the move. President Bill Clinton later argued against the ban, saying it was vital to train Indonesia's military leaders in human rights, and allowed the training to continue, but at the soldiers' own expense.

In 1995 graduate teaching assistants at Yale University attempted to unionize. They claimed that the stipends they received were insufficient and that holders of graduate teaching assistantships were used in place of higher-cost tenured faculty. Many of these students refused to submit grades on time, and three faced disciplinary hearings. The students protested, and 137 students and other supporters of the strike were arrested. After Yale threatened to expel some students and re-voke the teaching assistantships of others, the graduate students submitted their grades, since many of them relied on their stipends as their sole source of income. Some accused Yale administrators of trying to lock them out, as many were told they would not be offered assistantships in the future. Some union organizers have contended that Yale violated their First Amendment rights, punishing them for speaking out against poor working conditions.

See also Education; National Endowment for the Arts; National Endowment for the Humanities; Universities.

School dress codes

DEFINITION: Rules mandating what students can and cannot wear in public schools

SIGNIFICANCE: Faced with gang-related dress and clothing that provokes students in various ways, many public schools have chosen to censor student expression through clothing

After almost disappearing during the antiestablishment era of the 1960's, public school dress codes began to reappear during the 1980's and 1990's, largely in response to parental concerns about drugs, crime, and gangs on campus. Proponents have cited safety, economic, and academic reasons for such codes, while opponents have charged that such codes infringe upon students' constitutional rights.

For parents and school administrators, the most compelling argument for mandating school dress codes is safety. Schools have adopted codes that range from banning certain items of clothing, requiring that students wear identification tags, to mandating formal school uniforms. It has been argued that having students wear uniforms makes schools safer because any person not wearing a uniform on campus can be spotted quickly, making it easier to find potentially dangerous outsiders. Further, weapons are harder to conceal in uniforms, and students wearing uniforms are less likely to be accosted and robbed of expensive clothing and jewelry. Moreover, the influence of gangs on school campuses is diminished when gang members cannot set themselves apart by wearing distinctive clothing or colors.

Dress codes also make financial sense for many parents. Uniforms are more economical to purchase than school clothes and save daily arguments about what children should wear to school. Prohibiting the wearing of designer labels and other expensive status symbols eliminates on-campus peer pressure and competition over expensive clothes that many students cannot afford.

Many school officials favor dress codes in the belief that they can enhance academic performance and discipline. Administrators believe clothing regulations decrease distractions, help students to concentrate on learning, and reduce group conflicts. Teachers have expressed the opinion that students who dress better behave better, and administrators contend that distinctive school uniforms help create a sense of community within the school.

Banned Clothing. Garments banned by various school districts have ranged from the ordinary to the exotic. Commonplace items have included blue jeans and baseball caps. Less common items have included jewelry, gold chains, and designer sunglasses. Apparel designated as gang-related has included leather jackets, certain professional sports team jackets, bandannas, and earrings worn by men. Also prohibited are overly revealing attire and clothing of the opposite sex when worn to a prom. Other troublesome items have been T-shirts with printed messages.

Shirts bearing messages fall under the category of communicative dress, that is, dress that communicates speech. Shirts often convey political messages; sex-, alcohol-, drug-, or gang-related messages; caricatures of school administrators; threatening, offensive, or provocative messages; messages laced with double meanings; and totally innocuous messages. Banning any and all such messages when they appear on students' T-shirts raises the question of infringing on students' First Amendment rights to free speech. It is on this point that much of the opposition to school dress codes has rested.

Constitutional Issues. By the early 1990's the U.S. Supreme Court had made no clear rulings specifically addressing the constitutionality of school dress codes. There had been important lawsuits over these codes during the 1960's and 1970's, but these suits were filed in relatively gentler times when the issue was decorum in the schools and not the destructiveness of gang warfare. Most of the cases challenging school dress codes are arguments over the First Amendment right to freedom of speech; some challenges are brought under Fourteenth Amendment rights to privacy, due process, and equal protection.

Arguments that school dress codes infringe on First Amendment rights to free speech raise the question of whether there exists a constitutional right to control one's appearance. Further, if such a right exists, is it significant enough to require a compelling state interest to override it? In *Tinker v. Des Moines Independent Community School District* (1969) the U.S. Supreme Court established the right of students to freedom of expression in schools, unless exercising that right intruded on the rights of other students, a school's need for appropriate discipline, or the academic work of the school. The arguments in the Tinker case were used in the case of T-shirts that school officials banned because they believed that the vulgarity of the shirts in question interfered with the school's educational mission. In *Hazelwood School District v. Kuhlmeier* (1988), the Supreme Court reinforced its ruling by allowing schools to restrict freedom of expression for legitimate pedagogical reasons. These decisions placed individual student rights in a secondary position to the rights of students as a whole to an orderly educational process. The compelling state interest of safety in the schools, as fostered by dress codes, overrides students' rights to dress as they please.

In arguing against school dress codes on Fourteenth Amendment grounds, privacy rights proved a weak argument, since restrictions on clothing worn in public would not logically infringe on one's privacy. The right to due process is emphasized to insure that dress code requirements are specific and detailed, in an attempt to eliminate code infractions which are judged on the basis of taste or style. The right to equal protection in dress codes affects restrictions targeted at a particular race or gender. In *Olesen v. Board of Education of School District No. 228* (1987) the issue was male students' being prohibited from wearing earrings, which were considered symbols of gang membership. An Illinois court ruled that girls showed gang connections in ways other than earrings, and those other ways, which violated school policy, were also prohibited; therefore, the rule was not discriminatory.

Despite all the constitutional arguments over school dress codes, two significant factors in their acceptance by the courts have been reasonableness and effectiveness. Many courts, while acknowledging student rights, base their judgments on whether the rules in question are both reasonable and effective in accomplishing particular objectives—most often that of campus safety.

Opponents of school dress codes believe that restricting students' choice of clothing inhibits their individuality and freedom of expression, restricts their development, and cuts off productive avenues for debate. Most vocal in opposition is the American Civil Liberties Union (ACLU), which has decried the message sent by the censorship inherent in school dress codes: that students must give up their rights in order to be safe.   —*Peggy Waltzer Rosefeldt*

See also Campus speech codes; Education; Fear; Fourteenth Amendment; *Hazelwood School District v. Kuhlmeier*; Symbolic speech.

BIBLIOGRAPHY

Perry A. Zirkel's "Student Dress Goads." in *Phi Delta Kappan* 75, no. 7 (March, 1994) is a brief overview of court decisions on school dress codes. A more detailed, yet readable, study of dress code litigation can be found in James A. Maloney's "Constitutional Problems Surrounding the Implementation of 'Anti-Gang' Regulations in the Public Schools," *Marquette Law Review* 75, no. 1 (Fall, 1991). California public school dress code law and the ACLU's opposition are discussed in "Should Schools Adopt Dress Codes?" *Current Events* 94, no. 3 (September 19, 1994).

School prayer

DEFINITION: Formally organized prayers in public schools

SIGNIFICANCE: Although the U.S. Supreme Court has ruled that school prayer violates the First Amendment's establishment clause, many people have argued that it should be protected by the amendment's free exercise clause

The First Amendment to the U.S. Constitution guarantees freedom of religion by endorsing the separation of church and state. The Fourteenth Amendment assures that state governments cannot suppress any citizen's religious rights. Public schools in the United States are state-run institutions; opponents of organized prayer in public schools argue that separation of church and state means separation of church and public schools. Proponents of school prayer argue that if public schools allow time for nonsectarian prayer, no church intrudes into public schools. Proponents may also argue that restrictions on organized prayer in public schools violate the First Amendment's protection of the free exercise of religion, as well as Fourteenth Amendment rights to equal protection.

Formal school prayer was an issue in the Supreme Court

case of *McCollum v. The Board of Education* (1948), which concerned religious instruction in public schools during regular school hours. In 1952 the Court heard the *Zorach v. Clauson* case, which dealt with released time for religious education. In both cases, the Court ruled against mingling public schools and religion. A decade later, in *Engle v. Vitale* (1962), the Court ruled that having students begin the day with prayer in the New Hyde Park School District was unconstitutional. Five parents successfully argued that individual students should not be required to participate in prayer or available alternatives. After the verdict in *Engle v. Vitale* was announced, newspapers, politicians, and religious leaders were flooded with letters from angry constituents. Within the next two years sixty-two propositions for a school prayer amendment to the U.S. Constitution were submitted. All failed.

Bible reading in school was ruled unconstitutional in *Abington School District v. Schempp* (1963). The issue of school prayer returned to the Supreme Court in *Wallace v. Jaffree* (1985). The Court declared that a state law granting a daily moment of silence for individual prayer was also unconstitutional. During the 1990's some school districts initiated moments of silence with no reference to prayer. Federal courts upheld the moment of silence. In 1989 the Supreme Court ruled that prayers formally delivered at school graduation exercises were unconstitutional. Later the Court allowed graduation prayers, provided that such prayers were initiated and conducted by the students.

The legislatures of Mississippi, Florida, South Carolina, and Virginia, and interested scholars have taken the stance that the school prayer issue entails student's right to free speech rather than freedom of religion. Freedom of speech heralds the right of free expression, peaceable assemblage, worship, academic freedom, and the right of teachers to express their beliefs without fear of penalty or dismissal. Support for a constitutional amendment to allow school prayer continued. Evangelists and religious groups actively speak, publish, and distribute literature promoting school prayer, which has considerable popular support in the United States.

See also Atheism; Committee to Defend the First Amendment; Courts and censorship law; Education; First Amendment; Fourteenth Amendment; O'Hair, Madalyn Murray; Religion; Religious education.

Science

DEFINITION: Science is the practice of gaining knowledge through experiment

SIGNIFICANCE: The culture of knowledge, logic, and experiment has often run afoul of the culture of belief, creeds, and revelation; the people and institutions of science have also engaged in censorship

Cultures holding worldviews contrary to science may suppress valid science and science education. Additionally, scientists themselves have declared certain areas of investigation off limits, have denied funding to research that is outside current paradigms, have constrained the publication of opposing views, or have been constrained from disseminating scientific findings.

Science is a modern worldview based on using recorded, repeatable observation of fact to reach logical conclusions about the world. As such, science stands apart from many other human pursuits that do not test their intellectual models by constant reference to the verifiable world. Although tethered to the real world, the discoveries of science are portrayed in the language and cultural conditions present at the time and place of their elaboration.

Pre-Modern Science. Prior to printing and the use of publications as a main avenue for disseminating scientific theories and discoveries, science centered upon personalities who were skilled in posing new questions about real phenomena. Most such people had to rely on local position or a teaching post to support their inquiry, and were subject to social and political censorship of the time. Although Socrates asked a wide array of questions ranging well beyond the realm of science, and was considered dangerous to Greek youth of that time, many early scientific thinkers took similar risks when they dared espouse new views that better reflected the real world's cause-and-effect relationships. One clear early suppression of scientific observations and theory that contradicted the established worldview was the case of Galileo Galilei. Early scientists often lived in regions of limited tolerance and were particularly careful in such acts as securing cadavers to dissect or discussing controversial ideas. The availability of print expanded the outreach of scientific ideas and complicated the role of the censor.

Publication and Openness in Science Research. Science communication centers around the open dissemination of new research results in the short term by journals and the accurate generalization of proven concepts in textbooks. More than 80,000 science journals worldwide publish original science research following a general format of: introduction to the problem, detailed methodology, test results, and conclusions. Although Peter Medawar has correctly indicated that science research is often not conducted in this fashion, the open publication of science in this format allows for efficient peer review and all-important replication (or failure to replicate) research for future verification.

Modern scientists have agreed to not publish or disseminate science research in the public record in two broad cases: matters of national security and commercial discoveries of proprietary value. The central example of suppression of technological development for national security reasons is nuclear technology. As soon as early experiments indicated the possibility of a nuclear chain reaction, and before the Manhattan Project was established, Western physicists refrained from publishing results that could be used by the Axis powers to build an atomic bomb. As war became imminent, science secrecy extended to research in sonar, radar, cryptography and other fields, and wartime laws enforced the censorship of military science secrets. Today, across science disciplines, both science authors and journal editors continue to exert some degree of self-censorship on publication of articles that would allow the easy construction of an atomic bomb, the production of deadly biological warfare agents, and so on.

The distinction between sensitive military science facts and nonsensitive knowledge is not always clear. Developed countries have access to databases, such as detailed satellite imaging useful in predicting weather and crop failures, which they acquire with other intelligence data. But the United States government has deemed unclassified, nonsensitive data as potentially sensitive since it could be compiled into intelligence data. Most countries reserve the right to deny passports and thus restrict travel and discussion for military personnel who possess sensitive knowledge: This ban can extend to scientists.

Commercial scientists hired to develop specific products and processes are also committed by civil contract to maintaining the secrecy of their discoveries, and may have to submit their publications and presentations to internal review before their public release. While such censorship comes with the job and is therefore mutually agreed to, there is again a gray scale between specific applied research that produces patentable products and general discoveries that have broad value across the sciences.

The science publication process also permits the possibility of censorship of research results by peer reviewers, the journal editors, and by language restrictions.

Cyril Burt. Sir Cyril Burt, the powerful editor of a major British educational psychology journal and knighted in 1946, was also a proponent that IQ was preponderantly determined by heredity. When his study of identical twins reared apart was challenged as based on too few cases, he conveniently published a confirming article by two unknown female researchers that supported his work. Only after his death in 1971 was it discovered that this article was fraudulent, that the authors had never existed, and that Burt had merely inflated his earlier data. Only in retrospect did it become clear how a powerful editor could prevent challenges to weak research and manipulate the public discourse in science. His dominance in the field laid the foundation for the two-level tracking used in most British educational systems.

Peer review is a recent system used by most science journals for ensuring publication of research of value and quality. When an article is submitted for publication, the editor forwards it to a number of reviewers in the field for comment and assessment. Reviewers may recommend it for publication, suggest critical revisions, or recommend against its publication because it provides no new insights, has a faulty design, draws conclusions beyond what is supported by the data, or belongs in another journal. However, peer review cannot detect fraudulent data because reviewers are rarely in a position to repeat experiments themselves. Peer review also creates the opportunity for censorship, particularly for articles that do not support the predominantly accepted paradigms. In an age when university researchers are pressured to maintain a consistent publication record, some have protested that their papers have been rejected on ideological grounds, and that they are discouraged from reporting results that contradict current science understanding. The bureaucratic inertia that stifles bolder articles is contrary to science, which allows for the discarding of old understandings when more accurate ones are found. In several cases, the rejection of articles has led to the establishment of additional science journals. The distribution

of science journals, however, is not proportional to research being conducted in cultures worldwide, which reflects another problem.

Language Discrimination in Science Publishing. Non-Western scientists openly discuss and occasionally publish their concerns that only research published in English-language journals is cited and rewarded. Although English ranks behind various other major languages in first-language usage, science journals are predominantly in English, reflecting the British and American cultural, economic, and scientific dominance of the world during the nineteenth and twentieth centuries. Non-English-language researchers note that if they publish in local language journals, they are ignored and not cited; credit goes to others who publish later in an English language journal. If non-English-language researchers submit their work in translated English, it is more likely to be rejected for lack of fluency. Meanwhile, non-English-speaking scientists tend to cite the worldwide literature in all languages, while many Western scientists cite only English language articles, particularly reflecting the lack of language training among younger United States scientists. To combat this imperialism, several European journals require abstracts be provided in three languages.

Trofim Lysenko—A Case of Total Science Censorship. Trofim Lysenko Scientific debate and a system of publication and peer review can be overcome by censorship imposed by a greater political campaign. After the Russian Revolution in the early twentieth century, rulers Vladimir Ilich Lenin and Joseph Stalin promoted young scientists with worker and peasant origins. The young agronomist Trofim Lysenko was from this poor economic class and had developed a cold treatment for plants, such as peas and wheat, so they could supposedly be planted in winter rather than in spring. Such manipulation of plant variation would be exceedingly important for the future of Russian agriculture, if it worked. Lysenko, however, was a scientist who avoided statistical analyses and thus was unable to distinguish a normal capacity for survival in mild winters from genuine cold-hardiness.

The new science of genetics that was being built in North America and Europe proposed hereditary units called genes and contended that the inheritance of traits was determined by the laws of probability and the genetics of the parents. Inheriting qualities without regard to an individual's merit was, to the mind of Soviet thinkers, reminiscent of the monarchy system. Lysenko's belief (called "Michurinist science" after Michurin, an earlier Russian plant breeder) that acquired features could be inherited (for example that a father born with normal musculature but who worked to form strong muscles would produce a stronger baby) fit with the new communist system of thought. Although a hallmark of scientific thought is to discard a belief that does not fit the facts, scientists in the Soviet Union were obliged to make facts fit the belief. Lysenko also was politically correct in that he represented trial-and-error plant breeders, rural agronomists who viewed the Western genetics as terribly mathematical and abstract, divorced from the realities of farming. Lysenko's battle against Western genetics was therefore an anti-intellectual stance that gained Stalin's favor for its simplicity and its fit with communist political views.

Lysenko was rapidly promoted and successfully campaigned for his theories. Eventually, he became president of the Lenin All-Union Academy of Agricultural Sciences and held enough political power to proclaim scientists who were favorable to Western genetics as enemies. Such scientists were criticized in meetings, did not receive valuable posts, and were censored from publishing. The world famous Nikolay Vavilov, an early supporter of Lysenko, discovered the extent of Lysenko's exaggerations by 1937; Vavilov was arrested in August of 1940 and died in Saratov prison in 1943. Following the 1948 academy session meetings, more than 3,000 scientists were dismissed, completing the purge of Soviet scientists with any understanding of genetics. This sentenced the Soviet Union to twenty years of ignorance in a biological field critical to food production.

State censorship of schoolbooks was complete. Biology textbooks in schools supported only the Lysenko line and mentioned Western genetics only in derision. During this time, the People's Republic of China was making heavy use of Russian advisers. Since virtually all Chinese science textbooks were translations of Russian texts, Lysenko's influence reached far more people in China than in the U.S.S.R. Michurinist faculty remained at universities until the 1990's.

Immanuel Velikovsky. Western science has also held to scientific orthodoxy, although not to the extreme of sending rebel scientists to prison camps. The most blatant Western case involved Immanuel Velikovsky, who wrote *Worlds in Collision* (1950), a speculative manuscript that provided a rather sensational alternative explanation for many phenomena in geology and astronomy. Macmillan Publishing, a recognized printer of science textbooks, published the controversial text. In response, some members of the science community threatened to boycott Macmillan. The senior editor in charge was fired, as was a planetarium director who had recommended the book for publication. Science departments at some campuses would not allow Velikovsky to speak, in effect censoring or restricting the presentation of his unorthodox ideas.

The book was soon republished by Doubleday (not a science textbook publisher) which made the science community less worried. Nevertheless, librarians had to determine where to catalog the book; classifying the book with the pure or applied sciences provided more legitimacy

Science and Sex. Western society's reluctance to discuss matters of sexuality in public, based on the Judeo-Christian worldview, severely constrained research and publication in human reproductive biology. Basic anatomical and physiological research of reproductive organs lagged two centuries behind equivalent research with the stomach. Margaret Sanger faced official censorship when attempting to disseminate the most rudimentary information about birth control early in the twentieth century. Alfred Kinsey, an established entomologist, was asked to teach a basic sexuality class at Indiana University and was appalled at the lack of research available to present to his students. The studies he began as a means to establish reliable course content soon developed into his famous surveys; the controversy that resulted from his basic research

would have destroyed professors with lesser reputations.

The benefits of science research are rarely felt until incorporated into society at large through public education. In spite of the supposedly freer discussion of sexual matters during the sexual revolution of the 1960's, formal sex education did not become a regular part of the curriculum but was limited to isolated progressive teachers. Before 1980 and the arrival of AIDS, only one state mandated sex education. In 1990 twenty-eight states required some minimal sexuality and AIDS education curriculum, although extensive opposition in some communities substituted "Just Say No" alternatives to genuine sexuality education. Nearly all states mandating sex education also provided a clause permitting parents to withdraw their students from such classes—a political tactic that reduced opposition to the state mandate. In contrast to the rest of the compulsory curriculum, this allowed parents to censor this portion of the public school curriculum for their children alone rather than for all children in the school.

Parents and religious groups also protest the addition of factual, scientifically accurate sex materials in public and school libraries, especially accurate literature about homosexuality that fails to cast it in a bad light. Biology and sexuality textbooks do not directly espouse or condemn any sexual viewpoint, which is precisely, in the eyes of some, what is wrong with biology and sexuality textbooks. Such books' matter-of-fact presentations using scientific terminology are often accused of promoting secular humanism.

Although current definitions for personhood state that a person's life begins at birth, funding for fetal research has been severely curtailed under conservative federal administrations and has driven such research overseas. The availability of abortion procedures for pregnant patients is clearly a factual matter of scientific information provided by medical doctors in a professional setting. Nevertheless, a U.S. Supreme Court decision in *Rust v. Sullivan* in 1988 found that it was legal to require doctors to withhold such information from patients in family planning clinics and public health facilities receiving federal funds. Had the case involved banning private health care facilities as well, concerns about free speech would probably have prevailed. Nevertheless, the ruling provided the U.S. government with the right to utilize funding to censor legitimate professional discussion of medically scientific facts.

Evolution, Animal Rights, and Textbook Censorship. The teaching of evolution is also portrayed as a part of a secular humanism curriculum and often draws the same opponents as does sex education. Evolution is so central to biology that it permeates the textbooks and reference materials in a library. However, the most active censorship of evolution materials was self-censorship by textbook publishers during the 1960's and 1970's. About half the states utilize textbook adoption committees that establish a list of textbooks that can be used in that state. Originally established as buying consortia so the southern states could purchase in bulk, the textbook adoption committees—especially of Texas and California—have become important censors. If a national textbook is not adopted in these states, it loses a major portion of its market. Sadly, most publishers rewrote their biology textbooks with an eye toward the pressures of adoption, eliminating the concept and term "evolution." Over a decade, the science community working as committees of correspondence (later to become the National Center for Science Education) worked to counter the antievolution arguments and expose textbook censorship. Most science textbooks restored a discussion of evolution by 1990, only to begin a similar removal of dissection and animal experiments in response to the animal rights movement.

Self-censorship. In 1988 when the Environmental Protection Agency (EPA) had to determine safe levels for several chemicals, including the nerve gas phosgene, its agency report included data originating from Nazi experiments on French prisoners. The EPA administrator expunged the data at the request of twenty-two EPA scientists. Proponents for censoring the Nazi data contend that any use of the data justifies or condones the original experiments. Opponents of the censorship contend that usage in no way makes the original experiment legitimate, and they also note that failure to use the data may cost lives.

There is some research that poses no ethical dilemmas and yet one cannot expect to be pursued. Research into aphrodisiacs could serve aging patients; however, science has not sought aphrodisiacs. Objective research into IQ and race is

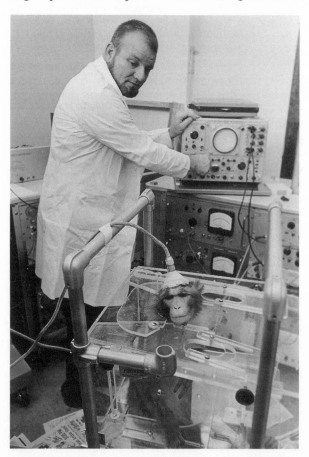

During the 1990's the debate over discussing evolution in science textbooks began giving way to pressures to remove discussions of animal research. (AP/Wide World Photos)

virtually impossible, given the controversy surrounding the issue; IQ and race research has often been a veiled way of "proving" white superiority, although Asian students generally are excelling in American schools. Thinkers contend that the lack of investigation into such questions indicates the extent that science is a product of its society.

—*John Richard Schrock*

See also Bacon, Francis; Galileo Galilei; Kinsey Report; Pesticide industry; Political correctness; Secular humanism; Sex education; Textbooks; Universities.

BIBLIOGRAPHY

The Anatomy of Censorship by Jay Elwood Daily (New York: Marcel Dekker, 1973) is somewhat judgmental and polemic, but includes details of the Velikovsky episode in American science as well as perspectives on science and sex education. *The Scientific Revolution: 1500-1800—The Formation of the Modern Scientific Attitude*, by A. R. Hall (Boston: Beacon Press, 1954), provides an accurate narration of Galileo's clash with the Roman Catholic church, including the force with which he was personally censored and the chilling effect the censorship had on the scientific movement regionally. *Censorship: The Knot That Binds Power and Knowledge*, by Sue Curry Jansen (New York: Oxford University Press, 1988), includes a brief discussion of relativism in science and its use as an excuse to censor science. David Joravsky's *The Lysenko Affair* (Chicago: The University of Chicago Press, 1970) details the tragedy of basing Soviet agricultural science on ideology. Joravsky documents the early simple work of Ivan Michurin, the rise of the essentially anti-intellectual and anti-science rural horticulturists, and the rejection of the new Western genetics. *Patterns of Censorship Around the World*, edited by Ilan Peleg (Boulder, Colo.: Westview Press, 1993), provides a broad view of censorship under the post-Cold War order, including totalitarian and authoritarian systems, and censorship in liberal democratic systems. Valery N. Soyfer provides a brief and accessible summary shedding "New Light on the Lysenko Era" (*Nature*, 339, June 8, 1989), citing previously unpublished documents that reveal the details of political maneuvering necessary for Lysenko to rise in power, suppress colleagues who believed in the new genetics, and continue to support a theory of inheritance of acquired characteristics that did not correspond with the realities of the research laboratory.

Scientology, Church of

FOUNDED: 1954

TYPE OF ORGANIZATION: Religious

SIGNIFICANCE: The Church of Scientology has been both a target of censorship and a force for censorship

The Church of Scientology is a religion based on the teachings of its founder, L. Ron Hubbard. Its basic tenets can be found in Hubbard's book *Dianetics: The Modern Science of Mental Health* (1950). Before establishing Scientology, Hubbard was a writer of science fiction novels.

After a personality test, prospective members of the organization are usually told they will derive benefit from the program. Members are "audited" and eventually cleared of "engrams," or mental aberrations. When this process is completed, members continue their assent through successive levels of enlightenment. At even higher levels, Scientologists are freed from the multiple spirits, or thetans, that inhabit their bodies. As the members graduate to higher levels, the money required to complete the current level increases. The top level is rumored to cost eleven thousand dollars; the sessions take place aboard Hubbard's yacht.

Hubbard lived on his yacht for about ten years, usually sailing in international waters. The church continued to prosper. When he returned to the United States, he went into hiding, dying under mysterious circumstances in 1986. His most avid followers continued the mission of the church and embarked on a heavy television and print advertising campaign. The church has even been accused of having members buy Hubbard's *Dianetics* and his science fiction novels in order to keep the books on the best-seller lists.

The Church of Scientology has been on both sides of the censorship issue. The church's scientific bent was denounced by the American Medical Association shortly after its founding. When a federal court upheld a Food and Drug Administration ruling that the scientific claims of the church were unfounded, Hubbard changed the names of Scientology officials and practices. Auditors became ministers and the auditing a religious sacrament. Internationally, Hubbard's yacht was denied docking at several ports in Europe in the 1970's. A court in France convicted him *in absentia* for fraud and the religion was banned in Great Britain. Australia also has been critical of Scientology, declaring it a nonreligion. The church's tax-exempt status as a religious institution in the United States was revoked in 1967 and this revocation upheld in 1988. In 1993 the status was reinstated. The Canadian Supreme Court upheld a libel judgment in excess of one million dollars against the church for criticizing a public official. Canadian laws were criticized for being more favorable to the target of libel than laws in the United States. In the late 1990's Scientologists in Germany faced government harassment.

As a force for censorship, the church has been active in filing lawsuits against real and perceived threats against its secrecy. Hubbard instructed his followers to use every means to resist enemies of the church, and the church leadership has filed lawsuits frequently against its critics. At one time, the church had seventy-one cases against the Internal Revenue Service alone.

In 1995 the church secured the name of an anonymous writer in Finland who was spreading the secrets of the church via the Internet. All documents pertaining to the church were recovered from the writer by Finnish police and returned to the church.

See also Copyright law; Internet; Religion; Technology.

Scopes trial

DATE: July 10-21, 1925
PLACE: Dayton, Tennessee
SIGNIFICANCE: A Tennessee law censoring the teaching of evolution led to a highly publicized trial of a high school teacher

On March 21, 1925, Tennessee enacted a law forbidding teachers in any state-supported school from presenting anything about the origin of humans that did not agree with the biblical creation story. Further, teachers were not to teach that humans had descended from lower animals. This was seen by the American Civil Liberties Union (ACLU) in New York as a clear contradiction of the constitutional rights of freedom of speech. The ACLU decided that a court case was needed to test the constitutionality of the Tennessee law.

Finding a Test Case. The ACLU advertised for a Tennessee teacher to challenge the law. In the small town of Dayton, Tennessee, about forty miles northeast of Chattanooga, town leaders decided to take up the ACLU offer. Not all of them were antievolution, but they saw a test case as a way to bring in visitors and this would be good for business. John T. Scopes, a twenty-four-year-old high school science teacher and football coach, volunteered to stand trial. The Dayton group informed the ACLU they were willing to test the Tennessee law. Local lawyers prepared to be the prosecuting attorneys while John Godsey, an elderly former judge, agreed to be Scopes's defense attorney.

Newspaper accounts of the coming trial attracted a number of volunteers to help on both sides. Some saw the state law as a direct infringement of free speech and academic freedom. Others saw the trial as a battle between Christianity and modern science, between good and evil. One volunteer was William Jennings Bryan, a sixty-five-year-old lawyer, former U.S. secretary of state, three-time candidate for the U.S. presidency, and a firm believer in a literal interpretation of the Bible. A self-professed expert on the Bible, he welcomed the chance to beat the nonbelievers at debate. Bryan soon became the lead attorney in a prosecution group that included six other attorneys.

Volunteers for the defense also quickly came forward, including Clarence Darrow, a widely respected sixty-eight-year-old criminal lawyer. Unlike Bryan, who was an active churchgoer, Darrow was an agnostic (some called him an atheist). He became the lead defense counsel with five assisting attorneys. The twelve lawyers were arrayed when, on July 10, 1925, Judge John T. Raulston opened the case of *State of Tennessee v. John Thomas Scopes* in the Rhea County circuit court, Dayton.

Tennessee was not the first state to try to censor teaching about evolution. In 1922 the Kentucky legislature defeated such a bill by only one vote. That same year, South Carolina considered but failed to pass an anti-Darwinism bill. In 1923 similar bills were raised in the legislatures of Florida, Georgia, and Texas but failed. In 1924 Oklahoma removed mention of evolution from textbooks but did not specifically forbid teaching the subject. An antievolution bill was defeated in 1924 in North Carolina, but high school textbooks mentioning the topic were removed from circulation.

A Circus Atmosphere. The Scopes trial succeeded in calling attention to Dayton but perhaps not in the manner that had been hoped. For weeks there had been stories in national newspapers about the coming trial, and, following the popular notion that Darwin's evolution theory stated that humans had descended from ape ancestors, the trial became known as the "Monkey Trial." People poured into town, and the courtroom

Although Clarence Darrow (leaning on desk) conducted an eloquent defense of John T. Scopes, he lost the case and his defendant was fined one hundred dollars. (Library of Congress)

was filled to capacity. Vendors set up lemonade and hot dog stands on the sidewalks. Others sold Bibles, antievolution books, and souvenir buttons. Sidewalk preachers proclaimed sermons to clusters of passersby. Some circus performers brought trained chimpanzees to cash in on the monkey theme.

A twelve-man jury was chosen, sworn in, and heard the charge. Some of Scopes's students were called as witnesses and testified he had indeed included evolution in his class curriculum. The case appeared to be complete. Darrow then surprised everyone by calling Bryan as a defense witness. Bryan agreed to this unusual step, although it was not required of him. The defense had recruited a number of scientists with the intention of having them testify about the truth of evolution. The judge refused to permit this but did allow their written testimony to be included in the documents of the trial but not in the transcript. This step would at least have the scientists' statements available for study when, if all went according to plan, the ACLU appealed the case to the state supreme court and, ultimately, the U.S. Supreme Court. The defense expected to lose in the county court and the Tennessee Supreme Court. Darrow's questioning of Bryan included references to inconsistencies and contradictions in the biblical account of creation, especially the origin of humans. Bryan's replies were simplistic and demonstrated shallow thinking and a narrow view of the world. Occasionally he contradicted himself and stated in effect that everything he needed to know he found in the Bible. His responses disappointed and shocked many of his Fundamentalist supporters in the courtroom. Bryan, who had hoped to outargue the evolutionists, was bested by Darrow.

The outcome of the trial was not unexpected. The jury found Scopes guilty of violating the Tennessee law and the judge sentenced him to pay a hundred-dollar fine. Five days after the trial, Bryan died in his sleep—friends said of a broken heart for the humiliation he had suffered on the witness stand. The school board offered Scopes his job back, but he instead chose to accept a scholarship to study geology at the University of Chicago. He spent the remainder of his life as a field geologist for several petroleum corporations.

The ACLU appealed the case to the state supreme court in 1927, but the court remanded it to the lower court on a technicality. The county court declined to retry Scopes, and the Tennessee antievolution law remained intact. In 1926 Arkansas and Mississippi had enacted similar legislation. Tennessee repealed its law in 1967, and test cases in Arkansas and Mississippi resulted in the U.S. Supreme Court's declaring those laws unconstitutional.

During the years the antievolution laws were on the books, textbook publishers and teachers kept mention of evolution to a minimum to avoid controversy. Long after the laws were repealed, open discussion and teaching of Darwinism and evolution remained under a real or perceived shadow of censorship. —*Albert C. Jensen*

See also American Civil Liberties Union; Courtrooms; Darwin, Charles; Evolution; First Amendment; Intellectual freedom; Science; Textbooks.

BIBLIOGRAPHY

Arthur Blake's *The Scopes Trial: Defending the Right to Teach* (Brookfield, Conn.: Millbrook Press, 1994) discusses balanced views of freedom of speech and worship as well as the rights to academic freedom and learning. The definitive account of the Scopes trial is L. Sprague de Camp's thoroughly documented *The Great Monkey Trial* (Garden City, N.Y.: Doubleday, 1968). Tom McGowen illustrates *The Great Monkey Trial: Science Versus Fundamentalism in America* (New York: Franklin Watts, 1990) with photographs of the trial and its principal figures. Personal views of the trial are offered in John T. Scopes and James Presley, *Center of the Storm: Memoirs of John T. Scopes* (New York: Holt, Rinehart and Winston, 1967). *D-Days at Dayton: Reflections on the Scopes Trial*, edited by Jerry R. Tompkins (Baton Rouge: Louisiana State University Press, 1965), is a collection of essays written forty years after the trial by surviving participants, including Scopes.

Screw

TYPE OF WORK: Magazine
FIRST PUBLISHED: 1968
PUBLISHERS: James Buckley (1944-   ) and Alvin Goldstein (1937-   )

SUBJECT MATTER: Adult sexuality and political satire

SIGNIFICANCE: When this magazine was tried under state obscenity laws and ruled obscene in 1973, the decision called into question the legality of all American sex magazines

In November, 1968, writer Alvin Goldstein and editor James Buckley, both of the underground newspaper *New York Free Press*, put together the first issue of *Screw* magazine. A sex magazine containing nude photographs, sex commentary, personal advertisements, and ratings of sexual aids, X-rated films and sex novels, *Screw* also commented on politics, war, and societal mores and fetishes. Within several years, the magazine doubled its physical size and had a circulation of more than 100,000 issues a month.

On May 30, 1969, New York City police raided the offices of *Screw* and confiscated copies of issues allegedly libeling local politicians. Buckley and Goldstein were eventually tried by the U.S. Supreme Court, which ruled that *Screw* was not obscene. Four years later, in *Miller v. California*, the Supreme Court decided that individual states could set their own definitions of obscenity. During that same year a jury in Wichita, Kansas, convicted Buckley and Goldstein on eleven counts of obscenity. They were also found guilty in the New York State Court of Appeals. An appeal to the Court was rejected. Despite these convictions, *Screw* continued to appear.

See also *Hustler*; Men's magazines; *Miller v. California*; Newspapers, underground; Nudity; Obscenity: legal definitions; Obscenity: sale and possession; *Penthouse*; *Playboy*; Pornography; Sex in the arts.

Secular humanism

DEFINITION: According to Christian Fundamentalists, a set of religious beliefs mistakenly glorifying all things human and unduly emphasizing the things of this world

SIGNIFICANCE: Fundamentalists have charged that public institutions such as schools and government, rather than being free from religion, as required by the Constitution, have adopted the religion of secular humanism

Considered separately, words such as "secular," meaning worldly, and "humanism," referring to the perfectibility of humans through reason and intellect, are innocuous. When paired, however, they become a derogatory label. To some Fundamentalist Christians, secular humanism is a religion, a cult of sorts, that has infiltrated the government, the justice system, and the classrooms of the United States. Some Fundamentalists have charged that secular humanism has infringed upon, perhaps usurped, traditional national values of Christianity. Although students of the founding and of the Constitution of the United States might be puzzled by such an assertion, it began to influence social and political life in the late twentieth century. Fundamentalists chastised the secular humanism of textbooks, curricula, and instructors. Secular humanism has been blamed for corrupting young minds, promoting self-serving ethics, and encouraging students to think for themselves.

Humanism was born of the Renaissance's resurgence of interest in classical works. Humanism has asserted a belief in universal truth and a belief that humans are perfectible through education and capable of self-fulfillment without recourse to supernaturalism. Humanism is a nontheistic, rather than an atheistic, theory. Humanism does not deny God but rather concentrates on humanity. Humanism encountered the disapproval of the church from the start. With the Reformation, humanism diminished as a topic of debate, although many of the Humanists' criticisms of the Roman Catholic church, particularly of monasticism and corruption, became points of contention for the Protestants. Humanist values arguably gained wide, if unacknowledged acceptance from the sixteenth century onward.

Modern Attacks. After the decline of communism as a threat to the United States, many Fundamentalists took up the battle cry of "secular humanist" to replace the epithet of "godless communist." The appellation was designed to quash argument and to silence those who disagreed. The most prominent Fundamentalists—Jerry Falwell, Phyllis Schlafly, Pat Robertson, Senator Jesse Helms, Mel Gabler, Norma Gabler, and others—shared certain religious convictions of the majority of the nation's populace. The difference, however, was the conclusions they drew from those convictions. Advocacy of those conclusions has contributed to the withdrawal of thousands of children from public schools into private or home schooling.

According to this group, textbooks, library books, curricula, films, and teachers have acted as subversive agents of secular humanism in the schools. Consequently, many Fundamentalists have been of the opinion that since class time was devoted to what they referred to as "values change," or indoctrination into secular humanism, no time was left for educating children in the basics, which had contributed to the decline in the late twentieth century in academic prowess, classroom discipline, and SAT scores. The Fundamentalists have campaigned to amend textbooks, prohibit sex education, remove books from libraries, mandate prayer, require the teaching of creationism, and eliminate any references they deemed anti-American or anti-Christian. They have also advocated removal of students from public schools and placement of students into private Christian schools or teaching children at home.

Multiple Definitions. Definitions of secular humanism have been wide and varied. However, there are several specifics on which Fundamentalists have agreed. When it has come to the education of their children, they have identified eight basic concepts that they prefer not to have discussed in classrooms. This list has been incorporated into the printed materials furnished by Educational Research Analysts, a Texas-based textbook review group headed by the Gablers. Under each point was a verse from the Bible, selected to add credence to their objections. The concepts they wish to exclude are evolution, which regards the universe as self-existing and not created; self-authority or individual autonomy—the belief that humans are their own authority and not accountable to any higher power; situational ethics or relativism—the belief that there are no absolute rules for conduct, other than what individual situations dictate; distorted realism—the exposure to diverse points of view, including profanity, immorality, and perversions as acceptable modes of self-expression; sexual permissiveness—the belief that all forms of sexual expression are permissible, including sex education; antibiblical bias—the notion that humans created God out of their own experience; opposition to free enterprise—the ideology that government control or ownership of the economy should replace private ownership; and one-world government—advocacy of global citizenship as a replacement for nationalism or any view that advocates world peace.

A popular pamphlet widely circulated among the group, *Is Humanism Molesting Your Child?*, describes humanism as a denial of the Bible, God, and moral values, and a belief in sexual freedom, incest, abortion, suicide, and a one-world socialistic government.

Growing Numbers. The Fundamentalist Christian movement against secular humanism has gained adherents through use of selected media, such as Pat Robertson's Christian Broadcasting Network, which has claimed a viewing audience of thirteen million households, and through the political machinations of such people as Senator Jesse Helms. Tim LaHaye, a San Diego minister and member of the Moral Majority, sold more than 350,000 copies of his pamphlet *Battle for the Mind*, primarily through direct mail. LaHaye contends that 275,000 committed secular humanists have infiltrated the government, the courts, the schools, and the media of the United States. Other Fundamentalists have asserted that the U.S. Supreme Court has effectively declared secular humanism the official religion of the United States, in violation of the First Amendment.

Teaching Religion. The U.S. courts have ruled that public schools can teach about religion, but not teach which religious beliefs are correct. Because parents, school systems, and many educators have confused culture with religion, school curricula have tended to exclude all mention of religion's influence on history, art, literature, and values. It was simply too difficult to address a diversity of traditions while remaining neutral, and textbooks and teachers began to distort history and literature to avoid discussing religion at all. This practice drew the attention of Fundamentalists.

One Fundamentalist school board member lamented that humanists were having church services in schools five days a week, while others compiled lists to alert parents to humanistic terminology in texts. Additionally, others insisted that since humanism centered on the self, the educational system tried to instill a positive self-image in the children, which eliminated their going to Christ for forgiveness of sin. Although Christian Fundamentalists and publishers and educators who eliminated material to avoid controversy have disagreed on many points, both have practiced censorship.   —*Joyce Duncan*

See also Atheism; Evolution; Gabler, Mel, and Norma Gabler; Moral Majority; Parents' Alliance to Protect Our Children; Religion; Textbooks.

BIBLIOGRAPHY

Bruce Grindal's "Creationism, Sexual Purity, and the Religious Right," in *The Humanist* 43 (March-April, 1983), is a humanist view of the Fundamentalist's objections. Edward Larson's *Trial and Error* (New York: Oxford University Press, 1985) offers a historical look at battles over evolution and creationism. Thomas Toch's *In the Name of Excellence* (New York: Oxford University Press, 1991) examines reasons why national school reform has failed. Paul Vitz's *Censorship: Evidence of Bias in Our Children's Textbooks* (Ann Arbor, Mich.: Servant Books, 1986) is a nearly definitive study on values and religious mentions in elementary texts.

Sedition

DEFINITION: Inciting resistance or revolution against a legal government

SIGNIFICANCE: Sedition laws, which are justified as necessary responses to the dangers of revolution, have pervaded human history; by stifling discussion of political issues, they have constituted one of the most powerful and repressive forms of censorship.

The concept of sedition generally, and of the common-law crime of seditious libel in particular, has eluded precise definition. Any expression that promotes disaffection toward, or hatred or contempt of, government—especially expression that advocates public disorder or rebellion—might be classified as seditious. Seditious libel implies the additional charge that the communication is defamatory or injures a person spoken of or otherwise represented. For a statement to be libelous in the United States it must be untrue as well as injurious. Sedition is distinct from treason—which is an action directed toward the overthrow or military defeat of a government. Roughly speaking, then, sedition is encouraging overthrow of the government, treason attempting to do so. Many antigovernment activities—such as burning draft cards or national flags—are problematic because they contain both speech and acts.

Sedition in Western Civilization. A succession of laws criminalizing sedition has characterized the history of Western civilization from ancient to modern times. The United States provides the broadest protections against the enactment and enforcement of laws regulating sedition, but the wide range of activities encompassed within the concept defies easy categorization and, thus, sure immunity against interference. In the early American colonies, proscriptions of seditious writings and utterances were intermittently but, in certain well-publicized cases, vigorously enforced. Surprisingly, however, the colonial press and public behaved as if these common-law traditions did not exist. Whether or not the First Amendment to the U.S. Constitution was intended to supersede the common-law crime of seditious libel has been the object of considerable historical debate. What is uncontested, however, is that the American experience with the Sedition Act of 1798 profoundly altered subsequent political thought regarding government censorship of free expression.

During a wave of censorship, the Federalist-dominated Congress in 1798 passed the Sedition Act, which criminalized "writing, printing, uttering or publishing any false, scandalous and malicious writing . . . against the government of the United States." The act also prohibited the publication of messages that would bring the government, Congress, or the President into "contempt or disrepute." At least twenty-five people were charged with, and ten convicted of, violations of the Sedition Act prior to its expiration in 1801. Most were newspaper editors critical of the Federalists. Popular opposition to the act contributed to the defeat of the Federalist Party in the elections of 1800. When the act expired in 1801, then-president Thomas Jefferson pardoned those imprisoned and repaid the fines of those who had been convicted. The lesson of the Sedition Act was that antisedition laws can be easily transformed into tools for stifling political dissent.

World War I and the Espionage Act of 1917. The consequences of the Sedition Act deterred government censorship until the United States entered World War I. In the interim, a number of states passed "criminal syndicalism" or "criminal anarchy" statutes to harass and censor various groups, including abolitionists, anarchists, and advocates of organized labor; enforcement, however, was sparse. America's entry into World War I precipitated the passage of the Espionage Act of 1917, amended and fortified in 1918 to empower the federal government to punish seditious expression. The act outlawed false statements intended to impair the operations of the military. It also criminalized attempts to incite insubordination or refusal of duty in the military and attempts to obstruct military recruitment. Amendments to the law in 1918 further proscribed disloyal or abusive criticism of the form of government of the United States and "language intended to bring the form of government of the United States . . . into contempt . . . or disrepute." The patriotic fervor behind the war led many states to pass or strengthen antisedition statutes that were often vigorously enforced.

Many enduring principles of free speech law were developed in judicial opinions written when sedition cases reached the courts. In *Schenck v. United States* (1919), for example, the U.S. Supreme Court announced a standard for deciding cases involving sedition: Communication was punishable if the words used create a "clear and present danger" of evils that government has a right to prevent. Invocation of this standard routinely resulted in conviction of defendants because their expression had a tendency to cause harm. However, in *Abrams v. United States* (1919), Justice Oliver Wendell Holmes invoked the standard in dissent, arguing that words should be protected "unless they so imminently threaten immediate interference with . . . the law that an immediate check is required to save the country."

State sedition statutes were also challenged in the courts. In *Gitlow v. New York* (1925), the Supreme Court held that the First Amendment's guarantee of free expression had been extended by the Fourteenth Amendment to apply to the states. The majority of the Court nevertheless upheld the conviction of defendant Abraham Gitlow for inciting the overthrow of the government, arguing that preventive action is essential to extinguish the spark of revolution before it kindles a revolutionary blaze. Holmes and fellow justice Louis Brandeis objected because Gitlow's communication "had no chance of starting a present conflagration." Holmes added that if, "in the long run, the beliefs expressed in proletarian dictatorship are destined to be accepted by the dominant forces of the community, the only meaning of free speech is that they should be given their chance and have their way." Justice Brandeis noted in *Whitney v. California* (1927): "If there be time to expose through dis-

cussion the falsehood and fallacies . . . the remedy to be applied is more speech, not enforced silence."

The free-speech theory of Holmes and Brandeis ultimately prevailed in 1969, when the Supreme Court ruled, in *Brandenburg v. Ohio*, that seditious and even threatening speech is protected "except where such advocacy is directed to inciting or producing imminent lawless action and is likely to incite or produce such action." The Court later invoked the First Amendment to protect a broad range of political expression. These have included anonymous messages (*Talley v. California*, 1960); criticisms of government officials—including false statements, so long as they are not made with knowledge that they are false or with reckless disregard of truth (*New York Times Co. v. Sullivan*, 1964); refusal to salute the American flag (*West Virginia State Board of Education v. Barnette*, 1943); and burning U.S. flags as a form of symbolic political expression (*Texas v. Johnson*, 1989). The Court has declined, however, to protect expression advising youth to oppose the military draft or to refuse or evade military service (*Gara v. United States*, 1950), and has refused to protect draft-card burning to express opposition to military service (*United States v. O'Brien*, 1968). —*Richard A. Parker*

See also Chase, Samuel; Clear and present danger doctrine; Coercion Acts; Draft-card burning; Espionage Act of 1917; Flag burning; Free speech; *Schenck v. United States*; Sedition Act of 1798; Smith Act; War; World War I.

BIBLIOGRAPHY

Franklyn S. Haiman's *Speech and Law in a Free Society* (Chicago: University of Chicago Press, 1981) provides thorough explanations and insightful critiques of American attempts to control seditious communication. Leonard W. Levy provides a somewhat unbalanced but insightful history of sedition prior to 1800 in *Emergence of a Free Press* (New York: Oxford University Press, 1985). The most thorough history of the Sedition Act is James Morton Smith's *Freedom's Fetters: The Alien and Sedition Laws and American Civil Liberties* (Ithaca, N.Y.: Cornell University Press, 1956). A concise explanation of the origins of seditious libel that summarizes the most important U.S. sedition cases can be found in Thomas L. Tedford's *Freedom of Speech in the United States* (2d ed. New York: McGraw-Hill, 1993).

Sedition Act of 1798

ENACTED: July 14, 1798

PLACE: United States (national)

SIGNIFICANCE: This act was the first seditious libel law passed by Congress after ratification of the Constitution; the controversy over its enforcement led to substantial developments in free-press theory

Formally titled "An Act for the Punishment of Certain Crimes against the United States," this act was one of four closely related laws generally referred to as the "Alien and Sedition Acts." The immediate impetus for the passage of these acts was the undeclared U.S. war with France. The Federalist Party, which controlled the presidency and had majorities in both houses of Congress, argued that such an act was a necessary element of the federal government's actions to protect itself against domestic and foreign enemies. By this reasoning, the Federalists were essentially following English common law as articulated by William Blackstone's *Commentaries on the Laws of England* (1765-1769), which held that antisedition laws did not infringe freedom of the press because they did not impose prior restraint on publication, but rather punished offenders after they published.

The Republican opponents of the Sedition Act argued that the powers given to Congress in the Constitution did not include the power to establish a federal common law, and that the punishment of seditious libel was the province of the states. Behind this debate over constitutional theory was the Republicans' recognition of the political reality that if a sedition law were passed, it would be directed primarily against them. Federalists often referred to Republicans as "Jacobins" and sought to connect them in the public mind with the French revolutionaries. Hysteria over the war crisis was part real and part exaggerated, but it was clearly used by the Federalists as a political weapon against their opponents.

Passage of the Act. Senator James Lloyd of Maryland introduced the Sedition Act into the Senate, where it passed on July 4, 1798. When the proposed act reached the House, Federalist leaders made several changes in it that represented substantial departures from English common law. Defendants in seditious libel cases were to be able to use truth as a defense, leaving the government to prove malicious intent; further, juries, not the judges, would be permitted to decide questions of law, as well as questions of fact. Moreover, the act was written to expire in three years. By the standards of the time, the Sedition Act was a comparatively liberal law of seditious libel. Nevertheless, Republicans argued against it. Representative Albert Gallatin of Pennsylvania, a leading Republican opponent of the act, told the House that "this bill must be considered only as a weapon used by a party now in power in order to perpetuate their authority and preserve their present places."

Republican fears were realized shortly after the Fifth Congress narrowly passed the Sedition Act, which quickly became a tool for the suppression of dissenting opinions. Under the provisions of the act, anyone who wrote or assisted in the publication of "false, scandalous and malicious writings against the government of the United States" could be fined up to two thousand dollars and jailed for up to two years. Within a month of the act's passage, arrests of Republican writers and newspaper editors began. President John Adams himself signed the arrest warrant for John Daly Burk, the publisher of the New York *Time Piece*. Other Republicans arrested under the act included Matthew Lyon, a Congressman from Vermont, for articles published in the *Vermont Journal*; Anthony Haswell, for an advertisement in the *Vermont Gazette*; and Charles Holt, editor of the New Haven, Connecticut, *Bee*. Dr. Thomas Cooper, a scientist from England who had sought refuge in Philadelphia from political prosecution, and James T. Callender, an English-born journalist living in Richmond, Virginia, were among other prominent figures tried under the act. Another target of the act was Benjamin Bache, the grandson of Benjamin Franklin and publisher of the Philadelphia *Aurora*; however, Bache died of yellow fever before being jailed. All told, twenty-five people were arrested and eleven were convicted.

Reaction to the Act. Opposition to the Sedition Act was led by Thomas Jefferson and James Madison, leaders of the Republican Party. At the time, Jefferson was vice president. Jefferson wrote resolutions that were intended for adoption by state legislatures in which he made a states' rights argument against the constitutionality of the act. He argued that because the Constitution had given no specific authority to Congress to regulate sedition, any such authority belonged to the states. The legislatures of two states adopted his resolutions: Kentucky, which passed them on November 10, 1798, and Virginia, which adopted a somewhat different resolution written by James Madison, on December 24, 1798. The passage of these state resolutions is often regarded as the opening salvo in Jefferson's successful presidential campaign of 1800. The furor over the Sedition Act and the perception that the Federalists were hypocritical in their attempts to imprison opponents, rather than debate them, undoubtedly contributed to Jefferson's election.

The Sedition Act expired on March 3, 1801, the day before President Thomas Jefferson took office. After becoming president, Jefferson issued pardons to all persons still serving sentences under the act and dismissed all pending prosecutions. Jefferson's own record as a defender of the First Amendment rights of the press, however, is not entirely clear. Unlike Madison, whose report to the Virginia legislature on the Sedition Act took a more expansive view of the First Amendment's protection of the press, Jefferson's criticism of the act relied heavily on the idea that the law represented a usurpation of a right that belonged to the states. Jefferson encouraged Pennsylvania's prosecution of a Federalist by the Republican state government, and he may have encouraged a similar prosecution in New York. The constitutionality of the Sedition Act was never tested before the Supreme Court. —*Steve Wiegenstein*

See also Federalist Party; First Amendment; France; Jefferson, Thomas; Madison, James; Prior restraint; Sedition; Smith Act.

BIBLIOGRAPHY

American Politics in the Early Republic: The New Nation in Crisis, by James Roger Sharp (New Haven, Conn.: Yale University Press, 1993), provides a good discussion of the political issues of the time. The development of the federal courts in this era is examined in *The Federal Court, 1787-1801*, by George J. Lankevich (Danbury, Conn.: Grolier, 1995). Two books examine the Alien and Sedition Acts specifically: *Crisis in Freedom: The Alien and Sedition Acts*, by John C. Miller (Boston: Little, Brown, 1951), and *Freedom's Fetters: The Alien and Sedition Laws and American Civil Liberties*, by James Morton Smith (Ithaca, N.Y.: Cornell University Press, 1956). The central texts of the debate over whether the Sedition Act was a serious threat to the Bill of Rights are discussed by Walter Berns in "Freedom of the Press and the Alien and Sedition Laws: A Reappraisal," in *The Supreme Court Review, 1970*, edited by Philip B. Kurland (Chicago: University of Chicago Press, 1970), and by Leonard W. Levy in *Emergence of a Free Press* (New York: Oxford University Press, 1985).

Seeger, Pete

BORN: May 3, 1919, New York, New York

IDENTIFICATION: American folksinger

SIGNIFICANCE: A pioneer composer and performer in modern folk music, Seeger is best known for protest songs that led to his blacklisting

Seeger developed an interest in American folk music at the age of sixteen, when he began learning to play the banjo. The banjo became his trademark instrument throughout his long career singing in support of labor unions, civil rights, and the ecological movement. With kindred spirit and fellow folksinger Woody Guthrie, Seeger "uncled" the modern folk music movement by merging traditional musical forms with populist politics that both energized and changed the direction of American folk music during the 1950's and 1960's.

During the 1930's Seeger explored folk music by studying the archives in the Library of Congress and by traveling on the road as a banjo-playing hobo. In 1940 he formed the Almanac Singers with Guthrie, Lee Hays, and Millard Lampell, and began performing songs such as "Which Side Are You On?" before occasionally violent audiences at labor rallies. During World War II he performed his overtly procommunist shows. Afterward, along with Guthrie, he created the immensely popular "hootenanny" sing-alongs. In 1948 Seeger formed the

Accompanied by his wife, Toshi, Pete Seeger enters a New York federal court building to be sentenced on contempt of Congress charges for refusing to answer questions about his political affiliations. (AP/Wide World Photos)

Weavers, the most important and influential of the American folk revivalists. Three years later the Weavers were slated for their own television series, but were dropped when the show's sponsor, Van Camp Pork and Beans, dropped the project because Seeger had been cited thirteen times in *Red Channels*, a listing of alleged subversive performers.

An unrepentant communist, Seeger was blacklisted in 1955 after refusing to testify before the House Committee on Un-American Activities. Although he later dropped his membership in the Communist Party and was acquitted of all charges in 1962, Seeger was banned from network television, including the American Broadcasting Company's *Hootenanny*. This popular 1963 show borrowed both Seeger's sing-along concept and its name, but refused to feature Seeger because of pressure from its advertisers. In response, fifty other performers boycotted the show. In 1967 and 1968, the Columbia Broadcasting System and its Detroit affiliate censored Seeger's two attempts to perform his song "Waist Deep in the Big Muddy" on *The Smothers Brothers Comedy Hour*. In 1971 Seeger's comeback appearance on Dave Garroway's local Boston show resulted in RKO's canceling that series.

During the 1960's Seeger's political activism expanded to incorporate civil rights, antiwar, and ecological issues in his music, and he participated in such events as the 1965 march in Selma, Alabama, led by Martin Luther King, Jr. For the growing protest movement, he wrote or popularized such anthems as "We Shall Overcome," "If I Had a Hammer," "Where Have All the Flowers Gone?" and "Little Boxes." He influenced younger performers such as Joan Baez, Bob Dylan, and the group Peter, Paul and Mary. Rock bands such as the Byrds sang Seeger's songs to protest the Vietnam War and advocate civil rights.

In later years, Seeger continued appearing at leftist activities and won numerous honors, including President Bill Clinton's invitation to perform at the White House in 1995. However, Seeger's past communist associations continued to draw criticism from conservative commentators who decried his unwillingness to denounce Russian communist history and policies.

See also Advertisers as advocates of censorship; Baez, Joan; Communist Party of the U.S.A.; Folk music; Guthrie, Woody; Music; Protest music; Vietnam War; Weavers, the.

Seldes, George

BORN: November 16, 1890, Alliance, New Jersey
DIED: July 2, 1995, Windsor, Vermont
IDENTIFICATION: American journalist, author, media critic, and muckraker
SIGNIFICANCE: The most censored journalist in American history, Seldes was the earliest known critic of the media's failure to report the dangers of cigarette smoking

In a career spanning nearly eighty years, George Seldes earned a reputation as one of the most original and independent reporters in the history of American journalism. It started in 1909, when he was hired as a cub reporter for the *Pittsburgh Leader*. He would soon have his first experience with censorship, when he reported on a son of the owner of a large department store, and advertiser, who thought he had the right to seduce every pretty female clerk. The story was censored and was not published; shortly thereafter, the store doubled its advertising in the paper. It was an experience Seldes never forgot.

Early Encounters with Censorship. While a freelance war correspondent in Europe at the end of World War I, Seldes and three other journalists drove into Germany on Armistice Day, in violation of the armistice regulations. They got an exclusive interview with German field marshal Paul von Hindenburg, who tearfully confessed that the Germans had lost the war to the American infantry on the battlefield. This story was censored by the U.S. Army under pressure from a group of journalists, including Edwin L. James of *The New York Times*, who did not want their papers to know that they had been scooped. Seldes always believed that if Hindenburg's statement had been widely publicized, Hitler would not have been able to appeal to the masses with false claim that Germany lost World War I, not on the battlefield but because it had been "stabbed in the back" by socialists, communists, and Jews. Years later, Seldes wrote that James, who had risen to the position of managing editor at *The New York Times*, had ordered his staff "never to mention" Seldes' books or name.

In 1927 Seldes was sent to Mexico by *The Chicago Tribune* to report on the unrest in the country. Seldes recalled that while the Associated Press frightened the public with reports of a possible communist revolution in Central America, he found that the real news story concerned representatives of American oil interests, who wanted to topple the government so they could appropriate Mexico's oil reserves. After winning a promise from *The Tribune*'s managing editor to publish both sides of the issue, Seldes wrote a series of ten articles describing what he found in Mexico—five reporting the official U.S. State Department version, and five reporting the other side of the issue, based on what he had observed or verified himself. *The Tribune* ran the first five, supporting American business interests, but never ran the second five. Seldes quit the paper in disgust and became a pioneering freelance journalist, launching his career with the aptly titled book, *You Can't Print That* (1929). It was the first of twenty-one books.

In 1937 Seldes and his wife went to Spain to cover the Spanish Civil War for *The New York Post*. Seldes later claimed that if the world's free press had printed the truth about what was happening in Europe and particularly in Spain, the democratic nations of the world would have rallied to support the Spanish Republic rather than abandoning it to be destroyed by Germany and Italy. After the *Post* bowed to pressure from Franco supporters and dropped his reports, Seldes quit newspaper reporting permanently and launched his own newsletter, *In fact*.

The *In fact* Newsletter. *In fact*, a weekly newsletter first published in 1940, was described as being published "for the millions who want a free press" and, later, as "an Antidote for falsehood in the daily press." It was the nation's first periodical of press criticism. Seldes was the first media watchdog to criticize the press for not reporting the connection between smoking and cancer. It started in 1938 when he tried, without success, to get the press to report the results of a five-year study involving nearly seven thousand persons at The Johns

Hopkins University. The study revealed that smoking decreased life expectancy. In 1940 *In fact* launched a ten-year crusade against tobacco, publishing some one hundred items on the subject. Few of his exposés ever appeared in the mainstream media.

Week after week, *In fact* castigated the mainstream media for failing to cover important issues. It reached a circulation peak of 176,000 and was the inspiration for *I. F. Stone's Weekly*. Stone originally wanted to restart *In fact* but Seldes warned him about the pressure it received from the government and the media. He urged Stone instead to start his own newspaper and gave him his subscription list to help him get started.

Ironically, despite Seldes' many years of outstanding journalism and media criticism, his most popular acclaim came from a brief appearance in a Hollywood movie and from a book that was not about the media. Seldes made a cameo appearance in Warren Beatty's film, *Reds*, in 1981, which brought him immediate national recognition. His best-known book, titled *The Great Quotations*, was originally rejected by twenty publishers but after publication in 1961 it sold more than a million copies worldwide.

A hallmark of Seldes' professionalism as a journalist was that he always went directly to the best sources for his stories, instead of depending on tips, rumors, or anonymous sources. Seldes' sources included William Jennings Bryan, Theodore Roosevelt, John Pershing, Douglas MacArthur, Albert Einstein, Woodrow Wilson, Sigmund Freud, Benito Mussolini, Leon Trotsky, J. Edgar Hoover, and Harry S Truman.

Although *The New York Times* and much of the other major media censored Seldes for more than half a century, they could not censor his unparalleled contribution to the press in America. Perhaps Seldes' most important tip for aspiring journalists first came from his father, who cautioned him to "question everything; take nothing for granted." Seldes also said that it was sometimes best to "tell the truth and run."

Following the death of his wife in 1979, Seldes lived alone with his cat in rural Vermont. One of his late books was entitled *Never Tire of Protesting* (1968). George Seldes never did.

—*Carl M. Jensen*

See also Associated Press; Communications Decency Act; House Committee on Un-American Activities; News media censorship; Smoking; Stone, I. F.; World War I.

BIBLIOGRAPHY

The most comprehensive resource about George Seldes is his autobiography, published when he was ninety-six years old, *Witness to a Century: Encounters with the Noted, the Notorious, and the Three SOBs* (New York: Ballantine Books, 1987). Other books by Seldes dealing with major historic events and the media include *You Can't Print That* (New York: Payson & Clarke Ltd., 1929), *Freedom of the Press* (New York: Bobbs Merrill, 1935), *You Can't Do That* (New York: Modern Age Books, 1938), *Tell the Truth and Run* (New York: Greenberg, 1953), *Never Tire of Protesting* (New York: Lyle Stuart, 1968), and *Even the Gods Can't Change History* (Secaucus, N.J.: Lyle Stuart, 1976). Randolph T. Holhut has compiled a comprehensive sample of Seldes' books and newsletters in *The George Seldes Reader* (New York: Barricade Books, 1994).

Sendak, Maurice

BORN: June 10, 1928, Brooklyn, New York

IDENTIFICATION: American author and illustrator of books for children

SIGNIFICANCE: Sendak's work has provoked controversy for dealing openly with children's emotions and especially for breaking taboos against nudity in picture books

Pointing out that fear and anxiety are "intrinsic" to children's daily lives, Sendak defended his widely debated—and wildly popular—picture book *Where the Wild Things Are* (1963) with the claim, "It is through fantasy that children achieve catharsis." Suggesting that children have aggressive impulses toward adults, this award-winning book was considered by one librarian as too disturbing "to be left where a sensitive child may come upon it at twilight."

While the psychoanalytic undercurrents of *Where the Wild Things Are* caused alarm, the nudity of *In the Night Kitchen* (1970) provoked open calls for censorship. Parents in Morrisonville, New York; Jacksonville, Florida; and Cornish, Maine, for example, demanded it be removed from school libraries, protesting that the nakedness of the book's young protagonist would promote child molestation. *In the Night Kitchen* was reinstated in each case; however, the book did end up being placed on a closed shelf in Indiana and removed from a library in Washington. Sendak responded that his pictures "aren't any more graphic" than "paintings of the Christ child."

Nudity—this time of goblins—caused *Outside over There* (1981) to be pulled from the shelves by a South Dakota school librarian. Noted Sendak, "The people who are frightened by my images and stories are adults, not children."

See also Books, children's; Libraries, school; Nudity.

Seneca the Younger

BORN: c. 4 B.C.E., Córdoba, Spain

DIED: April, 65 C.E., Rome

IDENTIFICATION: Roman philosopher, writer, and statesman

SIGNIFICANCE: As an adviser to Emperor Nero, Seneca helped to guide Rome's fortunes from 54 until 62 C.E., but was later charged with complicity in a political conspiracy and forced to commit suicide

Seneca was remembered by later generations of Romans as one of their most beloved and courageous philosophers and statesmen. Born of a wealthy Italian family of aristocratic rank in Spain, he received a first-rate education in rhetoric, law, and philosophy. Although he established an enviable reputation early on as a brilliant court orator and writer, it was as tutor and adviser to Nero that he exercised his greatest influence on Rome. As a Stoic philosopher, Seneca encouraged his pupil to follow the traditional ideals of duty, compassion, restraint, and seriousness of purpose in governing the Roman Empire. Unfortunately, Nero soon demonstrated that such lessons were lost on him, engaging in murderous excesses similar to those that had plagued his predecessors' reigns. In 62 C.E. Seneca asked to retire to his country estates and bequeath his vast fortune to the emperor. Following the unsuccessful Pisonian conspiracy against Nero, Seneca was accused of complicity in the plot and forced to commit suicide. There is little to suggest that Seneca was a conspirator, and Nero more than likely saw this as a convenient pretext for eliminating a man who had so recently and publicly served as his "conscience."

See also Cicero; Death; Ovid; Roman Empire.

Serrano, Andres

BORN: August 15, 1950, New York, New York

IDENTIFICATION: American artist

SIGNIFICANCE: Serrano's photograph *Piss Christ*, depicting a crucifix submerged in an effervescent veil of urine, became a catalyst of politically motivated actions intended to suppress public funding for projects deemed immoral

In 1988 Serrano received a fifteen-thousand-dollar award from a National Endowment for the Arts (NEA) funded exhibition coordinated by the Southeastern Center for Contemporary Art. The exhibition traveled to Los Angeles, Pittsburgh, and then Richmond, Virginia, where controversy arose in 1989. A letter to the editor of the *Richmond Times Dispatch* stated outrage that the museum would subsidize "hatred and intolerance" and that it was this type of "mentality that led to the unspeakable atrocities of the Holocaust." Serrano intended his work as a commentary on the commercialization of religion and the symbolic qualities of bodily fluids and the Eucharist.

A year earlier, a Richmond fundamentalist preacher, Donald Wildmon, had led national boycotts against Martin Scorsese's film *The Last Temptation of Christ* and Madonna's music video "Like a Prayer." Thinking that the immoral and pornographic natures of the film and video were echoed in Serrano's *Piss Christ*, Wildmon sent a letter to members of Congress vilifying both the artist and government support of such projects. Outrage culminated when Senator Jesse Helms initiated legislation that outlined subjects that would not be appropriate for NEA funding, including "material which degenerates the objects or beliefs of the adherents of a particular religion."

See also Helms, Jesse Alexander; *Last Temptation of Christ, The*; Madonna; Mann, Sally; Mapplethorpe, Robert; National Endowment for the Arts.

Sex education

DEFINITION: Formal instruction about human sexuality

SIGNIFICANCE: Sex education has been a constant target of censorship attempts

Whether focusing on reproductive facts and birth control, or gender, sexual experience, and sexual orientation, sex education has long been a controversial topic in the United States. This controversy has been exacerbated as sex education has moved out of the realms of family and church and into the curriculum of public school and government or other public agencies.

The Comstock Act of 1873 prohibited the distribution of birth control devices and the dissemination of information about such birth control. It was this law that the pioneer of American birth control, Margaret Sanger, broke in 1917. Similar attempts to restrict the availability of information regarding birth control and other sex education issues have continued.

Many local American schools and districts began sporadically and irregularly implementing various forms of sex education within their health and science curricula during the 1960's. Government legislation began the creation of a national family planning program in 1970, which has culminated in the mid-1990's with approximately 150 school-based clinics in which adolescents can get information about birth control and sexually transmitted diseases (STDs), as well as birth control devices.

Compared to other developed countries, the United States has been among the slowest to implement formal sexual education. Sweden is generally acknowledged to be the first country to make widespread information on sex education available to its students. On the other hand, the most highly developed Asian nation, Japan, has various restrictions, largely because the Unification Church has lobbied against such education. All textbooks used in Japanese schools must be cleared by the national Ministry of Education.

Some sex education has become available in more than 80 percent of school districts in the United States, but less than 10 percent of these programs are comprehensive. According to the Sex Education and Information Council of the United States (SEICUS), truly comprehensive programs are those including family life education for each year in school. The most comprehensive programs are the ones that potential censors have tended to challenge, because they go beyond the basic facts of life that virtually all Americans find acceptable into the social and psychological contexts of sexuality. Studies have found that as few as 3 percent of parents disapprove of sex education per se, but more than 20 percent have reservations about comprehensive sex education. These reservations are often magnified by the fact that truly comprehensive sex education starts much earlier than most parents believe to be necessary. A study issued in 1993 by S. S. Janus and C. L. Janus found that up to 89 percent of parents favored sex education, including birth control education for students ages twelve and up. However other studies have suggested that such education should start at younger ages to be effective. Some traditionally resistant parents have become more open to this early education because of fear of child molestation. The introduction of "good touch" and "bad touch" sex education has been generally lauded to help young children to protect themselves.

What makes comprehensive sex education offensive to conservatives is the relation of sexuality to the affective and skill domains. These involve such things as values clarification—which encourage adolescents to assess their own beliefs, rather than simply comply with authority figure demands; tolerance—which may be interpreted as promoting "deviant" lifestyles; self-esteem—which, again, is not necessarily predicated on pleasing parents and other authority figures; decision-making and interpersonal communication skills—which are certainly more involved than the "just say no" attitude that characterizes conservative perspectives on adolescent sexuality; and an integrated approach to sexuality—which may be at odds with a traditional perspective on its solely reproductive function. Consequently, the liberal approach to comprehensive sex education has often been strongly opposed by those who feel that it is the antithesis of a facts-based approach, which should emphasize traditional family values in sexual behavior and orientation.

Pro and Con on Restrictions. Conservatives tend to believe that sex education which fails to emphasize abstinence exclusively has been responsible for increased rates of premarital sex, STDs, premarital pregnancies, and abortions. They argue that such education encourages adolescents to experiment with sexual behaviors that might not even have crossed their minds otherwise. Since the formal sex education that occurs in public schools and other government facilities often fails to stress abstinence sufficiently, conservatives feel that this formal education should either be transformed or curtailed. Therefore, they often involve support efforts to replace the "permissive" sex education in schools with a restrictive and absolutist curriculum that dictates abstinence.

Liberals argue that American families have never formally taught sex education. They suggest that in the past such education as occurred was an accidental by-product of a lack of privacy in the home. Since the lack of privacy has largely been overcome, sex education no longer informally occurs in the home. Studies have found that less than 15 percent of adolescents report any meaningful sex education in their homes. These same studies indicate that adolescents report getting most of their sex education on the streets. It is this, health educators argue, that is responsible for the relatively high rates of undesirable sexual outcomes decried by almost everyone. Furthermore, they point to studies which suggest that sex education in America is too little and occurs too late. Those against restrictions argue that effective sex education has been found to have strong support from parents and the local community and reduces not only pregnancy, abortion, and STDs, but also the age at which first intercourse occurs.

Furthermore, they argue that while the abstinence-based curriculum may promote more traditional attitudes among students, there is no evidence that it produces behavioral differences superior to comprehensive sexuality education. Finally, comprehensive sex educators suggest that one can provide moral instruction without being moralistic (for example, by suggesting that those who engage in premarital sex will get AIDS and die).

Methods of Restricting Sex Education. While book banning has taken take place (the Eagle Forum got all six approved health texts in Alabama eliminated), it is not the most common tactic. Those who oppose comprehensive sex education often do so with legislative initiatives of one sort or another. In the early to mid-1990's more than fifteen states had moved to transform or restrict sex education in some fashion. These attempts have run the gamut from mandating the teaching of so-called "abstinence-only, fear-based" sex education curricula, to segregating such classes by gender, to making sex education essentially elective. In 1995 forty-seven states gave parents the opportunity to excuse their children from sex education classes. Since small numbers of parents have made this choice, opponents of comprehensive sex education have attempted to require families to elect to have their children take sex education classes.

During the mid-1980's about 150 U.S. communities had major sex education controversies in the mid-1990's. According to SEICUS, most of these controversies arose in only four

states: California, Massachusetts, Michigan, and New Jersey. These were not, however, the only states in which restrictions on sex education were pervasive. Indeed, there are indications that restrictions have been greatest in Southern states; however, since these restrictions are often popularly supported, there have been few public controversies.

What Gets Restricted? Studies have found up to 75 percent of American adults want sex education courses to include information about homosexuality and abortion—the subjects most likely to attract attempts at restriction. Indeed, Utah entirely restricts the consideration of sexual orientation and homosexuality in its schools. The books most opposed for use in classrooms or school libraries have pertained to same-sex relationships. Sex education materials relating to the deadliest STD, Acquired Immune Deficiency Syndrome (AIDS), are not exclusively directed at homosexual behavior; however, homosexuality has been so often seen as linked to AIDS that AIDS education has been restricted in many communities as a result. Opportunities for adolescents to understand their own sexual orientations, such as support groups for gay and lesbian students, have also been attacked by those who disdain such "nonnormative" lifestyles.

While decidedly not associated with homosexuality, information regarding abortion has also been restricted in classrooms and school libraries. The book *Our Bodies, Ourselves*, which examines abortion and other issues, has probably been the most restricted American publication relating to sex education. During Ronald Reagan's and George Bush's presidencies, federally funded abortion clinics—including some in schools—were prohibited from even providing information about abortion. The Congress elected in 1994 seemed inclined to pursue a similar course, despite President Bill Clinton's more open position on access to abortion information.

—*Scott Magnuson-Martinson*

See also Abortion gag rule; Birth control education; Comstock Act of 1873; Homosexuality; Kinsey Report; Obscenity: legal definitions; *Our Bodies, Ourselves*; Pornography.

BIBLIOGRAPHY

"Censorship Incidents in U.S. Schools Increased 50% for the 1991-92 School Year," in *Media Report to Women* (Winter, 1993), indicates most incidents related to sex education. Patti Britton's "Education Through Ignorance (Protection of Women's Reproductive Rights," *Index on Censorship* (January, 1993), asserts that sexual information restriction in America produces higher rates of reproductive dysfunction than in other developed countries. Cui Lili documents the expansion of sexual information in China in "Sex Education No Longer Taboo, *Beijing Review* (April 3, 1995). Shelley Ross and Leslie M. Kantor present the perspective on restrictions of the foremost American sexual information provider in "Trends in Opposition to Comprehensive Sexuality Education in Public Schools in the 1994-95 School Year," *SEICUS Report* (August-September, 1995). The conservative agenda's impact on sexual education is discussed in William L. Yarber's "AAHE Scholar's Address: While We Stood By . . . The Limiting of Sexual Information to Our Youth," *Journal of Health Education* (September-October, 1992). Parental opinions regarding sex education are presented in *Censorship* (New York: H. W. Wilson, 1989) by Robert Emmet Long, ed. Lisa Orr notes the incidence of comprehensive sex education across American school districts in *Sexual Values: Opposing Viewpoints* (San Diego: Greenhaven, 1989). For a conservative case against the premier providers of sexual information outside public schools, see Robert Marshall and Charles Donovan's *Blessed Are the Barren: The Social Policy of Planned Parenthood* (San Francisco: Ignatius, 1991). "The Flap over Gay Literature for Children" is explored in *CQ Researcher* (February 19, 1993). Herbert Foerstel explores school and library materials dealing with homosexuality in "Conflict and Compromise over Homosexual Literature." (*Emergency Librarian*, November-December, 1994).

Sex in the arts

DEFINITION: Written, drawn, photographed, filmed, or taped representations of human sexual activity

SIGNIFICANCE: Depictions of sex have widely been deemed offensive and have been censored by religious and civil authorities of various stripes

Formal attempts to limit expression on sexual matters go back at least as far as early Roman times. In 443 B.C.E. the office of the censor was established in part to control public morals. The office persisted until the fall of the Roman Empire. It was effective, but not infallible; it failed, for example, to suppress all copies of Ovid's *Art of Love*. The censorship of sex in literature through the mass burning of books began in the late fifteenth century, when the Florentine monk Girolamo Savonarola regularly organized the destruction of texts that depicted sexual and other offending subjects in the "bonfire of the vanities."

In the sixteenth century the Roman Catholic church became embroiled in a related controversy. Michelangelo's *The Last Judgment* in the Vatican's Sistine Chapel had shocked observers when it was unveiled in 1541. The pope considered having it destroyed, but in 1558 it was instead touched up, with drapery painted over human genitalia. Such alterations to art depicting nudity were not uncommon and would later be used in Victorian England. Similarly, touch-ups to sanitize offensive literature occurred when Thomas Bowdler and his family edited sexual innuendo from the writings of William Shakespeare and others. Likewise, American lexicographer Noah Webster changed or removed problematic biblical passages referring to sex.

American attitudes toward erotic expression had been largely influenced by the Puritan ideas that had originated in England in the early seventeenth century. Puritans, as their name indicates, were concerned with purity, and treated dancing, nonreligious music, and nonreligious literature with great suspicion. They had no toleration for sex in art. Concerned that their children were being corrupted in the Old World, many Puritans made their way to the New World, establishing a cultural tradition that has often since found itself in conflict with the American legal guarantee of freedom of expression

In 1787 King George III of Great Britain made a proclamation condemning licentious prints and publications. Publica-

tion of John Cleland's salacious novel *The Memoirs of Fanny Hill* in 1821 met immediate condemnation and censorship. In 1857 Britain's Parliament passed the Obscene Publications Act in an attempt to curtail sexually oriented literature. So-called sensation fiction, targeted at women, nevertheless flourished shortly thereafter. Themes incorporating adultery and bigamy were staples of the adventures of the heroines of sensation fiction. British explorer Sir Richard Burton's translation of the ancient Hindu work *Kama Sutra* reached limited audiences in 1875. Burton also translated an erotic literary work of another Eastern culture in his version of *The Arabian Nights*.

In the United States, the 1842 Customs Act was intended to regulate the distribution of what were called French postcards. The 1865 Mail Obscenity Statute and the Comstock Act of 1873 functionally made postal inspectors censors over depictions of sexual expression. It has been suggested that the poetry of Walt Whitman catalyzed some of this rush to regulate offensive materials.

Film. As early as 1896, with *The Kiss*, a short film of a couple kissing, Thomas Edison and other filmmakers scandalized the puritanical portion of the public, entertained others, and initiated the struggle between filmmakers and censors. Censorship boards in New York—then the center of the film industry—began attempting to regulate such provocative portrayals. The city of Boston and many state and local governments soon followed in similar censorship attempts, and the phrase "banned in Boston" became synonymous with pornographic depictions. In 1922 the Hays Office was established in an attempt to regulate obscenity in films nationwide. After half-hearted self-regulation (beginning in 1930) that was not widely followed and which led to Congressional hearings in 1934, film industry self-censorship ultimately resulted via the 1939 Motion Picture Production Code, which was enforced until the mid-1950's.

Between the two world wars, the League of Nations held an international conference on the suppression of the circulation of and traffic in obscene publications. In 1934 a U.S. court of appeals upheld the censorship of James Joyce's book *Ulysses* (1922). Similar fates befell D. H. Lawrence's sexually explicit *Lady Chatterley's Lover* (1928) and Henry Miller's *Tropic of Cancer* (1934). With the birth of the Irish Republic in 1949, literary and artistic censorship became pronounced in that predominantly Roman Catholic country.

The 1950's. Depictions of sex became easier to find in the 1950's. Both *Playboy* magazine, in Chicago, and Paris' Olympia Press began in 1953. Beginning with English translations of the work of the Marquis de Sade and other titles in English, such as Vladimir Nabokov's *Lolita* (1958), the Olympia Press became an international purveyor of many books widely censored in the English-speaking world until it was driven out of France in the mid-1960's. The press was re-established in New York in 1967.

In the mid-1950's U.S. senator Estes Kefauver held hearings on the corrupting effects of comic books. He forced publishers "voluntarily" to accept the Comics Code, which constrained immoral depictions. Comics thus remained clean until the 1960's, when what at first were called underground comics began to be published. In the early to mid-1960's, case-by-case challenges on previously censored books resulted in their unrestricted publication. These included such controversial classics as *Lady Chatterley's Lover*, *Tropic of Cancer*, and *Fanny Hill*.

In the late 1960's U.S. president Lyndon Johnson appointed a Commission on Obscenity and Pornography to review the scientific evidence on pornography's effects. The commission's findings were nothing from which political hay could be made; the committee recommended eliminating virtually all restrictions on depictions of sex. The recommendations were rejected by President Richard M. Nixon as morally bankrupt. Hays had resigned in 1945, and, in the 1950's, a few Hollywood films had successfully defied censors. The Motion Picture Association of America (MPAA) was revitalized in 1966 when Jack Valenti was chosen to lead the organization. The MPAA adopted a film ratings system that reflected the content of films, including their sexual content. The ratings system initiated the X rating, which designated especially violent or sexually explicit films. Persons under eighteen were not allowed to view films with an X rating. The ratings system replaced a system in which a film either did or did not receive a seal of approval; the more flexible ratings system was less censorious but still alerted audiences as to the nature of films.

With the X rating came films to exploit it; *Deep Throat* (1972) and *Behind the Green Door* (1972) were met with repeated censorship attempts that had some success. Another change in the American film industry that incorporated controversial depictions of sex was music videos. Many rock 'n' roll and rap artists used misogynist images and words. Such videos—often available on cable television—as well as increasingly explicit television shows and films broadcast on television, precipitated the call to develop a V-chip for televisions. This component would allow parents to program the television to censor material objectionable to them on the basis of sex, violence, or harsh language. This would require television stations and networks to provide ratings for all of their programming.

The U.S. Telecommunications Reform Act of 1996 mandated the inclusion of V-chips in all newly manufactured television sets by 1998. Additionally, this legislation outlawed the transmission of sexually explicit materials to minors over computer networks. How this could be done was entirely uncertain. Responding to similar legislation in Germany, one major on-line provider proposed to eliminate all service to German customers as the only viable way of meeting this requirement. Immediately after the U.S. legislation was passed, it appeared that it would face a court challenge from the American Civil Liberties Union and other interested parties.

Definition of Obscenity. The 1973 U.S. Supreme Court ruling in *Miller v. California* determined that material could be regulated as obscene if it met a three-part test: First, the average person, using community standards, finds it to be obscene; second, it depicts—in an offensive manner—sexual conduct as defined by state law; third, it lacks literary, artistic, political, or scientific value.

This demanding standard led to a decrease in attempts to censor films, and even fewer attempts to censor books. Consequently, pornography became widely available after the *Miller* decision. In response to the proliferation of pornography, Attorney General Edwin Meese appointed a pornography commission in 1986. Perhaps remembering Nixon's earlier difficulty, Meese appointed members of the Religious Right, antipornography activists, and antipornography feminists to the commission, which unsurprisingly gave the political official back recommendations that were very different from the earlier commission, but they sought an outright ban only on child pornography.

Antipornography Feminists. Feminists have been divided on the issue of depictions of sex. Almost no one speaks in favor of pornography, but many feminists argue that censorship is harmful to women and that obscenity is too difficult to define. Some feminists, however, have argued against pornography from a civil rights perspective, saying that pornography injures women's rights generally. The Minneapolis City Council banned pornography as a form of discrimination harmful to women, but the mayor of Minneapolis vetoed this 1983 ordinance. Feminists were successful in passing a similar ordinance into law in Indianapolis, but it was ruled unconstitutional by a U.S. court of appeals in 1985. This judgment was affirmed by the Supreme Court in 1986, when the Court refused to hear the case.

Later, antipornography feminists' legal arguments came into play in a 1992 Canadian Supreme Court ruling that redefined Canadian obscenity laws. As critics of the antipornography feminists had predicted, the new law, intended to protect women from pornography that—arguably—incites men to violence against women, was used by Canadian customs to seize gay and lesbian materials.   —*Scott Magnuson-Martinson*

See also Art; Books and obscenity law; Child Pornography Law; Film censorship; Internet; Men's magazines; Nudity; Obscenity: legal definitions; Obscenity: sale and possession; Ovid; Pornography; Savonarola, Girolamo; Sex education.

BIBLIOGRAPHY

For a French perspective on sexually explicit writings, see James Simpson's translation of Jean-Marie Goulemot's *Forbidden Texts: Erotic Literature and Its Readers in Eighteenth Century France* (Philadelphia: University of Pennsylvania Press, 1994). Carolyn Dean elaborates the transformation of French pornography into literature in "Pornography, Literature, and the Redemption of Virility in France" in *Differences: A Journal of Feminist Cultural Studies* 5, no. 2 (Summer, 1993). Richard Maltby examines early American prohibitions of pornographic films in "The Genesis of the Production Code" in *Quarterly Review of Film and Video* 15, no. 4 (March, 1995). For a historical perspective on film censorship, see Francis G. Couvares' "The Good Censor: Race, Sex and Censorship in the Early Cinema" in *The Yale Journal of Criticism* 7, no. 2 (Fall, 1994). Several authors explore erotic expression in various media in Catherine Itzin's *Pornography: Women, Violence, and Civil Liberties* (New York: Oxford University Press, 1992). Editors Lynne Segal and Mary McIntosh develop similar themes in *Sex Exposed: Sexuality and the*

Pornography Debate (New Brunswick, N.J.: Rutgers University Press, 1993). Censorship in film and literature across the United States and England are considered in Susan M. Eaton's *The Problem of Pornography: Regulation and the Right to Free Speech* (London: Routledge, 1994). The definitive work in this area is written by American Civil Liberties Union president Nadine Strossen: *Defending Pornography: Free Speech, Sex, and the Fight for Women's Rights* (New York: Scribner, 1995).

Sex manuals

DEFINITION: Books that offer sex education and instruction
SIGNIFICANCE: Courts have consistently rejected notions that manuals meant for sex education are obscene

Until 1957 the U.S. Supreme Court applied the standard of the 1868 English case *Regina v. Hicklin* to its definition of obscenity. The *Hicklin* decision found material obscene if it had a "tendency" to corrupt the sexual morality of vulnerable individuals. Under U.S. postal regulations, it was forbidden to send obscene matter through the mails. In 1930 a Pennsylvania housewife, Mrs. Dennett, decided that she wanted her two adolescent boys to know more about sexual relations. She searched her local library for help but decided that the materials available were not suitable; she thus wrote and published her own instruction book, a brief pamphlet called *The Sex Side of Life*. When she mailed a copy of the pamphlet to a friend in Virginia, she was arrested and convicted by a federal district court of violating postal law. Her lawyer argued that her manual was meant only for educational purposes. The judge, however, instructed the jury that the manual's purpose meant nothing; all they had to do was decide whether Dennett's work was "obscene, lewd, or lascivious" under the rule. The jury found her guilty, and Dennett was fined three hundred dollars.

Dennett took her case to a federal appellate court, which in *United States v. Dennett* (1930) reversed the decision. Judges on the appeal panel praised the work and recommended it as useful in instructing the young. The court described the *Hicklin* test as outdated and challenged its definition of obscenity. If the *Hicklin* standard were to continue to be used, the court noted, "much chaste poetry and fiction, as well as many useful medical works" would be banned.

In the same year, however, the U.S. Customs seized several thousand copies of *Married Love*, a manual by Marie Stopes, a British scientist and sex educator. The book, which had been sold in England for more than thirty years, was declared obscene by customs agents under provisions of the Tariff Act of 1930. The law required the Customs Service to take seized material to federal court for review for alleged obscenity. Stopes's book contained expressions of feminist philosophy along with explicit advice on making love. The judge deciding the case found against the Customs Service: "I cannot imagine a normal mind to whom this book would seem to be obscene or immoral within the proper definition of these words or whose sex impulses would be stirred by reading it," he concluded. The book was thus freed for sale in the United States; by 1939, more than one million copies had been sold.

A new standard was established in 1957 in *Roth v. United States*, in which the Supreme Court held that the effect of a work taken as a whole must be used to judge obscenity. The debate over sex manuals subsequently shifted largely to local school boards and their debates over what books to use in sex-education classes. In most cases, school boards have allowed parents who do not want their children to read sexually explicit material to excuse their children from sex-education requirements.

See also Birth control education; Family; *Joy of Sex, The*; Kinsey Report; Obscenity: legal definitions; *Our Bodies, Ourselves*; *Roth v. United States*; Sex education.

Shakespeare, William

BORN: April 23, 1564, Stratford-upon-Avon, Warwickshire, England
DIED: April 23, 1616, Stratford-upon-Avon, Warwickshire, England
IDENTIFICATION: English playwright and poet
SIGNIFICANCE: Shakespeare's plays have been censored, cut, altered, adapted, and abridged, both in print and performance, on political, religious, artistic, and moral grounds, and for alleged obscenity

Censorship of Shakespeare's plays began in the author's lifetime. In 1581 England's Queen Elizabeth I ordered that all plays to be performed should first be submitted to the Master of the Revels for examination for political and religious sedition. In 1607 this requirement was extended to the printing of plays. At least two of Shakespeare's plays are believed to have fallen foul of the censor: *Richard II* (1597) and *Henry IV*, parts I and II (1598). *Richard II* contains a scene in which Richard is deposed. After the Earl of Essex's unsuccessful revolt against Elizabeth in 1601, the queen complained that a certain play, probably Shakespeare's *Richard II*, had been publicly performed to encourage insurrection. On the eve of the rebellion Essex's followers had sponsored Shakespeare's company, the Lord Chamberlain's Men, to perform the play. The censor subsequently judged the deposition scene to be too politically sensitive to be performed. It was omitted from all editions of the play until 1608, after Elizabeth's death.

Henry IV provoked animosity because of its use of the names Oldcastle, Harvey, and Russell for characters. Descendants of these historical figures objected to the unflattering portrayals of their ancestors, so Shakespeare rechristened the characters Falstaff, Bardolph, and Peto.

In 1642, after the execution of Charles I, England became a Commonwealth under the governance of Oliver Cromwell. Cromwell, a Puritan, closed the theaters and banned the performance of stage plays, including Shakespeare's. The ban did not include musical entertainments, however, so Shakespeare's plays, along with others, were adapted to accommodate enough music to make them legal.

The Restoration. With the Restoration of the monarchy in 1660, stage plays made a limited comeback. Charles II licensed just two theaters in London (compared with the sixteen that had operated from 1576 to 1614). One holder of a license was Sir William Davenant, who was given Shakespeare's plays to "reform and make fit" for performance by the actors

William Shakespeare may be the most often censored literary figure in world history. (Library of Congress)

under his management. Davenant typified an attitude to Shakespeare that was born in the Restoration and survived into the nineteenth century—that Shakespeare was a genius who had the misfortune to live in a barbaric age and therefore lacked decorum. He portrayed unpleasant situations and placed rough language in the mouths of royalty. Accordingly, Davenant's version of *Macbeth* does not contain the death of Lady Macduff, and Macbeth's unkind words to a servant "The devil damn thee black, thou cream-faced loon!/Where gott'st thou that goose look?" became, "Now, Friend, what means thy change of Countenance?"

In another Restoration version of *Measure for Measure*, Angelo turns out to be a hero, declaring that he loved Isabella all the time and was only testing her. The poet and critic John Dryden adapted many of Shakespeare's plays according to contemporary taste, producing such works as *Truth Found too Late* (1679), a version of *Troilus and Cressida* in which Cressida is faithful. Another notorious adapter, Nahum Tate, rewrote *King Lear* with a happy ending, in which Lear and Cordelia survive, Lear is restored to his throne, and Cordelia is told that she will be a queen.

Women and Censorship. Shakespeare's portrayal of women was deemed inappropriate to the Restoration sensibility, which romanticized them as gentle, refined creatures innocent of sexual matters. Davenant's version of *Hamlet* "sanitizes" Ophelia, transforming her from a full-blooded and sexually conscious woman to a silent, coy creature. Shakespeare's Ophelia is aware of the sexual implications of Hamlet's banter, responding with double-entendres of her own.

Davenant's Ophelia responds only with silence, denoting either embarrassment or ignorance.

Ironically, the arrival in the Restoration period of female actors also led to a kind of reverse censorship, in that Shakespeare's plays were sometimes made bawdier. In his 1670 adaptation of *The Tempest*, Dryden gave Miranda a twin sister called Dorinda who specialized in sexual innuendo.

Restoration adaptations of Shakespeare became the standard acting texts of the eighteenth century. They were so widely used that many people assumed them to be Shakespeare's own words. When, in the mid-1700's, the actor-manager David Garrick announced a production of *Macbeth* "as written by Shakespeare," there was an outcry from those who had long loved the existing version, believing it to be Shakespeare's. In the end, Garrick compromised. He restored the original words in some scenes, but made some "improvements": He left out Lady Macduff's death scene, removed the crude Porter, had the witches sing and dance, and wrote a moralistic dying speech for Macbeth. In his version of *Hamlet*, Garrick cut out the grave-diggers because he thought low-life comedy inappropriate to tragedy. Colley Cibber's 1700 adaptation of *Richard III* remained the popular acting text until well into the nineteenth century, and some of Cibber's additions even survived into Laurence Olivier's film version of 1955.

An incident of 1795 revealed much about eighteenth century attitudes toward Shakespeare. A forger called William Henry Ireland printed an expurgation of *King Lear*, billed as Shakespeare's original manuscript. Ireland's forgery fooled many. He explained after he was caught that he had cleaned up the text because people found it hard to believe that Shakespeare himself had written such "ribaldry." *King Lear* also fell victim to political censorship when it was banned from the English stage from 1788 until 1820, out of respect to George III's insanity.

Protecting Women and Youth. The year 1774 was a landmark in the history of Shakespeare bowdlerization. A drama critic, Francis Gentleman, edited complete plays for the publisher Bell. Bell's Shakespeare aimed to make the plays "more instructive and intelligible, especially to the ladies and to youth." Gentleman objected to such "vulgarisms" as Macbeth's insult to his servant and Cleopatra's threat to her maid to give her "bloody teeth." This, Gentleman says, would be unworthy of a person "in a middling station," let alone of a "royal character." Bell's edition is curiously inconsistent, however. It omits some "glaring indecencies" altogether, but Bell's *Othello* has minor indecencies in italics, as a sign for ladies and youth to skip over them. Sometimes, he simply rebuked the objectionable lines in footnotes.

The most famous of all expurgated books, Dr. Thomas Bowdler's *The Family Shakspeare*, appeared in 1807. The edition was intended to remove "everything that can raise a blush on the cheek of modesty." Its success inspired a number of other expurgations, such as the Reverend J. Pitman's *School-Shakspere* (1822). Pitman aimed to provide a more rigorous expurgation than Bowdler's. In most cases he succeeded, cutting the drunken Porter's speech in *Macbeth* from twenty lines to three, as compared with Bowdler's six. He did

726 / Shakur, Tupac

not stop short of eliminating entire characters, such as Touchstone and Audrey in *As You Like It*.

The Backlash Against Expurgation. The nineteenth century saw the beginning of a countermovement to expurgation. Actor-managers such as Robert W. Elliston, William Charles Macready, and Samuel Phelps staged performances with partly restored texts. In 1823 Elliston restored the tragic ending of *King Lear*, and in 1838 Macready reintroduced the Fool after decades of absence from the play. Elliston's 1821 restoration of *Richard III* shocked some people, including a *Times* critic, who thought it a new arrangement, not a return to Shakespeare, and declared it dramatically inferior to the generally used Cibber version. Phelps finished the task that Elliston had begun, virtually eliminating the use of Cibber's *Richard III*.

Other actor-managers were less scrupulous in their fidelity to Shakespeare's texts, manipulating them to suit their own interpretations of roles and to protect the sensibilities of audiences. For example, in 1885 William Kendal adapted *As You Like It* so that the cantankerous Jacques "became more reasonable." Henry Irving's edition of *Macbeth* cuts the murder of Banquo and Fleance, and Lady Macduff's death scene.

Another blow for authenticity was struck in 1843, when Parliament removed the monopoly that, since the Restoration, had confined the performance of plays to two London theaters. To circumvent the ban (and feed the popular mania for elaborate spectacle), non-licensed theaters had disguised Shakespeare's plays with spurious elements—pageants, dancing, and singing. After the ban was lifted, a large number of theaters began to produce the plays "straight," with greater sensitivity to his original texts.

Censorship in Schools. Meanwhile, the Shakespeare expurgation industry was thriving in America, fostered by the growing demand for school texts. In 1849 the first American expurgation of the plays in dramatic form was published: the *Shaksperian Reader*, edited by Professor John W. S. Hows. Hows wrote an apologetic preface, confessing his veneration for the "pure unmutilated text," but explaining that without revision, Shakespeare could not be used as a class book or for family reading. Hows cut mercilessly, removing Falstaff completely from *Henry IV*, part I, and stopping *Othello* at the end of the third act. He also added four years to Juliet's age in *Romeo and Juliet* (Shakespeare makes her not quite fourteen).

Expurgation of school texts continued unabated into the twentieth century. Back in 1750, Garrick cut Juliet's ardent wish that Romeo would hurry and deprive her of her maidenhead. Bowdler removed the same lines. Nearly two centuries later, a 1985 survey revealed that American school texts, including those of Harcourt Brace Jovanovich; Scott, Foresman; Macmillan; Ginn; McDougal, Littell and Company; and McGraw Hill, had also cut the lines. Scott, Foresman's *Romeo and Juliet* cut more than three hundred lines, mostly sexual allusions. For example, Romeo's line, "Well, Juliet, I will lie with thee tonight" was changed to " . . . I will be with thee tonight." In 1985 a ninth-grade student in Vienna, Virginia, protested these cuts. His teacher responded by supplying the class with a full text and discussing the cuts with the students. In the media debate that followed, some school editions were criticized for failing to state that they were abridged. Ginn, for example, omitted four hundred lines from its *Romeo and Juliet*, yet claimed in its teachers' edition that the play was "presented here as Shakespeare wrote it."

Political censorship manifested in the twentieth century in the form of political correctness. Groups monitoring discrimination on grounds of sex, race, religion, and disability found plenty to object to in Shakespeare. In 1931 *The Merchant of Venice* was eliminated from high school curricula in Buffalo and Manchester, New York, in response to pressure from Jewish organizations, who believed it fostered anti-Semitism. On the twentieth century stage and on film, directors continued to cut Shakespeare—not because it was bawdy, but for reasons of length or obscurity. Often they "interpreted" plays to emphasize a political or philosophical standpoint, sometimes with acclaimed results, sometimes with a decidedly reductionist effect. There has been an antifascist interpretation of *Julius Caesar* with jack-booted crowds saluting Caesar, and a feminist version of *The Taming of the Shrew* in which Kate ends her speech of submission to her husband by spitting in his eye.

—*Claire J. Robinson*

See also Abridgment; Bowdler, Thomas; Drama and theater; Jonson, Ben; *MacBird*; Master of the Revels; Molière; Poetry; Political correctness; Puritans; Textbooks.

BIBLIOGRAPHY

For a survey of political censorship in Shakespeare's own day, see Janet Clare's " 'Greater Themes for Insurrection's Arguing': Political Censorship of the Elizabethan and Jacobean Stage" in *The Review of English Studies* 38, no. 150 (May, 1987). Transcripts of original documents of control affecting the stage are found in an appendix in E. K. Chambers' four-volume *The Elizabethan Stage* (Oxford, England: The Clarendon Press, 1923). Phyllis Rackin's *Stages of History: Shakespeare's English Chronicles* (Ithaca, N.Y.: Cornell University Press, 1990) provides an intelligent analysis of the political and social climate in which Shakespeare wrote. Noel Perrin's *Dr. Bowdler's Legacy: A History of Expurgated Books in England and America* (New York: Atheneum, 1969) devotes two chapters to Shakespeare. A chronological overview of adaptation and censorship of Shakespeare is found in Gareth and Barbara Lloyd Evans' *Everyman's Companion to Shakespeare* (London: J. M. Dent & Sons, 1978).

Shakur, Tupac

BORN: June 16, 1971, New York, New York
DIED: September 13, 1996, Las Vegas, Nevada
IDENTIFICATION: American rap musician and actor
SIGNIFICANCE: Shakur was sued for lyrics that allegedly incited a teenager to murder a Texas state trooper

Rap musician Tupac Shakur was born one month after his mother, a member of the Black Panthers, was acquitted of attempted murder. He eventually sold millions of records detailing his mother's drug addiction and welfare dependency, and his own rebellious childhood.

At the age of twenty, Shakur's solo debut album *2Pacalypse Now* (1991) went gold. The album's violent lyrics, including several songs about the murder of police officers, were at-

Shot in a robbery attempt several days earlier, rap musician Tupac Shakur is helped into a car after attending his trial on sexual abuse charges in December, 1994. (AP/Wide World Photos)

tacked after the fatal shooting of a Texas state trooper. The widow of the slain officer filed a civil suit against Shakur and his record company alleging that because a nineteen-year-old was listening to Shakur's album at the time he killed her husband, Shakur was responsible for inciting the teenager's violent action. In September, 1992, Vice President Dan Quayle requested that Interscope Records remove *2Pacalpyse Now* from stores.

Shakur's personal life imitated his lyrics. In March, 1993, he was convicted of assaulting a film director who had fired him from a film. In February, 1995, he was convicted of assaulting a woman in a New York hotel room. His third album, *Me Against the World*, became a number-one seller while he was serving time in prison on his 1995 assault conviction. In September, 1996, he died from gunshot wounds inflicted by an unknown assailant while he was riding in a car in Las Vegas with the head of his recording company, Marion Knight. Shakur also acted in several films, including *Juice*, in which he portrayed a remorseless teenager on a killing spree.

See also "Cop Killer"; Copycat crime; Fighting words; Rap music.

Shaw, George Bernard

BORN: July 26, 1856, Dublin, Ireland
DIED: November 2, 1950, Ayot St. Lawrence, England
IDENTIFICATION: Irish playwright and philosopher

SIGNIFICANCE: Shaw often attacked censorship, but his own works were regularly censored in England and elsewhere

Shaw's first major attack on censorship was *The Quintessence of Ibsenism* (1891), a tract defending Henrik Ibsen, the Norwegian playwright, some of whose work dealt with venereal disease and immoral marriages, against public reaction that demanded censorship or expurgated versions. Inspired by Ibsen's work, Shaw wrote *Mrs. Warren's Profession*; however, the Lord Chamberlain denied it a license in 1898. Shaw could not find a theater for private performances, or an actress willing to play the lead role of a successful but coarsened brothel madam. The play was finally produced privately in London in 1902, but was not licensed for public performance in England until 1925. At its New York City opening in 1905, New York police—urged by Anthony Comstock—secured warrants for disorderly conduct against its producer, leading lady, and manager. The latter was arrested but was acquitted in 1906. In 1955, the play was banned from the Salle Luxembourg in Paris by the selection committee of the Comédie Française. Meanwhile, Shaw had published the play in 1898 in a volume with a preface about censorship, supplemented by a second essay in 1930. He was to publish more than fifty papers on the topic.

In 1907 Shaw was among seventy-one prominent writers to form a committee of protest against censorship. His lengthy written testimony on the subject was itself censored. By this time, Austrian censorship had banned a 1903 production of

Shaw's *Arms and the Man* (1894); in New York, Comstock futilely tried to suppress production of *Man and Superman* in 1905, while the New York Public Library system restricted circulation of Shaw's work. In England, in 1909, two plays, *Press Cuttings* and *The Shewing Up of Blanco Posnet* were banned from public performance. The former showed the problems of women's suffrage campaigners and was banned because it burlesqued public figures; the censor found blasphemy in the latter. In 1913, the censor recommended that Catherine in Shaw's *Great Catherine* be made more temperate in her personal life for fear of offending the Russian government.

At the outbreak of World War I in 1914, Shaw's *Common Sense About the War* (1914) brought a storm of criticism. Newspapers advised readers to avoid it; libraries removed Shaw's work from their shelves. Pressure from peers forced Shaw to give up his Dramatists Club and Society of Authors activities. During the war Shaw withdrew a recruiting play, *O'Flaherty, V.C.*, from rehearsal upon being advised that its production might provoke rioting.

After the war, censorship continued. In 1923, the Lord Chamberlain offered to license *Back to Methuselah* (1920) if Shaw made certain changes, such as having Adam and Eve appear in conventional dress. In 1938, the American Motion Picture Producers and Distributors Association, reviewing a film version of Shaw's *Pygmalion* (1913), demanded cutting of references to the heroine's illegitimacy and to her father's offer to sell her. The 1941 film adaptation of *Major Barbara* (1905) was reduced from 137 to 115 minutes in the United States because censors objected to Shaw's attitude to religious institutions. In 1935, a scenario of *Saint Joan* (1923) was submitted to the Vatican Office for Catholic Action, which vehemently disapproved; that verdict ended hopes for a Hollywood production. Shaw's religious allegory, *The Adventures of the Black Girl in Her Search for God* (1932) was suppressed in Ireland until 1948. His work was also banned from Needham, Massachusetts, schools in 1924 and from Yugoslavian libraries in 1929. In 1939, shortly after the start of World War II, his 1938 play *Geneva* was banned in Germany, but, in 1940, the British Ministry of Information vetoed a BBC radio broadcast in which Shaw attacked Adolf Hitler's anti-Semitism.

See also Blasphemy laws; Comstock, Anthony; Drama and theater; Film adaptation; Ibsen, Henrik; Joan of Arc; Lord Chamberlain; Motion Picture Association of America; Prostitution; United Kingdom; World War I; World War II.

Shelley, Percy Bysshe

BORN: August 4, 1792, Field Place, Sussex, England
DIED: July 8, 1822, at sea, near Viareggio, Italy
IDENTIFICATION: English poet and philosopher
SIGNIFICANCE: Shelley was expelled from Oxford University for publishing a pamphlet on atheism, and his first major poetical work was later subjected to prosecution by the Vice Society

Born into a wealthy landed English family of conservative beliefs, Shelley developed such independence of thought that he earned the nickname "mad Shelley." By the time he entered Oxford University in 1810, he had already published juvenile verse and two Gothic romances. At Oxford he turned to more controversial subjects. His short theological polemic *The Necessity of Atheism* (1811), examined and refuted proofs traditionally offered for the existence of God, and then asked readers either to supply any deficiency in its reasoning or to embrace the truth that it contained, arguing that truth can never be detrimental to society.

Shelley's pamphlet—which he contentiously sent to bishops and heads of the colleges at Oxford—coupled with his political writings and conspicuous efforts to support an imprisoned Irish journalist, brought him to the attention of the masters and fellows of University College. They summoned him to a meeting in March, 1811. There, instead of acknowledging authorship and reiterating his stance as a pursuer of truth, he refused to acknowledge the pamphlet and argued that because it had been printed anonymously, his questioners had no legal right to interrogate him concerning its authorship. The university then expelled him, not for his published religious or political beliefs, but for his stubbornness in answering questions, a matter of college discipline.

Soon after his expulsion, Shelley eloped with Harriet Westbrook. The young married couple's itinerant lifestyle took them through England, Ireland, and Wales in pursuit of various political causes. In 1813 their first child was born and Shelley's first long poem, *Queen Mab*, saw publication. This poem attacked established religion, especially Christianity; political tyranny; and the destructive forces of war and commerce. It also attacked the institution of marriage, which, Shelley argued, polluted human love and gave rise to prostitution; however, the poem also gave an optimistic look at the future when these forces would be overthrown and subjugated by love. Even while his poem was being printed, Shelley recognized that it was too radical to be left unchallenged. Instead of offering its two hundred printed copies for general sale, he privately distributed seventy copies to friends and acquaintances he thought would appreciate the poem's worth.

The other copies of *Queen Mab* remained unsold until 1821, when a radical bookseller named Clark bought them and put them up for sale. Clark was immediately prosecuted by the Society for the Suppression of Vice. However, Richard Carlile, another printer brought out a new edition in late 1821 and a second edition in 1822. Ironically, twenty-five years after its first printing, *Queen Mab* had become the most popular and influential of Shelley's writing, hailed almost as a Bible by middle- and working-class reformers.

See also Atheism; *Index Librorum Prohibitorum*; Literature; Poetry; Society for the Suppression of Vice, U.K.

Shield laws

DEFINITION: Legislation that extends the concept of privileged communication to the relationship between journalists and their confidential sources
SIGNIFICANCE: By protecting journalists from having to reveal their sources in courtroom trials and other public hearings, shield laws encourage the news media to investigate news more freely

More than half of the states of the United States have shield laws that protect journalists from revealing their confidential sources when they are subpoenaed to testify under oath. For example, California's law is part of that state's constitution. Shield laws typically define not only what kinds of testimony cannot be forced from journalists, but also who is a "journalist." Opponents to these laws call such provisions de facto licensing requirements, harking back to early English forms of censorship and Star Chamber courts. The censorship argument bites both ways, however. Without shield laws, governments have greater power to harass journalists and to find means of damaging their sources. In contrast, shield laws give journalists and their sources greater freedom to harm defendants with anonymous accusations that cannot be cross-examined.

Shield law protections are not absolute. Some judges have ruled that these laws should yield to other interests, and that their use should be restricted to protecting limited kinds of information. New Jersey's state supreme court has made a ruling—which has not been seriously questioned elsewhere—that any state's shield law must fall when confronted by defendants' Sixth Amendment right to confront hostile witnesses. Some critics of the courts contend that because many judges do not like shield laws, they obey them in form but not in spirit.

Proponents of shield laws contend that when governments use subpoenas to intimidate the press, reporters must have the right to protect their sources; otherwise facts about government corruption and other matters will be suppressed, or censored, in fact if not in name. Opponents charge that such laws have the negative effect of separating reporters and from other members of the public by granting them special legal privileges.

Maryland was the first state to legislate a shield law, in 1896, but most modern shield laws arose from legal battles fought during the 1960's, when many reporters refused to testify in trials. The journalists argued that having to reveal their sources would violate the freedom of the press guaranteed to them under the First Amendment to the U.S. Constitution. The U.S. Supreme Court has never accepted that argument. In *Branzburg v. Hayes* (1972), the Court explicitly ruled that the press has no special right to withhold the evidence it gathers while reporting news. Lower federal courts, however, have constructed a principle that contributes to protecting confidential news sources. They base the principle not on the First Amendment, but on the need of the public to know. This construction assumes that the public is more likely to be fully informed when journalists report on news unfettered by any form of censorship—such as being forced against their will to reveal their sources.

See also Courtrooms; Courts and censorship law; First Amendment; News media censorship; Off-the-record information; Privileged communication.

Shih huang-ti
BORN: c. 259 B.C.E., Ch'in, China
DIED: 210 or 209 B.C.E., China
IDENTIFICATION: First emperor to rule a unified China
SIGNIFICANCE: In one of history's monumental acts of censorship, Shih ordered the destruction of every book in his realm that did not have immediate practical value

Shih huang-ti came to power in 246 B.C.E. as King Cheng of the state of Ch'in, one of many feudal states in China's Warring States period (481-221 B.C.E.). This state eventually overpowered its rivals, thereby unifying China in 221 B.C.E. To celebrate his success and his newly formed dynasty, Cheng adopted the title of Ch'in Shih huang-ti, First Emperor of the Ch'in dynasty. Both the Ch'in state and its royal dynasty were governed by Legalism, a totalitarian philosophy emphasizing discipline and complete obedience to the ruler. It contradicted the Confucian doctrine of filial piety by making loyalty to the ruler the supreme value. The Legalist philosopher Han Fei-tzu espoused strict laws and merciless punishment for a secure state.

The repressive political atmosphere in that era encouraged government censorship. Han Fei-tzu called for the regulation of thought and said that under an enlightened ruler, "there are no books; the only instruction is supplied by law." This philosophy was embraced by Emperor Shih's respected councillor Li Ssu, who also believed in an authoritarian government. In 213 B.C.E. the Confucian scholar Ch'un-yü Yueh made a speech in defense of feudal values at an imperial banquet. He stated that nothing endured which was not modeled after antiquity. Fearing an alliance between the old feudal aristocracy and the Confucian scholars, Li Ssu responded strongly to this attack. He countered that scholars study only the past that they use to oppose Ch'in Shih huang-ti's rule. Furthermore, by opposing the emperor's decrees and criticizing his orders, they encouraged disrespect among the population. This, he warned, would lead to factionalism and a decline in imperial authority. Li Ssu took advantage of Shih's willingness to strike at his adversaries by recommending that all works of literature, philosophy, and history be destroyed by their owners within thirty days. Those who failed to obey would be branded and sent to work as convicts. The only books to be spared were those on medicine, agriculture, and divination, and works concerning the history of the Ch'in dynasty. Anyone found quoting the old texts would be publicly executed. Shih accepted Li Ssu's recommendation, and the book burning took place in order to prevent past writings from discrediting his reign. Li Ssu most likely exempted works on divination from the burning because the emperor himself was interested in these matters, and also because the belief in the effectiveness of divination was so widespread that its suppression would be difficult. Under this decree, knowledge was considered to be an imperial monopoly and only the emperor was allowed to have a library. In a further act of control the following year, the emperor ordered the execution of 460 scholars who upheld Confucian teachings and who were said to be spreading rumors. It is believed that they were buried alive.

See also Book burning; China; Confucius.

Shostakovich, Dmitri
BORN: September 25, 1906, St. Petersburg, Russia
DIED: August 9, 1975, Moscow, Soviet Union
IDENTIFICATION: Prominent Soviet composer
SIGNIFICANCE: Shostakovich frequently encountered opposition from Soviet authorities for writing music that did not always conform to the Communist ideal

Widely regarded as the Soviet Union's greatest composer, Shostakovich spent his entire career within the oppressive Soviet system. Shostakovich's career demonstrates the possibility of artistic integrity and creative growth in the face of ferocious official censorship and repression. He enjoyed stunning youthful success as a composer, when his First Symphony (1926), written while he was a composition student, was performed throughout the world. His Seventh Symphony (1942) was widely hailed in the West as a depiction of the Soviet people's heroic resistance to the German siege of Leningrad.

Shostakovich frequently fell out of favor with Soviet officials. In 1930 his satirical opera *The Nose* was attacked as a product of "bourgeois decadence." He was twice the target of censorship schemes on the part of the Soviet government. In 1936 his opera *Lady Macbeth of the Mtsensk District* was greeted by a withering review in *Pravda* entitled "Chaos Instead of Music," which accused the composer of incoherence and selfish individual experimentation. The composer withdrew his Fourth Symphony during rehearsals as a result of the *Pravda* controversy. In 1948 Joseph Stalin's dislike of Vano Muradeli's opera *The Great Fellowship* led to a general indictment of the most prestigious Soviet composers, who were assembled by Andrei Zhdanov, Stalin's commissioner for the

arts, and accused of failing to provide positive music that would encourage the Soviet people in their postwar recovery. The composers were accused of "formalism"—excessive concern with artistic form for its own sake—as well as "modernism." Zhdanov's criticisms amounted to a brutal demonstration of Stalin's total control over every aspect of Soviet life and culture.

Although after each occasion Shostakovich worked his way back into official favor, the censorship and veiled threats of retribution increasingly pushed him into a darker and a more oblique style. While conditions for the arts improved somewhat during Nikita Khrushchev's tenure as the Soviet leader, the limits of artistic freedom were once again evident with the heavy-handed official response to Shostakovich's Thirteenth Symphony (Babi Yar) (1962), a setting of five poems by Yevgeny Yevtushenko on the subject of the Nazi massacre of the Jews during World War II. After the first performance, officials required Yevtushenko and the composer to soften the references to Soviet anti-Semitism. The appearance of Shostakovich's memoirs, *Testimony* (1979), showed the extent of the composer's victimization and helped to absolve him of charges made by critics in the West that he had passively participated in a deeply repressive system.

See also Khachaturian, Aram; Music; Opera; Prokofiev, Sergei; Soviet Union; Stalin, Joseph; Yevtushenko, Yevgeny Aleksandrovich; Zhdanov, Andrei.

Silverstein, Shel

BORN: 1932, Chicago, Illinois

IDENTIFICATION: American cartoonist and author of children's books

SIGNIFICANCE: Condemnations of Silverstein's children's books have run the gamut from protests against perverseness to charges of sexism

Well known as a cartoonist for *Playboy* and other magazines, Silverstein has become one of the most popular American authors of children's books—an achievement that he has claimed never to have sought. His most successful books have been eccentric collections of light verse, such as *Where the Sidewalk Ends: The Poems and Drawings of Shel Silverstein* (1974) and *A Light in the Attic: Poems and Drawings* (1981). Although the first of these books has frequently been used in middle-grade classrooms, both books were pulled from the shelves of Minot, South Dakota, public school libraries in 1986 by an assistant superintendent who objected to their "suggestive illustrations." Three years later, students in Duval County, Florida, public schools were required to obtain their parents' permission to borrow *A Light in the Attic* from school libraries—because the book contains a cartoon of a person whose bare buttock has been stung by a bee.

Also in 1989, *Where the Sidewalk Ends* was removed from library shelves in Riverdale, Illinois, public schools because its poem "Dreadful" was accused of being in bad taste. "Dreadful" was challenged again four years later at a Pennsylvania school district for suggesting that "someone ate the baby." A mother's complaint about allusions to suicide in *A Light in the Attic*'s "Little Abigail and the Beautiful Pony" led to that

Russian composer Dmitri Shostakovich works on a score around the time that he was beginning to feel censorship pressures from the Soviet government. (Library of Congress)

book's being banned from second-grade classes in Huffman, Texas. Both of these volumes of verse were challenged at various school libraries for encouraging rebelliousness.

In 1988 Silverstein's parable *The Giving Tree* (1964) was locked away in 1988 by a Boulder, Colorado, public librarian who considered it sexist because it glorified female selflessness.

See also Books, children's; Feminism; Libraries, school; *Playboy*; Socialist Realism.

Simon Wiesenthal Center

FOUNDED: 1974

TYPE OF ORGANIZATION: Center dedicated to preserving memories of the Holocaust

SIGNIFICANCE: This international body is dedicated to defending human rights and Jewish people in particular with the goal that another Holocaust will never be able to happen

Founded by Holocaust survivor Simon Wiesenthal, this center is dedicated to the preservation of the memory of the Holocaust through education and awareness. Its supporters believe that if recollections of the atrocities committed by Germany during World War II are kept alive through knowledge and imagination such atrocities are not likely to be repeated. To this end the center organizes educational outreach programs, researches and compiles histories of the Holocaust, and publishes magazines and newsletters on the subject.

In 1993 the center opened the Beit Hashoah-Museum of Tolerance in Los Angeles. This institution focuses on the Nazi Holocaust and offers interactive exhibits about racism and prejudice in America. The center has been involved in actively opposing groups that openly deny the Holocaust and many other supremacist organizations.

See also Holocaust, Jewish; Judaism; National Socialism; World War II.

Simpson, O. J., case

DATE: June, 1994-October, 1995

PLACE: Los Angeles, California

SIGNIFICANCE: Perhaps the most public in U.S. history, the trial renewed debate about the constitutional rights to a fair trial versus the constitutional right of freedom of the press

In June, 1994, Orenthal James (O. J.) Simpson, a sports commentator, actor, and former professional football star, was arrested and charged with the murders of his former wife Nicole Brown Simpson and her friend Ronald Goldman. By the time a Los Angeles jury acquitted Simpson of the murders in October, 1995, media coverage of the case had become a nationwide frenzy, illustrating the conflict in balancing the constitutional right to a fair trial with the constitutional right to freedom of the press.

The Sixth Amendment to the U.S. Constitution guarantees a person's right to a speedy and public trial before an impartial jury. The First Amendment, in turn, protects the media's right to report crime news, including information that may prejudice potential jurors against someone who has not yet stood trial and is presumed innocent by law. Before a jury had been selected in the Simpson case, the media had started revealing incriminating

PUBLIC VIEWS ON TELEVISING THE SIMPSON TRIAL

In October, 1994, shortly after O. J. Simpson's murder trial began, a CNN/*USA Today*/Gallup Poll surveyed a cross section of Americans on the question of whether television cameras should be allowed into his courtroom. Despite the extraordinary public interest in the trial, 69 percent of those interviewed expressed the view that television cameras should be banned. Only 27 percent favored allowing cameras, and 4 percent expressed no opinion on the subject.

details of the case. Millions of viewers watched the two-hour police pursuit leading to Simpson's arrest on live television. The media carried the tape or transcript of a 911 emergency call made by Nicole Simpson a few months before her death with a man identified as Simpson shouting obscenities in the background. The media also reported that Simpson had entered a no-contest plea to misdemeanor domestic abuse charges in 1989 and that Nicole Simpson had repeatedly called the police about earlier incidents in which Simpson allegedly beat her.

Media coverage of the Simpson case became so intense that a judge disqualified the Los Angeles County grand jury from hearing evidence and deciding whether to issue an indictment against Simpson. Millions of viewers watched the live television coverage of Simpson's preliminary hearing and nine-month trial. Judge Lance Ito, who presided over the Simpson trial, repeatedly chastised the media for leaking information about the case and threatened to remove the television cameras from the courtroom. There were efforts to censor media coverage of the case. Simpson tried but failed to prevent the broadcast and sale of a private videotape of his wedding to Nicole without his permission. Simpson's attorneys had argued that the broadcast and sale of the videotape invaded Simpson's privacy. A Los Angeles Superior Court judge, however, ruled that barring the media's use of the videotape would be prior restraint, violating the First Amendment.

The Simpson case also promoted state legislatures to introduce measures designed to control pretrial publicity in future trials. In response to potential witnesses in the Simpson case being offered large sums of money to sell their stories to media organizations, the California legislature passed a law barring witnesses to crimes from selling their stories to the media before trial.

See also African Americans; Courtrooms; Criminal trials; Prior restraint; Project Censored; Telephone law.

Sinclair, Upton

BORN: September 20, 1878, Baltimore, Maryland

DIED: November 25, 1968, Bound Brook, New Jersey

IDENTIFICATION: American author and reformer

SIGNIFICANCE: Despite repeated attempts to silence Sinclair, his muckraking journalism helped institute industrial and social reforms during the early twentieth century

Upton Sinclair early in his long writing career. (Library of Congress)

Sinclair started writing while a student at the City College of New York, which he entered at the age of fifteen. His early novels include *Springtime and Harvest* (1902, retitled *King Midas*); *Prince Hagen* (1903); *The Journal of Arthur Stirling* (1903); *Manassas* (1904); and *A Captain of Industry* (1906). He is best known, however, for *The Jungle* (1906), a brutally graphic exposé of Chicago's stockyards that led to the strengthening of federal food adulteration laws. True to his socialist beliefs, Sinclair invested the profits from this, his most successful book, in the Helicon Home Colony, a cooperative community in Englewood, New Jersey. Other early books included *The Metropolis* (1908); *The Money-changers* (1908); and the semi-autobiographical *Love's Pilgrimage* (1911). In 1915 Sinclair moved to California, where he wrote such books as *King Coal* (1917); *They Call Me Carpenter* (1922); *Oil!* (1927); and *Boston* (1928), which addressed the case of Nicola Sacco and Bartolomeo Vanzetti, robbery and murder suspects who many believe were executed because of their anarchist beliefs.

When the first publisher of *Oil!* asked Sinclair to delete sections describing the extramarital affairs of one of his characters, Sinclair suggested a compromise: On pages from which objectionable passages were removed, large fig leaves were printed to suggest to readers what they were missing.

During the Depression Sinclair took an active role in California politics. In 1934 he formed EPIC (End Poverty in California), an alliance of progressives and the unemployed that took control of the state Democratic Party and nearly won

him the governorship. After several other unsuccessful tries for public office, Sinclair returned to literary work in 1940 with the first of eleven novels tracing the career of a character named Lanny Budd from World War I to the Cold War. The third of these novels, *Dragon's Teeth* (1942), won a Pulitzer Prize.

See also Debs, Eugene; Mitford, Jessica; Morality; Seldes, George.

Skokie, Illinois, Nazi march

Date: March, 1977-October 16, 1978
Place: Skokie and Chicago, Illinois
Significance: When members of the American Nazi Party attempted to march in a largely Jewish community, their right to free expression clashed with the community's right to protect its members from ethnic and religious hatred

In March, 1977, Frank Collin, a leader of the American National Socialist Party, announced plans for the neo-Nazi organization to hold a rally before the Skokie Village Hall. A suburb of Chicago, Skokie had a large Jewish population, many of whom were survivors of the Holocaust in Europe. In order to prevent the controversial march, the village enacted three ordinances on May 2. The first required permits for parades and assemblies, and also required the applicants to purchase expensive liability insurance. The second prohibited dissemination of materials intended to incite racial or religious hatred. The third prohibited political leaders from participating in demonstrations in military-style uniforms.

On June 22, 1977, Collin applied for a permit under the ordinances, and after he made it clear that the demonstrators would wear Nazi-like uniforms complete with swastikas, the permit was denied. Supported by the American Civil Liberties Union, Collin then went to a federal district court and requested an injunction to prevent Skokie from enforcing its ordinances, with the argument that the ordinances violated the right to free expression as protected by the First Amendment.

In the resulting decision, *Smith v. Collin* (1978), the district court ruled in favor of the expressive rights of the Nazis. Based on the premise that the ordinances' purpose was to shield people from offensive ideas, the court's decision held that the concept of community standards of decency did not apply when the issue was content of political speech, and it emphasized that the Supreme Court in *Tinker v. Des Moines Independent Community School District* (1969) had established that any restriction on the "symbolic forms of expression" must be justified by compelling governmental interests, a test not met by Skokie. The decision was affirmed by court of appeals, and the Illinois Supreme Court issued a similar ruling. Although Collin and followers prevailed in these court decisions, they decided to hold their rallies in downtown Chicago on June 24 and July 9, 1978, and their small groups of demonstrators were shouted down by huge hostile audiences.

On October 16, 1978, the Supreme Court announced its refusal to hear Skokie's appeal in *Smith v. Collin*, but Justice Harry Blackmun, joined by one other member of the Court, dissented and argued that the Court should consider the issues of the case. Blackmun noted that the Court had never formally overturned *Beauharnais v. Illinois* (1952), a case which had upheld criminal sanctions for defamation of groups based on race or religion; in addition, he observed that a Nazi march in Skokie might constitute a "potentially explosive and dangerous situation," perhaps analogous to shouting fire in a crowded theater. Because seven members of the Court voted not to review the case, however, the Skokie controversy failed to resolve any of the difficult issues concerning "fighting words" and "hate speech."

See also American Civil Liberties Union; Armbands and buttons; Campus speech codes; Demonstrations; Fighting words; Hate laws; Holocaust, Jewish; Judaism; Marching and parading; National Socialism; Symbolic speech.

Slander

DEFINITION: False or defamatory speaking that injures another party

SIGNIFICANCE: The victim of slander may seek, in court, compensation for injury sustained as a result of slander, but the First Amendment limits to some extent the availability of this remedy, especially when the victim is a public figure

Slander is the oral twin of its written sibling, libel. Both are defamations that falsely or maliciously injure another. Prior to the 1960's, slander was widely viewed as posing no constitutional issue regarding freedom of speech. Nevertheless, the possibility of obtaining damages for allegedly injurious spoken or written words inevitably has a dampening effect on free expression. Accordingly, beginning with the 1964 decision of *New York Times v. Sullivan*, the Supreme Court has viewed defamation actions—whether for slander or for libel—as raising First Amendment issues. In the *New York Times* case, the Supreme Court held that the First Amendment prevented a public official from recovering damages for slander or libel unless the official demonstrated that a defamatory falsehood been made with actual malice—that is, with actual knowledge that a defamation was false or with reckless indifference to whether it was false or not. The Court has subsequently held that private individuals may in some circumstances be treated like public officials with respect to defamation, if they are famous or notorious or have somehow thrust themselves forward in the public eye.

See also Anti-Defamation League, The; Courts and censorship law; Defamation; Libel; *New York Times, The*.

Smith, Joseph

BORN: December 23, 1805, Sharon, Vermont

DIED: June 27, 1844, Carthage, Illinois

IDENTIFICATION: Founder of the Church of Jesus Christ of Latter-day Saints (Mormonism)

SIGNIFICANCE: Smith suppressed dissident Mormons, revised his own prophecies, suppressed knowledge of his personal involvement in polygamous marriages, and brought about his own death by destroying an opposition press; since his death, his church has striven to present his life in the best possible light

In 1830 Smith founded the Church of Jesus Christ of Latter-day Saints in New York after publishing the Book of Mormon—which he purported to be a true history of early America that he had translated from golden plates revealed to him by an angel. Despite the disappearance of those plates and Smith's local reputation as a creative treasure hunter, his new church grew rapidly. Smith soon took his fledgling church to Ohio, but controversy over his leadership forced him to flee

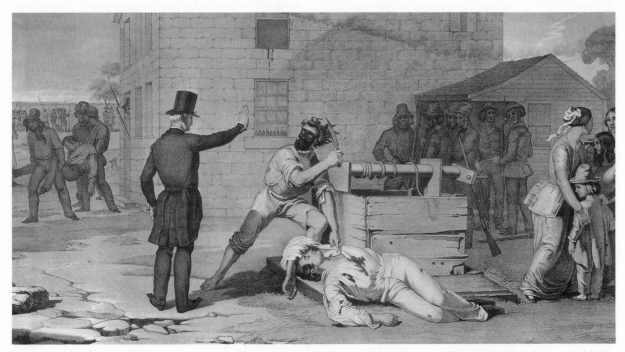

Mormon leader Joseph Smith was assassinated by an angry mob that took him from the Illinois jail where he was held after he destroyed the press of a newspaper whose criticisms he would not tolerate. (Library of Congress)

Ohio for Missouri. The church's growing paramilitary power and Smith's claim that he was a prophet of God, who had given his followers the region as a new Zion, provoked local hostility that forced him to move again in 1838, this time to Illinois. There his followers built Nauvoo into one of the most prosperous cities in the state.

At the height of Smith's power, he secretly engaged in plural marriage. However, not only did he deny being polygamous for the rest of his life, he denounced those who exposed him and often smeared their reputations. Decades later one of Smith's loyal followers claimed that Smith had even had dissident followers executed. Meanwhile, some of Smith's disaffected associates started a newspaper in Nauvoo dedicated to promoting church reform by exposing Smith's polygamy and autocratic rule. Smith ordered their press destroyed after only one issue of the paper had been printed. When the paper's owners sought redress in court, the case was dismissed because Smith controlled the courts. Nevertheless, Smith was jailed in Carthage, Illinois, for destroying the press.

Local citizens regarded Smith as a threat to democracy because he used his Nauvoo charter to nullify arrest warrants against himself and his followers; he also controlled local elections, outlawed criticism of his church, and challenged separation of powers by simultaneously being prophet, mayor, judge, city council member, and militia commander. In 1844 he even declared himself a candidate for president of the United States. Fearing his power and ability to evade prosecution, a mob stormed his Carthage, Illinois, jailhouse and killed him.

During his lifetime Smith revised some of his own prophecies, though he claimed them to have issued directly from the mouth of God. For example, he changed an early prophecy limiting his role to translator of the golden plates, and he obscured an associate's use of divining rods. He also suppressed his prophecy authorizing polygamy, publicly condemning polygamy, while secretly circulating the prophecy's contents to trusted associates and women whom he wished to marry while their husbands were sent on foreign missions.

Several controversial aspects of Smith's life have been suppressed in histories authorized by the Utah-based Church of Jesus Christ of Latter-day Saints, which allows only trusted members access to sensitive documents. The church's official early history—purportedly written by Smith himself—is now acknowledged to be a compilation of sources. Modern editions have been substantially revised. For example, they soften Smith's confessions of youthful indiscretions, and they reconcile contradictory statements—such as the name of the spirit who revealed the plates. These editions also delete Smith's many cursings of his enemies, his calling the president of the United States a "fool," his incorrect use of foreign phrases, at least four prophecies that failed, his "cure" for cholera, and his admissions of violating church prohibitions against tobacco and alcohol.

Modern printings of the Book of Mormon have also been heavily revised, despite the fact that there is no authoritative text except Smith's own version. Most of the modern edition's nearly four thousand changes correct Smith's grammar. More substantive changes include reconciliations of contradictions.

Two of these have substantive theological implications (a claim that baptism was an ancient practice and deletion of a statement that God's decrees are inalterable).

The best-known biography of Smith, *No Man Knows My History* (1944), was written by Fawn Brodie. Though she was raised in the church and was closely related to one of its highest-ranking officers, her critically acclaimed work attributed Smith's prophetic career entirely to natural, rather than supernatural, causes. Her book also gave full treatment to Smith's personal weaknesses and their effects on his movement. The church excommunicated her, allegedly for her views.

See also Christian Science; Christianity; Jehovah's Witnesses; Mormonism; Newspapers; Religion; Scientology, Church of.

Smith Act

ENACTED: June 28, 1940

PLACE: United States (national)

SIGNIFICANCE: This federal law made it a crime to advocate, or to conspire to advocate, the violent overthrow of the government

The Smith Act was a product of American anxieties during the late 1930's. As the world moved toward war, Americans grew more suspicious of foreigners and their ideologies. By 1939 opinion surveys revealed broad public support for new restrictions on aliens and for the hearings of the new House Committee on Un-American Activities, which had been created to investigate anti-American propaganda activities. Reflecting this suspicion, Congress considered forty different measures aimed at aliens and subversive propaganda. Representative Howard W. Smith of Virginia drew from several of those proposals to create an omnibus antiradical bill that he introduced in March, 1939.

Smith's bill contained new requirements for aliens, criminalized efforts to interfere with military recruitment and discipline, and sought to punish anyone advocating the violent overthrow of the government. The House of Representatives approved Smith's measure by a vote of 272-40 in late June, 1939, but Congress adjourned before the Senate could consider the bill. A year later the Senate passed a slightly modified version without a roll call vote, and on June 28, 1940, President Franklin D. Roosevelt signed the measure into law.

Sedition Clauses. The most controversial provisions of the Smith Act were contained in its sedition sections, which made it unlawful knowingly to advocate, advise, or teach the violent overthrow of any government in the United States. The act also provided penalties of up to five years in jail and fines of up to ten thousand dollars for anyone who published, distributed or displayed printed materials advocating the violent overthrow of the government or who organized or who knowingly joined any society advocating such a goal. The measure also contained a conspiracy section that carried the same penalties for any person who conspired with anyone else to commit the aforementioned acts.

The Smith Act was aimed principally at the purveyors of subversive propaganda. Since existing law already prohibited conspiracies to overthrow the government, the Smith Act added only the element of advocacy. Earlier proposals in Congress had called for restrictions on propaganda stemming from Nazi and communist sources, and Smith drew heavily on these proposals in drafting his measure. His law was designed to eliminate one category of expression from the American marketplace of ideas.

Enforcement of the Act. Under President Roosevelt, the Justice Department proved reluctant to enforce the advocacy sections of the Smith Act. In 1941 eighteen members of the Socialist Workers Party were convicted of violating the act's provisions outlawing attempts to promote disloyalty among the armed services, and in 1944 twenty-eight alleged pro-Nazis were indicted on similar charges. However, their case was dropped after the death of the trial judge.

After World War II the Cold War gave the Smith Act new life. Mounting frustrations over Soviet expansion abroad and growing public concerns over communist subversion at home convinced the Truman Administration to use the Smith Act against American communists. In July, 1948, the Justice Department brought charges against eleven members of the central committee of the Communist Party of the United States (CPUSA). Lacking proof of direct incitement or actual revolutionary deeds by the accused, the federal prosecutors sought conviction under the conspiracy section of the act. Members of the party's central committee were charged with conspiring to teach and advocate the overthrow of the government and with conspiring to form the CPUSA to achieve those ends. The stormy nine-month trial ended in October, 1949, with a guilty verdict. Each defendant was fined ten thousand dollars and sentenced to five years in jail.

The Dennis Case. In 1951 the U.S. Supreme Court affirmed, by a vote of 6-2, the constitutionality of the Smith Act in *Dennis v. United States*. Chief Justice Fred M. Vinson's majority opinion paid homage to the American tradition of freedom of speech, noting that it rested on the "hypothesis that speech can rebut speech, propaganda will answer propaganda, free debate of ideas will result in the wisest governmental policies." However, Vinson went on to declare that free speech "must, on occasion, be subordinated to other values and considerations," in this case, to the right of the government to protect itself. In his effort to balance the value of free speech against the authority of the government, Vinson relied on the Court's long-standing "clear and present danger" test. Prior rulings using this test had suggested that before the government could limit speech, it had to establish the existence of a serious danger that was both obvious and imminent. But Vinson concluded that the words "clear and present" did not require the government to "wait until the putsch is about to be executed." Even though a communist coup was unlikely to succeed, the "gravity of the evil" was sufficient to justify this "invasion of free speech."

Vinson's opinion elicited two vigorous dissents. Justice William O. Douglas denied that American communists represented any "clear and present danger to the republic." To him, they were the "miserable merchants of unwanted ideas," whose conviction should be set aside. Justice Hugo Black went further. He noted that the members of the CPUSA had

not been charged with overt acts against the government, or even with saying or writing anything subversive. Instead they were charged with conspiracy to form a political party that might use speech and other forms of communication to advocate certain ideas in the future. Black found their conviction "a virulent form of prior censorship of speech and press" that was forbidden by the First Amendment. He would have declared the Smith Act unconstitutional.

Later Prosecutions. With the Smith Act affirmed, the Department of Justice began prosecuting minor CPUSA leaders. By the spring of 1956, when the Supreme Court agreed to hear a second Smith Act case, 102 party functionaries had been convicted and twenty-eight other cases were still pending. In *Yates v. United States*, decided in June, 1957, the Court narrowed the implications of the *Dennis* ruling and made prosecution under the Smith Act more difficult. Justice John Marshall Harlan's majority opinion drew a distinction between advocacy of abstract doctrines, such as those contained in Marxist theory, and advocacy of illegal acts. Harlan concluded that the Smith Act had never been intended to prohibit advocacy and teaching of forcible overthrow as abstract principles, divorced from actions. Consequently, the government's prosecutions were flawed. Faced with this stricter standard, the Justice Department ceased all further actions under the advocacy section of the law. Charges were dropped, or the convictions reversed, in cases involving ninety CPUSA members. The Smith Act was dead. Nevertheless, the government's efforts to use the act to destroy the Communist Party had largely succeeded. By 1958 the party's leadership was in disarray and its membership had largely vanished.

—*Jerold L. Simmons*

See also Clear and present danger doctrine; Communist Party of the U.S.A.; First Amendment; Foreign Agents Registration Act of 1938; House Committee on Un-American Activities; Loyalty oaths; Pledge of Allegiance; Propaganda; World War II.

BIBLIOGRAPHY

The most useful on how the Smith Act was used against American communists are Michael R. Belknap's *Cold War Political Justice: The Smith Act, The Communist Party, and American Civil Liberties* (Westport, Conn.: Greenwood Press, 1977) and Peter Steinberg's *The Great "Red Menace": United States Prosecution of American Communists, 1947-1952* (Westport, Conn.: Greenwood Press, 1984). The Supreme Court's opinions in the *Dennis* and *Yates* cases are reprinted in many collections; however, that of Thomas I. Emerson, David Haber, and Norman Dorsen, eds., *Political and Civil Rights in the United States* (Boston: Little, Brown, 1967), contains additional details about these and other cases.

Smoking

DEFINITION: Inhaling or ingesting smoke from tobacco products, such as cigarettes and cigars

SIGNIFICANCE: Concern over health damage and deaths caused by smoking in the United States has prompted efforts to censor or restrict the advertising and promotion of tobacco products

Mounting evidence that smoking contributes to lung cancer and emphysema, resulting in serious health problems and even death, has lead to insistent calls for new laws banning or restricting the advertising and promotion of cigarettes, cigars, and other tobacco products in the United States. The issue has pitted the American Cancer Society, parent groups, and environmentalists against the Tobacco Institute, advertisers, and civil libertarians. It has tested the strength of First Amendment protection for commercial speech in a context in which the products being advertised have many users but few defenders.

From time to time Congress has considered banning advertising tobacco products. Generally, such laws would prohibit the advertising and promotion of cigarettes, cigars, and other tobacco products through any medium, including radio and television commercials, newspaper and magazine advertisements, billboards, sponsorship of athletic events, and the distribution of free samples. Such bans would cover truthful as well as false, deceptive, or misleading advertising.

Commercial Advertising. Historically, commercial advertising played a significant role in the establishment and growth of a free press. The Founders who wrote the Declaration of Independence and the Bill of Rights had come of age reading newspapers financed by advertising. Advertising served as a vital source of financial backing that made newspapers possible and kept them largely independent of political control, often exercised through favored appointments of official printers.

The values reflected in the First Amendment apply with equal force to advertising as to other forms of expression. Advertising expresses ideas and information that are useful and oftentimes necessary to the public. Learning about the availability, cost, and advantages of goods, including cigarettes, may be more vital to the everyday affairs of most people than reading about the theories of John Locke or the Senate's debates on grain subsidies.

Likewise, the First Amendment reflects confidence that the American people can be exposed to the art of persuasion and still make informed choices, regarding consumer goods or regarding candidates for office. The U.S. Supreme Court has held that "the State's fear that voters might make an ill-advised choice does not provide the State with a compelling justification for limiting speech." The state's fear that consumers might make an ill-advised purchase of cigarettes in response to a truthful advertisement does not provide the state with a compelling justification for limiting, let alone prohibiting, such advertisements. The Supreme Court has consistently invalidated restrictions designed to deprive consumers of accurate information about diverse products and services legally offered for sale, including contraceptives, housing, pharmaceuticals, legal services, and abortions.

Opponents of restrictions on cigarette advertising have argued that any attempt by Congress to prevent citizens from obtaining truthful tobacco advertising because of the effect Congress fears such information will have in encouraging the purchase and use of tobacco products cannot withstand constitutional scrutiny. "The people in our democracy are entrusted with the responsibility for judging and evaluating the relative merits of conflicting arguments," the Supreme Court has held.

The First Amendment presupposes that people will perceive their own best interests only when they are well informed, and that the best means to that end is to open channels for communication, not close them.

Gambling on Tobacco. Supporters of banning cigarette advertising rely on the decision in *Posadas de Puerto Rico Associates v. Tourism Company of Puerto Rico* (1986), in which the Supreme Court upheld a narrow restriction on advertising of lawful casino gambling aimed at residents of Puerto Rico, while allowing other advertising within and without Puerto Rico. Justice William H. Rehnquist wrote the Court's 5-4 opinion. Noting that the case involved "pure commercial speech which does no more than propose a commercial transaction," the regulation concerned a lawful activity neither misleading nor fraudulent; the "reduction of demand for casino gambling by the residents of Puerto Rico" was a "substantial" government interest; the regulation "directly advanced" the government's stated interest; and the restrictions were "no more extensive than necessary to serve the government's interest." The Court disagreed with the casino's argument that the way to reduce demand for casino gambling by residents was to promulgate more speech, not less, designed to discourage gambling. "It would surely be a Pyrrhic victory for casino owners . . . to gain recognition of a First Amendment Right . . . only to thereby force the legislature into banning casino gambling by residents altogether."

In dissent, Justice William J. Brennan, joined by justices Thurgood Marshall and Harry A. Blackmun, said that none of the differences between commercial and other speech "justify protecting commercial speech less extensively where, as here, the government seeks to manipulate behavior by depriving citizens of truthful information concerning lawful activities." Regulation of speech based on "fear that recipients will act on the information provided . . . should be subject to strict judicial scrutiny." Even if substantial government interests had been shown, Justice Brennan found no indication that the advertising regulation would satisfy concerns about corruption or organized crime.

Opponents of restrictions on tobacco advertising have argued that the law at stake in *Posadas* bears little resemblance to proposed prohibitions of all advertising of all tobacco products in all media at all times and in all places. Unlike casino gambling, which is legal in only two states, the sale of tobacco products is legal in every state of the union. Where traditionally lawful activity is concerned, the government's decision not to outlaw such activity is strong evidence that no substantial evil exists that would justify a complete ban on the advertising of that activity. The question remains, however, if U.S. society, which chooses not to outlaw tobacco products themselves, should allow for some lesser governmental right to ban tobacco advertising.

Children and Tobacco Advertising. Efforts to ban or regulate tobacco advertising have gained their greatest support by focusing on the impact of smoking on the health of young people. The natural desire to protect children, combined with objections to the perceived manipulations of advertisers, have led politicians, parents, health authorities, and community

Antismoking groups concerned about teenage smokers have targeted advertisement campaigns such as this attention-grabbing "Joe Camel" promotion that appeared in early 1996 magazines. (AP/Wide World Photos)

leaders to press for the elimination of tobacco advertising aimed at children. Joe Camel, the cartoon camel used to sell Camel cigarettes, came to symbolize crass attempts to induce young people to smoke. Proponents of restricting tobacco advertising argue that children are particularly gullible to the appeal of cigarette advertisements. The tobacco industry has responded that advertising does not cause children to begin smoking but rather only influences brand selection, but few in the public seemed convinced by such an argument, and the debate persists.

False and Misleading Advertising. The fact that advertising is constitutionally protected does not mean that deliberately false and misleading advertising is constitutionally protected. Existing agencies, such as the Federal Trade Commission, are authorized to deal with specific instances of false, deceptive, and misleading cigarette advertising.

If tobacco advertising were to be banned, civil libertarians ask what may be banned next. Advertising for foods containing saturated fats, red meat, or refined sugar might be banned. Advertisements for alcohol, contraceptives, war toys, real guns, insecticides, and nuclear energy may also be banned. If the First Amendment were to be interpreted to tolerate a total ban on the advertising of one thing, there might be no distinction that would protect the advertising of anything. —*Stephen F. Rohde*

See also Advertising as the target of censorship; Alcoholic beverages; Commercial speech; *44 Liquormart, Inc. v. Rhode Island*; Health epidemic news; Pressure groups.

BIBLIOGRAPHY

Rodney A. Smolla's *Free Speech in an Open Society* (New York: Alfred A. Knopf, 1992) is a highly readable and accessible discussion spanning such major First Amendment issues as the rationale of constitutional protection of freedom of speech and press, flag-burning, hate speech, libel, public funding of the arts and education, money and politics, prior restraint, censorship during the Persian Gulf war and the challenges of new technologies. Works on restrictions on advertising that discuss tobacco include Edwin P. Rome and William H. Roberts' *Corporate and Commercial Free Speech: First Amendment Protection of Business Expression* (Westport, Conn.: Quorum Books, 1985), Michael G. Gartner's *Advertising and the First Amendment* (New York: Priority Press Publications, 1989), and Richard T. Kaplar's *Advertising Rights: The Neglected Freedom: Toward a New Doctrine of Commercial Speech* (Washington, D.C.: Media Institute, 1991). Kaplar also edited *Bad Prescription for the First Amendment: FDA Censorship of Drug Advertising and Promotion* (Washington, D.C.: Media Institute, 1993), which analyzes the debate over the Food and Drug Administration's controls on drug advertising generally.

Smothers Brothers Comedy Hour, The

TYPE OF WORK: Television program
BROADCAST: 1967-1969
SUBJECT MATTER: Musical acts and comedy sketches
SIGNIFICANCE: The Columbia Broadcasting System canceled this popular variety show after failing to control its content

A year after the music and comedy team of Tom and Dick Smothers began their musical variety show, they began receiving complaints from senior CBS executives about its content. The network officials were uneasy about the show's barbed political and social satire, which was geared toward students, young adults, and minority groups. The network worried particularly about the show's irreverent references to such sensitive topics as drug use, homosexuality, and religion.

CBS objected to one March, 1969, episode in particular, claiming that its master tape had not been submitted in time for the network censors to review it—a claim that was disputed. In that episode, folk singer Joan Baez sang a tribute to her husband, imprisoned antiwar activist David Harris, and comic Jackie Mason made slightly risqué remarks. On another show, CBS objected to Tom Smothers' double-entendre remark, "Bolshoi!" in reply to his brother's praise of the famous Russian ballet of that same name. Two segments of an interview with controversial anti-Vietnam war spokesman Dr. Benjamin Spock and a satire of President Lyndon B. Johnson were not allowed to be aired. Another censored routine slated for an Easter broadcast had Tom, dressed as an Easter bunny, saying that Jesus Christ had risen from the grave, but that if he did not see his own shadow, winter would be extended. Tom Smothers later claimed that 75 percent of the twenty-six shows they did that season had been censored: "They don't beep out words—they edit. That's because they don't want people to know censorship is going on."

Later that spring, CBS dropped the show, despite the fact that its one-third share of American viewers made it the first show in eight years to top the rating of NBC's long-running *Bonanza* in the same time slot. The network complained specifically about an episode that lampooned Rhode Island's Senator John O. Pastore, who was then investigating television practices, and that featured a monologue by comic David Steinberg on Jonah and the whale. After a private screening of the episode for one hundred interested Federal Communications Commission (FCC) officials, reporters and congressmen, columnist Peter Brooks of *The New York Times* wrote that "there could not be the slightest objection to it." CBS claimed that the FCC had prohibited some of this material, but FCC commissioner Nicholas Johnson denied this as he praised the show's attempt to deal with issues on an adult level. He agreed with Tom Smothers, as well as lampooned figure Senator Pastore, that government was not involved in broadcast censorship, but rather that top network executives were exercising prior restraint by not allowing the network's affiliates the choice to air, edit, or censor shows in their own regions. Other critics pointed to CBS's other programming, particularly its daytime soap operas, as evidence of the network's lack of taste and hypocrisy. Ironically, the cancellation occurred after a speech the previous November by CBS chair Frank Stanton to the national convention of Sigma Delta Chi, a journalism honorary society. His speech had denounced censorship, saying the network would not engage in the practice.

In the summer of 1970 the Smothers Brothers hosted a new variety show for the American Broadcasting Company, and in the spring of 1975 they starred in the National Broadcasting Company's *Smothers Brothers Show*.

See also Baez, Joan; Federal Communications Commission; Folk music; Intellectual freedom; *Saturday Night Live*; Television; Television networks; Vietnam War.

Snepp v. United States

COURT: U.S. Supreme Court
DECIDED: February 19, 1980
SIGNIFICANCE: This decision held that agreements requiring government employees to submit their writings for review prior to publication did not violate their First Amendment rights

As a condition of employment, agents of the Central Intelligence Agency (CIA) are required to sign an agreement that they will not publish any information during or after employment without prepublication clearance by the agency. In 1977 former CIA employee Frank W. Snepp III published a book, *Decent Interval*, that described CIA activities in Vietnam, without first submitting his manuscript for prepublication review. The government then sued him for breach of contract, requesting that an injunction be imposed requiring him to submit all future publications for prepublication review. The government also sought to control all profits earned from the sale of Snepp's book. A federal district court in Virginia sided with the government in 1978. Two years later the U.S. Supreme Court upheld the district court ruling in *Snepp v. United States*.

Snepp argued that the prepublication agreement constituted an unconstitutional prior restraint upon his freedom of expression. The Supreme Court ruled, however, that such agreements are reasonable and appropriate to prevent unauthorized disclosure of CIA sources and methods, because the government has a "compelling interest" in protecting both national security secrets and the appearance of agency confidentiality. This ruling reaffirmed a previous decision of the Fourth Circuit Court of Appeals in *United States v. Marchetti* (1972), which had enjoined publication of *The CIA and the Cult of Intelligence* (1974) by Victor Marchetti and John Marks, until the manuscript was purged of classified information. A federal appeals court subsequently ruled that both secrecy agreements and prepublication agreements did not violate the First Amendment in *McGehee v. Casey* (1983).

The CIA cases involved government efforts to impose censorship upon massive quantities of information regarding government activities because of potential danger to national security. The government and the courts have routinely viewed these cases as matters of contract law. To defenders of free speech, however, these attempts to censor writings critical of the government raise several concerns. First, questions of whether material might endanger national security is left entirely to government agencies; the courts have been reluctant to intercede in these determinations. Therefore, the authority to weigh the arguments for and against censorship has been delegated to the censor. Second, because the information is relevant to government policies and decisions, opponents of censorship fear that both the right of authors to criticize the government and the people's right to know may be jeopardized by agency decisions. Third, these regulations constitute prior restraints upon publication. With few exceptions, the courts have overturned prior restraints because they impose direct burdens upon authors and publishers and because they deter critics from engaging in expression that might be deemed seditious. However, the CIA prepublication and secrecy agreements constitute one area where prior restraints have been upheld by the courts.

See also Central Intelligence Agency; *CIA and the Cult of Intelligence, The*; Classification of information; Free speech; National security; Prior restraint; Sedition.

Snuff films

DEFINITION: Films that purport to show actual killings of human beings

SIGNIFICANCE: Although rumors of the existence of such films have led to efforts to suppress them, their actual existence has not been proven

During the 1970's rumors spread throughout the United States that there was a new kind of sex film available in which women were actually killed on screen. These rumors caught the attention of the news media, and many stories were heard alleging the existence of such films—including the possibility of an actual 1977 film titled *Snuff*. Americans who advocated banning all pornography pointed to "snuff films" as the ultimate outgrowth of lawful pornography. Meanwhile, law enforcement agencies failed to locate purveyors or producers of such films.

The U.S. Customs Bureau also spent time examining packages from known European pornographers. Eventually the Federal Bureau of Investigation (FBI) concluded that if European pornographers were actually producing "snuff films," they had to be doing so on a small scale, and that any such films were not being shipped to the United States.

However, when the FBI followed leads to Mexico, it found what appeared to be at least one genuine snuff film, involving only two people: a man who was hooded throughout the film, and a woman identified as a Mexican prostitute who appeared to be killed after having sex with the man. In attempting to trace the origin of this film, agents found that the film appeared to have been made specially for a single customer, who had paid more than five thousand dollars for a copy. The producers, the customer, and the middlemen were never identified, however, and the case remained open. Since then the FBI has routinely checked with Mexican authorities, who trace pornography when prostitutes from California and other border states disappear, especially when they are found killed in Mexico.

New Yorkers concerned about violence against women protest the showing of an alleged "snuff" film in 1976. (Betty Lane)

See also Customs laws, U.S.; Federal Bureau of Investigation; Gangster films; Mexico; Pornography; Violence; Women Against Pornography.

Socialist Realism

DEFINITION: Art style officially dictated by the government of the Soviet Union from the early 1930's through the 1980's

SIGNIFICANCE: Socialist Realism was an attempt to have art adhere to the government's political and ideological agenda

The Soviet government officially defined "Socialist Realism" in 1932 and promoted it until the 1980's. After consolidating power in the early 1920's, the new leaders of the Soviet Union sought to press all social and societal institutions into the service of the state. The arts were no exception. General Secretary Joseph Stalin in particular recognized the power of the arts to influence the values, temperament, and motivations of the masses. At his instigation, the regime proclaimed the doctrine of Socialist Realism in 1932.

Socialist Realism was the name of the artistic style toward which Soviet artists were supposed to strive. It was meant to promote socialist ideals and values through the portrayal of allegedly ordinary Soviet life. The government developed detailed guidelines that specified the way the artist should treat subjects such as work and leisure, and how the artist should portray groups such as soldiers and families. Workers were to be presented as heroes, capitalists as exploitative and malevolent, and Stalin himself as a benevolent father or a brave leader—as political needs warranted. In all cases it was the state, rather than the artist, that chose the message to be expressed. Art therefore became formulaic, judged by its conformity with governmental standards rather than by any intrinsic quality as art.

As were virtually all other workers in the Soviet Union, artists were employees of the state. The government thus had considerable opportunity to enforce the standards of Socialist Realism. In one sense, then, Socialist Realism was a form of censorship. Artists who did not produce work that conformed to governmental standards were not permitted to publish, perform, or otherwise display their work. At the same time, Socialist Realism was more than mere censorship; not content with merely banning objectionable works, the Soviet authorities commissioned politically desirable ones.

Socialist Realism extended to all the arts. Films depicted such pedestrian events as road-paving and forest-clearing with exaggerated glory. Enormous statues of peasants and workers in heroic poses were erected. Even music followed the formula of Socialist Realism, with instrumental works that failed to satisfy the authorities being rejected as "bourgeois" or "degenerate."

Socialist Realism as an art form has been dismissed as petty, grotesque, and perverse. One might well ask whether works conceived and developed through coercion and regimentation can be considered art. Certainly many Soviets answered in the negative, and various Soviet artists defied the strictures of Socialist Realism by producing illegal works that not infrequently led to their imprisonment. With the onset of Mikhail Gorbachev's policy of openness in the mid-1980's, Soviet artists were largely freed from the constraints of Socialist Realism, and Soviet (and Russian) art returned to the direction of its distinguished, pre-Soviet heritage.

See also Akhmatova, Anna; Art; Bulgakov, Mikhail Afanasyevich; Communism; Degenerate Art Exhibition; Gorky, Maxim; National Security Decision Directive 84; Soviet Union; Stalin, Joseph; Zhdanov, Andrei.

Society for the Suppression of Vice, New York

FOUNDED: 1873

TYPE OF ORGANIZATION: Censorship organization founded by Anthony Comstock

SIGNIFICANCE: Following the passage of the Comstock Act in 1873, this society became a model for procensorship organizations in the United States and was instrumental in several significant censorship trials

During the 1800's reformers in the United States tackled issues such as temperance, prison reform, and slavery. With the wave of industrialization and urbanization following the Civil War, reformers feared that young people who came to the cities alone looking for work would be vulnerable to corruption and vice. These fears were confirmed when a Young Men's Christian Association (YMCA) survey of young men working in New York City in 1866 revealed widespread gambling, pornography, and prostitution. Besides their concerns about crime and morality, reformers feared that the rapid spread of venereal diseases then occurring might threaten public health. The YMCA immediately began campaigning for stricter obscenity laws; in 1872 a committee was formed to combat the spread of vice.

Anthony Comstock. One of the most vocal people involved in the YMCA campaign against vice was Anthony Comstock, the man primarily responsible for the passage of the federal Comstock Act of 1873. On May 16, 1873, Comstock's committee, renamed the Society for the Suppression of Vice, was chartered as an independent organization by the New York State legislature. Just as the Comstock Act set the standard for antiobscenity legislation in the United States, this group was the archetype for organized vice reform in America. Its most notable offshoot, the New England Society for the Suppression of Vice, was formed later in 1873 and soon became known as the Boston Watch and Ward Society.

Although its appeal was neither universal nor widespread, the New York Society for the Suppression of Vice did attract influential members. Those involved in the original incorporation included banker John Pierpont Morgan, copper magnate William E. Dodge, textbook publisher Alfred S. Barnes, lawyer William C. Beecher (the son of Reverend Henry Ward Beecher), feminist author Julia Ward Howe, and the country's first female licensed doctor of medicine, Elizabeth Blackwell. The society's first president, New Jersey soap manufacturer Samuel Colgate, served until his death in 1898; Comstock himself served as executive secretary until his own death in 1915. By law, the group received 50 percent of all fines collected from the successful convictions of cases prosecuted by its agents. Other funding came from hundreds of donors, including such notable figures as Andrew Carnegie, Mrs. Russell Sage, Louis C. Tiffany, John Wanamaker, and Charles Olmstead. The organization's largest benefactor was Comstock's close friend and society vice-president Morris Ketchum Jesup—the banker and railroad financier who became president of the New York State Chamber of Commerce in 1899. Jessup donated a million dollars to found the American Museum of Natural History.

The group's strongest opposition during its early years came from Robert G. Ingersol's National Liberal League, which by 1878 had collected fifty thousand signatures petitioning the repeal of the Comstock Act, and the National Defense Association, formed in 1879 to investigate questionable instances of prosecution under that law. Neither group had enough social or financial resources, however, seriously to deter Comstock's new organization.

The Society for the Suppression of Vice used a combination of legal pressure and social influence to attack obscenity and vice. The group's actions were generally affirmed by the city's two largest newspapers—*The New York Tribune* and *The New York Times*—and state and local courts convicted more than 90 percent of those prosecuted. Initially, the accused were mostly small-time publishers and importers of erotica and vulgar true-crime stories, materials deemed obscene by the genteel elite. Established publishing houses had little trouble with the society until the 1890's, when early naturalist fiction, such as Stephen Crane's *Maggie* (1893) and Theodore Dreiser's *Sister Carrie* (1900) came into question. The society worried that such books would incite readers to lust, thereby promoting crime and disease.

During the Progressive Era reformers tackled such issues as child labor, sanitation, housing, and social hygiene. A wave of prostitution reform began in 1910 with the publication of *The Social Evil in New York*, a report by a committee of fifteen people, several of whom were supporters of the Society for the Suppression of Vice. As Comstock's influence increased, along with public concern over vice and prostitution, the society started censoring more established writers and books. Around 1915, when U.S. involvement in the war in Europe began to look inevitable, the military feared that prostitution and venereal disease would cripple American troops. The Navy called for the closing of red-light districts, and combating vice became a patriotic occupation. At the same time, however, opposition to Comstock and his reformers grew among such intellectuals as George Bernard Shaw, who feared the suffocating effects "Comstockery" was having on literature and the arts. Comstock died on September 21, 1915, leaving leadership of the society to John Sumner.

John Sumner and the Later Years. During his first decade as president of the Society for the Suppression of Vice, Sumner launched two plans attempting to regain momentum for its procensorship cause: the "book jury" plan after World War I, and the "clean books" campaign of 1923-1925. However, these plans failed to attract much support. After the war a new generation of liberal publishing firms began printing books and periodicals with racier subject matter. Despite conservative opposition, authors such as Dreiser gained respect from the intellectual community and influential supporters such as Horace Liveright and H. L. Mencken.

Works charged with obscenity during Sumner's tenure as president included James Branch Cabell's *Jurgen* (1919), James Joyce's *Ulysses* (1922), D. H. Lawrence's *Lady Chatterley's Lover* (1928), and Edmund Wilson's *Memoirs of Hecate County* (1946). In 1924 Sumner announced that the society had confiscated an average of 65,000 pictures per year since its formation. By 1946 it had conducted 5,567 arrests and confiscated nearly 400,000 books and magazines, 3.5 million postcards, more than 3 million catalogs, and more than 8 million other items.

After World War II public opinion shifted away from systematic censorship, and by Sumner's retirement in 1950, the society had greatly diminished. While vestiges of its procensorship agenda continued to exist among some conservative organizations, the Society for the Suppression of Vice soon ceased officially to exist.   *—Geralyn Strecker*

See also Book burning; Book publishing; Books and obscenity law; Censorship; Comstock, Anthony; Comstock Act of 1873; Pressure groups; Sumner, John; World War I.

BIBLIOGRAPHY

Paul S. Boyer's *Purity in Print: The Vice-Society Movement and Book Censorship in America* (New York: Scribner, 1968) offers the most comprehensive overview of the society's relationships with similar groups throughout the United States, especially the Boston Watch and Ward Society. Heywood Broun and Margaret Leech's biography, *Anthony Comstock: Roundsman of the Lord* (New York: Albert and Charles Boni, 1927), explores Comstock's role in the formation and early activities of the society. Robert W. Haney's *Comstockery in America: Patterns of Censorship and Control* (Boston: Beacon Press, 1960) discusses the fervor of the procensorship movement, as does Morris L. Ernst and Alan U. Schwartz's *Censorship: The Search for the Obscene* (New York: Macmillan, 1964). Richard Hofstadter's *Anti-Intellectualism in American Life* (New York: Knopf, 1963) focuses on the stifling effects censorship has had on American scholars and artists. The best source for the society's influence on prostitution reform is Willoughby C. Waterman's *Prostitution and Its Repression in New York City, 1900-1931* (New York: AMS Press, 1968).

Society for the Suppression of Vice, U.K.

FOUNDED: 1801

TYPE OF ORGANIZATION: British procensorship body

SIGNIFICANCE: This organization played a leading role in opposing such vices as pornography and prostitution in nineteenth century Great Britain

Concerned with decline of an organization called the Proclamation Society in 1801, a British procensorship group published "A Proposal for Establishing a Society for the Suppression of Vice and the Encouragement of Religion and Virtue." The new group's concerns were initially broad, covering confidence games, honest measurements, fortune telling, cruelty to animals, prostitution, and various common amusements. The group's chief goal, however, was censoring obscene and blasphemous materials, such as literature, titillating reports of true crime, magazines, photographs, postcards, and art prints—anything offered for sale by London's notorious Holywell Street pornographers. Since pornography in nineteenth century Great Britain was not just a working-class amusement, but an elite obsession, the society drew most of its support from the growing bourgeoisie, who feared what kinds of dangerous materials the increasingly literate lower classes might begin reading. One early society success was the 1824 Vagrancy Act, which controlled street people and prohibited the sale or display of indecent materials.

The society was Great Britain's primary censoring body until passage of the Obscene Publications Act of 1857. Between 1845 and 1868, it was responsible for 154 successful prosecutions for obscenity. The group dwindled due to lack of funds through the 1870's and ceased its work in 1880. It was revived as the National Vigilance Association after an August 22, 1885, Hyde Park demonstration in support of journalist W. T. Snead's purity campaign against prostitution.

See also Hyde Park Speakers Corner; Obscene Publications Acts; Society for the Suppression of Vice, New York; United Kingdom.

Socrates

BORN: c. 470 B.C.E., Athens, Greece
DIED: c. 399 B.C.E., Athens, Greece
IDENTIFICATION: Ancient Greek moral philosopher
SIGNIFICANCE: Socrates was executed for corrupting the young, disbelieving in the official gods, and introducing new deities

One of the most influential figures in Western philosophy, Socrates is also the most perplexing. He is not known to have written anything, so his thoughts are known only from the works of his younger associates, Plato and Xenophon. He claimed to know only that he did not know, yet antagonized influential Athenians with reproaches that seemed to presume moral knowledge. He was tried and executed by the Athenian Democracy, which he criticized; yet he fought for that democracy, and both refused to obey and openly upbraided its oligarchic opponents. Both oligarchs and democrats threatened to silence him, yet Socrates himself appears to have been willing to censor others.

These apparent contradictions may be explained by considering Socrates' mission in life, which he believed to be divine in two senses. He possessed a personal deity that spoke to him to prevent him from doing wrong. Also, the god Apollo's oracle at Delphi had said that Socrates was the wisest and most just man. Socrates was puzzled by this, since he was aware of how uncertain his knowledge was. He resolved to spend his life "seeking wisdom." This entailed engaging in an activity that combined morality and philosophy. He asked questions of others both to discover and to test their moral opinions and to seek definitions of justice, moderation, and other moral qualities.

This left Socrates doubly endowed morally. His divine voice kept him from doing wrong: His moral questioning moved him toward goodness. He appears to have been convinced that he was blessed with leading the right life. But his

moral self-assurance made him appear arrogant to others, especially prominent figures stung by the sharpness of his critical questioning. Those figures included both oligarchs and democrats. However, Socrates was more threatening to the repressive oligarchy of the "Thirty Tyrants" (404-403 B.C.E.) than to the tolerant, freedom-loving democrats. The freedom accorded by what Socrates considered an inferior regime was necessary to his philosophizing: But when he himself designed a just regime in Plato's *Republic*, Socrates did not hesitate to censor traditional literature in order to keep corrupting influences from the young. Similarly, the tight oligarchic regime tried to silence Socrates by issuing a decree against teaching "the art of debate."

The oligarchy was overthrown, but Socrates had offended democrats as well, both individually and because he was hardly more sympathetic to democracy than to oligarchy. Both regimes failed to meet both Socrates' personal moral standards and his definition of justice. Finally, a group of democrats charged him with having undermined Athenian traditions. His "new gods" were certainly his personal deity, and perhaps also his moral "Ideas." He "corrupted the young" by critically examining both those in authority and the god-giving poets. He defended himself characteristically, saying that while he honored the Athenians his first duty was to the god, to continue his divine/moral mission. After he was convicted, he was executed by poison.

See also Athens, ancient; Death; Democracy; Morality; Plato.

Solzhenitsyn, Aleksandr

BORN: December 11, 1918, Kislovodsk, Soviet Union
IDENTIFICATION: Russian author and political dissident
SIGNIFICANCE: Solzhenitsyn's published criticisms of the Soviet system made him a powerful political dissident and resulted in his being exiled by the government

Solzhenitsyn achieved world renown as a writer of epic novels. His writings depict the struggle of humanity against modern totalitarianism. His criticism of the Soviet system under which he lived resulted in his censorship, repression, and exile. A facetious comment about Joseph Stalin that he made in a private letter in 1945 led to his arrest and imprisonment in a corrective labor camp. Only after Stalin's death in 1953 was he given his freedom. Solzhenitsyn's prison experience provided the material for his novella *One Day in the Life of Ivan Denisovich* (1962), which Stalin's successor, Nikita Khrushchev, permitted to be published. This gripping exposé of life in the Soviet labor camps made Solzhenitsyn a celebrity at home and abroad. At the same time, however, it brought criticism from conservatives in the Soviet Union who opposed the cultural "thaw" that permitted writers to examine previously forbidden subjects.

Following Khrushchev's ouster in 1964, Leonid Brezhnev's regime embarked upon a policy of political and cultural repression. In that atmosphere Solzhenitsyn became even more critical of the Soviet regime, which retaliated by prohibiting publication of his writing and harassing him. Solzhenitsyn created a sensation in May, 1967, when he made an impassioned public condemnation of censorship in the Soviet Union in an open letter to the Fourth Congress of Soviet Writers.

Although Solzhenitsyn's novels could not legally be published in his own country, they were widely read as *samizdat*, a form of publication by means of typed reproduction circulated to an underground readership. Copies of his novels *The First Circle* (1968) and *Cancer Ward* (1968) were smuggled to Europe, where they were published without the author's permission. In 1970 Solzhenitsyn won the Nobel Prize in Literature. When Soviet authorities refused to publish his novel *August 1914* (1972), Solzhenitsyn authorized its publication abroad. Angered, the Soviet government intensified its pressure on him, going so far as to seize copies of his writings. Soviet authorities even threatened his life and banned him from Moscow. The last straw for Soviet authorities was the publication abroad of parts of Solzhenitsyn's monumental history of Soviet labor camps, *The Gulag Archipelago* (1974-1978).

In February, 1974, Solzhenitsyn was arrested and summarily sent into exile. He initially settled in Switzerland, where he did research for his novel *Lenin in Zurich* (1976). Seeking greater privacy, he moved to the rural town of Cavendish, Vermont, in the United States in 1976. Occasionally he ventured out of Cavendish to lecture on the excesses of democracy and the evils of communism. His criticism of materialism and lack of spirituality in the West made Solzhenitsyn a controversial figure in the West, as well as in the Soviet Union.

With the collapse of the Soviet Union in 1991, Solzhenitsyn was free to return to his native land, which he did in May, 1994. On returning to Russia, he described his country as a land "tortured, stunned, altered beyond recognition." He took on the mission of an elder statesman seeking to warn his countrymen of the flaws of its fledgling democracy. Many Russians found his prescriptions for simplicity and honesty to be anachronistic, but few denied his unique moral authority.

See also Communism; Gorbachev, Mikhail; Intellectual freedom; Pasternak, Boris; Russia; Sakharov, Andrei; Soviet Union; Stalin, Joseph; Yevtushenko, Yevgeny Aleksandrovich.

Son of Sam laws

DEFINITION: Laws that seek to prevent criminal defendants from profiting from their crimes

SIGNIFICANCE: This restriction on the speech of criminal defendants has been declared unconstitutional by the U.S. Supreme Court

In 1977 David Berkowitz committed a series of brutal murders and was ultimately apprehended and found mentally incompetent to stand trial in New York. He became known as Son of Sam, because of conversations he claimed to have had with Sam, his spiritual father. Sam communicated with Berkowitz through the barking of a dog. When the New York legislature discovered that Berkowitz's notoriety seemed poised to make him rich from the sale of his memoirs, it responded by enacting its Son of Sam law. The law required convicted criminals to turn over the proceeds of any sale of their stories to the state, to be used to compensate the victims of the criminals' crime. Ironically, although the law was later amended to cover accused as well as convicted criminal defendants, it did not

apply to Berkowitz, who, having been declared mentally incompetent, was never convicted of his serial murders. Berkowitz apparently paid his share of royalties from a book about his crimes to his victims or their estates.

In 1991 the U.S. Supreme Court held in *Simon & Schuster, Inc. v. Members of the New York State Crime Victims Board* that New York's law violated the guarantee of freedom of speech by singling out expressive activity for a special burden. Faced with this discrimination against particular speech, the Court found that a law imposing such a discrimination could survive constitutional challenge only if there was a compelling state interest for the law and the law was narrowly tailored to serve that interest. The Court agreed that the state did in fact have a compelling interest in compensating victims of crimes and in seeing that criminals did not profit from their crimes. The Court insisted that New York's law restricted more speech than necessary, since it could be construed to apply to any works in which the criminal defendant made reference to a crime, no matter how inconsequential the reference might be in the context of the whole work. By the law's reasoning, Saint Augustine could be prevented from earning royalties on his *Confessions* (c. 400 C.E.) because he recounts there his childhood crime of stealing pears from a neighbor's tree.

The ruling against New York's Son of Sam law has not ended the issue of whether the participants in criminal proceedings can be stripped of profits made as a result of selling the stories of their participation to the highest bidder. California legislators, for example, in the face of enormous publicity surrounding the O. J. Simpson trial, enacted legislation that made it a misdemeanor for jurors or witnesses to receive compensation for providing information relating to a criminal case within specified time periods. A federal district judge declared the law unconstitutional in August, 1995.

See also Criminal trials; Simpson, O. J., case.

South Africa

DESCRIPTION: Independent republic occupying most of the southern portion of Africa

SIGNIFICANCE: Government censorship pervaded South African life through the late twentieth century until the dissolution of apartheid and ensuing advent of universal democracy in the 1990's brought about a significant reversal

To understand the repressive government that ruled South Africa from 1948, when apartheid was officially enacted to keep the races separate, until the early 1990's, one must understand the racial composition of the country. Black Africans representing a dozen language groups constitute 75.2 percent of a population that numbered about thirty-nine million by 1991. Whites account for 13.6 percent, slightly more than five million residents, with 8.6 percent being of mixed race. Asians comprise the remaining 2.6 percent.

While apartheid was in effect, the largest portion of the white population lived near the centers of large urban areas, whereas blacks were restricted by law to ten black homelands and to specified urban neighborhoods, forcing them to live great distances from their work. Educational facilities for blacks were far inferior to those for whites.

Despite their numbers, blacks were permitted to own only 13 percent of the land under legislation passed in 1936 to replace the already restrictive Native Lands Acts of 1913. The official establishment of the ten black homelands in 1970 further restricted the freedom of the black populace.

Imprisonment of Nelson Mandela. Black attorney Nelson Mandela joined the African National Congress (ANC) in 1944, and was active in the organization until 1962, when he was arrested and sentenced to a five-year prison term. In 1964, while serving this initial sentence, he was tried and convicted of treason and sabotage, which carried a life sentence. Mandela served twenty-nine years in prison before South Africa's president F. W. de Klerk, bowing to world-wide protests about Mandela's persecution, ordered him released in 1991. Immediately upon his release, Mandela resumed his political activity and became a highly visible international personage. He shared the 1993 Nobel Peace Prize with de Klerk in 1993 and was elected South Africa's first black president in 1994.

Under de Klerk South Africa enacted a new constitution, among the most liberal in the world, protecting not only freedom of speech and assembly, but also outlawing racial discrimination and specifically banning discrimination based on sexual orientation, thereby making it the only developed nation specifically to protect the civil rights of gays and lesbians.

Book Banning and Thought Control. By the time South Africa banned apartheid, more than a hundred of its laws suppressed freedom of the press. The country had enacted a Suppression of Communism Act prohibiting the publication or other distribution of material produced by members of the Communist Party or of any other organization designated subversive by the central government. Such people were banned from public gatherings as well.

This legislation was clearly racist because it effectively muzzled anyone who advocated the liberation of the African majority in the country, including most African writers of note. Members of the ANC were, under such laws, prevented from working publicly for the changes that would eventually outlaw apartheid.

Under South Africa's Customs and Excise Act, the importation of indecent, obscene materials or those otherwise objectionable in the eyes of the government was illegal. The Publications and Entertainments Act of 1963 banned the production and publication of objectionable materials within South Africa, while the amended Publications Act of 1986 extended the ban beyond publications to film, art, sculpture, and all forms of entertainment.

Banning was based on five essential criteria, any one of which was considered grounds for listing a given work in the *Government Gazette*, which was tantamount to banning. Works were prohibited if they were considered obscene, indecent, or harmful to public morals (as defined by those who did the banning), if they were considered blasphemous or were

One of the greatest negotiated political revolutions in modern history elevated Nelson Mandela from the status of "banned" prison convict to victorious candidate for president of South Africa in free elections in 1994. (AP/Wide World Photos)

offensive to any religious group, if they aimed any ridicule at white South Africa, if they impaired relations between segments of the country's people, or if they risked compromising public safety or national security.

Before the end of apartheid, banning was accomplished through the Publications Control Board and the Publications Appeal Board, both agencies of the white, minority government. The Appeals Board encouraged South African writers and their publishers to submit manuscripts for review prior to publication. Book store personnel were also encouraged to report to the Board materials that they deemed objectionable.

Under these repressive mandates, South Africans were officially kept from reading any materials that questioned apartheid, that explained communism or depicted societies in which it was practiced, that criticized racism, or that questioned the validity of colonialism. Under the ban, more than eighteen thousand titles were specifically prohibited from distribution in South Africa.

Nevertheless, during this period, fugitive books entered the country and were distributed clandestinely, perhaps hastening the cessation of book banning and other such repressive acts. Thought control in South Africa, however, extended far beyond book banning and affected the lives of every South African.

Censorship Versus Control. During the repressive era that officially ended with the abolition of apartheid in 1992, the South African government denied practicing censorship, contending rather that it practiced control of those media that most affected the public welfare and safety and that protected national security. Despite such protestations, freedom of the press was denied for nearly fifty years in South Africa and all of the arts endured under the ever-present threat of oppression.

Such oppression in South Africa has a long history. As early as 1914, the Riotous Assemblies Act gave the president the power to forbid the publication of any materials that might cause hostility between blacks and Europeans. This act required no proof of intent on the parts of the accused. The amended version of it in 1956 criminalized publicizing information about any assembly that was banned. In 1927 the Bantu Administration Act made it illegal for anyone to utter words or commit acts that might engender antagonism between the races.

The 1950's and 1960's. The Suppression of Communism Act of 1950 worked hand-in-hand with other repressive acts of censorship in South Africa. This act authorized the president to ban from the nation any person thought to espouse communist doctrine and to ban publication of materials by such people. The act, from which there was no appeal, allowed the government to suppress the materials of dead, as well as living, people with communist leanings. It banned such South Africans from writing for publication in places other than South Africa.

The Criminal Law Amendment Act of 1953—which was aimed directly at the ANC—criminalized actions that encouraged others to break existing laws. In the same year, the Public Safety Act declared a state of emergency that permitted the executive banning of any newspaper in the country. In another legislative measure aimed at the ANC, the Official Secrets Act of 1956 made it illegal to publish material relating to the military, the police, or the Bureau of State Security (BOSS). This act was followed in 1959 by the Prisons Act, which banned the publication of anything about prisoners or the administration of prisons that had not been previously approved by the commissioner of prisons.

The Extension of the University Education Act in the same year established separate tribal colleges for blacks and forbade the circulation of student publications not previously approved by the rector. The act also eschewed students' speaking to the media without similar approval.

In 1963 the Entertainment Act, later strengthened by the Publications Act of 1974, provided for a Board of Censors to monitor films and advertising and to ban imported as well as domestic materials considered politically controversial. The Publications and Entertainments Act of 1963 listed ninety-eight examples of materials the government considered objectionable. The Customs Act of 1964 gave the government full power to ban the importation of materials it thought to be objectionable in any way. The Defense Amendment Act of 1967 prohibited, in the name of national security, the publication of any material that provided information about the South African armed forces. By the end of the decade, the General Law Amendment Act of 1969 empowered the minister of justice to declare any geographical area officially protected, thereby prohibiting the press from referring to it in any way.

The BOSS Act of 1969 made illegal communications about any personnel of the Bureau of State Security or any of its detainees. Under this law, evidence in a legal case involving BOSS was banned from trials no matter how important it was to a defendant's case.

Last Decades of Apartheid. Repressive laws continued to be enacted as apartheid began crumbling as an institution and as South Africa's racial inequalities attracted world-wide notoriety. The Newspaper and Imprint Registration Act of 1971 forced all newspapers to make known their intended natures and contents and to provide personal information about their editors and staffs. They also were forced to make indemnity against the possibility that their staffs would breech the Suppression of Communism Act. The Internal Security Act of 1982 consolidated most of the security laws existing in South Africa. It specifically addressed publications government authorities thought subversive or potentially disruptive.

On June 12, 1986, the South African government declared a state of emergency against newspapers that threatened the violent overthrow of the state. A proclamation extended this state of emergency in 1987. A new Board of Censors was appointed to control the newspapers. Emergency regulations passed in 1986 and 1987 prohibited journalists from covering scenes of unrest or restricted gatherings.

Fall of Apartheid. In 1989 politically moderate F. W. de Klerk was elected president of South Africa, serving in that position until 1994. Within three years he led the parliament to abolish all laws that supported apartheid, thereby effectively ending this blight on South Africa's world image and paving the way for the enfranchisement of blacks. In March, 1992, two-thirds of the electorate voted for South Africa to draft a new constitution that would extend the franchise to black Africans, who first voted in a presidential election in 1994, electing Nelson Mandela to the presidency.

South Africa's new constitution is a model of political liberalism. Ironically, this country that banned television until 1976 is now a leader in producing television sitcoms that satirize racial problems, much as Norman Lear's *All in the Family* did in the United States in the 1970's.   —*R. Baird Shuman*

See also Books and obscenity law; Free speech; Intellectual freedom; Language laws; Lear, Norman; Literature; Mandela, Nelson; Military censorship; Race; Zimbabwe.

BIBLIOGRAPHY

South Africa: Human Rights Handbook 1992, edited by Neil Boister and Kevin Ferguson-Brown (New York: Oxford University Press, 1994), provides the most current account of the fall of apartheid in South Africa and the changes following its fall. Ike Rosmarin's *South Africa* (New York: Marshall Cavendish, 1994) is brief but covers the high points well, as does Claudia Canesso's *South Africa* (New York: Chelsea House, 1989), which addresses political problems still unresolved at the time of her writing. T. R. H. Davenport's *South Africa: A Modern History* (4th ed. Toronto: University of Toronto Press, 1991) is a standard work on South Africa and is extensive. Marina Ottaway's *South Africa: The Struggle for a New Order* (Washington, D.C.: Brookings Institution, 1993) serves to update Davenport's book in this rapidly changing political environment. Robert M. Price's *The Apartheid State in Crisis: Political Transformation in South Africa, 1975-1990* (New York: Oxford University Press, 1991) demonstrates well the economic implications of apartheid.

South America

DESCRIPTION: Western Hemisphere continent containing more than twenty independent nations

SIGNIFICANCE: Many of the independent countries of South America have retained the legacy of government and church control over information as a way to ensure uniformity of thought and action

The people of South America have experienced censorship in many forms over the centuries. Beginning with the Incas, and continuing through the colonial period into the national era of the nineteenth and twentieth centuries, those who have held ecclesiastical or political power have tried to control freedom of expression. While the form of censorship has changed, the goal has not: to enforce orthodoxy. Pluralism has not often been recognized as a desirable goal in South America, and opposition has rarely been loyal to established institutions. As a result, church and state have exercised their powers to limit freedom of speech, press, radio, film, and television.

Precolonial and Colonial Periods. During the fifteenth century the Incas, with their capital in Cuzco, high in the Andes, began to conquer most of the peoples of what became modern Peru, Ecuador, and portions of Bolivia, Chile, and Argentina. Two policies enforced by Inca rulers had the effect of limiting the actions and speech of the conquered peoples. The first of these policies was that of resettlement. Those defeated by the Inca were removed from their towns and villages and resettled in other parts of the empire. The goal was to destroy the identity of conquered tribes so that they would not rebel and would eventually blend with other peoples under Inca rule. The second policy assisted in this effort by banning local languages and enforcing the Inca language, Quechua, as the official language of the empire.

When the Spanish arrived and began their conquest of the Inca Empire in the 1530's, their goals were to enlarge their king's domains and to bring the Native Americans into the Christian church. When the Inca capital of Cuzco was captured, Inca temples were pulled down and churches constructed on their sites, symbolizing the suppression of earlier religious beliefs by Christianity. Through methods that included loving guidance and harsh punishments, natives were prohibited from worshiping their gods and instructed in Christian beliefs.

Spanish settlers were restricted by both the state and the church from obtaining printed material thought to be sinful or corrupt. The royal decree of April 4, 1531, prohibited the importation to the Indies of all romances and books other than those of a religious or moral nature. The Inquisition and the *Casa de Contratacion*, or Board of Trade, in Seville, were responsible for judging the value of written works sent to Spain's colonies. Many prohibited works reached the Americas, however, because oversight was lax. During the period of the Enlightenment in the eighteenth century, most of the works of the French philosophes, although banned, were readily obtainable in the Americas, and often found in the libraries of church or government officials. Many of these works praised individual liberties and were critical of censorship. While the writings of Thomas Jefferson and Thomas Paine were banned by the government because of their revolutionary nature, they too could be found throughout South America, and influenced leaders of the independence movements.

Nineteenth Century. South American countries freed themselves from Spain in the early nineteenth century, in most places, through wars of liberation. In the aftermath of independence, conflicts erupted among military leaders, called caudillos, who vied for control of the state, and governments were faced with armed opposition. In this atmosphere, newspapers were most often published for their polemics rather than news, and the dictators responded harshly to their critics. Perhaps one of the most effective and colorful such dictators was the Argentine, Juan Manuel de Rosas who, between 1835 and 1852, established a method of control over the population that embodied censorship and terror. Official documents were printed on government stationary which had in its letterhead a call for death to the Unitarist opposition. A secret police enforced the dictator's will through assassinations, leaving victims in the street with their throat cut as an animal in the slaughterhouse. Rosas also used symbolism to control opposition. Anything blue, the color of the Unitarists, was prohibited in public. Argentines, to show their loyalty to Rosas, had to wear red ribbons and hang red banners from their homes or stores. Liberty, in Rosas mind, led to unrestricted license, so the only education permitted was controlled by the church, and the press was restricted.

Nations of South America

The use of the press as a partisan tool, however, was not restricted to dictators. Politicians in the nineteenth century regarded newspaper editors and reporters as purveyors of an ideological point of view rather than objective journalists. The great statesman and president of Argentina, Domingo Faustino Sarmiento, used the presses under his control to vilify his enemies.

Colombia's president in the early 1800's, and hero of the independence movement, Francisco de Paula Santander, attempted to enact liberal legislation to restrict the power of the church. However, he also put pressure on the publisher of a liberal newspaper to cease publication after it had called for the suppression of all monasteries and caused the president political embarrassment.

Liberal regimes during the nineteenth century in Colombia passed laws to abolish libel and do away with restrictions on the free exchange of ideas in printed form. The Constitution of 1853, written by the liberals, abolished religious censorship, and the Constitution of 1863, another liberal document, abolished all restrictions on the freedom of speech. The Conservative Party, however, gained control of the government and, toward the end of the nineteenth century, began to silence opposition newspapers through occasional crackdowns. The Roman Catholic church in Colombia favored the Conservative Party and at times threatened excommunication or other religious penalties to those who voted for, or even read the newspapers printed by, the Liberal Party or dissident Conservatives.

Twentieth Century. Many South American countries have endured dictatorships and repressive military regimes during the twentieth century. One of the most repressive military regimes in the twentieth century was that of General Augusto Pinochet who headed the junta that overthrew President Salvador Allende in Chile in 1973. The Chilean military rounded up thousands, tortured and killed many hundreds, and kept political prisoners in jail for years. Many Chileans fled into exile in the face of Draconian measures.

The government of Juan Perón in Argentina attacked newspapers which opposed his government. In 1951, after denying sufficient newsprint for the paper to be published, *La Prensa*, the most prestigious daily newspaper in Buenos Aires, was taken over by state-dominated unions. The government also banned foreign journals which were critical of Perón. Another method of stopping newspapers was employed by conservatives in Bogota, Colombia, in the 1970's. There, the liberal newspaper *El Periodico* was punished for its political views by restricting its revenues. This was accomplished not by the government itself, but through private citizens who withheld their advertising to silence the newspaper.

Labor unions and working class organizations have often been limited in their activities and their freedom of expression. At the beginning of the twentieth century strikes invariably led to police or army intervention on behalf of employers. Workers by law were not permitted to organize or to strike and their press was censored or seized. *La Protesta*, the anarchist daily in Argentina, was often the target of police.

In Brazil, the 1937 constitution establishing the *Estado Novo*, or corporate New State, under Getulio Vargas banned all strikes, and union activity was more tightly controlled by the government. Employees were forbidden from owning newspapers, magazines, or radio stations. In addition, a Department of Press and Propaganda was created to censor newspapers.

In 1964 a military coup ended civilian government in Brazil for nearly two decades. Military governments passed laws that restricted political expression as well as freedom of the press. In 1968 the government of Artur de Costa e Silva tightened press censorship and suspended the right of habeas corpus for those accused of political crimes through Institutional Act Number 5. This led to the suspension of political rights for 294 people, among them congressional deputies, mayors, and journalists. Opposition was not permitted, and in 1973 the prestigious daily newspaper in Rio de Janeiro, *Jornal do Brasil*, was closed by the military government. In 1979 a National Security Law established heavy penalties for criticizing the government: thirteen years in prison for "subversive propaganda." In the face of such sustained pressures, much of the media in Brazil managed to survive only through self-censorship, avoiding topics that were sure to produce a reaction by the government.

Media Censorship. By the mid-twentieth century South American governments had to contend with more than newspapers, and acted to control broadcast media. Television presented a powerful way to inform or entertain as well as a means of government propaganda. To counter widespread opposition to the military regime in Brazil, government-controlled radio and television spread propaganda about the successes of the regime. Other countries passed legislation to license broadcast media and in some cases, to nationalize it. In Argentina, military-dominated governments of the late 1930's and early 1940's censored radio stations by denying them license renewal, and Perón's regime would eventually nationalize the industry, making all those who worked in broadcasting employees of the state. The Falcao Law in Brazil, in force for the elections of 1978 and 1982, restricted access to the media by political parties for two months prior to elections. In Colombia, where democratic regimes vied for power in relatively free elections, the government reserved the right to censor telecommunications during what it considered to be periods of national emergency. A Statute for the Defense of Democracy and amendments to the right of habeas corpus were enacted in 1988, at the height of the conflict with the drug cartels, to maintain public order in Colombia.

Films and performing arts have also been censored in South American countries. *The Last Temptation of Christ* could not be shown in movie theaters in Colombia because of church opposition. In Argentina, *Last Tango in Paris* was prohibited as pornographic, and *Jesus Christ Superstar* was not shown after a bomb went off outside one theater. The opera *Bomarzo* by the world-famous Argentine composer Alberto Ginastera, premiered in Washington, D.C., because it was forbidden to be performed in Argentina by the military government.

In the last decade of the twentieth century most South American nations achieved democratically elected regimes, which respect the rights of their citizens to a free press and expression of ideas. Nevertheless, the tradition of government control and censorship, especially in times of conflict, remains.

—*James A. Baer*

See also Argentina; Brazil; Central America; Chile; Cuba; Mexico; Spanish Empire; Spanish Inquisition; Timerman, Jacobo.

BIBLIOGRAPHY

C. H. Haring, *The Spanish Empire in America* (New York: Harcourt, Brace & World, 1963), is a classic account of Spanish America, with chapters on the church, education, and scholarship. David Bushnell, *The Making of Modern Colombia: A Nation in Spite of Itself* (Berkeley: University of California Press, 1993), is a clear history of Colombia that includes discussion of the press, films, literature, and music. Mark Falcoff's *Modern Chile, 1970-1989: A Critical History* (New Brunswick, N.J.: Transaction Publishers, 1989) analyzes Chile's transformation from democracy to dictatorship under Salvador Allende and the Augusto Pinochet. Jacobo Timerman, *Prisoner Without a Name, Cell Without a Number* (New York: Knopf, 1981), is the memoir of an Argentine publisher who was imprisoned and tortured by Argentina's military regime during the 1970's.

Southern, Terry

BORN: May 1, 1926, Alvaredo, Texas
DIED: October 29, 1995, New York, New York
IDENTIFICATION: American novelist and screenwriter
SIGNIFICANCE: Southern's satirical writings mocked pornography, attacked religious complacency, and explored fascist tendencies in the United States

One of Southern's first novels, *Candy*, parodies Voltaire's *Candide*; it was not published until 1959 because publishers were leery of its sexually explicit material. After it was published *The New York Times* refused even to review it; not until 1965 did the newspaper lift its self-imposed ban on advertising the book. In Great Britain *Candy* was issued in a shorter version that omitted several sexually graphic passages. These changes were prompted by the experience that a British publisher had with Hubert Selby, Jr.'s *Last Exit to Brooklyn*, which a 1967 British court ruled obscene (the ruling was overturned in 1968). In 1967, however, American publishers were concerned about possible British censorship. The situation in France was simultaneously more serious and more ludicrous. After *Candy* was banned as indecent by the French government, its Parisian publisher changed the book's title in order to resume publication: The new title was *Lollipop* (1962).

Southern's other books were less overtly censored. His novels *The Magic Christian* (1960), later transformed into a considerably tamer film, and *Blue Movie* (1970) offended the religious right and the right-wing media watchers, who feared the influence of film. Informal but organized efforts to keep these novels off library shelves and out of bookstores limited their reading audiences.

Southern was also interested in making films, as the story of *Blue Movie* suggests (the novel is about a serious filmmaker who makes an explicitly pornographic film). While he continued to write short stories and novels, he turned his attention to screenwriting. His film credits include *The Loved One* (1965), an adaptation of novelist Evelyn Waugh's satire on the

Among Terry Southern's screenplay credits is the 1969 cult film Easy Rider, *whose script earned an Academy Award nomination.* (Arkent Archive)

American funeral industry; *Easy Rider* (1969), the classic road/buddy film; *The End of the Road* (1969), an adaptation of John Barth's savage academic novel; and *Dr. Strangelove, or, How I Learned to Stop Worrying and Love the Bomb* (1964), an antiwar film suggesting American fascist tendencies. Of these films, only *Dr. Strangelove* received much criticism, not because of its quality, but because of its liberal stance on the Cold War. Southern was a satirist whose work was not understood or appreciated by American conservatives.

See also Abridgment; *Last Exit to Brooklyn*; *New York Times, The*; Voltaire.

Soviet secret cities

DEFINITION: Militarily sensitive cities in the Soviet Union whose existence was not officially disclosed

SIGNIFICANCE: The official hiding of entire cities demonstrates the magnitude of the Soviet leadership's obsessive secrecy and the extent of its power

In the early years of the Soviet Union, government leadership was especially anxious about its susceptibility to internal and external enemies. Joseph Stalin in particular raised official paranoia to unprecedented heights. One manifestation of that paranoia was obsessive official secrecy. This resulted in, among other things, the creation of secret cities in the Soviet Union.

Secret cities were communities built around nuclear research facilities and other sensitive weapons production plants. The regime created these towns in remote areas, relocating people to work and live there, building infrastructure, and otherwise developing self-sufficient communities. These communities were ringed with electrified, barbed-wire fences with watchtowers and guards. Some facilities and housing were even built underground. The secret cities were conceived by the Soviet Secret police and placed under the formal control of the euphemistically named Ministry for Medium-Machine Building. Comings and goings were strictly controlled. These secret cities were neither depicted on public maps nor officially acknowledged to exist. Even among the governmental elites, the secret cities were called by their code names.

The most valuable workers within the secret cities were physicists and other scientists who developed new technologies for nuclear, chemical, and biological weapons. Although the secrecy and security limited their movements, these workers enjoyed reasonably good living conditions. Far more numerous were the workers at production facilities, a large portion of whom were drawn from nearby prison camps. The secret cities thus could be considered part of the system of labor camps developed by Stalin.

With the collapse of the Soviet Union in 1991, the secret cities were acknowledged and identified. They were no longer supplied with slave labor, their budgets were cut, and the demand for their work slackened with the signing of new arms control agreements. They have been burdened with the monumental environmental problems that mounted during the Soviet period. Many of the cities were sites of then-unacknowledged nuclear tests and accidents. Others must contend with poisoned water tables and leaking nuclear storage facilities. Much of the research and some of the production continues. The secret cities have assumed a status closer to the old Soviet closed cities, whose existence was acknowledged but access to which was restricted. The restrictions may ultimately become obsolete. With the termination of labor camp coercion and the lack of attractive salaries, few Russians are volunteering for employment at the former secret cities.

See also Fear; Nuclear research and testing; Russia; Soviet Union; Stalin, Joseph.

Soviet Union

DESCRIPTION: Communist state that controlled the former Russian Empire from 1917 until its dissolution in the early 1990's

SIGNIFICANCE: Under the totalitarian leadership of the communist regime, censorship of all aspects of cultural and intellectual life thoroughly stifled creativity and freedom of expression

The totalitarian regime established in the Soviet Union in 1917 was an autocratic system which empowered the leadership to employ any methods necessary to create an ideologically driven movement, the purpose of which was the complete reconstruction of society. In such a political system every aspect of society was placed under absolute control. From the inception of the Soviet State, culture would be required to serve politics, to strengthen the dictatorial system, and to assist the masses in thinking and feeling "correctly."

In the V. I. Lenin years, from 1917-1924, Soviet culture experienced little repression or censorship. The absence of an official policy relating to culture was the result of the chaos prevailing at that time, as the Bolshevik elites were struggling to establish their control. Therefore, a reasonably liberal atmosphere permeated the cultural arena.

Stalin Era. With the advent of the Joseph Stalin era, marked by the total consolidation of power in the hands of the dictator, a "revolution from above" was initiated. The inauguration of five-year plans, forced collectivization, and other restructuring of society began in 1929. Such transformations required tighter controls and censorship on intellectual activity. Independence of thought, individuality, creativity, criticism of Communist Party ideology, and nonconformity were no longer to be permitted.

Joseph Stalin's principal target in achieving complete control over the minds of the Soviet peoples was the intelligentsia. They were compelled to serve the party by becoming "engineers of the human soul," by spreading the Leninist-Stalinist dogma, and by encouraging blind obedience to the party and the state.

That he might assert absolute control over all aspects of literature, Stalin created a single writers' union under the direction of the state. In 1934 the First Congress of Soviet Writers was convened. The delegates heard for the first time of the new obligatory style for literature, Socialist Realism. Soviet writers were required to nationalize literature, to swear an oath of loyalty to the party, state, and Stalin. A new age of party-oriented literature was born. All writers were to chant the glories of Stalin, to extol the successes of the five-year plans, to praise the loyalty and heroism of the peasants on the

NATIONS OF THE FORMER SOVIET UNION

collective farms and the city workers whose fierce dedication and hard work were assisting in the preserving of Mother Russia. Soviet culture was to become a weapon used by party elites to propagandize, motivate, and stir the workers. Socialist Realism stifled true artistic and literary genius.

The era of the Great Purges, 1935-1938, decimated the intelligentsia. In excess of six hundred writers vanished during this period. Labeled as "enemies of the people," denounced by friends as well as enemies, they lived in terror, awaiting arrest. One such victim was Osip Mandelstam, a poet of Jewish birth, who was considered one of the most brilliant authors of that era. Accused of "distorting reality" by decrying Stalin's evils, he was arrested and later died in a labor camp.

Every form of communication in the Soviet Union fell under the auspices of party control. The war against nonconformity included all newspapers, magazines, pamphlets, journals, music, radio broadcasts, education, and the cinema. They were ordered to espouse the party line. Ideas and works from the West were likewise blacklisted as the Soviet Union became increasingly isolated from any infusion of new ideas.

The Central Committee of the Communist Party announced in its own newspaper, *Culture & Life*, that every aspect of cultural activity of the party and state was mandated to serve the communist education of the people. Typical of party censorship in the field of music was the case against an opera by Dmitri Shostakovich. After viewing a performance, Stalin branded it "repulsive, obscene and raucous." In the wake of that criticism, further works by the composer were also denounced, virtually destroying his career. His fate became an ominous warning to all other composers and artists that nonconformity could be dangerous and life-threatening.

Following World War II, the fear of Western "contamination" of Soviet subjects became an obsession of Stalin. That Western ideas and influences might be permeating the country was to be an excuse for a new ideological offensive. This campaign, under the leadership of Andrei Zhdanov was known as Zhdanovshchina. Two of the nation's most prominent writers, Anna Akhmatova and Mikhail Zoshchenko, were singled out as "scum of the literary world." The composers Sergei Prokofiev and Shostakovich had their music branded as "too bourgeois." The Zhdanov era, typified by anti-intellectualism, was a major victory for Stalin and the party, destroying anyone with talent and creativity and forcing culture to serve the party.

Khrushchev Era. Soviet control and censorship in the post-Stalin regimes of Nikita Khrushchev and Leonid Brezhnev vacillated between "thaws" and repression. However, Socialist Realism remained the policy as both leaders fought against dissidents. In what initially appeared to be a more liberal, open atmosphere in Khrushchev's early years, Boris Pasternak submitted the novel *Doctor Zhivago* (1957) for publication in Moscow. Although published in the West, his book was not allowed to be printed in the Soviet Union.

In 1962 Khrushchev became embroiled in the Cuban Missile Crisis and the Sino-Soviet clash. Combined with mounting economic crises, these issues brought about a new policy of "ideological purity" which meant once again control and censorship.

Brezhnev Era. Upon Khrushchev's fall from power in 1964, Brezhnev continued the party policy of complete cultural control and absolute inflexible conformity. In response, a counterculture gradually appeared. Samizdat, or self-publication, meant writings were being produced on personal typewriters and copying machines and circulated surreptitiously by hand. Tamizdat were writings published outside the Soviet Union and then sneaked back into the Soviet Union. By these methods, the intellectuals could cheat the censor, while becoming internationally renowned.

Not all were successful in evading detection even when using pseudonyms. Andrei Siniavski and Yuli Daniel, young writers and critics, were arrested in 1965 and accused under what would become the most frequently used section of the Criminal Code, article 70, for disseminating "slanderous" and "defamatory" lies regarding the Soviet Union. Both were sentenced to years of forced labor. Joseph Brodsky, a poet, was convicted as a "parasite," or not being employed, a common allegation against writers.

Andrei Sakharov organized the Human Rights Movement in 1970 to fight against Party policies that contravened individual rights guaranteed not only by the Soviet constitution but also by covenants in international law to which the Soviet Union was a signatory. In the wake of protests by intellectuals spurred on by this movement, a major crackdown occurred. Sakharov was sent into internal exile in Gorky.

Yet dissent continued to grow as government repression and censorship increased. *The Chronicle of Current Events*, a samizdat pamphlet publication, kept the Soviet public aware of arrests, exiles, imprisonments, and court proceedings.

Aleksandr Solzhenitsyn, author of the *Gulag Archipelago* (1975), was arrested and sentenced for his works describing Soviet life in the labor camps. Once his books were published in the West, the party intensified its campaign against him. After being arrested and charged with treason in 1974, he was sent into involuntary exile to the West.

The Soviet Union's 1961 penal code declared that "dissemination of fabrications discrediting the Soviet State" was to be treated as a crime. This law made it simpler to arrest dissidents as criminals. For those who represented the most serious threat to the system there was a new and more insidious punishment—the mental hospital. Soviet psychiatrists, under state control, diagnosed dissidents with a new disorder—"creeping schizophrenia." *—LaRae Larkin*

See also Communism; Gorbachev, Mikhail; Lenin, Vladimir Ilich; Pasternak, Boris; Russia; Sakharov, Andrei; Socialist Realism; Soviet Union; Stalin, Joseph; Trotsky, Leon; Yevtushenko, Yevgeny Aleksandrovich; Zhdanov, Andrei.

BIBLIOGRAPHY

Dmitrii Volkogonov, *Lenin: A New Biography* (New York: Free Press, 1994), a biographical account of Lenin's rise to power, includes new materials from the national archives. Studies of the Stalin era drawing on post-glasnost period evidence include Robert Conquest, *The Great Terror: A Reassessment* (New York: Oxford University Press, 1990); Walter Laqueur, *Stalin: The Glasnost Revelations* (New York: Charles Scribner's Sons, 1990); and Roy Medvedev, *Let History Judge: The Origins and Consequences of Stalinism*, ed. and trans. by George Shriver (New York: Columbia University Press, 1989). The last is by a Soviet Marxist. Dmitrii Volkogonov, *Stalin: Triumph and Tragedy* (New York: Grove Weidenfeld, 1991), by the chairman of the Soviet archives, draws on documents from the Central Party, Supreme Court, Ministry of Defense, and Armed Forces General Staff. Aleksandr Solzhenitsyn's *The Gulag Archipelago* (New York: Harper & Row, 1975) chronicles thousands of incidents and personal histories from the Soviet Gulag system. A comprehensive biography of Khrushchev's public life written with the aid of numerous members of his family can be found in Roy Medvedev's *Khrushchev* (Garden City, N.Y.: Anchor Press/Doubleday, 1983). Mikhail Geller and Aleksandr M. Nekrich, *Utopia in Power* (New York: Summit Books, 1986) is a comprehensive survey of cultural and political trends throughout the history of the Soviet Union.

Soyinka, Wole

BORN: July 13, 1934, Abeokuta, Nigeria

IDENTIFICATION: Nigerian writer and Nobel Prize winner

SIGNIFICANCE: Nigeria's foremost advocate of human rights and artistic expression, Soyinka was persecuted by his own government

As a playwright and poet, Soyinka developed his voice and vision during Nigeria's most politically turbulent period, and he became the first black African to be awarded the Nobel Prize in Literature, in 1986. Throughout his career, Soyinka worked as both an artist and political activist, meshing the concerns of an emerging postcolonial Africa with authentic traditions and voices in Nigeria.

Soyinka's political stance shifted continually between the classroom and the theater, while his work often focused on the political corruption surrounding the slow emergence of Nigerian democracy. Plays such as *The Trials of Brother Jero* (1960) and *The Lion and the Jewel* (1960) placed Soyinka in opposition to the first national government, and his work was frequently denied official support and funding. By 1965 heavy censorship was being imposed on his work, and he was arrested on dubious charges that were ultimately dismissed.

In 1967 Soyinka was appointed director of the school of drama at the University of Ibadan, where he wrote against the government until he was arrested at the outbreak of the Biafra war in the same year. After his release in 1969, Soyinka left the country and produced a prison play, *Madmen and Specialists* (1970), and an autobiography, *The Man Died* (1972), both of which were blistering attacks on the Nigerian regime.

Though many of Soyinka's works sold poorly in Nigeria, mainly due to suppression, he remained a major African voice, and his continual defiance of corruption, compromise, and censorship continued to make him a focus for democratic expression throughout the continent. He was particularly criti-

Nigerian writer Wole Soyinka in Paris shortly after his Nobel Prize in Literature was announced in 1986. (AP/Wide World Photos)

cal of the military rulers of his own country. In March, 1997, a little more than a year after the Nigerian government executed Ken Saro-Wiwa, it charged Soyinka with treason. Conviction would carry a death penalty, but Soyinka was living in exile.

See also Drama and theater; Literature; Nigeria; Saro-Wiwa, Ken.

Spanish-American War

DATE: 1898-1899
PLACE: Cuba, Puerto Rico, and Philippine Islands
SIGNIFICANCE: The United States government imposed censorship restrictions on military personnel and on newspaper correspondents covering the military operations of the war

On April 25, 1898, the United States declared war on Spain. The declaration came after several years of repeated newspaper accounts of Spanish atrocities against the Cuban people and the sinking of the battleship USS *Maine* on February 15, 1898, in the Cuban harbor at Havana—an act most Americans believed was perpetrated by the Spanish.

In the several decades prior to the war with Spain, correspondents of the major American newspapers had freely covered both domestic and international events unhampered by any form of official censorship. In fact, the government often relied on reports sent by correspondents from around the world, and in some cases even used reporters in semiofficial capacities to deliver government information. When government censorship was finally imposed for reasons of military security, the press was shocked.

The first act of censorship during the war took place on April 23, 1898, just two days before the U.S. Senate officially declared war. On that day, the U.S. Navy Department took control of the Key West, Florida, cable office in order to monitor all cable correspondence passing through. Key West stood squarely in the path of American naval convoys sailing to the island of Cuba, some ninety miles away.

Two days later, on April 25, 1898, on President William McKinley's orders, the Army Signal Corps placed an official censor in each of the six cable companies located in New York City, the headquarters for most of America's major papers. Censorship by the government was not restricted exclusively to the press, but included reviewing all forms of cable correspondence and any mail going to or coming from Spain. Another form of censorship placed restrictions on the U.S. military itself. Orders from Navy Secretary John D. Long forbade naval personnel from speaking with representatives of the press on matters pertaining to the Navy. Secretary of War Russell A. Alger followed suit by issuing a directive making all War Department records confidential and unavailable for discussion with newspaper representatives.

Censorship of the press was enforced in several ways. Typically, stories were edited so that no information thought detrimental to the military was printed. Often the stories that correspondents cabled back to their home newspapers ended up on publishers' desks with so many details missing that they proved useless. Another method of enforcement employed by the Army was threatening newspaper correspondents with the loss of their military-issued press credentials if they were caught bypassing censorship rules. Loss of military press credentials precluded correspondents from accompanying troops into battle areas.

Although censorship restrictions worked well overall, persistent reporters found ways to get around them. Some sent messages to cable offices in Haiti or Jamaica, which were then forwarded to the United States. Other reporters sent their stories with stipulations that they were not to be published until they returned home. Given the fierce competition among the papers for fresh news from the front, especially the New York papers, some unscrupulous publishers, such as William Randolph Hearst of the *New York Journal* and Joseph Pulitzer of the *New York World*, printed stories that their correspondents had asked to delay without regard for the repercussions that their reporters would face.

See also Crimean War; Cuba; Hearst, William Randolph; Martí, José Julián; Pulitzer, Joseph; Spanish Empire; War.

Spanish Empire

DESCRIPTION: Those parts of North and South America, the Caribbean Basin, Africa, and the Philippine Islands that Spain ruled for varying lengths of time between the early fifteenth and twentieth centuries

SIGNIFICANCE: At its height one of the largest European colonial empires, the Spanish Empire played a major role in extending Spanish and Roman Catholic cultures and values to large parts of the world

Spain's colonial empire began with its expansion into North Africa and the Canary Islands in the early fifteenth century. Its major growth came after Christopher Columbus' American discoveries at the end of the century, when the crown of Spain claimed a monopoly over the entire Western Hemisphere. Unable to enforce these vast claims, Spain soon relinquished Brazil, the Lesser Antilles, and what later became Canada and the eastern United States to other European powers. The Spanish Empire later included the Philippines, several small Pacific islands, and parts of northwestern and equatorial Africa. Under Spain's rule, the Roman Catholic religion and Spanish art, literature, government, and political and social values greatly influenced development throughout these regions.

Spain retained most of its empire for nearly three and a half centuries. Mexico and Spain's Central American and South American possessions won their independence in the early nineteenth century. After the Spanish-American War of 1898 Spain lost the Philippines and Puerto Rico to the United States and Cuba became independent. Portions of Spain's African territories remained under Spanish control until after World War II.

The motives for Spanish overseas expansion have been epitomized in the phrase "God, Gold, and Glory." Although not all the Spanish conquerors concerned themselves with spreading Christianity, the Spanish crown consistently supported Roman Catholic missionary work in the colonies. Church and state collaborated closely to reinforce each other's powers and prerogatives. Each believed that it held supreme power in its domain and did not hesitate to censor and coerce colonial subjects to conform to its demands. Through royal officials, the Spanish crown tried to suppress all opposition and ideas that would undermine its royal prerogatives. Spain also limited the immigration of outsiders into its colonies in order to keep out unwanted ideas.

In cooperation with the church, the government censored education, books, and discussion or circulation of any ideas that were deemed possibly subversive to either the government or the church. Such censorship was, however, less effective during the late eighteenth and nineteenth centuries than it had been earlier. Improved communications throughout the world, the ability of colonial subjects to travel outside of the empire, the presence of greater numbers of foreigners in the colonies, illegal trade, and the close proximity of other European colonies in the Caribbean Basin all contributed to making it impossible for Spain to control the exchange of new ideas. The same Enlightenment ideas that helped to inspire the American and French revolutions found their way into Spanish America and played a significant role in the development of early nineteenth century independence movements.

The Roman Catholic church used the Inquisition and its index of prohibited books as tools of censorship in Spain and its empire. Since the church financed and staffed the institutions of higher education, it was easy to censor education. In general, however, the church was no more successful in enforcing censorship in the late colonial period than was Spain's government.

See also Argentina; Central America; Chile; Cuba; Exploration, Age of; *Index Librorum Prohibitorum*; Maya books, destruction of; Mexico; Philippines; South America; Spanish-American War; Spanish Inquisition.

Spanish Inquisition

DATES: 1478-1834

PLACE: Spain and its colonies

SIGNIFICANCE: For three and one-half centuries, this institution significantly limited dissemination of ideas that challenged religious and political orthodoxy and the interests of the ruling power

The roots of the Inquisition lie in Roman Catholic history and in the Spanish experience. In response to doctrinal challenges, the Fourth Lateran Council (1215) ordered a program of inquisition to condemn and eliminate opponents. The inquisitors had the authority to investigate and punish (with the arm of the secular forces) heretics—people whose religious ideas differed from those of the Church.

Within the papacy's sphere of religious and political power were the several kingdoms comprising Spain, the only land in Western Europe with a truly multireligious population. Even during peaceful times, relations between the dominant Christians and the Jews and Muslims were never amicable.

Throughout the fourteenth century, fostered by anti-Semitism and a changing economy, the growing number of urban poor attacked various Jewish communities. In response to these increasingly vicious and deadly attacks, large numbers of Jews converted to Christianity on the assumption that the pogroms would stop once Jews took on the dominant religious status. A parallel process—but of smaller proportion—occurred a century later for the Muslims.

Converted Jews were known as *conversos*. The subsequent economic, political, and academic success of the *conversos* aroused the jealousy and frustration of the Christians. In 1492, all non-Christians were ordered to leave Spain, convert, or die. Once the Jewish and Muslim communities were gone, generations of enmity turned on the *Moriscos*, or Muslim converts, and especially the *conversos*.

Historians do not agree on the exact reasons for the establishment of a distinct Inquisition in Spain. It was initiated when a call for a separate Spanish Inquisition resulted in a supportive papal bull in 1478. Unlike in the other European offices, in Spain it was the king and not the pope who made the appointments of the inquisitors (the first Spanish inquisitor general being Tomás de Torquemada) and who ultimately controlled the purse.

Trial and Sentencing. The Inquisitor, backed by the secular forces, had the power to try people for heresy. The Inquisition, also called the Holy Office, maintained spies in the community, who reported on unacceptable words and acts. In addition, people were encouraged to reveal incriminating information about their neighbors and their families. According to the Edict of Faith (1519), not only were secret practitioners of Judaism or other heretical faiths guilty but so were those who knew about the practices but did not report them. Thus one had to watch one's tongue among neighbors, casual acquaintances, and sometimes even among family. These hidden censors led to a profound climate of fear among the *conversos*. Among the Christians who were not of *converso* origin, there was tacit approval for the humiliation and the taking of the property of the *conversos*.

Once incriminating information was brought to the regional inquisitor, he and the committee had the power to try the accused. If the charge was serious, they had the right to imprison the accused until the trial and sentencing were finished. That incarceration typically would be accompanied by a seizure of the accused people's property, to pay for their upkeep as well as for the inquisitor's office.

Eventually, sentence was rendered. In the small minority of cases, the accused were set free. In most cases, even if innocent, the accused admitted to their transgressions—in vague terms, since they often did not know what the charge was—to avoid more serious punishment. The accused who received lesser punishments were fined and assigned to some forms of public penance, which sometimes lasted two or three years. It was not unusual to be whipped publicly.

In more serious cases, in addition to the whipping, people were not allowed to practice their previous livelihood and were confined to the village or even to their home. Penitents were often required to wear an outer garment of guilt and shame (called a *sanbenito*) or to have it hung in the church for public display and humiliation.

The most serious cases involved an unacceptable belief, especially by someone previously convicted or accused of wrong beliefs. Maintaining one's innocence raised the stakes. People were imprisoned; many men did slave labor, which in the early years meant rowing all day in galleys. In the most extreme cases the accused were burned to death.

The process was—surprisingly to modern people who might think that it was lawless—legalistic. The process was blatantly unfair but legal and in service to the state. The accused were treated as guilty until the tribunal was (infrequently) willing to proclaim them innocent. Although they were, at times, allowed to have legal advisers, only the rich could afford to pay for their own. Others had to use counselors who worked for the Inquisitor's Office and who pressured the accused to admit their guilt. Torture was used, even if only in a minority of cases, and confessions wrung out in the torture room were repeated in court. The trial often dragged on interminably, in many famous cases going on for seven years and longer. In a number of these serious cases, the accused died while in jail, usually a dreadfully unhealthy place.

The most pernicious aspect of the Inquisition was its secrecy. Presumably, in order to protect the inquisitorial process and the sources of information, the accused were not told who accused them or, often, of exactly what they were accused. The accused could not cross-examine witnesses nor challenge evidence, since witnesses remained unknown as often did the evidence. It was almost impossible for the accused to win the case.

The pervasive secrecy was part of a plan to instill fear in the populace, to control their religious and political behavior. This was displayed dramatically in the *auto-da-fé* (act of faith), a public sentencing, often leading to the burning of some of the accused. When the accused had successfully fled, they were burned in effigy; when they had already died, their corpses were unearthed and then burned. Not only did it provide entertainment for the masses, but it shaped their behavior. Spectators got the message to avoid any behavior that might land them on the executioner's woodpile.

The Inquisition initially intended to root out heresy in the form of Jewish practices—even washing linens on Friday could be incriminating evidence—and to weaken the *conversos'* economic and political position. The Inquisition succeeded. Over time, overt Jewish practices disappeared almost entirely. As is predictable for an institution, the Inquisitors did not then disestablish themselves and relinquish power. They moved on to punish those of unorthodox religious ideas and practices, those critical of the institutionalized church, humanists, Protestants, freethinkers, political opponents of the king, homosexuals, people engaging in sexual practices deemed unchristian, witches, and common criminals. The Holy Office was, above all, a powerful agent of social control.

Controlling Ideas. As part of its control, the Inquisition established a means of censoring to what ideas the people could be exposed, a job made more difficult by the introduction of the printing press. It did so initially by limiting who could print books; licenses were granted by eight sources, six of them bishops or archbishops.

Books had to be controlled because they were "silent heretics." The Holy Office moved to ban certain books and pamphlets, or parts thereof—in which case, the offensive parts required expurgation. Originally, the Index of Forbidden Books was borrowed from other Catholic Indexes but after 1551 it was produced internally, reflecting Spanish concerns. About three times a century until 1790, the Holy Office published an extensive list of ideas that were banned along with the titles of all the forbidden works.

Initially, the Inquisition engaged in burning books. One of the earliest instances was organized by Torquemada in his own monastery. In 1501 Ferdinand II ordered the burning of all Arabic books in Grenada, a campaign organized by Archbishop Cisneros, later the inquisitor general.

The lists of banned books were most restrictive—especially against Protestants—from 1551 to 1584. During that time of the Counter-Reformation, the list read like a sample of the great thinkers of Europe: François Rabelais, William of Ockham, Niccolò Machiavelli, Dante Alighieri, Thomas More, Giovanni Boccaccio (in Spanish), and sixteen works of Desiderius Erasmus. Martin Luther and all the other Protestant thinkers were anathema. When accompanied by interpretation, even the Bible itself became suspect. Sixty-seven different editions of the Bible were banned, primarily those in Spanish, along with a host of other religious texts in the vernacular.

The censors were sharpest in their supervision of religion and philosophy. Those texts that even slightly challenged the Church's scholastic approach to knowledge were circumspect in doing so. In addition to the Bible, access was also limited to some of the early church fathers and the classics.

More latitude was given to poets and to novelists, particularly those writing popular adventure novels. Authors were keenly aware, however, of the censors' constraints and undoubtedly followed them to the best of their abilities—for their own protection.

The Inquisition also developed its own bureaucracy of censorship implementation. The national office kept tabs on printers and the local officers monitored booksellers and private and public book collections. Surprise visits were made, sometimes to all the town's booksellers at one time to prevent them from warning one another. The censors then went through entire collections to remove the forbidden material.

During the virulent Counter-Reformation, extra precautions were taken in the northern port cities close to The Netherlands and Germany. Ships' bills of lading were checked against cargo contents. Foreign sailors and some travelers had their possessions searched, and a number were sentenced for possessing Protestant literature, including several who paid for their mistake by being burned at the stake. In order to eliminate foreign influence, Spanish students studying abroad were forced to come home from all places but a handful of closely monitored Catholic seminaries.

Even during the strictest period, books and ideas filtered through. Later, individual exemptions were granted to some scholars. The Inquisition did a good job of frustrating and, in some cases, terrorizing the universities. Mateo Pascual of the University of Alcalá was accused of having doubts about purgatory, for which the inquisitor took away all his possessions and exiled him. At the University of Salamanca, a handful of frustrated informers brought charges against colleagues, several of whom died in jail, while others were denied their jobs at release after two to six years. This was the original age of political and religious correctness in the university. Sometimes the best scholars, who earned the envy of others, were secretly accused and so lost their positions, which contributed to a decline in academic quality.

Inquisition apologists argue that Holy Office restrictions were not greater than those in other European countries, and they point to the expansion of military and political power and to the flowering of Spanish art and literature in the sixteenth century. The argument is not very convincing. Despotic governments are often strong militarily. The literature that flourished was limited to adventure novels, often of rogue heroes. Much of the traditional concerns of philosophy, religion, and later science waned. The Inquisition curtailed much, perhaps most, serious expression of ideas and art for several hundred years.

Although cracks appeared in its walls, clearly the Inquisition stifled public thought and expression. Books and pamphlets were periodically and systematically removed from public and private places. Booksellers had unacceptable books

taken from their property, without compensation. Readers and collectors could be fined and jailed. Many respected scholars were subject to the punishment of the Inquisition. The more serious their challenge to orthodoxy, the more serious their punishment. A number of important teachers and thinkers withered away in Inquisition prisons and died there or shortly after they were released. Some were burned. There can be no doubt that the censorship imposed by the Inquisition and the attendant climate of fear contributed to a Spain that was cut off from intellectual developments in the West. —*Alan M. Fisher*

See also Bible; Christianity; Erasmus, Desiderius; Judaism; Lateran Council, Fourth; Luther, Martin; Reformation, the; Spanish Empire; Torquemada, Tomás de; Vatican.

BIBLIOGRAPHY

Angel Alcala, ed., *The Spanish Inquisition and the Inquisitorial Mind* (Boulder, Colo.: Social Science Monographs, 1987), is useful scholarship. Richard Greenleaf, *The Mexican Inquisition of the Sixteenth Century* (Albuquerque: University of New Mexico Press, 1969), covers the Inquisition in the Americas. Stephen Haliczer, *Inquisition and Society in the Kingdom of Valencia, 1478-1834* (Berkeley: University of California Press, 1990), is a comprehensive overview of one court. Henry Kamen, *Inquisition and Society in Spain in the Sixteenth and Seventeenth Centuries* (Bloomington: Indiana University Press, 1985), is germane, readable, and informative, but contains contradictions. Henry Charles Lea's *A History of the Inquisition of Spain* (4 vols. New York: Macmillan, 1906-1907) is still the best, most comprehensive source. Jean Plaidy, *The Spanish Inquisition: Its Rise, Growth, and End* (New York: Citadel Press, 1967), is simplistic and emotional but fact-filled, well organized, and readable. Benzion Netanyahu, *The Origins of the Inquisition in Fifteenth Century Spain* (New York: Random House, 1995), focuses on *conversos* and is an enormous, detailed work.

Spellman, Cardinal Francis Joseph

BORN: May 4, 1889, Whitman, Massachusetts

DIED: December 2, 1967, New York, New York

IDENTIFICATION: Roman Catholic cardinal and archbishop of New York

SIGNIFICANCE: Spellman played a leading active role in advocating film censorship during the 1940's and 1950's

Spellman was the Roman Catholic archbishop of the New York diocese from 1939 until his death in 1967, and was elevated to cardinal by Pope Pius XII in 1946. Through these years he was embroiled in numerous censorship controversies in which he exerted his personal and religious influence. Although he supported the church's condemnation of films and theater entertainment that threatened moral standards of decency, he opposed censorship that limited political and religious freedom.

In the early 1940's Spellman began making fervent condemnations against the American film industry. His first noted attack was against the film *Two Faced Woman*, starring Greta Garbo, that happened to be produced by one of Spellman's film industry friends, Louis B. Mayer. The film had been condemned by the Legion of Decency, a Catholic organization that rated the moral acceptability of films, because of its passionate love scenes and Garbo's low-cut dresses.

Spellman's political influence was significant and he used it to restrict the showing of several films and plays in his diocese. Immediately after the Italian film *The Miracle* opened in New York City in 1950, Spellman called on the city's commissioner of licenses to halt its showing. The film's producers fought the censure appealing their case to the U.S. Supreme Court, where they eventually won. Spellman's political connections extended to the rank and file of the New York City police department. Predominately Irish Catholics, the city's police were willing to do their cardinal's bidding on request. When, for example, the Ambassador Theater opened the burlesque stage production of *Wine, Women and Song*, Spellman persuaded the police department to serve summonses on the theater's production crew and manager. City leaders saw nothing wrong with the way the police handled the matter.

In 1956 Spellman lashed out against producer Joseph Levine's controversial film *Baby Doll*, adapted from a Tennessee Williams play. Spellman's outspoken criticism ended up doing more to entice interest in the film resulting in successful box office sales. By this time Spellman's influence on the film industry was waning. After the U.S. Supreme Court affirmed the appeal of *The Miracle* producers, filmmakers in the United States ceased to be troubled by condemnations of the Roman Catholic church.

See also Cushing, Cardinal Richard James; Film censorship; Legion of Decency; *Miracle, The*; Williams, Tennessee.

Spinoza, Baruch

BORN: November 24, 1632, Amsterdam, United Provinces
DIED: February 21, 1677, The Hague, United Provinces
IDENTIFICATION: Dutch philosopher
SIGNIFICANCE: Spinoza's writings—which were banned during his lifetime—provided the basis for a thoroughly naturalistic cosmology and thus helped lay the philosophical foundations of the secular world

During the seventeenth and eighteenth centuries, Spinoza was widely denounced as an atheist, even though his views on religion were beginning to influence the thinking of Deists and French materialists and were paving the way for what became known as "higher criticism" of Scripture. Spinoza took the radical step of replacing religious tradition with rational, scientific reasoning and of subjecting religion to scientific inquiry. In *Tractatus Theologico-Politicus* (1670)—justification for intellectual and religious freedom—he rejected the basis for revealed religion by denying the supernatural. He presented the Bible as a document that was both historical and human, and concluded that its moral teachings were valid solely because of their compatibility with reason.

For Spinoza, supernatural events could not occur because they contradict natural laws; in effect, he equated "God" with "nature." In *Ethics* (1677) Spinoza developed the idea that everything in the world is an aspect of God, who cannot thereby be a purposeful being. The impossibility of historical interaction between God and humanity negated belief in prophecy, miracles, and revelation itself.

Spinoza published *Tractatus Theologico-Politicus* without putting his name on the book; nevertheless, the work was uniformly banned and sold with false title pages. Because his authorship of the work was an open secret, Spinoza was condemned as a notorious atheist. While he was negotiating to publish *Ethics*, rumors spread that a book proving God did not exist was in press and complaints were lodged with the Dutch magistrates. Spinoza responded by agreeing to delay publication of his book, which did not appear until shortly after his death in 1677. The book identified him only by his initials, so infamous had his opinions become.

Opprobrium for his radical, secularist views came early for Spinoza. At the age of twenty-four, he was excommunicated by Amsterdam's Jewish community. Some scholars consider it likely that Spinoza's heretical ideas developed out of heterodox controversies within the Jewish community itself. Others hold that synagogue leaders wished to enforce unity in the Jewish community to counter the spirit of skepticism and laxity fostered by the many Amsterdam Jews who escaped the Spanish Inquisition by pretending to convert to Christianity (Marranos). A generation earlier, one such man, Uriel de Costa, had been expelled twice for his unorthodox opinions.

Still others claim that Spinoza was excommunicated primarily for his involvement with Amsterdam's radical intellectuals, who advocated free trade, among other reforms. Members of the Jewish community—particularly its leaders—played a leading role in Amsterdam commerce. They not only derived income from Dutch trade monopolies, but their investments in them gave them leverage against the persecution of Jews abroad. For example, Jewish economic power in Amsterdam prevented the expulsion of Jews from New Amsterdam in the New World.

Following Spinosa's excommunication, hostility against the unrepentant philosopher apparently extended to an attempt on his life. By 1660, Spinoza had left Amsterdam. In 1673, denying control over religious dissent, he declined a position teaching philosophy at Heidelberg on condition he not disturb the established religion. Four years later, he died of consumption, which was possibly aggravated by the lens-grinding work that he did to earn his living.

See also Atheism; Bible; Bruno, Giordano; Heresy; Intellectual freedom; Judaism; Kant, Immanuel; Spanish Inquisition.

Sports news

DEFINITION: News media coverage of amateur and professional sports
SIGNIFICANCE: Despite the fact that sports news has traditionally been regarded less significant than other forms of news, sports journalists have faced at least as much censorship as other journalists

Los Angeles Times sports editor Bill Dwyre once described the sports department as the unwanted child of the newsroom, shunted into a corner so that it does not contaminate the true journalists. Perhaps as a result of such segregation, sports journalists have developed writing styles that differ significantly from other kinds of newswriting. This segregation may also have contributed to significant differences in how sports journalists perceive their roles and responsibilities.

Most censorship in sports journalism has been practiced by sports organizations or sports journalists themselves. Government censorship has rarely occurred. Instead, government has generally been more concerned with protecting the broadcast rights of networks that have contracted to show sporting events. The U.S. government did, however, censor films of African American boxing champion Jack Johnson's defeat of Jim Jeffries, the so-called Great White Hope, in 1912. Journalists covered the event, however, and reported on the outcome. Sports journalists have also faced censorship—particularly pressure to keep newsworthy stories from the public—from powerful organizations such as teams and leagues.

Self-censorship. Self-censorship has long haunted sports journalists. In the nineteenth century Henry Chadwick, considered the father of American sportswriting, not only coined common terms for baseball plays, but also worked closely with the game's leaders to advance the sport. Chadwick's coverage was designed to popularize the sport and it may have led to a symbiosis between sports journalists and sports promoters. In his stinging critique *The Jocks* (1969) sportswriter Leonard Shecter painted some of his modern colleagues as overgrown sports fans who would cover up a sports organization's flaws for "a set of glasses with the team logo."

Certainly in the 1920's—sometimes called the Golden Age of Sports—many sportswriters were willing to cover up negative news about the sports stars of the day. Writers who followed baseball hero Babe Ruth, for example, were allowed to accompany him on tours. In exchange, they kept silent about his paternity suits, heavy drinking, and other problems. In Jerome Holtzman's oral history of sportswriters, *No Cheering in the Press Box* (1974), writers boast of helping Ruth and others avoid bad publicity. Richards Vidmer, for example, claimed that he "could have written a story about the Babe every day if I had wanted. But I never wrote about his personal life, not if it would hurt him." Vidmer also boasted of keeping the news that baseball player Lou Gehrig was suffering from a fatal disease from his audience. He argued that the public had no right to know about the disease; it had only the right to know whether Gehrig would play or not.

Sports journalism, for the most part, eventually outgrew Vidmer's brand of self-censorship, but reporters have continued to face the self-censorship question in dealing with athletes, coaches, and other sports officials, all of whom have methods of intimidation that can be used against sports journalists.

The Locker Room. Coaches and athletic team administrators have some power to influence news content through their dealings with the managements of news organizations. The most common form of censorship coaches use is the threat of limiting access to sources. The threat is clear for many sports journalists: Print or broadcast something negative and get frozen out of the news loop. Though this practice may not fall as blatantly under the censorship banner as prior restraint, it nevertheless has a chilling effect on open reporting.

In 1995 Tom Osborne, coach of the University of Nebraska's powerhouse football program, barred two reporters representing the university's student paper from attending practices and from entering the team's locker room because the paper had printed editorial cartoons critical of Osborne and his athletes. Osborne later rescinded the ban, but said he would decline interviews with the student reporters and enforce stricter rules for all reporters. Osborne's philosophy is not strikingly different from that of other coaches. He claimed that attending team practices was "a privilege and not a right." Open access to locker rooms and practice sessions is vital to reporters' access to their sources.

Limited access to men's locker rooms and practices has been a thorny issue for women sports journalists. Women watched male reporters walk into locker rooms during the 1977 World Series while an order from baseball commissioner Bowie Kuhn kept them out. After reporter Melissa Luedtke filed suit, federal courts ruled that women journalists had the same right to access as male reporters. However, tradition did not wither easily under the court order. Particularly in collegiate sports, some athletic directors and coaches continued to bar women from male athletes' locker rooms. In 1988, for example, reporter Karen Rosen was told by Vanderbilt's athletic director, "We don't let girls in our locker room. We never have and we never will." Once admitted to the locker room, women sports journalists have, at times, faced harassment from athletes and coaches. Reporter Susan Fornoff, for example, once received a gift-wrapped dead rat from a baseball player.

Male reporters have also often received harassment in locker rooms. All reporters run the risk of receiving the silent treatment. In 1985, for example, Seattle columnist Steve Kelley criticized a Seattle Mariners baseball player and found the entire team refused to participate in interviews with him. Players can also use physical intimidation—hardly a surprise since many athletes are professionals at physical intimidation—to punish reporters for stories that they deem negative. In 1979, after reporter Dale Robertson wrote that quarterback Dan Pastorini appeared to have problems throwing the football, he had a locker room altercation with Pastorini—who later admitted that he did, in fact, have a shoulder injury.

After Columbia Broadcasting System (CBS) golf announcer Gary McCord remarked that the greens at the Masters golf tournament were slick like "bikini wax" in 1994, the tournament's directors demanded that CBS remove him from its telecast—or they would entertain bids from other networks for the rights to the telecast. CBS complied. Examples such as these and many others have repeatedly shown that sports reporters must often censor their own stories in order to do their jobs.

—*Randy E. Miller*

See also Ali, Muhammad; Journalists, violence against; News media censorship; Newspapers.

BIBLIOGRAPHY

Editor Jerome Holtzman's *No Cheering in the Press Box* (New York: Holt, Rinehart, and Winston, 1974) and Gene Wojciechowski's *Pond Scum and Vultures: America's Sportswriters Talk About Their Glamorous Profession* (New York:

Macmillan, 1990) offer inside stories on how sports journalists censor themselves. Readers can also find criticism of sports journalists among larger critiques of sports. Leonard Shecter's *The Jocks* (Indianapolis: Bobbs-Merrill, 1969) and Robert Lipsyte's more reasoned *SportsWorld: An American Dreamland* (New York: Quadrangle/New York Times, 1975) attack the status quo of the sports journalism of their days. Leonard Koppett's *Sports Illusion, Sports Reality* (Boston: Houghton Mifflin, 1981) is a valuable resource for anyone considering an academic approach to sports, and Lawrence A. Wenner's *Media, Sports, and Society* (Newbury Park, Calif.: Sage, 1989) develops a model of the symbiotic relationship between sports journalists and sports organizations.

Spycatcher

Type of work: Book
Published: 1987
Author: Peter Wright (1916-   )
Subject matter: Memoirs of a senior intelligence officer concerning his work in the British Secret Service
Significance: In its unsuccessful attempt to suppress publication of this book, the British government unintentionally increased its sales and brought Britain's Official Secrets Acts into disrepute

In 1985 Peter Wright, a senior officer in Britain's counterintelligence agency MI5, attempted to publish his memoirs. They detailed his work from 1955 to 1976 and advanced the largely discredited thesis that the former head of MI5, Sir Roger Hollis, was a Soviet spy. The British government denied Wright permission to publish on the grounds that he would be violating the Official Secrets Acts, which bound civil servants not to divulge without prior approval official information acquired in the course of duty. However, Wright was then a resident of Australia and intended to publish his book there.

The British government knew that it could not enforce the Official Secrets Act in another country, so it initiated a civil law suit in the Supreme Court of New South Wales, in Australia, to stop publication. Britain claimed that Wright was guilty of breach of contract, the contract being that he in effect had promised his superiors to maintain confidentiality of information acquired in the course of his work. Wright's defense attempted to demonstrate that no confidentiality was being broken and that Britain was trying indirectly to enforce its Official Secrets Act in Australia. During the trial, it was revealed that in 1980 and 1981, Wright had secretly given his information to Chapman Pincher, a British journalist, who in turn had published *Their Trade Is Treachery* (1981). The government, however, had taken no action against Pincher, apparently because it believed that the book's contents were not prejudicial to British interests.

On March 13, 1987, the Supreme Court of New South Wales ruled there was no breach of confidence in Wright's case, mainly on three grounds: that information on events occurring decades earlier could cause no harm; that the information contained in the book was already in the public domain; and that the government had failed to stop publication of the same material in previous books. Through appeals, the case eventually reached the High Court of Australia, which also ruled in Wright's favor on June 2, 1988, arguing that the British government was in effect trying to enforce its own penal laws in Australia.

Even before the Australian High Court's decision, the publication ban had been lifted. *Spycatcher* had already been published in the United States the previous July, and the book was selling well in both Australia and Europe as well. At the same time, legal action was proceeding in Britain, where the book was still proscribed. In October, 1988, however, Britain's House of Lords grudgingly allowed Wright's book to be published and legally sold in Britain, where it became a bestseller. This affair was a public relations disaster for the British government, which appeared intolerant, secretive, and foolish in attempting to prohibit circulation of a book the entire world was discussing. The affair also painfully exposed the limitations of the Official Secrets Act. In a final irony, reviewers found that Wright's book advanced a dubious hypothesis, and was generally dull, uninformative, and full of factual errors.

See also Australia; Book publishing; *CIA and the Cult of Intelligence, The*; Civil service; *Crossman Diaries (Diaries of a Cabinet Minister, The)*; Espionage; National security; Official Secrets Act (U.K.); United Kingdom.

Stag films

Definition: Underground 8 mm and 16 mm films of the prevideo period showing sexually explicit activities
Significance: Social and technological changes turned these heavily suppressed manifestations of fascination with adult sexual activity into anachronisms by the 1980's

Hard-core pornographic films were produced virtually from the invention of the motion picture camera. First introduced in the early 1900's, they were generally produced in a 16 mm film format. Due to the expense of the equipment and persistent legal suppression, they were typically produced by small numbers of people and rented to mostly male audiences for private "stag nights" or "smokes." Although the films were publicly outlawed, their audiences often comprised members of social, fraternal, business, veterans, and other mainstream organizations.

The introduction of inexpensive 8 mm film technology after World War II widened stag film audiences and shifted emphasis from rentals to sales. More people could make such films, but usually produced fewer of them and of lesser quality than in the 16 mm days. They were produced and distributed locally or regionally, usually in two-hundred-foot "loops." The content of these films typically reflected white middle-class male values. Predominantly heterosexual in content, the films showed some interest in group sex and female-female encounters, but there was little attention to male homosexuality, and pedophilia, bestiality, and fetishism were virtually nonexistent. The films flirted with the forbidden, while attacking certain social taboos such as miscegenation and oral sex. They also reflected a traditional double standard in regard to male and female sexual behavior. Phrases such as "stag films" and "training films" themselves suggested that sexuality was strictly a male domain.

During the 1960's the enlarged Super 8 format was introduced; by 1970 a new type of hard-core cinema known in the trade as "16 mm films" appeared. These films were graphic productions designed to be shown in limited numbers of decaying urban theaters to male audiences. These innovations, however, ran into countervailing social currents. Adult erotica became publicly more acceptable during the late 1960's. Pornography was legalized in Denmark in 1968 and in France in 1974. In *Stanley v. Georgia* (1969), the U.S. Supreme Court ruled that a bookmaker's mere possession of "obscene" films could not constitutionally be made a crime. The commercial film *Deep Throat*, released in late 1972, epitomized the new trend. Widely distributed in suburban theaters, it attracted large mixed audiences and soon became available on videotape.

The video revolution of the 1980's made access to lavish, sexually explicit 35 mm productions as convenient as one's home television set, and few American companies still even produced 8 mm film by the early 1980's. Adult erotica accounted for half of all video sales in 1981, and nearly half of its rentals in the 1990's were being made by women. These changes in technology and society made the social milieu of the titillating all-male rite of passage and the concept of the stag film passé.

See also *Deep Throat*; Film censorship; Obscenity: sale and possession; Pornography; President's Commission on Obscenity and Pornography; Sex in the arts.

Stalin, Joseph

BORN: December 21, 1879, Gori, Georgia, Russian Empire
DIED: March 5, 1953, Moscow, Soviet Union
IDENTIFICATION: Dictator of the Soviet Union
SIGNIFICANCE: Stalin's unrivaled control over practically all public expression in the Soviet Union helped give rise to the term "totalitarianism"

Born Joseph Vissarionovich Dzhugashvili, Joseph Stalin was the supreme leader of the Soviet Union from the late 1920's until his death in 1953. During those years he transformed V. I. Lenin's fledgling Soviet state from the largely rural, loosely integrated empire of nations inherited from the czarist regime, into one of the world's most powerful countries. The development of the Soviet Union under Stalin came at a brutal cost, however, involving the deaths of millions of citizens. The Stalinist system sought complete control over virtually all aspects of the people's lives, and a key element to that system of control was censorship.

The Nature of Soviet Censorship. Under Stalin government censorship was notable for its thoroughness. Various institutions were created at least in part to carry out the censorship task. In addition to Glavlit, the state body for "the preservation of state secrets in the press," publishing houses, editorial staffs, state propaganda agencies, the secret police, unions, and various other organizations were pressed into the service of monitoring and restricting the expression of ideas. "Political editors"—as censors were euphemistically called—were usually members of the Communist Party, and were always charged with protecting and promoting the regime.

Under Stalin censorship involved not only the restriction of

expression, but also the prescription of it. In other words, Stalin's regime insisted that the media convey the information, interpretations, and judgments desired by the Communist Party. Censorship applied to the past as well as the present: History books were revised to suit party purposes, and photographs were altered to corroborate changing party interpretations of the past. Toward the party's stated goal of creating a "new Soviet man," Stalin employed the tools of censorship to direct the masses in what to think, believe, and value.

Few aspects of communication and expression were overlooked by Stalin's censors. The government prescribed what could be taught in classrooms, and Communist Party members in the schools ensured that undesirable ideas were not surreptitiously—or inadvertently—being introduced. Book manuscripts often required a censor's stamp on every page, thus preventing the insertion of altered pages after review. Telephones were bugged and even carrier pigeons were registered by the state. A vast network of informants was cultivated. Mail was secretly examined. The visual arts and music (even instrumental works) were subject to censorship. Musicians and other performers were issued "artist's certificates," specifying which works they could perform. Filmmakers were confronted with numerous regulations, some of which were as arbitrary and trivial as prohibiting depictions of calendars with true dates.

Stalin's Personal Involvement. Throughout the Soviet censorship system, the vast array of institutions and bureaus was organized according to Stalin's personal orders. He personally initiated the founding of a Soviet publishing house to translate foreign scientific literature. Ironically, this turned out to be one of the few refuges from strict, formal censorship. It was presumed that material such as mathematical formulas and astronomical observations was relatively impervious to bourgeois influence, although introductions and author's notes to such works were closely scrutinized prior to their publication.

For military and nuclear research Stalin also authorized the creation of "secret" cities, whose existence was not officially acknowledged and whose residents were tightly controlled. He created the Central Committee's Secret Department, whose Special Sector infiltrated and spied upon all facets of Soviet society, including the other divisions of the government itself.

Stalin held a special personal interest in theater and opera, and he respected artists and writers of both. His personal tastes served often as the first, and always as the final, arbiter of censorship matters concerning the arts and literature. He insisted that writers and artists adopt a pedestrian and conservative approach called Socialist Realism. Persons working under these constraints found them stultifying. Under Stalin, even the works of as renowned a writer as Fyodor Dostoevski could not be published. Stalin recognized the importance of the arts in influencing societal values, and occasionally even personally censored and annotated manuscripts.

An intended result of the apparatus' reputation for efficiency and ruthlessness was that Soviet citizens practiced self-censorship. Particularly during the Terror of the 1930's (when millions of people were sent to labor camps or summarily killed by the state—the ultimate form of censorship). Few were inclined to test the limits of the regime's tolerance. Peo-

Despite Joseph Stalin's bloody record of oppressive tyranny, immense throngs turned out to mourn his death in 1953. (National Archives)

ple disappeared for transgressions as trivial as uttering an unflattering word about the regime or, most dangerous of all, about Stalin himself. Extreme secrecy, coupled with widespread fear, made for a potent censorship regime.

Despite the thoroughness of the Soviet censorship apparatus, however, daring writers and others devised ways to evade even Stalin's censors. Some would choose to write "historical" pieces about previous czars, such as Nicholas I, who perceptive readers understood to be metaphors for Stalin himself. Others resorted to samizdat (self-publishing), circulating works through underground networks. But these were dangerous and therefore rare actions. By and large published works toed the party line, and samizdat would not become a mass phenomenon until well after Stalin's death.

Rationale for Censorship. Under Stalin (and virtually all Soviet leaders) Marxism-Leninism was upheld as a "scientific" doctrine, and thus served as the yardstick by which truth was measured. Anything which ran counter to that doctrine, including social scientific reports, fictional works, and historical accounts, were deemed "unscientific," "irrelevant," "bourgeois," or otherwise unworthy of being published. It should be noted that Marx himself opposed censorship as "bad, even when it delivers good products." Yet under Stalin, the need for extensive censorship was underscored by the alleged presence of enemies of the state, whose noxious ideas had to be weeded out. It was, overall, a paternalistic rationale, in which state censors decided which material could safely be absorbed by the presumably simpler and weaker minds of the masses.

The nature of the Cold War, particularly during Stalin's time, could well justify some degree of censorship by the Soviet government. But the excessive and arbitrary nature of censorship under Stalin reveals his pathological suspicion and distrust of the masses and even his closest comrades. The extent of Soviet censorship under Stalin could not rationally be justified, any more than the brutal and arbitrary murder of millions of Soviet citizens. Stalin's successor, Nikita Khrushchev, revealed and criticized Stalin's excesses as senseless and obsessive. Censorship in the Soviet Union eased considerably, although it was not until Mikhail Gorbachev's policy of *glasnost* in the 1980's that the Soviet people would experience anything approaching free expression.   —*Steve D. Boilard*

See also Communism; Dostoevski, Fyodor; Gorbachev, Mikhail; Historiography; Lenin, Vladimir Ilich; Orwell, George; Russia; Socialist Realism; Soviet Union; TASS; Trotsky, Leon; Zhdanov, Andrei.

BIBLIOGRAPHY

Robert Conquest, ed., *The Politics of Ideas in the USSR* (Westport, Conn.: Greenwood Press, 1976), examines the control of public ideas throughout the Stalin years and slightly beyond. Harold Swayze's *Political Control of Literature in the USSR, 1946-1959* (Cambridge: Harvard University Press, 1962) covers the later years of Stalin's censorship. C. E. Black, ed., *Rewriting Russian History: Soviet Interpretations of Russia's Past* (New York: Published for the Research Program on the U.S.S.R. by Praeger, 1956), focuses on Stalinist revisionism. The anonymous "Censorship in Russia: A Note," in *Problems of Communism* 14, no. 1 (January-February, 1963), discusses a list of nearly ten thousand books that were banned in the Soviet Union from 1918 until 1941. *The Soviet Censorship* (Metuchen, N.J.: Scarecrow Press, 1973), edited by Martin Dewhirst and Robert Farrell, draws from a symposium on censorship in the Soviet Union. George Orwell's fictional work *Nineteen Eighty-Four* (New York: Harcourt, Brace, 1949) provides a chilling interpretation of Stalin-like censorship with "newthink" and "doublespeak."

Stamp Act
ENACTED: March 22, 1765
PLACE: Great Britain
SIGNIFICANCE: This revenue law made taxation a censorship tool in Britain's North American colonies

After Great Britain's victory over the French in the Seven Years' War, George Grenville's ministry directed Parliament to levy taxes on the colonies to defray the expenses of defending British North America. In March, 1765, Parliament passed the Stamp Act, requiring colonists to purchase government stamps for all legal and financial documents, as well as newspapers, pamphlets, almanacs, and even playing cards and dice. Prices of the stamps ranged from a half-penny to ten pounds; violators were to be tried in vice-admiralty courts. It was the boldest most widely felt action of the government and there was an immediate colonial response. When Patrick Henry denounced the tax, members of Virginia's assembly agreed to adhere only to those revenue bills which they had enacted.

In Massachusetts protests against the new law included pillaging a stamp agent's home and hanging him in effigy and ransacking the lieutenant governor's home. Bostonian James Otis, Jr., questioned the tax in a tract titled *The Rights of the British Colonies Asserted and Proved*, and Maryland attorney Daniel Dulaney challenged the British Crown in a widely read pamphlet, *Considerations on the Propriety of Imposing Taxes on the British Colonies*. Colonial protests came to a head when delegates met at an intercolonial congress in New York in October, 1765. Known as the Stamp Act Congress, this body petitioned Parliament to rescind the law. The Sons of Liberty rallied public support and Boston merchants resisted through nonimportation agreements. Parliament's repeal of the tax in 1766 set off many colonial celebrations.

Although the act was aimed at censorship, lawyers and printers refused to use the stamps. Since no stamps were sold in the colonies, no revenue was collected.

See also Revolutionary War, American; Tax laws; United Kingdom.

Steffens, Lincoln
BORN: April 6, 1866, San Francisco, California
DIED: August 9, 1936, Carmel, California
IDENTIFICATION: American journalist and author
SIGNIFICANCE: Considered one of the most talented journalists to emerge from the muckraking era of the early 1900's, Steffens found it difficult to publish in the United States because of his identification with leftist causes

A native Californian, Steffens studied psychology in Europe following graduation from the University of California at

Berkeley. When he returned to the United States, he found work as a reporter for the *New York Post*. In 1901 he became managing editor of *McClure's Magazine*, a periodical later renowned for its muckraking exposes. When Steffens became depressed at being trapped behind a desk, his publisher, S. S. McClure, took pity on him and told him to go out into the country to find a story in 1902. Steffens responded with his famous series detailing municipal corruption, "The Shame of the Cities."

Steffens remained with *McClure's* until 1906, when he left to start a new magazine, *American*, along with other muckraking journalists. His association with *American* lasted only two years. Because he was a progressive socialist, Steffens' radical views created conflicts with his more conservative colleagues. After he visited the Soviet Union in 1919, he wrote "I have seen the future and it works." For many editors, this statement confirmed that Steffens was communist and led to a blacklisting of his writings in the United States. Steffens remained influential in intellectual circles, particularly in Europe, where he associated with writers such as Ernest Hemingway and Gertrude Stein. *The Autobiography of Lincoln Steffens*, published in 1931, was widely read for many years, but fell out of favor during the Red Scare of the 1950's.

See also Communism; Magazines; Mitford, Jessica; Nader, Ralph; News media censorship; Seldes, George.

Steinbeck, John

BORN: February 27, 1902, Salinas, California
DIED: December 20, 1968, New York, New York
IDENTIFICATION: American novelist and screenwriter
SIGNIFICANCE: Steinbeck's writings, which were often characterized by sympathy toward the economically and socially dispossessed, have been widely banned and criticized by political and religious leaders

Born into a middle-class California family, Steinbeck was graduated from Salinas High School in 1919. He attended Stanford University to study English, but during five years there, he earned only half the credits needed to graduate because he often dropped out to work in various laborer jobs. Meanwhile, he published two short pieces in *The Stanford Spectator*.

Steinbeck's first three novels went largely unnoticed, but his fourth, *Tortilla Flat* (1935), won critical praise and became a best-seller. The book established him as one of America's major novelists. The following year, he published *In Dubious Battle* (1936), a story about strike organizers in the California fruit-picking industry. His sympathetic view of the "red" strikers led many conservatives to suspect that he was a communist. This novel and his Pulitzer Prize-winning *The Grapes of Wrath* (1939), about migrant workers, were Steinbeck's most controversial books; both were banned in many areas. However, both works also became major motion pictures, but before they were considered fit for the screen they were heavily edited for language and content. Sharp public debate over both films helped to increase Steinbeck's book sales.

In an effort to escape the controversy and publicity generated by his books, Steinbeck traveled to Mexico to film his first work written exclusively for Hollywood—the semidocumentary *The Forgotten Village* (1941). Release of this film was delayed by New York State censors who objected to its child-birth scene. When the film was finally released, it had little commercial success. Fearing reprisals, the studio provided the film with little publicity.

During the war years, Steinbeck continued to find himself under attack. His novel *The Moon Is Down* (1942) generated even more debate than *The Forgotten Village*. This story of Norwegian freedom fighters battling the German invaders was heavily criticized for its portrayal of German soldiers as essentially normal human beings who committed atrocities only because of pressure from their superior officers. After writing *The Moon Is Down*, Steinbeck felt compelled to support the American war effort and became a reporter for *The New York Herald Tribune* in 1943. He was fired, however, when his graphic depictions of the horrors of war led to charges that his ability to report simple facts was hindered by his literary tendencies and his emotions.

Although many of Steinbeck's postwar writings became best-sellers, they never reached the level of critical acclaim that his work had achieved in the 1930's. His major postwar works included the novels *Cannery Row* (1945), *The Pearl* (1947), *The Wayward Bus* (1947), *East of Eden* (1952), and *The Winter of Our Discontent* (1961); the film *Viva Zapata!* (1952); and the nonfiction book *Travels with Charlie* (1962).

In the 1950's Steinbeck launched caustic attacks on Senator Joseph McCarthy for his advocacy of censorship and his efforts to expose communists in the government. Steinbeck played a prominent role in Democratic presidential campaigns in 1952 and 1956, and later served as an adviser to Lyndon B. Johnson. He received the Nobel Prize in Literature in 1962 amid critics' protests that he was undeserving.

See also Communism; Film adaptation; *Grapes of Wrath, The*; Lewis, Sinclair; Literature.

Stendhal

BORN: January 23, 1783, Grenoble, France
DIED: March 23, 1842, Paris, France
IDENTIFICATION: French novelist
SIGNIFICANCE: Stendhal's writings were not censored during his time, but were later banned by several countries and the Roman Catholic church

Stendhal lived two lives: He was both a Napoleonic army officer and diplomat and the author of such sensitive novels as *De l'Amour* (1822), *The Red and the Black* (1830), and *La Chartreuse de Parme* (1839). It was his first life that caused him to run afoul of government authorities. While he was living in Milan after the defeat of Napoleon Bonaparte, his reputation as a "liberal"—as all opponents of the restored Bourbon regime in France were labeled—prompted the Austrian rulers of Milan to order his arrest in 1821. Forced to flee Italy, Stendhal returned to France, where he could not secure a government appointment because of his earlier association with Napoleon.

Official harassment for his political views prompted Stendhal to assume his second life as a writer. Always aware of the censors, he consciously avoided offending official sensibilities in his books. Yet although his works were not banned during his lifetime, his caution did not spare them problems after his death. The Roman Catholic church placed his novels on the *Index Librorum Prohibitorum* later in the century for their anticlerical content, and they were temporarily banned in Russia in 1850 and in Spain in 1939.

See also Balzac, Honoré de; Dreiser, Theodore; France; Hugo, Victor; *Index Librorum Prohibitorum.*

Stern, Howard

BORN: January 12, 1954, Roosevelt, Long Island, New York

IDENTIFICATION: American radio and television talk show host and author

SIGNIFICANCE: A pioneer in "sex talk" or "topless" radio, Stern has been the target of numerous listener complaints and has been investigated by the Federal Communications Commission

A communications graduate of Boston University, Stern began his career as a conventional radio deejay in Briarcliff, New York, in 1976. Two years later he moved to Hartford, Connecticut, where he began mixing music and uninhibited telephone conversations with his guests and listeners. The popularity of this format earned him shows in larger markets: Detroit and Washington, D.C., in 1980, and New York City in 1982. In the fall of 1986 he began syndicating his weekday

Talk-show host Howard Stern, who has built his career on shocking people, displays one of his books in October, 1993. (AP/Wide World Photos)

morning show from New York. By the mid-1990's the show reached more than thirty stations across the United States.

By deliberately flaunting outrageous remarks and bad taste, Stern earned the sobriquet "shock jock." In 1988, for example, he broadcast a Christmas party program that featured a man playing the piano with his penis. On another broadcast he led an ostensibly lighthearted discussion about dismembering a woman. Content such as that provoked many listeners to complain, calling him racist, misogynistic, homophobic, vulgar, and self-indulgent. Stern has claimed, however, that he does not intentionally try to shock audiences, but only to talk as men do off-the-air.

Chicago's WLUP removed his program from the air after many of its listeners had written to the Federal Communications Commission (FCC). The popularity of Stern's show has made it so profitable that his employer, Infinity Broadcasting, has paid nearly two million dollars in fines to the FCC for violating federal decency rules, rather than comply with them.

See also Carlin, George; Federal Communications Commission; Limbaugh, Rush; Obscenity: legal definitions; Offensive language; Radio; Talk shows.

Sterne, Laurence

BORN: November 24, 1713, Clonmel, Ireland

DIED: March 18, 1768, London, England

IDENTIFICATION: English novelist and Anglican cleric

SIGNIFICANCE: Sterne's novel *Sentimental Journey* was listed on the *Index Librorum Prohibitorum* because of its perceived attacks on the Roman Catholic church

A free-thinking, iconoclastic novelist and Anglican cleric, Sterne was a well-known critic of Roman Catholicism and the church's monastic orders. His second novel, *A Sentimental Journey Through France and Italy by Mr. Yorick* (1768), published shortly before his death, received the censure of the Roman Catholic church in 1819, when an Italian edition translated by Ugo Foscolo was listed on the *Index Librorum Prohibitorum.* By eighteenth century standards the novel was considered salacious, but it was its religious commentary that most concerned Catholic officials. At one point in the story, Sterne's protagonist—an Anglican priest named Yorick, based loosely on the author himself—refuses a Franciscan monk's request for alms, declaring, "we distinguish, my good Father! betwixt those who wish only to eat the bread of their own labour—and those who eat the bread of other people's, and have no other plan in life, but to get through it in sloth and ignorance, *for the love of God.*" Yorick also mocks Catholicism when discussing the three stages "in the empire of a French-woman": "coquette," "deist," and "devôte." In the last stage, he jests, she "re-peoples" her dominions "with the slaves of the Church." Ironically, *Sentimental Journey* expresses significantly more tolerance for Catholicism than much of Sterne's earlier work, including his collection of sermons, published as *Sermons of Mr. Yorick* (1760), and his first novel, *The Life and Opinions of Tristram Shandy, Gentleman* (1759-1767).

See also Fielding, Henry; Goldsmith, Oliver; *Index Librorum Prohibitorum*; Literature; Reformation, the; Religion; Vatican.

Stone, I. F.

BORN: December 24, 1907, Philadelphia, Pennsylvania
DIED: June 18, 1989, Boston, Massachusetts
IDENTIFICATION: Maverick American journalist
SIGNIFICANCE: For two decades Stone published a newsletter championing civil liberties and peace that became a major voice against censorship by exposing government chicanery and disinformation

The veteran gadfly journalist I. F. Stone has been characterized by Henry Steele Commager in *The New York Review of Books* as "a modern Tom Paine, celebrating Common Sense and the Rights of Man, hammering away at tyranny, injustice, exploitation, deception, and chicanery." A journalist since his teens, Stone published for nineteen years his independent newsletter, *I. F. Stone's Weekly* (later the *Bi-Weekly*), in which he spoke his mind on virtually any subject. Although Stone aimed his barbs primarily at the establishment, he managed, as Henry Allen put it in 1971, "to annoy some of the people all of the time, and all of the people at one time or another."

Stone had some 5,300 paid subscribers when he launched his four-page journal of fact and opinion, *I. F. Stone's Weekly*, in January, 1953. Among its early subscribers were Albert Einstein, Bertrand Russell, and Eleanor Roosevelt. Aided only by his wife, who handled the business end of the publication, Stone published the *Weekly* from a modest two-story house on the outskirts of Washington, D.C. Doing his own research, reporting, writing, editing, and proofreading, Stone achieved a high-quality publication. Accurate, well-written, and interesting, it was graced by Stone's idiosyncratic wit and humor.

Despite some initial difficulties, the *Weekly* soon began to prosper; by 1963 its circulation had nearly quadrupled. Stone curtailed operations somewhat in 1969, when the *Weekly* became *I. F. Stone's Bi-Weekly*. Although the number of its subscribers had grown to more than seventy thousand by the end of 1971, Stone ended publication of his newsletter on January 1, 1972. Afterward he became a contributing editor of *The New York Review of Books*.

An indefatigable researcher, Stone occasionally dredged up some significant revelations. In 1958, for example, he forced the Atomic Energy Commission to admit that its first underground nuclear test had been detected twenty-six hundred miles away, despite official claims that it could not be detected beyond a two-hundred mile radius. One of his favorite targets was the U.S. military establishment; he persistently dissected Pentagon budgets that had been inflated by spurious Defense Department claims of Soviet weapons superiority.

Despite having some leftist sympathies, Stone minced no words in pointing out the shortcomings he saw in the communist world. His unfavorable report on the Soviet Union following a visit in 1956 cost him four hundred subscribers. Perhaps his most controversial position was his criticism of Israel after its victory in the six-day Israeli-Arab war of 1967. Although Stone had supported the Jewish state since its creation in 1948, he rejected militant Zionism and believed that the Palestinian Arabs had valid claims against the state of Israel. As a solution to the Israeli-Arab conflict, he proposed that Israel take the initiative in compensating the Palestinian refugees and resettling them in a state of their own that would be linked with Israel in some form of federation. Stone's views were attacked in several leading American Jewish magazines, and he was accused of feeling self-hatred as a Jew, a charge that he emphatically denied.

See also Israel; Judaism; Mitford, Jessica; News media censorship; Nuclear research and testing; Paine, Thomas; Seldes, George; Soviet Union.

Stopes, Marie

BORN: October 15, 1880, Edinburgh, Scotland
DIED: October 2, 1958, near Dorking, Surrey, England
IDENTIFICATION: British paleobotanist, sex reformer, and playwright
SIGNIFICANCE: Stopes's books on marriage, sex, and birth control were banned in the United States and in several British Commonwealth countries

Stopes's work on marriage, sexuality, and birth control made her a household name in Great Britain and its colonies. Trained as a paleobotanist, she turned her energies to promoting sex education after the dissolution of a three-year marriage that was apparently never consummated. In her first sex education book, *Married Love* (1918), she argued that a knowledgeable, active and healthy sex life was critical to successful marriage. Arguing against Victorian stereotypes portraying women as passionless, Stopes insisted that women had the same sexual urges as men and needed fulfillment. Among the many topics she covered, she described birth control as an

Marie Stopes wrote sex education books that were suppressed in England, Ireland, Canada, and the United States. (Library of Congress)

essential aid to married bliss. With this assertion, Stopes became the leading birth control advocate in England.

Married Love was such a phenomenal success that its sequel, *Wise Parenthood*, also appeared in 1918. Aimed at a broad audience, this book provided simple but detailed instruction on birth control techniques. Although earlier birth control works had been classified as obscene, neither of Stopes's books were banned in Britain, nor were any of her nearly twenty other books and pamphlets on sex and birth control. Their publication in other countries was not, however, as easily accomplished.

American birth control reformer Margaret Sanger aided Stopes by convincing publisher William J. Robinson to risk issuing an American edition of *Married Love*. Although Robinson cut portions of the book to conform to American censorship laws, the New York State Court of Special Sessions judged the book as obscene under the Comstock Act in 1921 and banned it. Importation of British editions of *Wise Parenthood* and Stopes's *Enduring Passion* (1923) were also barred in the United States, and *Married Love* was banned in Ireland, Canada, Australia, and New Zealand.

Not only were Stopes's birth control tracts outlawed but her silent film, *Maisie's Marriage* (1923) and her play, *Vectia* (1926) were banned in Britain. In depicting the efforts of a working-class woman to rise from poverty, *Maisie's Marriage* contrasted the different family sizes of the poor and the upper classes as an argument for birth control. Although its screening was prohibited in London, the film was shown without a license in other parts of England and in parts of the British Commonwealth. *Vectia*, an autobiographical play describing Stopes's own disastrous first marriage and the dangers of sexual ignorance, was deemed unsuitable for the public and refused a production license in Britain.

Both the British and Irish press censored Stopes in subtle manners. Newspapers, especially *The London Times*, refused to carry advertisements for Stopes's books, lectures, or birth control clinic on the grounds that they were offensive. Despite the efforts of censors to restrict Stopes's message, her clinics, writings, and speeches made her one of the most popular and well-known figures of her day, and her views on sexuality later came to be widely accepted.

See also Birth control education; Comstock, Anthony; Comstock Act of 1873; Drama and theater; Kneeland, Abner; *New York Times Co. v. Sullivan*; Sanger, Margaret.

Strange Fruit

TYPE OF WORK: Book
PUBLISHED: 1944
AUTHOR: Lillian Smith (1897-1966)
SUBJECT MATTER: A novel about miscegenation in which a young Southern white man and an African American woman fall in love
SIGNIFICANCE: Although the novel was critically acclaimed and acknowledged to be a serious work, the state of Massachusetts banned it because it might titillate impressionable readers

Lillian Smith's first novel, *Strange Fruit*, tells the story of an interracial love affair in the South between a white boy and an educated African American woman. The novel contains several descriptions of sexual intercourse and masturbation and ends with a murder and a lynching. Massachusetts state authorities banned the book, but the literary scholar Bernard DeVoto challenged the ban. A judge found that Smith's book violated the state law barring material that either was "obscene, indecent, impure" or that tended to "corrupt the morals of youth." In his view, the work raised "lascivious thoughts" in the mind of the reader and aroused "lustful desire," so it should not be sold in the state. When the U.S. Post Office tried to prohibit shipping the book between states by mail, Eleanor Roosevelt intervened and got the order rescinded.

A few years later the author and her sister, Esther, adapted the novel into a play, which had a successful run on Broadway and in Canada. Irish authorities, however, refused to let the book be sold or the play be performed in Dublin. The original novel sold more than 200,000 copies in the United States, though most bookstores took it off their shelves after the ruling in Massachusetts and refused to sell it any more.

See also Drama and theater; Ireland; Literature; Miscegenation; Obscenity: legal definitions; Postal regulations; Race.

Street oratory

DEFINITION: Speeches given in streets, parks, or other public places
SIGNIFICANCE: Since the 1960's, the U.S. Supreme Court has given street oratory strong, but not unlimited, protection from censorship under the First Amendment

One of the classic symbols of free speech in Western civilization is in the Speakers Corner in London's Hyde Park. Every Sunday afternoon, this corner is filled with people listening to street orators declaiming on a wide variety of topics from lecterns or podiums provided by the government, unmolested from any censorship of the ideas expressed. This form of street oratory is such a well-known custom that, in the 1980's, Chinese students, faculty, and intellectuals created the same custom in one corner of Beijing's Purple Bamboo Park, but with limited success.

Whatever its value as a symbol, the U.S. street oratory issues are more complicated. While the U.S. Constitution's First Amendment promises the government shall make no law censoring speech or press, it promises this only for those who "peaceably assemble." The use of "peaceably" means the government does have a right to censor or exercise prior restraint over assemblies. Since street oratory means speech before an assembly, the assembly can be censored or regulated even if the speech itself cannot.

Over much U.S. history, speech before assemblies was regulated by the concept of "clear and present danger," and was guided by the example that no one was allowed falsely to shout "fire" in a crowded theater. Since the 1960's, the clear and present danger doctrine has fallen into disuse, and street oratory has become better protected. In *Feiner v. New York* (1951) the Court upheld Feiner's conviction for delivering a strong pro-black civil rights speech before a mixed race audience, some of whose whites took offense and threatened the speaker with violence. Policemen ordered Feiner to stop speaking, and upon his refusing, arrested him. Perhaps influenced by Feiner's uncooperative attitude, the Supreme Court upheld his conviction, although the Court had ruled in *Hague v. CIO* (1939) that government censorship of street oratory, demonstrations, and assemblies limited to "promoting the free movement of traffic in public areas" implied governments could not control speech content but only time, place, and manner of presentation.

By the 1960's the Supreme Court had eliminated the so called "heckler's veto" (in which a hostile audience stifles a speaker by threatening to riot, thereby provoking a police response against the speaker). Since *Brandenburg v. Ohio* (1969), the Court has rejected such a veto by insisting that police protect the speaker's free speech no matter what the audience response is—thereby effectively overturning *Feiner*. A related example can be found in the Court's reaction in the famous Skokie, Illinois, Nazi march case in which the courts firmly upheld the Nazis' right to march even though the townspeople threatened to riot if they marched. In the end, the Nazis chose not to march in Skokie, but the principle, so closely related to street oratory, was confirmed.

See also Assembly, right of; Fighting words; Fourteenth Amendment; Hyde Park Speakers Corner; Marching and parading; Offensive language.

Stubbs, John

BORN: 1541?, Norfolk, England
DIED: 1591, Havre, France
IDENTIFICATION: English Puritan pamphleteer
SIGNIFICANCE: A loyal monarchist, Stubbs suffered the loss of a hand for criticizing Queen Elizabeth I's proposed marriage

Stubbs is remembered primarily for the brutal punishment inflicted on him after he criticized Queen Elizabeth. As a Puritan, Stubbs showed clear enthusiasm for Protestant England and aversions to both Roman Catholicism and France—which he described as a "kingdom of darkness." In 1579 he grew anxious about England's negotiations with the French government to promote the marriage of Queen Elizabeth to the Duke of Alencon—the brother of French king Henry III, and he published an 86-page pamphlet, *The Discoverie of a Gaping Gulf Whereinto England Is Like to Be Swallowed Up by an Other French Mariage*.

From the beginning of her reign in 1558, Elizabeth had been pressured to marry any of several European sovereigns and aristocrats. The marriage of her half-sister, the late Queen Mary, to the Spaniard, Philip II, had soured many Englishmen on the prospect of their new queen's marriage to another Catholic prince. In the *Gaping Gulf*, Stubbs implored Elizabeth to reject the proposed marriage, arguing vehemently that the French hoped to infect the English with their vices through the proposed marriage. In Stubbs's view, Alencon (whom he calls "Monsieur") was a serpent sent "to seduce our Eve, that shee and we may lose this Englishe Paradise." Elizabeth was apparently offended by the suggestion that she—as the wife of Alencon—might fall under the control of the French and be like her sister in proving unable to conceive an heir.

A royal proclamation of September, 1579, insisted that the queen would not allow "the malice of some lewd, disordered persons . . . to irritate unjustly any foreign princes." In October Stubbs was tried, with his publisher, William Page, and the printer Hugh Singleton on the charge of disseminating seditious writings. Stubbs and his codefendants were found guilty and sentenced to have their right hands cut off (the printer was later pardoned). On November 3, 1579, Stubbs's hand was struck off by three blows of an axe. Immediately afterward, he astonished the crowd by removing his hat with his left hand and exclaiming, "God save the Queen." Although Stubbs was jailed for another eighteen months before his release, he remained a loyal monarchist. He was later elected to Parliament, and he died in France while on military duty in 1591. (Elizabeth's marriage negotiations were ended by Alencon's death in 1584).

Although Stubbs's book was frank in outlining the dire consequences of a French marriage for Queen Elizabeth, it was respectful toward the queen. The Crown's brutal response to his criticism clearly exposed the limits on free speech in Elizabethan England. Stubbs stands as a classic victim of censorship under a regime which reacted more out of pique than from any sober assessment of any damage done by publication of a pamphlet.

See also *Areopagitica*; Crop-ears; English Commonwealth; James I; Latimer, Hugh; Leighton, Alexander; Milton, John; United Kingdom.

Studs Lonigan : A Trilogy

TYPE OF WORK: Books
PUBLISHED: 1932-1935
AUTHOR: James T. Farrell (1904-1979)
SUBJECT MATTER: A young man grows to adulthood experiencing the vicissitudes of American society in Chicago's Irish American community
SIGNIFICANCE: This trilogy was pulled from bookstores and libraries after the courts failed to suppress it, demonstrating the unpopularity of its supposedly leftist views in the United States

After Vanguard Press published *Studs Lonigan* in 1935, the New York Society for the Suppression of Vice attempted unsuccessfully to halt its circulation because of its alleged obscenity (the organization also tried unsuccessfully to suppress Farrell's 1937 novel *World I Never Made*). Soon after *Studs Lonigan* was published, New York City's police began harassing Vanguard Press and city bookstores, angered by ties they perceived between the novel and a sensational murder case then going on. Farrell and Vanguard regarded the police actions as an attempt at political intimidation.

When legal censorship failed, many libraries and bookstores refused to carry Farrell's controversial works. A librarian at the Enoch Pratt Free Library in Baltimore, Maryland, for example, remarked that "hundreds of libraries are closed to him and his literary kind." In 1942 the American Library Association (ALA) dropped *Studs Lonigan* from its select list of books about life in the United States; because of the wartime paper shortage this decision had the effect of stopping publication of *Studs Lonigan* in Great Britain. Although the

ALA disavowed any attempt at censorship of Farrell's books, Farrell's left-leaning political views made critics skeptical of the ALA claim.

Farrell also had trouble with Canadian authorities; although Canadian customs reportedly cleared his book, it appears to have been banned in Canada. Farrell himself later responded to efforts to ban his books by writing, "We are still bedogged and bedeviled with impudent and antidemocratic efforts to censor our books."

See also American Library Association; Customs laws, Canadian; Libraries; Society for the Suppression of Vice, New York.

Subliminal messages

DEFINITION: Visual or aural stimuli presented below the conscious-awareness threshold of audiences

SIGNIFICANCE: Although the effectiveness of subliminal messages has been questioned, their use has been censored as being manipulative

Subliminal messages are words or images that are flashed on screens or played on recordings so quickly that audiences are unaware of receiving the messages. Subliminally transmitted images are generally embedded within other images, using an airbrush technique, so that the stimulus message is not recognized consciously. They reportedly have been used in advertisements, films, and records. They are also said to have been used in music played to customers in department and grocery stores to discourage shoplifting. The theory is that potential lawbreakers subconsciously hearing a message such as "do not steal" are supposedly less likely to shoplift. Cigarette and liquor advertisements in magazines have reportedly used subliminals to induce people to use their products. Some films, such as *The Exorcist* (1973), have used subliminal images of ghosts and skeletons to increase the fright of their viewers. Such uses are not against the law.

In 1957 James Vicary used a tachistoscope to flash the phrases "Drink Coca-Cola" and "Hungry? Eat Popcorn" on a cinema screen being watched by a audience. Every five seconds these phrases appeared on the screen for three-thousandth of a second throughout the film. Vicary claimed that Coke sales increased 18 percent and popcorn sales increased 57 percent. Despite lack of documentation, public uproar over these claims led the National Association of Broadcasters to adopt a rule in the television code stating that transmission of messages below the threshold of normal awareness is not permitted. Fifteen years later the Federal Communications Commission (FCC) reviewed a complaint that a toy manufacturer had run a commercial with the phrase "Get it" presented subliminally. In 1973 the FCC ruled that broadcasters presenting subliminal messages are not acting in the public interest and that such messages are deceptive and therefore not allowed.

In 1991 the families of two young people who attempted suicide sued the heavy metal band Judas Priest and CBS Records. The two adolescents were listening to one of the albums of the British rock group when they shot themselves in 1985. A Nevada court eventually ruled that the families had

failed to prove that subliminal suicide messages in the album were responsible. In 1991 Louisiana passed a law requiring warning labels on albums with themes of rape, murder, suicide, illegal drug use, child abuse, or satanic worship.

Controversy concerning the amount of subliminal messages used and the effectiveness of such use has continued. Advertisers do not cite any research involving such messages and in fact generally deny that such messages are used. Nevertheless, a growing body of evidence collected by academic research has found that people can, in fact, be affected by messages that they are not consciously aware of receiving.

See also Advertising as the target of censorship; Copycat crime; Federal Communications Commission; Obscenity: legal definitions; Rap music; Smoking; Suicide; 2 Live Crew; Violence.

Suicide

DEFINITION: Act of deliberately killing oneself

SIGNIFICANCE: Because suicide has long been seen as shameful, it has been a taboo subject in the arts, and the modern American news media have often censored news of suicides—particularly among the young—partly from fear that publicity may encourage imitators

During the 1990's suicide ranked as the ninth leading cause of death in the United States—immediately ahead of homicide. Nevertheless, suicide has been far less visible in the media than murder. It has also occurred much less often than murder in novels, in films, and on television—all of which has contributed to the misleading impression that suicide is less common than murder. Dying of murder is not necessarily shameful, and the rituals that follow it are public; such public acts are intended, in part, to heal the rift that murder creates in society. Suspected murderers are sought, captured, and brought to trial—leading to public discussion of guilt, innocence, and the justifications for their punishments. By contrast, a person who commits suicide is buried or cremated quietly, seldom with a discussion in public over whether the suicide was justified. Suicide is seen as shameful, something to be hidden from the public. The social damage of suicide is not compensated, in many cases, with public acts that seek to restore order.

News Reports. Suicides become public news when they are committed by famous or public persons, or when their circumstances are unusual. Marilyn Monroe's suicide, for example, received so much attention that her death was transformed into a cultural tragedy. Mass media textbooks have openly discussed the 1987 suicide of Pennsylvania state treasurer R. Bud Dwyer; he killed himself with a handgun during a live press conference. Suicides that are committed by people who are not famous, or that are not committed in striking ways tend to go unreported. Newspaper obituaries and death notices, which rely upon the cooperation of funeral homes and family members, typically omit cause of death in cases of suicide, or use vague euphemisms, such as "died at home" or "died suddenly."

Hiding suicide in the news media is particularly common when teenagers kill themselves. Newspaper editors and television news directors worry that reports of teenage suicides will lead to more suicides. They fear what has been called the

Students gathered outside of New Jersey's Bergenfield High School discuss the shocking multiple suicides of fellow students. (AP/Wide World Photos)

"Werther effect," so named after several readers imitated the suicide of a character in *The Sorrows of Young Werther*, a romantic novel written by Johann Wolfgang von Goethe in 1774. The Werther effect seemed to be present in 1987, when television news reports of the suicide of teenagers in Bergenfield, New Jersey, led to copycat suicides. Copycat suicides among the young also occurred in Japan after the production of *The Love Suicides at Sonezaki* (1703), by Chikamatsu Monzaemon, a popular play about two young lovers who commit suicide.

Suicide Manuals. Despite cultural taboos on discussing suicide publicly, a suicide manual topped *The New York Times* best-seller list for several weeks in 1991. Written for persons with terminal medical conditions, Derek Humphry's *Final Exit* spelled out in clear language and large type how to commit suicide efficiently. The Carol Publishing Group sold 550,000 hardback copies of the book, which also went into a paperback edition. *Final Exit* found its way into most U.S. libraries and bookstores; however, few outlets have displayed the book, and some independent bookstores refused to carry it. Bookstore chains acted differently. Waldenbooks and B. Dalton, for example, which earlier had been severely criticized for responding to threats by refusing to carry Salman Rushdie's

novel *The Satanic Verses* (1988), showed that they had learned their lesson by carrying *Final Exit*.

The sudden availability of hundreds of thousands of copies of *Final Exit* in bookstores and libraries prompted fears that the number of suicides would rise. Indeed, reports of attempted and successful suicides in which *Final Exit* may have played a part appeared soon after the book's publication. In Charleston, South Carolina, for example, a motel maid found the body of a healthy thirty-year-old man in his room. He was wearing a crucifix ring and was tattooed with "To Hell with Satan" across his shoulders and "777" on the back of his right hand. His last diary entry was a recipe for a cyanide cocktail copied from *Final Exit*. He died of cyanide poisoning.

In Oklahoma City the body of a healthy sixty-one-year-old man asphyxiated by carbon monoxide was discovered in his garage by his elderly mother. He showed that he had followed *Final Exit*'s advice by doing everything from putting his financial affairs in order and avoiding raising suspicions about when his suicide would occur to making sure that his Mercedes had a full tank of gas and that his garage was well sealed. In his living room next to his will and a note alluding to his suicide as his "final exit" was a copy of Humphry's *Final Exit*.

In the light of such alarming reports, several research projects were initiated to determine the effect of *Final Exit* on the suicide rate. One study compared suicides occurring in New York City during the years before and after *Final Exit* was published. It not only found a significant rise in the number of suicidal suffocations by plastic bag—a technique recommended in *Final Exit*—it also noted that few of the persons who had apparently used *Final Exit* before committing suicide suffered from terminal illnesses. However, the same study also noted that the overall suicide rate did not change. A comparison of national suicide statistics between 1990 and 1991 yielded similar findings. Suffocations by plastic bag and suicidal poisonings did increase significantly, but the total number of suicides did not increase. These studies collectively suggested that *Final Exit* influenced methods of suicide, not the suicide rate. In other words, the book may have given helpful instructions to suicidal people, but did not itself prompt their suicides. Nevertheless, family members of persons who followed advice in *Final Exit* to commit suicide called for measures to restrict access to the book.

Final Exit was published with the intent of forcing the issue of euthanasia into public discussion. The Hemlock Society, a euthanasia organization, has grown into an organization of thirty thousand members belonging to eighty-four chapters in thirty-nine states. The fact that *Final Exit* became a best-seller in a society that seems to be satisfied with the underreporting of suicide suggests that Americans view suicide as an option for elderly persons who are on the brink of their final suffering or mental or physical degeneration, but that they reject it as a solution for mental distress. —*John P. Ferré*

See also Book publishing; Copycat crime; Death; Goethe, Johann Wolfgang von; Intellectual freedom; Mayakovsky, Vladimir; Obituaries; Radishchev, Alexander; Rushdie, Salman.

BIBLIOGRAPHY

Derek Humphry's *Final Exit: The Practicalities of Self-Deliverance and Assisted Suicide for the Dying* (Eugene, Oreg.: Hemlock Society, 1991) is central to the discussion of the censorship of suicide in the late twentieth century. The book's effects are discussed in Peter M. Marzuk, Kenneth Tardif, and Andrew C. Leon, "Increase in Fatal Suicidal Poisonings and Suffocations in the Year *Final Exit* Was Published: A National Study," *American Journal of Psychiatry* 151, no. 12 (December, 1994). For an overview of this subject see Elizabeth B. Ziesenis, "Suicide Coverage in Newspapers: An Ethical Consideration," *Journal of Mass Media Ethics* 6, no. 4 (1991).

Sumner, John

BORN: September 22, 1876, Washington, D.C.
DIED: June 20, 1971, Floral Park, New York
IDENTIFICATION: Director of an American organization dedicated to censorship
SIGNIFICANCE: Sumner succeeded Anthony Comstock as the last head of the New York Society for the Suppression of Vice

The son of a U.S. naval officer, Sumner was educated in Washington, D.C., and New York City and was admitted to the New York Bar in 1904. Before practicing law in New York

City, he worked for a banking firm, and during World War I he was the secretary for the Young Men's Christian Association (YMCA) in France. Although he was politically an independent, he joined several conservative organizations, including the Order of Founders and Patriots of America, the Sons of the American Revolution, the New York Southern Society, and he belonged to the Episcopalian church.

Through his early career, Sumner published articles, engaged in public debates, and involved himself in numerous procensorship campaigns. In 1913 he became an associate secretary for the New York Society for the Suppression of Vice (SSV). When its executive secretary, Anthony Comstock, died in September, 1915, Sumner succeeded him in the post, which he held until he retired in 1950. During his first year in his new office he forced Theodore Dreiser's novel *The Genius* to be withdrawn from sale. Later he directed SSV efforts to initiate obscenity charges against such works as James Branch Cabell's *Jurgen* (1919), James Joyce's *Ulysses* (1922), D. H. Lawrence's *Lady Chatterley's Lover* (1928), and Edmund Wilson's *Memoirs of Hecate County* (1946). In 1927 Sumner helped get Mae West jailed for directing and acting in the play *Sex*.

Two important phases of Sumner's tenure as head of the SSV were his "book jury" scheme and the "clean books" campaign. After World War I, censorship was hotly debated, even within the publishing industry itself. Established conservative publishers clashed with newer and more liberal publishers over what criteria should be used to deem a work obscene. The National Association of Book Publishers (NABP) proposed a self-censorship plan monitored by a committee within the industry. Sumner saw this plan as an opportunity to increase SSV influence and proposed a "book jury" plan whereby the SSV would support works the NABP declared not obscene, while vigorously prosecuting anyone distributing materials that the NABP committee found obscene. Sumner retreated when his plan met opposition from both the publishing industry and the general public. His "clean books" campaign of 1923-1925 offered another opportunity for influence when New York Supreme Court justice John Ford and others expressed the need to amend New York State's obscenity law. Against opposition from Horace Liveright and other publishers, the SSV backed the amendment, sparking even further debates over censorship. Sumner lead the procensorship campaign.

See also Books and obscenity law; Cabell, James Branch; Comstock, Anthony; cummings, e. e.; Dreiser, Theodore; *Lady Chatterley's Lover*; Liveright, Horace; *Memoirs of Hecate County*; Society for the Suppression of Vice, New York; *Ulysses*; West, Mae.

Sunshine laws

DEFINITION: Legislation requiring government agencies to conduct their operations more openly
SIGNIFICANCE: These laws are designed to facilitate greater scrutiny of government decision making by increasing its exposure to the media and the public at large

Sunshine laws have arisen from the theory that the watchdog role of the media is seriously impeded when government decision-making bodies close their meetings to the public. The shielding of such meetings from public scrutiny might be construed as a form of media censorship. For some it conjures images of unscrupulous political horse-trading in smoke-filled rooms from which public accountability suffers. To address this perceived problem many local governments, all fifty U.S. states, and the federal government have adopted "sunshine laws," so named because they require that the work of government decision-making bodies be exposed to public view. Sunshine laws typically require that certain types of meetings are open to the public and that adequate prior notice of such meetings be disseminated. The first such law was adopted by Florida in 1975.

Another approach requires that the records or minutes of certain meetings be made available to the public. The federal Freedom of Information Act of 1966 requires federal agencies to fulfill requests for copies of documents and other information, with numerous exceptions. Some local laws require merely that the minutes of meetings be published or otherwise made available to interested persons.

The major federal sunshine law is the Government in the Sunshine Act, signed by President Gerald Ford in 1976. That act requires all federal agencies to give advance public notice of their meetings and dictates that certain meetings be made open to the public when quorums of their members are present. The law stipulates that such meetings be held in publicly accessible locations, and requires that minutes of proceedings be officially recorded. The act provides ten exemptions for especially sensitive meetings, such as those concerning personnel actions and national security matters. The act also exempts "predecisional" meetings.

Exemptions provided by sunshine laws typically are subject to a broad range of interpretations. Some critics have charged that government officials intentionally circumvent the open-meeting requirements by arriving at de facto decisions in earlier, closed-door meetings, leaving only the formal approval of policies already decided for the open meetings. Similarly, various subquorum groups of officials might meet privately to arrive at a consensus prior to holding a public meeting. For their part some officials have complained that open meetings inhibit the frank discussion of issues, while encouraging officials to play to their audiences (whom they might view as potential voters), rather than honestly grappling with issues at hand. Prohibitions on the informal or casual broaching of issues among officials also can be seen as unnecessarily inhibiting political discussion and reducing efficiency.

Overall, sunshine laws have generally been credited with making public decision-making processes more democratic. Their precise impact, however, has been difficult to gauge. A 1988 study by the U.S. General Accounting Office (GAO) found that federal agencies were adequately complying with the Government in the Sunshine Act. But the GAO subsequently admitted in Senate testimony that violations of the act were by their very nature difficult to detect.

See also Canadian Access to Information Act; Civil service; Classification of information; Freedom of Information Act; Press conferences; Privileged communication.

Sweden

DESCRIPTION: Northern European state with a constitutional monarchy and parliamentary form of government
SIGNIFICANCE: Since the mid-eighteenth century Sweden has prohibited censorship of the press, a liberal policy that has been extended to include all information media

Sweden appears to have been the first country in the world to establish freedom of the press when its parliament adopted a Freedom of the Press Act in 1766. A brief relapse into repression and censorship during the final decades of the eighteenth century was halted by constitutional reform in 1809. Another Freedom of the Press Act dates from 1949 and incorporates several subsequent amendments.

Swedish lawmakers have viewed and supported the media in the role of public watchdog, and public censorship of the press has been forbidden. Swedish law has required that the owner of any periodical appearing four times a year or more appoint a "responsible publisher," who is held solely accountable for any violation of the Freedom of the Press Act. A Press Ombudsman for the General Public, sponsored by the media organizations, investigates alleged violations. The law also explicitly prohibits the investigation or disclosure of newspaper reporters' sources of information. Exceptions include state employees who inform the media of information that could be detrimental to the security of the state. Legal actions against newspapers have mostly concerned libel. Except in special cases pornography has not been punishable by Swedish law. Part of the 1949 Freedom of the Press Act includes the principle of free access to public documents, except those relating to matters of national security and foreign relations, documents relating to criminal matters, and information concerning the personal integrity and safety of individuals.

Since electronic media was not included in the 1949 Freedom of the Press Act, the Radio and Broadcasting Liability Acts were passed in 1967. In 1977 these were superseded by Sweden's Mass Media Act in which the principles of noninterference, dating back to the mid-eighteenth century, were extended to all information media.

An exception to the general ban on prepublication censorship has involved the film industry. Movies intended for public showing are previewed by the National Board of Film Censorship, which is empowered to delete certain sequences or ban a film altogether. Censorship has been exercised mainly in the interest of young viewers, and it has generally been directed against excessive brutality or prurience. There have been unsuccessful attempts to abolish film censorship altogether. Despite demands for a careful scrutiny of video material there has been no censorship of videos, but video films, presented for public screening, have had to be vetted by the film censors.

At different times Swedish films have been banned in the United States. *I Am Curious—Yellow* was banned from entry into the United States and in numerous states in 1968-1971. *I, a Woman* was banned in 1967 in Indiana and Kentucky; *The Virgin Spring* was banned in Fort Worth, Texas, in 1962; and *The Language of Love*, a sex-education film, was banned from entry into the United States in 1969.

See also Denmark; Film censorship; *I Am Curious—Yellow*; News media censorship; Swedenborg, Emanuel.

Swedenborg, Emanuel

BORN: January 29, 1688, Stockholm, Sweden
DIED: March 29, 1772, London, England
IDENTIFICATION: Swedish religious teacher, mystic, and scientist
SIGNIFICANCE: Because Swedenborg's religious ideas departed from orthodox Christianity, censors often tried to prevent the distribution of his writings

After graduating from Uppsala University in 1709, Swedenborg became a recognized authority on human biology, mechanics, geology, metallurgy, and other scientific fields. He was also an active member of the upper house of the Swedish legislature. Around 1745 he underwent a mystical religious conversion that convinced him that God had commissioned him to present a new revelation to the world. Based on his visions and communications with heavenly spirits, Swedenborg believed that he understood the true meanings of the Bible (using an allegorical approach), and he devoted the rest of his life to writing lengthy books about religion.

Swedenborg rejected literal interpretations of most doctrines of traditional Christianity. He rejected orthodox ideas about the Trinity, the vicarious atonement, original sin, Hell as a place of future punishment, the Second Coming of Christ, and the authority of institutional churches. His theological system was human-centered, teaching that Christ was the highest manifestation of humanity and that the spiritual world is populated by deceased humans, who together form a collective deity. While he never tried to found an organized sect, he attracted dedicated followers during his lifetime, and beginning in 1787, his followers established the Church of the New Jerusalem, which was based on his teachings.

In a heresy trial of 1769, a lower court of the established Lutheran Church of Sweden condemned most of Swedenborg's teachings, and the government ordered that his works were not to be published or distributed. For the next few years, two of his most prominent disciples were not allowed to teach in Swedish universities. As Swedenborg's condemnation was appealed to a higher court, however, the theological faculty of Uppsala refused to rule that his teachings were heretical in 1774; the ban on his writings and ideas ended five years later.

Throughout Swedenborg's life, his works were censored on diverse grounds. In 1738, his mystical book about the origin of the universe, *Principles of Natural Things*, was placed on the *Index Librorum Prohibitorum* of the Roman Catholic church, where it continued to be listed as late as 1948. In 1909 U.S. Post Office authorities in Philadelphia seized Swedenborg's book *Conjugal Love* on the grounds of its presumed obscenity. In 1930, all of Swedenborg's works were banned in the Soviet Union, on the grounds that these works were incompatible with the materialistic metaphysics of official Marxism.

See also Christianity; Heresy; *Index Librorum Prohibitorum*; Postal regulations; Reformation, the; Religion; Sweden.

Swift, Jonathan

BORN: November 30, 1667, Dublin, Ireland
DIED: October 19, 1745, Dublin, Ireland
IDENTIFICATION: Anglo-Irish writer and philosopher
SIGNIFICANCE: Deeply involved in eighteenth-century Irish politics, Swift took satire and irony to new heights in his attempt to educate his readers while escaping prosecution

Swift has been well described as Ireland's "patriot-in-spite-of-himself." Born into an Anglo-Irish family, he always believed his rightful place was in the English court. However, he was destined to live out his life in Ireland, his only preferment being the Dean of St. Patrick's in Dublin. He fell out of favor with the ruling Tories by his own doing. His brilliant and most difficult satire, *A Tale of a Tub* (1704), was a parable of the development of Christianity. Although it was published anonymously, Swift was widely believed to be the author and Queen Anne became persuaded that he would never prove a reliable clergyman in the Church of England.

Serving as dean of St. Patrick's involved Swift heavily in Irish politics. Political censorship in the early eighteenth century usually took the form of criminal charges against publishers and printers rather than the prosecution of authors. The aim was to deprive writers of the means to communicate their works to the public. By charging those who bought, held the copyright, transported, or published certain of Swift's works with sedition, the government hoped to silence him.

The most egregious case of this form of censorship was directed against Swift's Irish political pamphlets. In 1720 Swift wrote a short pamphlet entitled *A Proposal for the Universal Use of Irish Manufactures*. Anonymously published, the pamphlet urged the Irish to boycott English manufactured goods in retaliation against discriminatory English trade policies. Swift's printer, Edmund Watters, was tried for sedition. While Swift was widely suspected to be the pamphlet's author, conclusive evidence could not be obtained from the printer. Moreover, the jury returned a not-guilty verdict for Watters—not once but nine times. Each time the judge refused to accept the verdict, until the jury finally returned a special verdict. It directed the judge to decide the case himself. Swift ultimately escaped prosecution.

Swift's criticism of English policy expanded to a full scale assault on the Walpole ministry in *Drapier's Letters* (1724). In the guise of a cloth merchant, Swift wrote a series of six letters harshly criticizing the ruling Whig Party. The fourth letter in particular was deemed treasonous, and a reward of three hundred pounds was offered for information leading to the arrest of the letter's author.

It is in the light of Swift's personal history of persecution that his most famous work, *Gulliver's Travels* (1726), should be read. Swift used it to draw contrasts between the political philosophy of the Ancients and the Moderns, while savagely satirizing English politics and profoundly criticizing modern philosophy and science. Swift's literary art can only be fully understood when his masterwork is read with the phenomenon of political censorship in mind. Like *A Tale of a Tub* and the *Drapier's Letters*, it is written in the voice of a fictional author who is not merely a substitute for Swift himself. The apparent

772 / SWINBURNE, ALGERNON CHARLES

shortcomings of each of his fictional authors gave Swift the room he needed convincingly to deny specific interpretations of his work that could be identified with his own personal views.

See also Book publishing; Boycotts; Fear; Ireland; Sedition; Symbolic speech; United Kingdom.

Swinburne, Algernon Charles

BORN: April 5, 1837, London, England
DIED: April 10, 1909, Putney, England
IDENTIFICATION: English poet
SIGNIFICANCE: Swinburne shocked Victorian society with the sadomasochistic and homoerotic poems included in his collection *Poems and Ballads*

While attending Oxford, Swinburne met and fell under the influence of the charismatic poet Dante Gabriel Rossetti. Rossetti lived a bohemian existence and believed in the principle of "art for art's sake." As a disciple of Rossetti, Swinburne expressed his disdain for conventional Victorian mores. While Swinburne had tried his hand at writing before meeting Rossetti, the association sparked Swinburne to take his writing far more seriously. He left Oxford without taking a degree and set off for a life away from the repression he had known during his school years. After settling in London, he made a complete break with Victorian conformity and lived the life of a bohemian. He was influenced by the poetry of French author Charles Baudelaire and the sexually explicit works of the Marquis de Sade.

Although some of Swinburne's earlier works touched upon sexual matters, it was the publication of his first collection of poetry, *Poems and Ballads*, in 1866, that thoroughly scandalized Victorian England. The collection was vehemently condemned by reviewers for being heretical and immoral. With such poems as "Anactoria," "Dolores," and "Laus Veneris," Swinburne used his vast technical skill to speak about finding pleasure in the inflicting of pain during sexual love. The collection was published in the United States in a pirated edition under the title *Laus Veneris and Other Poems and Ballads*. American reviewers condemned the volume as vigorously as those in England, yet the publisher G. W. Carlton had trouble keeping up with public demand. In England rumors circulated that the publisher, Moxon, was about to be prosecuted for obscenity. On the basis of the rumors alone, Moxon had *Poems and Ballads* removed from circulation. Swinburne was outraged at what his publisher had done. Another publisher, John Camden Hotten, approached Swinburne with an offer to republish the collection. Swinburne agreed to Hotten's terms, and *Poems and Ballads* was once again available in September, 1866. Because of the controversy surrounding his collection, Swinburne became a household name. In pushing the limits of public tolerance, he became known as the English Charles Baudelaire.

See also Baudelaire, Charles; Obscenity: sale and possession; Poetry; Sade, Marquis de.

Symbolic speech

DEFINITION: Any form of expression in which symbols or symbolic actions are used beyond purely spoken or written speech

SIGNIFICANCE: The First Amendment of the U.S. Constitution provides nearly absolute protection against censorship of the press or "pure" speech, but does not protect as strongly symbolic speech involving actions

Although the U.S. Supreme Court has interpreted the First Amendment to provide virtually absolute protection against prior restraint or most other censorship of "pure" speech or the press, the protection has not been as strong for either written or spoken symbolic speech that is frequently mixed or "briganded" (to use the Court's word) with action. These must be balanced against society's right to be protected against dangerous actions. Common sense indicates that the government has the right to prevent and to punish actions such as murders, thefts, and assaults that are harmful to public order. Historically there has been a clear line between words and actions.

History of Symbolic Speech Doctrine. The Supreme Court has long maintained a distinction between protected words and unprotected actions. The early view was that some words were so potent that they could themselves be considered "actions." In *Chaplinsky v. New Hampshire* (1942), the Court held that certain words in certain contexts constituted "fighting words" as potent to some listeners as a blow to the face. Such were "no essential part of any exposition of ideas" and the state could prohibit or punish their use. This decision continued a long-standing word and action dichotomy.

Because words are themselves symbols (or composed of letters that are symbols), this distinction was hard to maintain. There were some seemingly contradictory cases that set the stage for the development of the symbolic speech doctrine. In *Stromberg v. California* (1931), for example, the Court held that California had erred in banning the display of a "red" or "communist" flag since such a display was a valid exercise of free speech, thus developing a basis for the symbolic speech doctrine.

In its passive, written form, symbolic speech is usually a poster, placard, bumper sticker, button, or shirt on which words are printed. Even when written, symbolic speech is not thought of as a "press" issue since it is more in the nature of a slogan. The Court has increasingly protected more forms of these protests under the First Amendment, including some forms that clearly would have been unacceptable earlier. Since *Tinker v. Des Moines Independent Community School District* (1969), schools cannot stop students from wearing black armbands that protest U.S. government policies such as the Vietnam War. In *Cohen v. California* (1971), the Court overturned the conviction of Robert Cohen, a student who wore a jacket into a state court building with the words, "Fuck the Draft" emblazoned across the front. As an indication of how far the Court has progressed, Justice John Marshall Harlan, the most conservative member, wrote in *Cohen*: "While the particular four-letter word being litigated here is perhaps more distasteful than most of its genre, it is nevertheless often true that one man's vulgarity is another man's lyric."

The next logical question was what if a printed message contained no words at all. In *Spence v. Washington* (1974), the Supreme Court confronted a clash between two symbols: the

During the ceremony in which Tommie Smith (center) and Juan Carlos (right) were awarded medals for the 200-meter dash at the 1968 Olympics, they raised gloved fists to protest the oppression of African Americans in the United States. Their silent expressions of symbolic speech led to their expulsion from the Olympics and permanently branded them with a notoriety that hampered their later career choices. (AP/Wide World Photos)

American flag and the well-known peace symbol. The Court ruled that police cannot arrest someone for defacing an American flag, even if they display it or wear it in an unconventional way as a protest, as Spence did when he taped a peace symbol over the flag displayed from his window.

In its more active, spoken form, symbolic speech moves from words to actions which are said to be expressive. While the Court broadened the definitions of symbolic speech to the point that it seemed about to cross the boundary from speaking ideas to taking actions, it left some limits, at least in part. In *United States v. O'Brien* (1968), O'Brien protested the war by burning his draft card, claiming his action was symbolic speech. O'Brien was convicted for destroying a document that he was legally required to keep. The Court upheld his conviction stating, "We cannot accept the view that an apparently limitless variety of conduct can be labeled 'speech' whenever

the person engaging in the conduct intends thereby to express an idea." It thereby implied limits, such as violations of otherwise valid laws, beyond which it would not extend protections to symbolic speech.

The Status of Symbolic Speech. Later, the Supreme Court appeared to move away from the *O'Brien* case distinction and toward *Spence* by protecting flag-burning as a form of symbolic speech. A case arose in Texas, one of many American states that had a law against flag desecration, when a Communist Party member was arrested for burning an American flag outside the 1984 Republican National Convention. In *Texas v. Johnson* (1989) the Court, by a 5-4 decision, overturned Gregory Johnson's conviction on grounds that his action was a protected political protest.

It might seem that the distinction between thought and action would have been an easier test to follow than one that relied on determining motives. The *Johnson* decision set off a howl of protests calling for a constitutional amendment to remove flag burning from First Amendment protection, but this effort failed because Congress feared amending the Bill of Rights. Congress did attempt to ban flag burning with an ordinary statute. When test cases occurred, the Supreme Court struck down the federal statute as it had the Texas statute in the companion cases, *United States v. Eichman* (1990) and *United States v. Haggerty* (1990). Under the doctrine of selective incorporation of the Fourteenth Amendment, neither Congress nor the states can even punish the burning of the American flag as a form of protest.

There may also be a concern with the Court's rendering decisions that seem to go against deeply held cultural beliefs, such as respecting the national flag. Its decisions in this field have had the effect of using up some of the Court's reservoir of legitimacy. Beyond this, questions arise about several other issues. The freedom of persons to express themselves symbolically would seem to conflict with the doctrine of fighting words—an old concept that has been given new importance as the issue of prohibitions against racial epithets, hate laws, and sexual harassment have come to the fore. —*Richard L. Wilson*

See also Bumper stickers; Censorship; Fighting words; Flag burning; Fourteenth Amendment; Free speech; Offensive language; Prior restraint; School dress codes; Street oratory; *Texas v. Johnson.*

BIBLIOGRAPHY

The best book of general scholarship on this subject is Henry J. Abraham and Barbara A. Perry, *Freedom and the Court* (6th ed. New York: Oxford University Press, 1994). For a thoughtful analysis of free expression, see Kent Greenawalt's *Speech, Crime, and the Uses of Language* (New York: Oxford University Press, 1989). Greenawalt's *Fighting Words* (Princeton, N.J.: Princeton University Press, 1991) provides an excellent comparative analysis of Canadian and U.S. conceptions of symbolic speech. One of the best edited casebooks for general readers is Wallace Mendelson's *The American Constitution and Civil Liberties* (Homewood, Ill.: Dorsey, 1981). An interesting compilation of articles on flag burning is found in Michael Kent Curtis' *The Constitution and the Flag* (New York: Garland, 1993).

Syndicated television

DEFINITION: Programs produced for distribution to stations independently of the major networks, or programs redistributed to independent stations after being broadcast on networks

SIGNIFICANCE: The control of program distribution channels by media conglomerates can limit small producers' access to on-the-air opportunities

In American television, syndication is a large and amorphous market for independent program creators and producers and media conglomerates to develop and distribute programs. Syndicated programming encompasses series and specials sold to stations for airing in local areas. The largest market is commercial television stations; however, syndicated programming is also sold to radio stations, cable services, and noncommercial broadcast stations.

Of the three categories of syndicated programs, the most common is off-network syndication—the selling of previously aired network shows to local stations. Off-network syndication is popularly known as rerun syndication. First-run syndication sells programs created exclusively for sale to local stations. Game shows and talk shows predominate in this category. Theatrical films, made-for-television films, and one-time-only specials make up a third category of syndicated programs.

The television syndication market originated in complaints made by Hollywood film producers in the middle and late 1960's that the major television networks unfairly controlled the production of television programs. The Federal Communications Commission (FCC) responded by passing the Financial Interest and Syndication Rules (Fin-Syn), which prohibited the networks from owning and profiting from the programming produced by others. These rules also prohibited the networks themselves from selling programming to television stations. The FCC also created the Prime-Time Access Rule, which limited the networks to only three of the four prime-time hours (7:00 to 11:00 P.M.) in the fifty largest television markets.

These FCC rule changes created new markets for programming supplied by sources other than the networks. Existing Hollywood companies and new, independent companies began to supply station programming. The television networks were not, however, content to abandon the syndicated television business. Years of lobbying and changes in the FCC's stance, from regulator of broadcasting to deregulator of broadcasting, led to the elimination of the Financial Interest and Syndication Rules and the Prime-Time Access Rule. By the 1990's the television networks were producing their own programs and even selling programs to competing networks.

Network ownership provided more programming sales opportunities. Ownership of the programs and the stations that air them is a form of vertical integration. This can lead to renewed creative control and distribution problems and censorship for program creators, producers, and distributors. Media mergers place greater control of program creation, production, and distribution within several large companies and decrease the need for independent producers and syndicators. Mergers also force independents to seek unwanted business alliances. Creative control shifts from small to large firms.

Programs from independent producers often attract only small audiences. The combination of small audiences and demands to share production profits with major companies creates pressures that can lead to creative censorship before production, or after a show is produced and program distribution is being sought. Program creators and producers, unable to find suitable distribution for their programs, are often forced either to merge with the larger companies, or to go out of business.

Small production firms have continued to exist; however, as more and more television and radio stations are bought by large companies and media conglomerates control cable channel distribution, the small firms must seek alliances with the large firms or see their distribution channels shrink. Losing independent producers lessens program creativity.

See also Broadcast media; Cable television; Talk shows; Television; Television networks.

T

Talk shows

DEFINITION: Radio and television programming built around conversations among hosts, celebrity guests, and listeners

SIGNIFICANCE: Some talk shows have used controversial topics and coarse language to attract audiences; efforts to limit show discussions bring up censorship issues

The talk show is one of the oldest program genres. The programs allow the electronic media to do what they do best—provide listeners or viewers access to people with whom they normally could not meet or talk. The word "broadcast," drawn from agricultural vocabulary, means "sow" or "spread," and the broadcast media accomplish the job of presenting information through the talk show format. Talk shows are technically simple to produce. For radio or television only microphones and chairs are needed; a modest set, and perhaps an in-studio audience, may also be used for the television talk show.

Early radio and television talk shows included cooking, beauty hints, gossip, and other topics designed for the housewife. The character and content of talk shows has changed as the U.S. media have evolved. Over-the-air broadcasting has moved away from a public service function and toward an advertising-promotion function. Radio stations have increased in number from a few hundred in 1935 to more than twelve thousand licensed commercial and noncommercial radio stations. Television has become a ubiquitous home appliance. Cable television, created first in the 1950's to feed signals from the few operating television stations into the homes of viewers, has become a delivery conduit not for five or six over-the-air television signals but for fifty or more channels available through a cable subscription.

The novelty of broadcasting is no longer enough to attract listeners or viewers. Listeners' and viewers' appetites—and tolerances—have caused changes in programming formats and content. Multiple channels and the demand for the highest ratings possible have fueled the changes in talk show content. Syndicated and local radio, television, and cable talk show topics range from the tame (gardening talk shows, for example), to the controversial to the outrageous. Some talk shows provide needed platforms for discussion of controversial views. Others use the program only to draw an audience by appealing to prurient interests. A small portion of all talk shows, controversial shows draw the strongest discussions about content and censorship.

Talk Radio. Radio talk shows are typically aired live and afford listeners the opportunity to listen for controversial content and frequently allow listeners to participate through call-in segments. Radio, in the early 1970's, displaced by television as the public's primary entertainment medium, saw the emergence of a new genre of talk show. The candor with which sexual material was discussed led the programs to be referred to as "topless radio." The Federal Communications Commis-

sion (FCC), in the Sonderling Broadcasting case, fined a suburban Chicago radio station, WGLD-FM, two thousand dollars for airing material characterized as "indecent or obscene."

The Supreme Court has upheld the FCC's authority to limit indecent broadcasts. The government can ban indecent programming between 6 A.M. and 10 P.M. as a way of protecting children from offensive or sexually suggestive material. Still, no clear guidelines exist for what is acceptable or unacceptable. Station personalities tend to speak first and worry about the consequences later.

The other form of radio talk programming to emerge has focused not on sexual content but political content. Talk radio has become the new soapbox for political discussion. Until the late 1980's, it was thought that talk radio needed to be produced locally, featuring local hosts and local issues. The successful national syndication of radio personality Rush Limbaugh's program in the late 1980's demonstrated that listener interest could be sustained in a discussion of national politics and current events.

Television Talk Shows. Television talk shows have evolved from locally produced daytime chat programs aimed at housewives or weekend shows aired to meet FCC public affairs programming requirements to hour-long internationally syndicated talk programs. Early program hosts such as Merv Griffin or Mike Douglas provided a mixture of gossip and entertainment news. The television talk show genre changed in the 1970's when *The Phil Donahue Show* began to air nationally in program syndication on local television stations. Donahue's show featured controversial and noncontroversial guests and, more important, included a studio audience that achieved participatory status by questioning the guests. A new type of talk show was created, one that spawned a multitude of imitators, including Oprah Winfrey, Jenny Jones, Geraldo Rivera, Sally Jessie Raphael, Morton Downey, Jr., and Jerry Springer.

Most talk shows are recorded so that the studio audiences can react to the spontaneous and sometimes outrageous show content. Producers generally know how explicit the language used on the show can be and what will draw complaints but still keep the program on the air. Program excerpts are used to create teases to lure home viewers. Controversial topics on one show cause producers of competing shows to likewise select controversial topics. Talk show successes and the low production costs drive the creation of a fresh crop of shows and show hosts each fall. For new shows to be noticed by viewers, show producers push the limits of acceptability and feature more controversial topics in the quest to attract viewers.

Controversial and Outrageous Topics. Controversial topics did not appear overnight. In fact, topic escalation has been gradual and probably reflects both changes in society and competitive marketplace factors. Premarital or extramarital

British author Salman Rushdie—whose 1989 novel, The Satanic Verses, *brought down a death order from the Iranian government—discusses free speech on Phil Donahue's television talk show in January, 1996.* (AP/Wide World Photos)

affairs, AIDS, substance abuse, homosexuality, and spousal abuse are but a few of the topics that have become mainstream public awareness and discussion subjects. They are reflected in print and broadcast news coverage and on talk shows. Controversial and outrageous talk show topics have included makeovers for transvestites, pregnant women with cheating husbands, husbands afraid of losing their wives to lesbian lovers, and other material intended to draw strong emotional reactions from audiences.

A revolt by some television station managers, viewers, and advertisers began in March, 1995, after a male guest on Jenny Jones's talk show murdered another man who revealed his secret crush on him. The guest was told he had a secret admirer; he was not told that the admirer was a man. The episode never aired, but the television and cable trade magazine *Electronic Media* (December 11, 1995) labeled the event the shot heard around the dial.

Program genres follow a cycle of invention, imitation, and decline. A decision by television station general managers not to purchase national shows for local airing because of viewer reactions influences content. Fewer buyers will mean fewer shows and less pressure to air controversy. Similar influence may come from large national advertisers reluctant to advertise on the more controversial or derivative shows.

Government regulators in the United States and in countries importing U.S. programming have found it difficult to regulate program content in a manner that resists free-speech court challenges. Media mergers and deregulation may provide regulators with an indirect means of influencing programming. Companies merging or otherwise seeking regulatory approval sometimes promise to change programming. When Westinghouse purchased the Columbia Broadcasting System it pledged to the FCC to increase children's programming. Time-Warner abandoned its support of a controversial rap music distributor shortly after announcing its merger with Turner Broadcasting.   —*Gregory G. Pitts*

See also Call-in programs; Carlin, George; Federal Communications Commission; Limbaugh, Rush; Pacifica Foundation; Stern, Howard; Syndicated television; Television.

BIBLIOGRAPHY

Erik Barnouw's *A Tower in Babel: A History of Broadcasting in the United States, to 1933* (New York: Oxford University Press, 1966) provides a thorough chronology of the development of radio broadcasting in the United States through 1933. From the experiments of early scientists and engineers to the first efforts to regulate broadcasting by the Federal Radio Commission, Barnouw discusses the beginnings of the wireless medium. Susan T. Eastman's *Broadcast/Cable Programming: Strategies and Practices* (4th ed. Belmont, Calif.: Wadsworth Publishers, 1993) discusses the ability and need for news and entertainment programming to attract an audience. The impact of station ownership by media conglomerates and the effect such ownership has had on local and syndicated programming is also discussed. Frank J. Kahn, ed., in *Documents of American Broadcasting* (3d ed. Englewood Cliffs, N.J.: Prentice-Hall, 1978), provides a collection of primary source materials related to broadcasting public policy, regulation, and history. The book contains a thematic table of contents which includes sections on regulation of programming, broadcast journalism, regulation of competition, and the public's interest. Christopher H. Sterling and John M. Kittross provide a comprehensive review of the development and growth of radio and television broadcasting in the United States in *Stay Tuned: A Concise History of American Broadcasting* (2d ed. Belmont, Calif.: Wadsworth Publishers, 1990). The authors chronicle the technological development of broadcasting, review the regulatory history, and discuss programming development.

Talmadge, Eugene

BORN: September 23, 1884, Forsyth, Georgia
DIED: December 21, 1946, Atlanta, Georgia
IDENTIFICATION: Governor of Georgia, 1933-1937, 1941-1943
SIGNIFICANCE: Talmadge advocated the removal of books advocating racial equality from Georgia's public schools and universities

Talmadge was a vocal and aggressive defender of traditional Southern values and institutions, especially white supremacy in race relations. In 1941 as governor of Georgia, he proposed the removal of books advocating racial cooperation from public schools and state-supported colleges and universities. During a controversy over the dismissal of two college administrators accused of favoring racial equality in education, Talmadge authorized a citizens' committee to provide a list of books and publications deemed subversive of race relations. The committee identified twenty-three textbooks, which the state's board of education banned from the public schools. Also proscribed were books in college libraries as well as some texts assigned in college courses. Banned books included works advancing the theory of evolution, which was believed to contradict the Bible, and books judged to be critical of the South.

In August, 1941, Talmadge announced that he would ask the 1943 session of the Georgia legislature to require the burning of library books that advocated equality in race relations. However, the controversy over Talmadge's interference in the state's schools led to his defeat in the 1942 gubernatorial primary. After Talmadge lost the election, the pressures for censorship of books in Georgia's schools and universities diminished considerably.

See also Book burning; Libraries; Libraries, school; Race; Textbooks; Universities.

Talmud, The

TYPE OF WORK: Book
WRITTEN: Second century C.E. to the present
AUTHORS: Rabbinical scholars
SUBJECT MATTER: Compilation of oral traditions of Jewish law, touching on all aspects of life

SIGNIFICANCE: Understanding how the medieval Christian Church and modern totalitarian governments tried to destroy or censor the Talmud is essential to understanding Jewish-Gentile relationships

The Talmud is a vast compendium of rabbinic commentary on the 613 commandments set forth in the Five Books of Moses (the Pentateuch). It is known as the Oral Law because every generation took great care to attribute its contents to the original authors, avoiding putting it into writing lest it assume a status comparable to the Bible itself, the Written Law. However, during periods of bitter persecution, the rabbinic leadership took the lead in committing the Oral Law to writing, lest it be lost during the battle for survival. Thus, the oldest portion, the Mishna, written in Hebrew, was compiled late in the second century by Yehudah Ha-Nasi, during the Roman persecutions which followed the suppression of the last great Jewish revolt in 132-135 C.E.

Continued legal interpretation resulted in the growth of two great bodies of Oral Law, developed separately in Palestine and Babylonia. It was to be the Babylonian text which was ultimately set in writing, in Aramaic. This compilation is credited to Rabbi Mar Bar Ashi, (352-427). It, rather than the Jerusalem Gemara (Completion), has come to be regarded as authoritative and complete. Mishna and Gemara, together, constitute the Talmud.

This vast sea of legal commentary contains not only the definitive decisions of great rabbis over almost a millennium, but dissenting opinions, as well. In addition, this huge work contains a mass of *aggada* or narrative containing parables, legends, and proverbs. This material is sometimes only peripherally related to the actual legal decisions under discussion. Thus, religious considerations aside, the Talmud is a mirror reflecting contemporary Jewish opinions of the world from the time of Alexander the Great until the age of the Zoroastrian persecutions in Babylonia. These included comments about Judaism's increasingly hostile daughter, the new Christian faith.

Censorship in Medieval Christianity. As Christianity became the state church of the Roman Empire in the fourth century the Talmud became a symbol of the risks inherent in tolerating the old mother faith. Thus European medieval history is filled with repetitive attempts to censor or to destroy what had come to be regarded as a pernicious attack on Christianity. Attempts at the censorship of talmudic writings can be numbered in the hundreds. Pope Clement IV (1265-1268), censored not only the Talmud, but all Jewish books. Most dramatically, however, the Talmud was condemned to be burned at Paris in 1242, and in Italy in 1553. Complete censorship even forced the Jews to rewrite their synagogue service, to remove any references regarded as contradicting Christian doctrine. To this day, the *Olenu* prayer which concludes most synagogue services displays one text in services conducted by the descendants of European Jews, and another text in the services of Asran and Israeli Jews whose ancestors never suffered the censorship of the medieval Church.

Fortunately, copies of the Talmud existed in every land where Jews lived, so that it became impossible to destroy it.

The greatest danger of losing the Talmud ended when the printing press made possible mass reproduction. A printing of the Mishna was completed at Naples in 1492, and the Babylonian Gemara was printed at Venice in 1520-1523.

Until the fifteenth century, there were no Christian scholars in Europe who could translate Hebrew and Aramaic sufficiently well to understand the Talmud. Thus, the repetitive attacks were usually made possible by apostate Jews posing as talmudic authorities. Particularly serious threats to the survival of the work were posed in all Europe by Pope Gregory IX in 1239, in France a few years later, and in Spain early in the following century. Perhaps the worst example of the use of Jewish renegades to destroy the Talmud came when southern French rabbis who opposed the rationalist philosophy of Maimonides, petitioned King Louis IX of France to burn his writings. The king obliged them, and exceeded their request by ordering the burning of the Talmud.

Early Christian Defenders of the Talmud. A turning point came in 1509 when Johannes Pfefferkorn, a former kosher slaughterer who had a superficial acquaintance with the Talmud, published a booklet titled the *Judenspiegel* ("Jew's Mirror"), describing the Talmud as not merely critical of Christianity, but blasphemous as well. After converting to Roman Catholicism, Pfefferkorn attempted to ingratiate himself with his new coreligionists by such accusations, absurd in themselves because they took isolated talmudic references entirely out of context. Because of the sensational circumstances of his charges, however, Holy Roman Emperor Maximilian I was moved to convene a council to examine the charges. It was composed of Pfefferkorn, Jakob van Hoogstraeten, the Inquisitor of Cologne, and representatives of four universities. Johannes Reuchlin, professor of Hebrew at the University of Heidelberg, did not really have any expertise in talmudic law. His primary interest was in cabalistic, mystical writings. Nevertheless, he knew enough to defend the Talmud from Pfefferkorn's malicious charges. In the end, Reuchlin courageously declared that the Jews were subjects of the Holy Roman Empire who deserved to be protected in their independent religious rights. He added that there was much information in the Talmud which Christians interested in the history of their own religion should value.

Reuchlin's testimony ignited explosive controversy. An impressive gallery of authorities rallied to his defense. Martin Luther, not yet having begun the Protestant Reformation, achieved his first notoriety by supporting Reuchlin. Others who leaped into the fray as Reuchlin's advocates were Desiderius Erasmus, Ulrich von Hutten, England's Bishop Fisher of Rochester, Philip Schwarzerd (Melanchton), and fifty-three cities and sovereign German princes. Europe was convulsed with laughter at an anonymous published work titled *Letters of Obscure Men*, deliberately written in ungrammatical Latin, mocking the pretensions of Pfefferkorn and the Inquisition. The affair died as the Reformation caught the attention of Christendom. For the Jews, however, the Talmud had been spared, and even more significantly, a prominent Christian had defended their rights as citizens of the empire. The case dragged out until 1520 and ultimately ended with a rebuke and a small fine imposed upon Reuchlin.

The seventeenth century witnessed a widespread vogue for the study of the Hebrew language by scholarly Christians, such that King James I of England became personally involved in the Bible translation that bears his name. Once Jewish texts of all sorts were open to the examination of learned Christian scholars, it became more difficult for ignorant bigots to demand the censorship or suppression of the Talmud.

"Talmud" as a Generic Term. Over the past two centuries, as racial anti-Semitism has replaced religious anti-Semitism, bigots of all sorts have tended to use the word "talmudic" as a generic term for alleged Jewish plots to dominate the world. *The Protocols of the Elders of Zion*, the most infamous of those fictions, has been promoted by so varied a group of sponsors as automobile magnate Henry Ford, Nazi propagandists, and Israel's Arab opponents. In the Soviet Union, not merely the Talmud, but all Jewish religion was rigorously suppressed to the point wherein even the study of the Hebrew language was almost impossible for ordinary Jews. Only politically dependable students might study it at the university level.
—Arnold Blumberg

See also Anti-Defamation League; Bible; Book burning; Erasmus, Desiderius; Israel; Judaism; Koran; Luther, Martin; Religion.

BIBLIOGRAPHY

Salo W. Baron's *A Social and Religious History of the Jews* (in 16 volumes; New York: Columbia University Press, 1937) is the most thorough examination of the role of the Talmud in Jewish life, and the frequent effort to censor or threaten its existence. Eli Kedourie edited *The Jewish World: History and Culture of the Jewish People* (New York: Harry N. Abrams, 1979), which contains a vast collection of essays by outstanding authorities dealing with this subject. Hermann L. Strack's *Introduction to the Talmud and Midrash* (Philadelphia: Jewish Publication Society of America, 1931) is an essential description of the contents of the Talmud, with extensive notes on the history of printings of the work, as well as references to attempts to censor it. Max L. Margolis and Alexander Marx's *A History of the Jewish People* (Philadelphia: Jewish Publication Society of America, 1927) contains frequent references to this subject, and offers a fine chronology at the end. Almost all of the numerous textbooks covering Jewish history deal with this subject.

Tape-delay broadcasting

DEFINITION: Method of briefly delaying the broadcast of otherwise live material

SIGNIFICANCE: This technique permits broadcasters to delete or edit unwelcome words or ideas before they are transmitted to audiences

Tape-delay broadcasting is a system used by radio and television stations during call-in shows or any type of live broadcasts. The procedure is briefly to delay transmission of material before it airs, allowing the station to delete objectionable words or ideas. A "delay line" is a tape recording a few seconds long designed to retard playback and allow for censorship of questionable material. This technique is primarily used to monitor the language of call-in guests.

As television and radio have developed, audiences have shown a growing preference for interview and talk shows. The Federal Communications Commission (FCC) is a government agency that regulates broadcast media. Although the FCC may not interfere with basic freedom of speech rights, the Supreme Court has delivered a mandate concerning the content of broadcast speech. A 1978 Court decision states that broadcast speech must be treated differently than other forms of expression because children have access to programming without parent supervision. Also, radios are in homes where people's privacy interests are entitled to special deference, as unconsenting adults may tune into a station without any warning that offensive language is being broadcast. Because of the scarcity of broadcast spectrum space the government must license the broadcast media to protect the public interest.

The FCC has the power to punish stations for broadcasting indecent, profane, or obscene language. Stations use tape-delay broadcasting to protect themselves from inadvertently violating the broadcast rules.

See also Broadcast media; Carlin, George; Federal Communications Commission; Radio; Talk shows; Television.

Tarzan

TYPE OF WORK: Books
PUBLISHED: 1912-1940
AUTHOR: Edgar Rice Burroughs (1875-1950)
SUBJECT MATTER: Twenty-four novels about an aristocratic Englishman who lives in the jungles of Africa
SIGNIFICANCE: These books have been banned for a variety of reasons, including their implicitly Darwinian themes, their anti-German episodes, and their presumed sexual immorality

The author of more than seventy novels, Burroughs is best known for his books about Tarzan, a white man who lives in the jungles of equatorial Africa. *Tarzan of the Apes* (1912), the first novel in the series, begins the tale of a white child reared by an imaginary species of "great apes" after his marooned parents die. He learns the law of the jungle from animals and has almost no contact with other human beings until a party of Europeans enters his domain. From them he learns the ways of humankind, and he marries the Englishwoman Jane Porter. Thereafter he has adventures among both animals and humans.

In 1920—by which time six Tarzan novels were in print—an outcry was rising in England over the books' Darwinian themes. Several editors and printers expressed strong reservations regarding Tarzan as the evolution of Kayla the Ape. This led to a boycott of publication in England for several years.

The seventh novel in the series, *Tarzan the Untamed*, was published in English in 1921 and translated into German in late 1924. Its German title was equivalent to "Tarzan the German-Devourer." Written by Burroughs in 1915, when Germany and Great Britain were fighting in World War I, the story contains several episodes in which lions eat German "Huns"—including one scene in which Tarzan himself orders a lion to eat a German officer. Although the story has Tarzan avenging

the apparent murder of Jane, the German press began denouncing the Tarzan books and their author as representative of all the foreign powers that had humiliated Germany during the Great War. By the next year, all Tarzan books were banned from sale in Germany.

In the United States, the Tarzan books raised controversy from their first appearance until the early 1960's. The Los Angeles Public Library, for example, banned the books in 1918 out of fear that the books would contaminate the morals or literary tastes of its readers—because Tarzan and Jane were not married and because of the suspect relationship between Tarzan and the apes. During the early 1960's, Tarzan was again a target of censorship when a librarian captured national headlines by removing the books from the shelves because Tarzan and Jane were "living in sin." The librarian evidently had not read the books, for the couple were married in the first novel. Publicity from this incident revived interest in the series and began republication of all the original books.

See also Darwin, Charles; Evolution; Libraries; Morality; Race; World War I.

TASS

FOUNDED: 1925
TYPE OF ORGANIZATION: Official Soviet news agency
SIGNIFICANCE: TASS presented an official interpretation of news to the outside world

Among the primary means by which government of the Soviet Union maintained power were widespread propaganda and the strict censorship of virtually all forms of expression. TASS facilitated the government's control of information in both of these ways. TASS was at once the country's primary network for collecting general news and for disseminating sanitized versions of it.

TASS, the Russian acronym for "Telegraphic Agency of the Soviet Union," was established in 1925. It remained the official state news agency until the demise of the Soviet Union in 1991. TASS initially had been established to replace its Russian predecessor, *Rosta*, which had been set up by V. I. Lenin upon securing power in 1918. For most of its existence TASS operated under the formal supervision of the Soviet Council of Ministers, and thus was considered a government, rather than a Communist Party, organization. The party had established its own propaganda departments at the central and regional levels. TASS, like all government bodies, remained thoroughly controlled by the party apparatus, and was charged with promoting the party's ideology and interpretation of events. Other governmental agencies that controlled the media included *Novosti*, which produced news features and photos, largely for external consumption; *Goskino*, which concerned the domestic release of films; and *Gosteleradio*, which oversaw radio and television broadcasts.

Like *Rosta*, TASS was somewhat limited in its initial scope. Before long, however, it grew into a major news organization, with reporters and offices spread throughout the country, and with correspondents deployed around the globe. It became one of the Soviet Union's longest-lived and extensive tools for censorship and propaganda. With its network of foreign correspondents, TASS might have been well-suited for espionage and other illicit activities. It was *Novosti* (founded in 1961), however, that had direct ties to the Soviet Union's intelligence agency, the KGB, and thus which often served as a front for KGB activities. *Novosti* frequently supervised movements of foreign correspondents operating in the Soviet Union.

TASS was the main supplier of stories for Soviet newspapers. Newspapers traditionally had served as the people's primary source of news in the Soviet Union, and through them TASS was able to promulgate the government's version of news, define public debate, and inculcate party values. Stories provided through TASS seldom included outright falsehoods. Instead, news was generally purged of information that might be embarrassing to the government, while more positive events and data in the Soviet Union (as well as negative stories about the West) were emphasized. The result was a highly cohesive, coherent, and one-sided picture of reality that placed the Soviet Union and its government in the best possible light. Conflicting interpretations were not officially recognized. For example, until Mikhail Gorbachev assumed power in the 1980's, the government prohibited opposition publications, although underground publications existed throughout Soviet history.

TASS did more than provide stories to newspapers. As a major information-gathering arm of the government, TASS supplied less censored, and even uncensored, compilations of its information to authorized recipients. News reports were classified by the color of their cover page: "blue TASS" was for general distribution, and thus the most heavily censored. "White TASS" was distributed to public information officers and others whose jobs required a more accurate sense of events and such data as crime statistics and incidents of official corruption. White TASS also included reprints of articles and editorials from foreign publications. "Red TASS" was used by newspaper editors and various government officials who could be trusted with sensitive information. TASS "special bulletins," which contained the most sensitive information concerning crises and secret government policies, were reserved for Politburo members and other top officials.

For most of its existence, and particularly under Joseph Stalin's government during the 1930's and 1940's, TASS represented the quintessential ministry of information of an authoritarian communist state. Although not as omnipotent and malevolent as the Ministry of Truth portrayed in George Orwell's *Nineteen Eighty-Four* (1949), TASS carried out a censorship role that distinguished the press in the Soviet Union from the Western democratic ideal. The strict supervision by the Communist Party, the security classification of news, and the mandatory ideological guidelines, ensured that TASS institutionalized its censorship role.

Glasnost and Afterwards. Beginning in the mid-1980's, Mikhail Gorbachev's policy of *glasnost*, or openness, moved TASS closer to a credible, relatively unbiased source of news. For example, in 1986, after some initial hesitation, TASS reported relatively straightforward accounts of the meltdown at the Chernobyl nuclear power plant. While perhaps not a classic example of investigative journalism, TASS's handling of the Chernobyl disaster was unprecedented by Soviet stand-

ards, and illustrated quite clearly the changes that *glasnost* was bringing. Two years later TASS for the first time released to the newspapers official casualty figures for the war in Afghanistan. Until that time, military losses were a standard item for censorship by the Soviet authorities. By the end of the decade, TASS was reporting on such previously forbidden subjects as homelessness, homosexuality, drug abuse, domestic violence, and other social problems. Newspapers published letters to the editor that were critical of government policies, and some opposition newspapers were granted official permission to publish.

Perhaps partly as a result of *glasnost*, the party's hold on the Soviet government progressively weakened. By the end of 1991 the parliament had decreed the demise of the Soviet Union and Mikhail Gorbachev resigned the presidency. The country dissolved into its fifteen component republics, and the successor countries adopted varying degrees of multiparty government and democratic pluralism. Post-Soviet Russia in particular embraced the principles of free expression and governmental openness. Archives were opened and opposition publications flourished.

The new Russian government reorganized TASS as a legitimate news organization for a self-proclaimed democratic society. The new organization goes by the acronym ITAR, for Information Telegraph Agency of Russia. It focuses strictly on news within the Russian Federation, and supplies reports without the censorship for which its predecessor was known. News concerning the rest of the former Soviet Union is handled by a second successor to TASS, the Telegraph Agency of the Countries of the Commonwealth. This agency's Russian acronym also happens to be TASS. The two post-Soviet news agencies work in close cooperation, and news releases sent abroad are usually identified as originating from "ITAR-TASS."

—*Steve D. Boilard*

See also Communism; News media censorship; Propaganda; Soviet Union; Stalin, Joseph.

BIBLIOGRAPHY

For a deep analysis, see Theodore E. Kruglak, *The Two Faces of TASS* (Minneapolis: University of Minnesota Press, 1962). Many books concerning Soviet government and politics include sections or chapters describing the government's role in the collection and dissemination of news. Most make explicit reference to TASS, including Gordon B. Smith, *Soviet Politics: Continuity and Contradiction* (New York: St. Martin's Press, 1988). For a more focused look at journalism and the media in the Soviet Union, see Ellen P. Mickiewicz, *Media and the Russian Public* (New York: Praeger, 1981), Gayle Durham Hollander, *Soviet Political Indoctrination: Developments in Mass Media and Propaganda Since Stalin* (New York: Praeger, 1972), and Walter M. Brasch and Dana R. Ulloth, *The Press and the State: Sociohistorical and Contemporary Studies* (Lanham, Md.: University Press of America, 1986).

Tax laws

DEFINITION: Legislation relating to various forms of taxation

SIGNIFICANCE: Tax laws have sometimes been used as a censorship tool, particularly as a means of controlling the press

Taxes on the press have served as an important tool of censorship. In the nineteenth century, for example, many European nations enacted stamp taxes on newspapers and magazines, thereby placing the prices of the taxed publications beyond the means of the poor. Other government assessments have included taxes on advertising and paper. Additional forms of taxation have been requirements that newspapers deposit money as a condition of operation; such deposits are held in case newspapers are found guilty of libel. Practices such as these have generally been expressly intended to limit publication of news media to the members of the middle and upper classes, who alone could be entrusted to publish "appropriate" material.

Taxes on the Press. American jurisprudence has long recognized the potential dangers of taxation of the press. Thus, although restrictions on speech that take the form of taxation are not specifically outlawed, they are subject to judicial scrutiny under the First Amendment. The underlying First Amendment concern is that taxes not be used to force a publishing business—by reducing its profitability—to adopt the government's point of view. This is far from a frivolous concern. In 1934, for example, the state of Louisiana imposed a 2 percent tax on the gross advertising receipts of all newspapers with circulations greater than twenty thousand. Although only thirteen of the state's 124 newspapers were subject to the tax, all but one of the thirteen happened to be papers that had recently published negative information about the state's powerful senator Huey Long. Shortly afterward Long and Louisiana's governor complained to the state legislature about "lying newspapers," and described the new tax as a "tax on lying." Ultimately the U.S. Supreme Court held this tax unconstitutional, in *Grosjean v. American Press Co.* (1936), presumably because of its improper censorial purpose.

When an improper purpose does not appear to be present, however, the question remains whether taxes on press are constitutional. In *Minneapolis Star & Tribune Company v. Minnesota Commissioner of Revenue* (1980), the U.S. Supreme Court fashioned an approach to this question that focused first on whether a tax is one of "general applicability." A generally applicable tax is one applied to a broad group of taxpayers, who may include the press. Such taxes are constitutional as an acceptable economic regulation of the press under traditional First Amendment analysis. The rationale for this requirement is that because a generally applicable tax applies to taxpayers other than the press, it cannot easily be used to manipulate the views of the press or advertisers. Of particular concern in this arena is a state's ability to target specific members of the press or advertising community—ones whose views are not agreeable to its government. The test of general applicability effectively deals with this danger by requiring no discrimination among members of the press or among advertisers.

Differential Taxes. For taxes that are not generally applicable—known as "differential taxes"—the Supreme Court fashioned a two-step analysis. Under this approach, a court analyzing a differential tax must first weigh the burdens of the tax on the press against the asserted state interest. It must then exam-

ine the state's asserted goal to determine whether it could have been achieved without the differential tax. With respect to the first step, the very fact of singling out the press for taxation is an implicit and significant burden because of the traditional speech-related function of the press in a democratic society. This burden must be weighed against a compelling state interest. Mere collection of revenue is not a sufficient interest: The interest must be more important and significant.

In the second step of the test, the "fit" between the stated governmental interest and the means (differential tax) must be tested. In order to pass constitutional scrutiny, a state must show that its differential tax is the only means to achieve its goal—a difficult standard to meet. Extending this analysis, the courts have frowned upon attempts to differentiate among various types of press based on content of their publications. For example, the U.S. Supreme Court invalidated a statute exempting from a state sales tax religious publications, while subjecting other types of publications to the tax. However, in *Leathers v. Medlock* (1991), the Court approved a tax on cable television, while leaving other media exempt. In this case, the Court examined the potential of the tax for suppression of particular ideas or viewpoints. The tax at issue did not target a small group of operators, and did not discriminate on the basis of content—either on its face or in practice. Thus, the Court held this tax constitutional.

Free Speech and Tax Laws. Another important issue is the exercise of free speech in the administration of the tax laws. The Department of the Treasury promulgates various regulations interpreting the federal tax code. In doing so, it must offer adequate public notice and opportunity to be heard before regulations are made final. The degree of openness of the department to public comment is an important aspect of free speech in the administration of the tax system.

Another question that frequently arises is whether individual taxpayers can be punished for including with their tax returns information about political or social issues that relate to tax collection or budget expenditures. The federal Internal Revenue Service (IRS) has the power to invoke section 6702 of the Internal Revenue Code, which imposes a five-hundred-dollar civil penalty on taxpayers who file frivolous returns. When this section is used to deter inclusion of a taxpayer's views on political issues in a tax form, it might well be viewed as a form of censorship. For example, section 6702 was invoked when a taxpayer claimed a twenty-five-hundred-dollar "conscientious objection to war deduction," and enclosed letters explaining the taxpayer's objection to war and the reasons for taking the (illegal) deduction. Similarly, the penalty has been invoked when a taxpayer shared his opinion on the U.S. policy in Central America, instead of financial information, on a tax return. In such cases taxpayers have often invoked the First Amendment to combat imposition of the tax code's penalty, on the theory that they have a right to express themselves on their tax returns.

Courts have generally dismissed such claims on two grounds. First, it is not clear that the expression on a tax return of dissatisfaction with government policy is protected speech. Second, assuming that there is a protected First Amendment right to express oneself on one's tax return, this regulation of speech is evaluated under traditional First Amendment doctrine. Section 6702 usually passes constitutional muster in judicial eyes: The rule is within the constitutional power of the government; the rule furthers an important or substantial governmental interest (the administration of a sound tax system); the governmental interest is unrelated to the suppression of free expression; and the incidental restriction on alleged First Amendment freedoms is narrowly constrained to no more than is needed to accomplish the stated interest. Under this approach, section 6702's application has been found constitutional.

—*Gwendolyn Griffith*

See also Courts and censorship law; Customs laws, U.S.; News media censorship; Newspapers; Postal regulations; Stamp Act.

BIBLIOGRAPHY

For a discussion of the historical context of the taxation of the press, see Robert Justin Goldstein's *Political Censorship of the Arts and the Press in Nineteenth Century Europe* (New York: St. Martin's Press, 1989). Discussions of American jurisprudence can be found in Rodney A. Smolla, *Smolla and Nimmer on Freedom of Speech: A Treatise on the First Amendment* (New York: Matthew Bender, 1994); James L. Swanson, *First Amendment Law Handbook* (Deerfield: Clark Boardman Callaghan, 1995); and C. Edwin Baker, *Advertising and a Democratic Press* (Princeton, N.J.: Princeton University Press, 1994).

Technology

DEFINITION: Inventions and discoveries that promote communication, from the inventing of alphabets to the Internet

SIGNIFICANCE: The technologies that make human communication easier and more widespread have spawned attempts to suppress such communication, often by draconian means

Until written communication transformed sounds into symbols that could be comprehended visually, ideas, traditions, and folkways were transmitted orally, within narrow geographical areas. With the invention of writing, humankind was moving toward society as we know it today. Writing permitted ideas to be captured, preserved, and transmitted to people in distant places and in future eras.

The Impact of Writing. When writing first became feasible for humans, priestly enclaves developed among those who mastered the skills of literacy. Common people remained illiterate and had no access to written material, which, in the early days, was scratched on stone surfaces or on the walls of caves. In Babylon and Egypt, cuneiform, a form of writing in which the symbols were etched into soft clay that hardened into permanent records, was used by the elite, essentially for keeping tax records and other information that might be used against the common people. Hence, a suspicion of writing developed among the masses.

A single message on cuneiform tablets might require four or five carts to haul it from its writer to the person addressed. If one of the carts tipped and broke one or two of the brittle tablets, essential parts of the letter were lost. Therefore, when it was discovered that papyrus, and later animal skins, could be made into surfaces to write upon, another considerable technological advance was made. Written documents gained a portability not previously possible.

Still, the written word remained the property of the elite. Until the fifteenth century, less than 1 percent of the total world population was able to read and write. These people were generally holy men who considered it their duty to promote the religions of which they were members, so most documents, written by hand on vellum, were religious, particularly in Western cultures in which Roman Catholicism predominated.

The Printing Press. The invention of moveable type changed human history forever. Invented in Asia around 1400, moveable type was first used in Western Europe by Johann Gutenberg in 1454, when he set up Europe's first printing press. By 1474 William Caxton had established a similar press in England; in 1539 the first printing press on the American continent was set up in Mexico City.

With the invention of printing, the costs of printed materials plummeted. During the first century of printing, common people could even hope eventually to read. They could become their own interpreters of Scripture and moved toward doing so during the Reformation that Martin Luther led. In this period people began to question and reject authority. Those who had access to ideas through books became threats to established authority.

A year before Martin Luther bolted from the Church of Rome, the Fourth Lateran Council called for universal censorship for the good of society. By 1564 the church had released its first *Index Librorum Prohibitorum* of books that it proscribed. It moved toward licensing books through the Imprimatur, prohibiting books through the *Index*, and persecuting those who ignored its mandates through the Inquisition.

Telephone, Telegraph, and Radio. The proliferation of books and other printed materials helped to spawn further scientific developments during the eighteenth and nineteenth centuries as people could transmit and more easily disseminate their ideas and scientific findings. Inevitably the human need to communicate more quickly and over greater distances led to technological discoveries that again changed society forever.

Among these was the invention of electric telegraphy by Samuel F. B. Morse. Morse could tap out messages, using his special code, and transmit them by wire over considerable distances. In 1866 the first transatlantic telegraph cable linked the New World to Europe, and within a decade telegraphy became a practical mode of communicating. Invention of the voice-carrying telephone by Alexander Graham Bell in 1876 further enhanced human ability to communicate over distances. Invention of the radio by Guglielmo Marconi in 1896 gave humans the means of broadcasting ideas to large audiences.

As these advances were made, governmental controls were imposed. In the case of radio, standards of decorum, usually reflecting the morality of the communities involved, were imposed by censors who forbade the use of profanity, obscenity, and sexually explicit situations.

Films and Television. Early motion pictures were sideshow novelties until 1903, when the first mass distribution of motion pictures occurred. It was not until 1926 that sound was added to films, resulting in the sort of motion pictures common during the last half of the twentieth century. In the United States the film industry was self-regulating, adhering to the often-repressive Hayes Code that substantially restricted the language and content of films. Motion pictures reached huge audiences, bringing to small-town America films that depicted ways of life often foreign and frequently threatening to country folk. The advent of television, however, absolutely transformed the nation. Its influence has been felt everywhere. Through television American culture has become a powerful social influence upon most of the nations of the world.

Television was first conceived in the late nineteenth century, although it was not until 1926 that an operational television set was produced. During its infancy it was a curiosity that engaged those interested in electronics more than the general public. It was not until the late 1940's that television sets began to appear in average American homes. Broadcasting hours were limited and programming quality was low. Within a decade, however, many Americans had television sets. Broadcast hours were increased; programming improved greatly.

Pressure groups rail against immorality on television. The Federal Communications Commission, which controls the licensing of television stations, monitors the standards applied to broadcasters.

Computers, Fax Machines, and the Internet. The next step in the development of technologies came with the invention in the 1950's of computers. Although the earliest machines were large, cumbersome instruments designed for use by large corporations, miniaturization and the development of transistors soon reduced the size and the cost of computers. By the 1990's computers were in millions of homes, as well as in schools and other public places. To enter the twenty-first century without computer literacy is to limit substantially one's chances of flourishing economically in society.

The computer and the fax machine, through which messages can be transmitted in seconds to virtually any part of the world, have made effective thought-control by governments virtually impossible. When the government of the People's Republic of China attempted to suppress information during the Tiananmen Square uprising of 1989, for example, the dissidents communicated through fax machines; the government could not control this communication.

The Internet links people from throughout the world with each other and with huge stores of information contained in the world's most extensive repositories. Attempts to control the transmission of ideas through censorship have proved futile in an age when the electronic transfer of information is available in the remotest corners of the earth through modern technology.   —*R. Baird Shuman*

See also Broadcast media; Caxton, William; Communications Decency Act; Computers; Federal Communications Commission; Internet; Morality in Media; Printing; Telephone law; Tiananmen Square.

BIBLIOGRAPHY

Neil Postman's *Technology* (New York: Knopf, 1992) is a useful introduction to broad technology issues. For overviews of the relationship between communication, technological, and censorship issues, see Sue Curry Jansen, *Censorship: The Knot That Binds Power and Knowledge* (New York: Oxford University Press, 1988); John C. Merrill, *Global Journalism: A Survey of the World's Mass Media* (New York: Longman, 1983); and Ilan Peleg, ed., *Patterns of Censorship Around the World* (Boulder, Colo.: Westview Press, 1993). In *American Broadcasting and the First Amendment* (Berkeley: University of California Press, 1987) Lucas A. Powe, Jr., touches on the role of modern technological change in broadcasting. Redmond Buke's *What Is the Index?* (Milwaukee: Bruce, 1952) discusses the Roman Catholic church's *Index Librorum Prohibitorum*.

Telephone law

DEFINITION: Legislation regarding the uses of telephones and related telecommunications equipment

SIGNIFICANCE: Speech over telephones is generally protected, but public concerns about privacy, telemarketing, and the sale of sexually oriented conversations over phone lines has led to calls for legislating new restrictions on the use of telephones

The term "telephone solicitation" does not refer to fund raising or other kinds of calls by tax-exempt nonprofit organizations. There are no legal restrictions on fund raising by such organizations in the United States. There are, however, some restrictions on the use of telephones for commercial solicitation. For example, state laws typically restrict the hours that telemarketers may call private residences to between 9:00 A.M. and 9:00 P.M. There are also specific restrictions regarding the use of automated telephone equipment. For example, it is against the law to use an automated telephone dialing system to call the emergency number 911, patient rooms of hospitals, health care facilities or homes for older people, or any telephone numbers assigned to paging services, cellular telephone services, mobile radio services, or any services for which the parties being called would be charged for such calls.

More than half the American states have statutes restricting various telemarketing practices, but telemarketers can evade such prohibitions through interstate operations. The U.S. Congress has considered establishing a single national database to compile a list of telephone numbers of residential subscribers who object to telephone solicitations, but has not done so, leaving telemarketers free to call anyone listed in telephone directories.

The only recourse for those who strongly object to receiving telephone solicitations is to join an organization such as Private Citizen, based in Naperville, Illinois. For twenty dollars, telephone users can have their numbers listed in this company's directory, which is distributed to telemarketers. The directory notifies telemarketers that if they call anyone listed in it, they must pay those persons one hundred dollars for using their telephones. Whether anyone has ever actually collected fines from telemarketers, being listed in such directories has been claimed as effective in discouraging telemarketers from calling.

Aware of the fact that consumers consider automated or prerecorded telephone calls to be great nuisances, Congress passed the Telephone Consumer Protection Act, which prohibited sending prerecorded commercial messages to people's homes without the consent of those being called. However, this law was challenged and found unconstitutional in *Moser v. Federal Communications Commission* in 1993 because it was not a content-neutral time, place, or manner restriction. The statute was content-based not only because it distinguished between recorded versus live speech but also because it distinguished between commercial versus noncommercial messages (other users of prerecorded message machines have included schools, which use them to inform parents of their children's absences). Such distinctions were found to be unconstitutional.

It has been illegal to send unsolicited advertisements to telephone facsimile (fax) machines. Fax advertisers have challenged this law as unconstitutional, but a federal district court in Oregon held the law to be constitutional. Fax advertisements are commercial speech, so the government may legally prevent unfair cost-shifting to recipients of unsolicited advertisements (the cost-shifting occurs because fax recipients must pay for the paper on which the messages are printed). Therefore a ban on all unsolicited fax advertising was held reasonable in *Destination Ventures v. Federal Communications Commission* in 1994.

Aggressive Boycotts. In January, 1996, acquitted defendant O. J. Simpson released a video pleading his innocence in the murder of his former wife. Consumers could purchase his video by calling an 800 number. An immediate backlash against Simpson developed, with campaigns on radio talk shows, fax machines, and even in cyberspace to block sales of his video by keeping telephone operators so busy with questions that they would be unable to handle calls from actual buyers. Cautious radio talk show hosts did not actually advise their listeners to swamp Simpson's 800 number with calls to avoid being charged with conspiring to obstruct a business enterprise. Although it is clearly legal to organize a boycott of any product, an "aggressive boycott," in which people actively interfere with one's right to market, might indeed raise questions of legality.

Privacy. On October 25, 1994, Congress passed the Digital Telephony Act of 1994. Known officially as the Communications Assistance for Law Enforcement Act, the law was passed because of complaints by law enforcement agencies that new telecommunications technology was impeding their ability to conduct wiretaps and trace messages during criminal investigations. The act requires telephone companies to make it technically easier to conduct lawful wiretaps, and wiretapping capabilities must be incorporated (at the carrier's expense) into the new technology created by the telephone companies. Law enforcement officials may wiretap a private telephone line, provided that a judge has signed a valid warrant permitting the tap, and Federal Communications Commission (FCC) employees are permitted to monitor electronic communications.

It is, however, illegal for journalists or anyone else to tap someone else's telephone. The Omnibus Crime Control and Safe Streets Act, passed in 1968 and amended in 1986 as the Electronic Communications Privacy Act, also known as the Federal Wiretap Statute, prohibits the interception of any conversation carried over a wire or a nonwire conversation in a setting in which one expects privacy. Therefore anyone who uses a wiretap to record a phone conversation between other people would be liable for violating the statute.

There is an important exception. The statute expressly permits a participant in the conversation to record it secretly—provided that the person is not doing so for the purpose of committing a criminal or tortious act. This exception allows journalists to tape-record their telephone conversations with interview subjects because the consent of only one party to the conversation—in this case, the reporter—is required. However, if a reporter's purpose in taping a conversation is to commit a tort such as libel, the reporter would be violating the statute. California, Delaware, Florida, Illinois, Louisiana, Maryland, Massachusetts, Michigan, Montana, New Hampshire, Oregon, Pennsylvania, and Washington have outlawed such recordings. These states are all-party consent states, meaning that all parties to a telephone conversation must give prior consent before a conversation is tape-recorded. Other states are one-party consent states, meaning that participant recording is permitted provided there is no intent to commit a tort.

In addition to the Federal Wiretap Statute, the FCC's phone rule requires that before recording a telephone conversation for broadcast, a radio or television station must tell any party to the call that it intends to broadcast the conversation, whether the conversation is being taped or broadcast live.

Harassment and Obscene Telephone Calls. Any people who make telephone calls without disclosing their identity and with intent to annoy, abuse, threaten, or harass a person whom they are calling, or anyone who causes someone else's telephone to ring repeatedly with intent to harass that person may be fined up to fifty thousand dollars, or imprisoned for up to six months, or both. Anyone who makes any comment or request which is obscene, lewd, lascivious, filthy, or indecent may also be fined up to fifty thousand dollars, or imprisoned for up to six months, or both.

Dial-a-Porn. In 1982 "dial-a-porn" services became widely available through small telephone companies called "Baby Bells." Offered by a large number of small companies, these services differed in many respects, but shared the commonality of offering customers the chance to hear sexually oriented recordings or have uninhibited conversations about sex. Customers typically paid for such services by the minute. Although the Baby Bell companies began making large profits by sharing the revenues from dial-a-porn, some of them reacted strongly against being required to carry dial-a-porn. Several companies even sued dial-a-porn producers, seeking declaratory relief from having to distribute sex messages over their networks. Federal courts of appeal have dealt with this problem inconsistently. Whereas some Baby Bells were allowed not to carry dial-a-porn, others were required to carry it because telephone companies are common carriers. For example, the Baby Bells in Louisiana, Florida, and Arizona all refused to carry dial-a-porn, and the courts upheld their decisions. In contrast, California courts held, in 1989, that Pacific Bell had to carry dial-a-porn because it was a common carrier, despite Pacific Bell's objections. In Texas, Southwestern Bell permitted recorded messages only but prohibited live conversation on its information provider lines, and this was upheld by Texas courts in 1987.

In response to such controversy, Congress amended sections of the Communications Act of 1934 with the Telephone Decency Act (also known as the Helms Amendment after its principal sponsor, Senator Jesse Helms). This act contained a provision banning all dial-a-porn services, including indecent and obscene speech. Several dial-a-porn providers challenged the Helms Amendment as unconstitutional, but the only case to reach the U.S. Supreme Court was *Sable Communications v. Federal Communications Commission* (1989). The Supreme Court held that the 1988 Helms Amendment was constitutional in banning obscene speech but unconstitutional in banning indecent speech over the telephone. In a concurring opinion, Justice Antonin Scalia added that "while we hold that the Constitution prevents Congress from banning indecent speech . . . we do not hold that the Constitution requires public utilities to carry it."

The legal definition of obscenity was determined by the U.S. Supreme Court in *Miller v. California* (1973), in which the Court held that a jury must decide first whether the average person, applying contemporary community standards, would find that the material appeals to prurient interest; second, whether the work describes, in a patently offensive manner, sexual or excretory conduct defined by the applicable state law; and third, whether the work, taken as a whole, lacks serious literary, artistic, political, or scientific value.

The FCC issued two Notices of Apparent Liability to dial-a-porn providers for obscenity in 1988. The first was issued to Audio Enterprises. A second involved a dial-a-porn provider called Intercambio. Applying the *Miller v. California* test for obscenity, the FCC concluded that the messages were "consistently obscene"; it described in detail a scene in which an uncle sexually abused his nephew and a second scene in which a "doctor" sodomized a young boy during a physical exam. The FCC fined Intercambio $600,000 for making no attempt to restrict minors' access to its messages (dial-a-porn providers are legally required to restrict minors' access to their messages through use of credit cards or personal identification numbers which adults must apply for in writing).

The difference between indecent and obscene speech was not resolved. The only clue that sheds light on this question appeared in Scalia's concurring opinion in the *Sable* case, in which he suggested that "indecent" speech appeals to "normal, healthy sexual desires," as opposed to "shameful or morbid" sexual desires which are presumably obscene. Despite this clue, as a matter of practical application, the distinction in the *Sable* opinion between indecent and obscene speech ranges from vague to opaque. The dial-a-porn providers charged that the Helms Amendment unconstitutionally transformed telephone companies into a species of government-licensed but unguided and unsupervised censors, policemen, and prosecutors. If dial-a-porn is obscene, the Baby Bells can refuse to carry it, but this casts them in the role of censors, even if the Justice Department does not admit it. By being placed in the position of having to decide whether to carry dial-a-porn, just as a newspaper publisher may decide whether or not to print advertisements for pornographic films, the Baby Bells in effect had to take a small step toward the role of publisher rather than common carrier.

Three years after the *Sable* decision, dial-a-porn providers again asked the U.S. Supreme Court to declare the Helms Amendment unconstitutional in *Dial Information Services v. Thornburgh* (1991). The Supreme Court declined to hear the case, clearing the way for enforcement of the Helms Amendment. By the mid-1990's most of the Baby Bells had discontinued billing and collection on dial-a-porn, leaving the dial-a-porn providers to bill customers themselves by credit card.

—Juliet Dee

See also Commercial speech; Communications Decency Act; *Miller v. California*; Pornography; *Roth v. United States*; *Rowan v. U.S Post Office Department*; Simpson, O. J., case.

BIBLIOGRAPHY
Federal Telecommunications Law by Michael K. Kellogg, John Thorne, and Peter W. Huber (Boston: Little, Brown, 1992) is a large treatise analyzing legal issues in the area of telephone law. This work's substantive companion is *The Geodesic Network II: 1993 Report on Competition in the Telephone Industry* by Peter W. Huber, Michael K. Kellogg, and John Thorne (Washington, D.C.: Geodesic Company, 1992), which analyzes the policy implications of structural changes in the domestic telecommunications market since the 1982 Bell Consent decree. Daniel L. Brenner's *Law and Regulation of Common Carriers in the Communications Industry* (Boulder, Colo.: Westview Press, 1992) is a collection of excerpts from cases and materials with commentaries; it provides a basic introduction to the regulation of the telephone and other common carriers. Rohan Samarajiva and Roopali Mukherjee's "Regulation of 976 Services and Dial-a-Porn" in *Telecommunications Policy* 15 (April, 1991) analyzes the policy conflicts arising in the first decade of 976 services. It also identifies serious concerns regarding the move toward casting common carriers as censors with regard to dial-a-porn and other information providers. Juliet Dee's " 'To Avoid Charges of Indecency, Please Hang Up Now': An Analysis of Legislation and Litigation Involving Dial-a-Porn" in *Communications and the Law* 16, no. 1 (March, 1994) offers a history of the legal tug-of-war surrounding dial-a-porn.

Televangelists

DEFINITION: Christian Fundamentalists and evangelicals who proselytize by means of television and radio

SIGNIFICANCE: Religious broadcasting in the United States has experienced little overt censorship, but it has been shaped by a combination of government regulations and business practices

In 1925 U.S. secretary of commerce Herbert Hoover was trying to clear the "confusion in the ether" in part by stopping radio stations from using frequencies other than those assigned to them. When government inspectors applied federal rules to evangelist Aimee Semple McPherson, she resisted. "Please order your minions of Satan to leave my station alone," she wired to Hoover. "You cannot expect the Almighty to abide by your wavelength nonsense. When I offer my prayers to Him I must fit into His wave reception. Open this station at once." Government regulators learned early to tread lightly around religious broadcasters, who have always been as sensitive as anyone regarding issues of censorship, real or perceived.

Policies Favoring Mainstream Religious Groups. With its passage of the Radio Act of 1927, Congress empowered federal regulators to ensure that broadcasting was done "in the public interest, convenience, and necessity." This ambiguous phrase was soon put to the test by "Battling" Bob Shuler of Los Angeles' Trinity Methodist Church, South. An appellate court decision in 1932 upheld the right of the new Federal Radio Commission not to renew Shuler's license for his radio station because his slander, ethnic slurs, and blackmail threats were not in the public interest. A decade later the Roosevelt Administration worked behind the scenes to convince Father Charles Coughlin's archbishop to silence the popular demagogue, whose anti-Semitism and pro-Nazi sentiments were seen as a hindrance to American patriotism during World War II.

In 1970 the Federal Communications Commission (FCC) revoked evangelist Carl McIntire's license to operate a radio station in Media, Pennsylvania, because of his relentless attacks on all those unsympathetic to his ultraconservatism. Although the federal government could in such extreme cases silence religious broadcasters because of what they said, it preferred to resolve issues involving technology and leave content to market forces.

Pictured here at the height of his career as one of the most successful televangelists in soliciting cash donations, Jimmy Swaggart lost most of his following in 1988 after publicly confessing to having carried on a sordid affair with a prostitute. (Arkent Archive)

The FCC has seldom regulated content outright, but its requirement that stations broadcast noncommercial public affairs programs had a profound influence on the character of radio and television broadcasting. From the early 1930's every network, except the Mutual Broadcasting Network, refused to accept money for religious broadcasting. Instead, they donated air time to the three major religious groups in the United States: Protestants (who were represented by what would become the National Council of Churches), Roman Catholics (represented by the U.S. Catholic Conference), and Jews (represented by the New York Board of Rabbis). Except for Billy Graham, whose phenomenal popularity enabled him to secure regular air time on the American Broadcasting Company (ABC), Fundamentalists were relegated by this system to Mutual and any individual stations willing to sell time to them.

Policies Favoring Evangelicals. The tables turned after 1960, when the FCC decided that broadcasters did not have to give away time to fulfill their public service obligations. Radio and television stations quickly found entrepreneurs willing to buy the blocks of time that had formerly been given away: the evangelicals and Fundamentalists who had previously been stymied by the previous network policy. The new arrangement favored these evangelicals and Fundamentalists. Unlike mainstream groups encumbered with the high costs of denominational commitments, independent televangelists could afford to spend much of their income on production and the cost of air time.

The most vexing regulation for these religious entrepreneurs was the fairness doctrine, which required stations to present various perspectives on controversial political issues. In 1964 this doctrine came to a test. In a program aired on radio station WGCB in Red Lion, Pennsylvania, evangelist Billy James Hargis attacked Fred J. Cook, the author of a book critical of Republican presidential candidate Barry Goldwater. Hargis called Cook a left-wing ideologue who had once been fired from a newspaper for dishonesty. Cook's request for free time to reply to these charges under the fairness doctrine was ultimately upheld in court.

A similar case in 1979 involved evangelist James Robison. After one of his tirades against homosexuality—"a perversion of the highest order"—WFAA-TV in Dallas cancelled his program. After granting equal time under the fairness doctrine to the Dallas Gay Political Caucus, WFAA decided that Robison's program was simply too much trouble. Robison countered by holding a "freedom rally" that drew ten thousand people, and he retained flamboyant Houston attorney Richard "Racehorse" Haynes to press the FCC for a hearing. Shortly thereafter WFAA-TV reinstated Robison's program. Despite the notoriety of these fairness doctrine cases, the FCC hardly singled out televangelists as a means of enforcing the doctrine.

After the FCC's experience with the Lansman-Milam petition, the FCC gave a wide berth to religious broadcasters. In 1975 media consultants Jeremy Lansman and Lorenzo Milam asked the commission to reconsider issuing noncommercial FM and television licenses to sectarian groups. The public interest was not served by the narrow interests of such groups, they argued, and the incessant on-air fund-raising belied their claims to be noncommercial. The National Religious Broadcasters responded to this threat with a direct-mail campaign, arguing that the Lansman-Milam petition amounted to a wholesale attack on religion. The response of their audience was overwhelming. A campaign of protest ensued, producing several million letters and phone calls that continued for years and years after the FCC rejected the petition.

Televangelists and other mass communicators have coexisted mostly in peace. A grand exception occurred in 1983, however, when *Hustler* magazine published a parody cartoon depicting televangelist Jerry Falwell as a drunkard having sex with his mother in an outhouse. Outraged, Falwell sued the sexually explicit magazine for libel, invasion of privacy, and intentional infliction of emotional distress, and he mailed copies of the parody to thousands of supporters of *The Old Time Gospel Hour* in an effort to raise money for legal expenses. *Hustler* then tried to add injury to insult by suing Falwell for violation of copyright. *Hustler* lost its lawsuit, but Falwell lost his as well.

The Protestant reformer Martin Luther once observed that "it makes a difference whose ox is gored." The first forty years of broadcasting in the United States were dominated by an ecumenical consortium of mainstream Protestants, Roman Catholics, and Jews because of the ways that FCC policies combined with commercial pressures. The second forty years have seen Christian evangelicals and Fundamentalists rise to predominance because of changed FCC policies and commercial pressures. Fundamentalists suffered before, mainstream groups suffered after. Regardless of whose ox has been gored, however, the representation of religious faith and custom on radio and television has always been held artificially narrow by regulatory and market forces. —*John P. Ferré*

See also Broadcast media; Communications Act of 1934; Coughlin, Father Charles Edward; Fairness doctrine; Federal Communications Commission; *Hustler*; Moral Majority.

BIBLIOGRAPHY
The standard among books on televangelism is Peter G. Horsfield's *Religious Television: The American Experience* (New York: Longman, 1984). Jeffrey K. Hadden and Anson Shupe's *Televangelism: Power and Politics on God's Frontier* (New York: Henry Holt, 1988) focuses on political dimensions of televangelism, while Stewart M. Hoover's *Mass Media Religion: The Social Sources of the Electronic Church* (Newbury Park, Calif.: Sage Publications, 1988) emphasizes audience. William F. Fore treats televangelism as an element of television in general in *Television and Religion: The Shaping of Faith, Values, and Culture* (Minneapolis, Minn.: Augsburg, 1987). Quentin J. Schultze places televangelism in the contexts of both print and electronic media in *American Evangelicals and the Mass Media* (Grand Rapids, Mich.: Academie Books/Zondervan, 1990).

Television

DEFINITION: Visual broadcast medium
SIGNIFICANCE: Television's widespread presence in homes and its ready availability have made it a central fixture of censorship issues

Since television became widely available in the second half of the twentieth century, it has attracted a steady stream of critics. More than a few observers have doubted whether the various talents and interests responsible for television programming have made the medium anything other than a wasteland. Despite the fact that in the eyes of many critics, television has many channels but "nothing on," attempts to control the content of television programming have arisen from many quarters. Government, television networks, advertisers, local stations, grassroots groups and private individuals have all tried to censor television. Of attempts to control television, the role of government—at least in Western democracies—has generally been relatively minor. More significant have been the efforts of interests such as networks and advertisers. Networks and advertisers are motivated by the desire to attract and retain audiences. This desire has lead to a general policy of shunning controversy, which can alienate audiences and advertisers.

Although television censorship efforts have proceeded from several quarters, censorship efforts have tended to focus on a few areas. Since television's inception the most common areas in which efforts to restrict television programming have centered have been violence, sexual conduct, and objectionable language. The 1990's saw renewed attention to the issue of television violence especially, which renewed attempts to recruit government to a more active role in regulating the content of television programming.

Television and Children. Children may summon television's images and narration with the touch of a finger. Advocates of government restrictions on television have urged that since television—as does radio—reaches into the home and presents itself immediately to children, television should be subject to greater restriction than that to which the print media are subject; print media have traditionally been afforded far greater protections from attempted government regulation. Accepting the proposition that speech fit for adults might not be fit for children, the United States Supreme Court has generally been less protective of objectionable speech when young children are a part of an audience than when only adults are listeners. In *Federal Communications Commission v. Pacifica Foundation* (1978), for example, the Court upheld the Federal Communications Commission's (FCC) power to sanction a radio station which aired during the afternoon a comic monologue by the comedian George Carlin laced with "adult" language. A key factor in the Court's conclusion was its assumption that young children might be in the radio audience. It therefore held that the FCC was authorized to protect children from inadvertent exposure to indecent language, even when the language was not technically obscene. The presence of children in television audiences has also spurred efforts to enforce positive obligations on the part of programmers to include significant educational programming within their television schedules. These kinds of programming obligations may be seen as a kind of censorship, since they prevent broadcasters from airing the content of their choice in favor of the official desired educational programming.

Government Regulation of Television. In the United States, the FCC is the federal agency charged by law with the task of overseeing matters relating to radio and television. The Federal Communications Act prohibits the FCC from censoring broadcast programming. In general, however, federal law requires the FCC to grant licenses for broadcasting in a manner calculated to serve the public interest and to review the content of broadcast programming for its adherence to this same standard. Accordingly, courts in the United States have found that neither the ban on censorship nor the First Amendment to the Constitution prevent the FCC from attempting to assure that television programming (and other broadcast programming) serves the public interest. The rationale for this is that there is a limited number of frequencies on which to broadcast; these frequencies are viewed as a public resource, like water or publicly owned land. The government, therefore, has the responsibility to allocate the resources of the airspace in a manner that serves the public interest.

The Federal Criminal Code prohibits the broadcast of "obscene, indecent or profane language" and thus in theory justifies sanctions leveled against broadcasting stations who air such language. In the years after the Supreme Court's holding in *Federal Communications Commission v. Pacifica Foundation* that the FCC could monitor—at least to some extent—broadcast indecency, the FCC generally took the position that only the seven words highlighted in the *Pacifica* case were forbidden, and then only if used repeatedly. When the FCC did seek to police indecent broadcasting, it tended to focus its censorial energies predominantly in the area of radio broadcasting rather than television programming. Occasionally, though, the commission sanctioned television stations for overstepping the bounds of decency. For example, in 1987 the FCC fined a television station for airing during prime time an R-rated film. The United States has not been alone in finding room among the government's powers to oversee the decency of television broadcasting. In Great Britain, the Television Act of 1954 contained a provision banning programming offensive to good taste or likely to incite violence. Britain's Obscene Publications Act of 1959 was extended to broadcast media in 1991, and it forbids the portrayal of actual sexual intercourse.

Broadcasting Safe Harbors. The critics of government attempts to purge the airwaves of indecent material in the interests of children have often complained that these attempts threaten to make children the measuring rod of all programming suitability. Concern for protecting children from broadcast material unsuitable for their age has sometimes been accompanied by recognition that child viewers of television tend to decrease as evening progresses. This social reality has prompted the proposal that objectionable television programming be reserved for later hours of the evening, when most children have gone to bed. For example, in the United States, the television networks and the National Association of Broadcasters in the mid-1970's adopted a family viewing policy. This policy provided that programs aired from 7 P.M. to 9 P.M. would be suitable for the whole family unless the networks provided a specific warning advising parents otherwise. In 1976, however, a federal district court found this viewing policy to be a violation of antitrust law. By the end of the 1980's, the FCC had itself created a safe harbor between

midnight and 6 A.M., when indecent material might be broadcast so long as stations aired a warning concerning the offensive material. Shortly thereafter, however, the FCC—faced with increasing public pressure to restrict indecent programming—began to push for a ban on indecent programming until a federal appeals court ruled that such a ban would be unconstitutional. A year later, federal courts ruled that even the restriction of indecent material to the safe-harbor period of midnight to 6 A.M. was unconstitutional. The FCC relented somewhat in the face of this decision, but continued to enforce a ban on indecent programming from 6 A.M. until 10 P.M. Great Britain has also followed a similar pattern, treating 9 P.M. as a time after which programming unsuitable for children might be aired. Great Britain had enforced prior to 1957 the so-called toddlers truce between 6 P.M. and 7 P.M., when programming was expected to air with a special regard for children.

Censorship by Networks and Program Executives. Television censorship may take the form of enforced government prescriptions regarding the content of programming. More commonly, however, censorship occurs not as edicts descending from government but as self-imposed restrictions on programming. Thus, for example, Ed Sullivan required the Rolling Stones to change the lyrics of their song "Let's Spend the Night Together" to "Let's Spend Some Time Together" in the group's 1967 appearance on *The Ed Sullivan Show*. Similarly, the producer of the countercultural comedy show *Saturday Night Live*, though initially surprised by Sinead O'Connor's guest appearance in October, 1992, in which she tore up a picture of the pope, reasserted control when the program was reaired sometime later by substituting rehearsal footage in the place of the controversial episode. The *Saturday Night Live* program also illustrates the role of networks in television censorship. Over the years of its existence, *Saturday Night Live*'s writers and producers have regularly clashed with NBC's censors and executives. In general, the power of networks over the producers of particular programming has declined somewhat as the networks have lost segments of their audiences to cable television and to the use of videotapes by viewers.

Censorship by Sponsors and Advertisers. In the early years of television, popular television series such as the *Philco Television Playhouse* and *Kraft Television Theater* were, as their names suggest, sponsored by a single company whose products were advertised during the course of the series. This close relationship between sponsor and series created ample opportunities for a sponsor to exert control over the content of a series. Thus, although this period of television programming has sometimes been called the golden age of television, the sponsors of the programs during this period have earned criticism for their successful attempts to mold programming to suit the tastes of their intended audiences. Once television programming escaped the concept of a single sponsorship in favor of multiple commercial sponsors, the power of any one sponsor was lessened.

Television Violence. A concern for television violence has existed practically since television became widely available.

Television broadcasting began in earnest in the late 1940's, when few could have imagined the controversies about programming content that would come in the future. (AP/Wide World Photos)

Attempts to articulate standards for violence have varied considerably. In 1991, New Zealand's Broadcast Standards Authority issued a Code of Practices that caution against broadcasting the infliction of pain by unfamiliar methods or combining violence and sexual titillation. Great Britain's Code of Practices, published in 1989 by the Broadcasting Standards Council, warns producers against including gratuitous violence to bolster the appeal of otherwise weak material. However, assessments of the suitability of particular scenes of violence for children have not remained static. In Britain, for example, James Bond films were originally classified for adult audiences only, but by the closing years of the twentieth century they might be deliberately broadcast for a family audience. In the United States, critics of television violence have sometimes targeted for protest cartoon violence—such as that inflicted by the cat and mouse duo, Tom and Jerry, upon one another—that a previous generation had found more amusing than threatening.

In the United States, concern over violence on television has found expression since the beginning of television's widespread availability in the 1950's. Congress held hearings on

the effect of television violence on children during the mid-1950's, the early 1960's, and throughout most of the 1970's. Although the decade of the 1980's saw relatively little furor over this subject, a rising concern for reports of random violence in American society and reports of viewers copying events on television restored the issue of television violence to the public forefront toward the end of that decade. A five-year-old viewer of *Beavis and Butt-head* imitated the characters by setting his house on fire, killing his two-year-old sister. Two viewers of a film broadcast on television imitated a scene in which characters lay down in the middle of a highway to demonstrate their courage; both viewers were killed. Critics of government regulation pointed out that control of television violence would have done nothing to stop these copycat incidents, since *Beavis and Butt-head* airs on cable and the two who lay down on a highway were imitating a film rather than a television program.

One copycat incident that reached the courts resulted in a finding of no liability on the part of a television network. NBC broadcast a program in which a girl is raped with a plumber's helper. Four days later several boys who had seen and discussed the program raped a nine-year-old girl with a coke bottle. A California appellate court ultimately held that NBC could not be found to have incited the boys to this action and thus could not be found liable.

By the beginning of the 1990's, the critics of television violence in the United States had gained sufficient influence to persuade Congress to make some beginning of a search for greater restrictions. Congress passed the Television Program Improvement Act of 1990, which created a three-year antitrust exemption for various broadcast media interests. This exemption allowed broadcast media to work together to produce voluntary guidelines for reducing the amount of violence on television. The concern over television violence reached a crescendo in the mid-1990's and ultimately influenced the Telecommunications Act of 1996, federal legislation requiring television manufacturers to begin equipping all televisions with a V-chip. The V-chip is intended to enable parents to identify television programs with certain categories of objectionable material—including television violence—and to block these programs from being displayed by televisions in their homes. Canadian television had already begun experimenting with use of the V-chip prior to its adoption in the United States. The Telecommunications Act of 1996 did not require television programmers to rate their programs, but they have begun efforts to do so voluntarily, favoring such voluntary action over continued government involvement in this matter. Opponents of the V-chip provision claim that it will inevitably discourage programmers from including material that might cause parents to block a program, since advertising revenues would suffer from such a loss of viewers. Thus, these opponents argue, programmers will self-censor their broadcasts far more than they presently do.

Film Editing. Television programming includes not only programs created especially for that medium but films originally screened in cinemas. Films transferred from cinema to television are routinely edited for no more nefarious purpose than the need to fit a film within a particular time slot. Television producers also routinely edit film with the aim of censoring objectionable elements. As is true for many forms of external censorship, the censorship of film transplanted to television has the effect of encouraging filmmakers to engage in self-censorship from the outset of their production efforts. Film producers with an eye on an eventual television market may choose to exercise restraint regarding objectionable elements so as to avoid later cuts by television producers over which they will have no control and which might threaten the coherence of their films.

International Cultural Concerns and Television. Television transmissions effortlessly penetrate national boundaries, both when broadcasters in one nation deliberately target another nation to receive television signals or when signals inadvertently spill over from one territorial sovereignty to another. Residents of the northeastern United States may watch Canadian television. Texans may receive signals broadcast from Mexico. French television viewers may catch shows from Germany. The encroachment of uninvited television programming has prompted some nations to seek ways of curbing what

they see as threatening influences from beyond their borders. Especially in the light of new technologies such as direct satellite broadcasting, nations lacking access of their own to this technology have not always been enthusiastic when made the recipient of either satellite television signals intentionally targeted for these nations or signals which have unintentionally spilled over from another target. Satellite television signals may be used to communicate propaganda from one nation to another. This potential has fueled arguments, most prevalent among nonindustrial nations such as Cuba and certain of the former Soviet bloc nations which lack satellite television technology themselves, that the recipient nations should have the right of program control and be entitled to prior authorization before being made the target of these television signals. India has launched efforts to control foreign broadcast signals by investing in an expensive receiving station intended to monitor broadcasts that penetrate India's territory. A show such as *Baywatch*, for example, which features attractive young women in bathing suits, may be acceptable in the United States, but authorities in Iran have indicated that they are of a different opinion.

Nations fearful of being penetrated by unwanted television signals have used a variety of weapons to defend themselves. Certain television signals have been jammed, although newer satellite technologies have increased the difficulty of jamming television signals. Trade agreements restricting the flow of television and film across national boundaries are also common. These agreements effect a kind of censorship, often in pursuit of cultural objectives. The two most common reasons proffered by nations seeking to restrict the availability of foreign television and film to domestic viewers are the risks of polluting the domestic culture with foreign influences and the competitive danger posed to domestic media producers by foreign competitors. Cultural censorship of television in the international context has many illustrations. For example, the British Broadcasting Corporation (BBC) would not air the popular children's television program *Sesame Street* in Britain because of objections to its foreignness. The BBC apparently determined that *Sesame Street* communicated predominantly American values and declined to allow British youth to be inculcated with these values. —*Timothy L. Hall*

See also Academy Awards ceremonies; Blasphemy laws; Cable television; Copycat crime; Federal Communications Commission; Syndicated television; Television networks; Violence.

BIBLIOGRAPHY

Television: An International History, edited by Anthony Smith (Oxford: Oxford University Press, 1995) offers a useful historical survey of television technology and programming, including an essay by Colin Shaw titled "Taste, Decency, and Standards" that briefly explores censorship issues with an emphasis on British television. Colin R. Munro's *Television, Censorship and the Law* (Hampshire, England: Gower Publishing, 1983) explores television censorship in Great Britain. Lucas A. Powe, Jr.'s *American Broadcasting and the First Amendment* (Berkeley: University of California Press, 1987), explores the differences between regulation of print and broadcast media, and challenge government attempts to exert control over broadcast media. For a general review of the law of broadcast regulation, including the regulation of television programming, Kenneth C. Creech's *Electronic Media Law and Regulation* (Boston: Focal Press, 1996) is a helpful resource. *Prime-Time Television: Content and Control*, by Muriel G. Cantor and Joel M. Cantor (Newbury Park, Calif.: Sage Publications, 1992), surveys the various sources of attempts to control television programming. *Abandoned in the Wasteland: Children, Television, and the First Amendment*, by Newton N. Minow and Craig L. LaMay (New York: Hill & Wang, 1995) offers a spirited argument in favor of television regulation to protect the interests of children.

Television, children's

DEFINITION: Television programs designed primarily to be watched by children

SIGNIFICANCE: Television programs in general, and especially children's programming, are among the most highly regulated forms of entertainment

Since it first became popular in the early 1950's, television has been under close scrutiny from a number of sources. The Federal Communications Commission (FCC), a government agency appointed by the president, was created in 1934 to oversee broadcast media. The National Association of Broadcasters, created in 1952, set up a series of standards for radio and television broadcasts. The various networks and cable stations also have their own standards.

Throughout most of its history, television was dominated by its commercial aspects. Programming was determined on the basis of how well it would sell products to its audience. Generally, and especially after about 1970, the FCC has taken the stand that, in most cases, television is self-regulating: Sponsors will give the public what they want; thus if enough people object to a television program, it will be taken off the air because it will not be commercially successful.

The major battle in the regulation of television programming has been between those who insist the medium is protected by the free-speech clause of the First Amendment to the Constitution and those who insist that television has a responsibility to act in the public interest. An interesting test of this question came in 1973, when the FCC ruled that WBAI, a New York City radio station, could be fined for airing comedian George Carlin's "Seven Dirty Words" monologue, which contains obscene words. The Supreme Court heard the case in 1979 and ruled in favor of the FCC, in effect determining that radio and television were not protected by the First Amendment.

This ruling was based upon the conclusion that television and radio could easily be seen and heard by children at all hours of the day and night. Thus, a principle was established that the First Amendment was limited when it came to media to which children had access. Carlin's routine, however, was a rare instance. Radio, and especially television, had already adapted standards that were puritanical in many ways.

Early Television Programming. In the early 1950's, there was little television aimed directly at children. Early children's programming consisted mostly of old cartoons that had originally been shown in theaters; informational programs for children were occasionally carried on educational channels. The first really popular children's program was probably *The Mickey Mouse Club*, first broadcast in 1955. With the enormous success of this show, sponsors began to realize that there was a large potential audience of children. The immediate result was a large number of cartoons shown on Saturday mornings, a time at which few adults but many children were watching television.

During "prime time"—the evenings—most television programming was aimed at a massive audience, including both adults and children. In the 1950's and early 1960's, however, this seldom caused problems in censoring content. The most controversial subject matter in films of the time was sexual content, and this was virtually absent from early television. In the early situation comedies, married couples invariably slept in separate beds, and words such as "pregnant" were never spoken.

It was not until the mid-1970's that this situation changed significantly. Actual sexual acts were still not shown, except on a few premium cable services, but partial nudity, sexual suggestions, and prolonged kissing became common. There was some objection to such content, especially from religious fundamentalist groups, but the objections were never acted upon in any significant way by the FCC. In most cases, the First Amendment was considered to be more important than the supposed need to protect children from such content.

The Battle over Television Violence. Violence has been a mainstay of television since its beginning. Westerns, war

Although much television violence is make believe—as in this scene from an old Three Stooges film—many people are concerned that the negative images it conveys to young children may encourage them to imitate what they see. (Arkent Archive)

films, and slapstick comedy were among the most popular early programs. Children's cartoons were almost universally violent. Objections to violence first began to be heard in the late 1960's, especially after the 1968 assassinations of Robert F. Kennedy and Martin Luther King, Jr. Action for Children's Television (ACT) assumed an early position of leadership in opposing violence on television.

Studies of the effects of televised violence on children have had varied results. Most of the evidence points to a correlation between the amount of violent television children watch and antisocial activity, but this does not necessarily prove a cause-and-effect relationship. It has often been suggested that children who are already antisocial for other reasons are more likely to watch violent shows, so that the cause and effect may actually be the reverse of what those opposed to television violence would suggest. It has also been theorized that there may actually be an inverse effect: Watching fictional violence may allow children to release their frustrations vicariously, making them less likely to harm others.

In the 1990's, television stations began to announce warnings of violent content on television programs, and a computerized V-chip that would allow parents to screen out violent programs was developed. These partial solutions were objected to by both sides in the debate. Those opposed to violence suggested that announcing violent content might encourage children to watch programs, and the networks objected that the V-chip was a violation of the First Amendment.

Sexual Stereotypes. In early television programs, families were generally idealized according to traditional standards. Women were typically mothers or housewives; at most, they might be employed out of the house in clerical positions. Men ruled the household, had all the best jobs, and were more educated than their wives. This situation did not change significantly until the 1970's, when programs began to deliberately flout such stereotypes. A prime example was the 1980's comedy *Who's the Boss?*, which featured a male housekeeper employed by a female executive.

Nevertheless, men continued to dominate the airwaves, and women still tended to have more menial roles. In children's programming, depictions of boys greatly outnumbered those of girls. Commercial realities are often cited as an explanation of this phenomenon: Since men tend to have more economic power than women, and since boys tend to be more assertive than girls, programming is often aimed primarily at a male audience.

Public Television and Cable Networks. A final question to be considered is the quality of children's programming. Apart from eliminating violence and providing better images of minority groups, organizations such as ACT have attempted to improve children's programming by decreasing its commercial aspect. Public television, supported by government funds, was the first attempt to remedy the situation. Programs such as *Sesame Street* became enormously popular and were judged by many to be educationally sound and without violence or sexual content.

Nickelodeon, originally conceived as a cable network aimed entirely at children, was another attempt to improve children's programming. At first, this network was commercial free, relying entirely on fees paid by local cable companies. After a few years, however, Nickelodeon began to accept commercial advertising, thus raising protests that the network's original objectives had been forgotten.

—Marc Goldstein

See also Action for Children's Television; Clean Up Television Campaign; Federal Communications Commission; Public Broadcasting Service; Television; Television networks.

BIBLIOGRAPHY

Earle F. Barcus' *Images of Life on Children's Television: Sex Roles, Minorities, and Families* (New York: Praeger, 1983) is a study of children's television programs and their images of American lifestyles. George Comstock and Haejung Paik's *Television and the American Child* (San Diego: Academic Press, 1991) analyzes the possible effects television may have on young audiences. Robert M. Libert and Joyce Sprafkin's *The Early Window: Effects of Television on Children and Youth* (3d ed. New York: Pergamon Press, 1988) discusses the effects of television on viewers of various ages. William Melody's *Children's Television: The Economics of Exploitation* (New Haven, Conn.: Yale University Press, 1973) approaches the question of children's television on the basis of its commercial aspects. Newton N. Minow and Craig L. LaMay's *Abandoned in the Wasteland: Children, Television, and the First Amendment* (New York: Hill and Wang, 1995) discusses the dispute between those who wish to change the content of television programs aimed at children and those who oppose such changes as a form of censorship.

Television networks

DEFINITION: National organizations that distribute television programs to local stations or affiliates

SIGNIFICANCE: Television networks have been powerful forces in shaping the values, beliefs, and behaviors of viewers

Networks distribute programs to local stations or affiliates. Each network has a separate and distinct history. The American Telephone and Telegraph Company (AT&T) instituted the first television network in 1923. In 1926, this network became the National Broadcasting Company (NBC), which owned two networks, called the red network and the blue network. The red network proved stronger. Eventually NBC sold the blue network, which became the American Broadcasting Company (ABC). Another network that was developing when NBC was being established was the Columbia Phonograph Company in 1927. This network later became the Columbia Broadcasting System (CBS). These major networks evolved from radio and telephone networks.

The importance of television networks relative to censorship is related to their primary function. Specifically, television networks are essentially a programming service. They are designed to provide entertainment and information to the public. Networks exercise a considerable amount of control over the programs that are offered to mass audiences. Networks increase profits by increasing the number of viewers because advertising prices are based on the estimated number of viewers for any given program. Therefore, judgments must be made regarding the content and style of programs. In many cases, the values and lifestyles of the audience for whom programming is intended will dictate the content and format of the network's programs.

Network Programming. Prior to the 1970's, all three American networks exercised more direct control over the content of their programs. In 1972 the U.S. Justice Department filed an antitrust suit against the networks. When the litigation was concluded in 1980, all three networks purchased more independent programming. Nevertheless, since the three major networks represent a powerful vehicle for transmitting information, they continued to provide a lucrative service to independent producers and to advertisers. They therefore continued to wield significant influence over the content of the programs that they distributed.

In the United States, individual networks broadcast more than ninety hours of programming every week. Although each network offers unique programs, there is a fairly uniform programming schedule during prime time, or the peak hours of 7 P.M. to 11 P.M. Whatever the network, prime time programming usually consists of dramatic series, comedy series, variety or "magazine" programs, made-for-television films, and sports.

The extent to which such programs are included in a network's programming schedule reflects the best estimate of each television network regarding which programs will find wide audiences and therefore make profits. Critics of networks argue that the quest for wide appeal has led networks to fail to have a fair representation of members of minority racial and ethnic groups in their programming. For example, much of the networks' representation of African Americans has been stereotypical. This was especially pronounced prior to the 1970's. Further, in the 1970's, African Americans were conspicuously absent from network programming. It was not until the 1980's that the networks expanded their programming to include more representative images of African Americans. This effort to present more accurate and representative images, information, and news regarding African Americans and other racial and ethnic groups was not systematically continued in the 1990's, despite the objections of members of these groups and other critics.

Affiliates. Local stations that agree to carry some percentage of a network's programs are known as affiliates. The concept of affiliates was initially introduced by CBS. Generally, affiliates accept approximately 80 percent of the network's programs. The remainder of the affiliate's programming is determined and provided by the local station. Censorship occurs at the affiliate level as well. Local stations occasionally decide that the network's programming is unsuitable for their audiences. Historically, when decisions have been made by affiliates to omit the network's programs, the racial content of the program has been cited as being unacceptable to the local viewing audience. For example, many Southern states maintained and enforced antimiscegenation laws, and television programs including sitcoms and movies that contained interracial dating and marriage were often considered unacceptable by Southern affiliates.

Profits and Programming. The costs of producing programs is also a major determinant that influences the networks programming decisions. Critics cite the networks' intense interest in increasing profits as a major impediment to providing sound programming. Some believe that the networks relentless efforts to increase profits result in them focusing greater attention on ratings rather than on presenting interesting programs. Accordingly, it is suggested that programs of quality are not the primary concern of networks and that the value of programs is determined more by ratings than by programmatic content. Networks place a significant amount of emphasis on generating and maintaining profits, so they are quite competitive with one another. Therefore, the content of their programming is quite similar. The desire on the part of networks to satisfy the same kind of audience oftentimes results in the uniformity of content that is derived through the censorship of information and images. Moreover, the high costs of programming, particularly prime time programming, means that networks are rarely able to recover the costs of production by airing only one episode of a program. Therefore, repeats, using the same advertisers, along with syndication, allow networks to generate sufficient revenue and considerable profits. However, this type of programming reduces the diversification of networks' programs and increases the financial risk involved in creating a program. These economic considerations decrease the likelihood that network television will be representative on the basis of race, ethnicity, and social class.

Advertising is another area in which networks and advertisers control images, information, and news contained in the networks' programs. Advertisers have been known to refuse to purchase time from a network when they do not approve of the content of the network's programs. Advertisers generally play a significant role in influencing the content of the networks' programs because of the costs of producing programs, which operates in conjunction with the networks' overriding concern for maintaining and expanding their margin of profit.

—*K. Sue Jewell*

See also African Americans; British Broadcasting Corporation; Broadcast media; Canadian Broadcasting Corporation; Federal Communications Commission; National Association of Broadcasters; Public Broadcasting Service; Television, children's.

BIBLIOGRAPHY

William Adams and Fay Schreibman, eds., *Television Network News: Issues in Content Research* (Washington, D.C.: School of Public and International Affairs, George Washington University Press, 1978), examine the content of network news. Fred Czarra and Joseph Heaps, *Censorship and the Media: Mixed Blessing or Dangerous Threat* (Newton, Mass.: Allyn & Bacon, 1976), discuss the factors that influence censorship of media in the United States. K. Sue Jewell's *From Mammy to Miss America and Beyond: Cultural Images and U.S. Social Policy* (New York: Routledge, 1993) examines stereotypes and how they affect women. David Poltrack's *Television Marketing: Network, Local, and Cable* (New York: McGraw-Hill, 1983) discusses the varieties of broadcasters and how advertising affects them. Ella Shohat and Robert

Stam's *Unthinking Eurocentrism: Multiculturalism and the Media* (New York: Routledge, 1994) examines the deleterious effects of Eurocentrism in the media. Leslie F. Smith's *Perspectives on Radio and Television: Telecommunication in the United States* (New York: Harper & Row, 1990) is a broad overview, including discussion of television's rivals, including film, CB radio, and video games.

Temperance movements

DEFINITION: Groups and individuals who believe in moderation or abstinence in the use of alcohol

SIGNIFICANCE: As the temperance movement gained momentum in the nineteenth century, its emphasis shifted from a position of moral persuasion to coercive legislation

In the eighteenth century supporters of alcoholic temperance were a small minority of Americans. Many followed the instruction of the distinguished physician Benjamin Rush of Philadelphia. Through numerous pamphlets, he described the ill effects ardent spirits had on the mind and body, and encouraged moderation in the use of alcohol for a healthy life. Membership in temperance societies increased dramatically during the early 1800's. Local societies sprang up across the country. Rush's followers, mostly Quaker and Methodist ministers, were joined by Protestant ministers and nonsectarian groups, such as the Washingtonians and Cold Water Soldiers. By 1833 temperance societies claimed five thousand local organizations with more than a million members.

The message of the new movement changed from moderation to total abstinence. Temperance societies used moral persuasion through revivalistic methods to spread their message. Using many of the same techniques employed by contemporary Methodist and Baptist preachers, speakers traveled across the country delivering emotional lectures in tents, churches, and auditoriums. Their presentations included horror stories given by former alcoholics, threats of damnation, and fervent entreaties for audience members to sign pledges of abstinence. Women were recruited to boycott stores that sold alcohol. Temperance groups published thousands of pamphlets describing the negative effects of alcohol on personal and family finances and on a society which had to maintain jails, poor houses, and insane asylums for those afflicted.

In 1833 twenty-three state societies gathered for a convention in Philadelphia. Together they formed the American Temperance Union. Their emphasis changed from moral persuasion to more coercive measures. The new union campaigned for state and federal legislation that would prevent everyone from using alcohol. As a result of consistent ardent lobbying by temperance societies, eleven states and two territories enacted prohibition laws by 1855.

Opponents of coercive temperance legislation contended that a minority of Americans were trying to impose their morals on a majority. They saw temperance legislation as a violation of American liberties. Opponents asserted that imposing coercive legislation on a society did not change its morality. Rather, it diminished respect for government and encouraged usually law abiding citizens to break the law. Despite such criticisms, membership in temperance movements rose after the Civil War. They were joined by women's temperance movements, most notably the Women's Christian Temperance Union (WCTU). Members paraded, lectured, prayed, and sang in front of saloons trying to persuade patrons and owners to close down. Thousands of pamphlets were distributed and, in a few instances, personal property was destroyed. By 1880 virtually every state had enacted laws making temperance education in schools compulsory.

Though membership in temperance societies waned and most prohibition legislation had been repealed by the end of the century, this period saw the formation of the Anti-Saloon League. They were later joined by the WCTU and Prohibition Party. Their work ultimately led to the passage of the Eighteenth Amendment and national prohibition in the use of alcohol.

See also Advertising as the target of censorship; Alcoholic beverages; Environmental education; Propaganda; Street oratory.

Terrorism

DEFINITION: Violence undertaken, in part, to win publicity to a cause

SIGNIFICANCE: The emergence of the mass media as a dominant force in society presents governments and news organizations with the problem of handling news coverage of violence that is done to obtain publicity

Careless use of the term "terrorism" makes it difficult to comprehend terrorism. One person's terrorist is another person's freedom fighter. Neither the United States nor the United Nations has adopted official definitions of terrorism. Efforts to clarify the term in the United Nations have resulted in a stalemate between Western democracies and nonaligned nations. Western democracies tend to push for a definition of terrorism as acts performed to undermine the authority of legitimate, national governments. Nonaligned nations favor a definition that highlights acts by military regimes or ruling elites that suppress personal liberties.

Without a clear definition of terrorism, it is almost impossible for governments to draft coherent policy responses to such acts, to formulate appropriate counterterrorist strategies, or to design military and police force structures to combat terrorists. Without a clear definition of terrorism, it is difficult for public policymakers to cope with the publicity that terrorism generates. The Rand Corporation has helped to clarify the problem of defining terrorism by classifying terrorist incidents in terms of the nature of each act itself, and not by the identity of the actors or the cause to which they subscribe. There is at least some general consensus as to the elements involved in terrorist acts. First, the acts include violence or the threat of violence. Second, the acts are often coupled with specific demands. Third, the targets of the acts are often civilian. Fourth, political motives are behind the acts of violence. Fifth, the perpetrators are usually members of an organized group. Sixth, the act has a coercive purpose beyond the immediate infliction of physical damage. Seventh and finally, the goal of the act is to achieve maximum publicity.

Propaganda Goals. Utilizing the seven elements typically found in terrorist incidents, it is then possible to identify groups that engage in terrorist activities, to identify nations that train and sponsor such individuals, and to explore the propaganda goals of such organizations. Terrorists can be classified into three main categories: self-supported, state-sponsored, and individuals carrying out acts for tactical purposes. Terrorist groups are usually small, with a standard size of approximately 1,500 to 2,500 operatives. Terrorism does not require great levels of expertise, large quantities of materials, or even extensive personnel support, so small terrorist groups can prosper. In fact, only four or five members are needed in order to make up a viable terrorist subgroup. Bases of operations for terrorist groups are often in urban areas because urban environments usually provide ample places to remain unnoticed.

The terrorist mixes zealous devotion and brutality with sufficient knowledge of weapons, terrorist techniques, and media relations. Advocates of revolutionary terror call for members to sever ties with family and friends. Many terrorists are willing to die for their particular cause. Such individuals obtain money and mobility using funds from bank robbery, kidnapping, extortion, or government support to gain access to modern methods of travel. One of the most extensive public reports on terrorism was compiled by George Bush during his term as vice president of the United States under Ronald Reagan. Bush's report found that 50 percent of the total worldwide terrorist incidents were executed by groups located within the Middle East. Many of these acts involved militant religious groups supported or sponsored by countries such as Libya, Iran, Lebanon, and Syria. Incidents in Western Europe by groups such as the Provisional Irish Republican Army, the Italian Red Brigade, the French Direct Action, and the German Red Army Brigade made up approximately 25 percent of the total worldwide acts. The remaining 25 percent occurred in Latin America, Asia, and Africa.

Terrorism and Censorship. Modern communications technology provides terrorists with the mechanism for propaganda and psychological warfare. Furthermore, media coverage of terrorist acts has the potential to turn a group of criminal thugs into media celebrities by providing a platform for the political causes or grievances expressed by the group. In nations with closed political systems in which the mass media are under the control of the government, the problem of terrorist propaganda is minimal. In other words, these governments have the power and authority to completely censor coverage of terrorist acts from official news outlets. In nations with open political systems in which the mass media are apart from direct government control, news coverage of terrorist acts is of great concern. For example, as U.S. deputy attorney general Benjamin Civiletti stated before Congress in 1978: "Under the First Amendment, the U.S. government has no right to prohibit or limit coverage of a newsworthy event. However, it is appropriate to seek voluntary media cooperation in minimizing risks to life and to point out that certain media actions might exacerbate a dangerous situation."

The Iran Hostage Crisis. On November 4, 1979, approximately sixty American citizens were seized at the United States embassy in Teheran, Iran. On November 10, President Jimmy Carter instructed the attorney general to deport Iranian students who were living in the United States illegally. Two days later the president announced a suspension of oil imports from Iran. Months later on April 7, 1980, the United States officially broke diplomatic relations with Iran. Several weeks later, a military rescue mission was aborted when sandstorms in the center of Iran delayed the mission and resulted in a collision between a helicopter and a C-130 aircraft. Eventually, the hostages were released safely, but not until inauguration day for President Ronald Reagan; the Iranians did not allow either president to bask in the limelight.

Media coverage of the Iranian hostage crisis was extensive, with most major network shows opening their broadcasts each night with phrases such as "America held hostage" along with an exact tally of the number of days Americans had been held in captivity in Iran. As noted terrorism scholar Abraham Miller comments, "In the context of the Iranian hostage crisis, the question becomes, with respect to television and the press, whether event-oriented sensationalism is inextricably linked with mundane commercialism. Iran proved once again beyond any doubt, that terrorism is quintessentially the propaganda of the deed." As the Iranian hostage crisis demonstrates, terrorist propaganda can at times help sell newspapers and increase television viewers. All three major television networks, taking advantage of the Iranian hostage situation, developed a blind eye to professional and ethical considerations in a fervent competitive quest for audiences. The Iranian hostage situation continues to provoke debate over the proper balance of news coverage of terrorist incidents.

The Unabomber Manifesto. Most often the question of censorship and terrorism centers around government control of the news. In the case of the Unabomber, the controversy involved the question of voluntary censorship on the part of the free press. The Unabomber is the name assigned by the Federal Bureau of Investigation (FBI) to a serial mail bomber who is believed to have killed three people and injured twenty-three others since 1978. The Unabomber agreed to stop sending explosives through the postal service if *The New York Times* and *The Washington Post* would publish a 35,000-word manifesto that articulated the bomber's political philosophy. Upon the recommendation of Attorney General Janet Reno and FBI director Louis Freeh, the newspapers shared the cost of publishing the manuscript as a special eight-page section. Ironically, publication of the Unabomber's manifesto led directly to the identification and arrest of a prime suspect in 1996.

The decision to publish the manuscript touched off controversy among journalists, criminologists, and political commentators. The papers were criticized for acceding to terrorist demands and potentially encouraging others to blackmail the news industry. Members of the newspapers as well as members of the law enforcement community defended the decision, claiming that publication could lead to disclosure of the identity of the Unabomber. Relatives of a suspect in fact recognized a correlation between the manifesto and the suspect's writings, and an arrest was made.

According to the Bush report on terrorism: "The solution to this problem is not government-imposed restraint that conflicts with the First Amendment protection of freedom of speech and press. The media must serve as their own watchdog. Journalistic guidelines have been developed for use during wartime to protect lives and national security, and in some circumstances should be considered appropriate during a terrorist situation." The Bush report also suggests that certain media practices, such as saturation television coverage, political dialogue with hostages or terrorists, coverage of staged events, involvement in negotiations, payments to terrorist groups or supporters for interview access, and detailed coverage of military or police response plans to terrorist situations should be avoided. —*John W. Cavanaugh*

See also Bush, George; Clear and present danger doctrine; Espionage; Espionage Act of 1917; "H-Bomb Secret, The"; Hoaxes; Iran; Irish Republican Army; Israel; Military censorship; National security; National Security Decision Directive 84; Northern Ireland; Prior restraint; Sedition; Violence; War.

BIBLIOGRAPHY

Yonah Alexander and Seymour M. Finger's *Terrorism: Interdisciplinary Perspectives* (New York: John Jay Press, 1977) is a resource for advanced students or researchers looking for information across disciplines about terrorism. Vice President's Task Force on Combatting Terrorism, *Public Report of the Vice President's Task Force on Combatting Terrorism* (Washington, D.C.: Government Printing Office, February, 1986), explores policy responses to terrorism and issues concerning the media and censorship. Christopher Dobson and Ronald Payne, *Counterattack: The West's Battle Against the Terrorists* (New York: Facts on File, 1982), focuses on policy responses to the problem of terrorism. Michael T. Klare and Peter Kornbluh, eds., *Low Intensity Warfare* (New York: Pantheon Books, 1988), is an exceptional resource for students and researchers searching for an explanation of terrorism as a new modality of warfare. Klare and Kornbluh predict in this edited volume that the problem of terrorism will increase. Abraham H. Miller, ed., *Terrorism: The Media and the Law* (Dobbs Ferry, New York: Transnational Publishers, 1982), is an edited volume providing students and researchers with case law examples involving the topic of terrorism and censorship. Peter C. Sederberg, *Terrorism Myths: Illusion, Rhetoric, and Reality* (Englewood Cliffs, New Jersey: Prentice Hall, 1989), is a superior scholarly work for students who wish to explore questions revolving around definitions of terrorists, their political goals, and propaganda.

Tess of the D'Urbervilles

TYPE OF WORK: Book
PUBLISHED: 1891
AUTHOR: Thomas Hardy (1840-1928)
SUBJECT MATTER: Novel about an English peasant girl forced to give up her true love in order to be the mistress of a rich man, whom she eventually kills
SIGNIFICANCE: Hardy voluntarily cut and rewrote significant portions of this book in order to publish it as a magazine serial

Thomas Hardy began writing *Tess of the D'Urbervilles* in the fall of 1888, under contract to a large conservative newspaper syndicate in England. After reading drafts of the manuscript

this publisher decided certain scenes were indecent and asked Hardy to rewrite them. After Hardy refused, his publisher canceled his contract. For financial reasons Hardy needed to sell his book as a serial. He tried to sell the manuscript to two more magazine publishers, but both magazines rejected it.

Hardy undertook the revision of the text himself. His second draft won the approval of the *Graphic* magazine, except for two scenes. *Tess of the D'Urbervilles* appeared as a weekly serial between July 4, 1891, and December 26, 1891. It appeared in book form, with nearly all its original text restored, in November, 1891. The Wessex edition of 1912 was the first complete edition. The novel encountered mixed reviews upon publication, but sold quickly enough to go into a second edition within months.

The scene that had raised the strongest objections is Tess's seduction by Alec D'Urberville. Hardy revised this scene to have Tess believe that she is married to D'Urberville when he seduces her. The second objectionable scene is the baptism of Tess's illegitimate child, which Hardy fixed by simply removing the child from the story completely.

Hardy received many requests to dramatize *Tess of the D'Urbervilles*, but he never did. No London theaters were willing to risk the potential censorship to produce it, although several well-known actresses, including Sarah Bernhardt, offered to play Tess.

See also Abridgment; Adultery; Book publishing; Drama and theater; Literature; United Kingdom.

Texas v. Johnson

COURT: U.S. Supreme Court
DECIDED: June 21, 1989
SIGNIFICANCE: This decision affirmed that the First Amendment protects symbolic forms of expression, including the right to burn the U.S. flag as a political protest

While the Republican National Convention was meeting in Dallas, Texas, in 1984, Gregory Lee Johnson participated in a political demonstration protesting policies of the Reagan Administration and of certain Dallas-based corporations. In front of Dallas' city hall, Johnson doused an American flag with kerosene and set it on fire. As the flag burned, protesters chanted, "America, the red, white, and blue, we spit on you." Several witnesses testified that they had been seriously offended, but no one was physically injured or threatened with injury. Following this demonstration, a witness collected the flag's remains and buried them in his back yard. Johnson was then charged with the desecration of a venerated object in violation of the Texas penal code. He was convicted, sentenced to a year in prison, and fined two thousand dollars. A district appeals court affirmed Johnson's conviction; however, Texas' Court of Criminal Appeals then reversed the lower court decisions. Finally, the U.S. Supreme Court affirmed the reversal, by a 5-4 vote.

Associate Justice William J. Brennan, Jr., joined by justices Thurgood Marshall, Harry Blackmun, Antonin Scalia, and Anthony Kennedy, wrote the majority opinion. Brennan noted that the First Amendment protects "expressive conduct" as well as written and spoken words. While a state can prevent

A Seattle man burns a U.S. flag in October, 1989, shortly after Congress enacted a new anti-flag burning law in response to the Supreme Court's Texas v. Johnson *decision, which permitted flag burning.* (AP/Wide World Photos)

"imminent lawless action," Johnson's symbolic expression of dissatisfaction with government policies did not lead to a disturbance of the peace and did not threaten the state's interest in maintaining order. Instead, Johnson's expression was restricted because of the content of his message. "If there is a bedrock principle underlying the First Amendment," Brennan observed, "it is that the Government may not prohibit the expression of an idea simply because society finds the idea itself offensive or disagreeable." Toleration of Johnson's criticism reinforces the freedom that the flag represents. Brennan continued, "the way to preserve the flag's special role is not to punish those who feel differently about such matters. It is to persuade them that they are wrong. . . . We can imagine no more appropriate response to burning a flag than waving one's own, no better way to counter a flag burner's message than by saluting the flag that burns."

In a dissenting opinion joined by justices Byron White and Sandra Day O'Connor, Chief Justice William H. Rehnquist emphasized the unique role of the flag and the "profoundly offensive" nature of Johnson's conduct. In a separate dissent, Justice John P. Stevens argued that Johnson was prosecuted not for his criticism of government policies but for the method he chose to express his views.

Public outcries against this Court decision led to enactment of the federal Flag Protection Act. However, in *United States v. Eichman* (1990), the Supreme Court reaffirmed *Texas v. Johnson* by ruling that Congress was improperly trying to suppress expression because of its communicative impact.

See also Bush, George; Fighting words; Flag burning; Symbolic speech.

Textbooks

DEFINITION: Books written and designed specifically for classroom use

SIGNIFICANCE: Because of their central role in education, textbooks have been a continual target of censors

Behind textbook controversies are beliefs and values that encompass more than curriculum decisions in classrooms. Schools are community institutions and involve highly emotional issues concerning the upbringing of children. Additionally, financial support—through taxes—for public schools is mandatory, so they have been frequent targets for political machinations of one form or another.

From the beginning of American public education, schools have been buffeted by differing religious, political, and cultural viewpoints. In his plan for tax-supported schools in Virginia, first proposed in 1779, Thomas Jefferson emphasized secular academic subjects and citizenship and eliminated the Christian scriptures and religious doctrine that was commonly taught. Religious teaching and exercises continued unabated in most classrooms across the nation. To make schools at least nondenominational, Horace Mann, the person most responsible for opening free schools in the early 1800's, recommended that the Bible be read only in opening exercises, and that it be read without comment. An outcry greeted Mann's proposal. Conservative Christians wanted students to hear interpretations of the Bible, non-Christians objected to prayers directed to Jesus Christ, and Roman Catholics were incensed that the Bible used for readings was the Protestant version. This clash between religious faiths, brought on by a new wave of immigrants from Catholic countries, was further fueled in the late 1800's by the popular use of the McGuffey Readers, which contained anti-Catholic, anti-Jewish, and anti-immigrant statements.

Social Studies and History Texts. Issues such as what constitutes patriotism were early sources of contention. After the U.S. Civil War book publishers anxious to sell history texts often created two versions: one for the North and one for the South, each with a different slant on the war. Following World War I, all that was un-American became a central focus of censorship. In 1922 the Veterans of Foreign Wars fought for the elimination of all textbooks they deemed unpatriotic. The mayor of Chicago, William Hart Thompson, claimed that the discussions of British democracy, ideas, and achievements in textbooks made America look poor by comparison.

To make history more interesting and realistic, Professor Harold Rugg began publishing a series of texts on American society that dealt with such controversial issues as unemployment, immigration, class structure, and the effects of industrialization on everyday life in 1939. Widely acclaimed by educators, his books were used by half of the nation's school districts until they were attacked as socialist by the Advertising Federation of America, the National Association of Manufacturers, and the right-wing Hearst newspaper chain. The American Legion published a pamphlet, *Treason in the Textbooks*, charging that the books were telling students that the American way of life had failed. The texts were soon removed from schools and the series ended.

During the Red Scare era of the 1950's the primary concern of censors was communist infiltration in public education. The Soviet Union had become aggressive, communists had taken over China, America was involved in the Korean War, and Senator Joseph McCarthy was accusing intellectuals, politicians, artists, and clergy of being communist sympathizers. In 1949 the Sons of the American Revolution published a booklet called *A Bill of Grievances* charging that public schools were being converted by communist front organizations into agencies to disseminate radical propaganda to students.

During this period a retired English professor, Merrill E. Root, a liberal Quaker turned radical right, wrote a pamphlet, *Darkness at Noon in American Colleges*, in which he charged that such institutions were communist factories turning out robot collectivists. This was followed by *Collectivism on the Campus* (1954) and *Brainwashing in the High Schools* (1958), which made him a national leader in the assault on public education. Communism encompassed many perceived evils: racial integration, taxation, social security, unions, socialized medicine, fluoridation of water, the United Nations, and attempts at international cooperation.

Impressed by Root's book, the Daughters of the American Revolution published in 1961 *Textbook Study*, a pamphlet that blacklisted 170 social studies books for being subversive. Their objections included a description of the United States as a "democracy" rather than a "republic," emphasis on the Bill of Rights rather than the basic Constitution, discussion of the United Nations and international relations, pictures of slum areas and Great Depression-era unemployment lines, photographs of mushrooming nuclear bombs, too much realistic literature, and too many labor and folk songs.

A high school civics textbook called *American Government*, written and revised annually by Frank Magruder beginning in 1917 and, after Magruder's death in 1949, by William McClenaghan, was assailed by another popular critic, Lucille Cardin Crain, who claimed the book's purpose was to undermine students' belief in the efficacy of capitalism. Attacks by Crain and other conservative critics led to the book's temporary removal from schools in Georgia, Arkansas, and Texas.

The Gablers. From the early 1960's into the 1990's a married couple in Texas, Mel Gabler and Norma Gabler, exerted considerable pressure on publishers to alter textbooks to fit their Christian Fundamentalist viewpoints. They objected to historical personages depicted as having human faults. They also objected to criticisms of U.S. government actions, such as the internment of the Japanese during World War II, slavery, decisions that led to economic depressions, laws that discriminated against minorities or females, and U.S. involvement in the Korean and Vietnam wars. The Gablers also challenged the inclusion in social studies texts of such figures as César Chávez, Martin Luther King, Jr., Rosa Parks, and Mohandas Gandhi. The Gablers have strenuously objected to textbooks that ask open-ended questions and encourage independent thinking, instead of imparting factual information only. Such approaches lead students to believe, they have maintained, that there are no right answers or moral absolutes. The Gablers called the 1972 series *Man: A Course of Study*, developed by Professor Jerome Bruner and funded by the National Science Foundation, the "worst . . . imaginable." The series' purpose was to introduce students to a variety of cultures, such as the Netsilik Eskimos, with values and practices quite different from traditional American society.

In contrast to the attacks on books by those on the right, both Frances FitzGerald in *America Revised* (1979) and James W. Loewen in *Lies My Teacher Told Me* (1995) criticized history texts for their boring blandness, egregious misinformation, lack of intellectual standards and stimulation, and the manipulation of students into accepting particular ideological dogma.

Science Texts. At the heart of textbook censorship in science has been the theory of evolution. From 1900 to 1920 laws prohibiting the teaching of this concept were passed in Tennessee, Arkansas, and Mississippi. In 1925 Texas governor Miriam "Ma" Ferguson mandated that the word be deleted in all textbooks and any educator who taught evolution would be dismissed or prosecuted. In 1927 national attention focused on Dayton, Tennessee, when a young biology teacher, John Scopes, was convicted of flouting the state law prohibiting the teaching of evolution.

Thirty-five years later Susan Epperson defied a statute in Arkansas that forbade any state-supported school or university to teach that humans descended from a lower order of animals. The U.S. Supreme Court, in *Epperson v. Arkansas* (1968), ruled that the law violated the religious neutrality requirement of the First Amendment because it proscribed a particular body of knowledge on the basis that it conflicted with a sectarian interpretation of the Bible's Book of Genesis.

Because of the influence of the Biological Sciences Curriculum Study (BSCS) during the 1960's, evolution received an unprecedented emphasis in textbooks. This, however, was soon reduced or eliminated during the 1970's as a result of pressure from the Religious Right. Evolution gained again against the Religious Right in the late 1980's when California refused to purchase science books that did not adequately present the theory of evolution.

Having lost the battle to eliminate evolution from science classes, the Religious Right developed a new concept, "creation science." Claiming that evolution is unproved and a central tenet of the so-called religion of humanism, creationists maintained that the true scientific explanation of the earth's origin is in the Book of Genesis and demanded equal time in science classes for teaching creationism. In 1987 the U.S. Supreme Court ruled in *Edwards v. Aguillard* that a Louisiana law requiring science teachers to teach creationism if they taught evolution was unconstitutional because it put religious dogma into an academic, scientific curriculum. Justice Antonin Scalia argued for the dissent.

Literature Texts. Literature books were less targeted in schools than social studies or science texts, at least until the 1960's, for several reasons. First, prior restraint often occurred as teachers, librarians, administrators, and school boards refused to buy or place certain books on reading lists. Also, young adult novels and stories tended to be less realistic, negative, or controversial than works meant for adults. Finally, many texts containing works by William Shakespeare and other classic authors were—and still are—filled with alterations, bowdlerizations, and deletions, particularly regarding sexual matters or religious and political viewpoints.

From the 1960's into the 1990's, however, many books that conservative parents and right-wing organizations deem offensive were selected by teachers for required or supplemental reading. In short, teachers, writers, school librarians, and others developed a resistance to prior restraint. According to surveys done by the National Council of Teachers of English (NCTE), leading the list of censored literature books from 1965 to 1985 was J. D. Salinger's *The Catcher in the Rye* (1951), followed by John Steinbeck's *The Grapes of Wrath* (1939) and *Of Mice and Men* (1937), an anonymous teenage diary about drug use called *Go Ask Alice*, and George Orwell's *Nineteen Eighty-Four* (1949). Other books popular among adolescents that have been frequently censored by adults include *Lord of the Flies* (1954), *Adventures of Huckleberry Finn* (1884), *To Kill a Mockingbird* (1960), *Brave New World* (1932), *Manchild in the Promised Land* (1965), *Slaughterhouse-Five* (1969), *One Flew over the Cuckoo's Nest* (1962), *A Separate Peace* (1959), *The Scarlet Letter* (1850), and *I Know Why the Caged Bird Sings* (1970). Later additions to the frequently censored list have been Robert Cormier's *The Chocolate War* (1974) and Alice Walker's *The Color Purple* (1982).

The usual charges have been that the books are obscene, immoral, and blasphemous; they oppose the Bible, Christianity, religion, America, the family, and the free-enterprise system; are unpatriotic and socialistic; and espouse the "religion of secular humanism."

An irate superintendent ordered school copies of Kurt Vonnegut's *Slaughterhouse-Five* burned in Drake, North Dakota; elsewhere teachers were fired for teaching Albert Camus' *The Stranger* (1942). In 1987 sixty-four commonly used books were removed by the school superintendent in Bay County, Florida. Challenged by teachers, students, and parents, the superintendent reinstated most titles, but eleven English teachers resigned and the school was no longer listed by NCTE as a Center of Excellence.

In 1974 an eruption over new textbooks in Kanawha County, West Virginia, turned violent. Strikes and pickets disrupted the community, lives were threatened, and schools and buses firebombed as protesters, urged on by local Fundamentalist preachers and the Gablers in Texas, demanded that the godless textbooks be removed from schools. According to James Moffett, in *Storm in the Mountains* (1988), although many of the books remained in the schools by court order, teachers were afraid to teach from them, publishers reacted to the uproar by publishing extremely cautious texts, and school

districts across the country selected only books least likely to offend anyone.

Almost ten years later, a protest by eleven Fundamentalist families in Churchill, Tennessee, over a basic reading series began in 1983 and culminated in the 1987 Supreme Court decision *Mozert v. Hawkins County*. Objected to were such selections as *The Wonderful Wizard of Oz* (1900), King Arthur stories, "Cinderella," "Goldilocks and the Three Bears," and stories by Hans Christian Andersen. The case pitted two national organizations against each other: People for the American Way defended the school district and Concerned Women for America supported the parents, who charged that the books advocated witchcraft, Satanism, pacifism, feminism, environmentalism, vegetarianism, and one-world government, all of which offended their religious beliefs. In the opinion of the Sixth Circuit court, however, these books were not antireligious but taught a tolerance for divergent views, essential to democracy, and ruled for the books' continued use.

In an earlier case involving eleven library books, the U.S. Supreme Court said that school boards may not remove books because they dislike the ideas therein. In a school newspaper case, *Hazelwood School District v. Kuhlmeier* (1988), the Court granted administrators the right to make professional judgments about curriculum matters. With this as its basis, the Eleventh Circuit Court of Appeals in 1989 ruled in favor of board members who censured, because of vulgar language and sexual explicitness, a previously selected textbook that included Aristophanes' *Lysistrata* and Geoffrey Chaucer's "The Miller's Tale." Though expressing doubt that high school students would be harmed by reading such masterpieces of Western literature, the judges decreed that boards have the right to select whatever materials they deem appropriate.

Challenged works from 1991 to 1994 included a book intended for children about a young boy's positive relationship with a homosexual father, and the literature-based elementary series called Impressions, which includes selections from such writers as C. S. Lewis, A. A. Milne, Maurice Sendak, Rudyard Kipling, and Laura Ingalls Wilder. Critics from the Religious Right stated that stories about Halloween and ghosts, for instance, are satanic and promote the "religion of witchcraft," and drawings of rainbows inject mystical, New Age psychology into the classroom, which is dangerous to children's minds and souls.

Other Attacks on Texts. The Religious Right is not the only group to censor books. During the 1960's and 1970's, a dramatic shift took place in the censorship wars when new protesters appeared on the scene: the liberals, who before had generally resisted censorship. Many books were charged with being racist and sexist. To counter this, nonwhite faces were added to textbooks, African Americans and women were pictured as professionals rather than slaves and housewives, and the achievements and writings of minorities and women were included, although often tagged on at the ends of chapters. The Anti-Defamation League of B'nai B'rith, the National Association for the Advancement of Colored People, the Council on Interracial Books, the National Organization for Women (NOW), and other organizations denounced books deemed prejudicial and made their own demands for future texts, including nonsexist language. As a result, textbooks were watered down to the extent that they would offend neither a left-wing radical from Berkeley nor a right-wing radical Fundamentalist Christian from Texas; some critics judged such books to be so without anything that might be offensive that they were quite dull.

Adventures of Huckleberry Finn was removed from classroom reading in numerous school districts, including the Mark Twain Intermediate School in Fairfax, Virginia, and *The Autobiography of Miss Jane Pittman* was banned in a Texas town; both books were banned because of their use of racial slurs. Stepmothers and practicing witches objected to the reading of fairy tales that branded them as wicked, nutritionists decried stories containing junk food, and a Dr. Seuss book in which a greedy family devastates a make-believe forest was banned for its supposed attack on the logging industry.

A leading critic of public schools, Phyllis Schlafly, and her organization, the Eagle Forum, have maligned textbooks on sex, AIDS, health, and drug education, maintaining that such topics should be handled only by parents. They have also fought the use of psychology books that promote self-esteem and decision-making activities and the use of affirmations, visualizations, and cooperation, which they view as self-hypnosis and mind control.

Challenges to textbooks have varied in their focus over the years, but the critics' motivation and behavior remains constant: Individuals or groups vigorously and sometimes violently demand that their beliefs and values be imposed on all children. As Jack Nelson and Gene Roberts, Jr., state in their 1963 study of textbook censorship, *The Censors and the Schools*: "Since the early days of the Cold War, textbook crises have come in an almost unbroken stream, each controversy providing fuel for another. . . . The charges are essentially the same: the texts are blamed for what a censor dislikes about the world in which he lives."

—*June Edwards*

See also Abridgment; Daughters of the American Revolution; Eagle Forum; Gabler, Mel, and Norma Gabler; Kanawha County book-banning controversy; McGuffey Readers; Magruder's *American Government*; People for the American Way; Prior restraint; Scopes trial; Secular humanism.

BIBLIOGRAPHY

James C. Hefley, *Textbooks on Trial* (Wheaton, Ill.: Victor Books, 1976), provides a Religious-Right perspective on the Gablers' efforts to keep books off Texas' state-adoption lists and to influence publishers. The Gablers' own *What Are They Teaching Our Children?* (Wheaton, Ill.: Victor Books, 1985), written with James C. Hefley, details their many objections to texts in social studies, literature, science, and health. Niles Eldredge's *The Monkey Business: A Scientist Looks at Creationism* (New York: Washington Square Press, 1982) and Dorothy Nelkin, *The Creation Controversy: Science or Scripture in the Schools* (New York: Norton, 1982), examine the antievolution controversy. Joan DelFattore's *What Johnny Shouldn't Read: Textbook Censorship in America* (New Haven, Conn.: Yale University Press, 1992), discusses the people and organizations involved in censorship incidents. *The Censors and the Schools*, by Jack Nelson and Gene Roberts, Jr. (Boston: Little, Brown, 1963), and *America Revised: History Schoolbooks in the Twentieth Century*, by Frances Fitzgerald (Boston: Little, Brown, 1979), give historical overviews of school censorship. James Moffett's *Storm in the Mountains: A Case Study of Censorship, Conflict, and Consciousness* (Carbondale: Southern Illinois University Press, 1988) details the Kanawha County, West Virginia, textbook confrontation. *Preserving Intellectual Freedom: Fighting Censorship in Our Schools*, published by the National Council of Teachers of English (Urbana, Illinois, 1994), edited by Jean E. Brown, is a collection of essays on censorship by college and public school faculty, with suggestions on how to combat it. James W. Loewen's *Lies My Teacher Told Me: Everything Your American History Textbook Got Wrong* (New York: New York Press, 1995) is a compelling critique of twelve leading high school history texts that he finds boring, blindly patriotic, and filled with misinformation.

Theatres Act of 1968

ENACTED: September 26, 1968

PLACE: United Kingdom (national)

SIGNIFICANCE: By eliminating the Lord Chamberlain's powers to license theaters and approve all new plays, this law ended more than two centuries of stage censorship in Great Britain

After the passage of the Licensing Act of 1737, the offices of the Lord Chamberlain and the Examiner of Plays became responsible for approval of scripts for all new plays performed in Britain. With the Theatres Act of 1968, however, these powers were abolished, ending the nation's most restrictive form of stage censorship. At various points in history, theatrical professionals (including playwright George Bernard Shaw and critic William Archer) and the general public had opposed the censors' powers as too broad and idiosyncratic. The Lord Chamberlain had been the ultimate authority, responsible to no one else and able to censor for any reason. This sporadic opposition gained strength in the 1960's and eventually led to the overturning of previous laws governing theatrical censorship.

A pivotal event in the decision to overturn the existing law was the 1965 production of Edward Bond's play *Saved* at the Royal Court Theatre. The script had been denied approval by the Lord Chamberlain owing to a graphic scene in which a baby is stoned to death by youths. The English Stage Company proceeded with the production anyway, under a loophole in the law which allowed "private" performances of unlicensed plays. The police raided the theater, closed down the performance, and eventually won their court case against the company. However, public sentiment was aroused, and in 1966 Parliament was moved to create a joint committee on theater censorship. In 1967 a performance of another unapproved Bond play, *Early Morning*, was raided, but this case never came to trial. By then it was apparent that the parliamentary committee would recommend abolishing the Lord Chamberlain's powers of censorship. In due time, the 1968 law followed that recommendation.

After passage of this act, live dramatic performances in Britain finally enjoyed the same degree of freedom as did the press, television, and other forms of entertainment. Prior restraint—preventing the performance of a play before it was ever staged—was no longer possible. Prosecution after the fact was still possible if a play was deemed to break existing laws, such as those regarding libel, obscenity, or blasphemy. The most famous attempt to restrict theatrical performance after the passage of the law was the unsuccessful prosecution of Howard Brenton's *The Romans in Britain* (1980) because it depicted a homosexual rape.

See also Drama and theater; *Hair*; Licensing Act of 1737; Lord Chamberlain; Prior restraint; Shaw, George Bernard.

Thomas, Norman

BORN: November 20, 1884, Marion, Ohio
DIED: December 19, 1968, Huntington, New York
IDENTIFICATION: American Socialist Party leader
SIGNIFICANCE: Thomas wrote and edited articles censored under the Espionage Act of 1917, helped found the American Civil Liberties Union, and protested censorship of other leftist activists

During his career as a political activist, socialist Norman Thomas often encountered censorship. One early occasion was caused by the federal Espionage Act of 1917, which was used by Postmaster General Albert Burleson to revoke the mailing privileges of several socialists, thereby effectively halting publication of many left-wing periodicals. Among them was *The World Tomorrow*, a magazine published by the pacifist Fellowship of Reconciliation, which Thomas edited in 1918 when the U.S. Post Office outlawed its mailing. Thomas twice had the ban lifted, but on a third occasion, he was not so lucky. An issue containing his article entitled "The Acid Test of Our Democracy," which criticized American intervention in Russia, was deemed by the Post Office to be too pro-Bolshevik to be distributed. When Thomas rushed to Washington, D.C., to protest, he was told by Burleson that if he had his way he would not only kill Thomas' magazine, but would have Thomas himself sent to prison. President Woodrow Wilson disagreed with Burleson and ordered him to lift the ban, an order with which Burleson reluctantly complied. The next issue of the paper was also banned, but Thomas was able to send off a letter to Washington, defending the magazine, and was again able to have the ban lifted.

In 1920 Thomas helped form the National Civil Liberties Bureau, an organization which would become renowned for fighting censorship. Formed to aid conscientious objectors during World War I, it later became the American Civil Liberties Union (ACLU). Indeed, Thomas was a member when the ACLU itself had its papers confiscated under the Espionage and Sedition Act.

In 1938 Thomas traveled to Jersey City to protest Mayor Frank Hague's charge that the Congress of Industrial Organizations was controlled by communists. Hague also instituted a ban on public meetings of the organization. When the Socialist Party's request for permission to hold a meeting was denied, Thomas defied the order and tried to address a meeting of thirty-two hundred people on May Day. He announced another speech for that night. Before he could speak, he was seized by police, who escorted him to a ferry bound for Manhattan.

In addition to writing and speaking for the Socialist Party, Thomas was also the party's standard bearer in many electoral races. During the mid-1920's he ran for governor of New York and mayor of New York City, and he ran for president of the United States six times between 1928 and 1948.

See also American Civil Liberties Union; Debs, Eugene; Draft resistance; Espionage Act of 1917; Nonmailable matter laws; Sedition; World War I.

Thomas à Kempis

BORN: 1379, Kempen, near Cologne, the Rhineland, Germany
DIED: August 8, 1471, near Zwolle, Bishopric of Utrecht, Netherlands
IDENTIFICATION: German monastic and devotional writer
SIGNIFICANCE: Massachusetts Bay Colony censored his *The Imitation of Christ*

After being ordained to the priesthood in 1413, Thomas à Kempis entered an Augustinian monastery in the Netherlands, where he remained the rest his life. He is widely credited with having written the book, *Imatio Christi*, or *The Imitation of Christ* around 1427.

Although scholars have sometimes seen similarities between the thought of Thomas àKempis and the later Protestant reformer Martin Luther, any such similarity was apparently not obvious to the Puritans of the Massachusetts Bay Colony. In 1662 the Massachusetts General Court—the Colony's principal legislative body—created a licensing board to supervise printing within the colony. In 1669, however, the General Court discovered that the board had licensed the printing of *The Imitation of Christ*. It promptly instructed the licensing board to revise the work of this "popish minister" before going forward with the printing. The board declined the task of attempting a revision, and the publisher abandoned the printing of the book.

See also Abelard, Peter; Hus, Jan; Luther, Martin; Puritans; Religion.

Thoreau, Henry David

BORN: July 12, 1817, Concord, Massachusetts
DIED: May 6, 1862, Concord, Massachusetts
IDENTIFICATION: American philosopher and naturalist
SIGNIFICANCE: Thoreau's essay "Civil Disobedience" makes an eloquent case for freedom of conscience

Thoreau was an adherent of Transcendentalism, a nineteenth century New England movement that emphasized self-examination, religious feelings toward nature, individualism, and social reform. In order to come closer to nature so that he might arrive at a deeper understanding of himself, Thoreau withdrew from society in the 1840's to live at Walden Pond. He stayed there for two years and supported himself in solitude. The experience provided the background for his most famous work, *Walden, or Life in the Woods* (1854). On one level this book was a response to the utopian communes that had become popular in the nineteenth century. Alone at Walden Pond, Thoreau felt free of the self-styled reformers whom he considered great bores, claiming that he would rather be a bachelor in hell than live in a boardinghouse in heaven.

During his time at Walden Pond, Thoreau became convinced that majority rule was unprincipled because under it minorities were forced to compromise their ideas of right and wrong. Acting on this conviction, he refused to pay his poll taxes because he opposed the U.S. war against Mexico (1845-1848), which he considered no more than a poorly disguised scheme to expand U.S. slavery. For this he was jailed, but only for one night because a friend or relative quickly paid his delinquent taxes. In an essay he titled "Civil Disobedience" (1849, rev. 1866), Thoreau outlined his justification for refusing to pay the poll tax.

In "Civil Disobedience," Thoreau refused to recognize the moral authority of any government that permitted slavery or imprisoned just men. He did not expect the machinery of government to run perfectly or without friction. However, when a government allows friction to acquire its own machine to perpetuate immorality—in this case the institution of slavery—Thoreau proclaimed that it became time to bring the government to a halt. Instead of relying on the will of the majority, just persons should follow the dictates of their own consciences. Moreover, no person of conscience could be associated with a government that condones slavery. In fact, if the will of the majority requires someone to be an agent of injustice, the only place for that person to be is in prison.

Thoreau called upon the men of Massachusetts passively to resist the unjust laws that perpetuated slavery and to go to jail in mass. He was convinced that a government faced with the choice of placing all just men in jail or giving up slavery would not hesitate to choose the latter. Thoreau called this nonviolent technique of passive resistance to unjust laws "civil disobedience."

Thoreau's theory of civil disobedience later appealed to Mohandas Gandhi, and, through Gandhi, to Martin Luther King, Jr. Thus Thoreau indirectly helped shape the strategy for the only true mass movement in American history—the Civil Rights movement of the 1950's and 1960's.

See also Abolitionist movement; Civil Rights movement; Emerson, Ralph Waldo; King, Martin Luther, Jr.; Mexican-American War; *Utopia.*

Three Mile Island

DATE: March 28, 1979

PLACE: A nuclear power plant by the Susquehanna River, ten miles from the Pennsylvania state capital, Harrisburg

SIGNIFICANCE: The first major accident to a nuclear electricity-generating facility raised questions of whether government agencies were disclosing all relevant facts to the public

At 4 A.M. on Wednesday, March 28, 1979, a nuclear reactor at Three Mile Island generating electricity for the Metropolitan Edison Company began malfunctioning. As a result of mechanical and operator errors, the protective blanket of water surrounding the nuclear core dissipated, resulting in overheating and partial meltdown of the core. These developments created the potential for radiation to be released into the atmosphere.

On both that Wednesday morning and the following morning the utility company issued announcements about the accident, assuring the public that there was no danger to those outside the plant. However, on the Friday following the accident, the governor of Pennsylvania, Richard Thornburgh, recommended that pregnant women and pre-school children living within a five-mile radius of the plant be evacuated from the area. Schools in that same area were urged to close. National news programs on radio and television soon broadcast the story, with particular emphasis on potential radiation exposure. Although the evacuation recommendation applied to only about 12,000 persons, more than 140,000 left the immediate area. Both Governor Thornburgh and President Jimmy Carter visited the area immediately after the accident.

For ten days there was intense media focus on the Three Mile Island story. At the end of that time, when technical experts had brought conditions at the reactor fully under their control, the governor rescinded his evacuation recommendation. Most of those who had left returned to their homes, and media attention to the story diminished sharply. Because of its potential for widespread damage, the Three Mile Island affair

The "accident" that occurred at the Three Mile Island nuclear power plant in early 1979 soon brought out protesters concerned about safety in the region. (National Archives)

was immediately seized upon by the antinuclear movement as proof of their contention that all use of nuclear power was hazardous. The residents of the area were interviewed by the press, political activists, and political scientists in a series of public opinion surveys that were conducted immediately following the accident and at ever longer intervals thereafter. The most important of these surveys were those done by the Nuclear Regulatory Commission, a federal agency with the mission of monitoring and regulating nuclear plants, and by the Pennsylvania Department of Health.

Rumors abounded. Many centered on negative reproductive developments among farm animals in the area. Blame was leveled particularly at the utility company, which was almost universally believed not to be telling the truth about the risks, even though subsequent investigations revealed that most rumors had no foundation in fact. It was also widely believed that the Nuclear Regulatory Commission had failed to exercise proper supervision. The technology of nuclear electricity generation lost so much credibility that many nuclear plants under construction were canceled and no new nuclear plant contracts were let in the United States.

See also Chernobyl disaster; Nuclear research and testing.

Thurmond, Strom

BORN: December 5, 1902, Edgefield, South Carolina
IDENTIFICATION: American politician
SIGNIFICANCE: During his long career in the U.S. Senate Thurmond has been a leading advocate of censorship

An archetypal prosegregation, anti-civil rights Southern senator, Thurmond has led campaigns, including filibusters, against civil rights initiatives, and has campaigned against materials called indecent, antifamily, and the like. He has been a leader in various organizations promoting decency, including the Boy Scouts of America.

Elected governor of South Carolina in 1946, Thurmond, a Democrat, opposed the efforts of President Harry S Truman, also a Democrat, to end segregation. In 1948 Truman was campaigning for reelection and it appeared that he was going to lose to the Republican challenger. Truman had had limited success in pushing his legislation through a Republican Congress; the legislation included measures to expand social welfare policies and to shift the economy from a wartime to a peacetime focus. Frustrated liberals in the Democratic Party supported a dark horse candidate; and Southern Democrats, opposed to Truman's civil rights initiatives, also broke away and formed the States Rights' Democratic Party, known as the Dixiecrats. Thurmond became the Dixiecrats' presidential candidate. Truman won the election in a stunning upset, but his efforts toward progressive legislation, including civil rights, continued to meet limited success. Others—Democratic and Republican—proposing such legislation also found themselves stymied.

After becoming the only U.S. senator elected by a write-in vote in 1954, Thurmond, in 1957, made a record filibuster of twenty-four hours and eighteen minutes over a civil rights bill. In keeping with his conservative, states' rights principles, he switched from the Democratic to the Republican Party in

1964. Afterward he campaigned for censorship on various fronts, including the arts and abortion. He was reelected to the Senate in 1996 at the age of ninety-three.

See also Barnett, Ross Robert; Child Protection Restoration and Penalties Enforcement Act; Civil Rights movement; Congress, U.S.; Feminism; Political campaigning.

Tiananmen Square

DATE: April 15-June 4, 1989
PLACE: Beijing, China
SIGNIFICANCE: Seven weeks of public demonstrations against China's national government revealed dynamics involved in censorship

On April 15, 1989, Hu Yaobang, a former Chinese Communist Party chief who had been ousted for being "soft" on student demonstrations in 1986, died of a heart attack. His death set off a series of mass public demonstrations that ended abruptly with the Chinese army killing hundreds—perhaps thousands—of unarmed civilians who blocked streets as the army attempted to clear protesters from Tiananmen Square, a plaza in the center of the national capital.

The Chinese government, following the adage of its longtime communist leader Mao Zedong that a "single spark can ignite a prairie fire," has always imposed strict censorship on all media. This restraint has produced a constantly tense atmosphere among the people and helped to shape the character of opposition that has arisen. Lacking the opportunity to express themselves through open public media, the ordinary Chinese have long relied on word-of-mouth transmission of information; they realize that this may be unreliable, but they are certain that the official press is untrustworthy. At several moments in the Tiananmen Square demonstrations, the crisis worsened as the result of widespread but false rumors, which were given great credence by demonstrators. For example, the first report of Hu Yaobang's death was that he had been assassinated—an idea that was plausible because of political opposition he had faced from powerful opponents. Even though it was later generally accepted that Hu died from a heart attack, the cloud surrounding his death colored the early public reaction and gave those inclined to demonstrate a concrete focus to their cause.

The prevailing climate of censorship and the tight police control almost guaranteed that if the early demonstrations were not stopped, they would expand. While no individual person could stand against the Chinese government's power, growing crowds made the protest safer for each new person who joined. Furthermore, the Chinese government recognized that if it were weakened by early demonstrations, later demonstrations would be far larger and more threatening.

The flow of events in the early weeks aided the demonstrators and left the government off balance. As a high-ranking Communist Party official, Hu Yaobang was given an official state funeral, which allowed the students to mask their political intentions. For several months before Hu Yaobang's death, students had planned antigovernment demonstrations for 1989; the funeral simply gave them an opportunity to gather publicly by claiming—with some justification—to be in

A lone man momentarily halts the advance of army tanks as the Chinese government moves to crush the freedom movement at Tiananmen Square in June, 1989. (AP/Wide World Photos)

mourning. Before and during the funeral, the government attempted to quash the demonstrations by closing Tiananmen Square before the funeral, but the students were already encamped in the square before the government acted.

After Hu's funeral, some government leaders favored a crackdown on the students, but others advocated tolerance. With the government's leaders divided, its subsequent late April crackdown also failed, empowering the demonstrators still more. On May 4 the government tried to outmaneuver the demonstrators by pretending to join with them in celebrating the anniversary of a historic 1919 student demonstration by busing elementary-school students to the square in order to overwhelm the antigovernment forces, but this backfired when the younger students threw their support to their elders.

After the May 4 fiasco, the government faced another crisis with the long-awaited arrival of Soviet president Mikhail Gorbachev. No Soviet leader had visited China for thirty years, so Gorbachev's visit was regarded as a triumph for China's paramount leader, Deng Xiaoping. The presence of hundreds of foreign journalists made a crackdown unlikely—especially given Gorbachev's own reform initiatives in the Soviet Union. The students clever "hunger strike" gained them further sympathy.

After Gorbachev left Beijing, the government finally declared martial law, only to discover that ordinary citizens were now flocking to the demonstrator's defense. After two more weeks of maneuvering failed to dislodge the demonstrators, the government finally used deadly force on the night of June 3-4.

The widespread mass character of the demonstrations also meant that the first task of the government was to regain control of the media. Entirely unnoticed by the Western media covering the Tiananmen Square events was the government's clandestine seizure of the central television broadcasting studio about a week before the shooting occurred. This event almost certainly doomed the demonstrations, although even the student participants failed to appreciate its significance at the time. While the government no doubt felt the events proved the necessity of their strict censorship, the argument could be made that the demonstrations might have ended without bloodshed if alternative forms of political expression had been available. —*Richard L. Wilson*

See also Assembly, right of; China; Communism; Cultural Revolution, Chinese; Mao Zedong; Marching and parading; Wall posters.

BIBLIOGRAPHY

Published eyewitness accounts of Tiananmen Square would fill several bookshelves. While many are accurate as personal accounts, few are analytical. The three most accurate journalistic accounts are Michael Fathers and Andrew Higgins' *Tiananmen: The Rape of Peking* (London: The Independent, 1989); Yi Mu and Mark V. Thompson's *Crisis at Tiananmen: Reform and Reality in Modern China* (San Francisco: China

Books & Periodicals, 1989); and Scott Simmie and Bob Nixon's *Tiananmen Square* (Vancouver/Toronto, Canada: Douglas & McIntyre, 1989). Shen Tong's *Almost a Revolution* (New York: Harper/Collins, 1991) is an insightful account by a participant. A solid analysis of the event can be found in Bih-jaw Lin et al., eds., *The Aftermath of the 1989 Tiananmen Crisis in Mainland China* (Boulder, Colo.: Westview Press, 1992). An analysis set in the context of post-Mao Zedong reforms can be found in a volume edited by Richard Baum, entitled *Reform and Reaction in Post-Mao China: The Road to Tiananmen* (New York: Routledge, 1991).

Timerman, Jacobo

BORN: January 6, 1923, Bar, Ukraine, U.S.S.R.

IDENTIFICATION: Argentine journalist and author

SIGNIFICANCE: After Timerman was kidnapped and tortured by Argentine security forces for criticizing the government, his case became an international human rights issue

A Ukrainian by birth, Timerman emigrated to Argentina with his family when he was five years old. The family settled in Buenos Aires, and Timerman later became a naturalized citizen. After a year's study in an engineering school, he turned to journalism in 1947 and worked as a newspaper reporter. He became a prominent news commentator on radio and television before becoming publisher of two successful weekly news magazines in the 1960's. After selling his magazine interests in 1971, he cofounded the daily newspaper *La Opinión*.

The period during which Timerman edited and published *La Opinión* was among the most violent in Argentinean history. Although his own politics were left of center, he made his paper a voice for moderation that opposed extremism of all shades. As a result he and his paper became targets for violent harassment and bomb threats from both the Right and the Left. In July, 1972, his home was bombed by the Monteneros, an ultraleft guerrilla group. After a military junta took power in March, 1976, *La Opinión* condemned government violence, urged the release of prisoners taken without warrants, and published the names of those who had disappeared. When the government pressured the paper to desist, some reporters quit; others joined the scores of journalists who "disappeared."

In the early morning of April 15, 1977, twenty armed men in civilian clothes broke into Timerman's house and took him away. His family did not learn of his whereabouts for six weeks. For a year he was moved from place to place, beaten, subjected to electric shocks to his genitals, and held in solitary confinement. During intense interrogation sessions, his captors tried to force him to confess to taking part in a Zionist-Montenero guerrilla conspiracy. Timerman later described these experiences in *Prisoner Without a Name, Cell Without a Number* (1981). Timerman was certain he received especially harsh treatment because he was Jewish and a declared Zionist.

Although a military special war council cleared Timerman of all charges in October, 1977, he was not released from prison until the Argentine supreme court issued a writ of *habeas corpus* in July, 1978. He was then placed under house arrest until the supreme court issued a second, unanimous declaration of his innocence in September, 1979, whereupon the government stripped him of his Argentine citizenship, put him on a plane for Israel, and confiscated his property.

Timerman credited the worldwide attention aroused by his case, particularly efforts by the U.S. Carter Administration and the Vatican, for saving his life and securing his release from prison. When a democratically elected civilian government took power in Argentina in 1984, Timerman returned home. He was welcomed back by the new president, who helped restore his Argentinean citizenship and aided his efforts to win compensation for the loss of his newspaper.

See also Argentina; Fear; Journalists, violence against; News media censorship; South America.

Times Film Corp. v. City of Chicago

COURT: U.S. Supreme Court

DECIDED: March 20, 1961

SIGNIFICANCE: This case upheld the principle of prior restraint on films, thereby continuing a pattern of treating film differently than other media

The controversy surrounding this court case arose after the Times Film Corporation, a foreign-film importer and distributor, applied for a permit to show the Austrian film, *Don Juan* (1956), an adaptation of Wolfgang Amadeus Mozart's opera *Don Giovanni*. While the film contained no obscenities or sexual scenes, Chicago's municipal code required that films be submitted for censorship review along with applications before they could be publicly shown. The import company did not submit the film, claiming that the city's censorship statute was "null and void on constitutional grounds." They further stated that content of the film should not be subjected to censorship and if the city objected to the film, criminal process should not be brought against it until after *Don Juan* had been shown. The city denied them the permit because of the corporation's refusal to submit the film.

The film company filed suit in federal district court, asking that the film be permitted to be shown without prior censorship review, arguing that having a censor review films "amounted to a prior restraint on freedom of expression prohibited by the First and Fourteenth Amendments." The city argued that it could not protect the citizens of Chicago against "dangers of obscenity" if prior viewing and censorship were not permitted. The district court dismissed the case and an appeals court upheld the decision.

The Times Film Corporation's lawyers then petitioned the Supreme Court, which agreed to hear the case. The case was unusual in that most suits were filed because films submitted for review had been refused due to the content. The lawyers argued against permitting censorship prior to the film's viewing. In the Court's ensuing 5-4 decision, Justice Tom C. Clark said that the prior restraint in submitting a film did not violate the First Amendment. Chief Justice Earl Warren, one of the dissenting justices, warned that other forms of censorship on "newspapers, journals, books, magazines, television, radio or public speeches" might be invoked as a result of this decision. He also stated that the censor in offering judgment of the film's content does not have obligations to the public but to those who have hired him.

See also Censor; Censorship; First Amendment; Fourteenth Amendment; Opera; Prior restraint; *Roth v. United States*; Warren, Earl.

Titicut Follies

TYPE OF WORK: Film
RELEASED: 1967
DIRECTOR: Frederick Wiseman (1930-   )
SUBJECT MATTER: Documentary about a state prison hospital for the criminally insane
SIGNIFICANCE: Attempts by the state of Massachusetts to ban this film for invading the privacy of patients led to an important court ruling balancing the rights of free expression and privacy of filmed subjects

Titicut Follies is the first in a distinguished series of cinema verité documentaries about American institutions produced and directed by Frederick Wiseman. Photographed by John Marshall in 1966, it is both a shocking exposé of conditions at Massachusetts Correctional Institution at Bridgewater and a meditation on power and control. Its production required permission of state officials, who later went to court to prevent its release on the grounds that Wiseman had invaded the privacy of unconsenting or incompetent inmates and had violated an oral contract to allow state officials control over the final edit. Wiseman denied giving the state any such editorial control, however, and claimed that he had the oral consent of all subjects filmed or the consent of the prison staff to whom he looked for determinations of competency. He also argued that the state was more interested in protecting its reputation, and that of its officials, than in guarding the privacy of the men, whom it incarcerated, neglected, and abused at Bridgewater.

An attorney himself, Wiseman claimed First Amendment protection for his documentation of newsworthy activities filmed at a tax-supported institution.

Wiseman's claims of First Amendment rights met with vastly different results in a series of court decisions—two from the same judge—between 1967 and 1991. A judge in a New York federal court found Wiseman's First Amendment argument convincing and allowed the screening of *Titicut Follies* at the 1967 New York Film Festival. After a highly publicized and contentious legislative hearing regarding the film, the case of *Commonwealth v. Wiseman* was heard in a Massachusetts equity court. Superior Court judge Harry Kalus considered *Titicut Follies* "a crass piece of commercialism . . . excessively preoccupied with nudity," and ruled to ban the film. On appeal, the Massachusetts Supreme Court attempted to accommodate what it considered legitimate, but competing, First and Fourth Amendment rights in 1969 by devising a compromise whereby only specialized audiences would be allowed to see the documentary. Twice *Wiseman v. Massachusetts* was just one vote short of the needed four votes for review by the U.S. Supreme Court. For more than two decades *Titicut Follies* was the only American film to be burdened with court-imposed restrictions for reasons other than obscenity or threat to national security.

Unwilling to accept these restrictions, Wiseman returned to the Massachusetts courts. In 1989 Superior Court judge Andrew Meyer ordered blurring the faces of some men appearing in the film as a condition of general exhibition, an accommodation that had been unacceptable to Wiseman from the beginning. Urged to reconsider, the judge ordered all restrictions lifted in 1991. By then convinced that the privacy issue was of less concern to the court than the prior restraint issue and having seen no evidence of harm to any individual as a result of the film being exhibited, Meyer decided the time had finally come to free *Titicut Follies*. In April, 1993, twenty-six years after its initial release, *Titicut Follies* was broadcast on public television to a national audience.

See also Film censorship; First Amendment; Fourth Amendment; *Freaks*; Nudity; Prior restraint; Privacy, right to.

To Kill a Mockingbird

TYPE OF WORK: Book
PUBLISHED: 1960
AUTHOR: Harper Lee (1926-   )
SUBJECT MATTER: Novel in which race relations in the South during the 1930's are seen through the eyes of a child

In the film adaptation of To Kill a Mockingbird *Gregory Peck plays a southern lawyer assigned to defend an African American falsely charged with raping a white woman.* (Museum of Modern Art/Film Stills Archive)

SIGNIFICANCE: One of the most widely read novels in American junior high and high schools, this book has been challenged frequently by parents and school boards and even banned in some areas

When *To Kill a Mockingbird* first appeared in 1960, most critics praised it; the following year it won several awards, including the Pulitzer Prize. Set in a small Southern town in the 1930's, the novel focuses on the trial of an African American man accused of raping a white woman; it is narrated by the young daughter of the man's defense lawyer. The novel rapidly found a niche in young adult literature collections; by the mid-1960's it was widely read in junior and senior high school English classes. At the same time, however, some parents objected to the book's inclusion in school classes, calling it immoral and citing its use of profanity and explicit details of violence, especially rape. Some adults also complained that the novel depicted relations among blacks and whites unfairly by suggesting widespread bigotry by Southern whites. Others argued that the novel presented religion in an unfavorable light.

Most early complaints about the novel came from the South. In Hanover County, Virginia, for example, the local school board attempted to remove the book from county public schools on the grounds of its immorality. When national news coverage focused on the issue, however, the school board tried to dismiss the issue as a misunderstanding.

Meanwhile, attempts to censor the novel spread into the East and Midwest. In 1967 controversy over the novel arose at Lewis S. Mills Regional High School in Unionville, Connecticut. The issue was hotly debated, but a strong defense of the novel by the head of the school's English department defeated the bid for censorship. Attempts to ban the book continued elsewhere, however, and the novel tied for eighth place on the list of books most frequently banned from public schools between 1966 and 1975.

Attacks on Lee's novel continued throughout the 1970's and 1980's. A Vernon, New York, minister protested the availability of "filthy, trashy sex novels" such as *To Kill a Mockingbird* in public school libraries. In addition, a new line of attack emerged from African Americans who wanted the book banned because they felt it included bigotry and racial slurs. In the 1990's complaints centered again on the book's being a "filthy, trashy novel," which includes obscene words; the novel continued to appear on annual lists of works challenged in public schools and libraries. Meanwhile, the novel remained one of the most widely read among junior high and high school students in the United States.

See also African Americans; Banned Books Week; Books, young adult; Libraries; Literature; Offensive language.

Tokyo Rose

IDENTIFICATION: Nickname for Japanese radio propagandists who broadcast to U.S. troops in the Pacific theater of World War II

SIGNIFICANCE: A Japanese American woman was prosecuted in the United States after the war for participating in these broadcasts, even though she had done so against her will

Shortly after being taken into U.S. custody in September, 1945, Iva Toguri was grilled by military correspondents about her alleged activities as the notorious "Tokyo Rose." (National Archives)

On September 1, 1945, U.S. military police arrested California-born Iva Ikuko Toguri on suspicion of her having been one of at least five broadcasters whom GIs had dubbed "Tokyo Rose." The twenty-nine-year-old Toguri was transferred to Yokohama prison in Japan; in 1950 she was convicted of treason.

The "Tokyo Rose" broadcasts had been directed toward military forces stationed in the Pacific Ocean region. Overall, the goal of this propaganda was two-fold. First, it made American military personnel homesick in order to lower their morale and fighting spirit. Second, it was a form of censorship, designed for a captive audience to hear only one viewpoint, excluding any opposing ideas and expression. During wartime autocratic regimes such as Japan's restrict the broadcasting of all types of expression that might be considered attempts to undermine authority and the governing military order. During World War II the airing of opposing views by citizens of Japan was prohibited. Broadcasters such as the "Tokyo Rose" women were forced to do the programs from scripts and material written by the powers in charge.

Ironically, Japan's propaganda aims seem to have backfired. Tokyo Rose received a U.S. Navy citation for raising troop morale, by entertaining them "during those long nights," unknowingly bringing them "excellent music, laughter, and news about home."

In 1977 one of President Gerald Ford's last official acts was to pardon Toguri, who had served only six and a half years of her ten-year prison sentence. In a *New York Times* interview she said, "It is hard to believe. But I have always maintained my innocence—this pardon is a measure of vindication."

See also Armed Forces Radio and Television Service; Japan; Propaganda; War; Wodehouse, P. G.

Tolkien, J. R. R.

BORN: January 3, 1892, Bloemfontein, Orange Free State (South Africa)

DIED: September 2, 1973, Bournemouth, England

IDENTIFICATION: British author

SIGNIFICANCE: An exchange between Tolkien and a German publisher of *The Hobbit* reflected Nazi influence on the German publishing industry

During the summer of 1938, in anticipation of the projected publication of a German translation of *The Hobbit*, J. R. R. Tolkien was asked by the German publisher to provide a declaration that he was of *arisch* (aryan) heritage. Tolkien was annoyed by the request. He wrote to Allen & Unwin, his English publisher—which was acting as intermediary—that he was "inclined to refuse," and he noted that he "would regret giving any colour to the notion that I subscribed to the wholly pernicious and unscientific race-doctrine." In deference to Allen & Unwin, however, he enclosed drafts of two possible replies; the one sent by Allen & Unwin does not survive, but the unused draft was preserved in the firm's files. In it, Tolkien wrote that "if I am to understand that you are enquiring whether I am of *Jewish* origin, I can only reply that I regret that I appear to have *no* ancestors of that gifted people." He went on to remark that "if impertinent and irrelevant inquiries of this sort are to become the rule in matters of literature, then the time is not far distant when a German name will no longer be a source of pride." Whether because of the tone of Tolkien's response or the subsequent outbreak of World War II, the possibility of a German edition of *The Hobbit* did not surface again until 1946.

An entirely different issue was involved in the dispute over publication of the first American paperback edition of *The Lord of the Rings*. That edition was issued by Ace Books in May, 1965, without Tolkien's authorization, an act made possible by the failure of Tolkien's authorized American publishers, Houghton Mifflin, to establish proper copyright protection for the trilogy. Houghton Mifflin then commissioned Ballantine Books to publish a slightly revised and newly copyrighted alternative paperback version, which contained Tolkien's plea that readers "who approve of courtesy (at least) to living authors . . . purchase it and no other." The Tolkien Society of America and the Science Fiction Writers of America took up the author's cause, and Ace Books bowed to demands that it print no more copies of *The Lord of the Rings*.

See also Copyright law; Holocaust, Jewish; National Socialism; World War II.

Tolstoy, Leo

BORN: September 9, 1828, Yasnaya Polyana, Russia

DIED: November 20, 1910, Astapova, Russia

IDENTIFICATION: Russian author

SIGNIFICANCE: Because Tolstoy's writings were frequently at odds with Russia's governmental and religious authorities, they were often subject to censorship

Tolstoy is closely identified with the Russian character and conscience. Born into a wealthy and respected family, he became a prolific writer of both fiction and nonfiction. His novel *War and Peace* (1869) is almost universally counted among the greatest works of world literature. Tolstoy's fiction often portrayed Russian elites in an unflattering, critical light, but it was his nonfiction writings—essays and pamphlets on moral and political issues—that provided Russian censors with the most work.

As a champion of the Russian peasantry, Tolstoy agitated against the institution of serfdom. His efforts became the subject of a file kept on him by the czar's secret police. In 1862 the police conducted a destructive and intimidating (but nonetheless fruitless) search of his home for an illegal printing press. This only bolstered Tolstoy's opposition to the government. By the 1880's he had become a permanent antagonist of the czarist regime.

Tolstoy explained his evolving religious beliefs in *Confession* (1882), a book highly critical of the Russian Orthodox church. Its text was banned in Russia until 1906, and it helped get Tolstoy excommunicated from the church in 1901. The czarist authorities further considered that Tolstoy's writings made him a subversive, so he was placed under secret police surveillance from the time of *Confession*'s publication until his death in 1910. Moreover, the regime tightened its censorship of Tolstoy's publications. Although it remained relatively easy to control his literary works, most of his political and philosophical tracts were banned outright for many years. Some of his manuscripts were smuggled outside Russia, published abroad, and then smuggled back into the country. Others were circulated through underground presses.

Tolstoy's sympathies always remained with the peasants and the poor. For them cost and accessibility, more than government, stood in the way of their reading high-quality Russian literature. To remedy this, Tolstoy helped establish a successful publishing house that produced inexpensive booklets by Russian and foreign authors. This effort typified the charity and sense of mission that characterized his later years.

Many aspects of Tolstoy's philosophy fit within the Marxist-Leninist ideology that was being promoted by the Bolshevists in the early twentieth century. With the success of the Russian Revolution in 1917, seven years after Tolstoy's death, the new government debated whether to embrace his work or to revile it as bourgeois. On the one hand, Tolstoy's criticism of the Orthodox church and the czarist regime, as well as his treatises against private ownership of land, put him squarely in line with Marxist doctrine. On the other hand, his preaching of "nonresistance to evil" conflicted with the Bolshevist self-image as a "revolutionary party." Tolstoy's deeply held religious beliefs were also rejected by the atheistic state that deemed religion the "opiate of the masses."

Ultimately, the Soviet authorities permitted publication of Tolstoy's literary works, and even some of his political ones. By the time of World War II the regime had embraced Tolstoy as a patriot whose words might rally the public to the country's defense. However, the Soviet regime always made certain to keep a distance from the ideologically incompatible aspects of Tolstoy's philosophy.

See also Dostoevski, Fyodor; Gorky, Maxim; Kropotkin, Peter; Literature; Russia; Soviet Union; Zamyatin, Yevgeny Ivanovich.

Tonkin Gulf incident

DATE: August, 1964
PLACE: Gulf of Tonkin, off the coast of North Vietnam
SIGNIFICANCE: Facts concerning this incident, which was used to justify empowering the president of the United States to conduct warfare without Senate approval, were suppressed by the U.S. government in order to rally popular support for the Vietnam War

In early August of 1964, when U.S. forces in Vietnam still numbered only 25,000 troops, President Lyndon B. Johnson announced to the American public that two U.S. destroyers had been targets of unprovoked attacks by North Vietnamese torpedo ships. At the president's urging, Congress passed the Gulf of Tonkin Resolution on August 7, giving the president power to send U.S. troops into combat without asking Congress for a formal declaration of war. This resolution, in effect, contributed significantly to the subsequent escalation of the Vietnam War.

The American public was generally supportive of swift and decisive action. However, an inquiry conducted by Senator William J. Fulbright later raised serious doubts about the validity of Johnson's claims. Details of Johnson's account of what had transpired on August 2 and 4 conflicted with those of his own senior officials. When asked about the attacks, Secretary of Defense Robert McNamara often gave conflicting testimony, as did other military officials. Based on all testimony given at this inquiry, Fulbright concluded that the entire incident had been a "misrepresentation" of the facts and that conclusions based on military accounts and by the American press were suspect.

The U.S. press initially reported the Gulf of Tonkin affair in a positive light. In general, the American news media saw the incident and Johnson's reaction to the supposed attacks as a sign of American strength and decisiveness. In numerous press conferences reporters avoided asking hard and probing questions. The European press was less naïve. For example, a Denmark paper stated: "To create a pretext for an attack on Poland, Hitler ordered the Germans to put on uniforms and attack a German guard. What the Americans did in Vietnam is not the same. But the story sounds doubtful."

Although historians have continued to debate what actually occurred in that August off of Vietnam's coast, most agree that the Johnson Administration misled the public into thinking that American sovereignty had been attacked. The press, although it had not engaged in overt censorship, tacitly suppressed a more factual and detailed accounting of the incident by not following up on the numerous and varied inconsistencies in the accounts of the incident. The Gulf of Tonkin incident and its subsequent impact on international relations set a dangerous precedent; but perhaps the most damaging aspect of this affair was the blow it delivered to the public trust.

See also Hoaxes; My Lai massacre; News media censorship; Presidency, U.S.; Vietnam War; War.

Torquemada, Tomás de

BORN: 1420, Valladolid, Spain
DIED: September 16, 1498, Avila, Spain
IDENTIFICATION: Spanish inquisitor general of the Roman Catholic church
SIGNIFICANCE: Queen Isabella's confessor, Torquemada played a major role in launching Spain's campaign of terror against Jews

In the late 1480's Spain launched a campaign of terror against Jews and *conversos* (Jewish converts to Catholicism). Jealous of Jewish influence and wealth, Spaniards spread rumors that *conversos* secretly practiced their ancestral religion. Queen Isabella was initially reluctant to pursue forceful methods, but she decided that if she were to be an effective ruler, she could not allow heresy to continue. Years earlier she had sworn to Fray Tomás de Torquemada that if she became queen, she would eliminate heretics from Spain.

Torquemada, a Dominican prior in Segovia, and of *converso* descent himself, had spent his days in prayer and penance. In order to achieve spiritual grace, he wore hairshirts, abstained from meat, and fasted frequently. He preached hateful sermons against Jews and *conversos* and expressed a fervent desire that all Catholics be made loyal. In 1478 he persuaded Isabella to ask Pope Sixtus to issue a bull of inquisition. A second bull issued in 1482 unified the Roman Catholic church's Inquisition for both Castile and Aragón. Torquemada was appointed the first inquisitor general. In this position he had full power to appoint, dismiss, and hear appeals.

Between 1484 and 1498 Torquemada issued the four *Ordenanzas* that became the foundation for subsequent generations of inquisitors to investigate and punish Jews. Also condemned were the children and grandchildren of the accused, who could not serve in public office, or become priests, merchants, or lawyers. Those brought to trial had their money and property confiscated. Since inquisitors received one-third shares in confiscations, greed motivated many arrests and convictions. In 1488 two booklets dedicated to Torquemada urged that no mercy be shown to "relapsed" *conversos* who robbed "true Christians" of their money and property. During the eighteen years that Torquemada controlled the Inquisition, more than two thousand people were burned, and thirty-seven thousand were tortured into accepting conversion.

Torquemada denounced Jews generally for corrupting *conversos*, and publicized an alleged ritual murder to prove that Castile and Aragón would be forever threatened by heresy unless the Jews were expelled from Spain. In March, 1492, Queen Isabella and King Ferdinand signed the Edict of Expulsion, demanding that all Jews be baptized within three months or leave the country.

After 1494, when he began hearing complaints about Torquemada's abuse of his powers, Pope Alexander VI slowly stripped him of his authority. Torquemada retired to a convent in Avila that he had built. His legacy, the Inquisition, remained a working body in Spain for three centuries after his death.

See also Christianity; Fear; Heresy; Judaism; Spanish Inquisition.

Toxic waste news

DEFINITION: Industrial waste products that become chemically or biologically hazardous to human health or the environment generally when they are dispersed by seepage into ground water or released into the atmosphere

SIGNIFICANCE: Environmental watchdog groups have shown that mainstream news media have often suppressed, ignored, or underplayed news of toxic waste hazards

Toxic waste is usually classified in three categories. Solid waste consists of harmful industrial residue that is either released into the atmosphere through incineration, or into the ground by dumping. Chemical waste—usually liquid materials—are buried in containers of limited longevity. Nuclear waste consists of the contaminated by-products from electricity and arms production; it is usually stored in various manners, ranging from sea interment to above-ground dumping.

Although a survey taken by the American Society of Me-

chanical Engineers of Solid Waste Management Professionals in the early 1990's found that solid waste was America's primary ecological problem, content analysis of the news media revealed that solid waste issues were given a low priority in reporting.

One reason for the discrepancy between the seriousness of the solid waste issue and the lack of news coverage of it may be the concept of salability. Solid waste management is a dry and technically complex topic unlikely to appeal to the public. Also, reporters have long shied away from using terms such as "garbage" in their writing, so that the perceived quality of their work did not suffer. Solid waste issues have been given scant coverage by the news media, not because of their lack of importance, but because of their perceived inability to sell newspapers and attract television audiences.

One of the most famous cases of toxic waste pollution was Love Canal in New York. Discovered in the 1970's, and brought to national attention by extensive news coverage, the toxic waste infestation in a neighborhood near Niagara Falls, New York, resulted in the evacuation and condemnation of much of the nearby private housing. In August of 1978, President Jimmy Carter declared Love Canal a federal disaster area.

A sign of changing times is this warning at Times Beach, Missouri, where flood waters were dangerously polluted in late 1982. (AP/Wide World Photos)

In the mid-1990's clean-up efforts by federal and state environmental authorities persuaded the Environmental Protection Agency to announce that Love Canal was ready to be resettled. That resettlement program faced slow growth, however, because of the lingering public perception that Love Canal was still a death trap. Part of the reason for that perception was the paucity of news coverage of the clean-up. Many residents of Love Canal believed that the news media had exaggerated the original disaster in order to satisfy their own environmental agendas. There was also a suspicion that the news media preferred to concentrate on the dangers of Love Canal, rather than on its improvements, because bad news sells newspapers, and newspapers are, after all, a business. The practice of withholding certain information, or of stressing the importance of certain issues over others in order to realize self-interested goals, is a form of censorship.

See also Bhopal disaster; Environmental education; Health epidemic news; Nuclear research and testing; Pesticide industry; Pharmaceutical industry; Project Censored.

Translation

DEFINITION: The rendering of one language or dialect into another

SIGNIFICANCE: A necessity of cross-cultural communication, translation is often used as a means of abridging, distorting, or sanitizing an original work

Tradition has it that something is always lost in the translation. What that something is, and the significance of it, has been a matter of debate for as long as there has been a need for translation. The practical effects of the practice of translation, however, are much easier to judge and document. Translation is not just a literal recasting of a work from one language to another, but is also an adaptation of one culture's values and biases into another.

The Bible is perhaps the most translated work in the history of publishing. Beginning as a collection of Hebrew and Greek texts, the Bible first went through a process of canonization, in which some texts were selected as authentic, and others dismissed as inauthentic. It then underwent translation, in which the whole was brought into a single, standardized language. Further translations became necessary with the spread of Christianity, such as in the famous English King James version of the Bible, on down to the twentieth century, with such works as the "plain" English *Good News Bible*. This ongoing process of translation and re-translation is an example of cultural adaptation and abridgment of texts through translation.

Specific examples of censorship through translation abound in English. Works originally written in older versions of English, such as Geoffrey Chaucer's *The Canterbury Tales*, are often sanitized through translation to suit the tastes of modern audiences, or to placate school boards and textbook selection committees. Chaucer's scatological "Miller's Tale," for example, contains numerous examples of dilution through translation. Nicholas, the young Oxford student described in the tale, grabs the good wife Alison by the "queynte." This word has been translated textually as "middle" or "waist," but it literally and contextually refers to the female genitals, and is believed to be a pun on the etymological ancestor of the modern term "cunt." Few, if any, modern translators have taken it upon themselves to be as forthright as Chaucer and his lower-class Miller.

The record for translatory censorship most likely belongs to Giovanni Boccaccio's fourteenth century *Decameron*, sections of which remained untranslated into English for more than five hundred years. Of particular concern to the translators was the tenth story on the third day, the pornographic adventures of the religious hermit Rustico and his young female student Alibech, who receives instruction concerning "how to put the devil in hell." The earliest English translations of the work omitted the story entirely and even substituted stories by other authors in its place. The story was finally included in an 1822 edition, but its key passage was printed in Italian, though the bilingual could also refer to another version in the footnote, which was in French. Later nineteenth century editions printed large passages of the story in French. In 1930, however, the first publicly available complete translations of the tales were printed, and after a wait of almost six hundred years, the general reading public was finally allowed to find out what was lost in the translation.

See also Bible; Boccaccio, Giovanni; Books and obscenity law; Burton, Richard Francis.

Tropic of Cancer

TYPE OF WORK: Book

PUBLISHED: 1934

AUTHOR: Henry Miller (1891-1980)

SUBJECT MATTER: Sexually uninhibited novel about an American living a bohemian life in Paris

SIGNIFICANCE: Open publication of this novel and a ruling by the U.S. Supreme Court that it was not obscene dealt serious blows to the forces of censorship

Henry Miller's autobiographical novel *Tropic of Cancer* describes the experiences of a down and out American writer (also named Henry Miller) in Paris. After it was published by Obelisk Press in Paris in 1934, its vigorous writing secured for it an underground reputation among readers and critics able to visit France. However, the book's sexual content made its importation into the United States illegal. After U.S. Customs officials confiscated a copy the year of its publication, it was declared obscene in a federal district court.

In 1940 a pirated edition of *Tropic of Cancer* appeared in New York; however, it was not openly published in the United States until Grove Press issued it in 1961. Grove anticipated legal complications when it published the book; however, the process of legally defending it proved to be extraordinarily expensive and time-consuming. Grove was forced into court in state after state, and won decisively only in 1964, when the U.S. Supreme Court declared the book not obscene.

In *Tropic of Cancer* Miller had declared himself "the happiest man alive." He had defended his book as an expression of a life lived openly and honestly. Thus the Supreme Court's decision represented not only a legal victory for Miller and Grove Press, but also a measure of personal vindication.

See also Customs laws, U.S.; Grove Press; Miller, Henry; Obscenity: legal definitions.

Trotsky, Leon

Born: November 7, 1879, Yanovka, Kherson, Ukraine, Russian Empire

Died: August 20, 1940, Coyoacán, near Mexico City, Mexico

Identification: Russian author, revolutionary, and government leader

Significance: Trotsky's writings were banned by numerous governments of various political ideologies, and his estrangement from Joseph Stalin led to his assassination

Trotsky vigorously opposed censorship, both when he participated in the revolutionary movement against Russia's czarist government, and when he served in Stalin's later Soviet dictatorship. Trotsky argued that censorship was a tool of oppression under the czar. After he became a leading member of the revolutionary Bolshevist government, he argued for censorship as a revolutionary necessity. (The fact that he opposed censorship through most of his life, while supporting it in certain circumstances helps explain his portrayal as the pig Snowball in George Orwell's 1945 fable, *Animal Farm*, which depicts Snowball as unwittingly paving the way for the dictatorship of Napoleon.)

Trotsky's battle with censors began in 1903 when his "Report of the Siberian Delegation" was outlawed within the Russian Empire. After the Revolution, when he delivered a speech accepting his election as head of the Petrograd Soviet, he promised "full freedom for all factions, and the hand of the presidium will never be the hand which suppresses the minority." Seven years later, however, during the civil war, he argued in *Literature and Revolution* that "we ought to have a watchful revolutionary censorship."

After Trotsky was expelled from the Soviet Union by Stalin in 1927, he again found most of his work banned in Russia. In the years that followed, his attempts to promote his political views—critical of both Stalin and capitalism—were significantly hampered by censorship. For example, his writings were even banned in Boston, Massachusetts, in 1930, although they were freely available elsewhere in the United States. With Adolf Hitler's rise to power in Germany in 1933, Trotsky—who had been a bitter critic of Nazism—found his work outlawed in Germany. The following year, Benito Mussolini's Fascist Italy followed suit—but with the unusual exception of allowing deluxe editions. The Italian government possibly believed that the wealthy who could afford such editions would not be swayed by Trotsky's arguments. Meanwhile Trotsky's works were not only completely proscribed in the Soviet Union by 1933, but loyal members of pro-Stalin communist parties throughout the world were instructed to steal his books from public libraries and destroy them. Trotsky's supporters often faced violence at the hands of communists when they attempted to publicly sell his works.

Within Russia, all references to Trotsky's work and writings were deleted from publications—to the point of cutting pages out of encyclopedias in libraries. Nevertheless, Trotsky persisted in producing and distributing a large body of work highly critical of both Stalinism and fascism. The ultimate act of censorship occurred in 1940 when an agent of the Russian secret police murdered Trotsky in Mexico to silence his pen.

See also Death; Lenin, Vladimir Ilich; Orwell, George; Soviet Union; Stalin, Joseph.

Trumbo, Dalton

Born: December 9, 1905, Montrose, Colorado

Died: September 10, 1976, Los Angeles, California

Identification: American screenwriter and novelist

Significance: Convicted of contempt of Congress for refusing to answer questions about his political affiliation, Trumbo was sentenced to prison and blacklisted in Hollywood

After signing with Metro-Goldwyn-Mayer in 1943, Trumbo ranked as Hollywood's highest paid screenwriter. The following year he joined the Communist Party of the U.S.A. and participated in film industry labor disputes. While investigating these disturbances, the House Committee on Un-American Activities (HUAC) summoned Trumbo and nine other unfriendly witnesses to testify in Washington, D.C., in October, 1947.

HUAC eventually cited Trumbo for contempt for refusing to answer questions about his communist affiliations. Important to the case was the fact that witnesses before congressional hearings have fewer rights than defendants in criminal trials. Throughout the hearings Trumbo tried unsuccessfully to have his scripts entered into the record, arguing repeatedly, but futilely, that one should be accountable only for actions, not for purported thoughts.

Exiled from the Soviet Union after 1929, Leon Trotsky criticized Joseph Stalin's authoritarian regime from abroad until an assassin silenced him in 1940. (National Archives)

Convicted of contempt of Congress for not answering questions about his politics, screenwriter Dalton Trumbo waves farewell to a supportive crowd as he departs for jail in 1950. (AP/Wide World Photos)

After being blacklisted in the film industry as a member of the "Hollywood Ten," Trumbo later resumed his career, writing under assumed names for reduced fees. His script for *The Brave One* (1956), written under the pseudonym Robert Rich, won an Academy Award; the fact that Trumbo himself wrote it was not publicly known for years. In 1960, with the blacklisting finally over, he again wrote in his own name, and completed screenplays for such notable films as *Exodus* and *Spartacus* (1960), *Lonely Are the Brave* (1962), *Hawaii* (1966), and *Papillon* (1973). In surviving government censorship and industry blacklisting, Trumbo embodied the courage and idealism of many of his own characters.

See also Blacklisting; Communist Party of the U.S.A.; *Front, The*; Hollywood Ten; House Committee on Un-American Activities.

Turkey

DESCRIPTION: Predominantly Muslim nation that bridges southeastern Europe and southwestern Asia

SIGNIFICANCE: Part European and part Asian, Turkey experiences the conflicting pulls of Judeo-Christian and Muslim cultures

Although modern Turkey is notably Westernized, the bulk of its territory lies in Asia and most of its population is Islamic. The pull of Eastern and Western cultures has caused considerable unrest within the country, which has been, during the late twentieth century, a consistent ally of the West.

Modern Turkey was established in 1923 under the leadership of Mustafa Kemal Ataturk, who seized power after the fall of the Ottoman Empire following World War I. Modern Turkey remains mainly Muslim in its outlook, although religious courts were disbanded in 1924 and a secular state installed in 1928. It took until 1950 to establish a multiparty political system.

Political instability led to military takeovers in 1960 and 1980. When the latter takeover ended in 1982, General Kenan Evren was elected president, whereupon Turkey's National Security Council, staffed by military leaders in whom executive power had been vested, became the President's Council, serving until its disbanding in 1989.

Turkey is strategically located, bordering the former Soviet Union, as well as Iraq and Syria. In the 1980's the Armenian population of the Soviet Union sought independence and, occupying the portion of the Soviet Union closest to Turkey, became a threat. In 1986 Turkish forces massacred thousands of Armenians, reminiscent of the Armenian genocide during the 1920's.

To the southeast, Turkey is bordered by the part of Iraq settled by the Kurdish minority that Saddam Hussein has been attempting to eradicate. During the Persian Gulf War (1990-1991), thousands of Iraqi Kurds crossed into the Kurdish settlements of southern Turkey, where they endured considerable oppression.

Although Turkey's 1982 constitution assures adherence to human rights, it does so "within the concepts of public peace, national security, and justice." The constitution also includes limitations relating to public morals and health.

Under the New Police Law of 1985, an extension and toughening of the Police Duties and Powers Act of 1934, censorship of Turkish media is condoned. Turkish citizens are restrained by law from publishing or otherwise disseminating information that might incite violence and from making statements damaging to Turkey's international image. Article 163 of the penal code forbids the advocacy of religious sects.

Under the New Police Law of 1985 police may shut down dramatic performances and confiscate films and other media deemed harmful to Turkey's domestic tranquillity. They may arrest without warrant any person they consider threatening to the peace.

Book banning remains an accepted governmental practice in Turkey, where the Ministry of Justice in 1986 circulated a list of banned books to all educational institutions, with the result that thirty-nine tons of books were pulped. Among the banned titles were the *Encyclopedia Britannica* and David Hume's *On Religion*.

The Press Council has regulated Turkey's press since 1986. Between 1984 and 1987, 240 writers, publishers, and translators were charged with violations of the Press Act. Radio and television stations remain the property of the state, which censors strenuously what is broadcast. Film censorship, controlled by the Ministry of Tourism and Culture, carefully regulates which films the public can view. In short, despite alliances with the West, Turkey continues to place significant restraints upon freedom of expression.

See also Akhmatova, Anna; Armenian genocide; Crimean War; Islam; Pasternak, Boris; Russia; Sakharov, Andrei; Solzhenitsyn, Aleksandr; Stalin, Joseph; Zhdanov, Andrei.

Twain, Mark (Samuel Langhorne Clemens)

BORN: November 30, 1835, Florida, Missouri
DIED: April 21, 1910, Redding, Connecticut
IDENTIFICATION: American humorist, novelist, travel writer, and lecturer
SIGNIFICANCE: Mark Twain's position as a central figure in American literature lends special significance to the complex history of censorship of his works

Mark Twain's most famous work, *Adventures of Huckleberry Finn*, has been banned in classrooms and libraries since its first year of American publication, 1885. At the prodding of Louisa May Alcott, the public library of Concord, Massachusetts, banned the book, charging that it was unsuitable for impressionable young people. Such criticism died down until

the racially charged environment of the 1960's, when African Americans began calling the novel "racist trash." Attempts to ban the book achieved prominent attention as in 1989, when a black administrator of an intermediate school named after Mark Twain in Fairfax, Virginia, pushed to ban the book.

Other censored works by Mark Twain include *The Adventures of Tom Sawyer* (1876), which the Brooklyn Library in New York banned on its publication, calling it too coarse for young readers. During Mark Twain's brief 1864 stint as a news reporter for the *San Francisco Call*, his editor censored and suppressed his articles exposing social problems and police misconduct in order not to offend the paper's largely white and working-class readers. Anti-British sentiments expressed in the novel *A Connecticut Yankee in King Arthur's Court* (1889) and the travel book *Following the Equator* (1897) provoked mild attempts to ban these books in Great Britain. Communist nations, particularly the Soviet Union and China, have banned some of Mark Twain's work as "bourgeois" literature, while simultaneously lionizing his antireligious and anti-imperialistic writings.

Family and Friends. As a printer's apprentice on Missouri newspapers, the young Sam Clemens wrote occasional articles, but felt constrained by his older brother, Orion Clemens, who restricted his humorous jibes. Conflicts with Orion contributed to his leaving Hannibal in 1853 for the East Coast, where he worked as a printer. Mark Twain's real career as a writer began in Nevada in 1862, when he became a reporter for the *Virginia City Territorial Enterprise*. After one of his irreverent sketches that was reprinted in an Iowa newspaper offended his mother and sister, he asked to have his initials removed from later sketches republished in the East so not to upset his female relatives.

In later years friends such as fellow writer and *Atlantic Monthly* editor William Dean Howells and Mary Mason Fairbanks both provided editorial suggestions and cuts to his works they felt might offend potential readers. Fairbanks persuaded Mark Twain to tone down his barbs at religion in the 1867 travel letters he wrote from Europe and the Holy Land that became the basis for his hugely popular book *Innocents Abroad* (1869). In later years, when he became concerned with maintaining appearances of propriety, Mark Twain himself allowed friends and family members to suggest deletions and changes in his writings. However, he often rankled under their suggestions, which he did not always accept.

His wife, Livy, was particularly concerned about his use of coarse language. For example, she persuaded him to rephrase "combed it all to hell" to "combed it all to thunder" in *Adventures of Huckleberry Finn*. Despite later claims that Livy's censorship blunted Mark Twain's satirical potential, her suggestions helped him to improve his literary style and to retain his reading audience, and he was grateful for her assistance.

During Mark Twain's last years, his daughters provided editorial advice, particularly when his political essays grew too brutal and harsh. His polemic *King Leopold's Soliloquy* (1906), for example, was found so scathing it was determined unsuitable for magazine publication, and was instead issued as a pamphlet. His daughter Jean helped persuade him not to publish his bitter antiwar polemic, "The War Prayer." After Mark Twain died, another daughter, Clara, instructed the author of a short book about his time in Bermuda not to include potentially compromising photographs of him with young girls. She believed that readers might misconstrue his affection for the children.

Sex. As a Victorian era male, Mark Twain was uneasy about publishing overtly sexual material in his writings. He effectively censored himself by simply avoiding the subject. For example, his books *Roughing It* (1872) and *Life on the Mississippi* (1883) do not even hint at the existence of prostitution in western mining towns or on Mississippi steamboats. His autobiographical pieces, such as a memoir of Hannibal village residents that he wrote in 1897, deliberately sentimentalized his childhood, avoiding references to adultery and sexual practices of which he was clearly aware.

Mark Twain did, however, occasionally write scatological pieces privately, such as *1601* (written in 1876), a bawdy parody on Elizabethan manners. In 1879 he delivered a speech on masturbation, "Some Thoughts on the Science of Onanism," in Paris. Mark Twain had *1601* privately printed in the 1880's and many unauthorized editions followed, but his "Onanism" speech was not published until 1964—in *Fact* and *Playboy* magazines.

Philosophical Issues. Throughout his life, Mark Twain was interested in censorship. He observed the censorship of other authors, repeatedly decrying attackers of his philosophical mentor, essayist Thomas Paine. He defended poet Walt Whitman while advising that Whitman's *Leaves of Grass* be kept out of children's hands because of its sexual frankness. A "Pudd'nhead Wilson" maxim in *Following the Equator* summed up his feelings on free expression:

> It is by the goodness of God that in our country we have those three unspeakably precious things: freedom of speech, freedom of conscience, and the prudence never to practice either of them.

Central to Mark Twain's experiences with censorship were his views on Christianity. His attacks on religion resulted in a series of suppressions that continued fifty years after his death. For example, his anonymously published book *What Is Man?* (1906)—which he called his "Bible"—was tightly restricted; Mark Twain issued only 250 copies during his lifetime. He began writing *Extract from Captain Stormfield's Visit to Heaven* in 1881, but did not publish it until 1909 because he believed it could never be published "unless I trim it like everything."

One of the most egregious examples of censorship of Mark Twain's writings was his literary executor Albert Bigelow Paine's publication of *The Mysterious Stranger* in 1916. Although Paine represented this book as a novel written by Mark

This fanciful illustration of Mark Twain being cremated in the first printing of Life on the Mississippi *(1883) so upset his wife that it was stricken from all later printings.* (Kevin Bochynski)

Twain, the published book was in fact a heavily edited and substantially rewritten version of two different manuscripts that Mark Twain had left unpublished. Among the many changes that Paine and Harper editor Frederick Duneka made was replacing an evil Roman Catholic priest with a nonsectarian astrologer and removing all direct references to the Catholic church.

Five chapters of his autobiography that Mark Twain dictated in 1906 that were titled "Reflections on Religion" were suppressed by Mark Twain himself, Paine, and sole surviving daughter, Clara Clemens, until 1963. The selections finally appeared in the *Hudson Review* after two other magazines rejected them as too inflammatory. Mark Twain himself had directed that the passages not be published until a hundred years after his death. At the time he dictated them, he wrote to his friend Howells saying, "Tomorrow I mean to dictate a chapter that will get my heirs and assigns burnt alive if ever they venture to print it this side of 2006 A.D.—which I judge they won't." On some manuscripts, he prohibited publication for five centuries. These directives, which converged with the desires of his family and literary heirs, created one of the most interesting episodes of censorship in American literary history.

Posthumous Censorship. After Mark Twain died, his daughter Clara and his literary executor, Paine, suppressed and selectively edited for publication many of his previously unpublished manuscripts in order to preserve his image as a wholesome, kindly funnyman. Some of their efforts followed Mark Twain's own instructions. In other cases, however, decisions to censor arose from Clara's and Paine's own biases. For example, Paine's authorized biography of Mark Twain virtually ignores Mark Twain's personal secretary Isabel Lyon, whom Clara disliked. More often, however, Paine—who controlled publication of Mark Twain's manuscripts until his own death in 1935—was simply reluctant to publish anything negative about Mark Twain.

After Paine died, Clara frequently quarreled with Bernard DeVoto, who succeeded Paine as her father's literary editor. DeVoto—an accomplished scholar in his own right—wished to publish manuscripts that Clara feared might offend relatives of persons Mark Twain criticized in his autobiographical passages. DeVoto had earlier been hindered by Paine's refusal to let him inspect unpublished manuscripts. Unlike Paine or Clara, DeVoto understood the purely commercial value of keeping Mark Twain scholarship alive and controversial. He believed that Mark Twain's autobiography manuscripts—which he had composed with publication in mind—should not be edited or suppressed. After DeVoto published a selection of his material in *Mark Twain in Eruption* (1940), he discovered that Clara had suppressed passages without his knowledge. For this and other reasons, he resigned his position as editor of the Mark Twain Papers in frustration.

Clara also rigorously opposed publication of her father's *Letters from the Earth*, a savage satire on Christian beliefs that DeVoto prepared for publication in 1939. Mark Twain himself had worried about publishing this material. In 1909 he wrote to a friend saying that the book "will never be published—in fact it couldn't be because it would be a felony." Shortly before her own death in 1962, Clara finally consented to publication of *Letters from the Earth*. By then she realized that her father's religious ideas were well known, and that Americans were more tolerant of dissenting views of religion than in her father's time.

Meanwhile, Clara had refused to allow publication of the "Reflections on Religion" passages in Charles Neider's 1959 edition, *Autobiography of Mark Twain*. She believed that communists might find support for their ideology in her father's attacks on the Christian god, and she feared his sacrilegious opinions might provoke social turmoil and invite attacks on his reputation. She told Neider that publication of *The Mysterious Stranger* had already established her father's darker philosophical side, and that she did not want him perceived as "a dark angel." Clara was also privately unhappy with her father's negative writings on Mary Baker Eddy, the founder of Christian Science, as she was a member of that denomination.

After Neider noted Clara's refusal to publish the religion passages in the introduction to his edition of the autobiography, the Soviet Union's *Literary Gazette* published an editorial claiming that Mark Twain was being officially censored in his home country. These charges finally moved Clara to permit Neider to publish the "Reflections" passages—but not as part of the autobiography. Neider's publisher, Harper & Row, agreed that the material did not belong in a "family book." Even after Clara's death, and after publication of "Reflections" in the *Hudson Review* in 1963, another twenty-three years elapsed before the passages appeared in book form, in Neider's, *The Outrageous Mark Twain* (1987). A number of clergymen reacted against the piece, including Roman Catholic bishop Nor-

man Vincent Peale, who accused Mark Twain of cowardice for not having published the material in his own lifetime.

After Clara's death, other long-suppressed Mark Twain works—including many he had never intended for publication—began appearing in books edited by the Mark Twain Papers project at the University of California at Berkeley. Such project publications as *What Is Man? and Other Philosophical Writings* (1973), *Which Was the Dream? and Other Symbolic Writings of the Later Years* (1967), *Fables of Man* (1972), and *The Devil's Race-Track: Mark Twain's Great Dark Writings* (1980) contain unfinished novels, sketches, and literary fragments that had either never been previously published or that had appeared only in magazines or newspapers.

—*Wesley Britton*

See also *Adventures of Huckleberry Finn*; African Americans; Biography; Libraries; Libraries, school; Literature; Offensive language; Paine, Thomas; Race; Religion; Sex in the arts; Whitman, Walt.

BIBLIOGRAPHY

Van Wyck Brooks's *The Ordeal of Mark Twain* (New York: Dutton, 1920) has assumed classic status as an essay on Mark Twain's self-censorship. Bernard DeVoto rebutted Brooks in *Mark Twain's America* (Boston: Little, Brown, 1932). A modern echo of Brooks can be found in Guy A. Cardwell, "Mark Twain: A Self-Emasculated Hero," *Emerson Society Quarterly* 23 (1977). Charles Neider's introduction to *The Outrageous Mark Twain* (New York: Doubleday, 1987), a collection of previously suppressed Mark Twain material, chronicles the censorship of "Reflections on Religion," *1601*, "The Science of Onanism," and other short works. It also includes extracts from Clara Clemens' explanation of why she suppressed her father's religious writings. Henry Nash Smith's introduction to Mark Twain's *Letters from the Earth* (New York: Harper & Row, 1962) briefly describes the censorship of this volume and DeVoto's intentions in compiling this anthology. Howard G. Baetzhold and Joseph B. McCullough's *The Bible According to Mark Twain* (Athens: University of Georgia Press, 1995) collects all of Mark Twain's known writings on religion that have been suppressed in the past. For a comprehensive overview, see R. Kent Rasmussen, *Mark Twain A to Z: The Essential Reference to His Life and Writings* (New York: Facts On File, 1995).

2 Live Crew

FORMED: 1985

IDENTIFICATION: American rap music group

SIGNIFICANCE: In 1990 2 Live Crew became the first musical group to have one of its albums declared obscene in state and in federal courts

On June 6, 1990, a federal district judge, Jose Gonzalez, declared that the album *As Nasty as They Wanna Be* by 2 Live Crew violated community obscenity standards for the district including Broward, Dade, and Palm Beach counties in Florida. In his decision, the judge wrote that the album "has an appeal to dirty thoughts and the loins, not to the intellect and the mind." Skyywalker Records, the recording company that produced the album, initiated the civil case from which Gonzalez's decision originated. The company began legal proceedings after Broward County's sheriff warned local record store owners and managers that he thought that the album was obscene and that he might have to arrest them if the stores continued to sell the album. Skyywalker Records incorrectly reasoned that a federal judge would rule that the album had social value and therefore was not obscene.

Within two days of the decision almost all record stores in the three counties had removed the album from their shelves. An exception was a Fort Lauderdale, Florida, record store owned by Charles Freeman, who was arrested for violating a local obscenity law. The crackdown was not limited to record stores or to record stores in southern Florida. On June 10, two members of 2 Live Crew were arrested, including the group's lead singer, Luther Campbell, and warrants were issued for the arrest of other members. The charge was that the group had sung songs from the obscene album at an adults-only concert in Hollywood, Florida, and, therefore, had violated the obscenity statute. In fact, by September 28, 1990, a record store owner in Sarasota, Florida, was arrested for selling *As Nasty as They Wanna Be*.

Florida was not the only locality to act against 2 Live Crew. A Dallas assistant district attorney stated the recording was obscene under Texas law, and the town council of Westerly, Rhode Island, tried to prevent a concert by 2 Live Crew.

In addition to fighting in the courts, 2 Live Crew took their battle to the airwaves. In July, 1990, the band released an album titled *Banned in the U.S.A.*, containing songs denouncing censorship with the group's usual hard rap beat. *Banned in the U.S.A.* also faced censorship challenges because it contained a parody of Roy Orbison's "Pretty Woman."

The various challenges yielded different results. Even after appeal, record store owner Freeman was found guilty of violating the obscenity statutes. 2 Live Crew was found not guilty, and a federal judge prohibited the prevention of 2 Live Crew's concert in Rhode Island. On December 7, 1992, the U.S. Supreme Court let stand a federal appeals court ruling that *As Nasty as They Wanna Be* was not obscene. This decision ended the controversy.

See also "Cop Killer"; Copyright law; Obscenity: legal definitions; Obscenity: sale and possession; Prior restraint; Subliminal messages.

U

UFO evidence

DEFINITION: UFO is an acronym for "unidentified flying object"

SIGNIFICANCE: Many people who believe that UFOs are extraterrestrial spacecraft suspect that the U.S. government has deliberately suppressed evidence of their existence

UFO sightings have been reported in various cultures for centuries; however, a July, 1947, sighting in Washington State is considered to have been the beginning of the modern era of UFO sighting. Since then more than twenty thousand sightings have been reported from around the world. If the existence of alien spacecraft visiting the earth were verified, it would raise serious concerns about the planet's security until the intentions of the visitors were known. Travelers from other star systems would presumably have superior technology; if their intentions were hostile, they might pose a serious danger.

Most reported UFO sightings are explained as other phenomena, such as terrestrial aircraft, weather balloons, and cloud formations, but about 10 percent remain unexplained. More intriguing than sightings are occasional reports of spacecraft crashes from which alien bodies have been recovered. The most significant such event in modern times was an alleged UFO crash near Roswell, New Mexico, in July, 1947. Information about this incident was censored by the U.S. military, and the crash received little attention for several decades. Some researchers believe that President Harry S Truman began the secret Operation Majestic (MJ12) in 1947 to study the Roswell crash. The project's existence has been debated, with the government refusing to confirm or deny it, as researchers have debated its existence.

According to UFO researchers, known as "ufologists," a military project called Sign that began in December, 1947, concluded the following year that UFOs were indeed extraterrestrial. Ufologists have claimed that the military rejected this report and had it destroyed. The public was misled about the project name, the name was changed, and the project recommended its own termination, but was continued in 1949 as Project Blue Book.

After many people reported new UFO sightings over Washington, D.C., in July, 1952, the Central Intelligence Agency secretly convened the Robertson Panel to review the most promising incidents from Project Blue Book. The Robertson Panel viewed civilian interest in UFOs as threatening to orderly government, concluded that UFOs did not exist, and recommended covert surveillance of UFO organizations. Project Blue Book continued until 1969. Meanwhile, Project Moon Dust, a top-secret military project, conducted investigations in the 1960's, with Operation Blue Fly being the operational wing of the project. Moon Dust supposedly was involved in recovering spacecraft debris in Kecksburg, Pennsylvania, in 1965; in Sudan in 1967; in Nepal in 1968; and in other places. The U.S. government has, however, denied that Project Moon Dust ever existed.

Parts of thousands of documents obtained under the Freedom of Information Act suggest that governmental censorship of UFO issues began in 1947. Several reasons have been advanced for this censorship: that the government wants unilaterally to control any alien technological knowledge; that proof of the existence of aliens might cause people to distrust political or religious leaders; and that a malevolent alien presence might cause mass panic. Despite—or perhaps because of—censorship, and recognition by UFO believers that some reports are hoaxes, a 1990 Gallup Poll found that almost 50 percent of all Americans believe that UFOs are alien spacecraft. In contrast to the United States, the governments of some countries, including Mexico and Belgium, have encouraged UFO interest and open research.

See also Astronomy; Classification of information; Freedom of Information Act; Military censorship; Occult; Science; Technology.

Ugly American, The

TYPE OF WORK: Book

PUBLISHED: 1958

AUTHORS: Eugene Burdick (1918-1965) and William J. Lederer (1912-   )

SUBJECT MATTER: A series of fictional vignettes about untrained American bureaucrats mishandling foreign aid programs in Southeast Asia

SIGNIFICANCE: During the early Cold War U.S. government agencies occasionally attempted to suppress books such as *The Ugly American* that criticized U.S. foreign policies and operations

The Ugly American is an example of a novel that met with only modest commercial success until an effort was made to ban it. The United States Information Service tried to ban the book's sale overseas—especially in Asia—until adverse publicity forced it to rescind its ban. The book then gained further notoriety when the U.S. Department of State and Senator J. William Fulbright attacked the truthfulness of the authors, hinting they were traitors. Thanks to the ensuing publicity, the book jumped onto the bestseller lists for seventy-eight weeks and sold more than four million copies.

The book also stimulated the American public to question the effectiveness of U.S. foreign policies, and it may have influenced the shaping of foreign policy during the era. Both John F. Kennedy and Richard M. Nixon often cited the book's premise—that communism in Southeast Asia could only be defeated by small-scale actions in the field, not by bungling bureaucrats who preferred the cocktail circuit and schmoozing with political insiders.

When the book was adapted to the screen in 1963, its producers felt pressured by the Agency for International Development to tone down the theme of governmental incompetence.

See also Censorship; United States Information Agency.

Ulysses

TYPE OF WORK: Book
PUBLISHED: 1922
AUTHOR: James Joyce (1882-1941)
SUBJECT MATTER: Novel exploring the inner lives of lower-middle-class Dubliners on one day in 1904
SIGNIFICANCE: *Ulysses* became the subject of a court case that revolutionized the legal definition of what can be considered obscene in the United States

Unfolding in a single day—June 16, 1904—Joyce's novel re-creates the Dublin, Ireland, of his youth, as seen through the eyes of its inhabitants. With its individual sections patterned after Homer's *Odyssey*, the novel centers on that day in the life of Leopold Bloom—a Jew whose roots are in Hungary. Joyce's work was perhaps the most avant-garde of its time, but its most radical innovation is in the narrative format through which it unfolds. Informed by Sigmund Freud's theories about the subconscious, Joyce utilizes the stream-of-conscious technique to explore the innermost thoughts of his characters. It creates a polyphonic interplay of moods and impressions that were a radical departure from the work of Joyce's contemporaries. In it the unconscious mind is uncensored, and it is often prone to dwell on bodily functions—a subject that was taboo in the polite society of the early twentieth century. Therein lay the root of the book's censorship problems.

The Controversy. *Ulysses* was written over a six-year period, from 1914 to 1920; however, there were publication problems long before the novel was completed. Margaret Anderson and Jane Heap, who published *The Little Review* in New York City's Greenwich Village, were the first to try putting Joyce's new work into print. However, nearly all of New York's printers refused to accept a work that dealt frankly with such bodily functions as defecation and that used slang terms for sex organs. Fear of legal repercussions prompted them to refuse the commission. Anderson and Heap finally found a Serbian immigrant who was willing to undertake the task. Regarding censorship in America he observed: "Here the people are not brave about words, they are not healthy about words. . . . You can go to prison."

Censorship made itself felt soon after *The Little Review* released its first Joyce issue in March, 1918. Since this obscure publication was mailed to its subscribers, the U.S. Post Office intervened by seizing the magazine. It branded several issues obscene and burned them. Accounts vary, but from three to four such seizures took place, in which the Post Office destroyed all four thousand copies each time. Material known to have been seized included the "Lestrygonians" section in January, 1919; "Scylla and Charybdis" in May, 1919; and "Cyclops" in January, 1920.

The First *Ulysses* Trial. On October 4, 1920, John Sumner, head of the New York Society for the Suppression of Vice, had

Anderson and Heap arrested and charged with publishing obscene material. The offensive matter was the book's "Nausicaa" episode, appearing in the July-August, 1920, issue of the periodical. In that segment Leopold Bloom has a sexual orgasm when young Gertie McDowell exposes her legs on the beach. A three-judge panel heard the ensuing case in February, 1921, before the Court of Special Sessions. Defense witnesses failed to communicate the significance of Joyce's work, and two of the judges admitted that they could not understand the text. The standard for determining whether something was obscene at that time—the question of whether it had a tendency to corrupt the morals of young people—derived from an 1868 English case, *Regina v. Hicklin*. Anderson and Heap were convicted—barely avoiding jail time—fined fifty dollars each, and forced to cease publication.

The Repercussions. Once *Ulysses* was labeled "obscene," copyrighting it in the United States became impossible, effectively ending any chance for the book's legitimate publication in the United States for many years. The book's publication might have been left unfinished for many years, had it not been for the intervention of Sylvia Beach, the owner of the Shakespeare and Company bookstore in Paris. In France's more liberal atmosphere she was able to issue the first complete edition of the novel in February, 1922. Throughout the 1920's and early 1930's, the once-obscure novel gained an international reputation in literary circles and beyond. Censorship, however, continued unabated in many nations. In 1922 imported copies of *Ulysses* were burned in Ireland and Canada, and five hundred copies were burned by the U.S. Post Office. The following year saw the destruction of another five hundred copies at the port of Folkstone by British customs officers. Nevertheless, efforts to suppress the book ultimately failed. Pirated reprintings of the Paris edition continued to turn up in America, but without royalty payments for Joyce. Even after a 1928 customs court judge condemned the book, thousands of copies of the Paris edition found their way into the United States. *Ulysses* became the forbidden fruit: Daring Paris tourists smuggled blue paper-covered copies of the book out of France—under their clothes, or perhaps disguised as Bibles. By the early 1930's, this banned novel had even found its way into libraries as well as thousands of private homes. Since customs officials were unable to stop this smuggling, the task of censorship fell to individual librarians. In a 1930 address, George F. Bowerman, of the District of Columbia's public library system, wanted to relegate *Ulysses* "to a medical library or a library of abnormal psychology."

The Second Trial. Eventually Random House, an American publisher, decided to force a test case. After signing a contract with Joyce in 1932, Random House arranged to have a copy of *Ulysses* seized by customs officials in New York. The seized copy was bulging with copies of favorable reviews that had been pasted in—a ploy that was necessary in order to ensure that the reviews would be admitted as evidence in court. In the ensuing legal case, *United States v. One Book Called Ulysses*, the government declared that the book was obscene under the terms of the Tariff Act of 1930. Judge John M. Woolsey presided over book's trial, which opened in the fall of 1933 and closed with a decision lifting the ban in early December. Woolsey significantly liberalized the definition of obscenity in the United States. Whereas the Hicklin test could ban a book based upon a single paragraph, Woolsey decided that obscene intent should be determined by viewing the work as a whole—even if some passages could give offense. The decision was upheld by an appeals court, and Random House formally published *Ulysses* the following January.

While Woolsey's decision legalized publication of the book, censorship continued in other forms. In 1960, for example, Caedmon Records released recorded readings of two of the novel's characters, Leopold Bloom and his wife, Molly. The publisher made no mention of the fact that the recorded passages had been expurgated. A film adaptation of the book made by Joseph Strick in 1967 was heavily cut by the British Board of Film Censors—especially Molly Bloom's soliloquy at the end of the novel. However, the board later relented, and the excised material was restored in 1970. Ironically, a 1995 edition of the book in China—a country long known for censorship—was published intact.   —*Cliff Prewencki*

See also Book publishing; British Board of Film Censors; Cerf, Bennett; France; Hicklin case; Joyce, James; *Little Review, The*; Obscenity: legal definitions; Postal regulations; Society for the Suppression of Vice, New York.

BIBLIOGRAPHY

A substantial collection of legal material and personal responses to the Woolsey decision can be found in a volume edited by Michael Moscato and Leslie LeBlanc: *The United States of America v. One Book Entitled Ulysses by James Joyce: Documents and Commentary—A Fifty-Year Retrospective* (Frederick, Md.: University Publications of America, 1984). Morris L. Ernst and Alexander Lindey's *The Censor Marches On: Recent Milestones in the Administration of the Obscenity Law in the United States* (New York: Doubleday, Doran, 1940) includes a useful discussion of the meaning of Woolsey's ruling. Margaret Anderson's *My Thirty-Years' War: The Autobiography* (New York: Horizon Press, 1970) gives a full account of *The Little Review* and its struggles. An insider's view of *Ulysses*' publication in the United States can be found in Bennett Cerf's *At Random: The Reminiscences of Bennett Cerf* (New York: Random House, 1977). Edward de Grazia, *Girls Lean Back Everywhere: The Law of Obscenity and the Assault on Genius* (New York: Random House, 1992), provides much background material on the key players in *Ulysses*' many legal battles. For a concise narrative of the *Ulysses* controversy, see William Noble, *Bookbanning in America: Who Bans Books?—And Why?* (Middlebury, Vt.: Paul S. Eriksson, 1990).

Uncle Tom's Cabin

TYPE OF WORK: Book
PUBLISHED: 1852
AUTHOR: Harriet Beecher Stowe (1811-1896)
SUBJECT MATTER: This novel chronicles the evils of American slavery
SIGNIFICANCE: The novel exercised an enormous influence on American popular opinion in the decade prior to the Civil War; it was banned in several European countries, and it has remained a target of censors during the twentieth century

In 1851 Harriet Beecher Stowe began composing an antislavery novel that was serialized in the *National Era*, an antislavery journal. In 1852 the novel, which chronicles the fortunes of a kindly slave called Uncle Tom, was published in book form as *Uncle Tom's Cabin*. Appearing at a time when the abolitionist movement was gaining momentum, Stowe's novel broke the sales records of all earlier American best sellers. However, *Uncle Tom's Cabin* was not widely distributed in the South and was condemned as untruthful by Southern politicians, critics, and clergymen.

In 1853 Stowe's novel was banned in the papal states by Catholic officials in Rome, perhaps because one character in the book predicts a worldwide revolution of slaves and exploited workers. This ban led to censorship of the novel in several European countries.

Uncle Tom's Cabin has remained a victim of censorship during the twentieth century. A 1906 Kentucky law aimed at stage versions of Stowe's novel made it illegal to produce any play depicting antagonism between slaves and masters. Since 1950 the novel's sharpest critics have been African Americans, who have objected to Stowe's meek and passive protagonist. The term "Uncle Tom" has come to mean a black man who shamelessly curries favor with whites, or who sells out the interests of his own people; it is extremely pejorative. In 1954, for example, the National Association for the Advancement of Colored People attempted to block a stage production of *Uncle Tom's Cabin* in New Haven, Connecticut. During the 1970's, 1980's, and 1990's, school boards in many cities with large African American populations opposed the novel's appearance on high school reading lists.

See also Abolitionist movement; African Americans; Civil War, U.S.; National Association for the Advancement of Colored People.

United Kingdom

DESCRIPTION: Official name (since the early eighteenth century) for the sovereign nation encompassing England, Scotland, Wales, Northern Ireland, and several offshore islands
SIGNIFICANCE: Although the United Kingdom has a long tradition of democracy and respect for civil liberties, it has also had a history of government censorship over the arts

Censorship in the United Kingdom under the Tudors, from 1485 until 1603, reflected a close relationship between politics and religion. It considered religious heresy threatening to the state. Even after King Henry VIII broke from the Roman Catholic church and established the Church of England, the official government policy was to control the press, maintaining unaltered the bond between church and Crown.

Introduction of Printing. After William Caxton introduced the printing press into England in 1476, the state viewed printing as a royal privilege and became the licensing authority. Under Henry VIII, no book could be published without royal approval from the monarch or from the privy council or a bishop. As early as 1382 the British clergy were empowered to suppress heresy and, with the development of printing, its power was enhanced.

In the mid-sixteenth century King Edward VI forbade the publication and use of materials and prayer books that reflected Roman Catholic tenets. In 1556 the Roman Catholic queen Mary relaxed Edward's mandates but empowered the Stationers' Company to seize and destroy unauthorized books considered illegal or subversive. In return for its policing actions, the Crown granted the company monopolistic printing rights.

The Seventeenth Century. Under kings James I (1603-1625) and Charles I (1625-1649), censorship was largely at the whim of the archbishop of Canterbury. When the moderate George Abbot was succeeded as archbishop by the politically reactionary William Laud, harsh penalties were levied against those whose writing threatened the monarchy and the status quo. Some writers, besides being given long prison terms, were publicly flogged, had their ears lopped off, their nostrils split, and their cheeks branded. The Royal Star Chamber in 1637 strengthened the powers of the Stationers' Company, creating a new, more extensive licensing framework within it.

During the Restoration (1660-1685) following the fall of Oliver Cromwell, King Charles II reestablished rigid licensing laws with the enactment of the Licensing Act of 1662, designed to control sedition and similar to acts the Star Chamber had imposed in 1637. Under Charles II, theaters, closed by royal edict in 1642, were reopened.

The Licensing Act of 1662, renewed by James II's Parliament shortly after it lapsed in 1679 and renewed again during the reign of William and Mary, finally expired in 1695 and was replaced by secular authority more concerned with controlling obscenity than sedition. With the enactment of the Licensing Act of 1737, theaters fell under the control of the Theatres Royal of Drury Lane and of Covent Garden. These two companies regulated British theater until the Theatre Regulation Act of 1843.

In the modern United Kingdom, censorship has been imposed by various agencies. The customs and postal services are empowered by the Customs Consolidation Act of 1876 to seize materials considered obscene or indecent. When this act was rewritten in 1952, its powers were reinforced and included prints, paintings, photographs, books, cards, lithographic or other engravings, or any other indecent or obscene articles, essentially leaving definition and interpretation to the censors.

Victorian Britain. The Law of Confidence, originally devised by a British judge to prevent the publication of private etchings by Queen Victoria and Prince Albert, forbids the publication, if there has been a legal agreement to confidentiality, of private material that might damage people. This law, extended in 1967 to include corporations and corporate secrets, is unique to British jurisprudence and has been employed frequently against the tabloids of the United Kingdom.

Under the Indecent Advertisement Act of 1889, legislation originally promoted by Victorian England's National Vigilance Association, the posting or display within public view of any material considered obscene or indecent was punishable by fines and imprisonment, penalties that extended to those providing such materials as well as to those displaying them.

Later Acts Relating to Censorship. The Commissioners of Customs and Excise have, since 1978, covertly distributed a frequently updated, classified list, not publicly available, of materials banned from import. Although the Customs and Management Act of 1979 provides for appeals by those whose property is seized under the act, customs officers are not legally bound to inform such people of their rights.

This act is reinforced by the Indecent Displays Act of 1981, aimed primarily at adult bookstores, that makes it illegal to display any indecent material within public view. The Local Government Act of 1982 empowers local councils to regulate sex shops and sex cinemas and to define indecency in terms of local custom.

Censorship in Northern Ireland. Because the split in Northern Ireland between Catholics and Protestants has resulted in widespread acts of terrorism and continued strife, legislation unique to this part of the United Kingdom exists. Section eleven of the Prevention of Terrorism (Temporary Provision) Act of 1976 compels all citizens of Northern Ireland and the British mainland to report to the police information they have about impending acts of terrorism and to provide information that might lead to the arrest and prosecution of terrorists. This controversial act applies even to journalists who have interviewed members of dissident groups such as the Irish Republican Army (IRA).

The Emergency Provisions (Northern Ireland) Act of 1978 makes it illegal for anyone to collect, record, or publish information from which terrorists might benefit about the army, the police, judges, or prison officers. In Northern Ireland, it is forbidden to present television coverage sympathetic or favorable to the IRA. Irish television is banned from carrying interviews with IRA members even if the station states its opposition to the views expressed.

Library Censorship. Library censorship is practiced widely throughout the United Kingdom, with many such books as Geoffrey Chaucer's *The Canterbury Tales*, Giovanni Boccaccio's *The Decameron*, Henry Fielding's *Tom Jones*, Adolf Hitler's *Mein Kampf*, James Joyce's *Ulysses*, and Alfred Kinsey's *Sexual Behavior in the Human Male* widely banned. Film censorship in Britain is controlled by the British Board of Film Censors, established by the film industry in 1921. Under the Obscene Publications Act of 1959 and its amendments in 1977 and 1979, any film that might corrupt audiences is banned from import and may be withdrawn by the Director of Public Prosecutions.   —*R. Baird Shuman*

See also Book burning; Censorship; Free speech; Henry VIII; James I; Licensing Act of 1662; Licensing Act of 1737; Lord Chamberlain; Northern Ireland; Obscene Publications Acts; Privacy, right to; Puritans; Reformation, the.

BIBLIOGRAPHY

Julia Carlson, ed., *Banned in Ireland: Censorship and the Irish Writer* (Athens: University of Georgia Press, 1990), focuses on the most restrictive censorship environment in the United Kingdom. Alec Craig, *The Banned Books of England and Other Countries: A Study of the Conception of Literary Obscenity* (Westport, Conn.: Greenwood Press, 1977), provides vital commentary on how obscenity is defined and interpreted. A. L. Haight, *Banned Books: Informal Notes on Some Banned Books for Various Reasons at Various Times and Various Places* (3d ed. New York: Bowker, 1970), provides insights into book banning in the United Kingdom and elsewhere. D. M., Loades, ed., *Politics, Censorship, and the English Reformation* (New York: St. Martin's Press, 1992), discusses censorship in Britain during the seventeenth century. Annabel M. Patterson, *Censorship and Interpretation: The Conditions of Writing and Reading in Early Modern England* (Madison: University of Wisconsin Press, 1990), discusses cogently the laws affecting censorship in Victorian England. Geoffrey Robertson, *Obscenity: An Account of Censorship Laws and Their Enforcement in England and Wales* (Littleton, Colo.: Rothman, 1979), is one of the most complete accounts of censorship in the United Kingdom.

United Press International (UPI)

Founded: 1958

Type of organization: Press agency providing news and fillers to subscribing media

Significance: In conjunction with the Associated Press, Reuters, Agence France-Presse, and ITAR-TASS, UPI provides the majority of international and national coverage of news to local media

Although the first news gathering service was created in the mid-nineteenth century with the formation of Havas in France, press agencies and syndicates did not gain wide popularity until the American Civil War. During the Mexican War and American Civil War, several regional newspaper groups banned together and joined the New York Associated Press to provide news coverage of war events and activities. Through their collective activities, newspapers saved the expense of each sending individual reporters to cover the stories. By 1900 the small collection of regional newspapers had evolved into a nationwide cooperative, supplying foreign and domestic news and fillers for local media across the United States.

During the Great Depression of the 1930's competition between radio and newspapers had increased significantly. In 1933 United Press Association (UPA) caved into demands by newspaper clients to restrict the provision of news to radio stations. In an agreement with the Associated Press known as the Baltimore Agreement, UPA agreed to limit news reporting to radio to two broadcasts per day, and restrict broadcasts to commentary and interpretation only. This agreement was short-lived, and in 1935 United Press resumed unrestricted sale of news reports to radio stations and networks.

In 1958 UPI was created by the fusion of two influential press associations. The first was the United Press Association, created in 1907 by Edward Wyllis Scripps. The second was William Randolph Hearst's International News Service, formed in 1909. The two hoped to challenge the hegemony of Associated Press (AP). Although AP remained the largest news syndicate, UPI has risen to preeminence through its provision of information and stories to local newspapers and other media. Additionally, UPI pioneered many areas of news coverage, including the first wire transmission of photographs for news stories in 1925, transmission by telephoto, and by 1958, transmission by facsimile. UPI was also among the first news groups to provide election returns for the 1928 election and was the first news service to provide reports for radio in the 1920's and television in the early 1950's.

Although UPI has been bought and sold several times since its creation, and was reorganized in bankruptcy during the early 1990's, it has proven to be a powerful source and filter of information for the mass media. Its staff writers provide coverage and analysis of politics, business and economics, society, culture, and entertainment. As a result, it wields considerable influence and control over what information is presented to the public.

See also Associated Press; Civil War, U.S.; Hearst, William Randolph; Press-radio war; TASS.

United States

Identification: North American nation organized as a republic of separate states under a central national government

Significance: A multitextured example of both commitment to freedom of speech and press, especially as guaranteed by the First Amendment to the U.S. Constitution, and of numerous past and present instances of censorship

The federal system of government in the United States embraces both national and state sovereignties. This federal organization means that censorship issues may involve attempts by either the national government or by the various state governments—with their constituent local units—to limit freedom of expression. Furthermore, both provisions in the U.S. Constitution and in the state constitutions may shield citizens from particular forms of censorship.

Structural Limits on Government Power to Censor. The framers of the U.S. Constitution sought to create structural protections within the document that would minimize the possibility that the national government might infringe upon the rights of individuals, such as the right to freedom of expression. One key strategy for preserving liberty involved segregating spheres of power so that political action dangerous to liberty might be frustrated at several junctures in the political process. The system of checks and balances created by the Constitution included provisions that delegated only certain powers to the national government, reserving remaining political power to the states. Framers such as James Madison originally believed that by restricting the powers of the national government to specifically enumerated concerns only, the possibility of tyrannical action by the national government would be substantially lessened. Thus, at the national level at least, the limitation of national power to certain specifically enumerated matters in the Constitution acts as a restraint on government power to censor expression. Even at the time of the Constitution's original enactment, however, some observers believed that structural limitations on the powers of the national government were not a sufficient guardian of individual liberty and insisted that the Constitution be amended to include specific protections for liberties such as freedom of speech and press. Congress has, in fact, been able to censor speech in a variety of ways through the exercise of its constitutionally enumerated powers, such as its power to supervise matters relating to customs and the mail.

Limitation on the Power of States to Censor Expression. As originally framed, neither the Constitution nor its subsequently added Bill of Rights limited the power of state and local governments to censor expression. The First Amendment's guarantees of freedom of speech and press applied only to attempts by the national government to suppress expression. But ratification of the Fourteenth Amendment in 1868 added language to the Constitution that prevented states from depriving persons of "life, liberty, or property, without due process of law." The U.S. Supreme Court has understood this clause to make most of the provisions of the Bill of Rights applicable to state and local governments. In particular, the Court held, in *Gitlow v. New York* (1925), that the freedoms of speech and press were incorporated by reference in the due process clause's use of the word "liberty." The Court has understood this incorporation to mean that the Fourteenth Amendment's due process clause brings the protections of freedom of religion, speech, and press to bear upon state and local governments' attempts to suppress expression.

Government Censorship Generally. The First Amendment's guarantees of freedom of speech and press stand as a barrier to most forms of government censorship of speech. Nevertheless, the U.S. Supreme Court has never understood these guarantees to be absolute and has allowed restraint of speech in many circumstances. The modern Court has determined the degree of protection owed to particular speech by classifying it into several categories. For example, the Court has determined that obscenity is not protected by the First Amendment. The Court has viewed other categories of speech such as libel, commercial speech, and offensive speech as deserving of some protection, but not the same protection as afforded, for example, speech about matters of public concern. Furthermore, the Court has granted significant authority to government to regulate the timing, place of delivery, and manner of delivery of speech, so long as government does not simultaneously attempt to discriminate against the content of particular speech.

Censorship of Political Expression. Censorship of unpopular political ideas has not been unknown in the United States. Unlike nondemocratic regimes, such as South Africa prior to its own democratic revolution in 1992, the censorship of political expression in the United States has been mainly sporadic. The existence of the First Amendment's free speech clause has perhaps tempered but not altogether eliminated periodic government enthusiasm for suppressing speech deemed politically dangerous to the democratic order. However, among democratic societies, the United States has not been alone in determining that certain speech might threaten the very foundations of democratic order and thus might be legitimately censored. For example, the German constitution enacted after World War II generally prohibits censorship of expression, but provides that this freedom may be forfeited by those who abuse it to attack the democratic order itself.

The first important example of political censorship in the United States was the Sedition Act of 1798, enacted during the administration of John Adams, which provided criminal punishment for those convicted of conspiring to oppose the federal government. The act was used to punish critics of the Adams Administration, and its use may have contributed to the defeat of Adams by Thomas Jefferson in the election of 1800. The Civil War was also accompanied by a variety of efforts to suppress unpopular political expression, especially in the South. Southern defenders of slavery, for example, urged postmasters to suppress abolitionist literature mailed into the South, citing the threat of a violent uprising if such literature fell into the hands of slaves. During the twentieth century suppression of political speech has centered around federal and state espionage and sedition acts passed in connection with World War I, and later, by anticommunist sentiment expressed in a variety of laws criminalizing advocacy of the violent overthrow of the U.S. government and in the infamous congressional proceedings captained by Senator Joseph McCarthy.

In the first half of the twentieth century, the U.S. Supreme Court was generally supportive of laws punishing speech deemed threatening to the U.S. political order. Justice Oliver Wendell Holmes, for example, denied in *Schenck v. United States* (1919) that there was an absolute right to freedom of speech. Surely, he argued, a man who falsely shouts "Fire!" in a crowded theater should not be immune from punishment. He therefore concluded that seditious speech sometimes posed a "clear and present danger" to society and could be punished under these circumstances. Ultimately, however, the Court, in *Brandenburg v. Ohio* (1969), made prosecution of potentially dangerous political speech far more difficult by limiting prosecutions only to speech that threatened imminent lawless action and that was in fact likely to incite such action.

Censorship of Literature. The constitutional commitment to freedom of expression in the United States has from its beginning coexisted with laws prohibiting obscene or indecent forms of expression. By the early years of the nineteenth century states had begun to enact antiobscenity laws. Toward the middle of that century the federal government joined the lists against obscenity by passage of the 1842 Tariff Act—which included prohibitions against the importation of indecent and obscene materials—and the 1865 Postal Act—which banned such materials from the mails. Since then federal, state, and local indecency laws have been leveled against a variety of artistic and literary works. Federal postal officials have, at one time or another, banned from the mail such works as Aristophanes' *Lysistrata* and Geoffrey Chaucer's *The Canterbury Tales*, as well as works of modern authors, including Victor Hugo, Honoré de Balzac, Oscar Wilde, Ernest Hemingway, Eugene O'Neill, D. H. Lawrence, John Steinbeck, William Faulkner, and F. Scott Fitzgerald. Local schools and public libraries have purged their collections of an even longer list of works, ranging from Mark Twain's *Adventures of Huckleberry Finn* to the ever-popular object of censorial zeal, J. D. Salinger's *The Catcher in the Rye*.

More recently, increasing social distaste for the expression of racist expression has prompted efforts to censor literature felt to incite racist sentiments. *Adventures of Huckleberry*

Finn, for example, suffered criticism in the early years after its publication principally for presenting what some observers believed to be an unfitting example for America's youth. In the second half of the twentieth century, however, Twain's work has drawn fire more commonly for its use of the word "nigger" and its uncomplimentary characterization of Huck's black companion, Jim. Works such as Charles Dickens' *Oliver Twist* and William Shakespeare's *The Merchant of Venice* have drawn similar complaints because of their unfavorable characterizations of Jews, such as the thief Fagin in *Oliver Twist* and the money-lender Shylock in *The Merchant of Venice*.

Broadcasting Censorship. Television and radio broadcasting in the United States is subject to federal regulation. Broadcasters must obtain federal licenses and demonstrate to the satisfaction of the Federal Communications Commission (FCC) that their programming will serve the public interest. Although federal law prohibits censorship by the FCC in principle, in practice the commission has used the "public interest" standard to restrict the broadcast of objectionable programming, especially outside of late-night hours, when children might be in the audience. The U.S. Supreme Court, in *Federal Communications Commission v. Pacifica* (1978), upheld this exercise of authority on the part of the FCC. Although federal regulation of broadcasting has asserted itself most forcefully in connection with indecent programming, more recently federal legislative attention has turned to the matter of television violence. In 1996 Congress passed legislation requiring television manufacturers to include in new televisions a "V-Chip," that was to be used in connection with a ratings system to give parents the ability to screen objectionable material, especially violence, from being broadcast into their homes.

Journalism Censorship. The First Amendment's explicit guarantees of freedom of speech and press have generally foreclosed the possibility of widespread censorship of the press. Nevertheless, attempts to suppress particular news items is not unknown in the United States. Sometimes censorship efforts have tried to characterize news stories as entertainment to make them more amenable to regulation. In the 1920's, for example, New York enacted a state law that attempted to subject newsreels, which were shown in cinemas along with feature films, to prior review by a state censor, claiming that the newsreels were simply a form of entertainment. Early complaints that this form of review violated the First Amendment were generally unsuccessful, although evolving First Amendment law eventually rejected such attempts to regulate journalistic efforts. A more familiar, and successful, variant of press censorship has involved government attempts to limit access to information involving war-time activities and military secrets. —*Timothy L. Hall*

See also Congress, U.S.; Constitution, U.S.; Customs laws, U.S.; First Amendment; Fourteenth Amendment; Postal regulations.

BIBLIOGRAPHY

Thomas L. Tedford's *Freedom of Speech in the United States* (2d ed. New York: McGraw-Hill, 1993) provides a general overview of censorship issues in the United States, with a focus on the constitutional limits on attempts by government to suppress expression. *Banned in the U.S.A.: A Reference Guide to Book Censorship in Schools and Public Libraries* (Westport, Conn.: Greenwood Press, 1994) surveys late twentieth century book banning in the United States. Federal regulations of broadcasting and of materials sent through the mail are explored in *Regulating Broadcast Programming*, by Thomas G. Krattenmaker and Lucas A. Powe, Jr. (Cambridge, Mass.: MIT Press, 1995), and *Unmailable: Congress and the Post Office*, by Dorothy Ganfield Fowler (Athens: University of Georgia Press, 1977), respectively. Edward de Grazia and Roger K. Newman's *Banned Films: Movies, Censors and the First Amendment* (New York: R. R. Bowker, 1982) contains a general survey of film censorship in the United States, as well as a description and commentary concerning particular films that have been the object of censorship efforts.

United States Information Agency (USIA)

FOUNDED: 1953
TYPE OF ORGANIZATION: Propaganda agency
SIGNIFICANCE: The USIA has presented a positive image of the United States and U.S. foreign policy

The USIA is an independent agency of the executive branch. It is responsible for promoting American values and policies abroad. Particularly during the Cold War, USIA has been understood to be a propaganda arm of the U.S. government.

USIA was a creation of the Cold War. Its roots lay in World War II, when President Franklin D. Roosevelt established the Agency for Foreign Intelligence and Propaganda and the Office of War Information (OWI). Both agencies employed a variety of propagandistic devices. A division of OWI directed radio broadcasts into Germany and elsewhere as a wartime propaganda tool, and these broadcasts later became institutionalized as the Voice of America (VOA). Immediately after the war America's discomfort with the business of propaganda, as well as isolationism and fiscal conservatism, led to the severe reduction of such programs and agencies. The VOA survived, however, within the Office of Public and Cultural Affairs in the State Department.

The onset of the Cold War a short time later forced a rethinking of America's isolationism, and by 1947 the country had committed itself militarily and economically to Western Europe. In 1948 the Congress passed the Smith-Mundt Act, which added cultural promotion and information provision to the country's arsenal of Cold War tools. These were carried out through a new Office of International Information and the Office of Educational Exchange, both situated within the State Department. Additional programs and agencies were established in following years to fight the ideological dimension of the Cold War.

In 1953 the Cold War confrontation between Western democracy and Soviet Communism had reached new heights (in the form of the Korean War and the Berlin uprising, for example). In the United States, McCarthyism was near its peak. It was in this environment that USIA was created. The sense of a world communist threat had inspired American political leaders to more vigorously counter Moscow's ideological messages and propaganda with ideological propaganda of a Western, democratic, capitalistic sort. Senator McCarthy's attacks on the State Department, OWI, and propaganda operations in general made it politic to move the programs of the Office of International Information to an independent agency. The move also emphasized that USIA was in the business of providing information, rather than carrying out America's foreign policy. USIA emphasized people to people relations rather than the formal country-to-country diplomacy of the State Department. USIA information was required, however, to be consistent with overall American foreign policy objectives. USIA activities, however, were claimed to be more noble than mere counterpropaganda. Indeed, compared with earlier American postwar propaganda efforts, USIA programs were much less shrill and didactic, and frequently composed and reasoned.

Activities. Besides overseeing VOA, USIA has maintained an overseas presence by assigning personnel to American missions and by running a network of libraries and cultural centers around the world. At one point during the Cold War USIA was operating some 184 libraries in sixty-five countries. The America Houses that contained USIA libraries and cultural centers generally welcomed all visitors, and offered reading rooms, cultural programs, speakers, and other resources for communicating American ideas, information, and values. In carrying out these functions, USIA field operations had to consider their activities against the background of Cold War realities: the need to establish credibility with its target audience, and the necessity of retaining permission to operate from the host government.

Books in USIA libraries were meant to promote American cultural values and to undermine communist ideology. Deciding which particular books to purchase and make available were a small senior book committee. The committee considered recommendations made by the bibliographic division, whose half-dozen reviewers assessed thousands of books each year for possible adoption. Qualities considered by reviewers included whether the book supported U.S. policy and whether the book would be comprehensible to a foreign reader. The selection of books could be seen as a form of censorship, as works that were critical of the United States or that advocated communism were seldom made available at USIA libraries. At the height of McCarthyism, even the political orientation of an author (as distinct from the book) was enough to ban a book from libraries of USIA and its predecessors. Relatively pedestrian publications were construed to be anti-American, such as a 1957 pamphlet titled *Profile of America*, which included quotations by Henry David Thoreau. Individual issues of approved magazines were banned when an article within it failed to meet the criteria of the day. Some books which earlier had been approved were removed from USIA libraries and burned—an action that constituted a public relations nightmare for the United States and that was subsequently curtailed.

Even after the anticommunist frenzy abated, the lingering influence of McCarthyism discouraged the adoption of critical works, despite USIA's ostensible mission of presenting an accurate portrait of American life. Yet over time USIA's book adoption policies became more liberal. When a foreign group or a respected individual requested a rejected volume from the local USIA field library, special clearance was sometimes secured to provide the book at that library. These exceptions were meant to promote USIA's credibility and reputation for openness.

In addition to making books and other reading materials available at its libraries, USIA assisted foreign publishers in the production and distribution of books—again, with various conditions that restricted their content. The agency also produced magazines, including *Problems of Communism*, that were distributed abroad. At its peak USIA published five such magazines. The Smith-Mundt Act of 1948 prohibited the distribution of USIA publications within the United States.

Post-Cold War. The collapse of communism in Eastern Europe and the Soviet Union has weakened the justification for USIA's existence. Since the early 1990's USIA has undergone budget cuts and a retraction of its mission. Its broadcast operations have been placed under an International Broadcasting Bureau. Some of the agency's information dissemination functions have been adapted to electronic media, including the Internet. To overseas audiences, USIA now goes by the name United States Information Service (USIS).

—*Steve D. Boilard*

See also Libraries; News broadcasting; Propaganda; Radio Free Europe; Radio Martí; *Ugly American, The*; Voice of America.

BIBLIOGRAPHY

Martin Merson's *The Private Diary of a Public Servant* (New York: Macmillan, 1955) examines USIA and other information agencies during the McCarthy era. *The United States Information Agency*, by John W. Henderson (New York: Praeger, 1969), provides a detailed history of the agency and a full description of its functions. Robert E. Elder's *The Information Machine: The United States Information Agency and American Foreign Policy* (Syracuse, N.Y.: Syracuse University Press, 1968) offers a slightly less flattering description than Henderson's book. More recent research is presented in Shawn J. Parry-Giles' "The Eisenhower Administration's Conceptualization of the USIA: The Development of Overt and Covert Propaganda Strategies" in *Presidential Studies Quarterly* 24, no. 2 (Spring, 1994). For a description of challenges faced by the agency after the Cold War, see Dick Kirschten, "Restive Relic" in *National Journal* 27, no. 16 (April 22, 1995).

Universities

DEFINITION: Institutions of higher learning that award advanced degrees

SIGNIFICANCE: Censorship is an especially sensitive issue for universities, which ideally are charged with transmitting knowledge, encouraging inquiry, and exploring ideas

Universities can experience censorship in a variety of forms, including the censorship of curriculum, research, and speech. In some countries the application of censorship to universities is part of a broader use of the university as a tool for promoting government-approved doctrine. In other countries universities are relatively free from official censorship, revealing a commitment to the university's autonomy. In many cases, however, the issue of university censorship rests on a delicate combination of the university's several roles.

The University's Mission. Although their particular constitution varies over time and place, universities traditionally have played a central role in the development of civilization. The modern university is typically part of a country's educational system, which is designed to train, educate, and socialize citizens from childhood. The mission of universities, whose students generally are considered adults and for which matriculation typically is not compulsory, goes further.

Ideally, universities carry out three distinct roles. First, they provide a liberal education, transmitting an awareness of the civilization's scientific knowledge, literature, arts, and culture. Second, universities train their students for some specialized, professional occupation. Third, universities engage in basic research, pushing new boundaries of knowledge and challenging old ones.

The overall mission of the ideal university therefore can present something of a dilemma: How can an institution charged with transmitting the received wisdom also be charged with challenging it? How can the rather conservative task of training professionals be squared with the potentially revolutionary task of questioning prevailing norms? The issue of censorship stands at the center of these questions.

Censoring Faculty. Rules of tenure have been adopted by most American universities to protect faculty from arbitrary or politically motivated dismissal. Tenure rules are based on the logic that dismissal for espousing particular views is censorship. The threat of dismissal based on beliefs provides a chilling effect, thus restricting academic discourse. Tenure therefore has become an indispensable feature of the modern American university. Many countries, however, offer no such protections. The logic, shared by some critics even in the United States, is that tenure rules unduly tie the hands of university administrators. Tenure is sometimes used as a shield by unproductive or incompetent teachers, thus hurting rather than protecting constructive academic discourse.

Charges of de facto censorship of faculty have continued even after the widespread adoption of tenure rules. Some former faculty members have claimed that a university's failure to grant tenure in itself amounts to censorship. Attempts by some universities to minimize these battles by creating non-tenured lecturer positions also have brought some charges of censorship. For example, a former Chicano studies lecturer at a university in Southern California in the early 1990's claimed that his nonreappointment was tantamount to censorship of his controversial views. Many of these disputes ultimately have to be resolved by the courts.

Although universities long have been accorded a measure of autonomy, in the United States it was not until after World War II that the courts firmly recognized academic freedom as protected by the First Amendment. The courts were forced to examine the issue of academic freedom as the Cold War took form in the late 1940's, with the government using the cause of anticommunism to intervene in academia. The U.S. Congress and other bodies moved the balance between universities as a bulwark of the predominant culture and as a challenger of

received wisdom firmly toward the former role. Professors were required to sign loyalty oaths, were fired for belonging to organizations judged un-American, and were harassed for espousing socialist or communist views. The Supreme Court decisively ruled those practices unconstitutional.

Censoring Students. University students are presumed not to have achieved mastery of knowledge, so it is often argued that those students should be permitted, even encouraged, to make errors. If learning comes from failures, then students should feel safe to take intellectual risks—for example, proposing an unorthodox interpretation of history. A problem arises when a student's stated ideas intimidate or otherwise offend other students. For example, when a student makes offensive remarks about a racial group, students belonging to that racial group might experience a hostile environment. An environment of intimidation or hostility is antithetical to principles of learning, which are based on notions of tolerance and diversity.

During the 1980's and 1990's many campuses turned to speech codes, which prescribed punishments for hateful, demeaning, or otherwise unacceptable speech. "Unacceptable" was defined in different ways by various campuses, but in the main the speech codes banned words, actions, laughter, facial expressions, intonations, and other forms of expression that could be found demeaning or offensive to others on the basis of their race, creed, sex, handicap status, sexual orientation, age, national origin, or various other characteristics. These speech codes were intended to foster a tolerant atmosphere conducive to responsible academic discourse and student life. Yet some charged that tolerance could not be fostered by intolerance of intolerance. In terms of legality, the speech codes were a target for First Amendment challenges, and a number of the codes were declared unconstitutional.

Student expression through campus newspapers also has been subject to regulation. Obscene words and photographs in student-run, university-funded publications have long been restricted. Beginning in the 1960's those restrictions slackened but did not cease to be. In an atmosphere of what critics call political correctness, student groups and university authorities have attempted to regulate letters to the editor, political cartoons, editorials, and even news stories deemed to be offensive to racial, ethnic, and other groups. When those efforts have failed, some have resorted to confiscating newspapers from campus distribution points. Such vigilante censorship has not been affirmed by the courts.

Student demonstrations and protests pose another aspect of the censorship issue. From medieval times, students have led frequently disruptive, sometimes violent protests opposing governmental authorities and criticizing social mores. Although similar protests could well take place off college campuses, attention to campus protests is heightened by the image of the university as a generator of new ideas and a challenger of the status quo. Traditionally universities have enjoyed a broad latitude in addressing student demonstrations, adopting individual policies and procedures outlining permissible times, places, and means of protest. More broadly, for many years in the United States, the principle of *in loco parentis* authorized universities to restrict a range of student actions and behaviors. When the age of majority was lowered to eighteen in all states, however, *in loco parentis* no longer applied to most university students. University efforts to regulate the frequent student demonstrations during the 1960's and 1970's concerning the Vietnam War, civil rights, legalization of drugs, and other issues thus became more difficult. In general the courts held that violent or destructive behavior, trespassing, and the like were not constitutionally protected forms of expression; the First Amendment specifically allows, however, peaceful protest gatherings.

By the 1980's and 1990's the image of radical student protesters on American campuses was fading as students became more complacent. Different reactions to student protests could be found elsewhere in the world. In some countries, such as France, student protests remained common and generally tolerated. In other countries, such as the People's Republic of China, students pressed the limits of governmental tolerance to the breaking point, unleashing murderous state-sponsored crackdowns.

There are, of course, more subtle means of censoring student views. Since faculty possess power in the form of assigning grades, students might experience pressure not to challenge a professor's personal views in discussions and on examinations. Such was clearly the case in some countries ruled by ideological elites. In the Soviet Union, for example, Marxist-Leninist ideology was treated as scientific truth; believing otherwise could be construed as evidence that a student did not properly understand course material. Some dissidents were declared insane and placed in asylums.

Censoring Texts, Curriculum, and Research. Along with public libraries, elementary schools, and bookstores, universities have been a battleground for the debate over book censorship. Particularly controversial has been the assignment of required texts. The authority of a textbook, promoted as required reading by a professor or administration, heightens its influence. It is critical, therefore, that textbooks be accurate in their presentation of facts. In some disciplines especially, however, there is debate over facts, interpretations, and theories. Even the most venerable interpretations can have their critics. Controversies and censorship cases have arisen over how textbooks handle such issues.

In Western countries, text selection decisions have been made by university officials, either individual faculty members, departmental committees, or administrators. Selection has been seen as a matter of university autonomy, and outside forces seldom have been brought to bear. The tools of textbook censorship have not been entirely within the hands of the universities. Publishing houses decide what shall be included in their products. Market forces influence the type and content of texts offered, but ultimate editorial responsibility is not in the hands of the universities. Textbook selection therefore amounts to choosing from among several options, none of which might include the precise information or discussions desired by university officials.

At times universities have been charged with abusing their autonomy, and calls for some form of self-policing or greater regulation of textbook selection have arisen. In the United States during the 1960's and 1970's the university establishment came under attack. Arguing for a goal of balance, critics claimed the exclusion of certain points of view on topics such as evolution, militarism, and civil rights was systemic, amounting to censorship. Others opposed as paternalistic the exclusion of books for their use of vulgar words. Western countries came generally to accept the principle that no relevant views on controversial topics should be systematically excluded from university curricula. Textbooks including unorthodox views were adopted, and reading lists were expanded.

By the late twentieth century, however, calls arose in Western universities for a different kind of censorship. Coming largely from the political left, some have charged that certain depictions in literature and history, particularly depictions of racial and ethnic groups, perpetuate stereotypes and deserve to be eradicated from the curriculum. Sections of introductory textbooks, as well as a whole body of classic works by authors such as Mark Twain and Rudyard Kipling, have been held up as examples of racist works that only perpetuate bigotry. Increasingly, a multicultural approach was advocated in all areas of learning, especially the liberal arts.

In studies of literature, in which there is so much more that may be read than what can be read, the debate over what to include also entails a debate about what to drop. Some charge that the exclusion of certain perspectives or cultures in curricula amounts to censorship. In the social sciences, analogous debates have arisen over the teaching of perspectives such as feminism, radical environmentalism, or Afrocentrism. The resistance of mainstream departments to such perspectives, it is claimed, amounts to institutionalized censorship.

As one way of escaping this alleged censorship of certain theories and ideologies, some have sought to establish separate institutional bases within the universities. Women's studies, African American studies, Chicano studies, peace studies, and a variety of other academic departments and programs have been created to provide a forum for ideas and topics that some feel are systematically excluded from the academic mainstream. Even then, however, charges of censorship and discrimination are not necessarily eliminated. Resources (including faculty positions, office space, and budgets) may not be allocated equally among departments and programs. Whether this amounts to discrimination or censorship remains a subject of debate.

Curricula, research programs, and other aspects of universities are indirectly subject to another level of regulation through the accreditation process. Accreditation agencies use a variety of criteria to evaluate the performance of university programs. Traditionally such factors as the percentage of faculty with Ph.D.'s, number of classroom hours required for the conferral of a degree, and classroom equipment might enter into the accreditation decision. Toward the end of the twentieth century, various accreditation agencies increasingly applied standards less directly associated with instructional quality: retention rates of nonwhite students or percentage of nonwhite and female faculty, for example. Some universities have complained that such standards are irrelevant to the quality of education, and thus are an unacceptable infringement on university autonomy. Although most accrediting agencies in the United States are not governmental bodies, being denied accreditation can significantly harm a program's reputation and thus enrollment.

Public and Private Universities. The autonomy of universities is a tradition dating to medieval times. The precise degree of autonomy for a particular university is partly a function of whether it is public or private. Other things being equal, private universities are freer to make their own decisions regarding curriculum, hiring of faculty, codes of conduct, and other concerns. Private universities avoid the conditions that might be attached to state funding, and they avoid regulations and legal provisions that apply to agencies of the state. Private universities with religious affiliations, for example, might require student and faculty attendance at religious services, make signed pledges of conduct a condition for hiring or admission, or restrict administration positions to persons of certain faiths. Similarly, private universities with a mission to educate a particular racial group might restrict admissions and hiring to members of that group. Scholarships might be based exclusively upon race, ethnicity, or other factors.

At a public university, these practices could be, and have been, challenged as discriminatory. Many of them also could be construed as censoring particular points of view. This is not to say that private universities necessarily engage in censorship more frequently or more intrusively than their public counterparts; rather, the legal standards for private universities tend to be more lax.

Censorship works in both directions. While private universities have a broader latitude in matters of censorship, they are less subject to potential censorship from the state. In other words, public universities might construe some of the regulations and requirements placed upon them by the state to be an infringement upon academic freedom. This is especially true for public universities in countries whose governments are controlled by ideological elites.

Many of the broad range of censorship issues are experienced by universities, including the regulation of books, speech, and ideas; firing and expulsion as a means of censorship; constitutional questions; religious and secular heresy; and others. What makes these issues especially salient for the university is its presumed dual role as guardian and critic of a civilization's acquired knowledge.　　*—Steve D. Boilard*

See also Campus speech codes; Ethnic studies; Free Speech Movement; Intellectual freedom; Jeffries, Leonard, Jr.; Loyalty oaths; Multiculturalism; Newspapers, student; Scholarships; Yaqzan, Matan, affair.

Bibliography

Conrad Russell's *Academic Freedom* (New York: Routledge, 1993) examines the debate over the United Kingdom's Education Reform Bill of 1988. A different historical perspective is offered by Byron K. Marshall's *Academic Freedom and the Japanese Imperial University, 1868-1939* (Berkeley: University of California Press, 1992). This book examines attempts by the Japanese government to censor and dismiss

faculty who criticize government policy. A chapter on official regulation of speech on American college campuses appears in Annette Gibbs's *Reconciling Rights and Responsibilities of Colleges and Students: Offensive Speech, Assembly, Drug Testing, and Safety* (Washington, D.C.: School of Education and Human Development, George Washington University, ASHE-ERIC Higher Education Report, 1992). *The Courts and Higher Education* (San Francisco: Jossey-Bass, 1971), by John S. Brubacher, includes analysis of censorship from a legal standpoint. Ulysses V. Spiva's *Legal Outlook: A Message to College and University People* (Saratoga, Calif.: Century Twenty One Publishing, 1981) reviews a range of legal decisions concerning American colleges and universities during the 1970's. For an analysis of censorship of research, see Donna A. Demac's *Liberty Denied: The Current Rise of Censorship in America* (New Brunswick, N.J.: Rutgers University Press, 1990).

Unprotected speech

Definition: Forms of expression not protected by the First Amendment to the U.S. Constitution

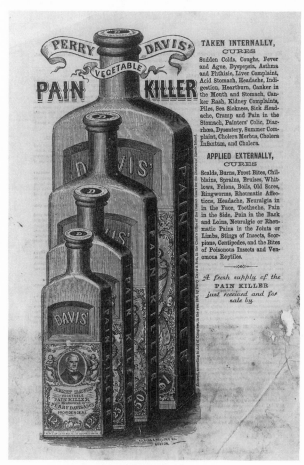

Exaggerated claims for products such as this early twentieth century "pain killer" contributed to the American view that commercial speech did not need constitutional protection. (Library of Congress)

SIGNIFICANCE: The U.S. Supreme Court established the unprotected speech category as a means to censor offensive or harmful speech

Although the First Amendment to the U.S. Constitution protects freedom of speech, not all forms of speech have constitutional protection. Political and some kinds of action (symbolic speech) have First Amendment protection, but the U.S. Supreme Court has ruled that some speech does not merit any constitutional protection because it contributes nothing to the robust debate the First Amendment is designed to foster. The types of expression that fall under the unprotected speech category are obscenity, fighting words, and false advertising.

The U.S. Supreme Court has supported censorship as necessary to protect public morality based on the belief that obscene publications lie outside the realm of ideas protected by the First Amendment. Significant debate has occurred about what defines obscenity. Fighting words do not have any First Amendment protection because the courts have found them to be so offensive that they are the equivalent to a person throwing the first punch in a fight. Thus, fighting words are those words or expressions that can be expected to bring about immediate injury or criminal acts. At one time advertising was among the categories of speech excluded from constitutional protection, but truthful commercial speech now enjoys some constitutional protection from government censorship. If the advertisement contains false information, however, then that form of commercial speech falls in the unprotected speech category.

See also Advertising as the target of censorship; Commercial speech; Fighting words; First Amendment; Obscenity: legal definitions; Offensive language.

Utopia

TYPE OF WORK: Book

PUBLISHED: 1516

AUTHOR: Sir Thomas More (1478-1535)

SUBJECT MATTER: Description of an imaginary ideal and unchanging society that owns everything communally

SIGNIFICANCE: When *Utopia* was first published, it was attacked for encouraging republican tendencies; in modern times it has been criticized for appealing to supporters of communist and other collectivist ideologies

In response both to the ideals of Renaissance humanism and the New World discoveries, Thomas More described an idealized, imaginary commonwealth in his most famous book, *Utopia*, which was first published in Latin in December, 1516. Utopia is the name of a highly authoritarian society that suppresses individualism and private property to secure the collective good. While the assertion of individual will is frowned upon in the imaginary Utopia, freedom of thought—but not of expression—is regarded as the chief happiness of life. Although the citizens of Utopia are encouraged to read, idleness is forbidden and hard work is strictly enforced by the state's agents, the syphogrants. Books that encourage citizens to engage in individualism or religious heresy or which threaten the stability of the Utopian system would presumably be suppressed. As England's chancellor under King Henry VIII, More led the efforts to suppress heretics, in the belief that heresy led to sedition and civil disorder. In *Utopia*, however, More playfully imagined a society which remained stable by restricting individualist tendencies to the minds of its citizens.

See also *Areopagitica*; Henry VIII; Latimer, Hugh; Milton, John.

V

Valachi Papers, The

TYPE OF WORK: Book

PUBLISHED: 1968

AUTHOR : Peter Maas (1929-   )

SUBJECT MATTER: Criminal activities of the Mafia

SIGNIFICANCE: The U.S. Justice Department's suppression of a criminal informant's memoirs led to Maas's publication of this third-person account

In 1964 Joseph Valachi (1904-1971), a Mafia informant, was urged by the U.S. Department of Justice to write a personal history of his underworld career with the so-called Cosa Nostra. Although Valachi was only expected to fill in the gaps in his formal questioning, the resulting account of his thirty-year criminal career was a nearly twelve-hundred-page manuscript.

In 1965 U.S. attorney general Nicholas Katzenbach authorized the public release of Valachi's manuscript, and gave author Peter Maas the job of editing the huge manuscript after he broke Valachi's story in *The Saturday Evening Post*. Katzenbach believed that publication of Valachi's story would aid law enforcement and possibly encourage other criminal informers to step forward.

In response to the book's pending publication, the Italian American newspaper *Il Progresso* denounced the book on the grounds that it would reinforce negative ethnic stereotypes. The American Italian Anti-Defamation Council then promoted a national campaign against the book, claiming the issue to be a civil rights matter. The Justice Department met with an Italian American delegation demanding that if the book's publication was not stopped they would appeal directly to the White House. Katzenbach reversed his decision on the book after a meeting with President Lyndon B. Johnson, in an action that embarrassed the Justice Department. On May 10, 1966, Katzenbach asked a district court to stop Maas from publishing the book—the first time that a U.S. attorney general had ever tried to ban a book.

Although Maas was never permitted to publish his edition of Valachi's original memoirs, he was allowed to publish a third-person account based upon interviews he himself had conducted. These formed the basis of *The Valachi Papers*, which Putnam published in 1968.

See also *Crossman Diaries*; Freedom of Information Act; *Pentagon Papers, The*; Presidency, U.S.; Prior restraint.

Vatican

DESCRIPTION: The center of the worldwide Roman Catholic church, the Vatican is an independent nation although it physically is only a tiny enclave within Rome, Italy

SIGNIFICANCE: As the official headquarters of Roman Catholicism, the Vatican makes the ultimate decisions concerning church censorship of print and nonprint materials, as well as issues of contraception, divorce, and priest celibacy

The headquarters of the Roman Catholic church is an independent state located within the city of Rome. Saint Peter's Basilica is the principal church of the Roman Catholic world. The city's civil administration is overseen by the Papal Commission for Vatican City. Canonic law is enacted by ecclesiastic authority to regulate church discipline. Vatican City and the Holy See are distinct entities; however, they are united in the person of the pope who is a head of state and is considered to be an infallible leader by Roman Catholics.

During the Middle Ages the Church established Canon Law and papal control over Western Christian nations. In the early sixteenth century Martin Luther led the Protestant Reformation against papal authority, the sacrificial nature of the mass, and the cult of the Virgin Mary. The Council of Trent (1545-1563) convened as a Counter-Reformation measure, and the council instituted the *Index Librorum Prohibitorum*, the official Vatican list of banned books, in 1559. While the council took steps to address abuses in the Church, it refused concessions to the Protestants and codified Catholic dogma. Tradition and Scripture were declared sources of spiritual knowledge with the Church as the sole interpreter of the Bible. Priest celibacy was maintained.

Vatican Council I (1869-1870) affirmed papal infallibility and reacted against modernism. In the 1920's concordatas (agreements) with several nations, especially in Latin America, ensured Catholic spiritual authority in these countries. Issues addressed by Vatican II (1962-1965) included the church in the modern world, the ministry and life of priests, the role of the laity, Christian education, and religious freedom. The *Index* ceased publication in 1966.

Catholic doctrine is based on the New Testament; the pope and bishops develop guidelines on doctrinal issues, as well as social justice and human rights. Censorship concerns involve print and nonprint materials, contraception, divorce, and priest celibacy. Some of these issues are decreed in Canon Law and implemented by Vatican councils.

Canon Law. Canon Law is the body of legislation (canons) that regulates the Roman Catholic church. In the twelfth century a Benedictine monk, Gratian, compiled the first systematic collection of canon law, based on papal decrees and the proclamation of synods. The Council of Trent laid the canonical foundation for church reform and codification. and further revision of church laws was put into effect in 1918. Pope John XXIII (1958-1963) initiated the modernization of the Code of Canon Law. Pope Paul VI (1963-1978) continued the task in consultation with world experts in social science and theology. A new draft of the code was completed in 1978.

Censorship Issues. According to canonic law, the Church has the right to censor by virtue of natural law and supernatural mission. The Catholic viewpoint is that the law is to be loved because it is rational and its origin is from God, and thus, it is the right and duty of the Church and society to exercise coercion for the good of the people. Freedom, in the Catholic view, is the freedom to act as one ought to, according to the reasonableness of the law.

Catholicism's concern for a balance between freedom of inquiry and purity of doctrine is documented in the *Index Librorum Prohibitorum*. The Council of Trent codified church regulations on book censorship and the first official *Index* was published in 1559. After Vatican I, a revised *Index* (of ten rules) was officially published in 1900. In 1948 the last edition of *Index Librorum Prohibitorum* was issued. After Vatican II the *Index* was declared primarily a historical document, with the new regulations emphasizing the positive value of books. Bishops are responsible for cooperating with authors and publishers to ensure that the church remains the custodian of divine revelation and the interpreter of the teachings of Christ. Catholic view of censorship also applies to other materials, such as films and television. Prior to Vatican II, community priests used to edit or expurgate objectionable portions of films, such as *Bitter Rice* (1953), before public viewing. Canon 1385, for example, addresses "censura praevia" (prior censorship); Catholic authors (clerics or lay) may not publish materials dealing with issues of faith and morals without permission from the diocesan bishop. An example of church censorship involved Galileo, who was tried by the Inquisition on suspicion of heresy because his scientific views were disputed by the Church. Galileo's *Dialogue* was banned and printers were forbidden to publish anything by him.

Although the Church has reserved the right to censor materials that are deliberately against Catholic theology, dogma, and moral teachings, canon 19 states that "laws which decree a penalty, or restrict the free exercise of one's rights . . . are subject to strict interpretation." This means that laws are not to be extended to other cases, but must be interpreted according to the meaning of the words. The Church has legislative, executive, and judicial authority as the divinely appointed carrier of Jesus Christ's revelation and of Christian morals.

—*Maria A. Pacino*

See also Christianity; *Index Librorum Prohibitorum*; Italy; Lateran Council, Fourth; Paul IV, Pope; Reformation, the; Spanish Inquisition.

BIBLIOGRAPHY

Adrian Hastings, ed., *Modern Catholicism: Vatican II and After* (New York: Oxford University Press, 1991), provides an authoritative guide to the Catholic church in the twenty-five years after the Second Vatican Council. Richard P. McBrien's *Catholicism* (Minneapolis, Minn.: Winston Press, 1980) provides a balanced and comprehensive historical perspective on the Catholic church with extensive notes and a glossary of terms. John L. McKenzie's *The Roman Catholic Church* (Garden City, N.Y.: Image Books, 1971) depicts a comprehensive, historical survey of the Catholic church and the implications for Catholics and Catholicism. Claud D. Nelson's *The Vatican Council and All Christians* (New York: Association Press, 1962) provides an interpretation of Vatican II—its goals, significance, and influences in pluralistic societies.

Venus de Milo

TYPE OF WORK: Sculpture
DATE: Created around 130 B.C.E.; discovered in 1820
SCULPTOR: Unknown
SUBJECT MATTER: Marble statue of the goddess of love and beauty from Greek and Roman mythology
SIGNIFICANCE: This sculpture has been subjected to censorship efforts because of its nude torso

Venus de Milo, the armless sculpture of the Greek love goddess, Aphrodite, received its modern name when it was discovered by a Greek peasant on the island of Milos. Fragments of arms and a pedestal were found at the same time, but have since disappeared. Since then the statue has been a victim of numerous censorship attempts, primarily because of its nudity. It is clothed only in a towel draped about its hips. In 1853, for example, a reproduction of Venus de Milo was tried for nudity in Mannheim, Germany, and was condemned. March, 1911, brought further criticism when Alderman John Sullivan of Buffalo, New York, wanted a copy of the statue covered or removed from public view. The 1920's found a reproduction of Venus on Palmolive soap labels, but with a white patch across its breasts. Hungarian police banned its picture from store windows around this same time.

In 1852 the Cyprus Tourist Office used the Venus on travel posters it sent to Kuwait. Kuwait's Sheik Abdullah al Salimal Sebah banned the posters because the figure lacked arms. The sheik was concerned that Kuwaitis would assume that Cypriot women were all hardened criminals when they saw the mutilated female figure. Censorship continued into 1955 when Indiana firemen discovered a full-scale replica of Venus covered with a robe of poison ivy. A midwestern shopping mall refused to allow Venus de Milo to be displayed in shop window in the early 1990's.

See also Art; Michelangelo; Nudity.

Venus in the Cloister: Or, the Nun in Her Smock

TYPE OF WORK: Book
PUBLISHED: 1683
AUTHOR: Jean Barrin(?)
SUBJECT MATTER: Imaginary dialogues between two teenage nuns discussing their sexuality
SIGNIFICANCE: Publication of this book in England contributed to the redefinition of obscene libel as a crime under common law, rather than ecclesiastical law

Originally published in Paris as *Venus dans le cloitre, ou, la religieuse en chemise* by a senior French clergyman, this short novel contains conversations between two nuns who believe that their religious devotion and sexual pleasure should be combined. The book says little about the nuns' own sexual activity; its purpose was to point out that religious orders were political establishments and that they did not truly follow the teachings of Christ.

The book gained its notoriety after it was translated into English and published in London in 1724 by Edmund Curll, who was notorious for publishing obscene books. Justices of the King's Bench had been looking for a reason to incarcerate

Curll and saw his publication of *Venus in the Cloister* as a large enough offense. The justices had difficulty in prosecuting Curll due to a discussion by Queen Anne, a few years earlier. She had dismissed another case involving a writer charged with publishing obscenity. The King's Bench decided to pursue the case as a civil, not religious, case declaring that Curll's publication was an offense against the peace, that intended to weaken the bonds of civil society and morality. This action set the precedent for prosecuting future pornography cases under common law.

See also Obscene Publications Acts; Obscenity: legal definitions; Printing; United Kingdom.

Vesalius, Andreas

BORN: December 31, 1514, Brussels, Spanish Netherlands
DIED: October 15, 1564, Zacynthus (Zákinthos), Greece
IDENTIFICATION: Flemish anatomist and physician
SIGNIFICANCE: As the author of groundbreaking works in anatomy, Vesalius exemplified self-censorship in the face of controversy and plagiarism

Andries van Wesel, known by his Latinized name Andreas Vesalius, was born into a family strongly associated with medicine. His father was apothecary to the Holy Roman emperor Charles V and at an early age he also decided to pursue a medical vocation. He studied at the universities of Louvain, Paris, and Padua. After receiving a doctorate in medicine at Padua in 1537, he joined the faculty there. While lecturing on human anatomy, he insisted on conducting his own dissections rather than turning them over to an assistant, which was then common practice.

His pioneering work in the dissection of human cadavers— often those of executed criminals—changed the field of anatomy profoundly. This, along with his detailed illustrations and careful descriptions, has led many to regard him as the "father of anatomy." His major work, *De humani corporis fabrica libri septem* (1543; *The Seven Books on the Structure of the Human Body*), the world's first comprehensive anatomy textbook, provoked widespread criticism initially. One of his greatest critics was Jacobus Sylvius (Jacques Dubois), his former professor at Paris who had originally encouraged him to study anatomy. Departing from the Galenic traditions on which anatomical studies had been based for thirteen centuries, Vesalius boldly declared that human anatomy could only be learned through dissection and observation. His opponents soon found that in order to refute him, they would need to pursue the same sort of practical and methodical studies he had. Others noted his significance, copied, and in some cases physically stole his charts, writings, and illustrations. Plagiarism of his work by others appears to have been a problem throughout his career. Frustrated by this state of affairs, he renounced anatomical studies.

With great misgivings, Vesalius chose to change his career by becoming the royal physician of Charles V and on the emperor's abdication served his son and heir, Philip II. Serving periodically as a military surgeon allowed Vesalius occasionally to pursue further anatomical research and proved to be some relief from treating the complaints of the high living

royal court. In 1564, wealthy but unsatisfied, he was permitted to make a pilgrimage to the Holy Land. On his way through Italy, he sought and was awarded his old chair at Padua, despite the fact that imperial service could not be abandoned once begun. However, he died on the Ionian island of Zákinthos on his return voyage.

The study of anatomy has been subjected to censorship and control throughout history, but Vesalius was fortunate in living in a period when such research was acceptable. His work was part of the humanistic revival of ancient learning that characterized his time. However, it went beyond mere copying of Greek and Roman learning. The thorough curiosity and disciplined inquiry that characterized Vesalius' career led to medicine becoming a learned and respected profession. By the dawn of the seventeenth century, Vesalian anatomy had received both academic and wider public acceptance. However, the narrow-minded and dishonest conduct of his colleagues and contemporaries clearly led him to suppress what could have been even greater genius.

See also Darwin, Charles; Film adaptation; Medical research; Science.

Video games

DEFINITION: Any games played on a microchip-controlled device, whether on a closed platform, personal computer, or coin-operated system
SIGNIFICANCE: As the technology and realism of the burgeoning multibillion-dollar video game industry have developed, concerns over the content of games and children's access to them have increased

With the introduction of Atari's game Pong in 1976, video games showed dramatic increase in popularity as a major recreational medium. Over the following two decades what had been first considered a fad grew into a multibillion-dollar-a-year industry in the United States alone. Meanwhile, the technology of the games had improved, transforming the games from the black-and-white block paddles of Pong to fully digitized interactive films.

As technology and the realism of the newer graphics increased, concern grew over violence, profanity, and sexual content found in this previously unrated and largely unrestricted medium. Many groups felt that violence in the entertainment media was responsible for increased violence in society. They felt that video games in particular would have a stronger effect on children's aggression because of its interactive nature. On the other side, publishers contended that their games should have as much protection under freedom of speech as other forms of media. They also asserted that video games were not being played only by children—especially games played on computers, the overwhelming majority of which were owned by adults.

Congressional Investigations. Between December, 1993, and July, 1994, three joint U.S. Congressional hearings were held on the violent content in video games. They were presided over by Democratic senator Herb Kohl of Wisconsin, chairman of the Subcommittee on Juvenile Justice, and Democratic senator Joseph I. Lieberman of Connecticut, chairman of the Subcommittee on Regulation and Government Information. These committees heard panels from both the industry and from concerned groups about content in video games. A statement on a bill to be proposed as the Video Game Rating Act of 1994 was also submitted. The act called for Congress to create the Interactive Entertainment Rating Commission, which would supervise an industry "voluntary" rating system. If the commission deemed this rating system unacceptable, it would install its own system. The idea of a government council approving material in this new medium, and forcing products to be labeled prior to their publication, was felt to be a violation of the First Amendment as a form of prior restraint. Defenders of the video games felt this bill submitted at the hearings was an ultimatum, and in itself a violation as it acted as a chilling effect on the industry with the threat of future legislation.

The senators aired excerpts from two controversial games, the popular Mortal Kombat (1993) and Night Trap (1993). Mortal Kombat, a martial arts combat game, features much bloodletting and finishing moves, such as ripping an opponent's heart out or removing his head and spinal cord. The even more controversial Night Trap features digitized films of live actors. In one of its scenes, vampires use a drill to drain the blood from a scantily clad girl's neck. Video game defenders felt that Lieberman's remark that Night Trap "ought not to be available to people in our society" was a direct attack on freedom of speech. Lieberman also twice asked why the game was not simply pulled from store shelves. The majority of both consumers and members of the industry agreed, however, that a rating system at least was needed. The industry representatives agreed to develop such a system and inform the subcommittees of their progress.

Following the December, 1993, session of hearings, Robert S. Peck submitted a statement on behalf of the American Civil Liberties Union (ACLU) that made several major points: For example, neither "sexually suggestive" nor "violent" expression should be singled out for restrictive legislative treatment. Further, the ACLU argued that requiring warning labels on expressive materials would violate the First Amendment, and that any such attempt could not overcome vagueness and overbreadth problems. The constitutional infirmities of this legislation were compounded by its impending threat of government regulation if the industry did not act acceptably. The ACLU also charged that the effort to label video games constituted a diversion from the problem of real violence in society. The ACLU compared the government ultimatum to *Bantam Books v. Sullivan* (1963), a case in which the U.S. Supreme Court found that seizure, banning, and prosecution were not necessary to constitute a violation of the First Amendment. The mere "threat of invoking legal sanctions and other means of coercion, persuasion, and intimidation" was a violation that produced a chilling effect. In the conclusion, the ACLU statement referred to the Court's *Erznoznik v. Jacksonville* (1975) decision, which stated that "the values protected by the first amendment are no less applicable when government seeks to control the flow of information to minors."

Divisions Within the Industry. The video game industry can be divided into three groups: closed-platform game systems, personal computer-based games, and coin-operated games. International Digital Software Association (IDSA), which represented the closed-platform cartridge and CD game systems, and the Software Publishers Association (SPA), which represented many personal computer platform software publishers, proposed to establish separate rating systems. The IDSA established the Entertainment Software Rating Board (ESRB). Available to all manufacturers, regardless of whether they were IDSA members, this board established a rating system for video games: EC (early childhood: ages three-six); K-A (kids to adults: ages six and up); T (teenagers); M (mature: ages seventeen and up); and AO (adults only: age eighteen and above).

The SPA, however, was not able to reconcile its own concerns about the new IDSA rating board. Its members feared that the ESRB might favor IDSA members' products. Also, they argued that the five-hundred-dollar fees charged for rating products were excessive for the many small publishers in the SPA. SPA publishers, especially shareware creators, included educators, new mothers, and other professionals who wrote programs in their spare time and might not gross as much as the fee it took to submit to the ESRB. The SPA, in cooperation with similar groups, instead created an entirely independent organization, the Recreational Software Advisory Council (RSAC), whose rating system differed from that of the ESRB in two important ways. First, applicants must only submit a filled out questionnaire on the content of the games. Second, RSAC did not adopt an age-based rating system but rather a content-based label. The label introduced the use of three thermometers each having values from one to four for content: violence, nudity/sex, and language. Products rated 0 in all three categories would receive separate labels indicating that their material is suitable for all audiences. Both the RSAC and the ESRB systems included economic reprisals in case of falsification of submissions.

The third group, the coin-operated games, were represented by the American Amusement Machine Association (AAMA). They worked closely with the IDSA to develop the latter's rating proposal. The problem with the coin-op based systems is that there is no practical way to enforce age limitations on arcade game players—a problem similar to stopping minors from buying cigarettes from coin machines. The AAMA did, however, promise to put advisory labels on their machines for parents' information. —*John Victor Heilker*

See also American Civil Liberties Union; Hays Code; Internet; Motion Picture Association of America; Prior restraint.

BIBLIOGRAPHY

The most pertinent publications on this rapidly changing subject can be found in periodical literature. For example, Michael D. Lemonick, "Erotic Electronic Encounters," *Time* (September 23, 1991), discusses the booming market in games with sexual content and the calls for product labeling. Useful overviews of the issues considered by the IDSA and SPA when they began developing product ratings include Graeme Browning, "Just Say No," *National Journal* (March 19, 1994), and Robin Raskin, "The Rating Game," *PC Magazine* (October 25, 1994). "Guidelines for the Gameboys," *Harper's*

Magazine (December, 1994), summarizes the RSAC's rating guidelines. A summary of the U.S. Senate hearings on video games was published in *Rating Video Games: A Parent's Guide to Games* (Washington, D.C.: Government Printing Office, 1995).

Vietnam

DESCRIPTION: Independent Southeast Asian nation reunified in 1975

SIGNIFICANCE: From the French colonial period to the war between the north and south that led to unification and communist rule, censorship has been used by every regime—colonial, republican, and communist—as a tool to enforce government control

The Vietnam War has been called the first uncensored war in American history. From the time that U.S. forces were dispatched to the Southeast Asian country in the early 1960's to the fall of Saigon in 1975, combat correspondents were given free reign to follow troops, enter hostile areas, and report from the battlefield. While correspondents working for U.S. media could broadcast and write about the political and military situation, and even question the legitimacy of the war, Vietnamese media on the two opposing sides, the north and the south, faced severe restrictions. The republican Saigon government and the communist government in Hanoi controlled the press to discourage dissent and criticism, and to sway public opinion to their respective sides. It is an irony that U.S. correspondents had more freedom in a foreign land than the nationals covering a bitter war that tore apart their homeland. Censorship of the Vietnamese media can be traced to the 1880's when the French introduced newspapers and magazines to Vietnam.

French Colonialism. The French solidified their control of Vietnam in the latter half of the nineteenth century. They published newspapers in the 1880's for colonials and their families to keep them abreast of French affairs and news within Vietnam. The idea caught on among Vietnamese nationals and within the next decade Vietnamese began publishing their own periodicals and newspapers, which often criticized French rule. The French had no tolerance of any Vietnamese questioning their authority or right to rule. Such criticism triggered censorship by a colonial administration that dismissed the notion of freedom of the press, although the French considered colonialism as a *mission civilisatrice* to enlighten backward nations about liberty. The French wanted Vietnamese newspapers and periodicals to popularize French culture and to promote harmonious colonial life. What the French permitted and sought were collaborationist newspapers that disseminated official statements and communiqués from the French authorities and Vietnamese imperial government ciphers. This set the stage for an ideological rather than an objective press, a press that served as an organ of government, rather than a voice of the people. The repression extended to literature in times of civil distress.

During World War II when Japanese forces attacked and occupied Vietnam, the French and Japanese governments clamped down on all periodicals and books published in Viet-

namese. When the French left Vietnam after their historic defeat at Dienbienphu on May 7, 1954, the two governments that were formed in the aftermath of French colonialism, the authoritarian republic in the south and the communist regime in the north, continued the French precedent of controlling the media and repressing free expression. Censorship became part of the legacy of French rule.

Republic of South Vietnam. The newly formed republic in 1954 wasted no time in shackling the press. The government adopted an old French decree that provided for prepublication review and censorship of the press. Government officials screened newspapers and as an additional threat controlled the distribution of newsprint. In 1957 the government of Ngo Dinh Diem issued orders for newspapers to deliver to the Ministry of Information two copies of each newspaper before publication. Furthermore, mobs attacked offices of newspapers known to be critical of the government. Diem extended his hard-line rule to ban all dancing, including folk dancing, and, in 1963, outlawed sentimental songs as detrimental to the war effort. After Diem was assassinated in 1963, subsequent governments continued to suppress the free exchange of ideas. Most of the problems were with newspapers because the government controlled the airwaves, including the one Vietnamese television network. Pro-Buddhist newspapers were confiscated in 1964, and a year later the government of Nguyen Cao Ky attempted to close all Vietnamese-language newspapers for a month. It became common to see large blank spaces on the pages of many Vietnamese-language newspapers because the censors removed the stories. But such tactics backfired because of the presence of a large, foreign press corps. Vietnamese reporters, often working for U.S. news agencies, tipped off American reporters about stories Vietnamese could never publish. Once the stories were broken by the world press, and broadcast on Voice of America and British Broadcasting Corporation (BBC) radio, the government had a difficult time withholding the information.

Democratic Republic of North Vietnam. The Vietnamese Communist Party has historically used the press as a propaganda tool and an organ in the fight to reunite the country. Communist ideology viewed the press as an instrument to serve the party. The party thus exercised tight control over all forms of media, including newspapers, film, and radio broadcasts. Only information approved by party censors is disseminated to the people; Vietnamese must listen to BBC or Voice of America broadcasting to gain other perspectives about the world. The North Vietnamese also reined in writers and intellectuals, purging newspapers of their ranks and prohibiting their works from being published. Such policies continued after the unification of Vietnam in 1975. Following the defeat of South Vietnam, military officers, government officials, and members of the intelligentsia, including actors, artists, journalists, writers, poets, publishers, and producers were forced to labor in reeducation camps for a period ranging from three months to more than fifteen years. Communist Party cadres held indoctrination sessions in the camps to prepare members of the old society for life in the socialist republic. The north maintained strict control over the south, which had been conditioned by French colonialism and twenty years of authoritarian rule to government control of the press and freedom of expression. Professor Jacqueline Debarats of the Australian National University reported that the first significant act of repression after the fall of Saigon was the burning of four million works in the Khai Tri publishing house. Religious institutions also came under attack. Buddhist, Catholic, and Protestant leaders have been arrested, sent to reeducation camps, or confined to house arrest. Seminaries have been closed and temples, pagodas, and other places of worship destroyed. Although Vietnam initiated free-market reforms in 1986, the Communist Party retains tight control over political affairs and has yet to liberalize restrictions on the press. The U.S.-based Freedom Forum Foundation of the Gannett Newspaper chain has been hampered by the government in its efforts to provide professional training for Vietnamese journalists. Programs to be led by Western journalists have been canceled, and Vietnamese journalists have been unable to obtain visas to study in the United States. Vietnam, which wants so much to modernize, even fears the Internet. Government officials worry that if they allow citizens access to the World Wide Web, they will be exposed to the same type of uncensored information from Western correspondents that they received during the war. —*Jeffrey Brody*

See also Burma; China; Communism; France; Indonesia; My Lai massacre; News media censorship; Police states; Vietnam War.

BIBLIOGRAPHY

Maurice M. Durand and Nguyen Tran Huan's *An Introduction to Vietnamese Literature*, trans. by D. M. Hawke (New York: Columbia University Press, 1985), discusses the development of the Vietnamese press in the nineteenth century and gives a detailed account of the newspapers during the French colonial era and the years of the Vietnam War. Harvey H. Smith et al., *Area Handbook for South Vietnam* (Washington, D.C.: U.S. Government Printing Office, 1967), is a comprehensive guide to the policies of the Republic of South Vietnam, with a section on press censorship. Bernard Fall's *The Two Viet-Nams* (New York: Frederick A. Praeger, 1963) explains the social structures of the two regions of the country. For a discussion of censorship and political repression after the Vietnam War, see Nguyen Van Canh's *Vietnam Under Communism, 1975-1982* (Stanford, Calif.: Hoover Institution Press, 1983), and Thai Quang Trung, ed., *Vietnam Today: Assessing the New Trends* (New York: Crane Russak, 1990).

Vietnam War

DATE: ca. 1961-1975
PLACE: Southeast Asia; Washington, D.C.
SIGNIFICANCE: This was the first large-scale military conflict closely covered on television; the relative absence of censorship controls was blamed by many for the failure of the U.S. military effort

After the United States defeat in the Vietnam War, a debate arose over the role played by newspaper and television reporters in that war. Censorship of the media by the United States government was undoubtedly less strict than in some earlier wars. Whether this relative absence of censorship was responsible for the American defeat in Vietnam has, however, been hotly disputed.

Contrasts with World War II. Because World War II began with a formal declaration of war, an Office of Censorship was set up almost immediately after the Japanese bombing of Pearl Harbor in December, 1941. Censors had to approve what appeared concerning the war in print (including combat photographs) and in motion picture newsreels. The American public was spared revelations about bungling or atrocities by the American military, although incidents of both occurred. Government censorship was supplemented by journalists' self-censorship; war correspondents believed it was their patriotic duty to help build up homefront morale. In contrast, the Vietnam War was an undeclared war, in which large numbers of American combat troops did not see action until 1965. Unlike in World War II, there were no war-bond drives, featuring stars of the entertainment world, to arouse homefront enthusiasm for the war and hatred for the enemy; nor was there an Office of Censorship.

During World War II television was not yet a commercial medium; Americans learned about the war through newspapers, radio reports, and motion picture newsreels. Television news broadcasts, which were still in their infancy during the Korean War (1950-1953), had become, by the time of the escalation of the Vietnam War in 1965, the major source of information about the world for most Americans. The existence of communications satellites and regular jet transportation in the early 1960's made the transmission of news faster than it had been in World War II or the Korean War, thereby making any government efforts to manage the news vastly more complicated than it had been in those earlier wars.

Although a ban on journalists' accompanying airmen limited the formers' coverage of the Vietnam air war, efforts by the United States and South Vietnamese governments to control news about the ground war were hampered by the guerrilla nature of much of the conflict, without clear frontlines, as were found in World War II. The military could sometimes keep bad news secret by denying reporters transportation to battlefields; but major battles could—as in 1968—erupt in unexpected places.

The contradictions of fighting a limited war made press self-censorship harder to maintain than in World War II, in which the aim had been the unconditional surrender of the enemy. During World War II journalistic self-censorship, and acceptance of official censorship, were encouraged by a national consensus that the war was necessary and just. The gradual breakdown of national consensus about the Vietnam War set media and government on the road to becoming adversaries rather than allies.

The Early Phase of the Vietnam War. The Geneva Peace Agreements of 1954, under which French colonial forces left Vietnam, divided the country into a communist north and a noncommunist south. By the early 1960's South Vietnam was troubled by a communist guerrilla rebellion in the countryside. When the U.S. military buildup was first begun by President John F. Kennedy in late 1961, only several hundred American military advisers were in South Vietnam; by the end of Kennedy's presidency, there were twelve thousand such advisers.

In the spring of 1963, it became clear that the South Vietnamese government of Ngo Dinh Diem had a dangerously narrow base of popular support. On November 1, 1963, after five months of protests by Buddhists angered at what they saw as Diem's favoritism to fellow Roman Catholics, Diem was overthrown and killed in a military coup. On November 22, 1963, President Kennedy was himself assassinated in Texas.

At first, the Vietnamese developments were overshadowed by other crises around the world, all seen by Americans as part of the Cold War between American democracy and Sino-Soviet communism. Although some American advisers were being killed and wounded in Vietnam in 1963, the relatively low American casualty figures and the fact that all the advisers were volunteers, rather than draftees, kept the Vietnam story from arousing controversy in the United States. Hence, the American media still had only a handful of representatives in South Vietnam. The wire services were represented, but only one newspaper, *The New York Times*. In 1963 there was still no full-time correspondent in Vietnam from any of the three major networks that then dominated television. Network evening newscasts were not even increased from fifteen to thirty minutes until September, 1963.

Meanwhile, three young reporters—Americans David Halberstam and Neil Sheehan and New Zealander Peter Arnett—ran into difficulty with the U.S. military mission in South Vietnam (which wished to minimize publicity for American efforts) because of their frank reporting. Frustrated by the bland optimism of the head of the U.S. military mission, these reporters sought information from lower-level American military advisers working in the field. In October, 1963, President Kennedy himself, unhappy about the pessimism he noticed in Halberstam's reporting, secretly—and unsuccessfully—urged *The New York Times* to recall him. Historians who have studied press-military relations for the 1961-1963 period can, however, detect no profound doubts among American reporters about the American goal of preserving a noncommunist South Vietnam.

However much frustration the American military mission caused them, American journalists faced much greater harassment from the South Vietnamese government during the Buddhist crisis of May-November, 1963. Relations became particularly bad after an American reporter photographed a Buddhist monk setting himself afire in protest. At one point, Arnett was physically beaten by Vietnamese police. To outwit Diem's censors, American reporters sometimes persuaded American military or civilian officials traveling back to the United States to serve as couriers for their film stories.

The Period of Escalation. Following Kennedy's assassination, his successor, President Lyndon Baines Johnson, at first tried to keep the military mission at the level that he had inherited. In the summer of 1964, Johnson won a resolution of support from Congress (the Gulf of Tonkin resolution) after an incident at sea between the U.S. Navy and North Vietnamese forces. Following his election in 1964 to the presidency for a full term, Johnson widened and deepened American involvement, ordering the bombing of North Vietnam in February, 1965, and in July, 1965, for the first time, sending large numbers of American combat troops into South Vietnam. As American casualties and draft calls increased sharply, more and more television reporters were sent to cover Vietnam full-time for the three major television networks.

A controversy that erupted over a single television story in August, 1965, clearly demonstrated both the risks of iconoclastic reporting and the limited ability of the Johnson Administration to censor reporters. A correspondent for the Columbia Broadcasting System (CBS) in South Vietnam, Canadian-born Morley Safer, produced a film piece with his own commentary, showing a detachment of American soldiers deliberately setting fire to the huts of a village from which enemy fire was supposed to have originated. After agonizing deliberation by Safer's CBS superior, news division chief Fred Friendly, the decision was made to broadcast the piece on the evening news. After it was aired, Press Secretary Arthur Sylvester wrote an angry letter to Friendly. President Johnson made an angry telephone call to Friendly's superior, CBS network president Frank Stanton, and angry telephone calls and letters poured in from viewers throughout the country. In the end, however, both Friendly and Stanton stood by Safer despite official pressure.

Further examples of dissenting journalism followed. In February, 1966, the voices of dissent from politicians were first heard when the television networks broadcast Arkansas senator J. William Fulbright's Foreign Relations Committee hearings on the war. During World War II no American journalist had reported from an enemy capital; hence, print journalist Harrison Salisbury was harshly criticized when, after returning from a trip to North Vietnam in December, 1966, he reported in *The New York Times* that—contrary to U.S. government statements—American bombing of the north had produced civilian casualties.

Yet as late as 1967 CBS refused to broadcast in full a documentary film on North Vietnam that it had commissioned British journalist Felix Greene to make, when it realized that the film criticized American bombing. Throughout 1966 and 1967, many television reports from South Vietnam still expressed empathy for the American military effort and hostility toward the North Vietnamese and the Vietcong.

Reporting on the Tet Offensive of January-March, 1968, in which the Vietcong launched bold (and ultimately unsuccessful) assaults against South Vietnam's major cities, bred distrust for the press in military circles. Film coverage of the Tet offensive, which was often transmitted by satellite in unedited form, was particularly disturbing to the average American viewer. Especially shocking was a film showing South Vietnam's chief of police, Brigadier General Nguyen Ngoc Loan, shooting a captured Vietcong insurgent in the head. In his report from the village of Ben Tre, Peter Arnett provided a catchy slogan for the American antiwar movement by simply relaying the conclusion of the American military commander, that American forces had had to destroy the village in order to save it. On February 27, 1968, Walter Cronkite, anchor of the CBS evening news broadcast, departed from his usual impartiality to urge the government to negotiate in good faith with the communist regime in North Vietnam. Shocked by the Tet offensive, Cronkite's defection, and setbacks in the primary elections President Johnson declared, on March 31, 1968, his decision not to run for re-election. Peace talks began in Paris, and Richard Nixon was elected president of the United States later that year.

The Last Years of the War. Under President Richard M. Nixon, the U.S. government tried gradually to shift the burden of fighting to the South Vietnamese. American casualties remained high, however, in 1969 and 1970. Nixon was able to hide enough information from the press so that the American entry into Cambodia in May, 1970, came as a surprise. Throughout his presidency, a markedly adversarial relationship prevailed between the administration and the media over Vietnam, one that contrasted strikingly with the government-media cooperation of the earliest phases of the conflict. There were reports in American newsmagazines of breakdowns of discipline in the American expeditionary force in Vietnam (nothing similar to that had ever been revealed in the newspapers during World War II); and in June, 1969, *Life* magazine put out a special issue listing—with photographs—all the American soldiers who had died in Vietnam in a single week.

President Nixon had his vice president, Spiro Agnew, publicly denounce the media, and also used threats to make the television networks more sympathetic to the administration's

Robert DeNiro and John Savage play American GIs in a Vietnamese prison in The Deer Hunter *(1978), a film that the Soviet Union and other communist nations objected to because of its harsh depiction of Vietnamese prison guards.* (Museum of Modern Art/Film Stills Archive)

viewpoint. After being violently criticized by the White House for allowing a television news reporter to speak favorably about a North Vietnamese peace proposal, the networks ended the policy of allowing instant analysis by television newsmen in front of the camera.

Yet the growing division of opinion over Vietnam in Congress had, by the early 1970's, emboldened at least some journalists to risk displeasing the executive branch of the government. In June, 1971, the Nixon Administration tried to prevent *The New York Times* from publishing the Pentagon Papers, U.S. government documents on the war's origins that had been stolen by Daniel Ellsberg, a Defense Department bureaucrat who had been involved in planning the war effort. The documents were embarrassing to American officials, but they endangered no American soldier's life; a Supreme Court decision guaranteed the people's right to see them in print.

As the number of American troops in Vietnam dwindled between 1971 and 1973, American media interest in the war also dwindled. American correspondents still in South Vietnam found themselves dealing less and less with American military censorship, and more and more with South Vietnamese government censorship. The Vietnam peace accords were signed in January, 1973. Nixon's resignation in August, 1974, in the wake of the Watergate scandal, ended all presidential attempts to pressure the media into supporting government policy on Vietnam. When Nixon's successor, Gerald Ford, asked for American aid to South Vietnam, a Congress mindful of popular war-weariness flatly rejected the idea. Coverage of the war ended after the North Vietnamese army overran South Vietnam in March-April, 1975.

Television Images and Public Opinion. Those who blamed the press for the U.S. defeat in Vietnam argued that excessively gory television coverage of the war so weakened popular support as to make defeat inevitable. Yet many scholars contend that the television coverage that critics of the medium remember most vividly—the burning of the village of Cam Ne and the police chief's killing of a captured Vietcong—was atypical of the combat scenes presented on the evening news. Television news broadcasts tried to avoid showing the bodies of dead American soldiers. Most combat footage simply showed American soldiers trudging onward, with enemy fire merely a menacing sound in the distance. Television reporters who tried to get combat footage were handicapped by the elusive nature of guerrilla foes, and by the fact that much combat occurred at night, when it could not be filmed. The most bloody American atrocity, the My Lai massacre of March, 1968, was not captured on film by a television journalist; it was uncovered a year after it happened by a United States-based print journalist. Revulsion against the war, many scholars contend, was caused not by images on the television screen, but by high American casualty levels sustained over a long period of time.

Legacy of the War. Although many scholars question whether any conceivable American strategy could have won the Vietnam War, the belief grew in some military and governmental circles that lack of press censorship had doomed the American effort in Vietnam to defeat. To prevent further such debacles, President Ronald Reagan decided that future military expeditions would be accompanied by tight controls over the press. Such strict censorship characterized the American expeditions in Grenada in 1983 (from which all newsmen were excluded) and Panama in 1989, and the Persian Gulf War of January-February, 1991.

Yet it is unlikely that strict censorship, by itself, assured victory. The more decisive role of air power in the Persian Gulf War, the complete absence of guerrilla warfare from that conflict, and Iraq's total diplomatic isolation may all be more important than censorship policy in explaining the difference between failure in Vietnam and success in the Persian Gulf.

—*Paul D. Mageli*

See also Agnew, Spiro T.; Draft-card burning; Korean War; *Last P.O.W.?: Bobby Garwood Story, The*; Military censorship; My Lai massacre; News broadcasting; Nixon, Richard M.; *Pentagon Papers, The*; Tonkin Gulf incident; Vietnam; World War II.

BIBLIOGRAPHY

Two insightful general works on the issue are media scholar Daniel Hallin's *The "Uncensored War": The Media and Vietnam* (New York: Oxford University Press, 1986), relying heavily on content analysis of television news footage preserved by the Defense Department, and historian Clarence R. Wyatt's *Paper Soldiers: The American Press and the Vietnam War* (New York: W. W. Norton, 1992). Both books challenge the notion of the media as a vanguard of the antiwar movement. William Prochnau's *Once upon a Distant War: Young War Correspondents and the Early Vietnam Battles* (New York: Random House, 1995) sheds light on the obstructions to reporting posed by both the U.S. military mission and the South Vietnamese government from 1961 through 1963. Readers interested in attempts to censor television should consult Erik Barnouw, *Tube of Plenty: The Evolution of American Television* (New York: Oxford University Press, 1975), and Robert J. Donovan and Ray Scherer, *Unsilent Revolution: Television News and American Public Life* (Cambridge, England.: Cambridge University Press, 1992). A first-hand account of the Cam Ne incident can be found in Morley Safer, *Flashbacks: On Returning to Vietnam* (New York: Random House, 1990). It is also discussed in the U.S. Army's official history, *Public Affairs: The Military and the Media, 1962-1968* (Washington, D.C.: Center for Military History, 1988), by William M. Hammond; in Gary Paul Gates, *Air Time: The Inside Story of CBS News* (New York: Harper & Row, 1978), and David Halberstam's *The Powers That Be* (New York: Alfred A. Knopf, 1979).

Violence

DEFINITION: Physical force used to kill or harm human beings, animals, or other entities

SIGNIFICANCE: Concerns over the effects of graphic portrayals of assault, murder, rape, and other violent behaviors in the arts, literature, drama, and film have prompted calls for banning or regulating its depiction

From comic books, paperback novels, and films such as *The Texas Chainsaw Massacre* and *Natural Born Killers* to advanced video games and Internet communications, crime and violent behavior have frequently been depicted in explicit detail. The increasing use of violence as a staple of entertainment has caused many parents, media watchdog groups, and social scientists to suggest links between such portrayals and antisocial behavior. In turn, these concerns have prompted calls for local, state, and federal laws to ban or regulate depictions of violence. However, although laws limiting portrayals of sexually explicit behaviors have generally been upheld in the United States, laws attempting to prohibit or even regulate violently explicit speech have not.

Role of the Courts in the United States. The U.S. Supreme Court has consistently held that "above all else, the First Amendment means that government has no power to restrict expression because of its message, its ideas, its subject matter, or its content"—the phrase used in *Police Department of Chicago v. Mosley* (1972). In its 1948 *Winters v. New York* decision, the Court invalidated a law that prohibited the distribution to minors of any publication "principally made up of . . . accounts of criminal deeds, or pictures, or stories of deeds of bloodshed, lust or crime." Although the justices saw "nothing of any possible value to society in these magazines," they held that the magazines were "as much entitled to the protection of free speech as the best of literature."

Using similar reasoning, a federal appeals court invalidated a Missouri law that prohibited the sale or lease of violent videocassettes to minors in *Video Software Dealers Association v. Webster* in 1992. Likewise, a federal circuit court has stated that "violence on television . . . is protected as speech, however insidious. Any other answer leaves government in control of . . . the institutions of culture, the great censor and director of which thoughts are good for us" (*American Booksellers Association v. Hudnut*, 1985).

As a matter of constitutional law, distinctions between "gratuitous" violence on the one hand and "legitimate" depictions of violence on the other, are subjective at best. Civil libertarians doubt that neutral First Amendment principles are useful in distinguishing between evening news broadcasts of events such as the police beating of Rodney King and television film reenactments of the same events. As one justice said in *Winters v. New York*: "What is one man's amusement, teaches another's doctrine." In *Cohen v. California* (1971) the Supreme Court pointed out that "it is precisely because government officials cannot make principled distinctions in [the arena of expression] that the Constitution leaves matters of taste and style so largely to the individual."

Proposals to restrict depictions of violence have raised serious vagueness problems. Statutes must provide explicit standards for those who apply them. A vague law impermissibly delegates basic policy matters to policemen, judges, and juries, or administrative agencies, for resolution on an ad-hoc and subjective basis. Such laws bring with them the dangers of arbitrary and discriminatory application.

Although supporters of regulating depictions of violence have suggested that all violence is gratuitous, some screen violence has been seen as generating positive consequences, such as that in *Schindler's List*, *The Deerhunter*, and *Apoca-*

To evade a film code ban on showing both a person firing a gun and a victim in the same frame at the moment of shooting, Little Caesar *(1931) showed killer Edward G. Robinson and the shadow of his off-camera victim in the same frame scene.* (Museum of Modern Art/Film Stills Archive)

lypse Now. Each of these films used violence to teach socially valuable historical lessons. Similarly, *Menace II Society*, a film about a Los Angeles ghetto, confronts viewers with real-life problems in contemporary urban society. Civil libertarians have argued that such depictions of violence are socially beneficial and should be encouraged not banned. They also assert that violent speech provides a safety valve for emotions that might otherwise explode as violent conduct. The Supreme Court has acknowledged the cathartic effect of violent expression: Without outlets to blow off steam through mere words or pictures "natural human reactions of outrage and protest are frustrated and may manifest themselves in some form of vengeful 'self-help'" (*Richmond Newspapers, Inc. v. Virginia*, 1980).

Defining violent expression subject to proposed regulations raises other difficult constitutional problems. The definition of "violence" must give broadcasters fair notice regarding what speech is subject to regulation. The Supreme Court struck down an ordinance that classified films as "not suitable for young persons" if they portrayed "brutality, criminal violence or depravity in such a manner as to be, in the judgment of the Board, likely to incite or encourage crime or delinquency on the part of young persons . . . [and thereby] create the impression on young persons that such conduct is profitable, desirable, acceptable, respectable, praiseworthy or commonly accepted" (*Interstate Circuit City of Dallas*, 1968).

The Overbreadth Doctrine. Regulations aimed at restricting violence on television or in films may also conflict with First Amendment overbreadth rules. Under this doctrine, laws that affect not only the speech that may legitimately be restricted but a substantial amount of protected speech as well are over-inclusive and thus unconstitutional (*City of Houston v. Hill*, 1987). If no constitutionally recognizable differences can be articulated among news programs, documentaries, dramatizations, sports, and pure entertainment programs, any regulation of violence would embrace many important forms of protected speech that could not legitimately be restricted.

The Supreme Court has held that First Amendment protections for television broadcasting are not as extensive as those for the print media. Nevertheless, "broadcasters are engaged in a vital and independent form of communicative activity. As a result, the First Amendment must inform and give shape to the manner in which Congress exercises its regulatory power in this area" (*Federal Communications Commission v. League of Women Voters*, 1980). Moreover, constitutionally valid speech restrictions, even in the broadcast media, may not be based on the viewpoint or subject matter of the expression regulated.

This approach applies to cable television as well. The Supreme Court has reaffirmed that "cable television provides to its subscribers news, information, and entertainment. It is engaged in 'speech' under the First Amendment, and is, in much of its operation, part of the 'press' " (*Leathers v. Medlock*, 1991). Cable television is therefore not subject to content regulation *(Home Box Office, Inc. v. Federal Communications Commission*, 1977).

Protecting Children. Supporters of proposed legislation restricting portrayals of violence often cite the need to protect children. But this legitimate and compelling governmental interest has been found insufficient to justify content regulations. A federal appeals court held, in *Pratt v. Independent School District No. 831* (1982), that a public school district had acted unconstitutionally when it removed from the curriculum a film version of Shirley Jackson's short story "The Lottery." This story was about a town whose inhabitants stone one resident to death each year in an unquestioning adherence to tradition. Teachers in the district had used the film in their classes for five years, but the film adaptation was abandoned after parents and other citizens complained about the story's violence and its negative impact on the students' religious and family values. Finding that the school board had failed to specify why the film was too violent, the appeals court decided that the board had "used its official power to perform an act clearly indicating that the ideas contained in the film are unacceptable and should not be discussed or considered" in violation of the First Amendment.

The Supreme Court has, however, also found that in some instances government may "adopt more stringent controls on communicative materials available to youths than on those available to adults" (*Erznoznik v. City of Jacksonville*, 1975). Nonetheless, "speech . . . cannot be suppressed solely to protect the young from ideas or images that a legislative body thinks unsuitable for them. In most circumstances, the values protected by the First Amendment are no less applicable when government seeks to control the flow of information to minors." Whatever restrictions can be adopted under a child-protection theory, the Court said, cannot be permitted to reduce the adult population to viewing only what is fit for children (*Butler v. Michigan*, 1957).

New Technologies. Television violence legislation must also surmount another legal hurdle: that the means chosen to regulate it be a "constitutionally acceptable less restrictive means" compared to others available "to achieve the Government's interest in protecting minors" (*Sable Communications of California, Inc. v. Federal Communications Commission*, 1989). Any regulatory legislation must employ "narrowly drawn regulations designed to serve those interests without necessarily interfering with First Amendment freedoms."

Parents who wish to protect their children from violent or other objectionable messages can use new technological de-

vices which do not endanger free speech. During the mid-1990's cable operators were required by law to provide lock-boxes to customers on request. Nearly two dozen models of television sets were available with built-in channel-blocking ability permitting parents to limit their children's viewing by blocking certain channels when the parents are not home. Some products permitted parents to block specific television programs or time periods. Lockboxes and similar devices place "the responsibility for making such choices . . . where our society has traditionally placed it on the shoulders of the parent" (*Fabulous Associates, Inc. v. Pennsylvania Public Utility Commission*, 1990).

Social Science Research. Social scientists disagree on whether steady diets of violent television and films, especially for young people, contribute to antisocial or even criminal behavior. Most studies show correlations rather than causal relationship. Indeed, it has been suggested that people who are prone to violent behavior may be attracted to violent films and television, rather than the other way around. The most scientifically prepared studies indicate that exposure to fictional violence increases the potential for violent behavior by 10 percent in otherwise normally adjusted people. Both proponents and opponents of censoring violent films and television can use such research to further their cause. Proponents of censorship might argue that a contributing factor of 10 percent is highly significant, thereby justifying further government control, while opponents urge that because a range of other factors—including family background, upbringing, education, and religious training—are, collectively, ten times more important, there is no valid or constitutional basis justifying prohibition of such fictional portrayals.

Pornography Victims Compensation Act. A coalition of conservative politicians and procensorship feminists have joined together to promote legislation which assumes a link between violent pornography and sexual assaults. The Pornography Victims Compensation Act of the mid-1980's was designed to create a new civil cause of action allowing victims of rape or sexual assault who can prove that their assailants were motivated—at least in part—by exposure to pornography to sue the producers or publishers of the videos, books, or magazines involved for money damages and attorney fees. Civil libertarians, anticensorship feminists, publishing and library associations, and many writers and authors have strenuously opposed such legislation. Opponents have urged that it would have a chilling effect on a whole range of expression, as there is no way of knowing what films, books, photographs, or other images may "motivate" criminal behavior and would shift responsibility for serious sexual assaults from the perpetrators to film producers and book publishers, encouraging a "porn-made-me-do-it" defense.

The depiction of crimes and violence is as old as Greek mythology and the Bible. Modern fears and anxieties over safety and order have prompted people to look for causes—or scapegoats. In such times, threats to security breed threats of censorship. —*Stephen F. Rohde*

See also *Blue Velvet*; Chilling effect; Comic books; Communications Decency Act; Cormier, Robert Edmund; *Deliver-*

ance; Gangster films; Hays Code; *King Kong*; *Mighty Morphin Power Rangers*; *Natural Born Killers*; *NYPD Blue*; Peckinpah, Sam; Pornography; *Pulp Fiction*; Snuff films; Television, children's; Women, violence against.

BIBLIOGRAPHY

Edward J. Cleary's *Beyond the Burning Cross* (New York: Random House, 1994) is a personal account of the landmark First Amendment decision in *R.A.V. v. St. Paul* written by the lawyer who represented the defendant. The book traces, in illuminating detail, the progress of a constitutional case through the courts, revealing the roles of the courts, prosecution, and defense counsel. Rodney A. Smolla, *Free Speech in an Open Society* (New York: Alfred A. Knopf, 1992), is an accessible discussion of major First Amendment issues. Violence is among the themes explored in Catherine Itzin's edited volume *Pornography: Women, Violence, and Civil Liberties* (New York: Oxford University Press, 1992). Catharine A. MacKinnon's *Only Words* (Cambridge, Mass.: Harvard University Press, 1993) is an extended essay addressing the need to make the law more receptive to protecting women from violence and discrimination.

Voice of America (VOA)

FOUNDED: February, 1942
TYPE OF ORGANIZATION: U.S. government broadcasting organization
SIGNIFICANCE: Voice of America transmits its broadcasts worldwide, providing information about the United States to international listeners

The U.S. government created Voice of America (VOA) during World War II as the radio division of the Office of War Information. The VOA had several objectives. One was to broadcast to populations in areas under totalitarian control, thereby to counter Axis propaganda and restricted access to alternative sources of information. Another goal was to reach America's wartime allies. Broadcasts to nonaligned nations, including Latin America, also presented information about the culture and history of the United States. These programs opposed the censorship practices of dictatorships and supported human rights and democratic political institutions. Begun in February, 1942, the VOA established a high level of credibility among listeners for the accuracy and quality of its programming.

The emergence of the Cold War between the Western democracies and communist nations following the end of World War II created new opportunities for the VOA as a part of the United States Information Agency. The goal remained the same: to provide objective news and balanced commentary as well as informing listeners in other nations about America's people, policies, culture, and history. Specialized organizations broadcast specifically to the Soviet Union (Radio Liberty) and to communist states of Eastern Europe (Radio Free Europe); the VOA generally expanded its programming to many world regions. This especially was directed to the Third World. Geographical transmission divisions in the VOA include East Asia, the Pacific, the Near East, North Africa, South Asia, Western Europe, Latin America, and Africa. By 1990 forty-three languages were included in regular daily broadcasts, with programs in other languages on an occasional basis.

Congressional legislation in 1976 reaffirmed the objectives of the VOA as the government's "global radio network" in the VOA charter. Satellite interconnect systems offer the ability to broadcast programs into remote areas of the world. The VOA's total budget in 1989 was $170 million. VOA programs include politics, economics, sports, music, history, current affairs, drama, commentary, and news. The original goal continues to provide information in an "open" forum. The VOA's importance as an opponent of broadcast censorship can be seen in authoritarian systems whose news censorship was jeopardized by these independent broadcasts reaching their citizens. These governments periodically have attempted to jam transmissions, attesting to the VOA's significance.

During the 1980's the United States criticized proposals introduced in the United Nations seeking to establish a worldwide supervisory committee to oversee international broadcasting, on the grounds this would interfere improperly with the free flow of information.

See also Broadcast media; News broadcasting; Radio Free Europe; Radio Martí; United States Information Agency.

Voltaire

BORN: November 21, 1694, Paris, France
DIED: May 30, 1778, Paris, France
IDENTIFICATION: French philosopher
SIGNIFICANCE: Voltaire's often-banned satires turned his pen into a weapon aimed at the religious intolerance, feudal privileges, cruel wars, and the irrationalities of France's Old Regime

The son of prosperous bourgeois parents, Voltaire had a first-rate education and developed a satirical wit that gained him early acceptance by aristocratic circles. In 1717, however, a poem he wrote lampooning the recently deceased King Louis XIV earned him nearly a year's confinement in the Bastille. Shortly after his release he adopted the pen name Voltaire and wrote a play titled *Oedipe* (1718) whose success established his reputation as a dramatist.

Eight years later Voltaire's witty reply to a high aristocrat led to his being beaten by the aristocrat's footmen and another term in the Bastille. By promising to leave the country, Voltaire gained release and went on a significant three-year journey to England. He compiled his laudatory observations of England as a land of liberty and tolerance in *Lettres anglaises ou philosophiques* (1734). Viewed as a direct and indirect criticism of France, this book was not allowed to be printed in France, where permission of the government's director of publications was necessary. Even with such permission, decisions could be reversed or bans imposed by local legislative bodies, or by a vote of the theology faculty of the University of Paris.

To avoid censorship complications in France, Voltaire followed a common practice of French writers by publishing *Lettres anglaises ou philosophiques* in Amsterdam, whence it was smuggled into France. In response the Parlement of Paris condemned his work to be burned by the Paris hangman. Fearful of yet another visit to the Bastille, Voltaire moved to Cirey, near the Lorraine border, where he could easily leave the country in case of difficulties. He remained at Cirey for nearly fifteen years; while there he wrote a multitude of works.

In 1759 Voltaire relocated in Ferney, near Geneva. Here the intensity of his attacks on religious intolerance and social injustice increased. More and more his trademark war cry "crush the infamous thing" appeared in his writing. In 1759 his immortal satire *Candide* was published abroad and smuggled into France. While the work satirized practically everything, its most vitriolic humor about human hypocrisy was reserved for the Inquisition and the Roman Catholic church. *Candide* was publicly burned in Paris and remained on the *Index Librorum Prohibitorum* of the Roman Catholic church until the *Index* itself was abolished in the mid-twentieth century. *Candide* was considered controversial even in the twentieth century and was banned by U.S. Customs in 1929.

Voltaire used every weapon in his satirical arsenal in his *Philosophical Dictionary* (1764) which was published anonymously. The book was burned in Paris, Geneva, the Netherlands, and Rome. Voltaire observed that they would like to burn the author as well. In 1774 Voltaire returned to Paris after a nearly three-decade absence. His last four years were spent writing voluminous letters. His published correspondence later filled nearly thirty volumes.

See also Book burning; Caricature; Daumier, Honoré; Diderot, Denis; France; *Index Librorum Prohibitorum.*

Vonnegut, Kurt

BORN: November 11, 1922, Indianapolis, Indiana

IDENTIFICATION: American novelist

SIGNIFICANCE: Vonnegut has been both a leading opponent of censorship and one of its most frequent targets

Noted for his accessible writing style—which is comprehensible even to young readers—Vonnegut combines uncompromising social criticism with a willingness to address such controversial issues as sex, religion, and politics. The mixture has made him one of the most frequently censored novelists in the United States. His most famous novel, *Slaughterhouse-Five* (1969), depicts the fire-bombing of Dresden, Germany, by British and American forces during World War II—an event that he witnessed firsthand as a prisoner of war. It combines fantastic elements, such as aliens and time travel, with the grim realities of war and the absurdities of human behavior. For various reasons, including the novel's sexual content— used primarily for satire—its realistic use of coarse language, and its graphic depiction of the devastating effects of American military power (the novel was written at the height of the Vietnam War), the book has been banned from school libraries throughout the United States.

A particularly famous case of Vonnegut censorship occurred in Island Trees, New York, in 1976. The local school board removed nine books from its libraries, including Bernard Malamud's *The Fixer*, Eldridge Cleaver's *Soul on Ice*, Desmond Morris' *The Naked Ape*, and Alice Childress' *A Hero Ain't Nothin' But a Sandwich*, as well as Vonnegut's *Slaughterhouse-Five*. Five high school students took the school board to court to challenge its right to remove books from school libraries. The plaintiffs argued that the board had denied them their First

A former General Electric employee himself, author Kurt Vonnegut joined a picket line in support of striking broadcast employees and technicians in New York City in July, 1987. (AP/Wide World Photos)

Amendment rights of free expression and had introduced "a pall of orthodoxy" into the school community. Although the board's lawyers argued that "bad taste" and "vulgar language" made the books objectionable, earlier attacks on the book that had been made by board members cited the books' political and religious views, as well as their language. In the case of *Slaughterhouse-Five* the board was offended by a character who insults the name of Jesus Christ.

Vonnegut's response to the many attempts to silence him and other writers can be found in his essay on the First Amendment, in which he writes: "Whenever ideas are squashed in this country, literate lovers of the American experiment write careful and intricate explanations of why all ideas must be allowed to live. It is time for them to realize that they are attempting to explain America at its bravest and most optimistic to orangutans. From now on, I intend to limit my discourse with dim-witted Savonarolas to this advice: 'Have somebody read the First Amendment to the United States Constitution out loud to you, you God damned fool!'"

See also First Amendment; Libraries, school; Literature; Offensive language; Savonarola, Girolamo.

Voznesensky, Andrey Andreyevich

BORN: May 12, 1933, Moscow, Soviet Union

IDENTIFICATION: Russian poet

SIGNIFICANCE: While carefully avoiding arrest in the Soviet Union's post-Stalin era, Voznesensky contributed to the rejuvenation of Russian poetry

Voznesensky first appeared on the Soviet literary scene in 1958, during the struggle for freedom in the Soviet Union after the death of Joseph Stalin. He quickly showed his promise, and, with Yevgeny Yevtushenko, became known as one of the "angry young men" of Russian letters. At mass readings Voznesensky excited listeners with poems of rebellion and hope for renewal. With his thinly veiled allusions to historical despots he warned of a possible return to a Stalinesque reign of terror. As a consequence, he was kept under police surveillance and was reprimanded for his iconoclastic stance. However, Voznesensky couched his poems in such obscure metaphors and allusions that authorities found it difficult to charge him with treason. Thus he was spared home detention and revocation of his passport, as happened to Yevtushenko. Voznesensky could travel abroad and write his poetry relatively uncensored.

Because of his popularity and reputation, both at home and abroad, Voznesensky was instrumental in the struggle for democracy in the late 1980's and early 1990's. He continued to write poetry of high caliber, while leading the rejuvenation of Russian poetry by bringing it closer to the mainstream of world poetry.

See also Akhmatova, Anna; Communism; Literature; Poetry; Police states; Russia; Socialist Realism; Soviet Union; Stalin, Joseph; Yevtushenko, Yevgeny Aleksandrovich.

W

Wagner, Richard

BORN: May 22, 1813, Leipzig, Saxony
DIED: February 13, 1883, Venice Italy
IDENTIFICATION: German author and operatic composer
SIGNIFICANCE: Wagner's writing and music have been banned by several governments, from nineteenth century Germany to modern Israel

Best known as the composer of German Romantic operatic music, including the four-opera cycle known as *Der Ring des Nibelungen* (*The Ring of the Nibelung*), Wagner is one of the few artists whose work has been banned by governments on both the Right and Left. During his lifetime, Wagner was known as an avowed advocate of the revolutionary political movements of nineteenth century Europe. He spent some years in exile from Germany because of his political activities, and his presence was met with hostility in countries such as France and England, because of his association with perceived dangerous ideas. In the twentieth century, his music became identified with the politics of Nazi Germany, which led to a long-standing performance ban by the state of Israel.

Wagner's avowed goal as a composer was to embody his social and political ideas in dramatic and musical forms. Because he wrote that his artistic ideas could not be fully realized without a concurrent social revolution, his operas were often perceived as a means of fomenting revolution. Wagner was actively involved in the February, 1848, worker's revolution in Paris, and later with the 1849 uprising in Dresden, Germany. A warrant for Wagner's arrest issued by the Dresden authorities led to his exile from Germany. Later, a similar brush with authorities led to his exile from the German state of Bavaria in 1865.

Wagner's famous work, the *Ring* cycle of operas, composed over a period of more than twenty-five years, illustrates many of his ideas. In mythical narrative form, the operas describe the construction of Valhalla, the elaborate castle of the gods, the life and death of Siegfried, a hero without fear, and of the ultimate destruction of Valhalla and the gods themselves. The opera's story has widely been interpreted as an allegory of socialist revolution, most notably and forcefully by Irish playwright George Bernard Shaw. Wagner had so much difficulty in staging the *Ring* that he founded his own opera festival at Bayreuth in 1872 in order to stage the entire cycle. His festival has since become an annual event. In 1882 Wagner established a special fund that would enable the poor to attend his festival. That fund also still exists.

As has happened with many artists, after Wagner died, various governments attempted to capitalize on the popularity of his work by adapting it to their own political purposes. The National Socialist government of Germany in the 1930's and 1940's used both Wagner's music and his often anti-Semitic political writings to serve as cultural icons for its own policies. The success of Nazi propaganda led to a ban on the public performance of Wagner's music in Israel that lasted until the 1980's.

See also Germany; Israel; Khachaturian, Aram; Mendelssohn, Felix; Music; National Socialism; Presidency, U.S.; Shostakovich, Dmitri.

Wales padlock law

ENACTED: 1927
PLACE: New York, New York
SIGNIFICANCE: This city ordinance gave New York City police authority to close down stage productions

The Wales padlock law was one of several ordinances that New York City enacted in 1927 under the broad title of Amusements and Entertainments; they were all sponsored by Mayor James Walker. The Wales padlock law dealt with public morals, authorizing the inspector of the Department of Licenses to investigate the character of exhibitions and report any offenses against morality, decency, and public welfare. The law gave one person authority to determine morality of all stage productions, including burlesque shows that included strip-tease dancing, and stage plays.

The ordinance was partly inspired by the high-profile case of actress Mae West, who was arrested in April, 1926, on morals charges while appearing in *Sex*, a long-running play that she had written herself. The play was raided and shut down by the police, at the urging of the Society for the Suppression of Vice, which had a voice on the ordinance committee. West was convicted of corrupting the morals of the youth because she exposed her gyrating navel during a belly dance.

See also Burlesque shows; Drama and theater; Lord Chamberlain; Morality; Society for the Suppression of Vice, New York; West, Mae.

Walker, David

BORN: September 28, 1785, Wilmington, North Carolina
DIED: June 28, 1830, Boston, Massachusetts
IDENTIFICATION: American abolitionist author
SIGNIFICANCE: Walker wrote one of the most powerful condemnations of slavery ever published in U.S. history; it was violently opposed by Southern slave states, and Walker himself died mysteriously

Because he was born to an enslaved African man and a free African woman in North Carolina, Walker's free status was determined by the law that stated that the status of the mother determined the status of the child. In 1815 he relocated to Boston, where he became heavily involved in the radical abolitionist movement. Fourteen years later he published, at his own expense, a pamphlet, *Appeal to the Colored People of the World*, which urged slaves to armed revolt. It was widely distributed and had great influence on African American social and political thought in the North and the South. More and more African American leaders were to echo Walker's words as they, too, called for resistance, violent if necessary, to slavery. Henry Highland Garnet acknowledged Walker's influence on his own political philosophy when he included Walker's text in his own militant manifesto, *Address to the Slaves of the United States of America*, in 1848.

Among white Americans, reception of Walker's *Appeal* was much less cordial than that of African Americans. Northern white abolitionists, committed to a philosophy of moral suasion rather than physical resistance, were appalled by Walker's violent rhetoric. For example, Benjamin Lundy, a leading white Quaker abolitionist, denounced it in the April, 1830, issue of his newspaper, *The Genius of Universal Emancipation*: "I can do no less than set the broadest seal of condemnation on it." William Lloyd Garrison, the leading white abolitionist, called the tract "a most injudicious publication," while acknowledging that slaveholders brought Walker's condemnation on themselves by their own violent actions.

White Southerners acted to suppress the pamphlet and blunt its impact. Because they considered the tract seditious, Georgia and North Carolina enacted laws against incendiary publications, making their possession and publication a capital offense. The mayor of Savannah and the governor of Georgia wrote to the mayor of Boston, demanding that Walker be arrested and his pamphlet suppressed. Boston mayor Harrison Gray Otis recognized the rights of Walker by refusing their demands, while noting that he personally held Walker's pamphlet in "deep disapprobation and abhorrence." Georgia went on to offer a ten-thousand-dollar reward to anyone who captured Walker alive and returned him to the South, and one thousand dollars if he were killed.

More stringent laws against teaching African Americans to read and write were enacted in several Southern states. Four African Americans were arrested in New Orleans for circulating Walker's tract. Louisiana passed a law that ordered the expulsion of all free blacks who had settled there since 1825 after copies of the tract were found throughout the state.

Walker realized the risk he was taking in producing such a document. He wrote that he "not only expect[ed] to be held up to the public as an ignorant, impudent and restless disturber of the peace [but] perhaps put in prison or to death." He died under unexplained circumstances in Boston in 1830.

See also Abolitionist movement; African Americans; Civil War, U.S.; Death; Douglass, Frederick; Fear; First Amendment; Free speech; Journalists, violence against.

Wall posters

DEFINITION: Large handwritten paper sheets used by Chinese people to express political ideas

SIGNIFICANCE: Wall posters have been a method of circumventing pervasive Chinese government censorship that is comparable to Russian underground newspapers and Western graffiti

China's people have long been governed by authoritarian governments—whether under the ancient emperors, Chiang Kai-shek's Nationalists, or the late twentieth century communists—all of whom routinely censored all media. The Chinese have responded by an interesting, sometimes effective, circumvention of control through the use of surreptitiously erected wall posters, or *dazhibao* (translated as "big character" posters), to criticize the government.

The use of wall posters amply demonstrates the motivation for governmental censorship and a natural resistance to it by people. The communist Chinese impose tight control on political self-expression, believing in the adage of Mao Zedong, their longtime leader, that "a single spark could ignite a prairie fire." Despite harsh penalties, some people have resisted, in some cases using wall posters to evade government censorship and to provoke rebellions. The prevailing climate of censorship and the tight police control have also increased the likelihood that if a mass rebellion were to exceed these initial restraints, as at Tiananmen in 1989, it would be more violent than if other forms of expression had been available.

With wall posters, as with graffiti, the opportunities to evade police control are reasonably numerous. In a society accepting their use, the posters can evolve into serious art including pictures as well as words (Chinese characters). Although they are inexpensive and can be posted almost anywhere, they normally do not allow for the presentation of lengthy discourse as might be provided by an underground book. While one poster was known to have reached over sixty feet in length, most are much shorter, making up in readability what they lose in length.

Procommunist wall posters in Beijing in the early 1950's. (National Archives)

Nevertheless, wall posters can only be read by a small percentage of the population, and can not reach the large audience of state-controlled media. Censorship, inefficient though it may be, is still effective enough to be heavily relied on in China.

Wall posters have also been used by rival governmental factions. Mao Zedong himself used wall posters to attack his opponents in the government when he launched the Cultural Revolution in 1966. His enemies responded in kind when they could. Wall posters acquired a reputation as vehicles for vicious libel and for causing turmoil. After Mao's death in 1976, many of those who had been attacked by his wall posters were "rehabilitated" and enacted new prohibitions against them. However, the nature of these posters has been hard to suppress. Wall posters remained widespread and were effective in stimulating demonstrations during the events leading up to the 1989 Tiananmen Square incident.

See also China; Cultural Revolution, Chinese; Graffiti; Mao Zedong; Mural art; Tiananmen Square.

War

DEFINITION: Organized armed conflict among nations or states, or among factions within a state

SIGNIFICANCE: Wartime situations have invariably led to increased censorship among belligerent factions

War and censorship are forms of state activity that have been closely connected for three reasons. First, the goal of censorship is to control what is thought and said. War encourages intense social controls in order to promote unity in facing an enemy. Second, after one side wins a war, censorship is one of the ways in which the victor can establish supremacy by forcing its own ideas on the loser and by suppressing dissent within the losing population. Third, states at war have used censorship to keep secrets about strategy and weaponry from being made available to their enemies.

Antiquity to the Modern Era. The ancient Greeks are often thought of as the first advocates of freedom of speech and opinion. The warlike Greeks of Sparta, however, banned all philosophical and speculative writing, and they allowed no study beyond functional literacy within their city-state. As a people perpetually in a situation of war readiness, the Spartans did not tolerate any questioning that might produce any degree of nonconformity.

During the Peloponnesian Wars of the fifth century B.C.E. the enemies of the Spartans, the Athenians, also censored the expression of opinions. Athens, considered the intellectual center of classical Greece, during war used exile, imprisonment, or execution to silence many of its leading artists and thinkers, including Euripides, Aeschylus, Phidias, Socrates, and Aristotle.

The word "censor" comes from another ancient people, the Romans, who created a vast empire through their proficiency at war. Under the Roman Republic, the censor kept track of the number of males of military age. He also oversaw the punishment of treason, as well as with the punishment of immorality, which was seen as related to treason, since it involved undermining Roman national virtues. With the fall of the Roman Republic, the emperors assumed the powers of censorship, and

suppression of treason and sedition was even more heavily emphasized. When Christianity became widespread, the refusal of Christians to participate in the army and their refusal to participate in religious ceremonies that expressed allegiance to the emperor were causes for the censorship and persecution of the new faith.

The Middle Ages saw the Crusades, warfare between Christian Europe and the Muslim Middle East, and attempts to suppress Muslim intellectual influences in Europe. The Church prohibited the translation of the Koran, the Muslim holy book, made by Peter the Venerable in the twelfth century. In the thirteenth century, ideas associated with the Arabic philosopher Averroës and with the Persian philosopher Avicenna were condemned.

With the rise of the modern state and the development of printing, governments became much more involved in censorship (which previously had been more the province of the Church), particularly during times of war. In England, for example, printing began in 1476 and the Tudor royal family, which came to power in 1485, became the first English sovereigns to maintain strict control over the press. King Henry VII, King Henry VIII, and Queen Elizabeth I, Tudor rulers of England, all acted decisively on their belief that government control of printing was necessary for state security.

During the English Civil War, in the mid-1600's, struggles for control of the state often took the form of struggles for control of information. After the king was executed in 1649, the English Parliament enacted a Printing Act limiting printing and requiring the licensing of all books and pamphlets. The goal was to silence the supporters of the king. When Oliver Cromwell became Lord Protector of England in 1653, he ordered the suppression and prosecution of all unlicensed printers and all unlicensed news publications.

Despite the gradual growth of the principle of freedom of the press in England over the course of the century following the English Civil War, individuals continued to be prosecuted for publishing writings considered to be seditious. During the time of the Napoleonic wars, in the late 1700's and early 1800's, when England was at war with France, English intellectuals who had been sympathetic to the French Revolution were suppressed and many were imprisoned.

Early American Censorship. The American government's first legislative act of censorship, the Sedition Act of 1798, was passed when the government was facing the possibility of war with France. The Sedition Act provided a maximum penalty of a two-thousand-dollar fine and a two-year jail term for any person who published anything against the U.S. government. The Sedition Act provoked strong opposition and this opposition helped win the presidency for Thomas Jefferson. Censorship in American life did not disappear, however, and it kept reappearing in times of war or fear of war. After Andrew Jackson's troops defeated the British at the Battle of New Orleans in January, 1815, Jackson imprisoned a Louisiana newspaper writer who refused to accept Jackson's censorship of war-related news.

During the Civil War, censorship was used to control public opinion regarding the war and to protect military secrets. The federal War Department at this time censored telegraph lines and the postmaster general refused to allow the use of the mail to newspapers seen as disloyal to the Union cause. In March, 1862, Secretary of War E. M. Stanton had soldiers seize the offices of a Washington paper, *The Sunday Chronicle*, that had been publishing information on troop movements. In Missouri, a state that contained large numbers of Southern sympathizers, in 1862 the U.S. army arrested and tried a newspaper editor for publishing articles that supported the Confederacy. In 1863 the Federal Army seized the offices of the *Chicago Times* for publishing opinions seen as disloyal. In 1864 the *New York World* was shut down on the order of President Abraham Lincoln himself and members of its editorial staff were arrested.

The World Wars. World War I produced the most severe censorship in American history. Many citizens did not understand the reasons for entering the war, or the goals of the United States in the war, and many citizens opposed American participation in the European conflict. The American government was therefore deeply interested in shaping public opinion and in eliminating opposition. In 1917 the U.S. Congress passed the Espionage Act, providing harsh punishment for anyone who spoke out against the U.S. government or military, and Congress strengthened this act a year later. The Espionage Act also empowered the postmaster general to deny use of the mail system to any writing or publication judged to be in violation of the act. This gave the power of censorship over all publications that moved through the mail to the postmaster general. Under the Espionage Act, Eugene V. Debs, founder of the Social Democratic Party and five-time presidential candidate, had his American citizenship revoked and was sentenced to ten years in prison for criticizing the war.

Congress also passed the Trading with the Enemy Act, which contained clauses that were intended to censor messages between the United States and foreign countries. This act authorized the establishment of a Censorship Board. The board contained representatives of the State Department, the War Department, the Navy, the Post Office, and the War Trade Board. It also contained George Creel, the chief of the Committee on Public Information. The Committee on Public Information was the primary source of war propaganda, so Creel's inclusion on the Censorship Board emphasizes the fact that the board was set up to attempt to shape public opinion and not simply to protect military secrets from disclosure to the enemy. Creel's committee told newspapers and magazines what kinds of material should not be printed, approved articles that were submitted to it, and it had the power to recommend that the postmaster general bar publications from the mail under the authority of the Espionage Act.

The Espionage Act continued to be used as a basis for censorship after the end of the war. The act was not repealed until 1921, and it was used, during the antiradical hysteria that followed the war, to suppress unpopular views. In 1919, under the Espionage Act, U.S. attorney general Mitchell Palmer raided the offices of the Seattle *Union Record* and closed the paper. Other newspapers were still being barred from the mails well after the Armistice. Militarization and enforced conformity have thus tended to turn the homeland of the victors into something resembling conquered territory.

Censorship was less severe in World War II than in World War I, perhaps because the war had such wide popular support that little control of public opinion was needed. Still, immediately after World War II began, the U.S. Congress established the Office of Censorship, headed by Director of Censorship Byron Price. The Director had authority to censor all communications passing between the United States and other countries. J. Harold Ryan, assistant director of censorship, was named to oversee the censorship of radio broadcasts. John H. Sorrells, the executive editor of the Scripps-Howard chain of newspapers, became another assistant director, charged with overseeing the press. In order to carry out the business of censorship, the Censorship Operating Board, consisting of sixteen government departments and agencies, was organized in January, 1942. The Espionage Act was revived to prohibit the mailing of subversive materials.

Government and press worked closely together in monitoring the flow of information and shaping public opinion. *Life* magazine, in April, 1942, published the article "Voices of Defeat," which denounced individuals, organizations, and publications that expressed seditious views. Much of the information in this article had been given to *Life* by the Post Office, a source that the magazine did not acknowledge to its readers.

The African American press received particular attention from the American government during the war. The Post Office and the Federal Bureau of Investigation (FBI), operating under the Espionage Act, followed black newspapers closely, since criticism of racial discrimination during the war was seen as undermining war unity. After a meeting with President Franklin D. Roosevelt, Walter White of the National Association for the Advancement of Colored People called a meeting of black editors in January, 1943. White urged the editors to tone down their social criticism in order to avoid prosecution by the U.S. government. Although J. Edgar Hoover, Director of the FBI, prepared lists of black papers that his organization considered were publishing unacceptable material, Attorney General Francis Biddle's support for freedom of speech prevented widespread attempts to suppress black publications.

The Vietnam War. The Vietnam War proved to be something of a turning point in American government-press relations. The news media had grown more sophisticated since World War II, and television had emerged. Television had the power to bring the horrors of war into every living room in America. American military and political leaders attempted to present the Vietnam War in a positive light, arguing that the war was being brought to a successful end and that U.S. forces, rather than being another in a long series of unwelcome foreign powers in Vietnam, were fighting on behalf of the beleaguered South Vietnamese military. A relatively uncensored news media made both of these positions difficult to maintain.

At the beginning of 1968 Vietnamese guerrillas known as the Viet Cong and the North Vietnamese army launched a major offensive in South Vietnam. Although the Viet Cong and North Vietnamese troops were driven back, the televised images of fierce fighting helped to convince many in the American public that the end of the war was not near, which, as it turned out, was the case. Television cameras and print reporters also continued to report on the enormous suffering the fighting was bringing to the Vietnamese people, in spite of military efforts to control the flow of news. For example, when more than three hundred civilian Vietnamese men, women, and children were murdered by American soldiers at My Lai in March, 1968, military officials deliberately withheld information from the press and attempted to minimize the atrocities. The news of the My Lai massacre became public, however, and many of the facts did emerge.

The ineffectiveness of the government's control over the press became even more clear with the attempt to stop publication of the Pentagon Papers. These papers consisted of secret documents on the history of American involvement in Vietnam, which had been compiled by order of Secretary of Defense Robert McNamara. These papers provided evidence that the U.S. government had systematically misled and deceived the American public during the course of the war. They were leaked to the newspapers by Daniel Ellsberg, a Defense Department employee. The government sued to block publication of the papers under the Espionage Act, but the Supreme Court eventually found in favor of the *The New York Times* and other papers involved in publishing the secret documents. The papers were published in book form and the government's attempt at censorship attracted attention to them.

After Vietnam. During the Vietnam War, information about the war, and particularly televised images of fighting and death, helped to provoke widespread opposition within the American public to the conflict. This made the American political leadership sensitive to the need to obtain positive coverage for any military involvement. The experience of Vietnam also stimulated American leaders, military and civilian, to develop sophisticated ways of manipulating reporting on war.

In 1983, when the United States invaded the island of Grenada, President Ronald Reagan used a photograph of a commercial airfield being built with Canadian funding to justify the claim he made on television network news that Cuba was building military facilities on Grenada. During the invasion, a news blackout was imposed, ostensibly for strategic reasons. By a combination of misinformation and blanket censorship, the U.S. leadership was able to obtain almost universal popular support for the venture.

The barring of reporters from the invasion of Grenada proved to be an effective means of controlling public opinion, but it resulted in dissatisfaction and criticism from those in the media. As a result, the Pentagon created the National Media Pool of rotating news organizations. Under the pool system, the military would decide, in time of armed conflict, when reporters would have to become part of the pool and the military could set ground rules for reporting. In this way, the U.S. government could avoid having unpleasant war news published and avoid accusations of censorship.

When U.S. Marines and Rangers led the invasion of Panama at the close of 1989, no journalists were allowed to accompany them. Under the pool system, reporters were brought into Panama by the military four hours after fighting began and they were not allowed to file dispatches for another six hours. News personnel were guided by the military; Panamanian civilian casualties appear, as a result, to have been vastly underreported.

A combination of misinformation and tight media control proved highly effective in the Persian Gulf War in 1991. The manipulation of the media was used not only to ensure popular support in the United States, but also to mislead the Iraqis. General Norman Schwarzkopf, after the successful campaign against Iraq, admitted that he had deliberately misled the media of his own country regarding where the major assault would take place, causing the Iraqis to concentrate their troops in the wrong places.

Reporters in the Persian Gulf depended heavily on American military Public Information Officers for their access to news. Since news about high casualties and the sight of civilian suffering, in photographs and on television, had contributed to the popular disillusionment with fighting in Vietnam, the Public Information Officers made an effort to represent the Persian Gulf conflict as a clean, high-tech war. The media were given low estimates of casualties among U.S. servicemen, and servicemen who had actually been killed or wounded in service were reported as "training casualties." The Public Information Officers also gave the television news networks tapes showing "smart bombs" zeroing in on specific, military targets to give the impression that all bombing was high-tech, with little death and destruction inflicted on Iraqi civilians. In fact, only about 7 percent of the bombs dropped were smart bombs and about 70 percent of all bombs dropped on Iraq missed their targets. A report critical of the effectiveness of smart bombs was not released until years after the war.

—Carl L. Bankston III

See also Athens, ancient; Civil War, U.S.; Crimean War; English Commonwealth; Espionage Act of 1917; Falkland Islands War; Korean War; Mexican-American War; Military censorship; Panama, U.S. invasion of; Persian Gulf War; Revolutionary War, American; Spanish-American War; Vietnam War; World War I; World War II.

BIBLIOGRAPHY

Men in Arms: A History of Warfare and Its Interrelationships with Western Society (New York: Holt, Rinehart and Winston, 1979), by Richard Preston and Sydney Wise, is a social history of war from ancient times through the Vietnam War era. Robert Summers' *Wartime Censorship of Press and Radio* (New York: H. H. Wilson, 1942) presents a useful, concise history of wartime censorship in the United States. *Red Scare* (Minneapolis: University of Minnesota Press, 1955), by Robert K. Murray, is a study of the attempts to suppress perceived radicalism following World War I. Patrick S. Washburn's *A Question of Sedition* (New York: Oxford University Press, 1986) offers a readable study of the U.S. government's investigation of the black press during World War II. *The Papers and the Papers* (New York: Dutton, 1972), by Sanford Ungar, is a detailed account of the conflict between the government and the press over the Pentagon Papers during the Vietnam War. Everette E. Dennis' *The Media at War: The*

Press and the Persian Gulf Conflict (New York: Gannett Foundation, 1991) describes how the press cooperated in its own censorship by the U.S. government during the Gulf War. *Freedom at Risk: Secrecy, Censorship, and Repression in the 1980's* (Philadelphia: Temple University Press, 1988), edited by Richard O. Curry, provides essays on military security and censorship during the Reagan Administration. The introduction to this last work also gives a good, succinct overview of censorship for the sake of security in American history.

War of 1812

DATE: 1812-1814
PLACE: North America
SIGNIFICANCE: The second American war for independence divided the United States into pro-French and pro-British factions, each with its own press attacking the actions of the other side

The First Amendment prohibited abridgment of freedom of the press because the Framers of the Bill of Rights wanted to guarantee rights enjoyed in Great Britain. When James Madison wrote the Virginia Resolution attacking the infamous Sedition Act of 1798, he wrote that attempts to curb speech could not be subjected to prior censorship and prosecution for seditious libel was inconsistent with American democracy. Therefore, it would have been intellectually and politically inconsistent for Madison, as president, to curb an active free press in the years preceding and during the War of 1812.

The American press of Madison's era published highly charged political commentary in newspapers, printed inflammatory political pamphlets, and, in a few instances, wrote political graffiti on town walls and offered bribes to British and U.S. political figures. In the years leading up to 1812 U.S. newspapers were divided into pro-Federalist and pro-Democratic-Republican camps. Washington, D.C.'s *National Intelligencer*, regarded as Madison's political mouthpiece, frequently contained articles written by Madison himself, or members of his staff, explaining their governmental views on issues affecting the nation. The Georgetown *Federal Republican* was run by Madison's archfoe, Alexander C. Hanson, who put aside his political rivalry with Madison long enough during the War of 1812 to warn the president about a plot to kill him.

President Madison made no formal effort, and did not encourage congressional action, to squelch press attacks on him during his presidency and the War of 1812. However, partisan politics exercised a form of press censorship when Madison supporters broke into opposition newspapers and destroyed their property. A particularly serious incident that occurred on July 27, 1812, was known as the "Baltimore Massacre." Former Virginia governor and Federalist Henry Lee was in Baltimore visiting William Hanson. Hanson, the editor of the *Federal Republican*, was a hard-core opponent of the war whose press regularly denounced the Madison Administration. Hanson's printing office came under attack by an unruly mob who destroyed his press. Hanson replaced the press and continued his criticisms. Lee was joined by additional Federalist Revolutionary War officers who came to defend Hanson. The new office was attacked and in the resulting melée, Lee was taken

for dead and left on the street. Found insensible, he was carried to the security of a jail, but, that, too, was attacked leaving Lee severely wounded. His health never fully recovered from these events and caused him to be disqualified from military service in the War of 1812. Such partisan violence and the inability of Federalist New England freely to trade with Great Britain only emboldened the minority Federalist Party and press to exercise their First Amendment rights in an active press war against the war, Madison, and the Democratic-Republican Party.

See also Censorship; First Amendment; Madison, James; Revolutionary War, American; Sedition Act of 1798; United States; War.

Warhol, Andy

BORN: September 28, 1928?, Forest City, Pennsylvania?
DIED: February 22, 1987, New York, New York
IDENTIFICATION: American artist and filmmaker
SIGNIFICANCE: Warhol's art was censored in several media, including film, sculpture, and silk screen/painting

An artist initially known for his serial photographic silk screen images of soup cans and celebrities, Warhol encountered censorship early in his career when a series of twenty-five large silk screened panels were painted over in silver for political reasons. The panels were displayed briefly in 1964 on the exterior of the New York State Pavilion at the World's Fair held in New York. The series, *13 Most Wanted Men*, depicted photographic images of thirteen men taken from eight-year-old Federal Bureau of Investigation most-wanted posters. The men, all of Italian descent and reported to have Mafia connections, had since been exonerated. Fearing lawsuits from their families, Governor Nelson Rockefeller had the images painted over in the dark of night without consultation with the artist.

The following year Warhol experienced another form of censure when the director of the National Gallery of Canada, acting as an adviser to the Canadian customs office, ruled that his grocery cartons and tin cans were not "original sculpture." Under Canadian customs regulations, these objects were subject to tariff regulations requiring a 20-percent merchandising duty to be paid by the Toronto gallery importing the works for an exhibition.

When Warhol turned his interests to film in the late 1960's, his experiments with the media brought a different level of censorship. His "factory films," as they have become known, featured a wide assortment of characters that frequented The Factory, his exclusive club in New York. His critically acclaimed 1968 film *Flesh* was followed by *Blue Movie/Fuck*, which took sexual intercourse from a mere scene, as in his earlier film, to become the entire focus with the stars, Viva and Louis Waldon, in a series of explicit sexual encounters. Warhol's intent was to use lovemaking as the backdrop for an afternoon in a couple's Manhattan apartment as they discussed mundane subjects of daily life. A New York County criminal court judge viewed the film; after finding probable cause for prosecuting it as obscene, he signed a search warrant for film seizure and "John Doe" warrants for the arrests of the theater manager, the projectionist, and the ticket-taker. After several appeals by Warhol's attorneys, an appeals court viewed the film in 1971 and upheld the police officer's seizure of the film and the lower court ruling that it was obscene under prevailing U.S. Supreme Court standards.

See also Art; Film censorship; Mural art; Obscenity: legal definitions; Rivera, Diego.

Warren, Earl

BORN: March 19, 1891, Los Angeles, California
DIED: July 9, 1974, Washington, D.C.
IDENTIFICATION: Governor of California (1943-1953) and chief justice of the United States (1953-1968)
SIGNIFICANCE: A zealous advocate of civil liberties, Warren opposed most forms of censorship but refused to accord constitutional protections to obscenity

As chief justice Warren presided over a period in the U.S. Supreme Court's history that saw civil liberties expand on a wide front. Warren generally allied with the Court's other liberal justices to favor protecting the freedom of individuals from government censorship. In *Times Film Corp. v. City of Chicago* (1961), for example, he joined justices Hugo Black, William O. Douglas, and William J. Brennan, Jr., in dissenting from the majority decision upholding a Chicago ordinance requiring films to be pre-approved by government censors. If such censorship was approved, he argued, there would be no basis for refusing to bless the censorship of other forms of communication.

Warren and his allies on the Court were successful in using the First Amendment's protection of speech to overturn legislation that attempted to restrict public interest litigation (*National Association for the Advancement of Colored People v. Button*, 1963) and to pry into the membership of politically unpopular organizations (*National Association for the Advancement of Colored People v. Alabama*, 1958).

Though opposed to censorship generally, Warren was nevertheless appalled at what he believed to be a flood of pornography sweeping over the country while he was chief justice. Society had a right to preserve decency, he thought, and sexually explicit materials challenged this right. He was thus prepared to uphold government restrictions on obscene materials, denying that obscenity could shelter its indecency beneath the First Amendment's fold. He saw that courts and legislatures could use the pretext of suppressing obscenity to regulate literary expression, and he was opposed to this kind of censorship. At the same time, however, his Court found it difficult to posit a definition that would distinguish unprotected obscenity from indecent literary works.

For a time it appeared that the Court had determined that obscenity was simply whatever at least five Supreme Court justices called obscene at a given moment. Warren was not happy with the idea of reviewing the allegedly obscene materials that were the subject of cases accepted for review by the Supreme Court. He generally preferred a deferential review of government decisions censoring obscenity, believing it to be the only way the Court itself could avoid sitting as a kind of super censor for the nation. However, a majority of his Court ultimately adopted a definition of obscenity that was considerably narrower than what he himself preferred in his public

discussions of this issue. In *Roth v. United States* (1957) the Court held that obscene materials were those sexual depictions that appealed to prurient interest; that had no serious literary, artistic, political, or scientific merit; and that were—taken as a whole—offensive to the average community.

See also Black, Hugo; Books and obscenity law; Brennan, William J., Jr.; Community standards; Courts and censorship law; Douglas, William O.; Obscenity: legal definitions; Pornography; *Roth v. United States*.

Watergate scandal

DATE: 1972-1974
PLACE: Washington, D.C.
SIGNIFICANCE: News media exposure of illegal activities of President Richard Nixon's reelection committee pitted the White House against the news media and the courts

During his reelection campaign in 1972, President Richard Nixon became concerned with information leaks from the White House. Frustrated by the inability of the Federal Bureau of Investigation (FBI) to stop the leaks, he authorized creation of an intelligence team called the "plumbers." A few months before he was reelected in a landslide, the plumbers were identified with a break-in at the Democratic National Headquarters at the Watergate hotel complex in Washington, D.C. It was also discovered that the break-in was financed by the Committee to Reelect the President (CREEP). Although James McCord, G. Gordon Liddy, and five others involved in the break-in were indicted prior to the election, the investigation, led by reporters Bob Woodward and Carl Bernstein of *The Washington Post*, continued to bring scrutiny closer to the president. Eventually Nixon's top advisers and Nixon himself were linked to the break-in and other "dirty tricks" perpetrated by the plumbers and the reelection committee.

Subsequent efforts to shield the president led to charges of obstruction of justice. Judge John J. Sirica determined that perjury had been committed and that political pressure was impeding the investigation. Eventually charges that the administration was attempting a cover-up superseded the break-in itself in the public eye. In 1973 the Senate established a special investigating committee, chaired by Senator Sam Ervin of North Carolina. The televised committee's hearings uncovered a series of illegal activities including further evidence of the cover-up. Special Counsel to the President John Dean, who had been given the job of shielding the president, became a key witness against the administration.

One of the tactics of the cover-up amounted to censorship through delegitimation: The administration allegedly used the FBI, Central Intelligence Agency (CIA), and Internal Revenue Service to discredit political opponents. One of the plumbers, Howard Hunt, had broken into the office of a psychiatrist to get records for a CIA psychiatric profile on Daniel Ellsberg. The administration wanted to discredit Ellsberg because he had leaked information about the forming of administration policy in Vietnam, called the Pentagon Papers, to *The New York Times*.

The delegitimation strategy was also used in an attempt to stifle the news media itself. The administration accused journalists of not following their own rules of objective reporting.

Sam Ervin (center), chairman of the U.S. Senate committee investigating the Watergate scandal, confers with Howard Baker (left) and Samuel Dash (right) during a break at the committee's televised hearings in May, 1973. (AP/Wide World Photos)

Nixon's defenders claimed coverage of the Watergate story was exaggerated and that journalists were carrying out personal vendettas against the president. Despite their failure to ward off the Watergate investigation, these charges initiated an ongoing debate about news media practices among public figures, professional journalists, and media scholars which resulted, at least in part, in eroding public trust in the news media.

Eventually it was disclosed that Nixon had routinely taped confidential conversations in the Oval Office. After a long legal battle the tapes were turned over to the Watergate Committee, and the extent of the president's involvement became more clear. When Nixon realized that a bipartisan congressional effort was underway to impeach him, he resigned from office.

See also Agnew, Spiro T.; Iran-Contra scandal; News media censorship; Nixon, Richard M.; *Pentagon Papers, The*; Vietnam War.

Weavers, the

FORMED: 1948
TYPE OF ORGANIZATION: Folk singing quartet
SIGNIFICANCE: The Weavers were blacklisted by conservative anticommunist groups

The Weavers (Pete Seeger, Ronnie Gilbert, Lee Hays, Fred Hellerman) became one of the most influential and popular folk singing groups in the United States in the period from 1949 to 1951, selling millions of recordings and gaining a large following. They were denounced as communists in 1952 by a Federal Bureau of Investigation informant—a former staff member of People's Songs who later recanted his testimony. Although the members of the Weavers had supported

progressive causes, only Pete Seeger had been on the rolls of the Communist Party, and he quit that organization. The Weavers disbanded in 1953 after finding it increasingly difficult to find engagements, encountering a series of rejections based on the assumption that they were subversives. Groups that refused to hire the Weavers included VanCamp beans, the National Broadcasting Company, and the organizers of the Ohio State Fair. Pete Seeger and Lee Hays were called before the House Committee on Un-American Activities in August, 1955. The Weavers reunited for a Carnegie Hall Christmas Eve concert that year at a time when many blacklisted performers were again finding work. They disbanded permanently in 1964 after several personnel changes and met for a last reunion at Carnegie Hall in 1980.

See also Blacklisting; Communism; Communist Party of the U.S.A.; Federal Bureau of Investigation; Folk music; Guthrie, Woody; House Committee on Un-American Activities; Protest music; Seeger, Pete.

Webster, Noah

BORN: October 16, 1758, West Hartford, Connecticut
DIED: May 28, 1843, New Haven, Connecticut
IDENTIFICATION: Pioneering American lexicographer
SIGNIFICANCE: Webster was the first American to expurgate the Bible

Well educated, Webster enjoyed writing on politics, economics, science, medicine and, most important, language. His works, including *American Spelling Book* (1783) and *American Dictionary of the English Language* (1828), helped to separate the British and American versions of English. Despite the inclusion of some slang in his works, Webster was cautious in his inclusion of colloquialisms and common language. As a result, he created linguistic and spelling standards that excluded many English, foreign, and common American words.

Although Webster is known primarily for his works on American English, he was also known for his editing of the Bible. In 1833 he published an expurgated edition of the Bible. While retaining the Bible's original stories, he changed much of their wording to reflect what he considered to be proper and decent values of the day. Webster's version of the Bible enjoyed early success and was adopted by the state of Connecticut and by Yale University. However, after the publication of the third edition in 1841, and substantial changes to many parts of the Bible, Webster's edition soon fell out of favor and was never published again.

See also Bible; Bowdler, Thomas; Dictionaries; Mencken, H. L.; Offensive language.

Well of Loneliness, The

TYPE OF WORK: Book
PUBLISHED: 1928
AUTHOR: Radclyffe Hall (1880-1943)
SUBJECT MATTER: Novel exploring the isolation of a lesbian struggling to find love and understanding
SIGNIFICANCE: While attempting to discuss "inversion" beyond the realm of morality, this novel was banned for its "obscene" thematic content

The lesbian protagonist of this novel, Stephen Gordon, fails to find love and understanding. After a series of rejections, her "inversion" is revealed to her mother, who orders her to leave her home. While serving in an all-woman ambulance corps during World War I, Stephen falls in love with Mary Llewellyn. Mary, however, later marries a man who had been Stephen's childhood friend.

Radclyffe "John" Hall considered herself an active or "congenital invert." Believing in sexologist Havelock Ellis' theories that "inverts" were biologically determined, Hall used scientific and medical concepts of inversion in literary discourse to discuss homosexuality outside the realm of morality.

In 1928 British home secretary Sir William Joynson-Hicks ordered the book banned in Britain. Representing the defense, John Holroyd-Reece of Pegasus Press and Harold Rubinstein invoked the Obscene Publications Act of 1857, which allowed books classified as "obscene" to be reconsidered in light of their "public good." Sir Charteres Biron presided over the trial and refused to allow testimony on the book's literary or scientific merit. Invoking a narrow definition of obscenity, Biron concluded that a book containing no indecent language might still be considered obscene for its theme or intent. Biron then ordered *The Well of Loneliness* "burnt as an obscene libel which tended to corrupt those into whose hands it fell." An appeal of this decision failed.

Meanwhile, in the United States the book was prosecuted under a federal law and acquitted in 1929. Although the book was banned in Great Britain, Pegasus continued to print it in France. In 1949, *The Well of Loneliness* was rereleased in England by Falcon Press.

See also Ellis, Henry Havelock; Homosexuality; Literature; Morality; Obscene Publications Acts.

West, Mae

BORN: August 17, 1893, Brooklyn, New York
DIED: November 22, 1980, Los Angeles, California
IDENTIFICATION: American stage and film actor
SIGNIFICANCE: After being jailed for obscenity in a stage production, West took her genius for sexual innuendo to the screen and helped provoke a move toward censorship in the U.S. film industry

A product of burlesque, West outraged American puritanical attitudes toward sex with her unabashed sexuality. She also shocked conventional notions of femininity by treating romance ironically and by seeming to regard men as mere sex objects. Jailed on obscenity charges for her 1926 play, *Sex*, she established herself as a personality. She also attracted the attention of Hollywood. After entering films West was dogged by censorship.

Six months after West's comedy *She Done Him Wrong* was released in 1933, the Roman Catholic Legion of Decency formed, with its founders intimating that West was largely the reason for the censorship body's existence. Nevertheless, the film (which was banned in Australia) helped save Paramount from bankruptcy. By West's third vehicle, *Belle of the Nineties* (1934), representatives of the Production Code Administration had become fixtures on her film sets.

Labeling West "a menace to the Sacred Institution of the American Family," newspaper tycoon William Randolph Hearst refused to let his papers carry advertisements for her film *Klondike Annie* (1937). Weary of battling censors, Paramount dropped West's contract in 1938, thereby virtually ending her film career. A year earlier, she had been banned from radio after her sexual double entendres provoked the radio network to cut off its live broadcast of *The Chase and Sanborn Hour*.

See also Film censorship; Hays Code; Society for the Suppression of Vice, New York; Sumner, John.

West Virginia State Board of Education v. Barnette

COURT: U.S. Supreme Court
DATE: June 14, 1943
SIGNIFICANCE: This decision invalidated compulsory state-sanctioned flag salutes as violations of freedom of expression under the First Amendment

In 1940 the U.S. Supreme Court upheld the constitutionality of a Pennsylvania school board regulation requiring teachers and students to participate in flag salute ceremonies. In *Minersville School District v. Gobitis* that year, the high court ruled in favor of the school board and against the Gobitis family, all of whom were Jehovah's Witnesses who refused to salute the U.S. flag. In that case the Court determined that because the concept of national unity outweighed interference with religious beliefs, the religious freedom of Jehovah's Witnesses could be abridged.

Three years later the Supreme Court reversed itself in *West Virginia State Board of Education v. Barnette*. This time the Court held that a compulsory flag salute resolution violated the free speech guarantee of the First Amendment. Barnette's lawyers argued that because their clients' religious convictions prohibited their children from "bowing down" to a "graven image," compelling their children to salute a flag would infringe on their religious liberties. After an injunction was issued against enforcement of the flag salute law in the lower court, the state of West Virginia appealed. In a 6-3 opinion, the U.S. Supreme Court upheld the lower court's injunctive relief, with justices Owen Roberts, Stanley Reed, and Felix Frankfurter dissenting. In his majority opinion, Justice Robert Jackson observed that "if there is any fixed star in our constitutional constellation it is that no official, high or petty, can prescribe what shall be orthodox in politics, nationalism, religion, or other matters of opinion and force citizens to confess by word or act their faith therein."

Both *Gobitis* and *Barnette* made clear, however, that free speech and religious toleration were not absolute; that, in some well-defined and narrowly drawn circumstances, both freedoms might have to yield to some form of censorship. For example, laws governing defamation, clear expressions of obscenity, and contempt may require that certain speech—verbal or symbolic—be censored for the common good.

See also Courts and censorship law; First Amendment; Flag burning; Intellectual freedom; Jehovah's Witnesses; Pledge of Allegiance; Symbolic speech.

Whistler, James Abbott McNeill

BORN: July 10, 1834, Lowell, Massachusetts
DIED: July 17, 1903, London, England
IDENTIFICATION: American Impressionist painter
SIGNIFICANCE: Whistler's avant-garde paintings were severely and publicly criticized when they were refused for major exhibitions

In 1862 Whistler painted a full-length view of a young woman clothed largely in white standing before a white background that he called *Symphony in White No. 1: The White Girl*. Its loose brushwork revealed few details. This painting was refused by the jury for an exhibition that same year at the Royal Academy in London and again the next year for the Paris Salon exhibition.

Because of the large number of rejections connected with the Paris Salon, Emperor Napoleon III ordered an exhibition of rejected works (Salon des Refusées) to be held at the same time and in the same building. The huge crowds that gathered to laugh at the rejected artworks created immediate controversy, as did the discussion of the works by art critics of Paris newspapers. Whistler's painting was one of their main targets. His painting attracted ridicule because of the deliberate lack of narrative inherent in its subject, as well as its loose impressionistic brushwork, which merely suggested what was there, instead of representing it in minute detail. The jurors as well as the public were unaccustomed to artworks without implicit storylines and little detail, which seemed to them to be incomplete. Whistler's intention was to explore a limited number of tonal values in his white on white composition thereby molding an abstract creation rather than telling a story.

See also Art; Beardsley, Aubrey; Dalí, Salvador; France; Manet, Edouard.

Whitman, Walt

BORN: May 31, 1819, West Hills, New York
DIED: March 26, 1892, Camden, New Jersey
IDENTIFICATION: American poet
SIGNIFICANCE: Whitman's work was often censored; he apparently lost his job in the U.S. Department of Interior for publishing *Leaves of Grass*

Leaves of Grass, Whitman's controversial book of poetry, grew over nine successive editions from a ninety-page folio in 1855 to a book of nearly 440 pages in 1892. Its celebration of the human body and sexuality in frank and explicit language, particularly in the original long poem "Song of Myself," and in two collections of poems added in 1860—"Children of Adam," which treats heterosexual love, and "Calamus," a work of a homoerotic nature—drew fire for the poems' "indecency." Ralph Waldo Emerson failed to convince Whitman that inclusion of "Children" would be fatal to his career, and Whitman—as he did throughout his life—remained true to his vision.

On June 30, 1865, Secretary of the Interior James Harlan fired Whitman from his post in the Bureau of Indian Affairs. After reading a copy of *Leaves of Grass* that he found at Whitman's work site, Harlan decided its author was immoral and must be dismissed at once. In response to this treatment of a poet whom he considered a national icon, the polemicist William Douglas O'Connor wrote *The Good Gray Poet*, a pamphlet denouncing Harlan's action and defending Whitman's character. The publication did much to defuse accusations of indecency and to implant a benign image of the poet in the American mind.

Whitman's early acceptance in England has been attributed to publication of a selected edition of his poems by London publisher William Michael Rossetti. Because of the book's controversial nature in the United States, Whitman rarely had the luxury of an American publisher, but had the book printed and promoted it himself.

In 1882 at the urging of the New York Society for the Suppression of Vice, Boston's district attorney threatened Whitman's publishers with prosecution if they attempted to distribute the current edition of *Leaves of Grass*. The fray that followed drew many voices on both sides of the debate. Citing the Comstock Act of 1873, the Boston post office refused to distribute a publication whose defense of Whitman reprinted his poem "To a Common Prostitute." The decision was eventually overturned and the item mailed, but the incident prompted Anthony Comstock, the nation's leading foe of so-called social vice, to issue a public threat against *Leaves of Grass*. O'Connor once again came to the book's defense, and in 1883 the libraries of Boston and Cambridge removed it from the category of restricted circulation. As a result of the controversy, *Leaves of Grass* began to earn steady royalties for the first time, and expanded its contribution to American and world literature.

See also Comstock, Anthony; Comstock Act of 1873; Poetry; Postal regulations; Sex in the arts; Society for the Suppression of Vice, New York; Twain, Mark.

Who's Afraid of Virginia Woolf?

TYPE OF WORK: Film

RELEASED: 1966

DIRECTOR: Mike Nichols (1931-   )

SUBJECT MATTER: Two married couples—university professors and their wives—share an evening together, during which they confront their hopes and illusions

SIGNIFICANCE: Hollywood film whose frank language and adult themes made a major assault on the standards of the Motion Picture Production Code, leading to the formation of a classification system segmenting audiences by age

In 1963 Jack Warner bought the movie rights to *Who's Afraid of Virginia Woolf?*, an award-winning Broadway play written by Edward Albee. Not unexpectedly, the Production Code Administration (PCA) found numerous violations of the profanity and obscenity sections of the rigid Motion Picture Production Code in the text of what was considered a groundbreaking play distinguished by the frankness and ferocity of its dialogue. The PCA recommended major alterations. Albee was unwilling to write substitute dialogue; screenwriter Ernest Lehman's final draft of the screenplay closely resembled Albee's original text. Warner, after exploring distribution channels outside PCA jurisdiction, decided that Warner Bros. would go forward with a high-visibility, high-cost production, gambling that such stakes would be advantageous for the studio in its inevitable confrontation with the PCA.

Although filmed on a closed set in an atmosphere of considerable secrecy, the production was surrounded by publicity, partly because of the casting of Elizabeth Taylor and Richard Burton in the leading roles as a volatile married couple whose

Richard Burton and Sandy Denis watch George Segal wrestle with Elizabeth Taylor in the 1966 film adaptation of Edward Albee's play Who's Afraid of Virginia Woolf? *(Museum of Modern Art/Film Stills Archive)*

verbal clashes drive the dramatic action. The film's director, Hollywood newcomer Mike Nichols, came to the project with Broadway credentials and no allegiance to the PCA. Nichols did not shoot alternative scenes with diluted dialogue, so when the PCA saw the completed film and found it unacceptable in May, 1966, there was no choice but to proceed with the film virtually intact or abandon it altogether.

Warner Bros. made only two minor deletions of language deemed offensive by the PCA and then appealed the PCA decision to withhold its seal of approval. Studio executives argued that the high quality and $7.5-million cost of the production merited special consideration. When the National Catholic Office for Motion Pictures (formerly the Legion of Decency) awarded the film an A-IV rating ("morally unobjectionable for adults, with reservations"), even more pressure was put on the Motion Picture Association and its new president, Jack Valenti, to find some accommodation.

While waiting for reconsideration, Warner Bros. devised an advertising campaign for the film that mandated an "adults only" audience. Heretofore, movie producers and exhibitors had strongly opposed all classification systems, presuming them to be economically disadvantageous. When the board eventually relented and granted the studio a seal of approval for *Who's Afraid of Virginia Woolf?*, the public announcements treated the decision as an exception, but the handwriting was on the wall: Changes in demographics, audience taste, and the law, in addition to the competition of television, pointed to the economic necessity of a classification system for Hollywood movies. Immediately after the film's release, the industry adopted a short-lived "revised code," which was soon replaced, in 1968, by the first industry-sponsored classification system in movie history.

See also Film adaptation; Hays Code; Legion of Decency; Motion Picture Association of America.

Wild Bunch, The

TYPE OF WORK: Film

RELEASED: 1969

DIRECTOR: Sam Peckinpah (1925-1984)

SUBJECT MATTER: Western story about an outlaw band that is destroyed in a spectacular violent climax

SIGNIFICANCE: The film's unprecedented levels of graphic violence forced its makers to fight against its being awarded a commercially damaging rating

Wishing to educate filmgoers about the true nature of the Old West, director Sam Peckinpah wrote the script of *The Wild Bunch* from an earlier draft by William Goldman. Its narrative follows an outlaw band led by a man named Pike Bishop (William Holden) as it is pursued in 1913 by Pike's old friend Deke Thornton (Robert Ryan), The film opens and closes with exceptionally bloody gunfights. However, Peckinpah's use of slow-motion montages gives this violence a balletic quality that seemed to transform mayhem into art. In the final battle scene, the remnants of Bishop's gang try to save one of their number from a Mexican army brigade that is torturing him. After the Mexican general slits the man's throat, all of Bishop's men die while killing hundreds of Mexican soldiers.

The Wild Bunch *ends as its begins: in violence, with William Holden (right), Ernest Borgnine, and other gang members dying in a shoot-out.* (Museum of Modern Art/Film Stills Archive)

During advance screenings, the film's preview audiences divided between those who fled the theaters, sick from the sight of blood, and those who stood up to applaud. Efforts of the Motion Picture Association of America (MPAA) to rate the film X for its violence failed. Jack Valenti, president of the MPAA, defended the film on First Amendment grounds. When the film was rereleased in 1993, the MPAA assigned it a new NC-17 rating; however, this rating was overturned two years later, when the film was rated R.

See also Film censorship; Motion Picture Association of America; Peckinpah, Sam; Violence.

Wilde, Oscar

BORN: October 16, 1854, Dublin, Ireland
DIED: November 30, 1900, Paris, France
IDENTIFICATION: Irish playwright, novelist, and poet
SIGNIFICANCE: Wilde was the best-known literary figure of his era to face censorship because of public disapproval of both his life and writings

By the 1890's, Oscar Wilde was the most popular playwright in London. His successes included *Lady Windermere's Fan* (1892), *A Woman of No Importance* (1893), *An Ideal Husband* (1895), and *The Importance of Being Earnest* (1895). Nevertheless, censorship of his work began with his very first play, *Vera, or the Nihilists*, scheduled for performance in 1881. Set in Russia around 1800, the play was based on the 1878

assassination of a St. Petersburg police official by an eighteen-year-old girl—who became the heroine of Wilde's play. Following the assassinations of Russian czar Alexander II on March 13, 1881, and U.S. president James A. Garfield—who died on September 9, 1881—unofficial pressure, reportedly from the Russian government, caused cancellation of the play's rehearsals. In 1892, Wilde's *Salomé* was being rehearsed for a London performance with French actress Sarah Bernhardt when the Lord Chamberlain refused a license because British law forbade theatrical depiction of biblical characters. Wilde published the play in Paris in 1893 and had it produced there in 1896. It was successful in Europe, especially after Richard Strauss produced a popular operatic version in 1905.

Wilde also wrote a controversial novel and is associated with another. *The Picture of Dorian Gray* first appeared in *Lippincott's Monthly Magazine* in 1890. W. H. Smith and Son, important British booksellers and news agents, withdrew that issue from stock and refused to handle it when a longer version appeared in book form. In 1895, Wilde sued Lord Queensberry (John Sholto Douglas) for criminal libel after Queensberry publicly accused him of homosexual activity. Queensberry's attorney cited *The Picture of Dorian Gray* and the aphorisms that prefaced it as evidence of Wilde's desire to subvert conventional morality.

Wilde's name also has been linked with the frankly erotic homosexual novel *Teleny, or the Reverse of the Medal: A Physiological Romance* (1893), which he brought to the attention of French bookseller Charles Hirsch in 1889. Scholars have divided over the question of who wrote the novel; some

Irish playwright Oscar Wilde got into trouble almost as much for his flamboyant lifestyle as he did for his frequently censored plays. (Library of Congress)

scholars have attributed it to Wilde, others have suggested that it was written by several different authors, including Wilde.

When Wilde's suit against Queensberry failed, the latter's charge against Wilde was proven correct, and Wilde was tried for homosexual activities under an 1885 British law. After he was sentenced to two years' imprisonment, some of his plays were taken off the stage and his name was removed as the author of others. Titles of his books were removed from publishers' lists, and his book sales decreased. Wilde's two sons were given a guardian and a new last name. In 1893, Wilde's name was omitted from an American Library Association list of titles suitable for small libraries; in 1904, the authorized ALA catalog banned his work. Local censorship occurred, as in Boston, where the Watch and Ward Society prevented a 1907 production of Richard Strauss's *Salomé*. That year, in New York, public reaction caused the Metropolitan Opera House to withdraw Strauss's work after a single performance.

See also American Library Association; Beardsley, Aubrey; Boston Watch and Ward Society; Drama and theater; Harris, Frank; Homosexuality; Lord Chamberlain; Morality; Opera; United Kingdom.

Williams, Roger

BORN: c. 1603, London, England
DIED: between January 16 and March 15, 1683, Providence, Rhode Island
IDENTIFICATION: Colonial American cleric
SIGNIFICANCE: Williams was driven from Massachusetts Bay Colony because of his religious beliefs

Williams graduated from England's Cambridge University in 1627 and shortly thereafter came to Massachusetts, where he became pastor of a church at Salem. There he immediately began attacking the right of magistrates to punish offences of the "first table," that is, the section of the Ten Commandments dealing with offences against God. The influence of John Calvin's ecclesiastical constitution at Geneva had come to Massachusetts, and Williams' opinions were highly unwelcome. First, pressure was brought to bear on members of the Salem church because they had allowed Williams to become their pastor without consulting with the magistrates.

This pressure escalated when Governor John Winthrop accused Williams of spreading unorthodox opinions concerning the role of civil officers in their relationship with the church. Then Boston refused to publish Williams' books. Williams insisted upon absolute liberty of conscience in religious matters and a "wall of separation" between church and state. These events led to Williams' banishment to Providence where, in 1639, he joined in forming a separatist church that embraced adult baptism and rejected civil jurisdiction over laws of the "first table"; it became the first Baptist church in America. Due to pressure from the magistrates, even Williams' own church in Salem finally withdrew fellowship from him.

From the standpoint of the governor of Massachusetts and the magistrates, the issue was their right to punish "heretics" and their belief that loss of this right would lead to anarchy, as well as schism within the church. From Williams' standpoint, the issue was liberty of conscience in religious matters without any intervention of government in purely religious affairs. Censorship was then imposed both in the refusal to print Williams' books and his banishment from Massachusetts because he refused to recant his opinions.

In 1643 Williams took his battle to England, where he hoped to find a printer for his books, a charter for his new colony, and support for his views. In July, 1644, he published a book entitled *The Bloody Tenent of Persecution for Cause of Conscience*, again setting forth his view that government had no right to interfere with the practice of religion according to one's conscience. When Parliament met the next month, it ordered the book to be burned. Had Williams not speedily departed the country, he might have been burned along with his book. He arrived back in Providence in late 1644 with a charter in hand and was quickly designated "chief officer." The charter specified that Portsmouth and Newport were to be part of the colony that became Rhode Island. Williams now had to practice what he had long proposed in theory—and he found that his task was no easy one. After a three-year struggle he succeeded, however, and a long beginning step was taken toward the constitutional guarantee of liberty of conscience by the later Constitution of the United States of America.

See also Calvin, John; Heresy; Hutchinson, Anne; Puritans; Reformation, the; Religion.

Williams, Tennessee

BORN: March 26, 1911, Columbus, Mississippi
DIED: February 25, 1983, New York, New York
IDENTIFICATION: American playwright and critic
SIGNIFICANCE: Several of Williams' plays have been attacked because of their violence and obsession with sexuality

Although Williams has been widely acknowledged as one of the leading modern American playwrights, his work has often been criticized for its violence and an obsession with sexuality. *A Streetcar Named Desire* (1947), for example, was a Broad-

Producer Irene Selznick (left), director Elia Kazan (center), and playwright Tennessee Williams (right) discuss their New York production of Williams' A Streetcar Named Desire *in 1947.* (AP/Wide World Photos)

way hit. It helped launch Williams' creative writing career when it won the Drama Critics' Circle Award and the Pulitzer Prize. However, it was criticized for being uncouth and overly violent. Williams publicly responded to such criticism by arguing that it was all right for a play to be violent and full of motion, so long as it has the "special kind of repose" that allows contemplation and produces a climate "in which tragic importance is a possible thing." In his preface to *Sweet Bird of Youth* (1959) Williams defended the violence in his plays by arguing that if there were any truth in the Aristotelian idea that violence is purged by poetic representations on a stage, then the violence in his own plays had a moral justification.

Controversy has also surrounded Williams' *The Rose Tattoo* (1951) and *Cat on a Hot Tin Roof* (1955). He wrote two endings for the latter play. He showed his first draft to director Elia Kazan, who made three suggestions. Kazan thought that the character of Big Daddy was too vivid and important to disappear from the play. He also suggested that the character of Brick should undergo some apparent mutation as a result of the virtual vivisection. Finally, Kazan argued that the character Maggie should be more clearly sympathetic to the audience. In order to persuade Kazan to direct his play, Williams accepted the last of his three suggestions. In so doing, he altered the play's thematic structure. In the play's published version Williams included both his original ending and the one that Kazan suggested. When Kazan directed a television adaptation of it in 1986, he focused on the relationship between Brick and Maggie, instead of that between Brick and Skipper—which is ostensibly homosexual.

Censorship took its toll on Williams' career and his life. He suffered several nervous breakdowns and was once committed to a St. Louis mental home. He was also reluctant to discuss his work with other people, comparing it to a "bird that will be startled away, as by a hawk's shadow."

See also Aristotle; Art; Drama and theater; Film adaptation; Film censorship; Literature; Sex in the arts; Violence.

Witnesses, protection of

DEFINITION: Activities that shield witnesses, generally from reprisals from friends or family of the accused

SIGNIFICANCE: Witness protection aims at reducing reluctance of witnesses to testify and has been criticized for allowing attorneys to prepare witnesses

The term "witness protection" is frequently associated with the famous U.S. Federal Witness Protection Program, which involves a complex and sometimes traumatic relocation of witnesses and their families. Protection of witnesses exists, however, at every judicial level and in many countries. Victims of crimes usually testify as witnesses, and since the 1960's U.S. courts have attempted to protect and compensate victims and other witnesses who, at least, are inconvenienced by their roles as witnesses, and in many cases are threatened with assault and death. If some effort is not made to protect witnesses, prosecutors may lose cooperation and the case may be weakened. On the other hand, criticism of witness assistance programs point out that such programs allow prosecuting attorneys to rehearse and smooth the testimony of protected witnesses.

Protection of witnesses and victims may include crisis counseling, referrals to appropriate agencies, contacts with employers, and actual physical protection. If the accused are threatening enough, the witness important enough, and the government responsive enough, protection may extend to such measures as relocation of families, name change, new employment, and establishment of a new identity.

Often, protection is inadequate. In Minneapolis, where a rash of murders challenged law enforcement, the solution rate dipped drastically. Police blamed this largely on the number of uncooperative witnesses. Witnesses feared retribution, and the Minneapolis Police Department was unable to protect them. When the Minnesota legislature fell short in providing funds, Hennipin County drew on other funds to protect witnesses. However, this protection amounted to minimum security measures for the witnesses' homes. In some few cases relocation meant simply a bus ticket to another town or a deposit on an apartment in another part of the city.

Even where stronger witness protection programs exist, they seem inadequate, and persons coming forth to testify are discouraged. Marilyn Ross, a Los Angeles mother who turned in her sons for murder, found that under the county's program only her first and last months' rent on a new apartment were paid. Because seeking a job would put her in jeopardy, she had little means of support. In addition, the California Right to a Fair Trial Act, which took effect on January 1, 1995, prohibits witnesses from profiting from information (by way of articles, books, or films) until one year after the date of the crime or until a final judgment is reached. This further narrows a witness's financial help. The law was enacted after witnesses—or people who claimed to be witnesses—to the marital troubles of O. J. Simpson and Nicole Simpson sold their stories to the media.

The Federal Witness Protection Program has been partially credited with the decline of the Mafia in the United States. The government reports that more than one hundred former Mafiosi are in the program, providing a large number of informants on the crimes of the bosses. Many of these witnesses, however, participated in many of the same crimes of which the accused are accused.

In South Africa a combination of an indemnity with a relocation program for police allowed the Nelson Mandela government to obtain information about crimes committed primarily against blacks during apartheid. As with the United States' compromises to weaken the Mafia, many guilty of the crimes were allowed to escape punishment under these programs.

See also Courtrooms; Criminal trials; Fear; Gouzenko, Igor Sergeievich; Police; South Africa.

Wodehouse, P. G.

BORN: October 15, 1881, Guildford, Surrey, England
DIED: February 14, 1975, Long Island, New York
IDENTIFICATION: Anglo-American writer and humorist
SIGNIFICANCE: While he was interned by the German government World War II, Wodehouse made several humorous radio broadcasts that led to attacks on him and his writings in Great Britain

Before World War II Wodehouse made a fortune—largely in the United States—from genial stories about English upper-class dimwits, and from his writing for Broadway and Hollywood. In 1940 he happened to be living in France when it was occupied by the German army and was captured and interned as an enemy alien. After a campaign to release him was mounted in America, he was removed to a hotel in Berlin, Germany, where he naïvely agreed to make a series of broadcasts to America over German radio.

Wodehouse's talks consisted of light-hearted descriptions of life in internment camps, but the mere fact of his consenting to broadcast under German auspices made him a traitor in British eyes. He was widely denounced in the British media, but a number of supporters also spoke out in his defense. The most prominent—and perhaps the most improbable—of these was the left-wing social critic and novelist George Orwell, who published an essay defending Wodehouse as a politically innocent dupe guilty of nothing worse than poor judgment.

After Germans released Wodehouse, he went to Paris. When France was liberated by the Allies, orders were issued to arrest him and return him to Britain for trial. He instead went to the United States, where he became an American citizen. He remained there for the rest of his life, continuing to write stories about England until the day of his death at age ninety-five. Despite wartime calls for Wodehouse's punishment in Britain, his literary reputation there was soon rehabilitated. Shortly before he died, Wodehouse was formally forgiven for his mistake when he was knighted (in absentia) by Queen Elizabeth II.

See also Orwell, George; Propaganda; Tokyo Rose; World War II.

Women

DEFINITION: Adult females

SIGNIFICANCE: Women have been barred, discouraged, and prevented from expressing themselves

People use symbols (language, art) to express themselves and interact with others. Over time, culture is passed from one generation to the next through these forms of expression. Language and other codes form sets of rules and conventions that determine what should be, and, in a sense, what can be said in a particular cultural tradition.

Women have trailed men in freedom of expression, which is the ability to create and transfer culture. At most times and in most places, a majority of women have lacked literacy. Women were excluded from learning to read or write in the symbols of their cultures. Since men constructed knowledge, they served as the gatekeepers, or controllers, of knowledge. They were able to decide what knowledge was and who had access to it.

Conditions surrounding cultural production, or the production of art, must be viewed in the historical context in which the work is produced. One must recognize the extent of political censorship in society to understand women's apparent absence in the history of art. The artist or author cannot be conceived of as an ideal, free, creative spirit, but precisely as someone with a given social and historical situation, confronted by the mundane conditions of artistic production. Whether or not authors are independent and free to sell their works to publishers, or how cultural producers are subject to certain constraints, depends on each society's hierarchical structure.

Patriarchy was derived from Greek and Roman law, in which the male head of the household had absolute legal and economic power over his dependent female and male family members. Many of the legal forms of patriarchy ended in the nineteenth century in the United States and other industrialized countries with the granting of civil rights to women, including married women. Patriarchy gave men control over culture in two ways: educational deprivation of women and male monopoly of cultural definitions. The economic basis of this control was no secret; hence its legal protection.

During the Middle Ages (roughly 500 to 1500 C.E.), culture was largely the province of male religious leaders. Most art, music, and drama had religious themes and was displayed or performed in church buildings. Most literature was written by male clerics and most musicians were clerics. During this time women were often excluded from schools and academies, and their writings were rarely accepted by men. The major art forms, including music and literature, were regarded as tied to characteristics deemed masculine. The work women artists, writers, and speakers produced was considered craft rather than art. The gender of the artist was the main factor in how a work was judged.

Women were to be chaste, silent, and obedient. Most women stayed close to home under the supervision of their fathers or husbands. Learning to read and write meant the ability to express one's ideas—an ability that few men regarded as important for women. Only royal women or cloistered nuns were allowed access to education and had sufficient leisure time. Consequently, little literature, music, or fine art produced by women dates from the Middle Ages.

During the seventeenth and eighteenth centuries more women artists and writers emerged. Spurred by the idea that education was important for the public good, men began to see women as important in their influence on children. In England, France, and Germany, a few boarding schools were opened for upper- and middle-class girls. These girls received education in the areas deemed to make them more attractive marriage partners: needlework, dancing, drawing and painting, moral instruction, domestic skills, and limited foreign language.

Women suffered censorship, however, because schooling was less available to them. Men continued to explain the world in their terms and define the important questions so as to make themselves the center of discourse. Industrialization, however, created the necessary conditions by which large groups of women could express themselves openly. Being allowed to participate fully in the control of the symbol system of a society, women became more able to develop their own forms of artistic expression.

Women's Writing. From 1640 to 1700, women's writing accounted for approximately 1.2 percent of the publications in England; studies in other countries suggest that less than 1 percent of the writing was done by women. The factors that kept women from publishing were their lack of educational opportunities, economic factors, and the cultural beliefs that women should remain silent.

Industrialization, which brought better educational opportunities for women, and suffrage were important turning points for women's expression. These events occurred in the nineteenth and twentieth centuries. Political participation opened the door for women to engage in the general exchange of ideas. Knowing that women's vote could decide an election, politicians became more open to what women were saying.

Women's Visual Art. During the Middle Ages in Europe, gender bias divided visual arts into arts and crafts. Women's art was what did not achieve the status of major arts. A good example of loss of status in an art form is embroidery, which in the Middle Ages was practiced by women and men in male-directed craft guilds. As time went on, embroidery became identified as a woman's craft and produced in the home. It was viewed as an individual creation rather than an art, and those who embroidered for pay (except the male designers of embroidery patterns) received lower wages.

In painting, there were few women. During the sixteenth century, several women became prominent painters in Italy, and a number of others are known to have painted regularly. During the seventeenth century the best opportunities for women painters were in The Netherlands, and by the middle of the eighteenth century in France.

Most women painters were the daughters of painters or intellectuals. Many were eldest daughters or came from families with no sons. Women were not allowed to study the male nude, which was viewed as essential if one wanted to paint large history paintings with many figures, so they generally painted portraits, smaller paintings with only a few subjects, or still lifes and interior scenes, which were viewed as lesser in importance.

In the twentieth century, there was an articulate and sustained objection to the way in which women had been excluded from the history of art. Social organization of artistic production over the centuries has systematically excluded women from participation in art.

Women's Music and Acting. Sixteenth century writers worried about women using music to lure men into the dangers of love, but by the seventeenth century singing and playing an instrument became suitable for middle- and upper-class young women. These girls were not allowed to play in public and could perform only for their own families. When women married, they often gave up their music.

Women were often the most well-known singers of all types of songs, adding verses, changing content, and altering tunes as they sang them.

As more elaborate forms of music developed over time in the West, more years of training to compose or perform were required. Church officials and nobles increasingly hired permanent professional composers and musicians and these people were typically men. Many female musicians, however, were the daughters of musicians or came from musical families, and their fathers not only trained them but also helped them to get their music published. By 1700, twenty-three women in Italy had had their music published, and during the early part of the eighteenth century women began to compose larger pieces as well. Of these, more than half were nuns who wrote secular and sacred music.

In 1686 Pope Innocent XI had extended a prohibition, forbidding all women—single, married, or widowed as well as nuns—to learn music for any reason from any man, including their fathers or husbands, or to play any musical instrument "because music is completely injurious to the modesty that is proper for the [female] sex." Evidently some men ignored this prohibition or never heard of it.

Many of the women who became noted as singers were also actresses. In general, actresses, opera singers, and ballerinas in the 1600's were not regarded as honorable women, and many were able to support themselves only by also being the mistress of an artistically inclined male. In modern times, women in the industrialized nations were as likely as men to perform musically and on stage. Women have played a much more prominent role in the modern music scene than they did in the past. They distinguished themselves not only as performers, a role in which they always had excelled, but also as composers, teachers, and conductors.

Women's Speech. Women's public speech during the seventeenth and eighteenth centuries was often linked with sexual dishonor. A woman who wanted her thoughts known by others was suspected of wanting to make her body available as well. Women were expected to remain silent in church and in public. In the home, a husband was legally permitted to silence his wife or children with physical force.

In the twentieth century, women became active in public speech. Although their representation in politics still lagged far behind men, women did hold more public offices than before. They were represented more in the mass media, and as a result of their increased participation in the workforce they continued to fill roles where they were able to participate in defining cultural values.
　　　　　　　　　　　　　　　　　　—*Carolyn Johnson*

See also Abolitionist movement; Feminism; National Organization for Women; Women, violence against; Women Against Pornography; Women Against Violence in Pornography and Media; Woodhull, Victoria.

BIBLIOGRAPHY

Stevi Jackson et al., eds., *Women's Studies: Essential Readings* (Washington Square: New York University Press, 1993), is a compilation on women's education and work, language and gender, and the media. Gerda Lerner's *The Creation of Patriarchy* (New York: Oxford University Press, 1986) provides a historical account of women's subordination in the world. Joseph Machlis' *The Enjoyment of Music* (New York: W. W. Norton, 1990) offers a historical account of women's participation in musical and acting expression. Merry E. Wiesner's *Women and Gender in Early Modern Europe* (New York: Cambridge University Press, 1993) gives a discussion of women's creation of culture during the Middle Ages. Janet Wolff's *The Social Production of Art* (New York: New York University Press, 1993) is a detailed discussion of the political and social forces that have historically determined cultural expression.

Women, violence against

DEFINITION: Physical harm caused to women, including assault, rape, and murder

SIGNIFICANCE: Violent depictions in the media and methods of reporting violence affect the levels of actual violence against women

There are three major issues concerning censorship and violence against women: reporting accuracy, media effect, and government censorship. The first issue concerns the accuracy of reports and estimates of violence inflicted on women. Official reports about the amount of violence that women endure vary worldwide. China, for example, reported to the United Nations in 1990 that it had a domestic violence rate of only 1 percent. In contrast, the National Family Violence Surveys has estimated that 16 percent of households in the United States experience some kind of spousal violence. However, because women demand official responses to the violence against them as they gain power politically and socially, official reports of violence against them increase. Low violence figures thus do not necessarily indicate low levels of violence.

The Debate over Measuring Violence. In addition to worldwide variation in reports of violence, there has been a debate about how to measure violence against women. In the United States violence against women is officially measured by the Department of Justice in its Uniform Crime Reports, which are compiled from data supplied by police departments throughout the country. A 1992 study financed by the U.S. government found that the number of completed sexual assaults in a given year is five times as high as that reported in the National Crime Survey. Because official reports underestimate actual violence, there have been numerous attempts to measure actual violence through victim surveys. However, victim survey estimates have been criticized as politically motivated exaggeration. In turn, the victim survey critics have been disparaged for mounting a politically motivated backlash. Author Susan Faludi has contended that official reports underestimate violence against women so greatly that it constitutes a form of censorship.

Two remedies have been attempted to address reporting and prosecuting problems in the United States at the state and local levels, and at the federal level. Because women victims of assaults often refuse to press charges after police have been called, many states and municipalities have begun requiring mandatory prosecution for all reports of domestic abuse. Subsequent studies, however, have found that arrest is not a deterrent for further abuse, and that as a result of these laws many women are arrested for assault because they were involved in mutual battery.

The second remedy is at the federal level. In 1995 the U.S. Congress passed the Violence Against Women Act. This legislation allows women to bring civil cases for attacks made against them because of their gender. The law also mandates educational programs against domestic violence and strengthens laws against spousal abuse. The law has been a significant step toward recognizing violence against women as a hate crime. The Hate Crimes Statistics Act of 1990 did not include sex as a category in its official definition; however, as a result of the Violence Against Women Act the Justice Department has begun compiling hate crimes motivated by the sex of the victim.

Media Effects on Violence. The media's effect on the prevalence of violence against women is another major issue. Depictions of violence against women have steadily increased on television, in advertisements, and in pop music lyrics and videos. This increase has matched increases in reported violence against women. Women have been disproportionately depicted as victims of violence in the media, while male characters have been portrayed as perpetrators of violence. Rape scenes have been particularly over-represented on television. Frequently rape is depicted in a manner that encourages rape-supportive attitudes, with victims portrayed as either deserving or enjoying the rape. Although many studies have demonstrated simultaneous rises in violence in the media and real violence toward women, this debate centers on whether media violence causes violent behavior in its audience.

There are three notable theories about causal relationships between media violence and violent behavior: cathartic effect, modeling effect, and catalytic effect. The cathartic effect theory, also known as the safety-valve effect theory, holds that viewing violence allows vicarious release of violent impulses, thereby reducing the need to be violent. Critics of this theory point out that the hypothesis lacks empirical support and that neither media violence nor real violence has declined. The modeling effect theory emphasizes the direct imitation of violent behavior. According to this theory media violence teaches and, in the case of some rap music, actually advocates violent behavior toward women. While several shocking cases of direct imitation have been widely publicized, critics of this approach point out that the overwhelming majority of viewers never attempt to imitate television violence. The catalytic effect theory, also known as the trigger effect theory, holds that under certain circumstances violent depictions can precipitate real violence. According to this theory violent viewing alone is not sufficient to explain episodes of real violence.

Government Intervention. Public concern over increasingly violent television programs has prompted debate about the government's responsibility to control violence in the media. In 1993, for example, the Radio-Television and Telecommunications Commission of the Canadian government imposed strict regulations over violent programming. These regulations restricted the manner in which violence could be portrayed and the hours when violent programming could be broadcast. The guidelines for children's programming were even more strict. The regulations banned all depictions that minimize the consequences of violence or that encourage violence.

There has been much concern expressed in the United States about the consequences of escalating violence on television, but no federal legislation has been passed. During the early 1990's President Bill Clinton and Attorney General Janet Reno asked the major television networks voluntarily to limit violent programming, threatening federal regulation if they do not.

Government has a responsibility to protect both the well-being and the rights of its citizens. Advocates of violence censorship contend that unchecked depictions of violence endanger women. Critics of censorship as a remedy for violence contend that restricting such depictions will not eliminate the real causes of violence. They argue that censorship dilutes the real responsibility of the men who commit these crimes. According to these critics, censoring violence in the media will not eliminate violence against women, but may, however, endanger free speech. Two nonlegislative solutions to this dilemma have been proposed. Technological solutions such as the V-chip have been suggested as an alternative to government censorship. The V-chip would enable individual viewers to block violent programming from their televisions. Others have suggested rating systems for television programs and music recordings as a means to inform consumers about violent content.

Although violence against women has continued to increase in official reports, in victim surveys, and in media depictions, debate about the amount of violence and accuracy of measurement can be viewed optimistically. The debate and countercharges of political motivation are signs that women have become powerful enough to define violence against them as a social problem.   —Von Bakanic

See also Canadian Radio-Television and Telecommunications Commission; Hate laws; Sex in the arts; Violence; Women Against Violence in Pornography and Media.

BIBLIOGRAPHY

Susan Faludi's *Backlash: The Undeclared War Against American Women* (New York: Crown Publishers, 1991) analyzes the media's effects upon women's minds and bodies. An excellent collection of feminist perspectives on violence against women is contained in Laurel Richardson and Verta Taylor, eds., *Feminist Frontiers III* (New York: McGraw Hill, 1993). A resource explaining the ways in which the justice system reports and prosecutes sexual assault is Gary D. LaFree's *Rape and Criminal Justice* (Belmont, Calif.: Wadsworth Publishing, 1989).

Women Against Pornography (WAP)

FOUNDED: 1979

TYPE OF ORGANIZATION: Feminist antipornography organization based in New York City

SIGNIFICANCE: This organization has worked to increase public awareness of connections between pornography and real-life violence against women

In her best-selling 1975 book *Against Our Will: Men, Women and Rape*, Susan Brownmiller wrote that "the case against pornography and the case against the toleration of prostitution are central to the fight against rape." As feminist awareness increased of the connection between violent pornography and sex-related crimes in the late 1970's, Brownmiller founded Women Against Pornography. She hoped to build on the success of the 1978 national convention of the San Francisco-based Women Against Violence in Pornography and Media (WAVPM). By protesting pornography through the media and other means, such as conducting guided tours through pornography districts in major cities, WAP aimed to raise the level of public consciousness of the pervasiveness of violent pornographic imagery. One of the organization's most publicized protests was directed against the magazine *Hustler* in 1983.

Members of Women Against Pornography march in New York City in October, 1979. (Betty Lane)

WAP contended that *Hustler* was responsible for the gang-rape of a woman in a Connecticut bar—an incident that occurred shortly after the magazine had published photographs depicting a similar event. Unlike the feminist antipornography movements that followed WAP in the 1980's, WAP neither tried to overturn laws governing pornography, nor advocated increased censorship. Rather, it consistently strove to persuade pornographers and producers of other media voluntarily to stop publishing images depicting sexual violence toward women.

See also Feminism; *Hustler*; Men's magazines; Snuff films; Violence; Women Against Violence in Pornography and Media.

Women Against Violence in Pornography and Media (WAVPM)

FOUNDED: 1976

TYPE OF ORGANIZATION: Feminist group opposed to misogynistic imagery in the arts and media

SIGNIFICANCE: This San Francisco-based organization with nearly four thousand members was one of the first to denounce pornography and negative portrayals of women in advertisements

In the past defenders of pornography have argued that pornography serves as a safe outlet for male sexual aggressions toward women. WAVPM challenged that hypothesis, asserting that pornography in fact teaches sexual aggressiveness toward women. WAVPM also voiced concern over the ways in which female bodies were used as objects for male viewing pleasure in advertising. WAVPM members were among the first to see pornography as a civil rights issue, arguing that its existence infringed on the civil rights of women because of the negative treatment of women that it promotes. It was not the display of women's bodies that offended the members of WAVPM, but the negative ways in which they bodies were used. Diana E. H. Russell, one of the group's founders, argued "that just as advertising succeeds in selling products, pornography sells sexism and violence against women."

WAVPM combated negative images of women in a variety of ways. The group's initial plan was simply to promote awareness and to conduct letter-writing campaigns to corporations that used misogynistic advertising. The group produced a letter-writing booklet that showed examples of advertisements that made women into objects of viewing pleasure and gave sample letters. WAVPM was also among a number of anti-pornography groups that advocated certain forms of civil disobedience, such as throwing food during objectionable scenes in film theaters, mutilating unsold magazines on newsstands, and—in one Canadian case—firebombing. Members of WAVPM also occasionally discouraged people from purchasing pornographic materials by openly photographing them as they entered pornography stores.

WAVPM and similar groups have been accused of being procensorship because they wish to deny many forms of pornography. This issue has produced a major schism among feminists, many of whom believe that denying people the right to buy pornography—regardless of the harm it may cause—constitutes unacceptable censorship. Feminist Anti-Censorship Task Force (FACT), a group that opposed WAVPM, is among the feminist groups that do not wish to censor pornography. Members of WAVPM see this issue as one of civil rights, as Russell says, "If racist and anti-Semitic movies are believed to inculcate or intensify anti-Semitism and racism, then it must be granted that movies that portray sexist stereotypes also inculcate or intensify sexism." WAVPM wished to censor insomuch as it would protect women.

Antipornography groups such as WAVPM have themselves been objects of censorship. Their activities are typically poorly covered in the news media, and often they are prevented from protesting or passing out their publications. Although WAVPM and its sister group, Women Against Violence Against Women, have stopped functioning, many other antipornography groups have continued to operate at local levels throughout the United States and Canada. Examples of such groups include Canada's Women Against Violence Against Women, Citizens Opposed to Media Exploitation, British Columbia Federation of Women, and the Minneapolis-based Organizing Against Pornography—which helped to pass one of the first U.S. antipornography laws.

See also Advertising as the target of censorship; Dworkin, Andrea; MacKinnon, Catharine A.; Pornography; Women, violence against.

Woodhull, Victoria

BORN: September 23, 1838, Homer, Ohio

DIED: June 10, 1927, Norton Park, Bremons, Worcestershire, England

IDENTIFICATION: American feminist, reformer, and newspaper publisher

SIGNIFICANCE: Woodhull's trial on charges of violating postal obscenity regulations provoked interest in giving the federal government authority to censor newspapers

From 1870 through 1872 Woodhull and her sister, Tennessee Claflin (1845-1923), published *Woodhull and Claflin's Weekly*, a newspaper that supported equality between the sexes, woman suffrage, and other reforms. Woodhull's outspoken advocacy of sexual liberation made her a frequent target of Protestant critics. In an effort to expose hypocrisy among her opponents, she published an article in her newspaper, in November, 1872, accusing Henry Ward Beecher, the most famous Protestant clergyman in the United States, of having committed adultery. Shortly afterward, Anthony Comstock of the New York Society for the Suppression of Vice appealed to federal authorities in New York to arrest Woodhull and Claflin for violating U.S. postal regulations banning obscene materials from the mail.

Federal authorities jailed Woodhull and Claflin for twenty-eight days before releasing them on bail. In June, 1873, the sisters were tried on federal obscenity charges. Benjamin Butler, a member of the congressional committee that had written the law under which they were charged, publicly stated that the law was not meant to apply to newspapers or to the kind of article that Woodhull had published. It was, he stated, aimed only at "licentious books and other matters . . . published by bad men for the purpose of the corruption of youth." The sisters' judge agreed, and their jury acquitted them.

"GET THEE BEHIND ME, (MRS.) SATAN!"—[SEE PAGE 141.]

WIFE (with heavy burden). "I'D RATHER TRAVEL THE HARDEST PATH OF MATRIMONY THAN FOLLOW YOUR FOOTSTEPS."

In early 1872 Thomas Nast—whose Harper's Weekly *cartoons helped topple New York City's corrupt politician Boss Tweed—pilloried Victoria Woodhull by depicting her as a devil offering salvation through free love.* (Library of Congress)

Beecher himself was acquitted on adultery charges after a well-published trial in 1875. Two years later Woodhull moved to England, where she lived another fifty years. Meanwhile, Woodhull's trial brought Comstock national attention. In 1873 he successfully lobbied Congress to enact tougher laws banning obscene materials from the mail. The new federal statute, known as the Comstock Law, added newspapers and books to the material subject to banning.

See also Comstock, Anthony; Congress, U.S.; Obscenity: legal definitions; Postal regulations; Society for the Suppression of Vice, New York.

World War I

DATE: August 4, 1914-November 11, 1918

PLACE: The war was fought primarily in Europe, but censorship occurred worldwide, notably in the United States and in European colonies in Asia and Africa

SIGNIFICANCE: This pivotal event of the twentieth century issued in a new era of modern media censorship, providing a proving ground for techniques of government control and propagandistic manipulation of the press which would be used in subsequent conflicts

During World War I, at the time the largest and most costly war in human history, censorship was pervasive, involving a complex web of ministries and laws in all belligerent nations. Thousands of censors were used on battlefields, in government offices, and in newspaper pressrooms to limit the access of press and public to the war's often terrible truths. As the war progressed, censorship in the principal combatant nations evolved in strikingly similar ways; for the sake of clarity, World War I censorship can be divided into three general phases, or periods.

First Phase. The beginning of the war witnessed the so-called eyewash period, nicknamed later by those who were appalled at tendentious lies and canards that had filled the press of all belligerent nations. This initial phase lasted through 1914, but the inaccuracies were most blatant in August and September. Editors and reporters filled news columns with misleading material, often because they were unable to obtain news from the war zones. Strict military censorship not only kept correspondents from the front but also kept a nearly complete silence regarding the major battles of fall, 1914. Faced with anxious readers clamoring for war news, editors responded with exhortations to patriotism and silly stories of doughty troops relentlessly advancing; one famous French headline, for example, optimistically reported that Allied soldiers were "only five steps from Berlin."

Editors in the belligerent nations, especially the democracies of Great Britain and France, accepted, with surprisingly little initial protest, the strict military censorship that made it almost impossible to obtain reliable information. In Britain, Lord Kitchener, commanding the British Expeditionary Force, intensely disliked the press. In France, General Joseph Joffre, commanding the French armies, believed, as did most of the French military, that press indiscretions had led to the country's defeat during the Franco-Prussian War of 1870-1871. He was not about to let such a hazard again befall French military operations.

In fact, neither Germany, Austria-Hungary, nor Russia generally allowed war correspondents at the front during this period. A partial exception was Germany, which, during the first weeks of war, allowed correspondents from neutral countries, such as the United States, to follow German troops as they advanced through Belgium and northern France. This meant that the press of neutral nations offered a more accurate perception of the fall battles than the press of combatant nations. Reporters who tried to sneak past military police risked being jailed or even executed as spies, although none apparently received the ultimate punishment for trying to evade military censorship.

Accompanying this silence from the front was a haphazard but determined effort to set up a censorship arm of government at home. Wartime press offices, designed to offer censorship guidelines and punishment for "betrayal," sprouted from all ministries. French censorship was typical: A day before France declared war, a "press office" was set up; two days later, before parliament adjourned to let the government fight unimpeded by politics, the Law of August 5, 1914, forbade publication of a wide variety of news. It covered news of military nature, such as troop and ship movements; mobilization, armament, and provision operations; and changes in high command. However, it also covered lists of killed and wounded, as well as any news "having a troubling influence on the spirit of the army or population." This last part was the origin of a new concept—that of political censorship during wartime. It would become the most controversial aspect of censorship during World War I.

In August, 1914, however, the press in most belligerent nations agreed with little protest to harsh limitations on freedom of expression. The key to understanding this, especially in nations such as France and Britain, which had enjoyed great press freedom, is the concept of a short but "sacred union." In every fighting nation, nearly everyone assumed that the war would be brief: a few weeks, perhaps; a few months, at most; "home by Christmas," for sure. For this short crisis period, nearly everyone agreed that the most effective and patriotic response was silence, a brief suspension of political discourse during a short war. If for a few weeks there could be no news other than patriotic hyperbole, it did not really matter, because after the war was over—and no country considered the possibility of a long struggle—normality would return.

The tight screws of censorship meant that few people, even in neutral nations, were aware of the scale of slaughter during the fall of 1914. As it became clear that the war would last longer than a few weeks, however, journalists began trying to reclaim their lost rights as reporters, especially in Britain and France.

The Allied military relented slightly at the end of 1914, when Britain, and then France, began to give journalists tours of the front. It was becoming clear to government and military leaders that carefully censored news articles could have a propagandistic effect more powerful than silence.

Second Phase. The second year of war inaugurated a new phase of censorship based not on the elimination of all war news but on the development of a structured system to carefully manage the news. At the beginning of the war, censorship generally developed haphazardly, with no underlying plan or structure. Of the conflict's major original belligerents, Britain had fought in other wars most recently, and therefore had more experience of press coverage during modern war. France, however, had a stronger central bureaucracy

and had enjoyed only three decades of press freedom, while Germany and Austria-Hungary were not committed to democratic principles of a free press, although prewar publications in those countries had been quite outspoken. Russia had never had a free press at all. As censorship coalesced into bureaucracy, France established the most pervasive of all systems. Censors were employed in every city, large and small, to review every publication in France, from the smallest rural magazines to the largest metropolitan dailies. Offending news columns could literally be scraped off the metal plates already molded, leaving huge blocks of blank space in the printed paper. No other country's press was physically so scarred by censorship.

The capriciousness of political censorship increasingly became an object of press protests. Governments discovered that their censors not only could stop military reports but also could offer a means to control morale on the home front.

The front page of this August 5, 1916, issue of the French newspaper Le Bavard *substitutes insincere patriotic homilies such as "Vive la Liberté" for the stories ordered removed by France's wartime censoring board. The "Germania" cartoon satirizes the drastic drop in optimism since the war had begun exactly two years earlier.* (Ross Collins)

France's censorship law against "troubling influence" left censors wide latitude to cut any sort of antigovernment criticism or negative news. Britain's Defense of the Realm Act provided the government broad powers to control criticism that might weaken morale, although Britain did not resort to on-site censorship as France did. However, as the terrible human and material costs of a stalemated war often ineptly fought over four hundred miles of front began to become clear, wartime governments also began to realize that, in order to win, public opinion would have to be mobilized for a long siege.

The need to mobilize public opinion, as well as industry, the economy, and men in uniform, became a significant new feature of this war, one which would heavily influence the century's later wars as well. By 1916 military commanders and government leaders were persuaded: The phases of great secrecy and begrudging acceptance gave way to the war's third phase of censorship, one in which the United States would play a major role.

Third Phase. Part of World War I lore is the story of the 1916 Verdun battle: The tenacious heroes of French forts, the "sacred way" supplying the front, and the ultimate sacrifices under the most difficult conditions became an inspiration for French and Allied morale throughout the rest of the war. This was, however, a legend produced by the French military's own correspondents, writer-soldiers in the field who dispatched battle stories to the press back home. The French military had replaced secrecy with an energetic publicity campaign designed to strengthen morale and sway world opinion to the Allied side. Britain, Germany, and soon the United States were also to build elaborate propaganda operations, which provided a blizzard of brochures, photos, articles, and reference materials to the world's press. A system of battlefield accreditation allowed Allied correspondents greater access to the front, and every government now encouraged reporters to publish more, and still more, about the war, as long as the press published the right kinds of story. Generally speaking, after 1915 no major battle was actually misrepresented in the Allied press.

The United States, outraged over renewed German submarine attacks on neutral ships as well as over the supposed "German atrocity stories" spread primarily by British propagandists, declared war on the Central Powers in April, 1917. The United States military had been little different from its European counterparts in its intense distrust of the press, but President Woodrow Wilson's government had learned from the trials and errors of its allies. The Committee on Public Information, directed by journalist George Creel, was charged with coordinating censorship and publicity but avoiding rigid controls; it encouraged the government to be as open and honest with the press as possible.

Still, the appearance of an American censorship more flexible than that of European powers belies the often coercive nature of U.S. censorship law. For accreditation, American war correspondents were required to take an oath not to disclose facts helpful to the enemy, and their sponsoring publications were required to post ten-thousand-dollar bonds to guarantee their proper behavior. Reporters in Europe chafed at the American general John Pershing's rigid control; in one case,

New York Tribune correspondent Heywood Broun, fed up with the enforced silence over the U.S. military's monumental supply blunders, broke the story in December, 1917, after evading on-site censors by returning to the United States. The newspaper forfeited its ten thousand dollars. Pershing was furious.

Another reporter determined to evade military censors, George Seldes, joined a group of five American correspondents shortly after the armistice to sneak into Germany from Luxembourg. The "adventure of the runaway correspondents" made the men celebrities, especially after Seldes and his group landed a short but sensational interview with the German field marshal Paul von Hindenburg. The reporters were arrested and tried in courts-martial on their return to the Allied lines, but they escaped punishment.

At home, American publications generally were not harassed as long as they reflected mainstream, patriotic concerns. Most did. Those that did not, particularly radical and socialist publications, were harassed not only by federal authorities but also by an extensive patchwork of state and local censorship laws designed, as per a government directive to accredited war correspondents, to withhold information liable to "injure the morale of our forces abroad, at home, or among our allies."

Three new federal laws limited free speech: the Espionage Act (1917), the Trading with the Enemy Act (1917), and the Sedition Act (1918). These formed the first set of U.S. laws controlling press freedom since the early 1800's, but, influenced by wartime patriotic fervor, few editors complained. Offending publications were denied access to the mails and confiscated from street corners. More than one thousand Americans were sentenced to banishment or long jail terms under the Espionage and Sedition acts, although most of their jail terms were commuted after the fear of German spies and postwar Bolsheviks faded in the early 1920's.

During World War I, the United States and other combatant nations established a sprawling web of censorship and propaganda unprecedented in its comprehensive influence. Germany was perhaps least skillful of the major powers in organizing this network to mobilize public opinion. Such Germans as Adolf Hitler and Joseph Goebbels, however, so obsessed with the control of public opinion, clearly learned from their enemies' successes in World War I; they would use these and other, similar techniques to great effect during the Nazi era, which would begin a mere fifteen years after World War I ended.

—Ross F. Collins

See also Debs, Eugene; Espionage; Espionage Act of 1917; France; Germany; Military censorship; Propaganda; Seldes, George; United Kingdom; United States; War; World War II.

BIBLIOGRAPHY

Stephen Vaughn's *Holding Fast the Inner Lines* (Chapel Hill: University of North Carolina Press, 1980) is a comprehensive account of George Creel's Committee on Public Information and of U.S. propaganda during World War I. An older discussion of the war's censorship and propaganda is Harold D. Lasswell's classic *Propaganda Technique in the World War* (New York: Alfred A. Knopf, 1927). James R. Mock is concerned with U.S. censorship in particular in *Cen-

sorship 1917 (New York: Da Capo Press, 1972). Phillip Knightley's *The First Casualty* (London: Pan Books, 1989) discusses censorship of war correspondents during World War I and generally, focusing on the British press. A fairly comprehensive account in English of French censorship during this period is Ross F. Collins, "The Development of Censorship in World War I France," *Journalism Monographs* 131 (February, 1992). The reminiscences of many former war correspondents and a few censors have also been published.

World War II

DATE: 1939-1945

PLACE: Worldwide

SIGNIFICANCE: During this conflict censorship was extended beyond military security material to delete, minimize, or classify any news conceivably useful to an enemy or damaging to home front morale

During World War II, censorship became part of a broader attempt on the part of combatant nations to develop an effective overall news policy that, in addition to protecting military information from the enemy, would also serve to bolster civilian morale. News of military victories, of course, required little censorship, while defeats were normally ignored, then denied, then explained as unimportant. Depressing news was generally taboo in all belligerent nations. Beyond such common factors, censorship varied from country to country.

United States. Censorship in the United States during the war avoided the heavy-handed bungling of World War I and caused relatively few media complaints. The war itself enjoyed broad public support, and antifascism was overwhelmingly endorsed by journalists, who wanted to be "on the team." The public was less ideologically oriented, but after Japan's surprise attack on Pearl Harbor, Americans were ready for extensive control of war news, including the Navy's refusal to reveal its losses at Pearl Harbor.

Under the War Powers Act, President Franklin D. Roosevelt named Byron Price on December 19, 1941, to head an Office of Censorship, which would develop guidelines for voluntary censorship by the producers of newspapers, magazines, radio shows, and films. Military plans, presidential trips overseas, intelligence operations, and new weapons (such as the atomic bomb) were secret, as were statistics concerning war production, shipping losses, and so on. The 1917 Espionage Act and the Trading with the Enemy Act were invoked to restrict use of the mails and to suppress, directly or otherwise, about thirty publications, most notably Father Coughlin's *Social Justice*. An attempt to prosecute the *Chicago Tribune* for revealing intelligence secrets failed to gain a grand jury indictment. The 1940 Smith Act, making it illegal to advocate the overthrow of the American government, was used more to prosecute individuals—mostly communists—than to censor the media. Most of the sixteen thousand employees assigned to censorship-related matters spent their time reading letters to and from servicemen stationed overseas.

Broadly speaking, bad news in the media was discouraged, and the government gave the African American press a particularly hard time for its supposed insufficient enthusiasm in

The U.S. military often discouraged news media from publishing pictures or information revealing the true extent of American casualties for fear of weakening morale on the home front. (National Archives)

support of the war effort. In war reports, censors deleted or minimized news of units refusing to go into combat, officers' cowardice, soldiers panicking or going AWOL, and casualties incurred from friendly fire, as well as of looting, black marketeering, rape, race riots, and mutiny. The tendency to sanitize the news obscured brutality and blunders and encouraged an ongoing tendency to "classify" inconvenient information.

The American Civil Liberties Union reported in 1945 that "wartime censorship raised almost no issues in the United States." Newsmen hailed what was widely called "the best reported war in history," although some admitted that they didn't always write the whole truth. Indeed, a Vietnam-era journalist might well have been surprised at the military misconduct that did not get reported.

United Kingdom. The Emergency Powers (Defence) Bill approved on August 24, 1939, authorized the renewal of the censorship powers contained in the Defence of the Realm acts of 1914 (DORA), apparently including many of DORA's well remembered faults. A new Ministry of Information provided voluntary censorship guidelines, but, with the outbreak of war, it was not clear who was in charge of releasing news. Ministry of Information censorship was largely entrusted to former navy officers whose instinct was to tell the public nothing and refer all problems to higher authorities, sometimes with incongruous results. American journalist John Gunther, for example, asking for a copy of a propaganda leaflet scattered by the millions in Royal Air Force flights over Germany, was informed that the government was not allowed to disclose information which might be of value to the enemy.

The fall of France in 1940 prompted a new spirit. The British mythologized the "Dunkirk Miracle," deleting from press reports all negative comments by returning troops. The tally of planes downed in the Battle of Britain was reported with a view to impressing public opinion in both Britain and neutral countries such as the United States. Making a favorable impression in America was considered to be worth security risks; Edward R. Murrow, for example, was allowed to do live and unscripted radio broadcasts critical of Britain during London air raids. On the other hand, any British public comments on the 1940 U.S. elections or the 1941 Lend-Lease Act were strictly forbidden. Among other countries, Canada was considered an especially important military and intelligence link with the United States, and the three countries often coordinated censorship operations.

British military censorship was successful in controlling news of advances in radar, details of the Normandy invasion, and the invention of the atomic bomb. It was a remarkable achievement to develop an effective news management system during a period of military defeats. Some confidential material remained classified after 1945, not by wartime censorship but under the Official Secrets Act of 1911.

France. French censorship from 1939 to 1940 by the information ministry under Jean Giraudoux was a model of ineffective news management. Compared to news from Berlin, Paris wartime bulletins were invariably late, vague, and misleading. French censorship did protect military secrets from the enemy, but it also promoted ignorance and complacency about the state of the country's defenses. From the debacle of 1940 to liberation in 1944, censorship in both occupied France, which was administered by Germany, and Vichy France, which was administered by a collaborationist French government, was under direct or indirect German control.

Russia. Czarist censorship, which ended in 1917, was soon followed by that of the Communists, and under the dictatorship of Joseph Stalin there was ample information for the censors to keep from public view—devastating famines, crippling production shortages, the ruthless purge of military and political opponents, and so on. In any case, the purpose of the Soviet news media was less to provide information than to define correct opinions and attitudes. World War II did not constrict the scope of Russian news but even slightly expanded it.

The major problem facing Soviet news agencies during World War II was explaining why the unpreparedness, defeats, and casualties of 1941-1942 were not the fault of Stalin and the Communist leadership. Censoring news about British and American war efforts made more plausible the emerging Stalinist interpretation that the British and Americans were covert partners in Adolf Hitler's treachery—an international conspiracy of fascists and imperialists attacking the Soviet Union again, as it had in 1919. Censorship left Stalin's leadership as the only hope of resistance. For the Russian people, wanting to believe in victory meant having to believe in Stalin.

China. The struggle against Japanese aggression in World War II was complicated by the intense internal conflict between Chiang Kai-shek's Nationalist party (Guomindang) and a rival offshoot, Mao Zedong's Chinese Communist party. Between 1927 and 1937, as Communist writers called for radical policies, the Guomindang censored or banned their

books and articles and bribed, shot, or beheaded their editors. The Sino-Japanese War (1937-1945) produced an official but uneasy truce between the Chinese rivals. In Chiang's wartime capital of Chongqing, the Communist activist Chou En-lai supervised *The New China Daily*'s attacks on the Guomindang, while Nationalist officials tried to prevent the paper from being delivered. Even the Guomindang papers depended on left-wing writers who had to be censored. After 1945 the government's obvious inability to control inflation, corruption, and inefficiency could not be disguised by censorship, and popular support as well as armed force brought the Communists to power in 1949.

Germany. In 1933 Adolf Hitler appointed Joseph Goebbels minister of propaganda in order to gain and keep control of German thought and opinion. While it was deemed important to advertise the positive objectives of Nazism, it was also considered essential to conceal a great deal about Hitler's character, associates, goals, and methods. A journalism law of October, 1933, systematized Goebbels' approach.

Censorship of foreign reporters kept the West from realizing the extent of antiwar sentiment in Germany during the West's calamitous appeasement of Hitler at the Munich Conference in 1938. However, newsreels showing Nazi Brownshirts attacking Jewish shops and homes in the 1938 riots known as the Night of Broken Glass were allowed to leave Germany, as was a 1939 film of Hitler rudely mocking Roosevelt in a speech to the Reichstag. Censorship also surrounded the staged incident in 1939 which Hitler used as an excuse to invade Poland and start the war.

German victories in 1939 and 1940 needed little censorship except to delete images of German dead from combat films. However, after the failure to take Moscow in 1941, soldiers' letters home began to be censored, and newspapers were limited to a "quota" of obituaries for local soldiers. As the war progressed, reporting on shortages of food, coal, and other necessities had to be censored, as did accounts of Allied air raids.

It was forbidden to report in the press on the extermination of the Jews and other victims of Nazi death camps. Nazi propaganda attempted to portray Germany's defeat as a tragic misfortune for Hitler and to conceal his indifference to German suffering. After the war ended, many Germans still found it impossible to blame Hitler for the Nazis' unspeakable crimes.

Italy. Statutes passed in 1923, the year after the Fascists seized power, proclaimed that "the press is free, but a law regulates the abuse thereof." In practice, editors applied censorship according to government directives. The primary specific goal was to present dictator Benito Mussolini as a great and infallible leader and conceal his many shortcomings and failures. Censorship helped to glamorize the conquest of Ethiopia in 1935-1936, minimize Italian defeats from 1936 to 1939 in the Spanish Civil War, and conceal Mussolini's mismanagement of the supposed conquest of Albania in 1939. However, after Italy entered World War II, the military's many failures—France in 1940, Greece in 1941, and the campaign against the British and Americans from 1941 to 1943—were impossible to hide from the Italian people. Censorship served only to further weaken confidence in Mussolini, who was ousted from power in 1943, prior to Italy's surrender.

Japan. Imperial Japan's traditionally nationalistic and authoritarian society favored unity rather than the ideological divisions encouraged by a free press. A government agency dictated which news would be available to the press. Censorship in the form of "token suppression" or jailing "token editors" in the 1920's became stricter as Japan's expansion into China became an undeclared war in 1937. The National Mobilization Law of February, 1941, tightened secrecy and censorship rules, assisting preparations for the December 7 attack on the U.S. Navy base at Pearl Harbor.

As war extended the Japanese Empire, propaganda and censorship, usually in English, were aimed at conquered peoples. The main attempts at thought control, however, were directed at the Japanese people themselves. Victory depended on loyalty and obedience to the hierarchy of authority in Japanese life—neighborhood groups, local officials, national leaders, and the emperor. The censors' task was to exclude ideas that might challenge this pattern of united action.

Following the war, Japan eventually lifted censorship on such topics as its wartime biological warfare research program, which was continued as a highly classified project by the U.S. armed forces. As the secret weapon changed hands, it was protected by a new shield of censorship.   —*Fred K. Gillum*

See also American Civil Liberties Union; Espionage Act of 1917; Holocaust, Jewish; Military censorship; News media censorship; Newspapers, African American; Office of Censorship, U.S.; Official Secrets Act (U.K.); War; World War I.

BIBLIOGRAPHY

No overall study of World War II censorship is widely available. Lee-hsia Hsu Ting's *Government Control of the Press in Modern China, 1900-1949* (Cambridge: Harvard University Press, 1974) is excellent, and Peter de Mendelssohn's *Japan's Political Warfare* (New York: Arno Press, 1944, reprint, 1972), although dated, is insightful. Useful information can be found in Michael Balfour's *Propaganda in War, 1939-1945* (London: Routledge & Kegan Paul, 1979), Jay W. Baird's *The Mythical World of Nazi War Propaganda, 1939-1945* (Minneapolis: University of Minnesota Press, 1974), Konstantin F. Shteppa's *Russian Historians and the Soviet State* (New Brunswick, N.J.: Rutgers University Press, 1962), and K. R. M. Short, ed., *Film and Radio Propaganda in World War II* (Knoxville: University of Tennessee Press, 1983). Chapters on the United States are included in Joseph J. Mathews' *Reporting the Wars* (Minneapolis: University of Minnesota Press, 1957), and Phillip Knightley's *The First Casualty* (New York: Harcourt Brace Jovanovich, 1975).

Worms, Edict of

DATE: May 26, 1521
PLACE: Germany
SIGNIFICANCE: Emperor Charles V denounced Martin Luther as a criminal and prohibited possession or printing of his works; the emperor's edict was largely ineffective

Charles V, ruler of The Netherlands, Germany, and Spain, convened the Diet of Worms ("diet" means "assembly";

Worms is a city in Germany) on January 18, 1521, to consider Martin Luther's attacks on the Roman Catholic church. Luther, given safe passage to and from the diet by Charles, appeared there to answer charges of heresy. When questioned about the books he had written and asked to recant his opinions, Luther responded by defending his writings and concluding: "Here I stand, I can do no other." On May 26 of the same year, Charles signed the Edict of Worms. The edict proclaimed Luther to be subversive of government, religion, and morality and forbade the emperor's subjects from having any dealings with Luther. He was to be seized if found and turned over to authorities, and his followers were likewise to be arrested and their property confiscated. The edict banned the buying, selling, printing, reading, and possession of Luther's works. Although the Edict of Worms was responsible for the burning of many copies of Luther's works, it ultimately failed to halt the rise of Protestantism in Germany and elsewhere. Luther himself was protected by friends and allies, and even most of his enemies realized that attempts to enforce the edict rigorously would have resulted in civil war.

See also Germany; Heresy; Luther, Martin; Reformation, the.

Wright, Richard

BORN: September 4, 1908, Natchez, Mississippi
DIED: November 28, 1960, Paris, France
IDENTIFICATION: American novelist, poet, and critic
SIGNIFICANCE: The first African American novelist to treat racial problems in Northern cities, Wright was criticized for his realistic portrayal of the horrors of racism

Wright was the first African American writer to reach a large white audience. His realistic and powerful portrayal of the African American experience in both the South and the northern cities of the United States brought the country's attention to African American suffering and hardships in the first half of the twentieth century. His masterpiece, *Native Son* (1940), marks a high point in the development of African American fiction. Its influence can be felt in the work of a whole generation of African American writers. Some black writers became imitators of Wright and consequently formed the Wright School of postwar black fiction. They are often referred to as protest novelists.

Wright's work, however, has also been strongly censured by both whites and other African American writers and scholars. *Native Son*, for example, has often been criticized for being too violent. Its protagonist, Bigger Thomas, is so alienated from all society that he kills both a white woman and a black woman. He is eventually sentenced to death. Wright's autobiography, *Black Boy* (1945), has been criticized for painting too negative a picture of the African American experience.

African American writers have also questioned Wright's frequent use of melodrama and the explicitness of protest in his fiction. James Baldwin, for example, suggested that the real cause of Bigger Thomas' tragedy in *Native Son* is not that he is cold, black, or hungry, but that "he admits the responsibility of his being subhuman and feels constrained, therefore, to battle for his humanity according to those brutal criteria

One of the first African American novelists to reach large numbers of white readers, Richard Wright was also one of the most heavily censored. (Library of Congress)

bequeathed him at his birth." Ralph Ellison, though critical of the aesthetic appeal of Wright's work, admitted that Wright's example "converted the American Negro impulse toward self-annihilation and 'going underground' into a will to confront the world . . . and throw his findings unashamedly into the guilty conscience of America."

Wright was introduced to Marxism through the John Reed Club and the Communist Party of the United States while he was working at odd jobs in Chicago. He joined the party in 1932 and first published many of his poems, stories, and essays in the party's press. The party, however, condemned the

publication of *Native Son*, asserting that its tone was too angry and its portrayal too violent. Feeling restrained, Wright broke from the party in 1942 and, after enduring racism all his life, decided to move to France with his wife. He never returned to the United States.

See also African Americans; Art; Baldwin, James; Communist Party of the U.S.A.; Literature; Race; Violence.

Wrinkle in Time, A

TYPE OF WORK: Book
PUBLISHED: 1962
AUTHOR: Madeleine L'Engle (Madeleine Camp, 1918-   )
SUBJECT MATTER: Novel about two children who are helped by three magical women to rescue their imprisoned father from a distant planet
SIGNIFICANCE: Christian evangelical groups have attacked this children's book because it features witches, fantasy, and supposedly anti-Christian values

Although Madeleine L'Engle is a devout Christian she has antagonized evangelical Christians with her children's novel *A Wrinkle in Time*. Her detractors have challenged the inclusion of her book in public schools primarily because its women characters—Mrs. Whatsit, Mrs. Who, and Mrs. Which—use magical powers to take twelve-year-old Meg and her brother Charles on a space trip through the fifth dimension. Objecting parents and pastors have claimed that characters are really witches practicing black magic under the guise of "New Age" religion, based on Hindu and Buddhist cultures. They have objected to children being indoctrinated with Eastern religions and mystical practices and to L'Engle's use of crystal balls, psychic healing, astral travel, and telepathy. Citizens for Excellence in Education in Waterloo, Iowa, for example, accused L'Engle of fostering occult practices, employing satanic suggestions, sadism, and—worst of all—by associating Jesus Christ with other great personages, implying that Christ was not divine. Most efforts to ban *A Wrinkle in Time* have failed, however. L'Engle has received strong support from her readers for her Newbery Award-winning novel and its themes of the power of love, respect for others, and the need for individuality.

See also Books, children's; Christianity; Libraries, school; Pressure groups; Secular humanism.

Y

Yaqzan, Matan, affair

DATE: November, 1993—January, 1995
PLACE: Fredericton, New Brunswick, Canada
SIGNIFICANCE: A national *cause célèbre* in Canada, this attempt to discipline a tenured university professor for expressing unpopular opinions challenged basic principles of free speech and academic freedom

On November 7, 1993, Matan Yaqzan, a mathematics professor with twenty-six years teaching experience at the University of New Brunswick, wrote an opinion piece titled "The Male Nature" for the student newspaper. Asserting that young men cannot control their sexual desires, he claimed that sexual intercourse is a "necessity" for them. He then argued that young women who are sexually experienced do not suffer as much from forced sexual encounters with young men—"so-called date rape"—as young virgins. "When a boy invites a girl to his bedroom," he stated, "she should consider it as an invitation for sexual intercourse." Finally, he asserted that "girls who use the word 'rape' to describe their dislike of a particular encounter in their endless sexual experiences, do a disservice to those who abide by the old traditions."

Yaqzan's article provoked instant protests from students, women's groups, parents, and some faculty. Complaining that he condoned date rape, many people demanded that he be fired and some students said that they would feel uncomfortable attending his classes. The university suspended Yaqzan on November 12, ordering him off the campus and calling for a full review of his academic performance and professional responsibilities before deciding on permanent actions. The university's president announced his concern about the "negative and incorrect impression of [the university] created by Yaqzan's article." In a widely reprinted article, he wrote that "free speech does not equal irresponsible speech. Prof. Yaqzan has abused his position by excusing and encouraging behavior that is not only unacceptable by standards of human decency but also subject to criminal charges."

Newspaper columnists and television commentators across Canada soon took up Yaqzan's story. Many argued that university authorities had overstepped themselves in punishing Yaqzan because academic freedom should allow even the expression of unpopular or repugnant views. The university's faculty association demanded that Yaqzan's suspension should be lifted and the university complied on November 20. In a joint statement with the faculty association, the university claimed that Yaqzan's suspension had not been intended as a disciplinary action, but as "a cooling-off period so that public safety and an orderly academic environment on campus could be maintained." The university reassigned Yaqzan's duties, however, and Yaqzan never returned to the classroom. The university also announced that it would convene a major conference to discuss issues of principle that arise when basic rights collide.

Meanwhile, rumors that Yaqzan was under pressure to resign circulated until January 1, 1994, when he took an early retirement. He reportedly was to receive his full salary for three years, followed by a pension. On learning of Yaqzan's retirement, a students' association officer said that Yaqzan's departure would "make for a safer learning environment."

The university's conference met on September 28, 1994. Its key speakers included the chief counsel for the Canadian Civil Liberties Association, Allan Borovoy, who called the university's handling of Yaqzan's punishment "repugnant." Calling a university campus, "a community of adults who are looking for truth," Borovoy said that opinions such as those expressed by Yaqzan "must receive not employment sanctions, but verbal and written debate. . . . That is what the university is about."

See also Campus speech codes; Canada; Free speech; Newspapers, student; Universities.

Yevtushenko, Yevgeny Alexandrovich

BORN: July 18, 1933, Zima, Soviet Union
IDENTIFICATION: Russian poet
SIGNIFICANCE: Yevtushenko won international fame for both his expressive poetry and his candid criticisms of the Soviet Union and the world

Yevtushenko gained national stature in the Soviet Union in

Yevgeny Yevtushenko was one of the most heavily censored writers under the Soviet regime. (Jean-Claude Bouis)

the early 1960's through his popular poetry readings to large audiences. His fame permitted him to travel to the West, enhancing his reputation. Many of his poems praised Soviet economic achievements, criticized United States involvement in the Vietnam War, and portrayed the Soviet Union as a peaceful nation. However, his poetry also criticized Russian anti-Semitism and the dangers of latent Stalinism within the communist leadership.

After unauthorized Western publication of Yevtushenko's outspoken and self-assured autobiography in 1963, Soviet authorities temporarily forbade him to travel out of the country. His independent voice was heard during the Leonid Brezhnev era, as when he openly supported Aleksandr Solzhenitsyn when the latter was deported in 1974—despite public and

official condemnation for his temerity in speaking out against Soviet censorship.

The Mikhail Gorbachev years raised Yevtushenko's hopes for genuine reform. Following the Soviet Union's dissolution in 1991, he urged Russians to break with the old servile obedience to those in power. His initial support of Boris Yeltsin as a reformer later diminished. Several of his books in the 1990's have focused more on the challenges facing Russia's population in the post-Soviet period. Yet optimism is characteristic of Yevtushenko's poetry and life.

See also Akhmatova, Anna; Communism; Gorbachev, Mikhail; Literature; Sakharov, Andrei; Solzhenitsyn, Aleksandr; Soviet Union; Stalin, Joseph; Voznesensky, Andrey Andreyevich.

Z

Zamyatin, Yevgeny Ivanovich

BORN: February 1, 1884, Lebedyan, Russia
DIED: March 10, 1937, Paris, France
IDENTIFICATION: Russian writer and romantic visionary
SIGNIFICANCE: Zamyatin's major work, the anti-utopian
novel *We*, has never been published in the Soviet Union

Devoted to an ideal Bolshevism, Zamyatin rejoiced at the
coming of the Russian Revolution in 1917. He had been jailed
and exiled for anticzarist activities in 1905 and 1911, and the
Petersburg District Court had interdicted publication of one of
his short stories in 1913. From 1917 to 1921 Zamyatin became
a leading figure in Leningrad intellectual circles, respected for
the virtuosity of his work as creative artist and critic. With the
introduction of the New Economic Policy in 1921, however,
he came under attack from communist critics, who characterized him as a decadent, apolitical individualist who was
hostile to the Revolution. The Leningrad Regional Administration of Literary and Publishing Affairs banned his verse
tragedy *Attila* in 1928 for its anti-Soviet character, shortly after
it had been warmly received by an audience that included
eighteen factory directors.

In 1929, with the purge of the All-Russian Union of Writers
consequent to the adoption of the First Five Year Plan, Zamyatin came under increasingly heavy criticism for the romantic
individualism of his major work, the anti-utopian novel *My*,
completed in 1921 and first published as a whole, in English
translation, as *We* (1924). As a result of that purge, Zamyatin's
books were removed from the shelves of many Soviet libraries, and dogmatic critics were prepared to stop publication of
anything new that Zamyatin might produce.

In June, 1931, Zamyatin requested of Joseph Stalin the
mercy of being exiled, since "being deprived of the opportunity to write is nothing less than a death sentence." He left for
France a few months later, never to return to Russia. His *We*
has not been published in his homeland.

See also Babel, Isaac Emmanuilovich; Bulgakov, Mikhail
Afanasyevich; Lenin, Vladimir Ilich; Mayakovsky, Vladimir;
Orwell, George; Soviet Union; Stalin, Joseph.

Zenger, John Peter

BORN: 1697, Rhenish Palatinate, Germany
DIED: July 28, 1746, New York, New York
IDENTIFICATION: American newspaper publisher
SIGNIFICANCE: Zenger's acquittal on a charge of seditious
libel after publishing criticisms of New York's government
was a landmark in the establishment of freedom of the press
in the American colonies

At age thirteen Zenger emigrated from his native Germany
to New York City, where he became a printer. After temporarily living in Maryland, he returned to New York City in
1723 and set himself up as an independent printer. He specialized in printing Dutch-language books and controversial materials that the official provincial government printer would
not accept.

In the early 1730's a party arose against the administration
of new governor William Cosby. Zenger was hired to print an
opposition newspaper, *The New York Weekly Journal* to
counter the official newspaper. The paper was written by two
talented men who had been dismissed by Governor Cosby:
lawyer and journalist James Alexander, who contributed most
of the articles, and former chief justice Lewis Morris. Their
stories and satirical advertisements were published anonymously, however, so Zenger was held responsible for the
newspaper's contents.

When Governor Cosby tried to prosecute Zenger, two grand
juries refused to indict him. Finally, Cosby had a warrant for
Zenger's arrest for seditious libel issued through the executive
council. On November 17, 1734, Zenger was arrested. He was
imprisoned when he could not post an excessively high bail.
He nevertheless managed to continue publishing his newspaper by issuing instructions to his wife and assistants through a
hole in his cell door.

Zenger's trial was a landmark in colonial jurisprudence for
the foundations it laid for freedom of the press. In holding
Zenger responsible for seditious libel, the government relied
upon the then accepted notion that truth is not a defense for
libelous writings. However, Zenger's brilliant defense counsel,
the distinguished Philadelphia lawyer Andrew Hamilton, argued otherwise. Hamilton, who was eighty and ailing, defended Zenger without fee.

Zenger's jury was instructed to find only the relevant facts
of the case: Whether Zenger had published the material in
question. The court itself would decide on the libel charge.
Hamilton countered by presenting a novel defense; he admitted that Zenger had published the paper but argued that the
jury—despite the court's clear instructions—had the right to
decide the question of libel as well. Above all, Hamilton insisted that if what Zenger published was true, he should be
exonerated. Hamilton also argued that liberty itself was at
stake, since writing the truth is one of the few ways available
to oppose arbitrary power.

Despite a stern admonition from the presiding judge, the
jury found Zenger innocent. Although truth was not accepted
as a defense against libel until the next century, Zenger's
acquittal struck a powerful blow for freedom from censorship.
Zenger's own name is most remembered for this case, but at
least equal credit for his legal victory belongs to Alexander
and Hamilton—the first for his trenchant political broadsides;
the latter for his ingenious and historic defense.

See also Constitution, U.S.; Libel; *Publick Occurrences*;
Sedition.

Zhdanov, Andrei

BORN: February 26, 1896, Mariupol, Ukraine, Russian Empire

DIED: August 31, 1948, Moscow, Soviet Union

IDENTIFICATION: Soviet government censor

SIGNIFICANCE: As commissar of the arts, Zhdanov presided over the purging of the arts in the last years of Joseph Stalin's repressive rule

Zhdanov set the tone for the official attitude toward the arts in post-World War II Soviet Union. Acting at Stalin's bidding, he was the driving force behind four ideological resolutions imposed by the Central Committee of the Communist Party. The Soviet Union's arts policies of the late 1940's have been dubbed "Zhdanovschina" because of his aggressive censorship and policing of the arts. Zhdanov intimidated and stifled the artistic communities until his sudden death in 1948.

Zhdanov's three resolutions of 1946 dealt with literature, theatre, and film, warning artists not to challenge the ideology of the Communist Party. The January, 1948, Conference of Musicians was allegedly summoned to discuss the shortcomings of Vano Muradeli's opera *The Great Fellowship*. Zhdanov called for an easily accessible style of music which would uplift the Soviet peoples in the difficult postwar period, but the real target of the conference was Dmitri Shostakovich, whose most recent symphonies had failed Zhdanov's banal criterion of instant popular comprehension. Zhdanov's criticisms were unsubtle reminders of Stalin's determination to control every aspect of Soviet cultural and artistic life.

See also Communism; Prokofiev, Sergei; Shostakovich, Dmitri; Socialist Realism; Stalin, Joseph.

Zimbabwe

DESCRIPTION: Independent central African republic formerly known as Rhodesia

SIGNIFICANCE: Among Africa's many newly independent nations, Zimbabwe has one of the oldest and most complex histories of government censorship

Zimbabwe takes its name from ruins of a civilization (the word "zimbabwe" means a stone dwelling) that thrived during the time of Europe's Middle Ages. The largest of these ruins is known as Great Zimbabwe. Europeans had long heard legends of a great city in southern Africa, reputed to be the biblical place Ophir and the site of King Solomon's mines. By the late 1800's the ruins took on a new political symbolism when the

Entrance to Great Zimbabwe's Hill Ruin, which colonial archaeologists gave the neoclassical name "Acropolis." To foster the myth of white superiority Zimbabwe's colonial rulers ignored or suppressed evidence that these ruins were built by black Africans. The disinformation tactic had the added benefit of making the ruins a deep "mystery" that enticed tourists to visit the country. (R. Kent Rasmussen)

British began active colonization. In 1890 the British businessman and imperialist Cecil Rhodes began bringing in pioneers and mercenaries for colonization, and the area became the self-governing colony of Southern Rhodesia in 1922.

The Zimbabwean ruins posed a problem for the white colonists. They justified taking control of land occupied by Africans by maintaining that the Africans were incapable of forming an advanced civilization without European direction. If Great Zimbabwe and the other ruined cities had been built by Africans, though, this would be evidence that Africans were capable of complex, urban societies. Cecil Rhodes saw the political importance of the ruins, and he hired the antiquarian Theodore Bent to excavate them to try to establish a non-African origin. Bent found no evidence of influences from any other continent, but he still concluded that Great Zimbabwe had been built by Mediterranean people. This official unwillingness to recognize that the cities were local creations enhanced the "Mystery of Zimbabwe," vague speculations that the cities had been constructed in ancient times by King Solomon, by the ancient Greeks, or by Arabs.

As movements for independence and black political rights became more active, white government support for the Zimbabwe myth became more intense. By the 1960's the colony of Rhodesia was under pressure from the British government to grant equality to black citizens. Complaining that whites and blacks were at vastly different levels of civilization, Rhodesia's prime minister Ian Smith issued the Unilateral Declaration of Independence (UDI) in November, 1965.

Government control of archaeology increased following the UDI. In the same year as the declaration, the National Historical Monuments Commission stated that there was little doubt that Great Zimbabwe was the work of indigenous African people. In response, a member of the Rhodesian parliament denounced the commission and demanded that its findings be "corrected."

In 1970 the Rhodesian government enacted censorship preventing all official publications from stating as fact that Great Zimbabwe had been an African creation. For many archaeologists, the extreme censorship of their discipline became unbearable. Peter Garlake, the leading expert on the ruins of Zimbabwe, left the country in protest, only to return in 1981, following the establishment of a majority black government.

Ian Smith's Administration. Ian Smith's Rhodesian Front party came to power in 1964. One of the new regime's first acts was the creation of the position of the parliamentary secretary for information, who was to control all information from the government. Government press releases and reports became little more than state propaganda. Smith also appointed new members of the Board of Governors of Rhodesian Broadcasting Corporation and established control over television broadcasting.

When Smith declared the independence of Rhodesia, the government also declared a state of emergency. The state of emergency gave the government the right to suppress criticism or opposition by force. Under the Emergency Powers Act, in 1967, the Rhodesian government enacted direct censorship of all news in the country. Even listening to disapproved radio broadcasts from abroad became illegal. At the end of 1967 the Smith government set up a Board of Censors to examine and regulate all types of media, and the board banned both domestic and foreign publications for moral as well as political reasons. Those who published objectionable materials could also be prosecuted, under the Official Secrets Act of 1970, for threatening national security.

The Rhodesian Printing and Publishing Company, the major newspaper publishing corporation in Rhodesia, was a subsidiary of the Argus newspaper chain in South Africa. Its newspapers were oriented toward the white inhabitants of Rhodesia. Nevertheless, the papers of the Argus chain were opposed to the UDI, and therefore were subject to heavy censorship. The *Daily News*, a paper not owned by the Argus chain, was owned and run by whites but sympathetic toward African nationalism and critical of the Rhodesian Front. As a result, the Smith government banned the *Daily News* in 1964. Reporters for the foreign media were also suppressed. In 1973 Rhodesian journalist Peter Niesewand was arrested for reports he had made to the British Press. He was sentenced to two years at hard labor for violation of the Official Secrets Act, and he was later deported to England.

Censorship Issues Since 1980. There appears to have been much less censorship in Zimbabwe, as the country became known with the establishment of the black majority government of Prime Minister Robert Mugabe in 1980, than there was under the Rhodesian Smith regime. The official government policy statement on the media, "The Democratization of the Media in Independent Zimbabwe," guaranteed the press freedom to publish. Nevertheless, there have been some incidents of government control of expression.

In February, 1981, the Zimbabwe Mass Media Trust took control of the country's main newspapers. In June, 1981, the government created the Zimbabwe Inter-Africa News Agency (ZIANA). Joshua Nkomo, chief political rival of Prime Minister Mugabe and then minister of home affairs, criticized the transfer of the press to the government, saying it would turn the press into the mouthpiece of Mugabe's party.

Political instability often raised threats to freedom of expression, since Mugabe's government has had to deal with antigovernment guerrillas. In 1984, as a result of guerilla activity, the government passed a ban on opposition party meetings in the center of the country. Criticism of the government's treatment of guerrillas has also provoked threats of censorship. In 1986 Enos Nkala, who succeeded Nkomo as minister of home affairs, denounced Amnesty International as an enemy of the state and threatened anyone who might pass information to Amnesty.

Two years later Nkala, by then defense minister, became the center of a censorship controversy regarding corruption, rather than state security. The *Bulawayo Chronicle* accused government officials of corruption in the affair known as the "Willowgate scandal." Nkala, the main target of the accusations, threatened to send the army to the newspaper headquarters to arrest the editor and deputy editor. Although the editors never suffered this fate, and the Zimbabwean government initiated an investigation of official corruption, the *Chronicle*'s editor was removed from his position and transferred to a nonreporting job. —*Carl L. Bankston III*

See also Archaeology; Colonialism; Exploration, Age of; National security; Race; South Africa.

BIBLIOGRAPHY

Peter S. Garlake's *Great Zimbabwe* (New York: Stein & Day, 1973) is a description of the ruins of Zimbabwe, written by one of the foremost archaeological experts on this subject. R. Kent Rasmussen's *Historical Dictionary of Rhodesia/Zimbabwe* (Metuchen, N.J.: Scarecrow Press, 1979) provides a wealth of information on the history of the country, including an entry on the history of censorship. A revised edition, coauthored by Steven Rubert, *Historical Dictionary of Zimbabwe* (Metuchen, N.J.: Scarecrow Press, 1990), adds information on the first decade of African majority rule. *Zimbabwe: A Land Divided* (Oxford, England: Oxfam, 1992), by Robin H. Palmer, is a readable discussion of the racial and ethnic conflicts that have troubled this newly independent nation. Readers seeking detailed information on the political and economic situation in Zimbabwe may want to look at the academic text by Jeffrey Herbst, *State Politics in Zimbabwe* (Berkeley: University of California Press, 1990).

Zola, Émile

BORN: April 2, 1840, Paris, France
DIED: September 28, 1902, Paris, France
IDENTIFICATION: French novelist
SIGNIFICANCE: Zola was prosecuted in both Great Britain and France for his writings, and his novels were later banned in several countries

Émile Zola took on the full power of the French government in his fearless defense of Alfred Dreyfus. (Library of Congress)

Zola was a pioneer in the naturalist school of writing that emerged in the late nineteenth century. In twenty interrelated novels that he wrote between 1871 and 1893, he employed scientific precision and careful attention to descriptive detail to portray the fortunes of individual members of the fictional Rougon-Macquart family. His novels such as *Germinal*, *Nana*, *La Terre*, and *L'Assommoir* focused on characters from the lower strata of society, describing every aspect of their often sordid lives with vivid and colorful detail. His honest approach to fiction frequently embroiled him in battles with various forms of censorship.

Serialization of Zola's novel *L'Assommoir* in the newspaper *La Bien Public* was suspended in 1876 in response to public outrage at his uncompromising examination of the ravages of alcoholism among the Parisian lower classes. Publication of an English translation of *La Terre*, a work describing greed, brutality, and jealousy in rural France during the Second Empire, provoked an excited public response and resulted in Zola's unsuccessful prosecution on obscenity charges in Great Britain in 1888.

Two later series of novels, *Les Trois villes* (1894-1898) and *Quatre evangiles* (1899-1903), provoked the animosity of the Roman Catholic church and resulted in all his works being placed on its *Index Librorum Prohibitorum*. Censorship even plagued Zola's work after his death: Yugoslavia banned his novels in 1929, Ireland banned them in 1953, and the American National Organization of Decent Literature condemned *Nana* in 1954.

The most notable episode of censorship in Zola's career occurred for political reasons, however. Convinced that the French army's Jewish officer Alfred Dreyfus had been framed during his trial for espionage in 1894, Zola wrote "J'Accuse" for the newspaper *L'Aurore* in 1898. Zola demanded that Dreyfus be given a new trial and accused many of the army's witnesses at Dreyfus' original trial of having deliberately lied. Right-wing supporters of the army raised such an uproar over this article that Zola was ultimately tried and convicted for libel. The original guilty verdict was overturned on a legal technicality but, when the government announced it intended to retry him, Zola followed his lawyer's advice and fled France for England. He was finally vindicated when some of the original anti-Dreyfus witnesses broke down and admitted they had lied. After Zola's own libel conviction was annulled in 1899, he returned to France that same year.

See also France; *Index Librorum Prohibitorum*; *Maggie: A Girl of the Streets*; National Organization for Decent Literature.

Zouaves

FOUNDED: 1868

TYPE OF ORGANIZATION: Quebec Roman Catholic association

SIGNIFICANCE: The main goal of the Zouaves was to create an elite group able to oppose the propagation within Quebec of liberal ideas formally condemned by the pope

Between February, 1868, and September, 1870, seven contingents of Canadians enrolled in the papal army to help defend

Rome from the Italian troops who wanted to bring about Italian unification. The last contingent of 114 recruits left too late and had to turn back because Rome surrendered. About 390 Canadians served as pontifical troops.

The troops' departure for Rome put the Canadian government in an embarrassing position, since the men were off to fight in a country with which Great Britain and Canada were not at war. The movement might have been forbidden but for George-Etienne Cartier (one of the Founders of Canadian Confederation whose great accomplishment was reconciling French Canadians to the Canadian Confederation), who stood up for the Zouaves because he feared that an attempt to ban the movement would alienate the clergy and voters of Quebec.

Most of the Canadian Zouaves were educated young men recruited in Quebec. The organizational committee set up by Bishop Ignace Bourget of Montreal had recruited them for their moral qualities. No other Canadian bishop of the time was as attentive to the directives from Rome or as fervent a supporter of the papal cult. Bourget's zeal inspired the raising of 507 Zouaves from his own diocese. Freedom of speech and conscience, popular sovereignty, and the separation of church and state were among the ideas that the Zouaves were to combat. Upon their return to Canada, the Canadian Zouaves formed an association that still exists and whose objectives have modified over time.

See also Canada; Religious education; Vatican.

Court Cases

Date	Case	Citation	Decision
1825	*Commonwealth v. Blanding 3 Pick.*	[20 Mass.] 304	Truth is not a defense in libel cases.
1845	*White v. Nicholls*	3 How. 266	Public officials suing for libel must show "express malice."
1868	*Regina v. Hicklin*	L.R. 3 Q.B. 360	Material is obscene if passages of the work (not necessarily the work taken as a whole) have a tendency to corrupt the sexual morality of depraved or vulnerable individuals (Hicklin rule).
1875	*Pollard v. Lyons*	91 U.S. 225	It is not slanderous to spread the truth about the fornication of others.
1877	*Ex Parte Jackson*	96 U.S. 727	Congress can prohibit information about lotteries from the U.S. Mail.
1878	*Bradlaugh v. The Queen*	3. Q.B.D. 607	The last serious court challenge in England to a publication dealing with birth control.
1895	*Grimm v. United States*	156 U.S. 604	The practice of government officials posing as interested parties offering obscene material through the mails is not entrapment.
1897	*Davis v. Massachusetts*	167 U.S. 43	Requiring a permit to speak on Boston Common is constitutionally permitted.
1907	*Halter v. Nebraska*	205 U.S. 34	State prohibition of using the U.S. flag in advertising is constitutionally permissible.
1907	*Patterson v. Colorado*	205 U.S. 454	It is constitutionally permissible to cite for contempt those who publish material impugning the motives of a judge.
1915	*Mutual Film Corp. v. Kansas*	236 U.S. 248	State boards of film censorship are a valid exercise of the police powers of states if they do not interfere with interstate commerce, abridge liberty of opinion, or delegate legislative power to administrative officers.
1917	*United States v. Motion Picture Film The Spirit of '76*	252 F. 946	Films exhibited during wartime that show a U.S. ally in a bad light are not protected despite the accuracy of their depiction of the ally's role in American history.
1919	*Debs v. United States*	249 U.S. 211	Speech by labor union leader opposing the U.S. war effort during World War I was not protected because it was intended to obstruct the war effort; whether it resulted in obstruction is not relevant.
1919	*Schenck v. United States*	249 U.S. 47	Speech is not constitutionally protected if it presents a "clear and present danger" that they will bring about the substantive evils that Congress has a right to prevent.
1919	*Abrams v. United States*	250 U.S. 616	According to Oliver Wendell Holmes's dissent, a constitutional commitment to free and open debate is essential to a free society.
1920	*Pierce v. United States*	252 U.S. 239	A pamphlet describing the horrors of trench warfare is not protected because it was intended to interfere with military conscription and recruitment.
1920	*Gilbert v. Minnesota*	254 U.S. 325	It is constitutionally permissible for states to prohibit advocating pacifism as a political philosophy, discouraging the war effort, or counseling against military service.
1925	*Gitlow v. New York*	268 U.S. 652	The Fourteenth Amendment incorporates First Amendment rights to freedom of speech and press, which therefore apply to state law.
1926	*Public Welfare Pictures Corp. v. Brennan*	124 A. 868	State or municipal government may not delegate the task of viewing films or plays for censorship purposes to police or voluntary committees.
1927	*Scopes v. State*	289 S.W. 363	It is permissible for the state of Tennessee to ban teaching of the theory of evolution.

Date	Case	Citation	Decision
1927	*Whitney v. California*	274 U.S. 357	Advocacy of the use of force to overthrow the government is not protected; concurring opinion suggests addition of imminence of danger to the "clear and present danger" test for constitutional protection of speech.
1929	*People v. Friede*	233 N.Y.S. 565	Radclyffe Hall's novel of lesbian love, *The Well of Loneliness*, is ruled obscene.
1931	*Stromberg v. California*	283 U.S. 359	Prohibition of a flag symbolizing opposition to the government is unconstitutional.
1931	*Near v. Minnesota*	283 U.S. 697	Statute banning publications of a "malicious, scandalous, or defamatory" nature found unconstitutional because the statute resulted in prior restraint; placed stringent limitations on prior restraint.
1934	*United States v. One Book Called "Ulysses"*	72 F. 2nd 705	A work of literature that contains erotic passages that do not amount to obscenity may be admitted into the United States from abroad; Hicklin rule is rejected for a rule that considers works in their entirety.
1935	*People on Complaint of Sumner v. Dial Press*	48 N.Y.S. 2nd 480	D. H. Lawrence's novel *Lady Chatterley's Lover* is obscene.
1935	*State of Wisconsin v. Arnold*	258 N.W. 843	A state statute banning use of condoms as contraceptives was violated by the sale of condoms in a gas station coin operated machine.
1936	*Grossjean v. American Press Co.*	297 U.S. 233	Taxes on newspapers based on their circulation violates the First Amendment.
1937	*Herndon v. Lowry*	301 U.S. 242	Statutes that prohibit attempts to incite insurrection do not violate the First Amendment.
1938	*Lovell v. City of Griffin*	303 U.S. 444	City ordinances prohibiting distribution of literature without the permission of the city manager are unconstitutional because such laws constitute administrative licensing of publications.
1939	*Hague v. Congress of Industrial Organizations*	307 U.S. 496	Activities related to speech such as leafletting, demonstrating, and speaking in public areas may not be prohibited.
1939	*Schneider v. Irvington*	308 U.S. 147	Laws are unconstitutional that curtail attempts to communicate with the public, such as by soliciting or distributing leaflets or anonymous pamphlets, by unpopular or weak groups whose access to other forms of communication is limited.
1940	*Thornhill v. Alabama*	310 U.S. 88	Picketing is a constitutional right.
1940	*Minersville School District v. Gobitis*	310 U.S. 586	States may require children to pledge allegiance to the U.S. flag.
1941	*Cox v. New Hampshire*	312 U.S. 569	A city ordinance requiring licensing and fees for public processions or parades as necessary to maintain public order and safety is constitutional.
1942	*Chaplinsky v. New Hampshire*	315 U.S. 568	Protected speech is distinguished from unprotected speech and "fighting words," libel, obscenity and lewdness are unprotected because they do not advance an exposition of ideas and their social value is too slight to outweigh society's interest in order and morality.
1942	*Valentine v. Chrestensen*	316 U.S. 52	Commercial advertisements are not protected by the First Amendment.
1943	*West Virginia State Board of Education v. Barnette*	319 U.S. 624	The First Amendment's freedom of speech clause forbids states from punishing those who refuse to salute the flag.
1944	*Prince v. Massachusetts*	321 U.S. 158	The state's right to regulate the activities of children takes precedence over their free speech rights.
1944	*Hartzel v. United States*	322 U.S. 680	Intemperate and malicious writing during wartime against government figures, wartime allies, and religious/ethnic groups involved in the war is protected by the First Amendment.

Date	Case	Citation	Decision
1946	*Hannegan v. Esquire*	327 U.S. 146	Revocation of second class mail privileges of a magazine on the grounds that it was not sufficiently contributing to the public good is unconstitutional.
1946	*Pennekamp v. Florida*	328 U.S. 331	When the First Amendment clashes with a criminal defendant's right to a fair trial, a balance must be struck, but "freedom of discussion should be given the widest possible range compatible with the essential requirement of the fair and orderly administration of justice."
1948	*Winters v. New York*	333 U.S. 507	The First Amendment protects publications on crime and crime stories.
1949	*Kovacs. v. Cooper*	336 U.S. 77	It is constitutional to curtail free expression that produces excessive noise.
1949	*Terminiello v. Chicago*	337 U.S. 1	Freedom of speech may serve its purpose best when it "induces a condition of unrest" or "even stirs people to anger."
1951	*Niemotko v. Maryland*	340 U.S. 268	Parks are traditional public forums where freedom of expression is protected.
1951	*Kunz v. New York*	340 U.S. 290	Requiring permits for street preaching is not justifiable under the First Amendment.
1951	*Feiner v. New York*	340 U.S. 315	A speech that angered a crowd into pushing and shoving, though not actual violence, is not protected by the First Amendment.
1951	*Dennis v. United States*	341 U.S. 494	Absolutist position on freedom of expression on public policy weakened by balancing the gravity of possible evil effects of speech with the probability of its occurring.
1952	*Joseph Burstyn, Inc. v. Wilson*	343 U.S. 495	City of New York policy denying movies found sacrilegious the right to be exhibited is unconstitutional.
1952	*Harisiades v. Shaughnessy*	342 U.S. 580	Deportation of aliens because they are members of the Communist Party is not unconstitutional.
1952	*Wieman v. Updegraff*	344 U.S. 183	Aliens proved to be former members of political party advocating the violent overthrow of the government can be deported.
1953	*Saumur v. City of Quebec*	[Canada]	The power of municipalities to prohibit the distribution of publications in the streets is legitimate in Canada.
1955	*Brattle Films v. Commissioner of Public Safety, Massachusetts*	127 N.E. 2nd 891	It is unconstitutional for states to ban Sunday gatherings such as movies and parades on the grounds that they are not in keeping with the religious observance of Sunday.
1956	*Adler v. Board of Education, City of New York*	342 U.S. 485	State loyalty oath requiring state school teachers to swear they do not advocate violent overthrow of the government or belong to the Communist Party is constitutional.
1956	*Pennsylvania v. Nelson*	350 U.S. 497	The Pennsylvania Sedition Act of 1952 which, inter alia, prohibited bringing the state or federal government into "hatred or contempt," is unconstitutional because the Smith Act takes precedence.
1957	*Butler v. Michigan*	352 U.S. 380	Statutes banning publication of works found "likely to corrupt the morals of a minor" are unconstitutional because such works are thereby unavailable to adults.
1957	*Konigsberg v. State Bar of California*	353 U.S. 252	Persons who fail to swear they do not advocate forcible overthrow of the government cannot for that reason be denied admission to the Bar.
1957	*Yates v. United States*	354 U.S. 298	Prohibition of the advocacy of forcible overthrow of the government in the absence of advocacy of acts to accomplish the overthrow is unconstitutional.

Date	Case	Citation	Decision
1957	*Roth v. United States*	354 U.S. 476	Obscenity is "material which deals with sex in a manner appealing to the prurient interest" and is "utterly without redeeming social importance." "Contemporary community standards" shall determine what is obscene.
1958	*Speiser v. Randall*	357 U.S. 513	State statutes requiring signing of a loyalty oath before individuals can receive a property tax exemption are unconstitutional.
1959	*Katzev v. County of Los Angeles*	341 P. 2nd 310	The First Amendment protects publications in which standard comic book characters commit crimes such as theft and abduction.
1959	*Barenblatt v. United States*	360 U.S. 109	The state's interest in forcing a congressional witness to testify may override the witness' First Amendment rights to free expression and association.
1959	*Farmers Union v. WDAY*	360 U.S. 525	Radio stations cannot censor political candidates' comments and stations cannot be held accountable for libel for such candidate comments.
1959	*Kingsley International Pictures Corp. v. Regents of the University of the State of New York*	360 U.S. 684	A state law banning films intimating that adultery may be justified under certain circumstances is unconstitutional because it attempts to ban an idea.
1960	*Regina v. Penguin Books Ltd.*		The uncensored version of D. H. Lawrence's *Lady Chatterley's Lover* is not obscene under Britain's 1959 Obscene Publications Act.
1960	*Grove Press v. Christenberry*	276 F. 2nd 433	D. H. Lawrence's novel *Lady Chatterley's Lover* is not obscene because its predominant appeal is not to the prurient interest.
1961	*Times Film Corp. v. City of Chicago*	365 U.S. 43	Legal requirements that films be submitted for possible censorship before public exhibition are not unconstitutional.
1961	*Scales v. United States*	367 U.S. 203	Punishment for active membership in the Communist Party is not a violation of the First Amendment.
1963	*City of St. Louis v. Mikes*	372 S.W. 2nd 508	Perpetrators of nightclub burlesque act considered "lewd and indecent behavior" can be punished.
1963	*Bantam Books, Inc. v. Sullivan*	372 U.S. 58	A state scheme to compose lists of books objectionable for minors and prosecute their distributors is unconstitutional.
1963	*Edwards v. South Carolina*	372 U.S. 229	The Due Process Clause of the Fourteenth Amendment, incorporating the First Amendment, does not allow states to prohibit peaceful expression of unpopular views in traditional public forums.
1964	*New York Times Co. v. Sullivan*	376 U.S. 254	Freedom of press and speech require public figures who sue for libel to show defendants' malice, the knowing or reckless disregard for truth.
1964	*Jacobellis v. State of Ohio*	378 U.S. 184	Under current interpretations of obscenity, the U.S. Supreme Court must determine in each individual case whether material is obscene.
1964	*Grove Press v. Gerstein, State Attorney*	378 U.S. 577	*Tropic of Cancer* by Henry Miller, having been found obscene by courts from 1934 onward is pronounced not obscene in a per curiam opinion by the U.S. Supreme Court.
1965	*Freedman v. Maryland*	380 U.S. 51	Government censorship of movies considered obscene is constitutional if strict procedures are followed and if there is opportunity for prompt review of decisions.
1965	*Lamont v. Postmaster General*	381 U.S. 301	Regulation permitting post office to require receivers of foreign political propaganda to request its delivery is invalid.
1965	*Griswold v. Connecticut*	381 U.S. 479	The First Amendment protects individuals' use of contraceptives.
1965	*Estes v. Texas*	381 U.S. 532	Television cameras can be banned from courtrooms.

Date	Case	Citation	Decision
1966	Regina v. Cameron		A work may be obscene in Canadian law even if it has artistic merit and the public good is served.
1966	Attorney General v. A Book Named Naked Lunch	218 N.E. 2nd 571	William S. Burroughs' novel *Naked Lunch* is not obscene under Massachusetts law, but advertising it for prurient appeal is subject to prosecution.
1966	Rosenblatt v. Baer	383 U.S. 75	The *New York Times v. Sullivan* libel test applies to government employees who have "substantial control over governmental affairs."
1966	Brown v. Louisiana	383 U.S. 131	Peaceful sit-ins on certain public property to protest racial segregation is constitutionally protected.
1966	A Book Named "John Cleland's Memoirs of a Woman of Pleasure" v. Attorney General of Massachusetts	383 U.S. 413	Material is obscene if its dominant theme is prurient, is "patently offensive because it affronts contemporary community standards," and is "utterly without redeeming social value."
1966	Ginzburg v. United States	383 U.S. 463	The use of double entendre place names, such as "Middlesex," in mailing erotic materials constitutes pandering, unprotected speech that openly appeals to erotic interests.
1966	Ashton v. Kentucky	384 U.S. 195	Criminal libel law focuses primarily on listener reaction rather than on message content.
1966	Sheppard v. Maxwell	384 U.S. 333	Judges should restrain attorneys from talking to the media to minimize pretrial publicity potentially adverse to defendants.
1966	Adderly v. Florida	385 U.S. 39	Demonstrating in the front lobby of a jail is not constitutionally protected speech.
1966	Bond v. Floyd	385 U.S. 116	Legislators cannot be denied their seats for statements made about federal government policies.
1967	United States v. Magazine Entitled "Hellenic Sun"	373 F. 2nd 635	A foreign magazine that appeals to homosexual interests by focusing on the male genitalia and has no other redeeming social value may be banned from importation.
1967	Time, Inc. v. Hill	385 U.S. 374	To win damages in invasion of privacy suits, newsworthy figures must prove malice by publishers.
1967	Keyishian v. Board of Regents	385 U.S. 589	Individuals cannot be denied public employment by states and municipalities because they are members of organizations advocating the violent overthrow of the government.
1967	Walker v. City of Birmingham	388 U.S. 307	It is constitutional for judges to cite for contempt of court individuals disobeying restraining orders, even if such restraints are likely to be found unconstitutional.
1968	Ginsberg v. New York	390 U.S. 629	Publications that may be sold to adults may be banned from sale to minors.
1968	St. Amant v. Thompson	390 U.S. 727	Proof of malice requires evidence that the defendant entertained serious doubts about the truth of a published assertion.
1968	United States v. O'Brien	391 U.S. 367	Burning draft cards as means of political protest is unprotected conduct rather than protected "symbolic speech."
1968	Rabeck v. New York	391 U.S. 462	Prohibition of sale to minors of erotic publications that "appeal to the lust" or to the "curiosity as to sex" or to the "anatomical differences between the sexes" is unconstitutionally vague.
1968	Epperson v. Arkansas	393 U.S. 97	A state statute banning the teaching of the theory of evolution is a violation of the First Amendment.

Date	Case	Citation	Decision
1969	*Commonwealth of Pennsylvania v. Stotland*	251 A. 2nd 701	Speech may be restricted in some circumstances to prevent civic disorders under "time, size, and area limitations upon peaceful public assemblies."
1969	*Tinker v. Des Moines Independent Community School District*	393 U.S. 503	Suspension of students wearing black arm bands to protest government policy is a violation of their First Amendment rights.
1969	*Gregory v. City of Chicago*	394 U.S. 111	Controversial speech in traditional forums of free expression may not be restricted unless police reasonably believe that disorder is imminent.
1969	*Stanley v. Georgia*	394 U.S. 557	The right to privacy allows individuals to use illegal obscene materials in the home.
1969	*Street v. New York*	394 U.S. 576	Burning the flag while speaking against racial injustice is constitutionally protected.
1969	*Red Lion Broadcasting Co., Inc. v. Federal Communications Commission*	395 U.S. 367	It is constitutional for the federal government to require broadcasters to allow time for reply in discussion of controversial issues.
1969	*Brandenburg v. Ohio*	395 U.S. 444	Speakers who advocate "crime sabotage, violence, or unlawful methods of terrorism" cannot be punished unless their advocacy is "directed to inciting or producing immanent lawless action and is likely to incite or produce such action."
1970	*Rowan v. U.S. Post Office Department*	397 U.S. 728	It is constitutional for the U.S. Postal Service to ban the mailing of erotic materials to individuals who complained about receiving them.
1970	*Schact v. United States*	398 U.S. 58	Criticism of the military while in military uniform in theatrical productions is protected speech.
1971	*Cohen v. California*	403 U.S. 15	Wearing offensive anti-draft slogans in a courthouse is constitutionally protected speech.
1971	*New York Times Co. v. United States*	403 U.S. 713	To justify prior restraint of the publication of classified documents government must show that disclosure would "surely" result in "direct, immediate, and irreparable" national security damage. (Pentagon Papers case)
1972	*Marchetti v. United States*	488 F. 2nd 1309	Prepublication review of former Central Intelligence Agency employees' writings is not a violation of the First Amendment.
1972	*Police Department of Chicago v. Mosley*	408 U.S. 92	Government may not place restrictions on some types of street demonstrations and not others; it is not constitutional for government to favor some types of speech over others.
1972	*Branzburg v. Hayes*	408 U.S. 665	Reporters do not have First Amendment rights to refuse to testify before grand juries.
1972	*California v. LaRue*	409 U.S. 109	Under the Twenty-First Amendment (repeal of Prohibition) states may regulate establishments serving alcohol, including denying licenses to those providing lewd entertainment.
1973	*Cincinnati v. Karlan*	298 N.E. 2nd 34	Using crude language to police is protected because such language is "fighting words."
1973	*Kleindienst v. Mandel*	408 U.S. 753	Government regulations prohibiting entrance to the United States of foreign nationals considered politically undesirable are constitutionally permissible.
1973	*Miller v. California*	413 U.S. 15	The idea was added to previous tests of obscenity that material is obscene if, taken as a whole, it "lacks serious literary, artistic, political, or scientific value."
1974	*Communist Party of Indiana v. Whitcomb*	414 U.S. 441	Statutes may not require loyalty oaths of political parties for those parties to be placed on the ballot.

Date	Case	Citation	Decision
1974	Smith v. Goguen	415 U.S. 566	It is constitutional to treat the U.S. flag "contemptuously," since contempt to one person may be art to another.
1974	Parker v. Levy	417 U.S. 733	The First Amendment does not protect a U.S. Army doctor's right to advocate that certain soldiers not fight in a war.
1974	Hamling v. United States	418 U.S. 87	An illustrated version containing obscene photographs of a government report on obscenity and pornography may be constitutionally unprotected if there is sufficient evidence of pandering.
1974	Miami Herald Publishing Co. v. Tornillo	418 U.S. 241	Laws requiring newspapers to publish replies to criticism of candidates for public office are unconstitutional.
1974	Lehman v. City of Shaker Heights	418 U.S. 298	A politician is not denied freedom of speech if his advertisements are rejected by a municipality's mass transit system, since its passengers are a captive audience.
1974	Gertz v. Robert I. Welch, Inc.	418 U.S. 323	Public figures involved in public controversy must show actual malice to win libel suits.
1975	Sanders v. Georgia	216 S.E. 2nd 838	The pornographic film *Deep Throat* is obscene.
1975	Southeastern Promotions, Ltd. v. Conrad	420 U.S. 546	Certain controversial plays may not be banned in publicly owned theaters.
1975	Bigelow v. Virginia	421 U.S. 809	A state statute forbidding publication of the encouragement of abortion violates the First Amendment.
1975	Erznoznik v. Jacksonville	422 U.S. 205	Overturns a local ordinance prohibiting drive-in theaters with screens visible from public areas from showing films containing nudity because government cannot shield all citizens from seeing nudity.
1975	Doran v. Salem Inn	422 U.S. 922	Topless dancing is symbolic speech protected by the First Amendment.
1976	Buckley v. Valeo	424 U.S. 1	Although federal limitations on contributions to candidates are constitutional, the First Amendment does not allow the federal government to limit the amounts candidates for public office can spend.
1976	Hudgens v. NLRB	424 U.S. 507	Shopping centers are not traditional public forums where free expression is protected.
1976	Greer v. Spock	424 U.S. 828	Free speech rights of presidential candidates in distribution of literature at a military base do not take precedence over requirements for the loyalty, discipline, and order of troops.
1976	Virginia State Board of Pharmacy v. Virginia Citizens Consumer Council	425 U.S. 748	Statutes banning the advertising of prescription prices are unconstitutional.
1976	Young v. American Mini Theaters, Inc.	427 U.S. 50	Zoning ordinances intending to regulate the sale of pornography which allow businesses to be closed but do not require a finding of obscenity may be constitutional.
1976	Nebraska Press Association v. Stuart	427 U.S. 539	Prior restraint is not permissible in publication of material obtained in open court that is possibly prejudicial to criminal defendants; made prior restraint of pretrial publicity difficult to justify.
1977	Wooley v. Maynard	430 U.S. 705	States may not force citizens to display state mottos to which citizens object on their license plates.
1977	Carey v. Population Services International	431 U.S. 678	It is unconstitutional for states to ban the advertisement and display of condoms.
1977	Bates v. State Bar of Arizona	433 U.S. 350	State restrictions on advertising by attorneys are unconstitutional.

Date	Case	Citation	Decision
1978	*Nova Scotia Board of Censors v. McNeil*	[Canada]	A Canadian province may regulate as a business the showing of films within its boundaries, but it may not make criminal the showing of films that it finds indecent.
1978	*Village of Skokie v. National Socialist Party of America*	69 Ill. 2nd 205	Regulations to license street demonstrations and parades aimed at restricting free expression by unpopular groups such as the American Nazi Party are unconstitutional.
1978	*Ratchford, President, University of Missouri v. Gay Lib.*	434 U.S. 1080	A university is not constitutionally justified in denying recognition to a group discussing the emotional needs of male homosexuals.
1978	*Federal Communications Commission v. Pacifica Foundation*	438 U.S. 726	The Federal Communications Commission may limit, but not prohibit completely, the broadcast of material that, although not obscene, is indecent; indecent broadcasts may be regulated by government at times when children may be among the audience.
1979	*Smith v. Daily Mail Publishing Co.*	443 U.S. 97	Only the strongest state interests can allow states to punish journalists who publish the names of juvenile criminal defendants.
1980	*Snepp v. United States*	444 U.S. 507	It is constitutional for the U.S. government to require certain former government employees to submit speeches and writings for reviews that might disallow publication of all or part of the material.
1980	*Central Hudson Gas & Electric Corporation v. Public Service Commission of New York*	447 U.S. 557	In commercial messages, only truthful advertising of legal products is protected under the First Amendment.
1980	*Richmond Newspapers, Inc. v. Virginia*	448 U.S. 555	The press has the right to attend judicial proceedings to gather information as part of its First Amendment rights.
1981	*Chandler v. Florida*	449 U.S. 560	Although the press has no First Amendment right to use cameras in courtrooms, states may permit cameras in state courts if they do not compromise the defendant's right to a fair trial.
1981	*U.S. Postal Service v. Council of Greenburgh Civic Associations*	453 U.S. 114	Mailboxes to deposit unstamped mailable matter are "off-limits" public property to which all groups are not entitled to equal access for First Amendment purposes.
1981	*Widmar v. Vincent*	454 U.S. 263	State universities may not prohibit a religious group from meeting on campus once other religious groups are allowed to meet, unless there is a compelling state reason.
1982	*Globe Newspaper Company v. Superior Court*	73 L.Ed. 2nd 248	A statute that mandates judges to hold closed trials in cases of sex crimes involving minors is unconstitutional.
1982	*Board of Education, Island Trees Union Free School District v. Pico*	73 L.Ed. 2nd 435	Boards of Education cannot summarily remove books believed to be "anti-American, anti-Christian, anti-Semitic and just plain filthy."
1982	*New York v. Ferber*	458 U.S. 747	States may prohibit non-obscene pornography in which minors are subjects.
1983	*Bolger v. Youngs Drug Products Corp.*	77 L.Ed. 2nd 469	The U.S. Postal Service cannot prohibit sending unsolicited advertisements for contraceptives.
1983	*Perry Educational Association v. Perry Local Educators' Association*	460 U.S. 37	It is constitutional for government to practice viewpoint discrimination in "off limits" public property because such public property serves a specific government purpose and is not a traditional forum for free expression.
1983	*United States v. Grace*	461 U.S. 171	"Time place, and manner" restrictions that make a substantial impact on free expression are constitutional only if they are narrowly tailored to protect a significant government interest and do not close alternative channels of expression.

Date	Case	Citation	Decision
1984	American Booksellers Association, Inc. v. Hudnut	598 F. Supp. 1316	Broad definitions of pornography that provide no provision for redeeming social value are unconstitutional.
1984	Press-Enterprise Co. v. Superior Court of California, Riverside County	464 U.S. 501	Judges may close court rooms to the press only if they have sufficient evidence of an overriding interest such as a defendant's right to a fair trial.
1984	Los Angeles City Council v. Taxpayers for Vincent	466 U.S. 789	City's prohibition of political posters on lamp posts is constitutional because lamp posts are not traditional public forums and a significant social interest is served in maintaining a litter-free environment.
1985	United States v. Albertini	472 U.S. 675	Military bases are "off-limits" public property to which all groups are not entitled to equal access for First Amendment purposes.
1985	Dun & Bradstreet v. Greenmoss Builders, Inc.	472 U.S. 749	Private individuals bringing libel cases can recover damages more easily if the contested issue "is not a matter of public concern."
1985	Cornelius v. NAACP Legal Defense and Educational Fund, Inc.	473 U.S. 788	Not all protected speech can be tolerated in all circumstances; government charitable fund campaigns are "off-limits" public property to which all groups are not entitled to equal access for First Amendment purposes.
1986	City of Renton v. Playtime Theatres, Inc.	475 U.S. 41	Zoning laws that are used to regulate businesses purveying offensive sexual materials that are not obscene do not violate the First Amendment.
1986	Philadelphia Newspapers, Inc. v. Hepps	475 U.S. 767	Truth is a defense against private individuals suing newspapers for defamation over matters of public interest.
1986	Los Angeles v. Preferred Communications	476 U.S. 488	The First Amendment rights of cable television operators are not violated if they fail to receive a license to broadcast.
1986	Posadas de Puerto Rico Associates v. Tourism Company of Puerto Rico	478 U.S. 328	Government may ban advertising for any activity that it can prohibit outright.
1987	Board of Airport Commissioners of the City of Los Angeles v. Jews for Jesus, Inc.	482 U.S. 569	Airport restrictions prohibiting all First Amendment activities are unconstitutional.
1987	Hustler Magazine, Inc. v. Falwell	485 U.S. 46	Opinions expressed about public figures by magazines motivated by ill-will are protected speech.
1988	Hazelwood School District v. Kuhlmeier	484 U.S. 260	Schools may censor articles written by students in school publications.
1988	Lakewood v. Plain Dealer Publishing Co.	486 U.S. 750	Licensing and antinoise regulations are unconstitutional if they are vague or give excessive administrative discretion to officials.
1988	Frisby v. Schultz	487 U.S. 474	Town ordinances that ban all demonstrations outside private residences are constitutional.
1989	Texas v. Johnson	491 U.S. 397	Prohibition of desecration of venerable objects such as the U.S. flag is a violation of First Amendment rights.
1989	Florida Star v. B.F.J.	491 U.S. 524	Publishing the legally obtained names of rape victims is constitutionally unprotected, absent a narrowly conceived state interest.
1989	Board of Trustees v. Fox	492 U.S. 469	To restrict commercial speech, government must show its grounds are reasonable but not that they are compelling.
1990	Miller et al. v. Civil City of South Bend		Nude dancing is constitutionally permissible in some circumstances.
1990	Osborne v. Ohio	495 U.S. 103	Prohibiting viewing or possession of child pornography does not violate the First Amendment.

Date	Case	Citation	Decision
1990	*Peel v. Attorney Registration and Disciplinary Committee of Illinois*	496 U.S. 91	Truthful advertising relating to a lawful activity is protected by the First Amendment.
1990	*United States v. Eichman*	496 U.S. 310	Prohibition of burning U.S. flag is a violation of First Amendment rights, serving no legitimate state interest.
1990	*Milkovich v. Lorain Journal Co.*	110 S.Ct. 2695	Requiring plaintiffs to prove newspaper stories false is a major protection regarding libel actions over critical opinion of government, art, and restaurants.
1991	*Cohen v. Cowles Media Co.*	111 S.Ct. 2513	States may punish reporters who break confidentiality promises made to sources.
1991	*Rust v. Sullivan*	111 S.Ct. 1759	Federal regulations prohibiting counsellors from discussing abortion or referrals for abortions do not violate the First Amendment.
1991	*Barnes v. Glen Theatre, Inc.*	501 U.S. 560	State statute prohibiting nude dancing does not violate the First Amendment.
1992	*Butler v. The Queen*	1 S.C.R. 452	Pornography may be banned in Canada on the grounds that it is "degrading" and "dehumanizing" to women.
1992	*R.A.V. v. City of St. Paul*	112 S.Ct. 2538	An ordinance outlawing certain forms of "hate speech" is unconstitutional.
1993	Wisconsin v. Mitchell	113 S.Ct. 2194	Laws that increase punishment of crimes of racial hatred do not violate the First Amendment's free speech clause.

—Charles F. Bahmueller

RESOURCE GUIDE

ANTIDEFAMATION GROUPS

Anti-Defamation League of B'Nai B'Rith
823 United Nations Plaza
New York, NY 10017
(212) 490-2525
Jewish group devoted to the eradication of anti-Semitism.

Hispanic Policy Development Project (HPDP)
36 E. 22nd St., 9th Fl.
New York, NY 10010
(212) 529-9323
fax (212) 477-5395
Works to remove what it sees as the long-standing neglect of the Hispanic population in American and wishes to increase awareness of Hispanic concerns.

Klanwatch
400 Washington Ave.
Montgomery, AL 36104
(334) 264-0286
fax (334) 264-0629
Collects and distributes information on the activities of the Ku Klux Klan.

Resisting Defamation
2530 Berryessa Road, No. 616
San Jose, CA 95132
(408) 995-6545
fax (408) 923-5836
Seeks to eliminate ethnic slurs and stereotypes of European Americans.

FAMILY ADVOCACY GROUPS

American Family Association (AFA)
PO Drawer 2440
Tupelo, MS 38803
(601) 844-5036
Conservative, Christian group that seeks to influence the media through letter writing campaigns and boycotts in order to produce better family entertainment.

American Society for the Defense of Tradition, Family and Property (TFP)
P.O. Box 1868
York, PA 17405
(717) 225-7147
fax (717) 225-7382
A civic group that wishes to peacefully and legally oppose socialist and Marxist views.

Eagle Forum (EF)
P.O. Box 618
Alton, IL 62002
(618) 462-5415
fax (618) 462-8909
Conservative organization that advocates traditional morality, national defense, and private enterprise as a way of strengthening the family.

Film Advisory Board (FAB)
1727 1/2 N. Sycamore
Hollywood, CA 90028
(213) 874-3644
fax (213) 969-0635
Promotes better quality family entertainment by evaluating films for all media, including television and videotapes.

Foundation to Improve Television (FIT)
50 Congress St., Ste. 925
Boston, MA 02109
(617) 523-5520
fax (617) 523-4619
Seeks to decrease the amount of violence that is shown on television due to it's impact on viewers.

Free Congress Research and Education Foundation (FCREF)
717 2nd St. NE
Washington, D.C. 20002
(202) 546-3000
fax (202) 543-8425
Organization concerned with the effects of direct democracy, public policy, and the judicial reform on traditional family values.

Parents' Alliance to Protect Our Children (PAPOC)
44 E. Tacoma Ave.
Latrobe, PA 15650-1141
(412) 459-9076
Works to protect the family and children from the mismanagement of the educational system and political structure.

Parents' Music Resource Center (PMRC)
1500 Arlington Blvd.
Arlington, VA 22209
(703) 527-9466
fax (703) 527-9468
Promotes more responsible production in the recording industry by using a "Parental Advisory" label for consumers.

GAY AND LESBIAN ADVOCACY GROUPS

Gay and Lesbian Alliance Against Defamation (GLAAD)
150 W. 26th St., Ste.503
New York, NY 10001
(212) 807-1700
fax (212) 807-1806
Works to replace bigoted representations, in the media and public, of homosexuals with more positive images of the gay community.

Gay and Lesbian Parents Coalition International (GLPCI)
P.O. Box 50360
Washington, D.C. 20091
(202) 583-8029
(201) 783-6204
Disseminates information regarding homosexual parenting. Works to end discrimination of sexual orientation.

Lesbian Feminist Liberation (LFL)
Gay Community Center

208 W. 13th St.
New York, NY 10011
(212) 924-2657
Women united to change views and institutions that proscribe lesbian and women's rights.

HISTORY/MILITARY

Center for Defense Information (CDI)
Library for Press and Public
1500 Massachusetts Ave. NW
Washington, D.C. 20005
(202) 862-0700
fax (202) 862-0708
Seeks to make available to the public informed analyses of U.S. defense policies.

Historians of American Communism (HOAC)
P.O. Box 1236
Washington Depot, CT 06793
(203) 868-7408
fax (203) 868-0080
Promotes interest in the history of communism in America.

International Military Archives (IMA)
c/o Lowell Anson Kenyon
5613 Johnson Ave.
Bethesda, MD 20817
(301) 897-0083
Archiving organizations grouped to promote better standards of evaluating military history and seeks the disclosure of all U.S. military records before 1946.

National Coordinating Committee for the Promotion of History (NCC)
400 A. St. SE
Washington, D.C. 20003
(202) 544-2422
fax (202) 544-8307
Coalition of historical organizations that work to protect historians' interests regarding federal policy.

National Women's History Project (NWHP)
7738 Bell Road
Windsor, CA 95492
(707) 838-6000
fax (707) 838-0478
Encourages the study of the history of American women.

JOURNALISM AND PUBLISHING GROUPS

AAP Political Action Committee (AAP/PAC)
c/o Association of American Publishers
1718 Connecticut Ave., NW, Ste. 700
Washington, D.C. 20009
(202) 232-3335
fax (202) 745-0694
Helps raise funds to elect persons to Congress who believe and support the right to know and free speech.

Accuracy in Media (AIM)
4455 Connecticut Ave. NW, Ste. 330

Washington, D.C. 20008
(800) 787-0044
(202) 364-4401
News media watchdog organization.

Alliance for Community Media
666 11th St. NW, Ste. 806
Washington, D.C. 20001
(202) 393-2650
Advocates responsible cable programming.

American Booksellers Foundation for Free Expression
828 South Broadway
Tarrytown, NY 10591
(914) 591-2665
fax (914) 591-2716
Free expression arm of the American Booksellers Association.

American Constitutional Law Foundation (ACLF)
P.O. Box 9383
Denver, CO 80209-0383
(303) 744-6449
fax (303) 744-6581
Seeks to uphold the First Amendment right to petition government.

American Library Association (ALA)
Office for Intellectual Freedom
50 E. Huron St.
Chicago, IL 60611
(800) 545-2433
(312) 280-4223
fax (312) 440-9374
The Office for Intellectual Freedom provides First Amendment support for the ALA and it's members.

Americans for Decency (AFD)
871 Post Ave.
Staten Island, NY 10310
(718) 442-6088
Conservative group that objects to free access to drugs, pornography, and vulgar music.

American Society of Newspaper Editors (ASNE)
P.O. Box 4090
Reston, VA 22090-1700
(703) 648-1144
fax (703) 476-6125
Managing editors of daily newspapers who are responsible for determining editorial and news policy.

Article 19: International Centre on Censorship
33 Islington High Street
London N1 9LH, England
011-44-171-278-9292
fax 011-44-171-713-1356
Prominent international organization dedicated to combatting censorship.

Asian Cinevision (ACV)
32 E. Broadway
New York, NY 10002

(212) 925-8685
fax (212) 925-8157
Encourages the presentation of positive alternatives to Asian stereotypes in the media.

Black American Cinema Society (BACS)
3617 Monclair St.
Los Angeles, CA 90018
(213) 737-3292
fax (213) 737-2842
Works to acknowledge the contributions of African Americans in the motion picture industry.

Christian Research (CR)
P.O. Box 385
Eureka Springs, AR 72632
(501) 253-7185
Serves persons who do not trust the media or U.S. public education system which they believe is controlled by secular humanists.

Committee on International Freedom to Publish
c/o Association of American Publishers
71 5th Ave.
New York, NY 10003
(212) 255-0200
fax (212) 255-7007
Committee that works to promote and protect the rights of publishers and authors.

Fairness and Accuracy in Reporting
130 W. 25th St.
New York, NY 10001
(212) 633-3700
fax (212) 727-7668
Group that promotes pluralism in the media, especially news coverage, and advocates freedom of the press and free speech.

First Amendment Congress
2301 S. Gaylord St.
Denver, CO 80208
(303) 871-4430
fax (303) 871-4585
Works to enhance awareness and understanding of what First Amendment rights are.

First Amendment Lawyers Association (FALA)
c/o Wayne Giampietro
125 S. Wacker Dr., Ste. 2700
Chicago, IL 60606
(312) 332-6000
fax (312) 332-6008
Union of lawyers who defend cases involving First Amendment rights.

First Amendment Press
8129 N. 35th Ave., No. 134
Phoenix, AZ 85051-5892
(800) 633-3274
(602) 561-9786
fax (602) 561-9786
Disseminates information of alleged government misconduct, conducts investigations, and offers legal advice about citizens' rights.

Free Press Association (FPA)
P.O. Box 63
Port Hadlock, WA 98339
(206) 385-5097
Network of news media professionals who oppose government censorship of the media.

Freedom of Expression Foundation (FOEF)
c/o Dr. Craig R. Smith
5220 S. Marina Pacifica
Long Beach, CA 90803
(310) 985-4301
Provides information to Congress and the public concerning First Amendment rights.

Freedom of Information Center
University of Missouri
20 Walter Williams Hall
Columbia, MO 65211
(314) 882-4856
A research service that acts as a clearinghouse for the dissemination of information.

Freedom to Advertise Coalition (FAC)
c/o Patton, Boggs, L.L.P.
2550 M St. NW, Ste.500
Washington, D.C. 20037
(202) 457-6313
fax (202) 457-6315
Coalition of advertising associations concerned with protecting the right to commercial free speech.

Freedom to Read Foundation (FTRF)
50 E. Huron St.
Chicago, IL 60611
(800) 545-2433
(312) 280-4226
fax (312) 280-4227
Works to protect and defend freedom of speech and freedom of the press especially where it relates to libraries or librarians.

Fund for Investigative Journalism (FIJ)
1755 Massachusetts Ave. NW, No. 324
Washington, D.C. 20036
(202) 462-1844
Offers grants to enable journalists to investigate systems that harm the public or abuses of authority.

Fund for Objective News Reporting (FONR)
422 1st St. SE
Washington, D.C. 20003
(202) 546-0856
Works to correct bias in the media.

Gap Media Project (GMP)
142 W.S. College Street
Yellow Springs, OH 45387
(513) 767-2224
fax (513) 767-1888
Works to increase access to information other than what is given by the media on commercially sponsored television.

Gay Media Task Force (GMTF)
71-426 Estellita drive
Rancho Mirage, CA 92270
(619) 568-6711
fax (619) 568-3241
Provides resources to the media on issues in the gay and lesbian community and monitors it on those issues.

Hispanic Public Relations Association
735 S. Figueroa St., Ste. 818
Los Angeles, CA 90017
(818) 793-9335
fax (818) 440-5263
Works to promote positive images of Hispanics in the media.

Inter American Press Association (IAPA)
2911 NW 39th St.
Miami, FL 33142
(305) 634-2465
fax (305) 635-2272
International group of publishers united to promote and protect freedom of the press in the Americas.

Media Access Project (MAP)
2000 M St. NW, 4th Fl.
Washington, D.C. 20036
(202) 232-4300
fax (202) 293-2672
Public interest law firm that works to insure that all forms of the media fully inform the public on important topics.

Media Action Research Center (MARC)
P.O. Box 320
Nashville, TN 37202
(615) 742-5451
(615) 742-5140
Seeks to inform the public of the content and influence on television of consumers and to bring about positive changes in the content and style of television.

Media Coalition/Americans for Constitutional Freedom (MC/ACF)
1221 Avenue of the Americas, 24 Fl.
New York, NY 10020
(212) 786-6770
fax (212) 997-4383
Trade Associations grouped to defend and protect First Amendment rights to produce, publish, and distribute various media.

The Media Institute (TMI)
1000 Potomac St. NW, Ste. 301
Washington, D.C. 20007
(202) 298-7512
fax (202) 337-7092
Foundation that promotes free speech and excellence in journalism.

Media Network (MN)
39 W. 14th St., No. 403
New York, NY 10011
(212) 929-2663
fax (212) 929-2732

Wishes to increase public awareness about influence of media and promote alternative views not being offered by mainstream media.

Media Watch (MW)
P.O. Box 618
Santa Cruz, CA 95061
(800) 631-6355
(408) 423-6355
fax (408) 423-6355
Group that works to promote a more positive image of women in the media.

Motion Picture Association of America (MPAA)
1600 Eye St. NW
Washington, D.C. 20006
(202) 293-1966
(202) 296-7410
Works as an advocate of the motion picture, home video, and television industries.

National Campaign for Freedom of Expression (NCFE)
1402 Third Ave., No. 421
Seattle, WA 98101
(800) 477-6233
(206) 340-9301
fax (206) 340-4303
Advocacy group primarily concerned with censorship issues involving the visual and performance arts.

National Coalition Against Censorship (NCAC)
275 7th Ave., 20th Fl.
New York, NY 10001
(212) 807-6222
fax (212) 807-6245
Coalition of organizations concerned with First Amendment issues.

Project Censored
Sociology Department
Sonoma State University
1801 E. Cotati Avenue
Rohnert Park, CA 94928-3609
(707) 664-2500
fax (701) 664-2108
Media watchdog group that seeks to expose bias and inconsistency in the media.

Reporters Committee for the Freedom of the Press
1101 Wilson Blvd., Ste. 1910
Arlington, VA 22209
(703) 807-2100
Provides legal assistance to journalists when their First Amendment rights are questioned.

Rutherford Institute (RI)
P.O. Box 7482
Charlottesville, VA 22906-7482
(804) 978-3888
fax (804) 978-1789
Gives free legal and educational advice to persons whose First Amendment rights have been imposed on.

Women's Institute for Freedom of the Press (WIFP)
3306 Ross Place, NW
Washington, D.C. 20008-3332
(202) 966-7783
Organization of women that are concerned about the lack of influence women have in raising issues with the media.

POLITICS

Anti-Censorship and Deception Union
Porter Square
P.O. Box 297
Cambridge, MA 02140
(617) 499-7965
Seeks to uncover deceptions that it believes have been perpetrated against persons and groups of people.

Center for Constitutional Rights (CCR)
666 Broadway, 7th Fl.
New York, NY 10012
(212) 614-6464
fax (212) 614-6499
Coalition devoted to promoting and protecting the United States Constitution and the "creative use of law" for positive social change.

Christian Coalition (CC)
1801 Sarah Dr., Ste. L
Chesapeake, VA 23320
(804) 424-2630
fax (804) 424-9068
Political organization that works to stop what it sees as the moral decline of government by electing conscientious persons.

Common Cause (CC)
2030 M St. NW
Washington, D.C. 20036
(202) 833-1200
fax (202) 659-3716
Lobby group of private citizens dedicated to making federal and state government accountable to citizens.

Communist Party of the United States of America (CPUSA)
235 W. 23rd St., 7th Fl.
New York, NY 10011
(212) 989-4994
fax (212) 229-1713
Political party dedicated to improving the interests of working-class people through socialist means.

Confederate National Congress (CNC)
HCR 33, Box 450
Elkins, AR 72717
Organization that has sought the independence of the Confederate States, since 1865, and that refuses to recognize the federal government of the United States.

Government Accountability Project (GAP)
810 First Street NE, Ste. 630
Washington, D.C. 20002-3633
(202) 408-0034
fax (202) 9855

Provides advice, legal and strategic, to individuals who seek to expose repressive, wasteful, and illegal government actions.

National Association of Pro America (NAPA)
2101 Connecticut Ave. NW
Washington, D.C. 20008
(202) 328-1244
fax (202) 328-1245
Women's group that has an interest in national defense, a strong national economy, and that seeks to influence local, state, and federal policy making.

National Committee Against Repressive Legislation (NCARL)
1313 W. 8th St., Ste. 313
Los Angeles, CA 90017
(213) 484-6661
Seeks to protect First Amendment rights, concerned especially with the control of federal intelligence agencies, and seeks to ban covert operations by the CIA and FBI.

PORNOGRAPHY

Adult Video Association (AVA)
270 N. Canon Dr., Ste. 1370
Beverly Hills, CA 90210
(213) 650-7121
Group that promotes the rights of adults to watch whatever they choose in their homes.

Citizens for Media Responsibility Without Law (CMRWL)
P.O. Box 2085
Rancho Cordova, CA 95741-2085
(408) 427-2858
Persons united to require the social responsibility of private enterprise and the media for the distribution of pornography.

Morality in Media (MIM)
475 Riverside Dr.
New York, NY 10115
(212) 870-3222
fax (212) 870-2765
Seeks to constitutionally put a stop to illegal trafficking of hard-core pornography and obscenity.

National Coalition for the Protection of Children and Families (NCPCF)
800 Compton Road, Ste. 9224
Cincinnati, OH 45231
(513) 521-6227
fax (513) 521-6337
Assists in uniting and training groups and individuals who wish to eliminate pornography.

Women Against Pornography
P.O. Box 845, Times Square Station
New York, NY 10108-0845
(212) 307-5055
Works to change public opinion about pornography believing that it is a form of prostitution and not free speech.

RELIGIOUS ADVOCACY GROUPS

Americans for God (AFG)
P.O. Box 20872
Damascus, MD 20872
(301) 253-3496
Group of persons distressed by the government ban on prayer and Bible reading in public schools.

Americans for Religious Liberty
P.O. Box 6656
Silver Springs, MD 20916
(301) 598-2447
Counter-group to the Moral Majority that seeks to uphold the separation of church and state.

Americans United for God and Country (AUGC)
P.O. Box 183
Merion Station, PA 19066
(215) 224-9235
Organization that works to revive the ideas of Christianity that they believe the United States was built on.

Americans United for Separation of Church and State (AUSCS)
1816 Jefferson Pl. NW
Washington, D.C. 20036
(800) 875-3707
(202) 466-3234
fax (202) 466-2587
Promotes public awareness of the importance of the separation of church and state.

Center for Law and Religious Freedom (CLRF)
4208 Evergreen Ln., Ste. 222
Annandale, VA 22003
(703) 642-1070
fax (703) 642-1075
Trains lawyers to deal with legal cases involving religious freedom and informs public of legal principles of religious freedom.

Christian Heritage Center (CHC)
1941 Bishop Ln., Ste. 810
Louisville, KY 40218
(502) 452-1592
fax (502) 452-1593
Organization that wishes to revitalize the Christian faith of the early Americans and include prayer and Bible reading in schools.

Church and School of Wicca
P.O. Box 1502
New Bern, NC 28563
(919) 637-5825

Works to increase public awareness of witchcraft as a religion, not a cult.

Cults Awareness Network (CAN)
2421 W. Pratt Blvd., Ste. 1173
Chicago, IL 60645
(312) 267-7777
Disseminates information and offers support concerning the mind control and deceptive recruitment used by cults.

Freedom From Religion Foundation (FFRF)
P.O. Box 750
Madison, WI 53701
(608) 256-8900
fax (608) 256-1116
Group that promotes the separation of church and state and is opposed to fundamentalist thought.

Institute for First Amendment Studies
P.O. Box 589
Great Barrington, MA 01230
(413) 528-3800
fax (413) 528-4466
Ex-members of fundamentalist churches that are dedicated to the separation of the church and state, monitors activities of fundamentalist right-wing groups.

National League for the Separation of Church and State (NLSCS)
P.O. Box 1257
Escondido, CA 92033
(800) 321-9054
(619) 432-0613
fax (619) 432-0613
Works to repeal all laws that are based on religious beliefs, especially those that restrict the civil rights of nonbelievers in an effort to promote the separation of church and state.

Religious Roundtable (RR)
P.O. Box 11467
Memphis, TN 38111
(901) 458-3795
fax (901) 324-0265
Group that promotes a "moral rebirth of America," and concentrates on such issues as abortion, pornography, and family.

Voice of Liberty Association (VLA)
692 Sunnybrook Dr.
Decatur, GA 30033
(404) 633-3634
Conservative, patriotic individuals and groups that oppose secular humanism in the nation.

—K. L. A. Hyatt

GLOSSARY

Abridgment: (1) Banning, restriction, or infringement of freedom of speech in a constitutionally impermissible manner. (2) Condensation of text, for purposes of saving space or removing unwanted material.

Academic freedom: Freedom of teachers to teach and of students to learn about any subject without fear of official reprisal.

Academic tenure: Freedom of college or university professors from dismissal for reasons other than gross dereliction in the fulfillment of their responsibilities.

Actual malice rule: Constitutional doctrine immunizing libel or slander against public officials or other public persons in the absence of a willful intent to harm the public person.

Adaptation: Conversion of an artistic work, such as a novel or play, into another form, such as a film.

Adult videos: Sexually explicit videotapes.

Advocacy: Form of speech supporting or encouraging others in a desired course of conduct that is constitutionally protected, as distinguished from unprotected incitement of others to imminent lawless action.

Aliens: Foreign-born persons who have not met the requirements of citizenship of the country in which they reside.

Antidefamation league: Organization founded by members of a racial or ethnic group to combat prejudice directed toward the group; the best-known such organization is the Anti-Defamation League of B'nai B'rith.

Antitrust law: Legislation regulating commerce by prohibiting monopolies and other practices that hinder business competition.

Apartheid: Official system of rigid racial segregation and oppression practiced in South Africa prior to its democratic revolution in the early 1990's.

Appeal: Application to a higher court to review a decision made by a lower court.

Assembly, right of: Constitutionally protected right of citizens to urge a concerted protest of government policies.

Bad tendency test: Legal test applied by U.S. courts in the early years of the twentieth century that allowed government to punish or restrict speech simply by demonstrating that it had a tendency to produce some harmful result.

Balancing test: Legal test in which the constitutionality of a restriction on a protected activity such as speech is evaluated according to whether it is justified by a sufficiently weighty governmental interest.

Banning: Prohibiting entirely a particular communication or form of communication.

Blacklisting: Designation of specifically named persons for avoidance or antagonistic treatment; a well-known example is the Hollywood Ten of the film industry.

Blasphemy: Speech expressing critical or irreverent ideas about a religion, or its deity or deities.

Book burning: Public burning of banned materials for the purpose of dramatizing their destruction.

Bowdlerization: Editing (often with abridgment) of another person's literary work to eliminate portions that the editor views as objectionable; the word derives from the name of Thomas Bowdler, a famous expurgator of Shakespeare's writings.

Boycott: Organized effort to refrain from doing business with designated persons or entities in order to protest their policies, views, or behavior.

Breach of the peace: Public disturbance of order.

Broadcast media: Radio and television.

Broadcast network: Cooperative arrangement among radio or television stations to produce and transmit programming.

Broadcasting: Over-the-air transmission of electronic signals through the media of radio and television; toward the end of the twentieth century the term was also beginning to encompass transmissions through cable.

Cable television: Television programming disseminated through hardwire connections, in contrast to broadcast television.

Call-in programs: Radio or television talk shows whose formats include live telephone calls from audience members.

Canvass: To go from person to person, or house to house, seeking to obtain political support or to discover the opinions of individuals on a particular matter, such as an election.

Captive audience: Persons exposed to a speaker's message who cannot readily avoid this exposure.

Caricature: Exaggerated artistic representation of a person or thing that ridicules its subject by distorting particular features.

Censor: Person who suppresses particular communications or the act of suppressing such communications; to act as a censor.

Censure: To criticize or find fault with something or someone.

Child pornography: Sexually explicit representations of children.

Chilling effect: Indirect tendency of a law or policy to frustrate or discourage speech.

Classification of information: Official designation of certain information as not to be disseminated beyond a limited audience, such as a designation of information as "Top Secret."

Clear and present danger: Constitutional standard for describing the magnitude of social danger that will justify suppressing particular speech.

Commercial speech: Speech, such as an advertisement, intended to do no more than propose a commercial transaction.

Community standards: Perceived consensus of a local community's definitions of what constitute morality, immorality, and obscenity.

Compelled speech: Forced affirmation of some expression, such as one's loyalty to country or belief in a deity.

Comstockery: Crusade against pornography; named after Anthony Comstock, famous nineteenth century opponent of pornography who helped to enact the federal Comstock Act of 1873.

Conduct regulation: Regulation of the timing, placement, or manner of delivery of speech, rather than the content of the speech.

Confidential news source: Source of information for a news reporter's story that is protected from disclosure.

Conspiracy: Combination of persons secretly plotting together to engage in an unlawful act.

Content discrimination: Regulation of speech based upon the content of the speech rather than its manner, timing, or placement.

Copycat crime: Criminal behavior suggested or motivated by real or fictional acts that a perpetrator has observed in the media.

Copycat lawsuit: Action for damages, typically against a musician or filmmaker, seeking to make a speaker liable for injuries or death caused when a listener or viewer copies events depicted in music or film.

Copyright: Legal protection of the creative work of authors, composers, and other artistic persons from unauthorized use by others.

Creationism: Christian Fundamentalism alternative to evolution that explains the development of life forms on the earth as the product of divine intelligence.

Criminal procedure: The set of rules governing the process of pretrial, trial, and appeal of litigation in criminal cases.

Criminal syndicalism law: Law making it a crime to advocate, teach, or aid in the commission of criminally violent acts, such as terrorism.

Customs laws: National laws regulating the materials that may be imported into or exported from a country.

Cyberspace: Colloquial expression for the global network of computers called the Internet and the exchange of information on this network.

Dashes and asterisks: Literary devices used to represent the omission of offensive words from a text.

Decency oath: Commitment made by applicant for a grant or other financial support that the funds received will not be used to produce any obscene work.

Defamation: Undermining of another's reputation or business through the communication of a falsehood.

Dial-a-porn: Telephone services that offer, for fees, sexually explicit prerecorded or live messages to callers.

Disorderly conduct: Criminal offense of breaching the peace or offending standards of public morality.

Draft (conscription): Selection of men or women for compulsory military service.

Draft-card burning: Common form of political protest against the United State's involvement in the war against North Vietnam and against the use of the draft to support the war.

Drive-in theater: Public motion picture screen viewed by an audience comprising persons seating within their own motor vehicles.

Due process of law: Guarantees in the Fifth and Fourteenth amendments to the U.S. Constitution providing that individuals may be deprived of life, liberty, or property only in accordance with fair and regular legal procedures.

E-mail: Direct electronic communications among individual computers through the computer network known as the Internet.

Equal time rules: Regulations of broadcasting media that require broadcast stations to grant similar access to competing political candidates to express their views.

Erotica: Literary or artistic communications with predominately sexual themes.

Espionage: Spying, or using spies, to collect secret information from a government, corporation, or other person or entity.

Euphemism: Socially agreeable or unobjectionable ways of referring to matters that others might otherwise regard as objectionable or offensive to mention; for example, to "powder one's nose" is one of many euphemisms for relieving oneself through bodily excretions.

Evolution: Scientific theory accounting for the progressive development of life forms on the earth.

Exploitation film: Trade name within the motion picture industry for low-quality films, whose chief quality is their ability to shock the viewer, often through scenes of nudity, sexual activity, or violence.

Expurgation: Removal of objectionable content or language from an artistic work.

Fairness doctrine: Federal Communications Commission policy enforced from 1949 to 1987 requiring broadcasters to provide balanced and impartial news coverage of controversial community issues.

Federal Communications Commission (FCC): Federal agency with responsibility for regulating radio and television broadcasting.

Feminism: Advocacy of women's rights.

Fighting words: Profane or abusive speech directed at a particular individual that is calculated to incite a violent response.

Flag desecration law: Law making it a crime to burn, deface, or otherwise abuse a national or state flag.

Four-letter words: Short words for sexual or excretory functions that most people would consider vulgar or offensive.

Fraud law: Law that punishes as a crime or allows individual citizens to recover losses occasioned by false statements of fact.

Free speech: General liberty of people to speak without fear of government reprisal; exceptions are sometimes made for circumstances in which strong governmental interests justify restricting or otherwise limiting speech.

Gag order/gag rule: Order or rule adopted by a court that prohibits attorneys, witnesses, or parties in a case from discussing the case with news reporters or other third parties; the term also may refer to an order or rule prohibiting news reporters from reporting matters concerning a case, although the U.S. Supreme Court has held that such orders are an unconstitutional abridgement of freedom of the press.

Gangsta rap: Form of popular music often criticized for glorification of violence, drugs, and offensive attitudes toward women.

Graffiti: Handwritten or drawn inscriptions on walls, buildings, or other structures or stationary objects.

Group libel: Public ridicule or defamation of the members of a group, generally on the basis of the race, ethnicity, national origin, or religion of the group's members.

Hardcore pornography: Sexual materials so explicit that they leave nothing to the imagination—in contrast to softcore pornography.

Hate laws: Legislation outlawing speech or behavior expressing hatred of ethnic, religious, or other minority groups.

Heavy-metal music: Fusion of rock and "electric blues" styles of popular music, with lyrics that frequently involve topics such as sex, drugs, alcohol, violence, suicide, and the occult.

Heckler's veto: Disruptive conduct by an audience that prevents a speaker from effectively communicating or that causes law enforcement officials to suspend the speech to avert riotous behavior.

Heckling: Attempting to disrupt a speech with questions, challenges, or other comments.

Heresy: Doctrines or opinions that contradict an official religious doctrine.

Hicklin rule: Test devised from a nineteenth century British legal case that once measured obscenity by whether the tendency of a communication was to deprave those susceptible to immoral influences.

Hypocrisy: Profession of beliefs or convictions inconsistent with one's own behavior.

Incitement: Direct influence of a speaker on a person or audience to engage at once in particular conduct, distinguished in constitutional law from more abstract advocacy of particular conduct.

Incorporation: Constitutional doctrine by which most provisions in the Bill of Rights have gradually been made applicable to state governments through the Fourteenth Amendment's due process clause.

Indecent: Morally offensive.

Index Librorum Prohibitorum: Roman Catholic church's index of books, the reading of which constituted a mortal sin.

Information highway: Colloquial expression describing the convergence of telephone, television, and computer technologies that will provide a broad spectrum of information and communication possibilities to consumers.

Injunction: Court order requiring a person or entity to act or refrain from acting in a particular manner.

Inquisition: Tribunal appointed to discover and punish heresy.

Internet: Worldwide communication network linking computers.

Jehovah's Witnesses: Religious group whose evangelistic efforts in the first half of the twentieth century were the frequent targets of local censorship efforts.

Junk food news: News that resembles "junk food" in being empty of useful content.

Knowledge tax: Tax on the distribution or publication of current public information such as news reports.

Leaflet: Single sheet of published information typically distributed by hand.

Libel: Written defamation of another's reputation, generally by the publication of a falsehood that injures one's reputation; distinguished from slander, which is oral defamation.

Licensing: Legal regulations that forbid publication of expression without prior approval from a government office or official.

Lobbying: Attempts to influence legislators or other government officials to initiate or support legislation or government policies that benefit the interests that the lobbyist represents.

Loyalty oath: Legal requirements that teachers or other public employees or officials formally affirm their loyalty to a particular government as a condition of employment, service, or other public benefit.

McCarthyism: 1950's campaign to identify and blacklist alleged communist sympathizers, championed by its namesake, Wisconsin senator Joseph McCarthy.

Marketplace of ideas: Metaphorical method of describing the exchange of ideas among citizens, for which freedom of speech is thought essential.

Mass media: Forms of communication capable of reaching great numbers of people, such as television networks and news services.

Media (sing., medium): Various modes of mass communication, such as the press, radio, and television.

Memoirs standard: Test for obscenity derived from the U.S. Supreme Court's 1966 *Memoirs v. Massachusetts* decision holding that material could be judged obscene only if taken as a whole it appeals to prurient interest in sex.

Miller standard: Test for obscenity derived from the U.S. Supreme Court's 1973 *Miller v. California* decision holding that material is obscene if an average person applying local community standards would find that it appeals to prurient interests.

Misdemeanor: Crime of a less serious nature than a felony that is generally punishable by a fine or imprisonment in a county jail.

Misogyny: Demonstration of hatred or scorn of women.

Music labeling laws: Regulations requiring music recording companies to label records, tapes, and compact disks with an indication of whether the music recorded contains sexual, profane, or other objectionable lyrics.

National security: The safety of a nation or government from external threat or domestic subversion.

News media: All print and broadcast media involved in collecting and disseminating news.

Nonmailable matter laws: Laws specifying kinds of materials that may not be carried by the postal service.

Obscene libel: Communication making use of sexually explicit images or language to defame an individual.

Obscenity: Patently offensive and sexually explicit communication that lacks any serious artistic, literary, political, or scientific value.

Offensive language: Vulgar, insulting, profane, or sexually explicit language.

Overbreadth: Constitutional defect of laws that restrict protected as well as unprotected speech.

Pandering: With respect to sexually explicit materials, to display or advertise openly these materials to prompt interest in potential customers of the materials.

Perjury: Intentionally false statement made under oath.

Phallic symbol: Symbols or representations of the male sex organ.

Picketing: Protest in which individuals bearing placards and signs attempt to inform others of their position in a dispute or to discourage others from patronizing particular businesses or institutions.

Plagiarism: To pass off another's ideas or writings as one's own.

Plaintiff (petitioner): The party instigating a lawsuit or court action in civil matters.

Police power: General power of state and local governments to make and enforce laws designed to preserve the comfort, safety, morals, health, and prosperity of citizens.

Political correctness (PC): Concept that arose in the United States around 1989 to encompass language, ideas, and behaviors relating to social issues that would be considered acceptable according to changing current majority views.

Pornography: Sexually explicit materials; sometimes distinguished from more offensive forms of such materials, which are generally referred to as obscenity.

Press, the: Newspapers and other print media used to communicate news.

Pressure group: Body of persons organized to advance a common interest through such mechanisms as letter-writing, lobbying, and boycotts.

Prior restraint: Legal requirement that written or spoken communications be submitted in advance of its delivery or publication to a government official with power to grant or deny permission to utter or publish the speech based upon its contents.

Privileged communication: Communication between two parties—such as a physician and a patient or an attorney and a client—that may not be disclosed under compulsion in a court of law or other official context.

Profanity: Language that offends the religious beliefs or values of other persons.

Protected speech: Speech that government may not ban on the basis of its content without some overwhelming justification.

Prurient interest: Interest in aspects of sex or excretion that many persons might regard as unwholesome.

Pseudonym: Fictitious name, usually used to conceal the true identity of a person, such as an author.

Public figure: Either a public official or someone who has deliberately sought public prominence.

Public forum: Public property such as a street or park traditionally open to speakers.

Public good: Generic interest cited historically to justify punishment of objectionable speech.

Rating systems: Procedures requiring that forms of communication such as music, television, cable programming, or films be labeled with indications of whether, and to what degree, they contain material that might be considered objectionable.

Red Scares: Periods during which the American public was conditioned to fear communist conspiracies, such as occurred in 1917 and in the early 1950's.

Redeeming social value: Artistic, literary, political, or scientific value in an otherwise obscene work justifying the work's protection from censorship.

Restraining order: The order by a court to the respondent to refrain from doing a particular action.

Right of reply: Right of one politician or partisan in a political dispute to gain access to a media forum such as radio or television after an opposing politician or partisan has been allowed to use the forum.

Right to know: Right asserted by a listener rather than by a speaker, based on the asserted interest in having information freely available.

Roman à clef: Fictional work depicting actual events or persons in a disguised fashion; for example, the 1940 film *Citizen Kane* has been regarded as a depiction of the life of newspaper publisher William Randolph Hearst.

Roth standard: Test for obscenity derived from the U.S. Supreme Court's 1984 *Roth v. United States* decision holding that for material to be obscene it must be "utterly without social value."

Sadism: Form of sexual arousal involving the infliction of pain or humiliation on other persons in order to obtain sexual release; from the name of the Marquis de Sade.

Safe harbor: Used in broadcasting to describe legal provisions that allow a broadcaster to transmit material within a particular time period that would otherwise be punishable, such as the broadcast of offensive material late at night when children are likely to be asleep.

Scatological expression: Any expression that refers to bodily excrement.

Seditious libel: Criminal offense punished widely during the colonial period that consisted of spoken or written criticism of government or its officials.

Self-censorship: Conscious decision of a person to limit the content of his or her speech to avoid undesirable consequences, such as public disapproval, legal action, or criminal punishment.

Sex crimes: Crimes involving sexual acts, such as rape or prostitution.

Shield laws: Laws protecting journalists from having to disclose the identities of the sources they use to gather news.

Shock radio: Form of broadcast in which announcers attempt to generate controversy by shocking or offending their audience, frequently through the use of indecent materials and comments.

Sit-in demonstration: Form of protest involving the peaceful occupation of some public place or establishment, such as the protests in which African Americans during the Civil Rights movement occupied lunch-counter seats to protest the refusal of proprietors to serve them.

Slander: Oral defamation of another's reputation, generally by the utterance of a falsehood that injures one's reputation; distinguished from libel, which is written defamation.

Speech: Spoken expression; or, more broadly, all forms of human expression.

Speech code: Regulations adopted by a government or an institution such as a university that prohibit certain kinds of speech, typically those involving racist and sexists remarks or those demeaning of other minority groups.

Stag films: Privately screened short films with graphic scenes of adult sexuality, usually without color or sound, prevalent most in the years between 1920 and 1970.

Street oratory: Impromptu public speaking on a street corner, park, or other public place in which such speaking has traditionally occurred.

Strict scrutiny: Standard used by courts to evaluate the constitutionality of laws restricting or punishing particular speech on the basis of its content, requiring that government demonstrate exceedingly persuasive grounds for so restricting speech.

Subliminal message: Message communicated through visual or aural stimuli undetected at the conscious level.

Symbolic speech: Expression that relies on some act of conduct such as burning a draft card in protest of a military draft or of a particular war to convey its meaning.

Taboo: Conduct or practice banned because of its perceived immorality or likelihood of offending a deity or the society at large.

Talk shows: Radio and television programs built around live interviews with guests, and which often include telephone calls from audience members.

Time, place, and manner (TPM) restrictions: Laws regulating the circumstances attendant to speaking rather than the content of the speaking.

Unprotected speech: Forms of expressions such as obscenity or fighting words that may be freely restricted by government because these varieties of expression are not deemed protected by constitutional guarantees that generally safeguard freedom of speech.

V-chip: Television component that, when coordinated with a system of rating television programs for objectionable conduct, allows parents to block access to such programs by their children.

Vice: Conduct officially defined as immoral, such as illegal gambling and prostitution.

Viewpoint discrimination: Form of speech regulation that seeks to suppress particular ideas or positions.

Vigilantism: Concerted action by private citizens to enforce what they perceive to be the requirements of justice.

Void for vagueness: Grounds for invalidating restrictions on speech that do not sufficiently specify the kinds of speech punishable or the circumstances in which speech will earn punishment.

Witch-hunt: Highly charged attempt to identify allegedly subversive elements in a community, named for the notorious attempts in colonial America to locate and destroy purported witches.

World Wide Web: Part of the global computer network known as the Internet.

Zoning law: Law organizing a city into various geographic zones and then regulating the kinds of property uses and architectural designs that may be present in each zone.

—*Timothy L. Hall*

BIBLIOGRAPHY

The book titles listed here pertain to general censorship issues. For more specialized titles, see the bibliographies appended to individual essays.

THE ARTS

Carmilly-Weinberger, Moshe. *Fear of Art: Censorship and Freedom of Expression in Art*. New York: R. R. Bowker, 1986.

Clapp, Jane. *Art Censorship: A Chronology of Proscribed and Prescribed Art*. Metuchen, N.J.: Scarecrow Press, 1972.

Dubin, Steven C. *Arresting Images: Impolitic Art and Uncivil Actions*. New York: Routledge, 1992.

Kramer, Margia. *Andy Warhol et al: The FBI File on Andy Warhol*. New York: UnSub Press, 1988.

Laufe, Abe. *The Wicked Stage: A History of Theater Censorship and Harassment in the United States*. New York: F. Ungar, 1978.

Rickards, Maurice. *Banned Posters*. London: Evelyn Adams & MacKay, 1969.

Trager, Oliver, ed. *The Arts and Media in America: Freedom or Censorship?* New York: Facts on File, 1991.

Zeigler, Joseph W. *Arts in Crisis: The National Endowment for the Arts Versus America*. Chicago: A Cappella Books, 1994.

THE COURTS

Bosmajian, Haig. *Freedom of Expression*. New York: Neal-Schuman, 1988.

————, ed. *The Freedom to Publish*. New York: Neal-Schuman, 1989.

————, comp. and ed. *Obscenity and Freedom of Expression*. New York: Burt Franklin, 1976.

Buranelli, Vincent, ed. *The Trial of Peter Zenger*. New York: New York University Press, 1957.

Campbell, Douglas S. *The Supreme Court and the Mass Media: Selected Cases, Summaries, and Analyses*. New York: Praeger, 1990.

Cohen, Jeremy. *Congress Shall Make No Law: Oliver Wendell Holmes, the First Amendment, and Judicial Decision Making*. Ames: Iowa State University Press, 1989.

De Grazia, Edward. *Censorship Landmarks*. New York: R. R. Bowker, 1969.

Devol, Kenneth S. *Mass Media and the Supreme Court: Legacy of the Warren Years*. 4th ed. New York: Hastings House, 1990.

Friedman, Leon. *Obscenity: The Complete Oral Arguments Before the Supreme Court in the Major Obscenity Cases*. New York: Chelsea House, 1970.

Friendly, Fred W. *Minnesota Rag: The Dramatic Story of the Landmark Supreme Court Case That Gave New Meaning to Freedom of the Press*. New York: Random House, 1981.

Gavin, Clark. *Foul, False, and Infamous: Famous Libel and Slander Cases of History*. New York: Abelard, 1950.

Hemmer, Joseph J., Jr. *The Supreme Court and the First Amendment*. New York: Praeger, 1986.

Hurwitz, Leon. *Historical Dictionary of Censorship in the United States*. Westport, Conn.: Greenwood Press, 1985.

Inglehart, Louis E. *Press Freedoms: A Descriptive Calendar of Concepts, Interpretations, Events, and Court Actions from 4000 B.C. to the Present*. New York: Greenwood Press, 1987.

Irons, Peter. *The Courage of Their Convictions*. New York: Free Press, 1988.

Katz, Stanley N., ed. *A Brief Narrative of the Case and Trial of John Peter Zenger*. Cambridge, Mass.: The Belknap Press of Harvard University Press, 1963.

Kauper, Paul G. *Civil Liberties and the Constitution*. Ann Arbor: University of Michigan Press, 1962.

Konvitz, Milton R. *First Amendment Freedoms: Selected Cases on Freedom of Religion, Speech, Press, Assembly*. Ithaca, N.Y.: Cornell University Press, 1963.

Lewis, Anthony. *Make No Law: The Sullivan Case and the First Amendment*. New York: Random House, 1991.

Mencken, H. L. *The Editor, the Bluenose, and the Prostitute: H. L. Mencken's History of the "Hatrack" Censorship Case*. Boulder, Colo.: R. Rinehart, 1988.

O'Brien, David M. *The Public's Right to Know: The Supreme Court and the First Amendment*. New York: Praeger, 1981.

Polenberg, Richard. *Fighting Faiths: The Abrams Case, the Supreme Court, and Free Speech*. New York: Viking Press, 1987.

Smolla, Rodney A. *Jerry Falwell v. Larry Flynt: The First Amendment on Trial*. New York: St. Martin's Press, 1988.

Sunderland, Lane V. *Obscenity: The Court, the Congress, and the President's Commission*. Washington: American Enterprise Institute, 1975.

EDUCATION

American Library Association, Office of Intellectual Freedom. *Censorship Litigation and the Schools*. Chicago: Author, 1983.

Archer, Jules. *Who's Running Your Life? A Look at Young People's Rights*. New York: Harcourt Brace Jovanovich, 1979.

Arons, Stephen. *Compelling Belief: The Culture of American Schooling*. New York: McGraw-Hill, 1983.

Bosmajian, Haig. *Academic Freedom*. New York: Neal-Schuman, 1988.

Brigman, Greg, and Peggy Moore. *School Counselors and Censorship: Facing the Challenge*. Alexandria, Va.: American School Counselor Association, 1994.

Brown, Jean E., ed. *Preserving Intellectual Freedom: Fighting Censorship in Our Schools*. Urbana, Ill.: National Council of Teachers of English, 1994.

Buckley, William F., Jr. *God and Man at Yale: The Superstitions of "Academic Freedom."* Chicago: Henry Regnery, 1951.

Burress, Lee. *The Battle of the Books: Literary Censorship in the Public Schools, 1950-1985*. Metuchen, N.J.: Scarecrow Press, 1989.

DelFattore, Joan. *What Johnny Shouldn't Read: Textbook Censorship in America*. New Haven, Conn.: Yale University Press, 1992.

D'Souza, Dinesh. *Illiberal Education: The Politics of Race and Sex on Campus*. New York: Free Press, 1991.

Estrin, Herman A., and Arthur M. Sanderson, eds. *Freedom and Censorship of the College Press*. Dubuque, Iowa: W. C. Brown, 1966.

Foerstel, Hebert N. *Banned in the U.S.A.: A Reference Guide to Book Censorship in Schools and Public Libraries*. Westport, Conn.: Greenwood Press, 1994.

Hentoff, Nat. *American Heroes: In and Out of School*. New York: Delacorte Press, 1987.

Inglehart, Louis E. *Press Law and Press Freedom for High School Publications*. Westport, Conn.: Greenwood Press, 1986.

Jenkinson, Edward B. *Censors in the Classroom: The Mind Benders*. Carbondale: Southern Illinois University Press, 1979.

_____. *The Schoolbook Protest Movement*. Bloomington, Ind.: Phi Delta Kappa Educational Foundation, 1986.

Kristof, Nicholas D. *Freedom of the High School Press*. Lanham, Md.: University Press of America, 1983.

Lewis, Lionel S. *Cold War on Campus: A Study of the Politics of Organizational Control*. New Brunswick, N.J.: Transaction Books, 1988.

Moffett, James. *Storm in the Mountains: A Case Study of Censorship, Conflict, and Consciousness*. Carbondale: University of Southern Illinois Press, 1988.

Nelson, Jack, and Gene Roberts, Jr. *The Censors and the Schools*. Boston: Little, Brown, 1963.

O'Neil, Robert M. *Classrooms in the Crossfire: The Rights and Interests of Students, Parents, Teachers, Administrators, Librarians, and the Community*. Bloomington: Indiana University Press, 1981.

Parker, Barbara. *Protecting the Freedom to Learn: A Citizen's Guide*. Washington: People for the American Way, 1983.

Reichman, Henry. *Censorship and Selection: Issues and Answers for Schools*. Chicago: American Library Association/American Association of School Administrators, 1988.

Rubin, David. *The Rights of Teachers: American Civil Liberties Union Handbook*. New York: Discus Books, 1972.

Schimmel, David, and Louis Fischer. *The Civil Rights of Students*. New York: Harper & Row, 1975.

Schlafly, Phyllis, ed. *Child Abuse in the Classroom*. Alton, Ill.: Pere Marquette Press, 1984.

Sherrow, Victoria. *Censorship in Schools*. Springfield, N.J.: Enslow, 1996.

Simmons, John S., ed. *Censorship: A Threat to Reading, Learning, Thinking*. Newark, Del.: International Reading Association, 1994.

Vitz, Paul C. *Censorship: Evidence of Bias in Our Children's Textbooks*. Ann Arbor, Mich.: Servant Books, 1986.

Woods, L. B. *A Decade of Censorship in America: The Threat to Classrooms and Libraries, 1966-1975*. Metuchen: Scarecrow Press, 1979.

Woodworth, Mary L. *Intellectual Freedom, the Young Adult, and Schools: A Wisconsin Study*. Rev. ed. Madison: University of Wisconsin Extension, 1976.

FILM

Black, Gregory D. *Hollywood Censored: Morality Codes, Catholics, and the Movies*. New York: Cambridge University Press, 1994.

Bouzereau, Laurent. *The Cutting Room Floor*. Seacaucus, N.J.: Carol, 1994.

Carmen, Ira H. *Movies, Censorship, and the Law*. Ann Arbor: University of Michigan Press, 1966.

Ceplair, Larry, and Steven Englund. *The Inquisition in Hollywood: Politics in the Film Community, 1930-1960*. Garden City, N.Y.: Anchor Press/Doubleday, 1980.

Couvares, Francis G., ed. *Movie Censorship and American Culture*. Washington: Smithsonian Institution Press, 1996.

De Grazia, Edward, and Roger K. Newman. *Banned Films: Movies, Censors, and the First Amendment*. New York: R. R. Bowker, 1982.

Facey, Paul W. *The Legion of Decency: A Sociological Analysis of the Emergence and Development of a Social Pressure Group*. New York: Arno Press, 1994.

Federman, Joel. *Film and Television Ratings: An International Assessment*. Studio City, Calif.: Mediascope, 1993.

Feldman, Charles M. *The National Board of Censorship (Review) of Motion Pictures, 1909-1922*. New York: Arno Press, 1975.

Fleener-Marzec, Nickieann. *D. W. Griffith's "The Birth of a Nation": Controversy, Suppression, and the First Amendment as It Applies to Filmic Expression, 1915-1973*. New York: Arno Press, 1980.

Gardner, Gerald C. *The Censorship Papers: Movie Censorship Letters from the Hays Office, 1934-1968*. New York: Dodd, Mead, 1987.

Hunnings, Neville M. *Film Censors and the Law*. London: Allen & Unwin, 1967.

Jacobs, Lea. *The Wages of Sin: Censorship and the Fallen Woman Film, 1928-1942*. Madison: University of Wisconsin, 1991.

Keough, Peter, ed. *Flesh and Blood: The National Society of Film Critics on Sex, Violence, and Censorship*. San Francisco: Mercury House, 1995.

Kuhn, Annette. *Cinema, Censorship, and Sexuality, 1909-1925*. New York: Routledge, 1988.

Leff, Leonard J., and Jerold L. Simmons. *The Dame in the Kimono: Hollywood, Censorship, and the Production Code from the 1920s to the 1960s*. New York: Grove Weidenfeld, 1990.

Mathews, Tom Dewe. *Censored!: History of British Film Censorship*. London: Chatto & Windus, 1994.

Miller, Frank. *Censored Hollywood: Sex, Sin, and Violence on Screen*. Atlanta: Turner, 1994.

Phillips, Baxter. *Cut, the Unseen Cinema*. New York: Bounty Books, 1975.

Randall, Richard S. *Censorship of the Movies: The Social and Political Control of a Mass Medium*. Madison: University of Wisconsin Press, 1968.

Richard, Alfred C. *Censorship and Hollywood's Hispanic Image: An Interpretive Filmography, 1936-1955*. Westport, Conn.: Greenwood Press, 1993.

Schumach, Murray. *The Face on the Cutting Room Floor: The Story of Movie and Television Censorship*. New York: William Morrow, 1964. Reprint. New York: Da Capo, 1975.

Skinner, James M. *The Cross and the Cinema: The Legion of Decency and the National Catholic Office for Motion Pictures, 1933-1970*. Westport, Conn.: Praeger, 1993.

Vizzard, Jack. *See No Evil: Life Inside a Hollywood Censor*. New York: Simon & Schuster, 1970.

Walsh, Frank. *Sin and Censorship: The Catholic Church and the Motion Picture Industry*. New Haven: Yale University Press, 1996.

GENERAL ISSUES

Article 19. *The Right to Know: Human Rights and Access to Reproductive Health Information*. Philadelphia: University of Pennsylvania Press, 1995.

Baker, C. Edwin. *Human Liberty and Freedom of Speech*. New York: Oxford University Press, 1989.

Barron, Jerome A., and C. Thomas Dienes. *Handbook of Free Speech and Free Press*. Boston: Little, Brown, 1979.

Beahm, George W., ed. *War of Words: The Censorship Debate*. Kansas City, Mo.: Andrews and McMeel, 1993.

Bennett, James R. *Control of Information in the United States: An Annotated Bibliography*. Westport, Conn.: Meckler, 1987.

_____. *Control of the Media in the United States: An Annotated Bibliography*. New York: Garland, 1992.

Berger, Melvin. *Censorship*. New York: Franklin Watts, 1982.

Bollinger, Lee C. *The Tolerant Society: Freedom of Speech and Extremist Speech in America*. New York: Oxford University Press, 1986.

Bosmajian, Haig, comp. *The Principles and Practices of Freedom of Speech*. Boston: Houghton Mifflin, 1971.

Broun, Heywood, and Margaret Leech. *Anthony Comstock: Roundsman of the Lord*. New York: A & C Boni, 1927.

Burstyn, Varda. *Women Against Censorship*. Vancouver, B.C.: Douglas & McIntyre, 1985.

Busha, Charles H. *An Intellectual Freedom Primer*. Littleton, Colo.: Libraries Unlimited, 1977.

Canavan, Francis. *Freedom of Expression: Purpose as Limit*. Durham, N.C.: Carolina Academic Press and Claremont Institute for the Study of Statesmanship and Political Philosophy, 1984.

Coetzee, J. M. *Giving Offense: Essays on Censorship*. Chicago: University of Chicago Press, 1996.

Coldrick, Jack. *Dr. Marie Stopes and Press Censorship of Birth Control*. Belfast, Ireland: Athol Books, 1992.

Cozic, Charles P., ed. *Civil Liberties: Opposing Viewpoints*. San Diego, Calif.: Greenhaven Press, 1994.

Daily, Jay E. *The Anatomy of Censorship*. New York: Marcel Dekker, 1973.

Davis, James E., ed. *Dealing with Censorship*. Urbana, Ill.: National Council of Teachers of English, 1979.

Downs, Robert B., and Ralph E. McCoy, eds. *The First Freedom Today: Critical Issues Relating to Censorship and to Intellectual Freedom*. Chicago: American Library Association, 1984.

Dworkin, Andrea. *Letters from a War Zone: Writings, 1976-1989*. New York: E. P. Dutton, 1989.

Emerson, Thomas I. *The System of Freedom of Expression*. New York: Random House, 1970.

Fiss, Owen M. *The Irony of Free Speech*. Cambridge, Mass.: Harvard University Press, 1996.

Garry, Patrick M. *An American Paradox: Censorship in a Nation of Free Speech*. Westport, Conn.: Praeger, 1993.

_____. *The American Vision of a Free Press: An Historical and Constitutional Revisionist View of the Press as a Marketplace of Ideas*. New York: Garland, 1990.

_____. *Scrambling for Protection: The New Media and the First Amendment*. Pittsburgh, Pa.: University of Pittsburgh Press, 1994.

Gordon, George N. *Erotic Communications: Studies in Sex, Sin, and Censorship*. New York: Hastings House, 1980.

Green, Jonathon. *The Encyclopedia of Censorship*. New York: Facts on File, 1990.

Harer, John B. *Intellectual Freedom: A Reference Handbook*. Santa Barbara, Calif.: ABC-Clio, 1992.

Harer, John B., and Steven R. Harris. *Censorship of Expression in the 1980s*. Westport, Conn.: Greenwood Press, 1994.

Hart, Harold H., ed. *Censorship: For and Against*. New York: Hart, 1972.

Heins, Marjorie. *Sex, Sin, and Blasphemy: A Guide to America's Censorship Wars*. New York: New Press, 1993.

Hentoff, Nat. *Free Speech for Me—But Not for Thee: How the American Left and Right Relentlessly Censor Each Other*. New York: HarperCollins, 1992.

Hoffman, Frank W. *Intellectual Freedom and Censorship: An Annotated Bibliography*. Metuchen, N.J.: Scarecrow Press, 1989.

Hoyt, Olga G., and Edwin P. Hoyt. *Censorship in America*. New York: Seabury, 1970.

Hudon, Edward G. *Freedom of Speech and Press in America*. Washington: Public Affairs Press, 1963.

Jansen, Sue C. *Censorship: The Knot That Binds Power and Knowledge*. New York: Oxford University Press, 1988.

Jennison, Peter S. *Freedom to Read*. New York: Public Affairs Committee, 1963.

Johnson, Claudia. *Stifled Laughter: One Woman's Story About Fighting Censorship*. Golden, Colo.: Fulcrum, 1994.

Kalven, Harry, Jr. *A Worthy Tradition: Freedom of Speech in America*. Edited by Jamie Kalven. New York: Harper & Row, 1988.

Kerr, Walter. *Criticism and Censorship*. Milwaukee, Wis.: Bruce, 1956.

Ladenson, Robert F. *A Philosophy of Free Expression and Its Constitutional Applications*. Lanham, Md.: Rowman & Littlefield, 1983.

LaHaye, Tim F. *The Hidden Censors*. Old Tappan, N.J.: F. H. Revell, 1984.

Lang, Susan S. and Paul Lang. *Censorship*. New York: Franklin Watts, 1993.

Liston, Robert A. *The Right to Know: Censorship in America*. New York: Franklin Watts, 1973.

McCormick, John, and Mairi MacInnes, eds. *Versions of Censorship: An Anthology*. Garden City, N.Y.: Doubleday/Anchor, 1962.

Minor, Dale. *The Information War*. New York: Hawthorn Books, 1970.

Oboler, Eli M. *The Fear of the Word: Censorship and Sex*. Metuchen, N.J.: Scarecrow Press, 1974.

Pally, Marcia. *Sense and Censorship: The Vanity of the Bonfires*. New York: Americans for Constitutional Freedom and the Freedom to Read Foundation, 1991.

_____. *Sex and Sensibility: Reflections on Forbidden Mirrors and the Will to Censor*. Hopewell, N.J.: Ecco Press, 1994.

Peleg, Ilan, ed. *Patterns of Censorship Around the World*. Boulder, Colo.: Westview Press, 1993.

People for the American Way. *Attacks on Freedom to Learn, 1985-86*. Washington: People for the American Way, 1987.

Phelan, John M., ed. *Communications Control: Readings in the Motives and Structures of Censorship*. New York: Sheed & Ward, 1969.

Rauch, Jonathan. *Kindly Inquisitors: The New Attacks on Free Thought*. Chicago: University of Chicago Press, 1993.

Schauer, Frederick F. *Free Speech: A Philosophical Enquiry*. New York: Cambridge University Press, 1982.

Snyder, Gerald S. *The Right to be Informed: Censorship in the United States*. New York: Julian Messner, 1976.

Spitzer, Matthew L. *Seven Dirty Words and Six Other Stories: Controlling the Content of Print and Broadcast*. New Haven, Conn.: Yale University Press, 1986.

Steffens, Bradley. *Censorship*. San Diego, Calif.: Lucent Books, 1996.

Swan, John, and Noel Peattie. *The Freedom to Lie: A Debate About Democracy*. Jefferson, N.C.: McFarland, 1989.

Taylor, C. L. *Censorship*. Robert B. Morris, consulting ed. New York: Franklin Watts, 1986.

Tedford, Thomas L. *Freedom of Speech in the United States*. New York: Random House, 1985.

Theiner, George, ed. *They Shoot Writers, Don't They?* Winchester, Mass.: Faber & Faber, 1984.

Tribe, David. *Questions of Censorship.* New York: St. Martin's Press, 1973.

Van Alstyne, William W. *Interpretations of the First Amendment.* Durham, N.C.: Duke University Press, 1984.

Weiss, Ann E. *Who's to Know?: Information, the Media, and Public Awareness.* Boston: Houghton Mifflin, 1990.

HISTORY

Bentley, Eric. *Are You Now or Have You Ever Been: The Investigation of Show Business by the Un-American Activities Committee, 1947-1958.* New York: Harper & Row, 1972.

Curry, Richard O., ed. *Freedom at Risk: Secrecy, Censorship, and Repression in the 1980s.* Philadelphia: Temple University Press, 1988.

Demac, Donna A. *Liberty Denied: The Current Rise of Censorship in America.* New York: PEN American Center, 1988.

Fried, Richard M. *Nightmare in Red: The McCarthy Era in Retrospective.* New York: Oxford University Press, 1990.

Hentoff, Nat. *The First Freedom: The Tumultuous History of Free Speech in America.* New York: Delacorte Press, 1980.

Hohenberg, John. *Free Press/Free People: The Best Cause.* New York: Columbia University Press, 1971.

Levy, Leonard W. *Jefferson and Civil Liberties: The Darker Side.* New York: Quadrangle Books, 1973.

_____. *Legacy of Suppression: Freedom of Speech and Press in Early American History.* Cambridge, Mass.: The Belknap Press of Harvard University Press, 1960.

Murphy, Paul L. *The Meaning of Freedom of Speech: First Amendment Freedoms from Wilson to FDR.* Westport, Conn.: Greenwood Press, 1972.

Navasky, Victor S. *Naming Names.* New York: Penguin Books, 1980.

Pivar, David J. *Purity Crusade: Sexual Morality, and Social Control, 1868-1900.* Westport, Conn.: Greenwood Press, 1973.

Schultz, Bud, and Ruth Schultz, eds. *It Did Happen Here: Recollections of Political Repressions in America.* Berkeley: University of California Press, 1989.

Vaughn, Robert. *Only Victims: A Study of Show Business Blacklisting.* New York: Putnam, 1972.

JOURNALISM AND PUBLISHING

Bagdikian, Ben H. *The Effete Conspiracy and Other Crimes of the Press.* New York: Harper & Row, 1972.

Baker, C. Edwin. *Advertising and a Democratic Press.* Princeton, N.J.: Princeton University Press, 1994.

Barron, Jerome A. *Freedom of the Press for Whom? The Right of Access to Mass Media.* Bloomington: Indiana University Press, 1973.

Benzason, Randall P. *Taxes on Knowledge in America: Exactions on the Press from Colonial Times to the Present.* Philadelphia: University of Pennsylvania Press, 1994.

Bollinger, Lee C. *Images of a Free Press.* Chicago: University of Chicago Press, 1991.

Collins, Ronald K. L. *Dictating Content: How Advertising Pressure Can Corrupt a Free Press.* Washington: Center for the Study of Commercialism, 1992.

Emery, Edwin. *The Press and America: An Interpretive History of the Mass Media.* Englewood Cliffs, N.J.: Prentice-Hall, 1972.

Evans, J. Edward. *Freedom of the Press.* Minneapolis, Minn.: Lerner, 1990.

Galt, Thomas F. *Peter Zenger: Fighter for Freedom.* New York: Thomas Y. Crowell, 1951.

Gerald, J. Edward. *The Press and the Constitution, 1931-1947.* Minneapolis: University of Minnesota Press, 1948.

Gora, Joel M. *The Rights of Reporters: The Basic ACLU Guide to a Reporter's Rights.* New York: Sunrise Books/E. P. Dutton, 1974.

Hemmer, Joseph J., Jr. *Journalistic Freedom.* Metuchen, N.J.: Scarecrow Press, 1980.

Jensen, Carl. *Censored: The News That Didn't Make the News—And Why.* New York: Four Walls Eight Windows, 1995.

Levy, Leonard W. *Emergence of a Free Press.* New York: Oxford University Press, 1985.

_____. ed. *Freedom of the Press from Zenger to Jefferson: Early American Libertarian Theories.* Indianapolis, Ind.: Bobbs-Merrill, 1966.

McCoy, Ralph E. *Freedom of the Press: An Annotated Bibliography.* Carbondale: Southern Illinois University Press, 1968.

_____. *Freedom of the Press: A Bibliocyclopedia. Ten Year Supplement (1967-77)* Carbondale: Southern Illinois University Press, 1979.

Rips, Geoffrey, comp, Ann Janowitz, and Nancy J. Peters, eds. *The Campaign Against the Underground Press.* San Francisco: City Lights Books, 1981.

Rogers, Donald J. *Press Versus Government: Constitutional Issues.* New York: Julian Messner, 1986.

Seldes, George. *Freedom of the Press.* New York: Garden City, 1937. Reprint. New York: Da Capo Press, 1971.

Smith, Jeffrey A. *Printers and Press Freedom: The Ideology of Early American Journalism.* New York: Oxford University Press, 1988.

Stevens, John D. *Shaping the First Amendment: The Development of Free Expression.* Beverly Hills, Calif.: Sage Publications, 1982.

Zerman, Melvyn B. *Taking on the Press: Constitutional Rights in Conflict.* New York: Thomas Y. Crowell, 1986.

LIBRARIES

Anderson, Arthur J. *Problems in Intellectual Freedom and Censorship: Problem-Centered Approaches to Librarianship.* New York: R. R. Bowker, 1974.

Berninghausen, David K. *The Flight from Reason: Essays on Intellectual Freedom in the Academy, the Press, and the Library.* Chicago: American Library Association, 1975.

Berns, Walter. *The Case of the Censored Librarian.* Chicago: American Foundation for Continuing Education, 1959.

Bielefield, Arlene, and Lawrence Cheeseman. *Library Patrons and the Law.* New York: Neal-Schuman, 1995.

Bosmajian, Haig, comp. *Censorship, Libraries, and the Law.* New York: Neal-Schuman, 1983.

Bryson, Joseph E., and Elizabeth W. Detty. *The Legal Aspects of Censorship of Public School Library and Instructional Materials.* Charlottesville, Va.: Michie, 1982.

Busha, Charles H. *Freedom Versus Suppression and Censorship.* Littleton, Colo.: Libraries Unlimited, 1972.

Foerstel, Herbert N. *Surveillance in the Stacks: The FBI's Library Awareness Program.* Westport, Conn.: Greenwood Press, 1991.

Garrison, Dee. *Apostles of Culture: The Public Librarian and American Society, 1876-1920.* New York: Free Press, 1979.

Gellathy, Peter, ed. *Sex Magazines in the Library Collection: A Scholarly Study of Sex in Serials and Periodicals*. New York: Haworth Press, 1981.

Geller, Evelyn. *Forbidden Books in American Public Libraries, 1876-1939*. Westport, Conn.: Greenwood Press, 1984.

Jones, Frances M. *Defusing Censorship: The Librarian's Guide to Handling Censorship Conflicts*. Phoenix, Ariz.: Oryx Press, 1983.

Lowenthal, Marjorie F. *Book Selection and Censorship: A Study of School and Public Libraries in California*. Berkeley: University of California Press, 1959.

McDonald, Frances B. *Censorship and Intellectual Freedom: A Survey of School Librarian's Attitudes and Moral Reasoning*. Metuchen, N.J.: Scarecrow Press, 1993.

McShean, Gordon. *Running a Massage Parlor: A Librarian's Medium Rare Memoir About Censorship*. Palo Alto, Calif.: Ramparts Press, 1977.

Merritt, Leroy C. *Book Selection and Intellectual Freedom*. New York: H. W. Wilson, 1970.

Moon, Eric. *Book Selection and Censorship in the Sixties*. New York: R. R. Bowker, 1969.

Moore, Everett T., ed. *Issues of Freedom in American Libraries*. Chicago: American Library Association, 1964.

Oboler, Eli M. *Defending Intellectual Freedom: The Library and the Censor*. Westport, Conn.: Greenwood Press, 1980.

Pope, Michael. *Sex and the Undecided Librarian: A Study of Librarians' Opinions on Sexually Oriented Literature*. Metuchen, N.J.: Scarecrow Press, 1974.

Robotham, John, and Gerald Shields. *Freedom of Access to Library Materials*. New York: Neal-Schuman, 1982.

Schrader, Alvin M. *Fear of Words: Censorship and the Public Libraries of Canada*. Ottawa: Canadian Library Association, 1995.

Selth, Jefferson P. *Ambition, Discrimination, and Censorship in Libraries*. Jefferson, N.C.: McFarland, 1993.

Symons, Ann, and Charles Harmon. *Protecting the Right to Read: A How-to-Do-It Manual for School and Public Librarians*. New York: Neal-Schuman, 1995.

Thompson, A. H. *Censorship in Public Libraries in the United Kingdom During the Twentieth Century*. Epping, England: R. R. Bowker, 1975.

Weigand, Wayne A. *An Active Instrument for Propaganda: The American Public Library During World War I*. New York: Greenwood Press, 1989.

LITERATURE AND BOOKS

Blanshard, Paul. *The Right to Read—The Battle Against Censorship*. Boston: Beacon Press, 1955.

Bosmajian, Haig. *The Freedom to Read: Books, Films, and Plays*. New York: Neal-Schuman, 1987.

Boyer, Paul S. *Purity in Print: The Vice-Society Movement and Book Censorship in America*. New York: Charles Scribner's Sons, 1968.

Cleaton, Irene and Allen. *Books and Battles: American Literature, 1920-1930*. Boston: Houghton Mifflin, 1937.

Craig, Alec. *The Banned Books of England and Other Countries*. London: George Allen & Unwin, 1962.

Daniels, Walter M. *The Censorship of Books*. New York: H. W. Wilson, 1954.

Fellman, David. *The Censorship of Books*. Madison: University of Wisconsin Press, 1957.

Ferlinghetti, Lawrence. *Howl of the Censor*. 1961. Reprint. Westport, Conn.: Greenwood Press, 1967.

Gillett, Charles R. *Burned Books*. 1932. Reprint. 2 Vols. Westport, Conn.: Greenwood Press, 1974.

Goodman, Michael B. *Contemporary Literary Censorship: The Case History of Burroughs' "Naked Lunch."* Metuchen, N.J.: Scarecrow Press, 1981.

Haight, Anne L. *Banned Books—387 B.C. to 1978 A.D.* 4th ed. New York: R. R. Bowker, 1978.

Haney, Robert W. *Comstockery in America: Patterns of Censorship and Control*. 1960. Reprint. New York: Da Capo Press, 1974.

Hentoff, Nat. *The Day They Came to Arrest the Book*. New York: Delacorte Press, 1982.

Homstad, Wayne. *Anatomy of a Book Controversy*. Bloomington, Ind.: Phi Delta Kappa Educational Foundation, 1995.

Hutchinson, Earl R. *"Tropic of Cancer" on Trial: A Case History of Censorship*. New York: Grove Press, 1968.

Kaplan, Justin. *Born to Trouble: One Hundred Years of "Huckleberry Finn."* Washington: Library of Congress, 1985.

Karolides, Nicholas J., and Lee Burress. *Celebrating Censored Books*. Racine, Wis.: Wisconsin Council of Teachers of English, 1985.

Lawrence, D. H. *Sex, Literature, and Censorship: Essays*. Harry T. Moore, ed. New York: Twayne, 1953.

Lehr, Susan S. *Battling Dragons: Issues and Controversy in Children's Literature*. Portsmouth, N.H.: Heinemann, 1995.

Malik, Akbar Ali. *"The Satanic Verses," Was It Worth All the Fuss?: A Muslim Lawyer's Viewpoint*. London: Unique, 1993.

Mitgang, Herbert. *Dangerous Dossiers: Exposing the Secret War Against America's Greatest Authors*. New York: Donald I. Fine, 1988.

Noble, William. *Bookbanning in America: Who Bans Books?—and Why*. Middlebury, Vt.: Paul S. Eriksson, 1990.

Perrin, Noel. *Dr. Bowdler's Legacy: A History of Expurgated Books in England and America*. New York: Atheneum, 1969.

Thomas, Cal. *Book Burning*. Westchester, Ill.: Crossways Books, 1983.

Thomas, Donald S. *A Long Time Burning: The History of Literary Censorship in England*. New York: Praeger, 1969.

Walker, Alice. *Alice Walker Banned*. San Francisco: Aunt Lute Books, 1996.

West, Mark I. *Trust Your Children: Voices Against Censorship in Children's Literature*. New York: Neal-Schuman, 1988.

Widmer, Eleanor, ed. *Freedom and Culture: Literary Censorship in the '70s*. Belmont, Calif.: Wadsworth, 1970.

Widmer, Kinglsey, and Eleanor Widmer. *Literary Censorship: Principles, Cases, Problems*. San Francisco: Wadsworth, 1961.

Williams, Gordon. *Shakespeare, Sex, and the Print Revolution*. Atlantic Heights, N.J.: Athlone Press, 1996.

Yuill, Phyllis J. *"Little Black Sambo:" A Closer Look*. New York: Racism and Sexism Resource Center for Educators, Council on Interracial Books for Children, 1976.

MILITARY AND WARTIME

Aukofer, Frank, and William P. Lawrence. *America's Team: The Odd Couple: A Report on the Relationship Between the Media and the Military*. Nashville, Tenn.: The Freedom Forum First Amendment Center, 1995.

Braw, Monica. *The Atomic Bomb Suppressed: American Censorship in Occupied Japan*. Armonk, N.Y.: M. E. Sharpe, 1991.

Curry, Richard O. *Freedom at Risk: Secrecy, Censorship, and Repression in the 1980's.* Philadelphia: Temple University Press, 1988.

Dennis, Everette E. *The Media at War: The Press and the Persian Gulf Conflict.* New York: Gannett Foundation, 1991.

Koppes, Clayton R., and Gregory D. Black. *Hollywood Goes to War: How Politics, Profits, and Propaganda Shaped World War II Movies.* New York: Free Press, 1987.

Linfield, Michael. *Freedom Under Fire: U.S. Civil Liberties in Times of War.* Boston: South End Press, 1990.

MacArthur, John R. *Second Front: Censorship and Propaganda in the Gulf War.* New York: Hill & Wang, 1992.

Roeder, George H., Jr. *The Censored War: American Visual Experience During World War Two.* New Haven, Conn.: Yale University Press, 1993.

Summers, Robert. *Wartime Censorship of Press and Radio.* New York: H. H. Wilson, 1942.

OBSCENITY

Chandos, John, ed. *To Deprave and Corrupt . . . Original Studies in the Nature and Definition of Obscenity.* New York: Association Press, 1962.

Clor, Harry M., ed. *Censorship and Freedom of Expression: Essays on Obscenity and the Law.* Chicago: Rand McNally, 1971.

_____. *Obscenity and Public Morality: Censorship in a Liberal Society.* 1969. Reprint. Chicago: University of Chicago Press, 1985.

Craig, Alec. *Suppressed Books: A History of the Conception of Literary Obscenity.* Cleveland, Ohio: World Publishing, 1963.

De Grazia, Edward. *Girls Lean Back Everywhere: The Law of Obscenity and the Assault on Genius.* New York: Random House, 1992.

Ernst, Morris L., and Alan U. Schwartz. *Censorship: The Search for the Obscene.* New York: Macmillan, 1964.

Ernst, Morris L., and Alexander Lindey. *The Censor Marches On: Recent Milestones in the Administration of the Obscenity Law in the United States.* 1940. Reprint. New York: Da Capo Press, 1971.

Frank, John P., and Robert F. Hogan. *Obscenity, the Law, and the English Teacher.* Champaign, Ill.: National Council of Teachers of English, 1966.

Lewis, Felice Flanery. *Literature, Obscenity, and Law.* Carbondale: Southern Illinois University Press, 1976.

Murphy, Terence G. *Censorship: Government and Obscenity.* Baltimore: Helicon Press, 1963.

Paul, James C. N., and Murray L. Schwartz. *Federal Censorship: Obscenity in the Mail.* Glencoe, Ill.: Free Press, 1961.

Rembar, Charles. *The End of Obscenity: The Trials of "Lady Chatterley," "Tropic of Cancer," and "Fanny Hill."* New York: Random House, 1968.

Schauer, Frederick F. *The Law of Obscenity.* Washington: Bureau of National Affairs, 1976.

Sharp, Donald B., comp. *Commentaries on Obscenity.* Metuchen, N.J.: Scarecrow Press, 1970.

POLITICS AND GOVERNMENT

Berns, Walter. *The First Amendment and the Future of American Democracy.* New York: Basic Books, 1970.

_____. *Freedom, Virtue, and the First Amendment.* Westport, Conn.: Greenwood Press, 1969.

Boyle, Kevin. *Article 19 World Report 1988.* New York: Times Books, 1988.

Capaldi, Nicholas, comp. *Clear and Present Danger: The Free Speech Controversy.* New York: Pegasus, 1969.

Demac, Donna A. *Keeping America Uninformed: Government Secrecy in the 1980s.* New York: Pilgrim Press, 1984.

Donner, Frank. *Protectors of Privilege: Red Squads and Police Repression in Urban America.* Berkeley: University of California Press, 1990.

Fowler, Dorothy G. *Unmailable: Congress and the Post Office.* Athens: University of Georgia Press, 1977.

Freedman, Warren. *Freedom of Speech on Private Property.* New York: Quorum Books, 1988.

Gordon, Andrew C., and John P. Heinz, eds. *Public Access to Information.* New Brunswick, N.J.: Transaction Books, 1979.

Greenawalt, Kent. *Speech, Crime, and the Use of Language.* New York: Oxford University Press, 1989.

Haiman, Franklyn S. *Speech and Law in a Free Society.* Chicago: University of Chicago Press, 1981.

Katz, Steven L. *Government Secrecy: Decisions Without Democracy.* Washington: People for the American Way, 1988.

Levin, Murray. *Political Hysteria in America: The Democratic Capacity for Repression.* New York: Basic Books, 1971.

Miller, John C. *Crisis in Freedom: The Alien and Sedition Acts.* Boston: Little, Brown, 1951.

Norwich, Kenneth P. *Lobbying for Freedom: A Citizen's Guide to Fighting Censorship at the State Level.* New York: St. Martin's Press, 1975.

Pember, Don R. *Privacy and the Press: The Law, the Mass Media, and the First Amendment.* Seattle: University of Washington Press, 1972.

Robins, Natalie S. *Alien Ink: The FBI's War on Freedom of Expression.* New Brunswick, N.J.: Rutgers University Press, 1993.

Belknap, Michal R. *Cold War Political Justice: The Smith Act, the Communist Party, and American Civil Liberties.* Westport, Conn.: Greenwood Press, 1977.

PORNOGRAPHY

Berger, Fred R. *Freedom, Rights, and Pornography: A Collection of Papers.* Boston: Kluwer Academic Publishers, 1991.

Byerly, Greg and Rick Rubin. *Pornography, the Conflict over Sexually Explicit Materials in the United States: An Annotated Bibliography.* New York: Garland, 1980.

Cline, Victor B., comp. *Where Do You Draw the Line?: An Exploration into Media Violence, Pornography, and Censorship.* Provo, Utah: Brigham Young University Press, 1974.

Copp, David, and Susan Wendell, eds. *Pornography and Censorship.* Buffalo, N.Y.: Prometheus Books, 1983.

Cornog, Martha, ed. *Libraries, Erotica, and Pornography.* Phoenix, Ariz.: Oryx Press, 1991.

Cotham, Perry C. *Obscenity, Pornography, and Censorship.* Grand Rapids, Mich.: Baker Book House, 1973.

Day, Gary, and Clive Bloom, eds. *Perspectives on Pornography: Sexuality in Film and Literature.* New York: St. Martin's Press, 1988.

Donnerstein, Edward, Daniel Linz, and Steven Penrod. *The Question of Pornography: Research Findings and Policy Implications.* New York: Free Press, 1987.

Downs, Donald A. *The New Politics of Pornography.* Chicago: University of Chicago Press, 1989.

Dworkin, Andrea. *Pornography: Men Possessing Women*. New York: G. P. Putnam's Sons, 1981.

Gerber, Albert B. *Sex, Pornography, and Justice*. New York: Lyle Stuart, 1965.

Griffin, Susan. *Pornography and Silence: Culture's Revenge Against Nature*. New York: Harper & Row, 1981.

Gubar, Susan, and Joan Hoff, eds. *For Adult Users Only: The Dilemma of Violent Pornography*. Bloomington: University of Indiana Press, 1989.

Hawkins, Gordon, and Franklin E. Zimring. *Pornography in a Free Society*. New York: Cambridge University Press, 1988.

Holbrook, David, ed. *The Case Against Pornography*. La Salle, Ill.: Open Court, 1973.

Hughes, Douglas A., ed. *Perspectives on Pornography*. New York: St. Martin's Press, 1970.

Hyde, H. Montgomery. *A History of Pornography*. New York: Farrar, Straus & Giroux, 1965.

Kendrick, Walter M. *The Secret Museum: Pornography in Modern Culture*. New York: Viking, 1987.

Kilpatrick, James J. *The Smut Peddlers*. 1960. Reprint. Westport, Conn.: Greenwood Press, 1973.

Kirk, Jerry R. *The Mind Polluters*. Nashville, Tenn.: Thomas Nelson, 1985.

Kronhausen, Eberhard, and Phyllis Kronhausen. *Pornography and the Law*. New York: Ballantine, 1959.

Kuh, Richard H. *Foolish Figleaves?: Pornography In and Out of Court*. New York: Macmillan, 1967.

Larsen, Otto N. *Voicing Social Concern: The Mass Media, Violence, Pornography, Censorship, Organization, Social Science, the Ultramultiversity*. Lanham, Md.: University Press of America, 1994.

Lederer, Laura, ed. *Take Back the Night: Women on Pornography*. New York: William Morrow, 1980.

Loth, David G. *The Erotic in Literature: A Historical Survey of Pornography as Delightful as It Is Indiscreet*. New York: Julian Messner, 1961.

Lynn, Barry W. *Rushing to Censorship: An Interim Report on the Methods of Evidence Gathering and Evaluation by the Attorney General's Commission on Pornography*. Washington: American Civil Liberties Union, 1986.

Moretti, Daniel S. *Obscenity and Pornography: The Law Under the First Amendment*. London: Oceana, 1984.

National Coalition Against Censorship. *The Meese Commission Exposed: Proceedings of a National Coalition Against Censorship Public Information Briefing on the Attorney General's Commission on Pornography, January 16, 1986*. New York: Author, 1986.

Nobile, Philip, and Eric Nadler. *United States of America vs. Sex: How the Meese Commission Lied About Pornography*. New York: Minotaur Press, 1986.

Nordquist, Joan, comp. *Pornography and Censorship*. Santa Cruz, Calif.: Reference and Research Services, 1987.

Osanka, Franklin M., and Sara L. Johann. *Sourcebook on Pornography*. Lexington, Mass.: Lexington Books, 1989.

Peckham, Morse. *Art and Pornography*. New York: Harper & Row, 1969.

Randall, Richard S. *Freedom and Taboo: Pornography and the Politics of a Self Divided*. Berkeley: University of California Press, 1989.

Segal, Lynn, and Mary McIntosh, eds. *Sex Exposed: Sexuality and the Pornography Debate*. New Brunswick, N.J.: Rutgers University Press, 1993.

Sellen, Betty-Carol, and Patricia Young. *Feminists, Pornography, and the Law: An Annotated Bibliography of Conflict, 1970-1986*. Hamden, Conn.: Library Professional Publications, 1987.

Sobel, Lester A., ed. *Pornography, Obscenity, and the Law*. New York: Facts on File, 1978.

Strossen, Nadine. *Defending Pornography: Free Speech, Sex, and the Fight for Women's Rights*. New York: Charles Scribner's Sons, 1995.

RELIGION

Alley, Robert S. *School Prayer: The Court, the Congress, and the First Amendment*. Buffalo, N.Y.: Prometheus Books, 1994.

Bates, Stephen. *Battleground: One Mother's Crusade, the Religious Right, and the Struggle for Our Schools*. New York: Henry Holt, 1994.

Carmilly-Weinberger, Moshe. *Censorship and Freedom of Expression in Jewish History*. New York: Sepher-Hermon Press, 1977.

Gardiner, Harold C. *The Catholic Viewpoint on Censorship*. Rev. ed. Garden City, N.Y.: Doubleday, 1961.

Ide, Arthur F. *Evangelical Terrorism: Censorship, Falwell, Robertson, and the Seamy Side of Christian Fundamentalism*. Irving, Tex.: Scholars Books, 1986.

Klausler, Alfred P. *Censorship, Obscenity, and Sex: The Christian Encounters*. St. Louis, Mo.: Concordia, 1967.

Pell, Eve. *The Big Chill: How the Reagan Administration, Corporate America, and Religious Conservatives Are Subverting Free Speech and the Public's Right to Know*. Boston: Beacon Press, 1984.

Quinn, A. James. *Censorship of Obscenity: A Comparison of Canon Law and American Constitutional Law*. Rome: Officium Libri Catholici—Catholic Book Agency, 1963.

Smith, Rodney K. *Public Prayer and the Constitution: A Case Study in Constitutional Interpretation*. Wilmington, Del.: Scholarly Resources, 1987.

Williams, Tom M. *See No Evil: Christian Attitudes Toward Sex in Art and Entertainment*. Grand Rapids, Mich.: Zondervan, 1976.

SCIENCE, MEDICINE, AND TECHNOLOGY

DeVolpi, A., et al. *Born Secret: The H-Bomb, the Progressive Case, and National Security*. New York: Pergamon Press, 1981.

Emord, Jonathan W. *Freedom, Technology, and the First Amendment*. San Francisco: Pacific Research Institute for Public Policy, 1991.

Ginger, Ray. *Six Days or Forever?: Tennessee v. John Thomas Scopes*. Boston: Beacon Press, 1958.

Kaplar, Richard T., ed. *Bad Prescription for the First Amendment: FDA Censorship of Drug Advertising and Promotion*. Washington: Media Institute, 1993.

Morland, Howard. *The Secret That Exploded*. New York: Random House, 1981.

Rose, Lance. *NetLaw: Your Rights in the Online World*. Berkeley, Calif.: Osborne McGraw-Hill, 1995.

TELEVISION AND RADIO BROADCASTING

Charren, Peggy, and Martin W. Sandler. *Changing Channels: Living (Sensibly) with Television*. Reading, Mass.: Addison-Wesley, 1983.

Cirino, Robert. *Don't Blame the People: How the News Media*

Uses Bias, Distortion and Censorship to Manipulate Public Opinion. New York: Random House, 1972.

Cowan, Geoffrey. *See No Evil: The Backstage Battle Over Sex and Violence on Television.* New York: Simon & Schuster, 1979.

Emery, Walter B. *Broadcasting and Government: Responsibilities and Regulations.* East Lansing: Michigan State Press, 1971.

Foley, Karen Sue. *The Political Blacklist in the Broadcast Industry: The Decade of the 1950s.* New York: Arno Press, 1979.

Friendly, Fred W. *The Good Guys, the Bad Guys, and the First Amendment: Free Speech vs. Fairness in Broadcasting.* New York: Random House, 1976.

Kronenwetter, Michael. *Free Press v. Fair Trial: Television and Other Media in the Courtroom.* New York: Franklin Watts, 1986.

Labunski, Richard E. *The First Amendment Under Siege: The Politics of Broadcast Regulation.* Westport, Conn.: Greenwood Press, 1981.

Montgomery, Kathryn C. *Target, Prime Time: Advocacy Groups and Entertainment TV.* New York: Oxford University Press, 1989.

Powe, Lucas A., Jr. *American Broadcasting and the First Amendment.* Berkeley: University of California Press, 1987.

Rowan, Ford. *Broadcast Fairness: Doctrine, Practice, Prospects.* New York: Longman, 1984.

Shapiro, Andrew O. *Media Access: Your Rights to Express Your Views on Radio and Television.* Boston: Little, Brown, 1976.

WORLD NATIONS

Califia, Pat. *Forbidden Passages: Writings Banned in Canada.* Pittsburgh, Pa.: Cleis Press, 1995.

Carlson, Julia, ed. *Banned in Ireland: Censorship and the Irish Writer.* Athens: University of Georgia Press, 1990.

Dewhirst, Martin, and Robert Farrel, eds. *The Soviet Censorship.* Metuchen, N.J.: Scarecrow Press, 1973.

Dillon, Ken. *Brought to Book: Censorship and School Libraries in Australia.* Melbourne: ALIA/Thorpe, 1993.

Girja, Kumar. *Censorship in India: With Special Reference to "The Satanic Verses" and "Lady Chatterley's Lover."* New Delhi: Har-Anand, 1990.

Hyland, Paul, and Neil Sammells. *Writing and Censorship in Britain.* London: Routledge, 1992.

Merrett, Christopher E. *A Culture of Censorship: Secrecy and Intellectual Repression in South Africa.* Macon, Ga.: Mercer University Press, 1995.

Myers, Robin, and Michael Harris, eds. *Censorship and the Control of Print in England and France, 1600-1910.* Winchester, England: St. Paul's Bibliographies, 1992.

Ohles, Frederik. *Germany's Rude Awakening: Censorship in the Land of the Brothers Grimm.* Kent, Ohio: Kent State University Press, 1992.

Sperling, Gerald B., and James E. McKenzie, eds. *Getting the Real Story: Censorship and Propaganda in South Africa.* Calgary, Alberta, Canada: Detselig Enterprises, 1990.

—Kevin J. Bochynski

CENSORSHIP

List of Entries by Category

Subject headings used in list

African Americans
Art
Books
   Children's and young adult
   Fiction
   Nonfiction
Broadcasting
Business and economics
Canada
Censorship tools
Court cases
Drama and theater
Education

Family and sexuality
Film
Films
Forms of expression
Government and
   politics
Historical events and
   eras
Laws
Libraries
Literature and publishing
Music and dance
News media

Obscenity and indecency
Organizations
People
   Artists
   Broadcasters and entertainers
   Journalists and publishers
   Justices and legal figures
   Moral crusaders
   Musicians and composers
   Philosophers and scientists
   Political figures
   Religious figures
   Social and political activists

Writers, American
Writers, British
Writers, French
Writers, German
Writers, Italian
Writers, Russian
Writers, Other
Periodicals
Places
Religion
Science
Wars
Women

AFRICAN AMERICANS

African Americans
Ali, Muhammad
Amos 'n' Andy
Baldwin, James
Birth of a Nation, The
Black Like Me
Chicago Art Institute furors
Civil Rights movement
Color Purple, The
Confessions of Nat Turner,
  The
"Cop Killer"
Davis, Angela
Douglass, Frederick
Farrakhan, Louis Abdoul
Garvey, Marcus
Jackson, Michael
Jeffries, Leonard, Jr.

King, Martin Luther, Jr.
Little Black Sambo
Lovejoy, Elijah Parish
Malcolm X
Miscegenation
Murphy, Eddie
National Association for the
  Advancement of Colored
  People
Newspapers, African American
Pinky
Race
Robeson, Paul
Shakur, Tupac
Simpson, O. J., case
2 Live Crew
Uncle Tom's Cabin
Walker, David

ART

Art
Beardsley, Aubrey
Butler v. The Queen
Caricature
Chicago Art Institute furors
Comic books
Cover art
Crumb, Robert
Dalí, Salvador
Daumier, Honoré
Degenerate Art Exhibition
Dine, Jim
Doonesbury
Drama and theater
Far Side, The
Graffiti
Grosz, George
Kent, Rockwell
Manet, Edouard

Mann, Sally
Mapplethorpe, Robert
Michelangelo
Mural art
National Endowment
  for the Arts
Nolde, Emil
Nudity
Performance art
Photographic film processing
Postage stamps
Regina v. Cameron
Rivera, Diego
Serrano, Andres
Socialist Realism
Venus de Milo
Warhol, Andy
Whistler, James Abbott
  McNeill

BOOKS: CHILDREN'S AND YOUNG ADULT

Alice's Adventures in
  Wonderland
Day They Came to Arrest the
  Book, The
Horror series controversy
How to Eat Fried Worms

Impressions reading series
Little Black Sambo
Little House on the Prairie
Robin Hood, The Merry
  Adventures of
Wrinkle in Time, A

BOOKS: FICTION

Adventures of Huckleberry
  Finn
All Quiet on the Western
  Front
American Psycho
Arabian Nights, The
Catcher in the Rye, The
Children's Hour, The
Citizen Tom Paine
Clan of the Cave Bear, The
Color Purple, The
Confessions of Nat Turner,
  The
Death of a President, The
Deliverance
Elmer Gantry
Fahrenheit 451
Fanny Hill, The Memoirs of
Farewell to Arms, A
Grapes of Wrath, The
Handmaid's Tale, The
Lady Chatterley's Lover

Last Exit to Brooklyn
Last Temptation of Christ, The
Lolita
Lord of the Flies
MacBird
Maggie
Naked Lunch
Peyton Place
Portnoy's Complaint
Red Badge of Courage, The
Sapho
Satyricon, The
Studs Lonigan
Tarzan
Tess of the D'Urbervilles
To Kill a Mockingbird
Tropic of Cancer
Ugly American, The
Ulysses
Uncle Tom's Cabin
Venus in the Cloister
Well of Loneliness, The

BOOKS: NONFICTION

Areopagitica
Black Like Me
CIA and the Cult of Intelligence,
  The
Crossman Diaries
Diary of Anne Frank, The
Dictionaries

I Know Why the Caged Bird
  Sings
Inside the Company
Joy of Sex, The
Kama Sutra
Kinsey Report

LAWS

Alberta Press Act Reference
Archival laws
Atomic Energy Act of 1954
Blasphemy laws
Canadian Access to Information Act
Child Pornography Law (Canada)
Child Protection Restoration and Penalties Enforcement Act
Cinematograph Act
Coercion Acts
Communications Act of 1934
Communications Decency Act
Comstock Act of 1873
Constitution, U.S.
Convention for the Protection of Human Rights and Fundamental Freedoms
Copyright law
Criminal syndicalism laws
Customs laws, Canadian
Customs laws, U.S.
Equal Access Act
Espionage Act of 1917
First Amendment
Foreign Agents Registration Act of 1938
Fourteenth Amendment
Fourth Amendment
Freedom of Information Act
Hatch Act
Hate laws
Hate laws, Canadian
Helsinki Agreement
Immigration laws
Intelligence Identities Protection Act
Language laws
Licensing Act of 1662
Licensing Act of 1737
National Security Decision Directive 84
Nonmailable matter laws
Obscene Publications Acts
Official Secrets Act (Canada)
Official Secrets Act (U.K.)
Padlock Act
Postal regulations
Privacy Protection Act of 1980
Public Broadcasting Act of 1967
Sedition Act of 1798
Shield laws
Smith Act
Son of Sam laws
Stamp Act
Sunshine laws
Tax laws
Telephone law
Theatres Act of 1968
Wales padlock law

LIBRARIES

Alexandria library
American Library Association
Banned Books Week
Book and Periodical Council Statement on the Freedom of Expression and the Freedom to Read
Book publishing
Books, children's
Books, young adult
Canadian Access to Information Act
Canadian Library Association Statement on Intellectual Freedom
Freedom to Read Foundation
Freedom to Read Week
Horror series controversy
Jeremiah's Book of Prophesies, burning of
Libraries
Libraries, Canadian
Libraries, school
Library Bill of Rights
Maya books, destruction of
United States Information Agency

LITERATURE AND PUBLISHING

Abridgment
Biography
Book burning
Book publishing
Books, children's
Books, young adult
Caxton, William
Cerf, Bennett
Comic books
Cover art
Fairy tales
Film adaptation
Ginzburg, Ralph
Girodias, Maurice
Index Librorum Prohibitorum
Literature

Liveright, Horace
Mythology
Nonmailable matter laws
Obscene Publications Acts
Occult
Poetry
Postal regulations
Pseudonyms, male
Regina v. Penguin Books Ltd.
Roman à clef
Roth, Samuel
Textbooks
Translation

MUSIC AND DANCE

American Society of Composers, Authors & Publishers
Baez, Joan
Beach Boys, the
Beatles, the
Broadcast Music, Inc.
Bryant, Anita
Burlesque shows
"Cop Killer"
Folk music
Foster, Stephen Collins
Guthrie, Woody
Hair
Jackson, Michael
Khachaturian, Aram
Lennon, John
Lewis, Jerry Lee
"Louie Louie"
Madonna
Mendelssohn, Felix
Mikado, The
Miller et al. v. Civil City of South Bend
Miss Saigon
Morissette, Alanis
Music
Music TeleVision
Nude dancing
O'Connor, Sinead
Oh, Calcutta!
Opera
Parents' Music Resource Center
Presley, Elvis
Prokofiev, Sergei
Protest music
Rap music
Recording industry
Redd v. State of Georgia
Reggae music
Robeson, Paul
Rock 'n' roll music
Rolling Stones, the
Seeger, Pete
Shakur, Tupac
Shostakovich, Dmitri
2 Live Crew
Wagner, Richard
Weavers, the

NEWS MEDIA

Accuracy in Media
Airline safety news
Alberta Press Act Reference
Associated Press
Automobile safety news
Bhopal disaster
Bolles, Donald F., Jr.
Bradlaugh v. The Queen
Campaign for Press and Broadcasting Freedom
Caxton, William
Chernobyl disaster
Douglass, Frederick
"H-Bomb Secret, The"
Health epidemic news
Hearst, William Randolph
Howe, Joseph
Iran-Contra scandal
Journalism reviews
Journalists, violence against
Junk food news
Kennedy, John F., assassination of
Letters to editors
Lovejoy, Elijah Parish
Magazines
Military censorship
Mitford, Jessica
New York Times, The
News media censorship
Newspapers
Newspapers, African American
Newspapers, student
Newspapers, underground
Newsreels
Obituaries
Off-the-record information
Office of Censorship, U.S.
Pentagon Papers, The
Pesticide industry
Pharmaceutical industry
Photocopying
Press conferences
Press-radio war
Printing
Publick Occurrences

PEOPLE: JUSTICES AND LEGAL FIGURES

Black, Hugo
Blackstone, William
Brennan, William J., Jr.
Chase, Samuel
De Grazia, Edward

Douglas, William O.
Ernst, Morris Leopold
Frankfurter, Felix
Holmes, Oliver Wendell, Jr.
Warren, Earl

PEOPLE: MORAL CRUSADERS

Comstock, Anthony
Coughlin, Father Charles Edward
Cushing, Cardinal Richard James
Gabler, Mel, and Norma Gabler

Spellman, Cardinal Francis
    Joseph
Sumner, John
Torquemada, Tomás de

PEOPLE: MUSICIANS AND COMPOSERS

Baez, Joan
Beach Boys, the
Beatles, the
Bryant, Anita
Foster, Stephen Collins
Guthrie, Woody
Jackson, Michael
Khachaturian, Aram
Lennon, John
Lewis, Jerry Lee
Madonna
Mendelssohn, Felix

Morissette, Alanis
O'Connor, Sinead
Presley, Elvis
Prokofiev, Sergei
Robeson, Paul
Rolling Stones, the
Seeger, Pete
Shakur, Tupac
Shostakovich, Dmitri
2 Live Crew
Wagner, Richard
Weavers, the

PEOPLE: PHILOSOPHERS AND SCIENTISTS

Anaxagoras
Aristotle
Bentham, Jeremy
Confucius
Copernicus, Nicolaus
Darwin, Charles
Democritus
Descartes, René
Ellis, Henry Havelock
Erasmus, Desiderius
Galileo Galilei
Hume, David
Kant, Immanuel
Kropotkin, Peter

Leary, Timothy
Locke, John
Marcuse, Herbert
Marx, Karl
Mead, Margaret
Mercator, Gerardus
Plato
Rousseau, Jean-Jacques
Sakharov, Andrei
Sanger, Margaret
Seneca the Younger
Socrates
Swedenborg, Emanuel
Vesalius, Andreas

PEOPLE: POLITICAL FIGURES

Agnew, Spiro T.
Barnett, Ross Robert
Bush, George
Cicero
Devlin, Bernadette
Dole, Robert
Franklin, Benjamin
Giddings, Joshua Reed
Gorbachev, Mikhail
Helms, Jesse Alexander
Henry VIII

Hoover, J. Edgar
James I
Jefferson, Thomas
Lenin, Vladimir Ilich
Lyon, Matthew
Madison, James
Mandela, Nelson
Mao Zedong
Meese, Edwin III
Morison, Samuel Loring
Nicholas I

Nixon, Richard M.
Reagan, Ronald
Royal family, British
Seneca the Younger
Shih huang-ti
Stalin, Joseph

Stubbs, John
Talmadge, Eugene
Thurmond, Strom
Trotsky, Leon
Zhdanov, Andrei

PEOPLE: RELIGIOUS FIGURES

Abelard, Peter
Bacon, Roger
Biddle, John
Calvin, John
Coughlin, Father Charles Edward
Cushing, Cardinal Richard James
Farrakhan, Louis Abdoul
Ghazzali, al-
Hus, Jan
Hutchinson, Anne
Joan of Arc
King, Martin Luther, Jr.
Knox, John
Latimer, Hugh
Leighton, Alexander

Luther, Martin
Malcolm X
Mani
Muhammad
O'Hair, Madalyn Murray
Paul IV, Pope
Richelieu, Cardinal
Rutherford, Joseph Franklin
Savonarola, Girolamo
Smith, Joseph
Spellman, Cardinal Francis
    Joseph
Thomas à Kempis
Torquemada, Tomás de
Williams, Roger

PEOPLE: SOCIAL AND POLITICAL ACTIVISTS

Bakunin, Mikhail Aleksandrovich
Berrigan, Daniel, and Philip
    Francis Berrigan
Debs, Eugene
Devlin, Bernadette
Douglass, Frederick
Garvey, Marcus
Goldman, Emma
Gouzenko, Igor Sergeievich
King, Martin Luther, Jr.
Malcolm X

Mandela, Nelson
Martí, José Julián
Metzger, Tom
Mindszenty, József
Nader, Ralph
O'Hair, Madalyn Murray
Pankhurst, Emmeline
Sanger, Margaret
Sumner, John
Thomas, Norman
Woodhull, Victoria

PEOPLE: WRITERS, AMERICAN

Andrews, V. C.
Baldwin, James
Blume, Judy
Cabell, James Branch
Caldwell, Erskine
Chomsky, Noam
Cummings, e. e.
Dahl, Roald
Dreiser, Theodore
Dworkin, Andrea
Emerson, Ralph Waldo
Faulkner, William
Ferlinghetti, Lawrence
Franklin, Benjamin
Ginsberg, Allen
Helper, Hinton
Hemingway, Ernest
Hinton, S. E.
King, Stephen

Lewis, Sinclair
London, Jack
MacKinnon, Catharine A.
Mencken, H. L.
Miller, Henry
O'Hara, John
O'Neill, Eugene
Paine, Thomas
Parker, Dorothy
Paterson, Katherine
Sendak, Maurice
Silverstein, Shel
Sinclair, Upton
Southern, Terry
Steinbeck, John
Thoreau, Henry David
Twain, Mark
Vonnegut, Kurt
Webster, Noah

Whitman, Walt
Williams, Tennessee

Wodehouse, P. G.
Wright, Richard

Tolstoy, Leo
Voznesensky, Andrey
Andreyevich

Yevtushenko, Yevgeny
Aleksandrovich
Zamyatin, Yevgeny Ivanovich

PEOPLE: WRITERS, BRITISH

Bacon, Francis
Blyton, Enid
Bowdler, Thomas
Burton, Richard Francis
Defoe, Daniel
Dickens, Charles
Fielding, Henry
Gibbon, Edward
Glyn, Elinor
Goldsmith, Oliver
Harris, Frank
Hobbes, Thomas
Huxley, Aldous
Jonson, Ben
Joyce, James
Kipling, Rudyard
Lawrence, D. H.
Mill, John Stuart
Milton, John

Moore, George
Morgan, William
Orwell, George
Paine, Thomas
Prynne, William
Pynchon, William
Raleigh, Sir Walter
Rushdie, Salman
Russell, Bertrand
Shakespeare, William
Shaw, George Bernard
Shelley, Percy Bysshe
Sterne, Laurence
Stopes, Marie
Swift, Jonathan
Swinburne, Algernon Charles
Tolkien, J. R. R.
Wilde, Oscar
Wodehouse, P. G.

PEOPLE: WRITERS, OTHER

Aristophanes
Cormier, Robert Edmund
Djilas, Milovan
Gárcia Márquez, Gabriel
Havel, Václav
Ibsen, Henrik
Laurence, Margaret
Lee, Dennis

Mahfouz, Naguib
Munsch, Robert
Nasrin, Taslima
Ovid
Saro-Wiwa, Ken
Soyinka, Wole
Spinoza, Baruch

PERIODICALS

Green Sheet, The
Hustler
Index on Censorship
Little Review, The
MAD magazine
Men's magazines
New Worlds

New York Times, The
Penthouse
Playboy
Publick Occurrences
Realist, The
Screw

PEOPLE: WRITERS, FRENCH

Babeuf, François Noël
Balzac, Honoré de
Baudelaire, Charles
Beaumarchais, Pierre-Augustin
    Caron de
Diderot, Denis
Dumas, Alexandre, *père*
Flaubert, Gustave
France, Anatole
Gautier, Théophile
Gide, André
Hugo, Victor
Maupassant, Guy de

Molière
Montaigne, Michel de
Montesquieu
Pascal, Blaise
Proudhon, Pierre-Joseph
Rabelais, François
Sade, Marquis de
Sand, George
Sartre, Jean-Paul
Stendhal
Voltaire
Zola, Émile

PLACES

Alabama
Albania
Argentina
Australia
Boston
Brazil
Burma
Canada
Central America
Chile
China
Cuba
Denmark
France
Georgia
Germany
Haiti
Hyde Park Speakers Corner
India
Indonesia
Iran

Iraq
Ireland
Israel
Italy
Japan
Mexico
Nigeria
Northern Ireland
Pakistan
Philippines
Poland
Russia
South Africa
South America
Soviet Union
Sweden
Turkey
United Kingdom
United States
Vietnam
Zimbabwe

PEOPLE: WRITERS, GERMAN

Brecht, Bertolt
Goethe, Johann Wolfgang von
Heine, Heinrich

Hochhuth, Rolf
Schiller, Friedrich von

PEOPLE: WRITERS, ITALIAN

Boccaccio, Giovanni
Bruno, Giordano
Casanova, Giovanni Giacomo

D'Annunzio, Gabriele
Dante Alighieri
Machiavelli, Niccolò

RELIGION

Abelard, Peter
Anti-Defamation League
Atheism
Bacon, Roger
Bible
Biddle, John
Blasphemy laws
Buddhism
Calvin, John

Christian Science
Christianity
Coughlin, Father Charles Edward
Cushing, Cardinal Richard James
Dead Sea Scrolls
Farrakhan, Louis Abdoul
First Amendment
Ghazzali, al-
Halloween

PEOPLE: WRITERS, RUSSIAN

Akhmatova, Anna
Babel, Isaac Emmanuilovich
Bulgakov, Mikhail Afanasyevich
Dostoevski, Fyodor
Gogol, Nikolai Vasilyevich

Gorky, Maxim
Mayakovsky, Vladimir
Pasternak, Boris
Radishchev, Alexander
Solzhenitsyn, Aleksandr

INDEX OF COURT CASES

Page numbers in boldface type indicate full articles devoted to the topics. Page numbers in italic type indicate photographs, drawings, maps, tables, charts, and graphs.

INDEX OF BOOKS, FILMS, AND OTHER ARTISTIC WORKS

This index includes books, essays, plays, films, songs, paintings, and other works discussed in the text. Page numbers in boldface type indicate full articles devoted to the topics. Page numbers in italic type indicate photographs, drawings, maps, tables, charts, and graphs.

SUBJECT INDEX

Page numbers in boldface type indicate full articles devoted to the topics. Page numbers in italic type indicate photographs, drawings, maps, tables, charts, and graphs.

Street oratory, **765-766**, 896
Street v. New York, 292, 882
Streetcar Named Desire, A, 278-279, 287, 437, 856
Strick, Joseph, 820
Strict scrutiny, 896
Strike at Coaldale, The, 281
Striptease, 106, 568
Stromberg v. California, 772, 878
Strossen, Nadine, 274
Stubbs, John, **766**
Student Nonviolent Coordinating Committee, 471
Student Press Law Center, 551, 558
Studies in the Psychology of Sex, 240
Studs Lonigan, **766-767**
Sturges, Jock, 605
Sturm und Drang, 327
Styron, William, 168
Subliminal messages, **767**, 896
Subversive Activities Control Act, 164
Sudan, 396, 551
Suharto, 385, 552
Suicide, 103, 167, 178, 284, 352, 381, 483-484, 523, 558, 613, 665, 719, **767-769**
Sukarno, 552
Sulistrowski, Zygmunt, 529
Sullivan, Arthur S., 496
Sullivan, Ed, 522, 633, 788
Sullivan, John, 831
Sullivan, L. B., 442, 546
Sulzberger, Arthur Hays, 545
Sumerians, ancient, 32
Summerfield, Arthur, 426
Sumner, John, 106, 194, 433, 702, 741, **769**, 819
Sun Also Rises, The, 352
Sun Records, 440
Sunday, Billy, 171
Sunshine and Health, 91
Sunshine Book Company v. Summerfield, 91
Sunshine laws, 127, **769-770**
Support for the Learning and Teaching of English, 90
Supreme Court, U.S., 75-76, 96, 181-183, 223, 301, 361, 823, 850
Surette, Ray, 176
Surrealist movement, 198
Swaggart, Jimmy, 375, 386, *786*
Sweden, 32, 197, 283, 522, 720, **770-771**
Swedenborg, Emanuel, **771**
Sweet Bird of Youth, 857
Swift, Jonathan, 530, **771-772**
Swinburne, Algernon Charles, 613, **772**
Switzerland, 359, 426, 689
Sylvius, Jacobus, 832
Symbolic speech, 304, 578, **772-773**, 829, 896
Symons, Arthur, 65

Syndicated television, **774**
Syntex, 603
System of Nature, 50
Szulc, Tad, 64

Taboo, 896
Taft-Hartley Act of 1947, 147
Tailor and Antsy, 393
Taiwan, 138, 552, 626
Tale of a Tub, A, 771
Talk radio, 451-452, 763
Talk shows, **775-777**, 779, 896
Talley v. California, 715
Talmadge, Eugene, **777**
Talmud, 82, 407-409, 673, **777-778**
Taming of the Shrew, The, 726
Taming the Star Runner, 354
Tanzania, 396
Taoism, 137
Tape-delay broadcasting, **778-779**
Tarantino, Quentin, 543, 657
Tarare, 583
Tariff Act of 1842, 31, 823
Tariff Act of 1930, 81, 196, 325, 412, 659, 819
Tarkington, Booth, 89
Tartuffe, 506
Tarzan, **779**
Tasmania, 53
TASS, **779-780**
Tate, Nahum, 725
Tax laws, **780-782**
Taxi Driver, 176
Taxpayer for Accountability in Government, 637
Taylor, Elizabeth, 288, *854*
Taylor, William Desmond, 282, 346
Technology, 126, **782-783**
Telecommunications Act of 1996, 111, 159, 546, 723, 790
Telecommunications law, 158-159, 258-259, 655
Telegraphy, electric, 782
Telemarketing, 783-784
Telephone, 782; law, **783-785**
Telephone Consumer Protection Act, 783
Telephone Decency Act, 785
Televangelists, **785-787**
Television, 99-102, 112-113, 152, 297, 503, 531, 546, 774-777, 779, **787-791**; cable, 110-111; children's, 5, **791-792**; closed-circuit, 188; networks, 774, **792-794**
Television Act of 1954, 788
Television news, public confidence in (chart), *548*
Television Program Improvement Act of 1990, 790
Temperance movements, 740, **794**
Tempest, The, 725

Tempier, Etienne, 49
Temple, William Franklin, 302
Temptation, *345*
Ten Commandments, 70
Ten North Frederick, 581
Ten Thousand Maniacs, 668
Tennessee, 66, 252, 711-712; Chattanooga, 569; Churchill, 799; Dayton, 711, 798; Hawkins County, 636; Memphis, 286-288; Pulaski, 422
Tenth Amendment, 174, 242
Terminiello v. Chicago, 223, 879
Terre, La, 875
Terrorism, **794-796**
Terry, Luther L., 9
Tess of the D'Urbervilles, **796**
Testament des Dr. Mabuse, Das, 284
Tet Offensive, 836
Tex, 354
Texas, 66, 71, 218, 253, 287, 292, 313-314, 447, 470, 494, 523, 596, 599, 608, 636, 709, 711, 773, 784; annexation of, 517; Austin, 491; Dallas, 627, 786, 796, 817; El Paso, 684; Houston, 137, 588; Huffman, 731; Longview, 636; Plano, 6; San Antonio, 149; Waco, 270
Texas v. Johnson, 108, 292, 715, 773, **796-797**, 885
Textbooks, 61, 88, 238, 412-414, 465, 636-637, 709-710, **797-800**, 827
Textualism, 76
Thailand, 626
Thalberg, Irving, 284, 303
Thalidomide, 603
That Was Then, This Is Now, 354
Thatcher, Margaret, 580, 693
Thayer, H. E., 148
Theater, 226-230
Theatre Regulation Act of 1843, 254, 821
Theatres Act of 1968, 254, 339, 450, 458, **800-801**
Their Trade Is Treachery, 758
Them, 683
Then Again, Maybe I Won't, 80, 89
Theocracy, 395
Theodosius, 19
These Three, 136, 285
They Won't Forget, 285
Thiers, Adolphe, *120*
Thirteenth Amendment, 174
Thirty-Seven Photographs, United States v., 412
"This Land Is Your Land," 295
Thomas, Clarence, 537
Thomas, Isaiah, 640
Thomas, J. Parnell, 285, 359-360, 368-369, 379
Thomas, Lewis V., 40
Thomas, Norman, **801**
Thomas à Kempis, **801**